ip. 57 –   25 –

SONS OF THE MOUNTAINS

SONS OF THE MOUNTAINS

Ethnohistory of the Vietnamese
Central Highlands to 1954

Gerald Cannon Hickey

New Haven and London
Yale University Press

Published with the generous assistance of the Earhart Foundation.

Designed by Sally Harris
and set in Monophoto Bembo type by
Asco Trade Typesetting Ltd., Hong Kong.
Printed in the United States of America by
Vail-Ballou Press, Binghamton, N.Y.

Library of Congress Cataloging in Publication Data

Hickey, Gerald Cannon, 1925–
    Sons of the mountains.

    Bibliography: p.
    Includes index.
    1. Montagnards (Vietnamese tribes)—History.
2. Vietnam—History. I. Title.
DS556.45.M6H53   959.7'0049992   80-21819
ISBN 0-300-02453-3

10   9   8   7   6   5   4   3   2   1

CONTENTS

MAPS

CHARTS

ILLUSTRATIONS

Unless otherwise indicated, photographs were taken by the author.

PREFACE

The present study really began in 1953 when I went to Paris on a fellowship to research the ethnology of Indochina. Although my primary interest was Vietnamese culture, I soon found myself intrigued with works on the ethnic groups of the northern and central highlands in Vietnam. I returned to Chicago carrying file folders bulging with data on their societies.

When I went to Saigon in 1956 as a member of the Michigan State University Advisory Group, I interviewed some refugee northern highland leaders from Tai-speaking groups and made one field trip to the uplands of northern Laos. But my interest in the people of the central highlands intensified considerably when I was able to visit the region in 1956 and 1957. As I gathered ethnographic data I had the good fortune to meet some of the young leaders who—as a reaction to the Saigon government's policy of forced assimilation—were fermenting a new spirit of ethnonationalism. In a report to the Michigan State group I suggested that the government accommodate the highland people's desire to preserve their ethnic identity. High-ranking Vietnamese officials, however, reacted negatively, so I was prevented from further travel in the region. I therefore turned to my original interest in Vietnamese peasant society and through 1958 and 1959 conducted field research in the Mekong river delta village of Khanh Hau.

During the early 1960s I prepared an ethnographic compendium of mainland Southeast Asia for the Human Relations Area File in New Haven, co-authored a book entitled *Ethnic Groups of Mainland Southeast Asia* with Frank Le Bar and John Musgrave, and completed the manuscript of another. *Village in Vietnam* was published by the Yale University Press in 1964. By that time I had left the faculty of Yale University to return to Vietnam. I continued research on the people of the central highlands, under an arrangement with The RAND Corporation, from February 1964 until March 1973. During that wartime period I was able to work with highland leaders, acting as an unofficial intermediary between them and Saigon (in particular, the American mission). I also conducted ethnographic research with a focus on the historical emergence of an inter-ethnic group leadership (part of which is represented in the kinship charts in this volume). Although the Advanced Research Projects Agency (ARPA) of the Defense Department was financing some RAND projects in Vietnam, I experienced no attempts to influence or to direct my work.

After leaving Vietnam in 1973, I went to Cornell University as a visiting associate professor, and in the quiet atmosphere of Ithaca I began the manuscript for this book. It was completed in the stimulating surroundings of the Woodrow Wilson International Center for Scholars at the Smithsonian Institution, to which I had received a fellowship from 1975 to 1977.

I would like to express my appreciation to a number of individuals and organizations who were of assistance to me in conducting ethnohistorical research on the highlands prior to 1954. Sally Cassidy and Paule Verdet obtained the Paris fellowship for me, and the late Wesley Fishel and Father Emmanual Jacques arranged for my position with the Michigan State University Advisory Group. Frank Le Bar, Karl Pelzer, and Harry Benda made possible the research associate appointment at Yale University. George Tanham, Joan Allen, Guido (Yogi) Ianiero, and Rita McDermott helped make my time with The RAND Corporation productive and rewarding. In Vietnam, highland people too numerous to mention lent help in gathering field data. I would, however, particularly like to thank Y Thih Eban, Touneh Han Tho, Nay Luett, and Y Char Hdok. Others who aided my field work were Laura and Gordon Smith, the researchers of the Summer Institute of Linguistics, the priests of the Missions Etrangères de Paris, and members of the Christian and Missionary Alliance.

In Saigon and Phnom Penh I was assisted in my research by Nghiem Tham, Tran Van Tot, Do Van Anh, and the late Martine Piat. Pierre-Bernard Lafont kindly provided documents from Paris and arranged for the Musée Guimet to send the photograph of a Cham statue found near Kontum. George McT. Kahin and Thomas Kirsch invited me to come to Cornell University, and I was assisted there by Giok Po Oey and Jay Scarborough. At the Woodrow Wilson International Center for Scholars, James Billington, Prosser Gifford, and Michael Lacey were most helpful.

The Earhart Foundation of Ann Arbor, Michigan, generously provided valuable support in funding a fellowship for Touneh Han Tho to spend a period as my research assistant in Washington and in granting a subvention for the final preparation of this book and the companion work. Mary Connor assisted with the preparation of the manuscript, which was typed by Joan Allen, Tazu Warner, and Eloise Doane. The maps were drafted by Christopher Mueller-Wille and Dan Greenway. Nguyen Van Tam did the sketches and the genealogy charts. At Yale University Press, the professional guidance of Adrienne Suddard and Edward Tripp has been invaluable in transforming the manuscript into the final product—the book.

I would like to thank my family, particularly my mother and my sisters, Catherine and Carole, for their support during the long period of research and writing.

Finally, I would like to extend my most heartfelt gratitude to the people of the central highlands for their unfailing kindness and for all I have learned from them.

INTRODUCTION

Ever since a remote time long before the advent of history, human societies have existed in Southeast Asia, and the drama of change in the course of centuries has produced a rich variety of peoples and cultures. In many respects this evolution has been like the constantly altering profusion of a luxuriant tropical garden with its old and new growths, its struggles and symbioses, florescence and death. There have been small human groups that settled in ecological niches well suited to their needs, and they changed relatively little over the years. Other groups migrated often, adapting to varying physical environments, so that they eventually fissioned, giving rise to many new and distinct societies. Other new societies resulted from groups that came together and fused. Then there were those human groups that lost the struggle for survival and died out.

In time, some societies, for a variety of reasons, experienced vast transformations and attained that level of cultural evolution we call civilization. Great kingdoms rose and fell, and in the more recent period national states as we know them today were created. But despite the fact that some ethnic groups have advanced more rapidly than others and have come to dominate these political states, the mosaic variety that has always characterized Southeast Asia has remained until our time.

This study is concerned with those people who in the distant past settled the central highlands of what is now the Socialist Republic of Vietnam. Geographically this would be the southern portion of the mountain range we know in English as the Annam Cordillera. (The French call this range the Chaine Annamitique, while the Vietnamese know it as the Trường Sơn, "Long Mountains.") Scattered through valleys, slopes, and plateaus of these green uplands are populations which number anywhere from 500,000 to 1 million (see appendix A). They speak languages of the Mon Khmer or Austronesian (Malayopolynesian) stocks. Physically, they resemble other Southeast Asians, such as the Cambodians, Malays, and Indonesians, who also speak languages of these stocks. They are further differentiated into a number of ethnic groups (which are described in chapter 1).

This book traces the ethnohistory of this region and its people from prehistoric times to 1954 (a companion book covers the period from 1954). Throughout both works these people will be referred to as the *highlanders* (various other generic designations found in the literature will be noted later). Use of this term reflects their being mountain dwellers who share many common ways and values that distinguish them from the lowland people. To begin with, the highlanders are culturally less advanced than the lowland Cham, Khmer, and Vietnamese. Relatively isolated in their forested mountains, the highlanders historically remained aloof from the Chinese great tradition that molded the society of the Vietnamese and also from the Indian influences diffusing eastward that brought civilization to the Cham and Khmer. Until recent times, all but one highland group (the Chru, who employed a Cham script) were without writing.

Up to the early part of the twentieth century there were no urban centers in the highlands (they were established by the French), and even with their appearance the people have remained village-oriented. Their small communities are characterized by close social relations, particularly among those of the same family group, reflecting the importance of kinship. Unlike the civilized lowland people, the highlanders have relatively little differentiation among their social, political, economic, and religious systems. This is exemplified in the roles of their village leaders (many of whom attain their positions because of their being favored by the spirits), who commonly perform religious rituals that have numerous social overtones as well as economic functions, e.g., assuring abundant harvests. All of the highland people have livelihoods based on agriculture with rice (upland dry rice or paddy) the staple crop, and they farm similar secondary crops. Fishing in nearby streams and hunting in the vast forests are supplementary economic activities. The division of labor is very similar in all of the societies. Finally, until the advent of Christianity in the mid-nineteenth century, all of the highland religious systems had similar pantheons of animistic spirits. In addition, many of their rituals have common characteristics (such as offering sacrificial animals and drinking alcohol from jars).

The use of the term *highlanders* also calls attention to the major thesis of this study that for a long period of time the mountain people have been developing a common ethnic identity. It has been a process of sociocultural change due to a number of interrelated economic, political, religious, and geographic factors, all of which are reflected in the events of history. As a result of such a process a group of people at some point experience a "we-they" distinction and come to identify themselves, and are identified by others, as being members of an ethnic group. In the case of the highlanders there has been for a long time a growing awareness that they collectively are different from the outsiders (usually lowlanders) with whom they have come into contact.[1] It is in many ways comparable to the process of ethnicity that historically occurred among the diverse indigenous groups of Americans who came to think of themselves as "Indian." Among the highlanders of Vietnam no such generic term has yet been adopted, although an intergroup elite instrumental in the rise of highlander ethno-nationalism has been using several designations from different languages. The one most favored is *Ana Chu* (or a cognate thereof) meaning "Sons of the Mountains," found in the Austronesian languages of the most populous groups—from which most of the elite come. It is a most appropriate term, capturing the almost mystical relationship that exists between the highlanders and their surrounding mountains, which for them is a world where they know that they will survive or die out as a people.

The emergence of a new ethnic identity among the highlanders was not an original focus of this study. Initial interests included a general ethnographic survey (with emphasis on the little-known groups), leadership, and socioeconomic change. When field research began in the mid-1950s, however, it became readily clear that in certain parts of the uplands ethnonationalism was on the rise. The prime movers were relatively young, educated highlanders, most of them of elite families descended from chiefs of the late nineteenth century. Although they were from different ethnic groups they identified themselves as "montagnards" (the French designation) and they espoused the cause of the highland people in general. During the period that followed, the ethnic identity of being a

1. The highlanders have some common designations for certain lowland people. The Vietnamese are known as *Yuan*, and the Lao as *Lao*. Those highland people who have had contact with the Khmer call them *Kur*. For the Cham, however, there are several designations. The Koho-speaking groups as well as the Mnong, Bahnar, Jarai (west of Cheo Reo) and Rhadé (west of M'drak) call them *Prum*, while the eastern Jarai and Rhadé, the Chru, and Roglai refer to them as *Cham*. On the western side of the mountains the French are known as *Prang* and on the eastern side they are called *Tay* (a Vietnamese term). The Chinese are *Khach* on the western side and *Lo* in the eastern region of the mountains. Indians (usually merchants in towns) are *Yawa*.

highlander deepened and spread among the villagers as the remaining isolation of the mountain region vanished.

What was observable in the mid-1950s had been evolving for a very long time, so a thorough understanding necessitated a reconstruction of the highlanders' ethnohistory, i.e., their role in the history of Indochina. For the period covered in this book a wide range of sources was consulted. Documentary materials included archeological data, historical linguistics, Cham stone inscriptions, Khmer and Vietnamese annals, explorers' accounts, missionaries' records, French administrative and military reports, ethnographies, private papers, and general histories. Oral sources were largely concerned with legends, genealogies, and reminiscences.

Archeological information and historical linguistics provided some very provocative insights concerning the primordial ties between the highlanders and the Cham, Khmer, and Vietnamese, but they shed no real light on the character of early relationships. It is with Cham petrographs of the mid-twelfth century that we encounter the first historical information about highland-lowland contacts. Cham armies were sent up the river valleys into the mountains, where many local chiefs submitted and sent tribute to the Cham capital. The king bestowed upon these vassals the title *potao*, which can be translated as "king," "lord," or "master."[2] He also

2. Pierre-Bernard Lafont in his *Lexique Jarai* (Paris: Ecole Française d'Extrême-Orient, 1968), p. 253, translates *potao* as "roi" (king) and lists the Potao Pui (King of Fire), Potao Ia (King of Water), and Potao Angin (King of Wind), while Jacques Dournes in his *Coordonnées structures Jörai familiales et sociales* (Paris: Institut d'Ethnologie, 1972), pp. 7, 51, 307, refers to *potao* as meaning "maitre" (master) or "seigneur" (lord) and describes three "masters of the elements": Potao Apui (Fire Master), Potao Ia (Water Master), and Potao Angin (Air Master).

The word *potao* or cognates thereof also are found in other Austronesian languages. In Georges Coedès, "La plus ancienne inscription en langue Cham," *New Indian Antiquary*, Extra Series I (1939): 46–49, it is noted that the earliest known inscription in the Cham language contains the term *putauv*, which Coedès interprets as an early version of the Cham word *patau* or *putau* meaning "king." In E. Aymonier and A. Cabaton, *Dictionnaire Čam-Français* (Paris: Imprimerie Nationale, 1906), pp. 260–61, *patau* or *putau* is translated "king," and it also is noted that this title indicates "one of the 'sadetes' (Khmer, *sdec*; Laotian, *sadet*) or 'god-king of the Jarai.'" Three "sadetes" are listed: (1) the King of Water (Jarai, *patao ya*; Khmer, *sdec tik*; Laotian, *sadet nam*; Vietnamese, *thủy xá*); (2) the King of Fire (Jarai, *potao apui*; Khmer, *sdec phlon*; Laotian, *sadet fai*; Vietnamese, *hỏa xá*); and (3) the King of Wind (Jarai, *potao angin*). The authors also note that the cognate *pauté* is found in the Atjehnese language, spoken in northern Sumatra.

Mathew L. Charles, a linguist specializing in Austronesian languages, related in a discussion on 13 January 1975 that Aymonier and Cabaton may have based their observation concerning Atjehnese from information contained in George Karel Niemann, "Bijdrage tot de kennis der verhouding van het Tjam tot de talen van Indonesië," *Bijdragen tot de Taal-, Land-, en Volkenkunde van Nederlandsch-Indie* 40 (1891): 41, where it is pointed out that the Atjehnese word for "king" or "ruler" is *pautĕ*. Another possible source is Karel Frederik Van Langen, *Handleiding voor de beoefening der Atjehsche taal* (The Hague: Martinus Nijhoff, 1889), p. 33, where the word *pautĕ* is translated "king, ruler, his majesty." Also in J. Kreemer, *Atjehsch handwoordenboek* (Leiden: E. J. Brill, 1931), p. 235, the word *po* is listed as meaning "master" or "boss," while *poteu radja* is "our king," and Poteu Alah is "god."

presented them with seals and sabers as symbols of their new authority as his upland representatives. With this, the chiefs and their people were initiated into the network of tributary relations that crisscrossed the Indochinese peninsula. They also found themselves embroiled in the wars between the Cham and Vietnamese. The later annals of the Khmer and Vietnamese reveal that their rulers established tributary relations with two powerful Jarai shamans—the Potao Apui (or Pui) and the Potao Ea (or Ia). In the Jarai language *apui* is "fire" while *ea* is "water." In this work potao will be translated as "king," so these leaders will be referred to as the King of Fire and the King of Water. The title potao strongly suggests a Cham imprint, and this is further substantiated by the fact that the King of Fire derives his power by virtue of being guardian of a sacred saber.

Tributary relations between the Jarai shamans and the Khmer and Vietnamese ended with the French conquest of Indochina during the latter half of the nineteenth century. The vassalage of the Jarai to the Court of Hue, however, provided the rationale for the French, as protectors of Annam, to assume control of the central highlands. With the twentieth century and French colonization of the region, the isolation of the highlanders began to diminish rapidly, and their leadership underwent vast changes. Repeating the earlier Cham pattern, the French colonial authorities used local chiefs as intermediaries between the administration and the indigenous populations. Isolation of the highlands began to diminish after the French established their presence and built "penetration routes" with corvée from the villages. French administrators in the settlements of Kontum, Ban Me Thuot, and Dalat were soon joined by Chinese and Vietnamese merchants. The children of the chiefs were predominant among the students in the first primary schools in these locales, and by the 1930s they had become the first highland teachers, civil servants, and technicians—representing a new type of leader familiar with the language and ways of the colonial regime while retaining their ties with the village societies from which they came. Marriage among them was a vital step in the emergence of a new highlander elite. Through the 1925–1939 period the French sought to consolidate their control and expand their economic exploitation of the mountain region. Wild forests gave way to coffee, tea, and rubber estates. Kontum, Ban Me Thuot, and Dalat grew into market towns. As a result of taxes, the detested corvée, and land grabbing, however, discontent among the highlanders with French rule was fostering ethnonationalism, which was manifest in the bizarre Python God Movement during the late 1930s.

With the Japanese takeover of the administration of Indochina on 9 March 1945, the highlanders were plunged into a long night of international conflict. The world that had existed prior to that date vanished forever. The highlanders now found themselves "a people in between" as some joined the French and some the Viet Minh while most became unwitting victims of the war. Nonetheless, their leadership developed further as the French, in an attempt to win their support, improved secondary schools. Increased marriage among members of elite families of different ethnic groups also resulted in a constantly expanding sociopolitical network that eventually would link all of the genealogies presented in charts 1, 2, 3, 4, and 5.

The Geneva Agreements did not bring a lasting peace to Vietnam, and the highlanders were to face even greater trials than they had in the past. In 1954, however, the process of ethnonationalism that had been set into motion so many years before was now irreversible. The contact with the outside world which had been so important to its inception would intensify and would heighten the highlanders' determination to preserve their own identity. In addition, the intergroup leadership that had become so vital in sustaining and defining ethnonationalism would crystallize further. Despite all that the future would bring, by 1954 the highlanders were well on their way to becoming the "Sons of the Mountains."

ABBREVIATIONS USED IN NOTES

BEFEO *Bulletin de l'Ecole Française d'Extrême-Orient*
BSEI   *Bulletin de la Société des Etudes Indochinoises*
IIEH   *Institut Indochinois pour l'Etude de l'Homme*
SA   *Southeast Asia*

References in the text to the kinship charts are given as a parenthetic number in which the first digit is the chart number and the digits following the decimal point identify the individual. For example, Pim (1.5) means that the highlander named Pim is shown on chart number 1 as person number 5.

1 THE TRADITIONAL WORLD
OF THE HIGHLANDERS

Through many long centuries before the appearance of civilization in Southeast Asia the warm Indochinese peninsula, with its fertile valleys and deltas, its dense forests so rich in game, and its rivers and coastlines alive with aquatic life, sustained human existence. Archeological research continues to shed more and more light on the mode of this human existence and to uncover the roots of the diverse cultures that would evolve from this prehistoric matrix. One of the earliest links between archeological and historical evidence is to be found in the vestigial ruins of the kingdom of Champa which lie scattered along the mountainous coast of what is now central Vietnam. These ruins contain a number of inscriptions, most of which relate the deeds of the Cham rulers. A few, however, refer to a people who lived in the remote hinterland west of Champa—a people who were not as advanced as the Cham and who were regarded with disdain. These inscriptions constitute the first recorded mention of the highlanders.

The most ancient such inscription, dated A.D. 845, appears on a stele not far from the Po Nagar temple (see map 4) in the vicinity of the present coastal town of Phan Rang, although the stele predates the temple by centuries.[1] This epigraph, written in Sanskrit, records that King Vikrantavarman, who was ruling at the time, dedicated to the deity Vikrantarudresvara a field called Rudraksetra located in a place inhabited by the *Vrlas*—a word Georges Maspéro interprets as a generic designation for the ethnic groups living in the mountains immediately to the west of Phan Rang.[2]

1. Etienne Aymonier, "Première étude sur les inscriptions Tchames," *Journal Asiatique* 17 (1891): 24–25.
2. Louis Finot, "Notes d'épigraphie," *BEFEO* 3, no. 2 (1903): 633; Georges Maspéro, *Le royaume de Champa* (Paris and Brussels: G. Van Oest, 1928), pp. 6–7.

An inscription at the Po Nagar temple in Nhatrang dated A.D. 1170 proclaims the victories of King Jaya Harivarman I in the mid-twelfth century over his enemies the Khmer, Vietnamese, Randaiy, Mada, and other Mlecchas.[3] Both Aymonier and Maspéro feel that the word *Randaiy* is a variation of Rhadé, the designation for one of the major Austronesian-speaking ethnic groups in the highlands west of Nhatrang.[4] Maspéro also speculates that the *Mada* were ancestral to the Jarai, another large upland Austronesian-speaking group, and he translates *Mlecchas* as "savage." Another epigraph from the same period also describes these victories, but the vanquished are the Vietnamese, Khmer, and the *Kiratas*, which Maspéro reports is a designation in India for primitive highland people.[5]

Centuries later, some of the first western travelers in Vietnam and Cambodia mentioned the highland people in their accounts. In his work on the kingdom of Cochinchina (Vietnam) published in Rome in 1629, Italian Jesuit Cristoforo Borri describes the mountainous interior as being "inhabited by the Kemois, which signifies savages, for although they be Cochinchinese, they will not acknowledge the king nor obey him in anything, cantoning and fortifying themselves in those mountains almost inaccessible."[6] The term *kemois* is clearly a variation of the Vietnamese *mọi* (savage), a pejorative term used for the mountain people, particularly those who inhabit the central highlands.

One of the early missionaries, Jesuit priest Alexandre de Rhodes, published a map of the kingdom of Annam in 1651, and on it the designation *Rumoi* is written across the area that approximates the central highlands.[7] In his 1666 account of his travels through Tonkin and Laos, another missionary, Father Giovanni Marini, notes that in Tonkin "one counts five princes there who are sovereigns, and if one wants to include certain people who live in the more remote and wild mountains and who follow two small *Roys* that are called the *Roy* of Water and the *Roy* of Fire, then there would be seven." Later he specifies that "the sixth and seventh (sovereigns) are found in the *Rumoi*, where the savages live, and some of them obey the two little *Roys* of Fire and Water as I noted above."[8]

3. Aymonier, pp. 41–42; A. Bergaigne, "L'ancien royaume de Champa dans l'Indo-Chine d'après les inscriptions," *Journal Asiatique* 11 (1888): 86; Finot, pp. 638–39.

4. Aymonier, pp. 43–44; Maspéro, pp. 6–7.

5. Louis Finot, "Notes d'épigraphie," *BEFEO* 15, no. 2 (1915): 6, 50.

6. Cristoforo Borri, *Cochinchina: Containing Many Admirable Rarities and Singularities of That Countrey*, translation (London: Robert Ashley for Richard Clutterbuck, 1633), pp. Bl, B2.

7. This map is reproduced in Henri Maitre, *Les Jungles Moi* (Paris: Larose, 1912), p. 552.

8. G. F. Marini, *Relation nouvelle et curieuse des royaumes de Tunquin et de Lao*, translation (Paris: Gervais Clouzier, 1666), pp. 34–35.

In 1641 a Dutchman named Gerrit Van Wusthoff traveled through Laos and Cambodia, and his account of the journey was annotated by Francis Garnier.[9] On 5 August 1641 Van Wusthoff reached the Cambodian town of Sambok on the east bank of the Mekong river near the present city of Kratie (see map 4), and he described how the Chinese merchants traded with a place in the remote interior called Phnough. Garnier interprets this as a deformation of *Phnong*, a Cambodian designation for the highland people, which, now spelled *Pnong*, is still used, particularly to refer to those in northeastern Cambodia. In his annotation, Garnier notes that *Phnong* would include the "Bnong, Cedar, Banar, etc.," which more than likely are references to the Mnong, Sedang, and Bahnar. Van Wusthoff noted that the Chinese traded salt, Chinese faience, and iron for slaves, gold, deerskin, wax, rhinoceros horns, elephant tusks, and gamboge.

During the latter part of the nineteenth century, French sources on the highlands invariably referred to the inhabitants by the pejorative Vietnamese term *mọi* or the French *sauvages*. It was not until the 1950s that the French began using *montagnards* (mountaineers or highlanders) in their literature and official documents. This term also became the common designation found in English-language newspapers and magazines. Some French social scientists have more recently begun to use the term *Proto-Indochinois* (Proto-Indochinese), although it is not clear what they mean by "Indochinese." The Viet Minh movement for a long time designated all of the upland people as *dân tộc thiểu số* (minority peoples), while the South Vietnamese in the 1950s began calling the highland people *người thượng* (highlanders) or *đồng bào thượng* (highland compatriots). More recently the official designation was broadened to *sắc tộc*, a term meant to embrace all of the ethnic minorities.

Since the beginning of the twentieth century there has been considerable reporting on the highlanders. Taking some of the available data in the literature, along with information resulting from my own ethnographic survey, it is possible to present a general view of highland societies, specifically of settlement patterns and house types, some aspects of religious beliefs and practices, livelihood activities, kinship and marriage patterns, and village leadership. However, prior to that, it is important to consider the matter of ethnic differentiation—the individual ethnic group identities of these peoples.

9. Francis Garnier, "Voyage lointain aux royaumes de Cambodge et Laouwen par les Neerlandais et ce qui s'y est passé jusqu'en 1644," *Bulletin de la Société de Géographie*, September-October 1871, pp. 253–55.

ETHNIC DIFFERENTIATION

The present study included an ethnographic survey of the highlands (see map 3). This involved an examination of ethnic boundaries based on views expressed by highland informants concerning their own and other ethnic identities. The initial question in the matter of ethnic differentiation is whether all of the people found in the central highlands can be said to have ethnic identities (that is, whether they all are aware of belonging to ethnic groups). On the basis of his research in highland Burma, Leach observes that all too often there is an erroneous notion that "in a 'normal' ethnographic situation one ordinarily finds distinct 'tribes' distributed about the map in orderly fashion with clear-cut boundaries between them." Noting that many ethnographic monographs suggest this is the case, he adds, "My own view is that the ethnographer has often only managed to discern the existence of a 'tribe' because he took it as axiomatic that this kind of cultural entity must exist. Many such tribes are, in a sense, ethnographic fictions."[10]

Where it appears that ethnic identities do exist, the next task is to differentiate one from the other and to determine the ethnic boundaries. Barth defines these as "social boundaries, though they may have territorial counterparts," which are "maintained by a limited set of cultural features."[11] To this end it is necessary to review first the ethnic distinctions that have been proposed by previous investigators, and this raises the question of ethnic labels. Most of the highland groups are called by a variety of names and the transcriptions of these names usually vary. Often the ethnic label commonly used in the literature is not the name by which the members of the group refer to themselves, although in many cases they recognize and accept the designation used by others. Each case must be considered individually, and the general rule in this study will be to retain the ethnic labels and transcriptions that have occurred very frequently in the literature, so as to avoid further complicating the already confused ethnic picture. There seems to be no point at this time in changing the name or spelling of a label such as *Rhadé*, which has been used in the literature for eighty years, to the more exact *Edê* or the more phonetic *Raday*.

10. Edmund Leach, *Political Systems of Highland Burma* (Cambridge: Harvard University Press, 1954), pp. 290–91.
11. Fredrik Barth, ed., *Ethnic Groups and Boundaries: The Social Organization of Culture Difference* (Boston: Little, Brown, 1969), intro. pp. 15, 38.

Sorting out the ethnic groups involves an examination not only of ethnographic literature but also of some of the more recent linguistic research, particularly since there has been a tendency on the part of some of the researchers to treat language groups as ethnic groups. Leach found this in Burma, noting that there often is an assumption by investigators that "a group which speaks a distinct language or dialect is, by definition, a separate tribe or tribal section," so that "each such section is then treated as a distinct cultural and ethnographic entity with a distinct history and a separate continuity in time." [12]

There has been, however, more linguistic than ethnographic research done in the central highlands, and it has included considerable lexicostatistical analysis. The result is a comprehensive identification of language groups and historic relationships still manifest among these groups. Since any discussion of ethnic group identity must invariably consider language groups, it would be wise to review the linguistic picture.

The languages spoken by the highlanders belong either to the Austronesian (Malayopolynesian) or Mon Khmer families. The Austronesian languages include Hroy, Rade (Rhadé), Jarai, Chru, Rai (Seyu), and Roglai (which has three dialects—Northern Roglai, Southern Roglai, and Cac Gia); together with the Cham language, they form the Chamic group within the Austronesian family. Dyen notes that "a somewhat rough lexicostatistical count for Rade [Rhadé], Jarai, Chru, Cham, and Roglai indicates beyond question that these languages are at least very closely related and in some cases may even be dialects of the same language; the latter is strongly suggested for Rade and Jarai." [13] On the basis of lexicostatistical evidence, Dyen places the Chamic languages in the West Indonesian group of languages, so their nearest relatives are the languages of Borneo, Sumatra, Java, and Bali.

Research by the Summer Institute of Linguistics (SIL) has intensely focused on the Mon Khmer languages. The Mon Khmer family is one of four that comprise the Austroasiatic stock (the other three families are Munda, Malacca, and Nicobarese). On the basis of lexicostatistical and other supporting evidence, Thomas and Headley divide the Mon Khmer languages into nine branches—Pearic, Khmer, Bahnaric, Katuic, Khmuic, Monic, Palaungic, Khasi, and Viet-Muong. Mon Khmer languages spoken

12. Leach, *Political Systems*, p. 291.
13. Isidore Dyen, "The Chamic Languages," in *Current Trends in Linguistics*, ed. E. Sebeok (The Hague and Paris: Mouton, 1971), 8: 200–10.

by the highlanders belong to either the Bahnaric or the Katuic branches. Thomas reports that within the Bahnaric branch, the North Bahnaric subgrouping contains Bahnar, Rengao, Sedang, Halang, Jeh, Monom, Kayong, Hre, Cua, Takua, and Todrah. Smith, a member of the SIL, proposed that within the North Bahnaric there be an Eastern North Bahnaric subdivision, composed of Cua and Kotua. The South Bahnaric subgrouping, according to Thomas, includes Stieng, Central Mnong (Preh, Biat, etc.), Southern Mnong (Nong, Prang), Eastern Mnong (Gar, Chil, Kuanh, Rolom), Koho, and Chrau. The Katuic branch contains seventeen languages, five of which are spoken in the Vietnamese highlands. These are Katu, Kantu (High Katu), Phuang, Bru, and Pacoh.[14]

The question of whether the Vietnamese language basically is Tai or Mon Khmer has long been discussed by investigators. In 1912 Henri Maspéro concluded that the Vietnamese language evolved through a fusion of Mon Khmer and Tai dialects with a third, unknown dialect, and subsequently there was considerable borrowing of Chinese words. He saw the dominant influence on modern Vietnamese as being Tai, and he felt that therefore Vietnamese should be considered to have been originally a Tai language.[15] French linguist Haudricourt, however, considers the long centuries of Chinese domination over the Tai groups and the Vietnamese as accounting for their evolutionary linguistic convergence. He would classify Vietnamese as an Austroasiatic language, closely related to the Mon Khmer.[16]

In 1942 Benedict put forth a scheme in which Vietnamese and Mon Khmer would comprise one group of the three that make up the Proto-Austric languages in Southeast Asia. (One of the other groups would include Thai, Kadai, and Indonesian, while the third group would be composed of the Miao-Yao languages.) More recently, Benedict has re-iterated this alignment, noting that the Vietnamese language "seems to represent the old northeastern 'anchor' of the Austroasiatic bloc, heavily

14. David Thomas and R. K. Headley, Jr., "More on Mon-Khmer Subgroupings," *Lingua* 25, no. 4 (1970): 398–418; David Thomas, "A Note on the Branches of Mon-Khmer," *Mon-Khmer Studies IV*, Language Series no. 2, Center for Vietnamese Studies and Summer Institute of Linguistics (Saigon, 1973), pp. 138–41; and Kenneth Smith, "Eastern North Bahnaric: Cua and Kotua," *Mon-Khmer Studies IV*, Language Series no. 2, Center for Vietnamese Studies and Summer Institute of Linguistics (Saigon, 1973), pp. 138–41.

15. Henri Maspéro, "Etudes sur la phonétique historique de la langue Annamite," *BEFEO* 12, no. 1 (1912): 117–18.

16. A. G. Haudricourt, "La place du Vietnamien dans les langues Austroasiatiques," *Bulletin de la Société Linguistique de Paris* 49 (1953): 122–28.

overlain from early times with Thai elements, including the old Thai (and Chinese) tonal system." [17]

In a 1973 article, Thomas classifies the Viet-Muong branch, which includes Vietnamese, Muong, May, Arem, and Tay Pong, within the Austroasiatic stock. While Muong, May, Arem, and Tay Pong are placed "solidly within Mon-Khmer, Vietnamese is 'slightly apart from Mon-Khmer.'" He concludes that this divergence of Vietnamese is due to heavy outside, mainly Chinese, influences. [18]

The next step in this analysis is to determine whether these linguistic groupings correspond in any way to ethnic distinctions discerned by my own survey and/or those proposed by other investigators. Among Austronesian language groups (those reported are the Jarai, Rhadé, Chru, Roglai, and Rai) only the first four are identified as ethnic groups. The status of the Rai cannot be determined because of insufficient research on them.

The Jarai, sometimes spelled Djarai or Jorai, are the most numerous of the highland groups (see appendix A). While the Jarai are clearly an identifiable ethnic group, there is considerable variation on the part of investigators as to subgroups. This raises the question of whether those identified as subgroups actually are groups at all in terms of identity or whether the labels simply indicate a location. Then, too, there is the question of whether those that are subgroups have any unique cultural features that set them apart from the other Jarai.

Henri Maitre, the French explorer who was one of the first to report extensively on the highlanders, describes the major Jarai groups as the He Drong (or He Grong), Habau, and Arap. He also notes that to the east of these groups there are smaller groups that display both Jarai and Rhadé characteristics: the Krung, Chur, Mdhub, and Blao (or Bloo). A 1959 North Vietnamese source reports that the Jarai are subdivided into the Hdrung, Hbau, A-rap, and To-buan. A South Vietnamese work lists the Arap, Hdrung, Tobuan, Mada, Chochom, Hedrong, Hebau, Chur and Bloo. [19]

---

17. Paul Benedict, "Thai, Kadai, and Indonesian: A New Alignment in Southeastern Asia," *American Anthropologist* 44 (1942): 576–601; idem, "Austro-Thai," *Behavior Science Notes* 1, no. 4 (1966): 227–61.

18. Thomas, "Branches of Mon-Khmer," pp. 139–41.

19. Maitre, *Les Jungles Moi*, pp. 398–99; Nhóm Nghiên Cứu Dân Tộc (People's Study Group), *Các Dân Tộc Thiểu Số Ở Việt-Nam* (Minority Peoples of Vietnam) (Hanoi: Nhà Xuất Bản Văn Hóa, 1960), p. 248; and Nguyễn Trắc Dĩ, *Đồng Bào Các Sắc-Tộc Thiểu Số Việt-Nam* (Vietnamese Ethnic Minority Compatriots), Bộ Phát-Triển Sắc-Tộc (Ministry for Ethnic Minority Development) (Saigon, 1972), p. 63.

French anthropologist Lafont divides the Jarai into the Arap, Habau, Hedrung, Sesan, Chu Ty, and Plei Kly. Dournes, another French anthropologist, reports a number of widely scattered Jarai subgroupings. In the vicinity of the Hodrung mountain, close to Pleiku city, are the Hodrung, and to the northwest of them, extending into neighboring Kontum province, are the Arap. The Pouh also are in the same general area. The Cebuan (or Tobuan) are on the western limit of the Jarai country, where they spill across the border into Cambodia. To the southeast of Pleiku in the vicinity of Cheo Reo (the name was changed to Hau Bon by the Vietnamese government, but it continues to be known by all as Cheo Reo) at the confluence of the Ayun and Apa (Ba is the Vietnamese name) rivers are the Cor, the subgroup studied by Dournes. Southeast of the Cor are the Mthur (or Mdhur), and still farther south are the Bblo, Ronying, Kodrao, and Koah. Southwest of the area occupied by the Cor, Dournes reports, are groups called the Trung and Tham, both of which represent a mixture of the Jarai and Rhadé. To the east of Cheo Reo in the mountains are the Hroai (or Hroy), a Jarai subgroup, and Dournes mentions a group called Hroai-Cham, a mixture of the Hroai and Cham.[20]

Jarai informants from varying locations only identify the Hodrung, Arap, Tobuan, Cor, Mdhur, and Hroy as subgroups. Other designations, such as Plei Kly, Chu Ty, and Sesan, all refer to locations; they are not subgroup names. They note that *Cor* is a term used to refer to a small number of villages in the Ayun river area not far from Cheo Reo. Jarai leader Nay Luett, whose mother is Mdhur and whose father is Hroy, considers both groups "Jarai in all respects." It was noted at the beginning of this chapter that a Cham inscription from the mid-twelfth century mentions a highland group called the Mada, which Georges Maspéro interpreted as a variation of Mdhur. Given their location as one of the easternmost groups of the Jarai, it is quite possible that historically they had contact with the Cham, who called them Mada.

The Jarai informants also identified the Hodrung, Arap, and Tobuan as subgroups located in the western Jarai country. Finally, they pointed out that the Trung are a mixture of Jarai and Rhadé, but their language is closer to that of the Rhadé, who call them Krung. Some informants from this

20. Pierre-Bernard Lafont, *Toloi Djuat: Coutumier de la tribu Jarai* (Paris: Ecole Française d'Extrême-Orient, 1963), p. 11; Jacques Dournes, *Coordonnées structures Jörai familiales et sociales* (Paris: Travaux et Mémoires de l'Institut d'Ethnologie, 1972), pp. 17–22; and idem, "Recherches sur le Haut Champa," *France-Asie* 24, no. 2 (1970): 157.

group identify themselves as Krung, but when the matter was discussed with Nay Ri, a Jarai, he said that some fellow students from this group became irate if called Krung or Trung, insisting that they were Jarai. Further investigation may well reveal that the Krung (or Trung) are in the process of diverging from the Rhadé and Jarai and developing their own ethnic identity.

Arap and Tobuan informants identify themselves by those names, adding that they are Jarai. In his study of the Jarai, Dournes emphasizes the importance of affiliation to matrilineai clans and the role of women as cultural features essential to being Jarai.[21] Yet the Arap and Tobuan do not have descent through the female line; nor do they have matrilineal clans, although older members recall some clan names that were used in the past (see below for further discussion of kinship systems). There are also other cultural features, such as communal men's houses, which are not shared by other Jarai. These variations raise the question of whether the Arap and Tobuan should properly be considered part of the Jarai ethnic group, and my view is that further investigation might reveal that both subgroups are in the process of developing ethnic identities separate from the Jarai.

The Rhadé, sometimes transcribed as Rade or Raday, call themselves Êdê, taken from *Anak H'de* or "Children of H'de." Informants point out that the neighboring Jarai refer to them as Rodé, from which the French derived the name Rhadé, and this has come to be the designation used in most western literature. The Vietnamese, however, have always called them Êdê and this continues to be the name used in Vietnamese sources.

Maitre reports that the subgroups of the Rhadé are the Kpa, Atham, and Dle-Rue and that neighboring groups include the Ktul, Bih, Epan, Blo, K'ah, K'drao, and H'wing, all of whose languages are close to Rhadé.[22] Jouin, a French doctor who practiced for many years in Ban Me Thuot, lists the Kpa, Mdur, A'dham, K'tul, Epan, Blo, K'ah, K'drao, and H'wing as subgroups.[23] In his unpublished study of Rhadé customs, civil servant Y Dhuat Nie Kdam describes the Êdê-Kpa as the group in the vicinity of Ban Me Thuot (the Vietnamese government changed the name to Lac Giao, but it is still generally known as Ban Me Thuot). Northwest of the town are the

21. Dournes, *Coordonnées structures Jörai*, pp. 7–13; idem, "Patao, les maîtres des états," *Asie du Sud-Est et Monde Insulindien*, 4 (1973): xix–xxvi.

22. Maitre, *Les Jungles Moi*, pp. 399–400.

23. Bernard Jouin, *La Mort et la tombe: l'abandon de la tombe* (Paris: Institut d'Ethnologie, 1949), pp. 132–93.

Adham. To the east are the Ktul, also called the Dlie-rue, the Blo, and Epan. The Rhadé Mdhur are in the northeastern part of the Rhadé country, and their dialect is closer to that of the Jarai Mdhur. To the south of Ban Me Thuot are the Bih. Rhadé informants invariably agree with Y Dhuat's view of the Rhadé subgroups.[24]

The Chru are also referred to as Churu and Cado, and according to information in their oral tradition related by Touneh Han Tho the Chru ethnic identity evolved as a result of intermarriage between Cham, who took refuge in the Danhim valley as the Vietnamese threatened their last coastal enclaves, and the indigenous Roglai and Koho-speaking people. The Cham on the coast referred to the group in the Danhim valley as the Cham-Ro or "Cham in Refuge," and this eventually became Chru. The Indian script traditionally used by the Cham also was employed by the Chru but, though it still is known by a few elderly men, it has for the most part been replaced by a romanized script. Condominas reports that in the area of Fyan at the south end of the Danhim valley there is a group called the Kudduu, but anthropologist Sister Albina Afferreiros points out that, according to Chru informants, *Kudduu* is a designation which the Chil and Lat use to refer to the Chru (it would appear to be a variation of the name *Cado* noted above).[25]

The Roglai call themselves Orang Glai (People of the Forest) and are dispersed in three groupings. The northern group of Roglai in the mountains west of coastal Nhatrang are sometimes called Radlai or Adlai. The southern group is scattered in present Thuan Hai province, while another small grouping, called Cac Gia by the Vietnamese, are in the highlands northwest of the coastal city of Phan Rang.

Turning now to the Mon Khmer-speaking groups, we shall begin with the northernmost, the Katuic branch, which contains five languages— Bru, Pacoh, Katu, Kantu (High Katu), and Phuang. The Bru and Pacoh are relatively well identified as ethnic groups, and it appears that the Kantu (High Katu) are ethnically Katu. Given their geographic inaccessibility, the Phuang have not been subject so far to ethnographic research so it is not possible at this time to determine their ethnic identity.

24. Nie Kdam, Y Dhuat, "Customs of the Rhadé Highlanders in Darlac Province" (translation from Rhadé), 1967, pp. 1–3.

25. Georges Condominas, *Nous avons mangé la forêt de la Pierre-Génie Goo* (Paris: Mercure de France, 1952), p. 15; Albina Afferreiros, "Les Kon Cau de la Da-Nying," mimeographed (Paris, 1971), pp. i–v.

The Bru, as they refer to themselves, are known variously as the Muong Leung, Kalo, Khua, Tri, Leu, and Mangoong. The Vietnamese refer to them and the neighboring Pacoh as the Van Kieu, and one South Vietnamese source explicitly describes the Bru and Pacoh as being one ethnic group called Pacoh.[26] While conducting research on the Bru and Pacoh in 1966 and 1967 in collaboration with SIL researchers John Miller and Richard Watson, Bru and Pacoh informants unanimously expressed the view that these were separate groups. Pacoh (People of the Mountains) informants pointed out that some of their people who live at lower elevations and whose dialect is influenced by Vietnamese are called Pahi, but they still are considered part of the Pacoh.

While the Katu are now identified as an ethnic group, there are indications that this ethnic label and perhaps their ethnic identity are of recent origin. Le Pichon reports that in 1913 Sogny, a French official in Quang Nam province, sought to prove that the highlanders who had been harassing Vietnamese settlements were "Mọi" who formed a distinct "race" with its own dialect.[27] Sogny conducted a survey of 250 villages and reported a population of 10,000 to which he gave the name Ka-Tu (which in their language means "savage"). This designation was accepted by the French administration and subsequently appeared on documents and ethnolinguistic maps. Le Pichon also notes that when he visited the area in the mid-1930s he inquired of the villagers whether they were "Katu." Invariably they denied that they were, quickly declaring that the "Katu" were those who lived at higher elevations. They identified themselves by the names of the villages from which they came. I encountered a similar situation when in 1957 I visited the villages in the vicinity of the Ben Giang river, an area said to be inhabited by the "Katu." The villagers claimed that they did not call themselves Katu but rather by the names of their natal communities. But the name Katu continued to appear on maps as well as in North Vietnamese and South Vietnamese censuses and books. By 1964 the informants from both the Communist-controlled and Saigon government-controlled areas of Quang Nam province who assisted SIL researcher Nancy Costello were identifying themselves as Katu. Since then, delegates to various ethnic minorities gatherings in Saigon also have called themselves Katu.

26. Nguyễn Trắc Dĩ, *Đồng Bào Các Sắc-Tộc*, p. 11.
27. J. Le Pichon, "Les Chasseurs de sang," *Bulletin des Amis du Vieux Hué* 25 (1938): 359–64.

Katu trading party at a Giang river settlement (1957)

This poses the question of whether prior to 1913 a Katu ethnic identity existed. It is quite possible that the population now called Katu lived in their villages without any group identity or any common designation for themselves. As contact with outsiders who called them Katu increased, they may have come to accept this designation (as the Anak H'de came to know themselves as Rhadé), and an ethnic group identity coalesced.

Costello describes the "two main groups of Katu" as the High Katu living at higher elevations close to the border of Laos and the Low Katu living in the lower areas near the coastal plain.[28] The Katu also are known as the Teu, Attouat, Kao, Khat, Thap, Nguon Ta, Ta River Van Kieu, Phuong Katu, and Kato.

To the south of the Katuic linguistic branch of the Mon Khmer family is the North Bahnaric branch, which includes the Bahnar, Rengao, Sedang, Halang, Jeh, Monom, Kayong, Hre, Cua, Takua, and Todrah languages. I have indicated previously that recently another language of the North Bahnaric branch called Kotua has been identified. On the basis of ethnographic research done thus far, the Bahnar, Rengao, Sedang, Halang, Jeh, Monom, Hre, and Cua are the ethnic groups that can be identified. Lack of ethnographic research prevents our determining whether the Kayong, Kotua, Todrah, and Takua speakers belong to any of the ethnic groups

28. Nancy Costello, "Socially Approved Homicide among the Katu," *SA* 2, no. 1 (1972): 77.

already identified. For example, are those who speak Takua actually of the Cua ethnic group, and by the same token are the Todrah speakers really Sedang?

The Bahnar are the largest and most widespread of the Mon Khmer-speaking groups in the highlands. French administrator Guilleminet reports that the subgroups of the Bahnar include the Alakong and Tolo north and south of An Khe respectively. To the west of An Khe are the Bahnar Bonom (Bahnar of the Forest) and the Bahnar Golar. East of Pleiku city are four small groups known collectively as Bahnar To Sung. Those in the immediate vicinity of Kontum town are known as Bahnar Kontum, and just to the northeast are the Jolong. Guilleminet also reports additional small subgroups—the Bahnar Ho Drong of Dak Doa, some thirty kilometers southeast of Kontum town; the Bahnar Krem north of An Khe; and

Cua children at Tra Bong

Bahnar Jolong pirogues along the Bla river near Kontum (1956)

the Bahnar Kon Do De in the immediate vicinity of An Khe. He also considers the Rengao a subgroup of the Bahnar.[29] A South Vietnamese source lists the subgroups of the Bahnar as the Bonam, Hrui, Jolong, Konko, Krem, Roh, Tolo, Monam, Rengao, and Alakong.[30]

Bahnar informants in Kontum do not distinguish between those in the Kontum area and the Jolong. The Jolong refer to all Bahnar farther south collectively as "Tolo," although Bahnar Golar and Bonom informants, as well as Christian and Missionary Alliance members with long experience in the area, distinguish the Tolo as a specific Bahnar subgroup located south of An Khe. These sources also identify the Bahnar Kon Kodreh, located along the Ba river south of An Khe, and the Bahnar Krem to the north of the Mang Yang pass and An Khe (although sometimes the latter are described as being a mixed Bahnar-Cham group).[31] The Golar are located east of Pleiku, closer to the city than are the Krem, while to the northeast are the Bonom. In the vicinity of An Khe are the Alakong, but informants note that some Bahnar use this designation to include the Krem and Kon Kodreh.

29. Paul Guilleminet, "Recherches sur les croyances des tribus du Haut-Pays d'Annam, les Bahnar du Kontum et leurs voisins les magiciens," *IIEH* 4 (1941): 12–13.

30. Nguyễn Trắc Dĩ, *Đồng Bào Các Sắc-Tộc*, p. 38.

31. Rolf A. Stein, "Le Lin-Yi," *Han Hiue: Bulletin du Centre d'Etudes Sinologiques de Pékin* 2 (1947): 227–29.

The Rengao are sometimes referred to as Reungao or Rongao, and there has been some disagreement as to whether they are a subgroup of the Bahnar or a separate ethnic group. It was noted above that Guilleminet considers them Bahnar, and this also is the view of Father Kemlin, a member of the Kontum Mission.[32] More recently, however, Gregerson has hypothesized from new ethnographic research that the Rengao are a separate ethnic group.[33] Two of the subgroups of the Rengao are the Rengao Homong and Kon Hongo, and there are villages north of Kontum whose residents describe themselves as Sedang-Rengao and Bahnar-Rengao.

According to Devereux, the designation *Sedang* is the name the French used for the group that call themselves Ha(rh)ndea(ng).[34] Smith reports that the word *roteang* (highlander) is the name by which they refer to themselves.[35] Informants report that other designations are Rotea (or Sotea), Hadang, and Hoteang. A North Vietnamese source reports that subgroups of the Sedang (Xó-đăng is the Vietnamese transcription) include the Duong, Cor (or Ta-Cor), Hre, and Halang, although these last two are considered by every other source to be separate ethnic groups.[36] This North Vietnamese work also describes the To-drah or "those who live in the sparse forest" as a subgroup of the Sedang. (It was noted previously that SIL researcher Smith classifies the Todrah language as distinct from the language of the Sedang.)

While conducting periodic ethnographic research on the Halang with James Cooper of the SIL between 1965 and 1972, informants reiterated that they, the Halang, are a distinct ethnic group: Halang is their only designation and they have no subgroups. During this same period, research on the Jeh in cooperation with Pat Cohen and Dwight Gradin of the SIL revealed that they are a separate ethnic group with no subgroups. Monom informants affirm that although they are a small group (seven villages), they consider themselves separate from their neighbors. Also in the late 1960s, research on the Cua by Eva Burton and Jacqueline Maier ascertained that the Cua identify themselves as a separate group. Among

---

32. J. E. Kemlin, "Alliances chez les Reungao," *BEFEO* 17 (1917): 1–10.

33. Marilyn J. Gregerson, "The Ethnic Minorities of Vietnam," *SA* 2, no. 1 (1972): 12–15.

34. Georges Devereux, "Functioning Units in Ha(rh)ndea(ng) Society," *Primitive Man* 10 (1937): 1–8.

35. Kenneth Smith, "More on Sedang Ethnodialects," *Mon Khmer Studies IV*, Language Series no. 2, Center for Vietnamese Studies and Summer Institute of Linguistics (Saigon, 1973), p. 43.

36. Nhóm Nghiên Cứu Dân Tộc, *Các Dân Tộc Thiểu Số Ở Việt-Nam*, p. 246.

themselves they refer to those at higher elevations as Kor, Koh, Dot, and Yot, and Cua in the valleys are known as Traw and Dong.

Research conducted with Hre-speaking informants in collaboration with Oliver Trebilco, an Australian missionary who was affiliated with the World Evangelization Crusade, revealed that the designation *Hre* came to be applied to this language group by the French earlier in the century and became the ethnic label used for the population in the larger area. Previously the term *Hre* was only used by the indigenous population for those who lived along the Hre river (called the Song Re by the Vietnamese). Similarly, other segments of the population were known by the rivers on whose banks their villages stood. It is not clear whether they had distinct ethnic identities, but it appears that in the course of time, as contact among themselves and with the outside increased, most of the population came to refer to themselves as Hre, although there are some relatively isolated villagers who call themselves Rabah (Tava), Creq (Kare), and Taliang. The Vietnamese for many centuries have referred to the Hre as Đá-Vách and Mọi Dỗng.

The South Bahnaric linguistic branch encompasses the Stieng, Central Mnong (Preh, Biat, etc.), Southern Mnong (Nong, Prang), Eastern Mnong (Gar, Chil, Kuanh, Rolom), Koho, and Chrau. On the basis of ethnographic research done thus far, the Stieng and Mnong are relatively well identified, but the Koho language group should be divided into various ethnic groups. Those that are well identified are the Maa, Sre, and Lat, while the Tring, Nop, Rdaa, Koyon, Jroo, and Dalaa are less so. Also, it is doubtful that the Chrau language group can be considered an ethnic

A Stieng woman with ivory earplugs

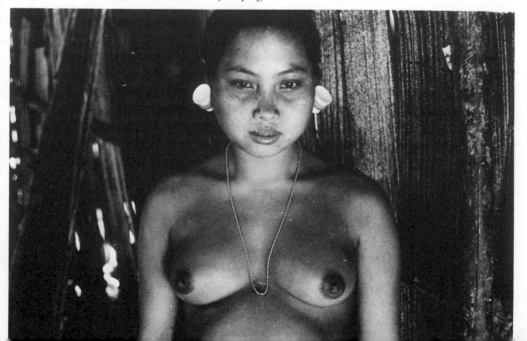

group. On the basis of present research, it appears that this language group is divided into several separate but related ethnic groups which may have fragmented from a larger ethnic group as the result of long contact with the Vietnamese. The Stieng have a well-defined ethnic identity, and while conducting research among them in 1966 and 1967 with Ralph Haupers of the SIL informants identified the Bulach, Budip, and Bulo as subgroups.

Those speaking languages of Central, Southern, and Eastern Mnong appear to belong to one widespread ethnic group called Mnong, which is composed of several subgroups. Condominas focused his research on a group he identifies as Mnong Gar, although he notes that they call themselves Phii Bree (People of the Forest). He also mentions the Mnong Cil, Mnong Rlam, and Mnong Prong. In an earlier brief study on the Mnong Rlam, Condominas refers to the Mnong Kuen and Mnong Dlie Rue.[37] Huard and Maurice list the Gar, Kil (Chil), Rlam, Preh, Bunor, Kpreng, Budong, and Biet. Jouin not only describes some Mnong subgroupings but makes further divisions within these. The Bu Nor are a grouping within the Mnong Nong; the Mnong Preh has within it the Preh Rlam, which in turn is divided into the Bu Rung, Dih Brih, Prong (R'but), and Bu Dong; and the Mnong Gar are divided into the Gar Cu and the Rlam.[38] One South Vietnamese source considers the Chil a separate ethnic group.[39]

Boulbet reports that in the vicinity of Di Linh (Djiring) and Bao Loc (Blao) in Lam Dong province, members of various ethnic groups refer to themselves collectively as Koon Cau (Sons of Men), a designation that differentiates them from the lowlanders—explicitly, the Koon Prum (Sons of Cham), Koon Kur (Sons of Khmer), Koon Yuon (Sons of Vietnamese), and Koon Toi or Parang (Sons of French).[40]

At the same time, however, the "Sons of Men" distinguish separate ethnic groups among themselves. The group located in the middle basin of the Dong Nai river is referred to as the Maa, and Boulbet lists the subgroupings as the Cau Maa, Maa Too, Cau Coop, Maa Huang, Boloo,

37. George Condominas, *Nous avons mangé la forêt*, pp. 13–19; idem,"Notes sur le Tam Bo Bae Baap Kuong (échange de sacrifices entre un enfant et ses père et mère) Mnong Rlam," *International Archives of Ethnography* 47, pt. 2 (1955): 127–30.

38. P. Huard and A. Maurice, "Les Mnong du plateau central Indochinois," *IIEH* 2 (1939): 27–30; Jouin, *La Mort et la tombe*, p. 167.

39. Nguyễn Trắc Dĩ, *Đồng Bào Các Sắc-Tộc*, p. 45.

40. Jean Boulbet, *Pays des Maa domaine des génies Nggar Maa, Nggar Yaang* (Paris: Ecole Française d'Extrême-Orient, 1967), pp. 132–37.

Two elderly Lat women

Preng, and Krung. He also reports that there are some small neighboring ethnic groups which he identifies as the Dalaa (or Talaa), Jroo, Koyon, and Nop. The ethnic map included in Boulbet's work contains another group called the Rdaa. Boulbet also identifies the Sree (normally spelled Sre) as a large group located to the east of the Maa. This group had earlier been identified by Queguiner and Dournes, and it is also identified by Sre informants.[41]

Informants from among the Lat (sometimes spelled Lac) describe their group as being separate from any neighboring ones. Their villages are located on the Lang Bian mountain near the city of Dalat ("Lat Water" in their language). Informants also report the identity of the Tring, although no ethnographic research has been conducted among them.

David Thomas of the SIL uses the term *Chrau* (which means "high-lander") to identify this language group, but he reports that those who speak this language have no general ethnic designation for themselves. Rather, they refer to themselves by local names, and there is some evidence that these may at one time have been names for kin groups—either matrilineages or matrilineal clans. Thomas reports that these groups are

41. Ibid., pl. 2; Dr. Queguiner, "Notes sur une peuplade moi de la Chaîne Annamitique sud: les Cau S're," *IIEH* 6 (1943): 395–97; Jacques Dournes, *Nri: recueil des coutumes Sre du Haut-Donnai* (Saigon: Editions France-Asie, 1951), pp. i–vi.

dispersed in the area east of Bien Hoa, with many of their villages interspersed among Vietnamese settlements. The local groups he describes include the Palay Jre, Palay Vajieng, Voq Twaq, Palay Mhat, Palay Mro, Palay Dijo, Palay Dijao, Palay Prang, Palay Swai, Vla, Dor, Boham, Jawan (or Chawang), Chalah, Chalun, Thuyuc, Yo Quang, Vato, and Vangot.[42]

THE HIGHLANDERS' WAY OF LIFE

Settlement Patterns and House Types

In many areas of the highlands, the disruptions since 1945 have drastically changed settlement patterns and house types. Vast numbers of highlanders were forced to leave their villages to live in resettlement and refugee camps built according to the specifications of outsiders. Before these things happened, the highlanders had always depended on knowledge handed down through past generations to select an efficacious site for their villages and build livable houses that would provide protection from wild animals and shelter from the elements. With some groups, these practical considerations were combined with ideational principles that dictated certain aspects of settlement pattern, as well as house form and decoration, with the aim of bringing well-being to the inhabitants. Further research might well reveal that some of these cultural features are important in maintaining ethnic identity.

Generally, the highlanders prefer to locate their villages on level, well-drained ground, near water sources, and accessible to forests. Until the arrival of outsiders, there were no towns in the highlands and, with some exceptions, most of the villages were relatively small. According to Cobbey, before events forced them into resettlement camps, the Northern Roglai did not cluster in villages but lived in isolated longhouses occupied by extended families. Reporting on Mnong Gar society in the early 1950s, Condominas describes the village of Sar Luc as having nine longhouses and a population of 146. Sedang informants report that their villages normally have between ten to twenty houses. Some High Katu informants claim that most of their settlements have around five or six dwellings, but the larger villages may have ten. In his 1938 publication on the Katu, however,

---

42. David Thomas, personal correspondence, 4 April 1974.

French administrator Le Pichon reported that some communities in the High Katu area included as many as fifty houses.[43]

Long-established Rhadé Kpa villages usually have between twenty to forty longhouses. Recently, Dournes described the Jarai village of Plei Pa as having sixty-five longhouses with 409 inhabitants and the village of Buon Ama Jong as having 276 residents in fifty-one longhouses.[44] According to Cua informants, before their villages were relocated in the 1960s, they had anywhere from ten to a hundred dispersed longhouses, and it was not unusual for one to have as many as 100 residents. An elderly Cua recalled that, in the past, some longhouses had around 500 inhabitants each, necessitating the use of a gong by the household head in order to assemble them all. Equally varied in size are the settlements of the Bahnar Golar. Some have two or three houses, others have over two hundred. One informant reported that his natal village had one hundred and eighty houses.

Among some groups the orientation of dwellings is based on weather patterns or the position of the sun, while with others the placement of houses in a village has to do with certain ideational guidelines. There are also groups whose dwellings have no particular orientation at all.

The Sedang are in the first category; they prefer not to have the morning sun strike the main entrance of the house. The Mnong Chil build their dwellings backed to the prevailing wind. Dournes points out that the longhouses of the Jarai Cor have a north-south orientation because of wind and rain patterns (they have the southwest and northeast rainy seasons) and the main entrance always faces south so that the sun may dry the rice, cotton, and other things they place out on the veranda.[45]

Among some highland groups the men's house—which in several cases functions more as a communal house—is an important institution, and its location often affects the orientation of dwellings in a settlement. Among the Halang all the houses in the village must face the men's house. High Katu informants report that their villages usually are shaped like a tilted "ell" with the top to the north and a row of dwellings oriented in a line from north to southwest. The "corner" of the "ell" is due west, and a second row of houses is oriented along a line to the southeast. Due east of

43. Vurnell Cobbey, "Some Northern Roglai Beliefs about the Supernatural," *SA* 2, no. 1 (1972): 125; Condominas, *Nous avons mangé la forêt*, pp. 16–21; Le Pichon, "Les Chasseurs de sang," p. 370.
44. Dournes, *Coordonnées structures Jörai*, pp. 22–29.
45. Ibid.

the "corner" is the stake where sacrificial animals are tied, and east of the
stake is the men's house. It is very important, the informants emphasize,
that at dawn the sun ascend behind the men's house.

The concept of "village" may incorporate a given territory in which the
residents farm, hunt, fish, and cut wood. For the Jeh this is the *sal ja*, for the
Sedang it is the *cheam bang*, and for the Pacoh it is the *cruang*. The Bru and
the Maa also have such territories. According to Guilleminet, those found
among the Bahnar are called *torings*, the ownership of which is shared by
several villages whose leaders cooperate in controlling any activities within
their boundaries.[46]

Most houses in the highlands are shared by more than one nuclear family
(parents and children), and some aspects of the kinship system, particularly
prescribed residence, affect the form of the house and interior floor-plan.
Generally, among those highland groups that have unilineal descent
systems—that is, descent traced through either the female line (matrilineal)
or the male line (patrilineal)—the living arrangements in the house tend to
be more rigidly defined than they are among those who trace descent
through both the male and female lines (bilateral). This is directly related to
the prescription, adhered to among those with unilineal descent, for the
married children to remain either with the wife's parents (matrilocal
residence, the rule when descent is matrilineal) or with the husband's
parents (patrilocal residence, the rule when descent is patrilineal). Among
those with bilateral descent, the pattern in the highlands is for the married
children to reside alternatively with both sets of parents (ambilocal residence), eventually settling with one or the other depending on which
needs them more. But many couples establish their own households
(neolocal residence). (For details on kinship and marriage see below and
appendix B.)

In spite of these and other variations, there are numerous common
features in house construction and use of available space throughout the
highlands. House construction is a cooperative effort of kin and neighbors,
and until recently all of the dwellings were constructed of locally available
building materials (roofing of tin and aluminum has become widespread).
The frame of the house most commonly consists of timber, often hardwood, and most houses are built on piling, which also provides the main
support for the roof. Bamboo is used extensively for floors, walls, and

46. Paul Guilleminet, "La Tribu Bahnar du Kontum," in *Actes du XXIe Congrès des Orientalistes*
(Paris: Imprimerie Nationale, Société Asiatique de Paris, 1949), pp. 383–84.

New thatching for a Jarai longhouse near Cheo Reo

interior partitions. Light and ventilation is provided in many houses by windows (which can be closed with bamboo screens) in the outside walls. Roofs are thatched with dried long grass, bunches of which are tied together and fixed to the roof frame with rattan cord.

Regardless of some differences in floor-plans, all highland houses devote the area along the walls to storage. In most cases, the things stored include personal belongings, such as clothes (particularly traditional garb worn during celebrations), blankets, mats, and looms. Invariably, there are the jars for alcohol and sets of gongs, both of which are prestige items that reflect the relative wealth of the family. In some houses, bins of paddy and firewood also are stacked along the walls. Farm tools, baskets of various types, traps, and weapons are placed on the rafters, and drying tobacco leaves will often be found hanging from the beams. All of the highland houses have open hearths for heating and cooking. Those used for preparing family meals usually have suspended over them several shelves of bamboo, which offer a convenient place to keep some cooking utensils as well as a good dry storage place for salt, tobacco, maize, rice ready for cooking, cooked meat wrapped in banana leaves, areca nuts, betel leaves, and dried fish. Pots for cooking, baskets for serving food, and gourds of drinking water sit near the hearth.

At the front entrances of many highland houses there are verandas of varying sizes. These verandas normally serve as storage areas for tools and chicken baskets, and they provide an excellent spot for sunning paddy, cotton, coconut shells (used for kindling), and the many kinds of roots and bark used in making alcohol. Very often paddy is husked on the veranda. This is done throughout the highlands by placing it in a hardwood mortar and pounding it with a long-handled wooden pestle. The area under the houses built on piling is usually used for storing firewood, and in some villages part of it serves as a pigsty.

It was indicated previously that among some highland groups every village has a men's house, and these are very similar in form and floor-plan. Invariably constructed on piling, all have high, sloping thatched roofs which are often graced with symbolic decorations. The frame of the men's house is of solid timber, and the walls are of bamboo. Inside are several hearths but no partitions, and the sleeping areas are carefully prescribed.

The Rhadé, Jarai, Roglai, Chru, Mnong, Sre, and Lat have matrilineal descent. In each of these groups a house is occupied by an extended family consisting of married daughters and their families. In most instances they have longhouses, the length of which is determined by the number of nuclear families in residence.

Religious Beliefs and Practices

In many respects, religion is omnipresent in the lives of the highlanders, and further research on ethnic boundaries would undoubtedly reveal that religious beliefs and practices frequently rank among those cultural features that help maintain such borders. The importance of religious beliefs in such things as settlement patterns and house construction among some groups has already been noted. With all of the highlanders, however, the house is, in addition to an abode, the place where religious celebrations are held. Supernatural beings play an important role in all of the origin myths recorded thus far, and all highlanders believe that supernatural forces guide the individual's destiny. An infant enters the world protected by a set of birth practices attuned to these forces, and there are amulets and rituals to sustain this protection throughout one's life. Since these supernatural forces determine whether crops will flourish or fail, they must be propitiated at planting time and given thanks at the harvest. If health fails or misfortune strikes, there are prescribed offerings to these forces so they will make things right. Those who attain power and wealth only do so because they are favored by the supernatural beings (see below). Celebrations that mark puberty and marriage have religious overtones. A complex of rituals surround death and the tomb, and the religious beliefs of all highland groups include some concept of a hereafter.

Traditional religious practices vary from one highland group to another but there are some common characteristics. By and large, religion is the affair of the family and village, and both family heads and village leaders organize and usually officiate at rituals, whether those held annually or those prescribed for times of stress. All of the highland pantheons include animistic spirits of varying kinds, and most groups have a particular variety called *yang*, or a cognate word thereof, regardless of whether their language is of the Austronesian or Mon Khmer stock.[47]

Among all of the highlanders there are shamans and sorcerers, and witchcraft is found in some groups. Macfarlane draws a useful distinction between witchcraft and sorcery that is applicable to the situation in the highlands: "Contrasting means to ends, 'witchcraft' is predominantly the pursuit of harmful ends by implicit internal means. 'Sorcery' combines harmful ends with explicit means."[48] In some highland groups there are those who have the inherent power to cause ill to others without performing any rituals or employing any kind of special medicines, and these individuals, in Macfarlane's definition, would be witches. There also are villagers who because of their *actions* (such as performing a special rite) can cause harm to others, and these are sorcerers. Then, too, there are individuals who are capable of communicating with supernatural beings, and their actions (which usually take the form of a ritual) are directed toward a beneficent end such as healing. They generally are described in the literature as shamans.

47. The Cham word *yang* is listed as meaning "spirit" in Gerard Moussay, *Dictionnaire Čam-Vietnamien-Français*, s.v. *yang, esprit*, and *génie*. In a discussion about the word *yang*, Frank Huffman, Professor of Linguistics at Cornell University, noted that in a survey he had conducted among Mon Khmer-speaking groups in Laos he found that the Ngeh, Alak, and Souei use the word *yaang* to indicate certain types of deities. In a similar discussion, Mathew Charles, an authority on Austronesian languages in Southeast Asia, pointed out that cognates of *yang* are found in some of the languages in Indonesia, Malaysia, and Malagasy. He explained that the old Javanese word *hyang*, meaning "godhead," is listed in H. N. Van der Tuuk, *Kawi-Balineesch-Nederlandsch woordenboek*, 1 (1897), s.v. *hyang*, and in R. J. Wilkinson, *A Malay-English Dictionary* (romanized), s.v. *yang*, the word *yang* is translated as "divinity." or "godhead," usually being used in compounds such as *sangyang* (to indicate a major Hindu divinity) and *sembahyang* (prayer). In G. Ferrand, *La Langue Malgache*, 2 vols., Feestbundel uitgegeven door het Koninklijk Bataviaasch Genootschap van Kunsten en Wetenschappen (Weltevreden: G. Kolff & Co., 1929), 1: 182, 186, it is noted that in Arabic-Malagasy manuscripts the Old Malagasy word *yang* is used to mean "divinity."

48. A. D. J. Macfarlane, "Definitions of Witchcraft," in *Witchcraft and Sorcery*, ed. M. Marwick, Penguin Modern Sociology Readings (Middlesex, England: C. Nicholls & Company; 2d ed., 1972), pp. 41–44.

For example, both witchcraft and sorcery exist among the Jarai. Lafont describes the *molai* as one whose head is the abode of a malevolent spirit that departs in the night to devour the soul of a victim.[49] By the above definition this person would be a witch. Jarai Arap informants point out that the molai does not perform any rites or employ any talismans and may not even be aware of this power. They add that some of these witches "eat the liver" of the victim and carry away blood in a gourd. Usually, if the shaman determines that illness is due to a witch, he or the victim makes an accusation, and anyone found guilty of witchcraft is subjected to severe punishment. If the victim dies, the witch is taken to the forest and executed. It is not uncommon throughout the Jarai country for the victim's family to take revenge on the accused witch. In 1957, in a discussion of witchcraft, Jarai leader Nay Moul expressed concern over the number of such incidents in the vicinity of Cheo Reo and blamed the shamans who, he felt, were using their power to take revenge on their enemies. The solution, he thought, would be to put all of the shamans in one village where they could be kept under surveillance. In 1965 an epidemic struck villages near Cheo Reo, and when the residents of one village pressured their shaman for a solution he revealed that a woman of the village was a molai causing the illness. In a rage the villagers stormed her house, chopping off her head as well as those of her husband and three children. Lafont also describes a sorcerer (*rohung*) who makes an alliance with an evil spirit that enables him to eat the soul of a victim, causing death, and notes that there are magicians who, it is said, receive their initiation in Laos.[50]

There are among the Jarai three special shamans: the King of Fire (*Potao Apui*), the King of Water (*Potao Ea*), and the King of the Wind (*Potao Angin*). The King of Fire and King of Water, both of whom are considered to be more powerful than the King of the Wind, also are better known in the highlands and more frequently mentioned in the literature. The King of Fire, who must be of the Siu clan, derives his power by being guardian of a sacred saber, and his authority extends over the eastern side of the cordillera. The King of Water is of the Rcom clan, and his talisman is a sacred rattan whip that has remained green through the long centuries. The western side of the mountain chain is his domain of authority. Whereas after death a Jarai normally is buried, the remains of these three shamans are cremated.

49. Lafont, *Toloi Djuat*, p. 234.
50. Ibid.

Dressing out a sacrificial buffalo in a Jarai village

Throughout the highlands there is a similarity in the format of ceremonies performed in conjunction with religious beliefs and practices. All
of them involve invocations to explicit deities, and these invariably are
accompanied by offerings of food and a jar (or jars) of alcohol. Normally
an animal is slaughtered as an offering, and depending on the type of ritual
it may be a chicken, goat, pig, buffalo, or occasionally a dog. Smaller
animals are killed swiftly by cutting the throat, but the larger animals,
particularly buffalos, are tied to a stake and killed more slowly with sabers
and/or spears. In a typical Jarai ceremony, several men with sabers dance
around the sacrificial animal and then one of them suddenly cuts the
tendons of the rear legs. The dance continues, and finally the buffalo is
killed with a blow to the back of the neck. The flesh and blood of the
sacrificial animals are served in the feasting that is part of highland ceremonies, and the alcohol, which also is part of the offerings, is drunk from
the jars through bamboo tubes. Gongs and drums are played when the
animals are being slaughtered as well as during the feasting. Gongs, jars,
and jar alcohol are discussed in appendix B.

Most of the highlanders bury their dead. The only exception is the Jarai
Mdhur, who Dournes reports cremate their dead, and he notes that in the
past this was the practice of the Rcom clan in the vicinity of Cheo Reo
too.[51] Usually there are ritual offerings made at the time of burial, and

51. Dournes, "Recherches sur le Haut Champa," p. 157.

some groups have subsequent ceremonies several years after the burial to "abandon the tomb."

Both Costello and Le Pichon report that among the Katu there are several forms of socially approved homicide.[52] One is related to the spirits of the "dog stone" and the black cobra. A "dog stone" is any white stone with a shape that suggests a dog. It is believed to be the manifestation of a particularly powerful spirit. Should someone come upon such a stone, the spirit may compel him to slaughter a victim so as to offer his blood to the spirit. Similarly, if one should encounter a black cobra in the forest, he must decide to do so, then he must offer human blood to this spirit. The blood may be obtained from a newly slaughtered victim or a live victim, and either victim is sought by organizing a raid on a distant village. If the blood of a dead person is to be offered, the killing is done in the victim's village, and that is the task of the one who must appease the spirit. Only males are considered appropriate victims in this type of raid, and there is great prestige to be gained by killing a village headman. After the person is slain, the one who must make the offering dips a spear in the blood. If the victim is a headman or someone of equal status, his head is severed. When the raiding party return to their village, the head is placed in a special hut that is entered only when the villagers need the help of the spirits associated with the heads. There also is a three-day celebration during which the blood is offered to the spirit while everyone dances to gong music and drinks from the jars. After the blood is offered on the first day, the killer and his raiding party retreat to the men's house where they remain for a month, during which it is taboo for them to communicate with anyone or to bathe.

Live victims usually are children kidnapped by the raiding party and carried back to the village. The child is forced to squeeze the blade of a knife with his hand, and his blood is offered to the spirit. Afterward the child is slaughtered and his head placed in the special hut for heads.

Economic Activities

The highlanders survive through the successful exploitation of their physical surroundings, and tradition has provided them with a wealth of knowledge about rainfall patterns, soils, flora, fauna, and aquatic life. Their subsistence is based on agriculture with rice the staple crop, and rice

52. Costello, "Homicide among the Katu," pp. 77–81; Le Pichon, "Les Chasseurs de sang," pp. 391–94.

farming methods vary considerably. Swidden farming to produce upland
dry rice is found throughout the highlands, but in many places the highlanders cultivate wet rice in paddy fields.[53] A great many secondary crops
also are grown in the fields and in kitchen gardens. In addition, most
highlanders gather food and other products in the forest, and practically all
of them engage in some kind of hunting, trapping, or fishing. Trade is
traditional in local areas and, historically, some groups traded with the
lowlanders: those adjacent to the coastal plain with the Cham and
Vietnamese; those on the western side of the Annam Cordillera with the
Khmer, Lao, and Chinese. As mentioned earlier, in 1641 Van Wusthoff
described how Chinese merchants from the Cambodian town of Sambok
exchanged goods with the highlanders, listing slaves among the items
traded.[54] In recent years, trading activity has become more widespread
among the highlanders, and in some areas cash cropping and petty commerce have been on the rise. (More detailed information will be found in
Appendix B.)

The area occupied by the highlanders is generally designated as the
central highlands, although physiographically it can be divided into two
regions: the mountain range and a terrace region which forms a transitional zone between the mountains and the flat, low-elevation Mekong
river delta. All of Vietnam lies within the northern tropical zone, with
distinct dry and rainy seasons. From late April or early May until October
the southwest monsoon rains sweep over all of the terrace region and the
large western portion of the central highlands. From October until mid-
March the northeast monsoon brings rains to the eastern part of the central
highlands adjacent to the coastal plain. In the South China Sea typhoons
frequently occur, usually in the month of October, and as in 1964 they can
bring heavy winds, rains, and destructive floods to the highland villages on
the eastern side of the coastal mountains.

The annual average rainfall in the central highlands and the terrace
region is about 2,000 mm. However the pattern varies, with places such as
the Bru country in southern Binh-Tri-Thien province receiving a great

---

53. This form of agriculture is also known variously as slash-and-burn, primitive horticulture, field-
forest rotation, shifting agriculture, and brand tillage. Often in the literature it is called by a native
name; for example, in many works on Indochina it is called *rẫy*, a Vietnamese term. The revived
English dialect word *swidden* for "burned clearing" has been favored in a number of works and has the
dual advantage of being a general designation not linked to any particular region and of functioning as
a noun.

54. Garnier, "Voyage lointain," pp. 253–55.

deal of rain, while the Jarai country in the area of the Ayun and Apa (Ba) rivers is relatively dry and from time to time even experiences droughts. In the terrace region the temperatures are similar to those in Saigon, with an annual mean of 27.5°C, while in the highlands it is cooler, averaging 24.0°C at Kontum, 22.4°C at Pleiku, 24.6°C at Ban Me Thuot, 21.7°C at Bao Loc (Blao), and 19.1°C at Dalat.[55]

A complex of mountain soils, mostly red and yellow podzolic and lithosolic soils, dominates the central highlands and the terrace region.[56] This unit of soils comprises several types of physiographic landscapes. First, there are the true mountains, some of which are over 2,000 meters—Ngoc Linh, the highest peak, rises 2,598 meters—above sea level. Then, there are isolated mountains, hills, and ridges, which are surrounded by flatter basalt plateaus and old terraces on recent alluvial plains. Finally, there are some strongly eroded plateaus with scarcely any remaining flat or undulating areas, for example, the plateau south of the Fimnon-Don Duong road southeast of Dalat.

The red and yellow podzolic soils are relatively infertile and have a low water-holding capacity, causing them to become very dry in the dry season and susceptible to erosion. Most of these soils are under forest (both broadleaf and pine) or savannah, which lend themselves to swidden farming. In some areas these soils are used for such crops as manioc, peanuts, and sweet potatoes, and in central Vietnam for cinnamon (see information on Cua economic activities below). Also, in the Dalat area, most of the truck gardening is done on these soils, and they are well suited for tea and rubber cultivation.

Large areas of reddish brown latosols on basalt are found southwest of Pleiku city along the Cambodian border, in the vicinity of Ban Me Thuot from Buon Ho in the north to Lac Thien in the south, in a large area around Song Be, and in the vicinity of Xuan Loc. These soils are developed on the weathering products of basalt, and they are associated with plain to rolling topography. Although not very fertile, they do have a fair reserve of plant nutrients, and the natural vegetation is secondary forest or savannah. Shifting agriculture is found on this soil, as are most of Vietnam's coffee and rubber plantations.

55. R. Champsoloix, *Rapport sur les forêts des P.M.S.* (Saigon: République du Viet-Nam, Ministère de la Réforme Agraire et de Développement en Agriculture et Pêcherie, 1952), p. 15.

56. F. R. Moorman, *The Soils of the Republic of Vietnam* (Saigon: Republic of Vietnam, Ministry of Agriculture, 1961), pp. 6–11.

Rhadé Kpa women sowing upland dry rice (rainfed) in a swidden

There are two kinds of red latosols. The first is associated with the higher parts of the ancient basalt plateaus in Song Be and southern Dac Lac provinces, and the second is found in the area between Ban Me Thuot and Pleiku on a basalt plateau. Most red latosols are less fertile than the reddish brown latosols, and the vegetation cover is secondary forest and savannah grass. Swidden agriculture is practiced in the red latosol areas. It also is found on the earthy red latosols of the large basalt plateau in the Pleiku-Kontum region. This is the site of the vast Catecka Tea Plantation, which utilizes a sprinkler system to increase its yield. On flat sections of the basalt plateau in the vicinity of Bao Loc (Blao) in Lam Dong province, there is compact brown latosol soil, and much of the area is planted to tea.

Smaller scattered areas of other soils are found throughout the central highlands and the terrace region. Peat and muck soils, associated with poorly drained depressions, are found in southwestern Gia Lai-Cong Tum province as well as along the rivers where Phu Khanh and Dac Lac provinces meet and in the border area of Thuan Hai and Dong Nai provinces. Regurs, also called black tropical clay, is found in the Cheo Reo depression in Gia Lai-Cong Tum province, and there are undifferentiated alluvial soils along some rivers and in the large swampy area in the vicinity of Lac Thien, Dac Lac province.

Most highland groups cultivate upland dry rice by the swidden method. Although this method varies from one highland group to another and even within individual groups (see appendix B), there are some basic common characteristics. Essentially, it is a system of rotating agriculture wherein a given field is cleared, and the cut wood and brush are dried and burned. After the rains begin, the field is farmed. The duration of the farming period depends on the adjudged fertility of the soil. Following the farming period, the field is left to fallow until a new growth has appeared, and then it is farmed again.

The Bahnar Jolong, Rengao, and Chru cultivate dry rice in permanent fields. Near Kontum town, along the banks of the Bla river, the Bahnar Jolong and Rengao have extensive fields on the higher ground, and after the rains have begun in late April or early May they begin to plow and harrow. No fertilizer is used, and the seeds are broadcast. During the growing period the weeding is done with a harrow-like instrument pulled by cattle. Varieties of three-month (higher quality) and four-month dry rice are grown, and harvesting normally begins in September. These fields can be farmed for five or six years, after which they are left to lie fallow. When some wild growth appears, the fields are fenced in and used for pasturage. On high ground in the Danhim valley, the Chru cultivate several varieties of dry rice, including glutinous rice in permanent fields. These fields are plowed and harrowed, and animal dung is used for fertilizer.

Where water is available, either from rainfall or from other water sources, and where they regard the soil as suitable, the highlanders usually cultivate wet rice in paddy fields. In most cases the paddy fields are on level or near-level land, but some groups also have them on hillside terraces. The Lat, who live in the vicinity of Dalat, are the only highlanders who practice wet-rice cultivation exclusively. Located at a high elevation, their paddy fields cover the small areas of level land, and their terraces sweep up the slope of Lang Bian mountain. To the southeast, the Chru in the Danhim valley farm wet rice on bottom land and in terraces. They have an elaborate irrigation system that taps water from the tributaries that feed the Danhim river and channel it through a system of canals and dikes. Every Chru village has a "water chief," who is responsible for mustering villagers to clear the canals and repair the dikes before each planting season. He also meets with other water chiefs to coordinate the maintenance of the whole system. Traditionally the Chru broadcast their seeds, but in recent years many of them have adopted the transplanting techniques used by the Vietnamese, who have moved into the valley since 1955. The Sre also have

paddy fields on level land and terraces, and they too have begun transplanting their wet rice, a method they have adopted from the Tai-speaking
people who settled in the area after coming south as refugees in 1955.

The Hre and Cua have bottom land and terraced paddy fields, and both
use rainwater in conjunction with irrigation systems that tap springs on the
hillsides. They employ a Vietnamese-type plow pulled by water buffalo in
the preparation of their fields. Many of the Chrau-speaking people use
Vietnamese-type plows and harrows and Vietnamese cultivation techniques. They are the only highlanders who produce rice as a cash crop,
selling some of it to the Vietnamese and to other Chrau-speaking people
who work in nearby plantations.

Extensive paddy fields are farmed by the Mnong Rlam in the swampy
area around Lac Thien in Dac Lac province, but they use neither buffalo
nor plow, breaking the earth with hand tools. The Bahnar Golar have
sizable wet-rice fields west of Pleiku city, and in the immediate area of the
city some of the Jarai Hodrung farm paddy fields in the volcanic depressions. Small paddy fields, some of them on low terraces arranged on gently
sloping terrain, are worked by the Jarai Arap, Jarai Mdhur, Rhadé Kpa,
Monom, Bahnar Jolong, Rengao, Maa, and Sedang.

The highlanders cultivate numerous secondary crops in kitchen gardens,
sometimes in paddy fields, and also in the swiddens. The most common
crop is maize. The Jarai and Katu, for example, plant maize in their
swiddens and then sow dry rice between the rows of young maize plants.
The Rhadé Kpa devote a section of the swidden exclusively to maize. The
Lat farm their maize in separate fields, as do the Mnong Rlam and Roglai.
Another common secondary crop is tobacco, which is sometimes grown in
the swidden but more often in a garden near the house and is chiefly for
family consumption. On the edges of their paddy fields the Bahnar Jolong
cultivate green leafy vegetables such as spinach; the Mnong Rlam grow
bananas, sugar cane, pineapples, papaya, manioc, and yams; and the Jarai
Arap and Banhar Jolong cultivate cotton. Many groups farm secondary
crops in the swiddens; for example, the Halang grow various types of
tubers, yams, watermelons, eggplant, cabbage, chili peppers, manioc, and
cucumbers amidst their dry rice.

In addition to these secondary crops, the kitchen gardens found in every
highland village contain squash, gourds, tomatoes, various types of beans,
melons, lettuce, pumpkins, lemon grass, taro, ginger, onions, mushrooms,
peanuts, carrots, and garlic. Scattered around most villages are such fruit

trees as lime, orange, coconut, banana, guava, jack fruit, grapefruit, papaya, mango, and avocado. Kapok trees also are grown in many villages, and the Bru, Pacoh, Katu, Hre, Cua, Chru, Roglai, and Mnong Rlam cultivate graceful areca palms with betel vines climbing the trunks. Coffee trees often are found near some of the Rhadé Kpa houses, and the Hre and Cua grow tea plants in their villages.

For hundreds of years there has been trade between some highlanders and lowland people, and this trade included a few cash crops. Those mentioned explicitly in historical accounts are areca nuts, betel leaves, and cinnamon. Since the Bru, Pacoh, Katu, Hre, Cua, Chru, and Roglai—all of whom are located in areas accessible to the coastal plain—are cultivators of areca nuts and betel leaves, it seems more than likely that some of these groups traded such products with the lowlanders. The Cua are the only highland group that has cultivated and gathered cinnamon, which used to be sold on the world market as saigon cinnamon. Some cinnamon is obtained by stripping bark from trees that grow wild in the mountain forests of the Cua country, but according to informants most of it is cultivated by the villagers. Although since 1964 the cinnamon trade has been badly disrupted by the war in Vietnam, the Cua still carry their cinnamon to the market at the district town of Tra Bong in Nghia-Binh province for sale to Vietnamese dealers. According to Jarai informants, sesame has traditionally been a cash crop of the Jarai Mdhur in the Ba river valley. For many years, at harvest time, Vietnamese traders have come to the area to bargain for the sesame crop. Also, in his 1938 publication on the Katu, Le Pichon noted that the Katu gathered betel leaves, medicinal plants, and fruit that they sold to the Vietnamese.[57]

In their past trade with the lowland people the highlanders also included a number of products gathered in the forests. Maspéro's list of gifts sent by the Cham kings as tribute to the Chinese court between the fourth and eleventh centuries mentions cardamom, wax, lacquer, various kinds of resins, and such precious woods as sandalwood, camphorwood, and eagle-wood, which historically were gathered by the Roglai and sold to the Cham and later the Vietnamese.[58] Van Wusthoff's 1641 account of the Chinese merchants records among the trade items brought back from the

57. Le Pichon, "Les Chasseurs de sang," p. 367.

58. Maspéro, *Champa*, pp. 57, 67, 87–88, 92, 120, 128, 133, 138. Eaglewood, also known as aloeswood, is the heart of the *Aquileria agallocha*, a tree found in tropical Asia. When burned, the wood emits a fragrant odor, making it a highly valued offering in Cham, Vietnamese, and Chinese rituals.

highlands gold, slaves, deerskins, wax, gamboge, rhinoceros horns, and elephant tusks.[59] Panning for gold continues to be an economic activity for a few highlanders, particularly in Halang and Jeh villages. Informants report that in the pre-1960 period it was a full-time activity for some of them. One man from Dak Rode recalled spending his days at the nearby river bank sifting through the auriferous sands. The negotiable measure was a morsel of gold the size of a rice kernel; five such morsels would buy a buffalo. The buyers were Lao traders who periodically visited the Halang country to purchase gold.

As will be discussed later in another context, slavery was widespread among the highlanders in the past. Until the early twentieth century some of the "great chiefs" among the Rhadé, Jarai, Bahnar, and Hre still had slaves, most of whom were war captives. Raiding villages to capture slaves to sell to the Lao and Cambodians was not uncommon. Slavery resulting from debt still exists. Gerber describes a type of debt slavery among the Stieng which is not a form of indentured servitude because the slave's labor does not count as recompense; the payment of the debt in full is the prerequisite to his release.[60] Stieng informants describe situations where slaves are passed from one family to another as part of the bride price. In Stieng villages it appears that slaves live more or less like members of the family, taking their meals with the family and participating in celebrations.

Kinship and Marriage Patterns

Patterns of kinship and marriage among the highlanders vary considerably, a situation well illustrated by the different rules of descent. Among most of the ethnic groups that have Austronesian (Malayopolynesian) languages, descent is traced through the female line. These groups are the Rhadé, Chru, Roglai, and some Jarai subgroups. Matrilineal descent also is found among some groups whose members speak languages of the South Bahnaric branch of the Mon Khmer family, namely, the Mnong, Sre, Lat, and some of the local Chru-speaking groups. Descent reckoned through the male line is the rule among some of the Mon Khmer-speaking people. These include the Stieng, Maa, Cua, Bru, Pacoh, Katu. The Bahnar, Rengao, Sedang, Halang, Jeh, and Hre, and some Austronesian-speaking Jarai subgroups such as the Arap and Tabuan trace descent through both the male and female lines. Since

59. Garnier, "Voyage lointain," pp. 253–55.
60. T. Gerber, "Coutumier Stieng," *BEFEO* 45 (1951): 230–32.

there has been no ethnographic research among the Austronesian-speaking Rai and the Mon Khmer-speaking Monom, Dalaa, Rdaa, Koyon, Jroo, Tring, and Nop, their kinship systems are unknown.

Most of the groups with matrilineal descent have exogamous clans so that those related through the female line are members of the same clan identified by a common name and in some cases by a common food taboo. Marriage within a clan is viewed as incestuous. One group, the Rhadé, have two phratrics into which all of the clans are grouped, and marriage within a phratry is forbidden.

Marriage patterns vary accordingly with similar practices found among those groups with the same descent rule. All of the highland groups, however, have the custom of taking plural wives (polygyny) for those who have the means, and with some groups this involves marrying sisters (sororal polygyny). Also some are reported to have the practice where on the death of a man his younger brother has either the right or obligation to take the widow as his wife (the levirate) and a woman has the right or duty to take her older sister's widower as her husband (the sororate).

All of the highland groups have teknonomy, a practice best described through an example: a couple names their first child "X" and henceforth the parents are known as "Father of X" and "Mother of X." When the first grandchild named "Y" is born, the grandparents are called "Grandfather of Y" and "Grandmother of Y." Numerous examples of this will be found in later chapters.

Inheritance varies according to the descent rules. Generally, where there is matrilineal descent, the females own the family goods (houses, jars, gongs, farm tools, animals, and crops) and these are passed down through the female line. As already indicated, among the Rhadé the eldest woman in the local clan group is guardian of clan land, and this role is inherited by her eldest daughter. With those groups that have patrilineal descent, family goods are transmitted through the male line. Less structured is the matter of inheritance where there is bilateral descent; both male and female children inherit from their parents and the distribution of goods is a decision for each individual family.

Traditional Village Leadership

All of the highland societies are village-oriented, and village leaders traditionally have been responsible for coping with the social, religious, economic, legal, and, at times, military needs of the community. In the past

A Rhadé village chief at the front entrance of his longhouse

some changes in village leadership were introduced by the Vietnamese in those ethnic groups with whom they came into contact as they expanded southward along the coastal plain. More widespread changes were effected by the French when they organized their colonial administration in the highlands. Nonetheless many elements of traditional village leadership seem to have been retained. To some extent this was due to a recognition by the officials that as long as there was relative stability, it was more efficacious to let local leaders run their own affairs. Among groups where basic changes in leadership patterns have occurred, whether due to outside influence or to indigenous developments, very often some memory of past leadership is preserved in the oral tradition.

Among most highland groups traditional leadership either rested with the headman selected by adult villagers on the basis of age, wealth, and wisdom or was a prerogative of local elites. In most instances of the latter type, leadership remained with certain unilinear descent groups, particularly matrilineal descent groups.

Leadership in villages of the matrilineal Jarai Cor and Trung, as reported by Dournes, is often rooted in entrenched elite kin groups.[61] Among the Jarai there is a distinction made between those who are "strong" (*kotang*) and those who are "weak" (*rodu*), and this is manifested in village society by a dichotomy between the well-to-do (*podrong-sah*) and the poor (*rin-*

---

61. Dournes, *Coordonnées structures Jörai*, pp. 1–10, 32–43.

bbun). Leadership is in the hands of the strong and wealthy. Dournes cites Jarai oral history that relates how in the past there were recurring wars among the Jarai themselves as well as between the Jarai and the neighboring Bahnar. Fortified villages were formed by strong individuals who gathered about them people seeking protection as well as war captives and indentured servants (who were equivalent to serfs). These strong leaders were known as *oi potao*, which Dournes translates as *seigneur local* (local lord) or *maître* (master) while the villagers were his *clients* (clients). The local lord had absolute authority. Following Jarai custom, this role passed to the husband of the eldest daughter so that ruling power became rooted in certain matrilineal clans. Although in time the power of these local lords diminished, the elite status of particular clans in some villages has remained, and it is these clans that inevitably provide the *po bbon* (village master) or headman. Dournes points out that in Plei Ama Rin it is the husbands of the Romah women who are the headmen while in Bon Phum it is the Ksor and in Plei Rongol Ama Corong it is the Nay. Although Dournes fails to mention it, another element in local leadership is the Jarai belief that the spirits bestow on some individuals a power called *kdruh*, which is a well-defined type of charisma. While "grand charisma" and "big charisma" enable people to attain positions of high rank, "small charisma" permits one to become something like a village headman.

Others active in village affairs are the *tha* (older men at least forty years of age) who are heads of families and active farmers. They form no council or assembly, but they influence village affairs. Dournes also notes that some others influential in village society are the *khoa yang*, a specialist who officiates at the rituals for the spirits; another specialist who is concerned with justice; the midwife (*po bbuai*); and the shaman (*pojau*).

In his introduction to the Rhadé poem, *Le chant épique de Kdam Yi*, Condominas notes that prior to the arrival of the French highlander villages were autonomous, and from time to time a leader in one village would gain ascendancy over several other villages, forcing them to supply him with warriors. Such developments were for the most part temporary, and on the death of the powerful leader the villages regained their autonomy. He notes that Kdam Yi, the hero of the Rhadé poem, embodies many of the qualities of these powerful leaders in being portrayed as a robust nonconformist who disdained work in the fields and by his personal strength and bravery became a famous leader.[62]

62. Georges Condominas, "Introduction to 'Chant épique de Kdam Yi' by F.-P. Antoine," *BEFEO* 47 (1955): 555–66.

Condominas goes on to say that this poem describes how the families of the chiefs intermarried, forming military alliances for war against other chiefs. When these chiefs were defeated, Kdam Yi took not only their belongings but also their serfs and all the inhabitants of the villages they ruled. Condominas sees in this a strongly cohesive family and social organization that permitted the Rhadé to develop a rudimentary form of feudalism. The ruling class of chiefs reinforced its position by intermarriage, and each marriage alliance was further guaranteed by the sororate and levirate wherein a deceased partner was replaced by his brother or her sister. The circuit of alliances was in effect a kind of endogamy among the elite families, and their function was to afford protection for the families who were engaged in farming.

Rhadé informants cite oral tradition in reporting that in the past the Rhadé village was led by a chief who was married to a woman of a clan that had been for a long time established as an elite family. At times one of these chiefs would gain control over a neighboring village and become the chief of a given area. As will be pointed out later, one elderly informant contends that this was the case at the end of the nineteenth century. This pattern of retention of leadership at the village level by certain clans is borne out in the Rhadé customs and traditions that were collected by French administrators and used as a basis for legal decisions in the indigenous law courts. These specify that on the death of a village chief he is to be replaced by someone related to the widow, preferably a husband of the widow's sister. Should the replacement be too young, then the eldest adults in the household will assist him, and the role of chief remains with the family as long as there are heirs.[63]

Rhadé informants also describe the whole matter of leadership at all levels as being affected by beliefs concerning a type of charisma bestowed by a spirit named Yang Rong. This charisma, called *dhut*, is not inherited but can be manifested in early life. A person who has dhut is described as *knuih*, and he is predestined to authority (*kohun*).

The elite status of certain clans in local areas also appears to be related to the Rhadé land tenure system. According to legend, the original owners of all land were members of the Nie Kdam clan, who, since they did not work hard in their fields, were in time forced to relinquish land to other clans. A given area of land claimed by a clan is well defined, with its boundaries

63. Dominique Antomarchi, *Recueil de coutumes Rhadées du Darlac* (Hanoi: Imprimerie d'Extrême-Orient, 1940), pp. 55–56.

known by clan members. The guardian of this territory is the *po lan* (proprietor of the land). Normally the eldest female of that part of the clan that claims ownership and lives in the area, the po lan protects the land for the clan members, designating who can farm, hunt, fish, and cut timber in the territory. Her other responsibilities include marking the boundaries of the land, periodically performing rituals for clan ancestors, and dealing with any violations of clan land (particularly such things as incest by clan members within the territory).

Chru informant Touneh Han Tho described religious beliefs concerning a spirit's ("spirit that bestows chieftainship") favoritism of certain individuals as being intertwined with some concepts of leadership. This spirit inhabits a person's body from birth, creating a condition that predestines that person for a role of leadership. People become aware of it through a type of external charisma (*gonuh seri*) manifested not only in physical appearance but also in a definite allure characterized by a majestic air and a voice that commands attention. Such persons lead charmed lives and invariably rise to become leaders among the Chru. Some assume the role of village headman, others become more regionally recognized chiefs. Han Tho also points out that among the Chru, village leadership has tended to remain in the hands of the Touneh, Touprong, Jolong, Banahria, Sahau, and Klong Drong clans.

Reporting on the matrilineal Mnong Gar, Condominas notes that the term *kuang* means a "rich and powerful adult male" and that it is these individuals who are the village leaders, although he does not associate them with particular elite clans. It is the kuang who serve in each village as "the three sacred men in the forest and village" (*croo weer toom brii toom bboon*). These are Rnot, who distribute the farm plots; Rnut, who oversee the burning of the swidden; and Rnoop, the "sacred man in the village" who decides the location of houses and the placement of the settlement. Condominas also reports that the shaman (*njau*) has an important place in village society.[64]

Lafont received information from Mnong Rlam informants indicating that in the past a village consisted of members of the same clan, and clan leaders functioned as village leaders. In time most villages contained more than one clan, but they segregated themselves in their own section of the settlement. The informants also reported that clans with a large number of

---

64. Condominas, *Nous avons mangé la forêt*, pp. 22–23, 378.

members predominated village society, providing leadership and controlling land distribution. If one of the "minor clans" needed land, it had to
arrange a "purchase" from one of the "major clans."[65]

The Roglai, who have matrilineages and not clans, had according to
informants no headman in their villages because each lineage occupied its
own house, and the lineage head was the group leader. Among the Maa,
descent is patrilineal, and Boulbet has described the "great lineages" which
trace their ancestry through the male line to very remote times as having
elite status.[66] They function as an aristocracy, and in the villages they
provide the leadership. The term *kuang* indicates an important male in the
village society (just as Condominas used the same term for the Mnong Gar
elite), and it also is a modifier to indicate the head of a great lineage (*cau
kuang*). It is the great lineages that provide the "master of the land" (*cau
toom bree toom nggar*) who regulates the farming in the village territory, and
they also produce the most skilled specialists as well as those who recite the
traditional chants at the rituals. Members of smaller lineages constitute the
common villagers, the "clients" of the great lineages.

The Bru, farther to the north, have patrilineal descent and exogamous
patrilineal clans, and the clan head, selected by the adult members, has a
wide range of social, economic, and religious responsibilities within the
clan. The role of the village chief (*ariaih*) is comparable. He regulates the use
of the village territory, approving new swiddens and the felling of large
trees, and he has begun functions that include arbitrating conflicts unresolved within and between clans and meting out punishment to those
who violate village taboos. He organizes village rituals, and his approval
must be had for any marriages. The role of village chief does not require
that a man be well-to-do or elderly but rather that he be considered capable
of performing his duties. Informants point out that in most villages the role
remains within a particular clan and is passed down from one generation to
another.

Although the neighboring Pacoh have a kinship system very similar to
the Bru's, their traditional village leadership appears to vary somewhat.
According to informants, there is no village chief but rather village elders
(*areiah xaxai*) who are selected by the adult villagers. They need not be
elderly but they should be men of good standing in the community—men

65. Pierre-Bernard Lafont, "Notes sur les structures sociales des Mnong Rlam du Centre Vietnam,"
BEFEO 53 (1967): 676–78.
66. Boulbet, *Pays des Maa*, pp. 39–63.

who can wisely regulate the use of the village territory (*cruang*) and wisely make the necessary decisions for the community, such as arbitrating conflicts and punishing those who do not adhere to Pacoh customs.

The Katu also have patrilineal descent and patrilineages (*kabuh hama*), and there appears to be a difference in village leadership among the High Katu and Low Katu. The High Katu are relatively isolated, and often a village will consist of one longhouse occupied by members of the same lineage, whose head, the eldest male, makes all decisions for the group and arbitrates any conflicts. In larger villages, lineage heads are the village leaders, and many of their activities are centered around a men's house. Located in the center of the village, this house is forbidden to females but it is the gathering place for the males. Young unmarried males sleep here, village leaders meet here, and some important village rituals are held here, particularly, as indicated previously, the human blood offerings to the spirits. The men's house also is found among the Low Katu, but village leadership is in the hands of a headman (*ta-ka*) who is selected by the adult villagers for his personal qualities, including such things as his bravery in having led a blood hunt, rather than for his age or wealth. But should any calamities like an epidemic or crop failure befall the village, the chief is expected to resign and a new one is selected.

An elderly Cua informant reports that in the past a village commonly consisted of only one longhouse inhabited by the members of a patrilineage, who, in many instances, numbered around five hundred. The role of lineage head (*dyalan*), which is passed on to either his eldest or youngest son, was extremely important, for he made all decisions affecting the group and was responsible for resolving all conflicts, maintaining good relations with neighbors, and officiating at rituals. As most villages came to have more than one patrilineal group, the pattern, which continues to the present, was to have all adult residents select a headman, but the lineage chiefs continued to influence decision-making. A similar pattern is found among the Stieng, who also have patrilineages; a village headman is selected by the villagers but lineage leaders have a voice in village affairs.

Traditional village leadership among groups with bilateral descent appears to be less entrenched in specific kin groups than is the case with most of the unilinear descent groups. Available information indicates that the common pattern is for the leaders to be selected by the villagers on the basis of such things as good personal qualities, age, and perhaps wealth. None of these leadership roles is hereditary. Village leadership is associated with communal men's houses which function as social and religious centers, and most of these groups have village territories, the use of which is regulated by the village elders.

Guilleminet describes Bahnar villages as being governed by a group of older men called the *kra*, and one of their major responsibilities is regulating, in conjunction with elders of neighboring villages, the use of the *toring*, an administrative entity that is shared with villages in a particular geographic area.[67] Land, hunting, and fishing rights are shared by all those residing in the area, and non-toring people (*tomoi*) are regarded as outsiders whether Bahnar or not. Guilleminet also reports that traditionally there were four classes in Bahnar society: (1) the freeman, which includes most Bahnar; (2) debtors (*dik*); (3) foreigners (tomoi); and (4) war prisoners, who are slaves.[68]

Bahnar Jolong informants elaborate, noting that the village elders (*kra polei*) must be fifty or more years of age and are considered the wisest and most experienced men in the village. They know the customs and traditions and are trusted to make decisions and arbitrate conflicts. A Bahnar Golar informant reports that the elders select an adult male villager to act as their spokesman; for example, if the elders declare a taboo, it is the spokesman who announces it to the villagers. All informants affirmed that the elders perform rituals for the Spirit of the Village Water Source and the Spirit of the Communal House. The unmarried males sleep in the communal house, and it is the gathering place for the elders in addition to being the site of village rituals. Among the Bahnar Jolong, women can enter to participate in rituals, but among the Bahnar Golar it is taboo for women to enter.

The pattern of leadership in Rengao villages appears to be very similar to that of the Bahnar. Gregerson reports that Rengao elders govern the village and act as its representatives in any conflicts with neighboring villages.[69] Kemlin describes a variety of different alliances that exist among the Rengao, one of which involves a blood oath that brings about an alliance between warring villages.[70] Each Rengao village has a communal house which serves as a sleeping place for unmarried males as well as the place where village rituals are held. Women are free to enter this house during the ritual celebrations.

67. Guilleminet, "La Tribu Bahnar du Kontum" (Congrès des Orientalistes), pp. 383–84.
68. Paul Guilleminet, "La Tribu Bahnar du Kontum," *BEFEO* 45 (1951–52): 513–15.
69. Gregerson, "Ethnic Minorities," p. 15.
70. Kemlin, "Alliances chez les Reungao," pp. 1–119.

Sedang village elders also are known as *kra*, and they have a collective voice in running community affairs. With the approval of adult villagers they select a headman (*kan polay*), who must be a man of good reputation: he is a good parent, he does not argue or use bad language, and he is a "wise man". He can make decisions without approval of the elders, although he usually is aware of their sentiments. The headman and elders oversee the use of the village territory (*cheam beng*), organize rituals in the communal house, arbitrate conflicts, and are consulted on marriage arrangements. A similar situation is found among the Halang, with a group of elders (*ghe*), numbering seven or eight, the village leaders. They in turn select one of their group as the headman, referring to him as "elder brother." Halang villages have no set territory, but the elders and headman are responsible for making decisions affecting the community, performing rituals in the communal house where the unmarried males sleep, and arranging alliances with other villages to avoid conflicts.

Among the Jeh, village leadership is associated not only with age and wisdom but also with wealth, and the leaders include females. The elders (*dradra*) must be older, and wisdom is equated with wealth; as one informant put it, "Poverty and wisdom do not live in the same person." Wealth, the informants also noted, means having a well-constructed house, four or five pigs, and three good alcohol jars. Women in the village who are qualified may join the ranks of the elders. One of the male elders who is particularly talented and well-to-do—an informant noted that this would be one "who has gold from the rivers"—is designated the headman (*yau*). As among some of the other groups, the leaders regulate village affairs, control the use of the village territory (*sal ja*), and officiate at rituals held in the communal house (*mrao*), where both unmarried males and females sleep and where some of the initial marriage rituals are held.

In the Hre household the eldest male is the head, and in village society these household heads assist the village chief (*ca-ra*) in making decisions affecting the whole community. The *ca-ra* is selected by all adult villagers on the basis of his personal qualities and knowledge of Hre ways.

This, then, has been a summary of the ethnographic characteristics of the people who for centuries lived in the central highlands of the Annam Cordillera relatively undisturbed by historical events in the world at their feet.

2 THE PREHISTORIC AND EARLY HISTORIC PERIODS

Toward the end of the first millennium B.C. the Chinese began to record their observations of the people and cultures they encountered in the Indochinese peninsula, and it is these accounts that provide the earliest historical information on the region. They tell us about the principalities that existed in the Red river delta when it was brought under Chinese control and about China's relations with the state of Lin Yi (later called Champa) and the Indianized states of Funan and its successor Chenla (out of which grew the kingdom of Angkor). Examining the origins of these Indochinese states, scholars put forth the hypothesis that the indigenous populations initially were composed of preliterate groups which, due to the civilizing influences of China and India, were welded into more culturally homogeneous populations with common ethnic identities. For example, the people of the Red river delta, civilized in the great tradition of China, became known as the Vietnamese, while those who came to be identified as Cham and Khmer were of the Indian great tradition.

Located in the mountainous interior, the populations that were ancestral to the highlanders of our time are mentioned briefly in some of the early Chinese accounts, although they remained aloof from the civilizing influences of China and India. As indicated in the previous chapter, they did retain their linguistic affiliations with the Cham, the Khmer, and to some extent the Vietnamese. These deeply rooted ties, combined with their relative cultural conservatism, have given the highlanders a place in some of the hypotheses formulated by French scholars concerning the origin of the Vietnamese and the people who founded the early kingdom of Lin Yi.

THE PREHISTORIC PERIOD

Traditional View of Prehistoric Migrations

Until recently most theories concerning the origin of prehistoric populations in Southeast Asia were based on the hypothesis put forth by Heine-Geldern in 1932 proposing a series of migrations from the north, i.e., from China and Japan.[1] Coedès accepted this hypothesis in his discussion of the prehistory of Indochina.[2] The terms palaeolithic and neolithic used by archeologists to designate two time periods in Europe—distinguished by the exclusive use of chipped stone artifacts and the predominance of polished stone tools respectively—cannot, Coedès maintains, be used to indicate two chronological periods in Indochina but only to describe two types of stone culture which cannot as yet be dated with any certainty. The palaeolithic type of chipped stone tool is represented by the early industry—Coedès puts it in the Lower Pleistocene—known as the Anyathian from the site in Burma which yielded pebbles chipped into the form of choppers. Similar stone tools have been found in Fing Noi in Thailand and at Phu Loi in northeastern upland Laos. In the latter site there also were human remains but they unfortunately were too fragmented to relate to any known type of human or hominid.

The next stage, known as the Hoabinhian, is named for the numerous sites in Hoa Binh province of northern Vietnam where archeological research unearthed a mixture of two stone tool cultures. Later, specimens of these cultures also were found in the northern Vietnamese provinces of Thanh Hoa and Quang Binh as well as in Thailand and northern Laos. The earlier levels of the Hoabinhian are characterized by paleolithic-type stone tools shaped in the natural form of the pebbles from which they were fashioned. They were usually worked on one side only. This suggests to Coedès a relationship between the Hoabinhian and the earliest industries of Southeast Asia. The later period is represented by protoneoliths: stone tools polished only at the cutting edge. In northern Vietnam the intermediate

1. R. Von Heine-Geldern, "Urheimat und fruheste Wanderungen der Austronesier," *Anthropos* 27 (1932): 543–619.
2. Georges Coedès, *The Making of South East Asia*, trans. H. M. Wright (London: Routledge & Kegan Paul, 1966), pp. 10–22; idem, *The Indianized States of Southeast Asia*, ed. Walter F. Vella, trans. Susan Brown Cowing (Honolulu: East-West Center Press, 1968), pp. 4–8. A detailed description of the prehistoric period in Vietnam can also be found in L. Bezacier, *Le Viet-Nam* (Paris: A. et J. Picard, 1972), pp. 21–77.

layer with the protoneoliths has over it another layer containing palaeolithic type tools, suggesting some kind of mixture or intrusion of the
palaeoliths.

Human remains have been found in association with some of these
Hoabinhian artifacts. Coedès cites Fromaget's analysis of the skull found at
Tham Pong in the Phu Loi massif of northeastern Laos as a "prototype
combining the characteristics of the earliest Europoid (such as Ainus,
Polynesians, and later Indonesians), the Papuan negroids, and the Veddo-
Australoids." [3] Fromaget also posits the hypothesis that the ancestors of this
human type must have had their habitat in southern China, somewhere in
the Yunnan-Tibet border area. From there they spread toward the east and
south throughout all of Southeast Asia where remains of their culture are
found. In other Vietnamese sites, skulls found at this layer display
Melanesian or Indonesian affinities (such as would be found among the
highlanders) and Coedès concludes that it indicates that they are more
differentiated than the Tham Pong skull.

The upper level of the Hoabinhian is known as the Bacsonian, named for
the sites in the limestone massif in the northern Vietnamese province of Bac
Son. The Bacsonian is related to the lower neolithic, and Coedès feels that
it was a culture introduced sometime during the fourth millennium,
marking a turning point in the prehistory of Southeast Asia. The characteristic tool of the Bacsonian is the "short axe," made by splitting a bifacial
tool and polishing it along the cutting edge of one side only. In Vietnam
this tool is usually found in association with palaeoliths, but this is not the
case in Laos. Sometimes there are bone or shell artifacts, and in the
Vietnamese province of Thanh Hoa there is a primitive kind of pottery
with markings that appear to have been made by basketwork. The numerous skulls and skull fragments at the Bac Son sites indicate that several racial
types may have coexisted in the area. The lower levels contain proto-
Melanesian and proto-Australian skulls, and above them some Indonesian
type skulls. Coedès notes that the site at Pho Binh Gia in Bac Son province
confirms the coexistence of Indonesian and Melanesian types in some
locales. In the Bacsonian site at Da But in the plains of Thanh Hoa province
there are burials containing Melanesian type skulls. Some of the dead had
axes and pendants by their side, others had their flesh removed and appear
to have been tied in a crouching position. A few were partially cremated,

3. Coedès, *Making of South East Asia*, p. 13. "Veddo" would be a racial type drawn from the Vedda
people of Ceylon.

and sometimes bones and burial objects were painted with red ochre.

Coedès estimates that the earliest neolithic could be no earlier than the second millennium.[4] One of the characteristic neolithic artifacts is the rectangular axe, which is found in such widespread areas as Indonesia, the Yellow river valley in China, Japan, and Korea. Another tool, the oval axe, is found in Cambodia and Burma. But the most typical neolithic artifact in Indochina is the shouldered axe. Neolithic sites in Vietnam are quite rare, but they contain skulls of the Indonesian type along with shouldered axes. In Cambodia, at Samrong Saen at the head of the Tonle Sap, there is a neolithic site with a variety of artifacts and skulls resembling those of the present inhabitants of the area. The artifacts include richly decorated pottery in different shapes, bracelets, rings, pendants, and beads, along with some bronze objects. The presence of bronze leads Coedès to speculate whether this site is contemporary with the beginning of the bronze age, and in the same vein he raises the question whether the whole Indochinese neolithic, characterized by the shouldered axe, was not contemporary with the bronze age.

Bezacier, citing the earlier research by European archeologists at Dong Son on the Ma river in the northern Vietnamese province of Thanh Hoa, suggests that the bronze age began in that area around the fourth or third century B.C.[5] (It is noted below that, more recently, North Vietnamese archeologists have found bronzes that are dated 3405 ± 100 by the carbon-14 method.) Research at Dong Son, which began in 1924, has yielded a large number of bronze objects and kettledrums of different types and sizes. Some of these drums contain elaborate stylized motifs of humans and birds. Their area of distribution extends from China to Indonesia, but their place of origin is thought to be northern Vietnam, particularly the vicinity of Dong Son where the oldest drums were found. There also are remains of structures built on piling. Nearby are graves containing bronze objects, fragments of iron weapons and tools, and numerous ornaments (some of them jade).

Coedès raises the question as to whether the Donsonians were Indonesians. He notes that it is tempting to think that they were and to consider them the ancestors of the "backward people of Indonesian type to inhabit the Vietnamese mountains."[6] By the same token he speculates

4. Coedès, *Making of South East Asia*, pp. 15–16.
5. Bezacier, *Le Viet-Nam*, pp. 79–253.
6. Coedès, *Making of South East Asia*, pp. 18–19.

whether it might have been Indonesians who constructed the dry stone-work tanks found in the vicinity of Gio Linh inland from Quang Tri. Since they predate the arrival of the Vietnamese, who now use these tanks, the builders might well have been the ancestors of the ethnic groups now found in the highlands west of Quang Tri.

Taking the available archeological and linguistic data, Coedès summarizes the hypotheses concerning the successive waves of migration in Southeast Asia during the neolithic times.[7] The first wave is based solely on the distribution of the ellipsoidal axe, carried by a branch of the human race that moved from either China or Japan, passing through Taiwan, the Philippines, Celebes, and the Moluccas in the direction of New Guinea and Melanesia, eventually introducing a neolithic culture into Australia. The second wave brought people, possibly of a Mongoloid race, who spoke Austroasiatic languages (which includes Mon Khmer languages) and possessed a culture characterized by the shouldered axe, out of some unknown center into the south coast of China, Indochina, Taiwan, the Philippines, North Celebes, Japan, northeastern Korea, and part of eastern India. The third, dating around the middle of the second millennium B.C., consisted of a migration from China of "primitive Austronesian peoples" (which would include Malayopolynesian-speaking people) with a culture similar to that of the late Northern Chinese neolithic Yangshao (characterized by a rectangular axe) who moved in the direction of Indochina. A number of culture traits belonging to different cultural stages have been attributed to the people of this migration. These include basket pottery or that made with coil techniques, bone utensils, rings made of stone or shell, necklaces of glass beads or small bead tubes, houses built on piling, cultivation of rice, domestication of the pig and the ox, construction of megaliths, headhunting, and a primitive form of the outrigger canoe.

The fourth migration consisted of people of mixed Austronesian and Austroasiatic stock with a culture that combined characteristics of the rectangular axe and shouldered axe cultures. They established settlements in Indochina. Before they could become firmly established, however, the fifth migration brought a group of primitive Austronesians southward and settled them among the people inhabiting the southern part of the Malay Peninsula who were still in the late paleolithic and early neolithic stage of development. The final wave was of Austronesians who had acquired skill

7. Ibid., pp. 22–26.

in navigation, and they moved out from the Malay Peninsula eastward into the islands and eventually to the Philippines, Taiwan, and Japan.

The "New Look" of Prehistoric Migrations

This traditional view that the people and cultures of the Southeast Asian neolithic originated outside the region is now being questioned by some investigators, notably archeologists, on the basis of discoveries made since the early 1960s. Recently, Solheim has outlined what he calls the "new look" of Southeast Asian prehistory.[8] It amounts to a reinterpretation of the archeological record formulated in five hypothesized stages and periods: Lithic, Lignic, Crystallitic, Extensionistic, and Conflicting Empire. Solheim's "new look" questions not only the past interpretations of the data on the neolithic in Southeast Asia but also the widely accepted notion that the appearance of civilization in the region was due exclusively to influences from China and India.

Solheim visited five areas in Southeast Asia where archeological excavations have produced evidence of cultural sequence that date back 40,000 years or more. He notes that, while in most of these archeological sites there have been additions to the cultural inventory, there is little indication of a replacement of one culture group by a new or different culture group. This evidence, he adds, does not mean that there were not movements of people large enough to be called migrations, but it does indicate that most of the cultural evolution in Southeast Asia was internal. He cites the findings at the Niah Caves in Sarawak and the Tabon Caves on the island of Palawan in the Philippines as containing evidence supporting the theory that humans have been living in Southeast Asia for a longer time than hitherto thought. The Niah Caves have a sequence that goes back over 40,000 years, and at the earliest levels the skull of an adolescent *homo sapiens* was found. In the Tabon Caves, Robert Fox has unearthed a sequence of cultures that dates back over 30,000 years.

Solheim then focuses on two sites in Thailand—Non Nok Tha and Spirit Cave—with which he is personally familiar. At Non Nok Tha, discovered by Chester Gorman in 1964 and excavated under the supervision of Solheim, evidence dated by carbon-14 reveals a sequence that begins before 3600 B.C. and continues up until one or two hundred years

8. W. Solheim II, "The 'New Look' of Southeast Asian Prehistory," *Journal of the Siam Society* 60 (1972): 1–20.

ago. At the very bottom of the site Solheim reports that they found
evidence of bovines, probably zebu cattle, which he concludes were
"probably domesticated." Also there were potsherds containing impressions of *Oryza sativa*, the rice most commonly cultivated in Asia, and he
expresses the opinion that it was a dry, domesticated rice. The site includes
a burial dating about 3600 B.C., and it contains a copper-socketed tool that
Solheim judges was very likely heat-worked at some stage in its manufacture. From levels just above the burial are numerous remnants of bronze
dating just prior to 3000 B.C. and including whole and fragmentary
crucibles, many small nodules of bronze, and several bronze axes as well as
remains of pairs of sandstone molds for casting the axes. These findings
would indicate that there had been bronze manufacture some two
thousand years before the Dongson, a thousand years before bronze appeared in China, and five hundred years before bronze was produced in
India.

The other site in Thailand is Spirit Cave, located in the northwest and
excavated during 1965 and 1966 by Chester Gorman, who describes the
findings as "a subcultural assemblage of the Hoabinhian technocom-
plex."[9] At the upper level of the site, dating around 6600 B.C., there are
cord-marked, incised, and burnished pottery, polished slate knives, and
rectangular polished stone tools. Throughout the site there are remains of
plants, including the bottle gourd, a species of cucumber, the Chinese
water chestnut, and leguminous beans, all of which suggest to Gorman "a
botanical orientation beyond simple food gathering." Solheim notes that
in Spirit Cave "the very possibly domesticated plants go back to 10000 B.C.
or earlier."[10] He also cites research conducted in Taiwan by Kwang-chih
Chang in which two distinct cultures dating to about 2500 B.C. were
identified. Below the levels of these two cultures Chang found an earlier
cord-ware culture, which led him to hypothesize that there had been a
horticultural society in existence for a long time.

Solheim describes several sites in Vietnam as yielding evidence supporting his "new look" theory.[11] At Hang Gon I, east of Saigon, Saurin

9. Chester Gorman, "Excavations at Spirit Cave, North Thailand: Some Interim Interpretations,"
Asian Perspectives 13 (1972): 79–107.

10. Solheim, "New Look," p. 12.

11. W. Solheim II, "Northern Thailand, Southeast Asia, and World Prehistory," *Asian Perspectives*
13 (1972): 148–49.

uncovered the fragment of a mold and other evidence of bronze working, and a carbon-14 date for charcoal fragments in potsherds is 3950 ± 250, but Solheim reports that Saurin thought this date unexpectedly old. In North Vietnam he cites evidence from Viet Thien, where there is a bronze culture older than Dongson and of a different tradition. Finally, Solheim notes that these North Vietnamese sites present some evidence of "centralization of power and political organization," and he also regards the site at Chansen in eastern central Thailand as indicating a relatively advanced social organization.[12] Excavated by joint Thai-University of Pennsylvania groups, this site gives evidence of use as a village and later a city. Carbon-14 and thermoluminescence dates indicate a settlement period from prior to 200 B.C. until about A.D. 1050.

Solheim's new interpretation of the archeological record begins with what he calls the Lithic stage, identified with the first appearance of man in Southeast Asia. This is manifest in the chopper-chopping tool tradition such as is represented in the Tampanian culture of Malaya (which dates from the Lower Pleistocene). Noting that nothing is known about the people of this time, he nonetheless states that "we can assume that they were living in small family groups and were dependent on hunting and gathering."[13] This stage is followed by the Lignic period, starting about 42,000 years ago, with the Hoabinhian culture developing directly out of the chopper-chopping tool tradition. According to Solheim, this period is marked by the development of wooden tools, the invention of the bow and arrow and blowpipe in Southeast Asia, the use of baskets and traps for trapping animals and/or fish, and, possibly, the beginning of cordage manufacture.

Solheim suggests that, at least as far as their material culture was concerned, both the Lithic and Lignic periods were generalized and very similar throughout Southeast Asia. With the next period, the Crystallitic, however, very distinct cultures began to appear. This period began about 22,500 years ago with the warm stadial stage of the final glaciation and is marked by the Middle Hoabinhian and the first polishing and grinding of stone tools. Solheim hypothesizes that in the early portion of this period, possibly as early as 15000 B.C., people were on the verge of domesticating plants and inventing pottery. Next is the Extensionistic period, a time of

12. Solheim, "New Look," pp. 13–14.
13. Ibid., p. 14.

movement and changing cultures. People were overflowing some of the small upland valleys associated with the limestone formations that had supported the Hoabinhian hunting, gathering, and incipient horticultural societies. The rising seas at the end of the Pleistocene were also forcing those living along the shores of the Sunda shelf up the rivers. At this time, around 6000 B.C., the groups in the mountain valleys were developing dry-land farming as their hunting and gathering proved insufficient for their growing populations. This new mode of food production was accompanied by domestication of the bovine and possibly the pig.[14] By 4000 B.C. the outrigger canoe had been invented by river people and they moved up major waterways into the interior. Some also ventured out to sea, and Solheim speculates that one such outward movement began from the shores of South China and central Vietnam. Storms and currents carried some to the southern islands of Japan while others were swept to the Philippines, Indonesia, and Melanesia. Ultimately, bands of people reached the Pacific Islands and Madagascar. By the first millennium B.C. some large villages had grown up on the mainland of Southeast Asia and it is possible, Solheim feels, that in a few places there was also the beginning of urbanization.

The final period was the Conflicting Empire, which is identified with protohistory and history, although prehistoric societies continued to exist in the more remote areas of Southeast Asia. With the beginning of centralization of power and political organization, empires began to emerge, and eventually they came into conflict with one another. These empires rose because of outside influences from China and India in the early centuries and from the western colonial powers in more recent times. A major event of this period was the migration of Malayo-Polynesian speaking peoples from southeastern China, beginning around 500 B.C., who carried with them pottery with geometric, impressed patterns, paddy farming, and the custom of burying their dead in large earthenware jars.

---

14. Chester Gorman, in his article "The Hoabinhian and After: Subsistence Patterns in Southeast Asia during the Late Pleistocene and Early Recent Periods," *World Archeology* 2, no. 3 (1971): 300–20, carefully examines all of the available evidence relating to subsistence patterns in Southeast Asia during the late Pleistocene and early recent periods and concludes that by 6500 B.C. a new technological complex entered or developed in Southeast Asia. As a result, over the next 1500 years the population density shifted from the karst riverine intermontane valleys to the plains. The most important factor in this development probably was the introduction of cereal grain, making the plains the most favorable environmental zone. By 3500 B.C. there is evidence of rice (*Oryza sativa*) on the plains, and at least one good sequence at the site of Non Nok Tha (in Thailand) traces rice cultivation from this time to the historic period.

Some of these groups settled in the Philippines, Indonesia, and southern Malaya while others made their way to Korea and Japan.[15]

THE EARLY HISTORIC PERIOD

Vietnam

Le Thanh Khoi writes that the legendary kingdoms of the Vietnamese appeared in the misty past, around the time of the bronze age.[16] The lore surrounding these kingdoms is rooted in the Vietnamese oral tradition. The first known written mention is found in the fourteenth century *Việt-Sử-Lược*, by an unknown author, but only a few lines are devoted to the kingdoms. A more complete collection of legends first appears in Ngo Si Lien's *Đại Việt Sử-ký Toàn-thư*, written in the fifteenth century. As recounted by Le Thanh Khoi, the earliest legend begins with De Minh, the great grandson of Than Nong, the "ancestor of agriculture," who was traveling in the country near the Chain of the Five Passes when he encountered an exquisite female immortal. He fell in love with her and they had a son named Loc Tuc. Later De Minh divided his kingdom, giving the northern part to De Nghi, his elder son by another woman, and the southern part to Loc Tuc, his younger son. Loc Toc married the daughter of the Lord of Dong Dinh and his wife Than Long (Dragon Spirit), and they had a son. When the son succeeded his father he took the name Lac Long Quan (Lord Dragon Lac) and married the beautiful immortal Au Co, who bore him one hundred sons. These one hundred sons were the ancestors of the Bach Viet or "One Hundred Viet" tribes (called Yue by the Chinese). One day the king informed his wife that since he was of the dragon race and she was an immortal they, like fire and water, could not exist together and so would have to part. Half the sons followed their mother into the mountains while the other half went with their father to the shore of the Southern Sea (Nam Hai), where they remained.

15. B. Y. Jouin, "Les Traditions des Rhadé," *BSEI* 25, no. 4 (1950): 357–400, relates several Rhadé origin myths. One describes five periods that marked the beginning of the world. First there was a period during which the world was consumed by fire. This was followed by a time when the earth was a wasteland which became inundated. When the flood subsided there was a great earthquake. Following this the Rhadé emerged from an underground existence through a hole called Adrenh and dispersed. A related myth describes how the ancestors of the Rhadé at one time lived on islands and constructed large rafts (*ki*) on which they made their way to the coast of what is now Vietnam.

16. Le Thanh Khoi, *Le Viêt-Nam: histoire et civilisation* (Paris: Les Editions de Minuit, 1955), pp. 82–85.

Lac Long Quan passed his throne on to his eldest son Hung Vuong, who called his kingdom Van Lang (The Country of the Tattooed Men) and ruled from his capital at Phong Chau, said to have stood not far from Hanoi. The territory of his kingdom extended from the Dong Dinh lake (Hunan) in the north to Ho Ton (identified with Champa and present Quang Nam-Da Nang province) in the south. The kingdom was divided into fifteen provinces (*bộ*), and the king governed with the aid of civil chiefs called Lac Hau (Lac Marquis) and the Lac Tuong (Lac Generals). Power was transmitted from the king to his eldest son, and the dynasty, called Hong Bang, included eighteen sovereigns.

Le Thanh Khoi notes that tattooing, a custom which would last until the rule of Tran Anh Tong at the beginning of the fourteenth century, came into being under the reign of Hung Vuong. Since his subjects were fishermen and susceptible to attacks by crocodiles, Hung Vuong decreed that they tattoo themselves with sea monster motifs for protection. Also for their protection he directed the fishermen to build their boats in the shape of fish and paint fish eyes on the prow for protection, a practice that survives to this day.

The ruler of the neighboring kingdom of Thuc approached Hung Vuong to ask for the hand of his youngest daughter, a girl of great beauty. Hung Vuong, however, fearing his neighbor's territorial ambitions, refused to give his consent. Two other suitors appeared—Son Tinh (Spirit of the Mountains) and Thuy Tinh (Spirit of Water). Only Son Tinh brought the gifts Hung Vuong had specified and so won the girl in marriage. He took her to his kingdom on Tan Vien mountain but the jealous Thuy Tinh unleashed winds and water to overwhelm his rival. Son Tinh, undaunted, retaliated with lightning bolts that defeated Thuy Tinh.

The king of Thuc, who continued to harbor resentment at having been rejected by his neighbor, instilled a hatred for Hung Vuong in his descendants. Years later one of the Hong Bang rulers sank into soft complacency, overconfident that the defenses against his aggressive neighbors were adequate. Realizing this, Thuc Phan, the ruler of the kingdom of Thuc attacked. His forces entered the Hong Bang capital and in the confusion of the fighting the Hong Bang ruler fell to his death in one of the wells. This event ended the Hong Bang dynasty in 258 B.C. Annexing the Hong Bang lands, Thuc Phan called his new kingdom Au Lac and took the title An Duong Vuong. His capital was established at Phong Ke where with the assistance of the deity Kim Quy (Golden Tortoise) he raised the citadel of

Loa Thanh with three extensive walls enclosing a massive spiral-shaped structure.

Before departing, the GoldenTortoise gave Thuc Phan a crossbow with a special claw as a trigger, noting that if the crossbow were used in battle it would render the bowman invincible because of this talisman. This proved to be the case when Thuc Phan used the crossbow in defeating the invading Chinese general Trieu Da (*Chin.*, Chao T'o). Subsequently, however, the wily Trieu Da arranged a marriage between his son Trong Thuy and My Chau, the exquisite daughter of An Duong Vuong. After gaining the confidence of his father-in-law, the new groom made off with the magic claw and presented it to his father. Trieu Da then launched an attack against An Duong Vuong, who, when he discovered that the claw trigger was missing from his crossbow, fled with his daughter My Chau. When they reached the edge of the sea he implored the Golden Tortoise to come to his aid. The tortoise appeared among the waves and declared, "Your enemy is at your back," whereupon An Duong Vuong cut off his daughter's head. Then, clutching a rhinoceros horn, he followed the tortoise into the sea. The blood from My Chau's body seeped into the water and there the oysters transformed it into pearls of extraordinary brilliance. Trong Thuy carried the body back to Loa Thanh where he buried it. Soon he became overwrought with regret, and one night he threw himself into the well in a courtyard where My Chau loved to sit and listen to the songs of the birds. Le Thanh Khoi notes that at the site of the ancient capital of Co Loa, not far from Hanoi, there are portions of three earth ramparts thought to be the remnants of the Loa Thanh citadel. Nearby there is a temple dedicated to An Duong Vuong, and under a very old banyan tree stands a shrine honoring My Chau.

Both Le Thanh Khoi and Coedès begin their discussions of early Vietnamese history based on Chinese sources with the year 221 B.C. when the Chinese emperor Ch'in Shih Huang-ti decided on an expedition against the country of the Viet (*Chin.*, Yuëh)—the "land of the barbarians of the south." [17] Coedès feels that the primary motivation for the south-ward expansion was to gain control over the Viet areas that provided the Chinese court with such luxury items as ivory, rhinoceros horns, tortoise shell, pearls, peacock and kingfisher feathers, spices, and aromatic woods in return for Chinese silk. The campaign did not begin until 218 B.C. when

17. Ibid., pp. 91–101; Coedès, *Making of South East Asia*, pp. 39–46.

the armies under the command of General Trieu Da (*Chin.*, Chao T'o) reached the western part of the Viet kingdom only to find that the indigenous Tay Au (*Chin.*, Hsi Ou) tribes had retreated into the hinterlands, leaving small armed bands to harass the Chinese. General Trieu Da called for reinforcements, but the new troops turned out to be largely men that the Chinese considered to be undesirable elements. As the campaign continued these undesirables were left in the conquered territories to found military colonies.

By 214 B.C. the Chinese forces had crossed the passes leading to the valley of the West river and had conquered the eastern territory extending to the sea. The area was divided into the three commanderies of Nan-hai, Kuei-lin, and Hsiang, and the forts established in them eventually became the chief towns of Canton, Hsun-chou, and Nan-ning. To the south of these commanderies, the Red river delta remained under the authority of hereditary indigenous chiefs called Lac (*Chin.*, Lo) in principalities described by Coedès as having a "feudal organization." The southward expansion of the Chinese came to a temporary halt when in 210 B.C. the death of Ch'in Shih Huang-ti initiated a period of anarchy in China. His only son reigned until 207, after which the military leaders fought among themselves to gain ascendancy. General Liu Peng was victorious and founded the Han dynasty (202 B.C.–A.D. 220). During the period of confusion just prior to this, the governor of the Viet, Nham Ngao (*Chin.*, Jen Ngao), attempted to become independent but was prevented from doing so by a fatal illness. As he died, he called upon General Trieu Da to succeed him. Once in authority, Trieu Da launched a purge, executing all officials loyal to the Ch'in regime and replacing them with his own followers. By the time the Han dynasty was founded, Trieu Da had declared himself king of Nam Viet (*Chin.*, Nan-yue), which embraced the three commanderies, and in return for recognition as ruler he accepted the suzerainty of the new dynasty.

In 183 B.C. Trieu Da broke off relations with Empress Lu, widow of the first Han ruler, when she forbade him to trade in iron. He assumed the title of emperor of Nam Viet. The Empress Lu sent an army to the south but heavy rains and epidemics of fever brought the campaign to a disastrous end. Trieu Da then lost no time in bringing his southern neighbors under his control. These included the Lac of Tay Au Lac, the feudal lords of the Red river delta and the coastal plains immediately to the south. He divided this newly acquired territory into two commanderies, Giao Chi (*Chin.*,

Chiao-chih), which included the Red river delta, and Cuu Chan (*Chin.*, Chiu-chen), the area farther south which included the lowland portions of the present provinces of Thanh Hoa and Nghe Tinh. In Giao Chi the Lac princes retained their authority and accepted their role as vassals to Trieu Da, who founded the Trieu dynasty. When in 112 B.C. the Trieu dynasty broke its ties with the Chinese court, the Han ruler, Wu-ti, sent armies southward and conquered Nam Viet, which was incorporated into the empire as the province of Giao-chi and divided into nine commanderies. Six of these included the present Chinese provinces of Kwangsi and Kwangtung, as well as the island of Hainan, while the remaining three corresponded to what had been Giao Chi and Cuu Chan with the addition of Nhat Nam (*Chin.*, Jih-nan), the coastal area from present Hoanh Son, where a mountain spur juts into the sea north of the city of Ba Don, to Deo Hai Van (Col des Nuages) just north of the present city of Danang.

Initially the Han made no attempt to alter the existing institutions in these acquired areas. The two legates of Viet at Giao Chi and Cuu Chan were confirmed in office and the people continued to be governed by their native lords, the Lac. With the first century, however, the Chinese governors began a systematic attempt to sinicize the population. Tich Quang (*Chin.*, Hsi Kuang), who served as governor between A.D. 1 and A.D. 25, set out to "change the people through rites and justice," which presaged an official policy of introducing Chinese institutions. Also at this time, there was a steady increase in the number of Chinese settlers—exiles, deported criminals, and fugitives—into the southern commanderies. These settlers were carriers of Chinese customs and language. When Wang Mang seized power from the Han in A.D. 9, Governor Tich Quang refused to recognize the usurper, and as a result many scholarly mandarin families who remained loyal to the dynasty sought refuge in the south. During this period Tich Quang founded schools, introduced the use of the metal plow, made the natives wear Chinese footgear and headgear and observe Chinese marriage customs, organized a militia trained in the Chinese manner, and launched a program for training native subordinate officials of all kinds.

In the view of the indigenous leaders, the program for preparing Chinese-trained administrators posed a threat to their traditional authority, and when in A.D. 25 Tich Quang was replaced by To Dinh (*Chin.*, Su Ting) the new governor encountered hostility from the local aristocrats. In the year 40 this culminated in an open rebellion led by two sisters named Trung (*Chin.*, Cheng) who were the daughters of the Lac chief in Me Linh.

Trung Trac, accompanied by her younger sister Trung Nhi, gathered the support of other Lac leaders and moved against Lien Lau, the capital. Governor To Dinh fled, and the rebels occupied the capital. When sixty-five more citadels had been captured, the rebels declared the area to be independent of China and raised Trung Trac (*Chin.*, Cheng Tse) to the status of queen. The imperial court in China was at this time preoccupied with other internal dissensions, and it was two years before an expedition could be sent to the troubled south. Commanded by seventy-year-old General Ma Vien (*Chin.*, Ma Yuan), the army of 20,000 moved into Giao Chi, penetrating as far as the Red river delta without encountering serious resistance. At Lang Bac there was a decisive battle, but the badly disciplined Lac troops were no match for the Chinese veterans. The Trung sisters fled, but several months later Trung Trac was captured, probably in present Son Tay province, and her sister was subsequently taken in present Hai Duong province.

Following his defeat of the rebels, Ma Vien organized new commanderies and prefectures modeled after the system established by the Han in China as the first phase of integrating the area into the empire. The Lac lords lost their privileges and many of them fled to the highlands where they eventually became petty chiefs of districts and villages, probably under Chinese authority. Hundreds of the aristocratic families were deported to southern China. Those who remained were reduced to low status, although in some areas they intermarried with the Chinese colonists who flooded into Giao Chi and formed new local elites. By the end of A.D. 43, Ma Vien had brought the area of Cuu Chan under control. Le Thanh Khoi notes that this area south of the Red river delta is described as having been a wild place of swamps and forests, the abode of elephants, rhinoceros, and tigers.[18] The inhabitants lived for the most part by hunting, using bows and arrows with bone arrowheads to kill beasts. They ate the flesh of pythons, fished, and also supplemented their diets with meager crops farmed in small swiddens. It was only around the administrative centers that some paddy fields were farmed, a cultivation technique learned from the Chinese colonists. A sequence of governors tried, with varying degrees of success, to apply the Chinese policy of assimilation. One outstanding governor was Si Nhiep (*Chin.*, Shih Hsieh), who administered from 187 to 226. He is remembered for having organized an effective program of

18. Le Thanh Khoi, *Le Viêt-Nam*, pp. 102–03.

bringing Chinese studies to the population of the Red river delta. He also is reputed to have received the first Buddhist missionaries, allowing them to spread their teachings and build monasteries. This too was a period when the followers to Taoism and Confucianism were allowed to teach their doctrines.

Although there were vast political changes in China brought about by the fall of the Han dynasty in 220 and the breakup of the empire into the three kingdoms, the policy of assimilation of the south continued. The troubles in China, however, did encourage some resistance to Chinese rule in Giao Chi and some incursions into the southern commandery of Nhat Nam by the rulers of the newly established kingdom of Lin Yi (early Champa, see below) to the south. The first revolt against Chinese authority occurred when Governor Si Nhiep's son, Si Huy (*Chin.*, Shih Hui), tried to succeed him when he died in 226. The new governor, Lu Dai (*Chin.*, Lu Tai), prevented this and had Si Huy executed. In 248 a twenty-three-year-old woman (called Trieu Au by the Vietnamese) led a force of one thousand in a six-months-long revolt in Cuu Chan. This too was repressed. Between 541 and 603 there were three uprisings led by chiefs bearing the name Ly, which has given rise to the theory that a local dynasty referred to as "the former Ly" reigned locally during this period. In 622 the T'ang ruler in China reorganized the former southern commanderies into the government of Chiao, which in 679 became the protectorate of An Nam (*Chin.*, An-nan, "the pacified south"). It included the area from the present Chinese border to Hoanh Son and was placed under the Chinese administration in the capital like other provinces of the empire.[19]

Le Thanh Khoi is convinced that "Lac" is the most ancient designation for the Vietnamese and that later the term "Giao Chi," the name for the first commandery founded by Trieu Da, became the name for the Vietnamese used in the Chinese literature.[20] Coedès also feels that Lac is the earliest ethnic designation for "the group of peoples who were later to form the nucleus of the Vietnamese."[21] More recently a similar conclusion was expressed by the North Vietnamese historian Nguyen Luong Bich, who notes that in the recent past Chinese scholars have taken the position that the Lac Viet were ancestral to a number of different ethnic groups,

---

19. Coedès, *Making of South East Asia*, pp. 46–49.
20. Le Thanh Khoi, *Le Viêt-Nam*, pp. 86–88.
21. Coedès, *Making of South East Asia*, pp. 41–42.

particularly the Tai-speaking people and the Chuang.[22] Their view is that "Lac Viet" evolved into Lao, Ly, O Hu, Lang, and Chuang. Citing early Chinese documents and works by other Vietnamese investigators, Nguyen Luong Bich calls the Lac unquestionably the ancestors of the Vietnamese.

As reconstructed from Chinese documents by Maspéro, the Lac society of the kingdom of Van Lang seems to have had a "feudal" social organization with a structured hierarchy similar to that found among the Muong, the Tai-speaking groups in the highlands of northern Vietnam.[23] At the local level the Lac Marquis (Lac Hau) held hereditary positions of authority, while below them were the Lac chiefs, who were of noble village families. The Lac were sedentary people who lived in small communities, where they farmed the land with polished stone hoes (plows later were introduced by the Chinese). They knew how to use the tides to irrigate their paddy fields and produced two crops a year. They tattooed their bodies so as "to avoid the crocodiles," they chewed betel and areca, and they blackened their teeth. Although the Chinese describe them as wearing no clothes, Maspéro feels that they more than likely wore some kind of garment. Religion was centered on agriculture with a large celebration at spring planting. Betel and areca were prescribed offerings for the bride at marriage, and the levirate was practiced. In warfare they used bows and arrows with bronze heads on which poison was smeared.

The use of bows and poisoned arrows with bronze heads also is mentioned by Nguyen Luong Bich in his discussion of the identity of the Lac Viet.[24] He notes that several Chinese sources record that in A.D. 43 General Ma Vien took 10,000 Lac troops from Me Linh northward to assist in putting down a revolt in Yunnan. Some 3,000 of these troops were adept at using bows and arrows with bronze heads smeared with poison and are described as having fired a rain of arrows at one time, killing many of the enemy.

In North Vietnam there was an attempt to relate the bronze age archeological finds to what have thus far been considered legendary kingdoms. Since 1959 considerable archeological research has been conducted

22. Nguyễn Lương Bích, "Lạc Việt, Lạc Vương, Lạc Hầu, Lạc Tướng, Lạc Dân là tổ tiên người Việt chúng ta hay là tổ tiên chung của nhiều dân tộc khác" (The Lac Viet, Lac Kings, Lac Marquis, Lac Generals, and Lac People: Were They the Ancestors of the Vietnamese People or Were They the Common Ancestors of Many Varied People?), *Nghiên Cứu Lịch Sử* (Historical Research) 56 (1963): 3–12. Translated by Mai Elliott.

23. Henri Maspéro, "Le Royaume de Van Lang," *BEFEO* 18, nos. 3 and 4 (1918): 8–10.

24. Nguyễn Lương Bích, "Lạc Việt, Lạc Vương," pp. 4–5.

by the North Vietnamese, and one of the important sites is at the location of the ancient capital of Co Loa, thought to have been the citadel of Loa Thanh established by An Duong Vuong, ruler of the kingdom of Au Lac. At this site, not far from present Hanoi, there are ruins of three ramparts which possibly are remnants of the citadel. At this site on 17 July 1959 archeologists unearthed some 10,000 bronze arrowheads, large in size with three edges, similar to those found in China dating from the time of the Warring States (468–200 B.C.).[25]

Also in 1959, the Phung Nguyen site in Vinh-Phu province was discovered and classified as upper neolithic. It yielded over five hundred chisels of all sizes, finely worked stone bracelets, awls, hoes, and a large number of vases and pots. In 1960, some three kilometers away, a related site was found at Viet Hung. In addition to containing stone bracelets and many potsherds, it had twenty-one stone axes, thirteen of which were shoulder axes.[26] More recently, two articles in the North Vietnamese newspaper *Nhân Dân* describe the Phung Nguyen as a period transitional from the neolithic (ending around 4000 years ago) to the bronze age (ending some 2000 years ago).[27] These authors also equate the bronze age with the Hung Vuong culture and the Hong Bang dynasty. Pham Huy Thong notes that there is a new archeological site at Lang Vac in Nghe-Tinh province that is thought to contain vestiges of the Hung Vuong period. More explicitly, Nguyen Lam Cuong and Vu The Long list some Hung Vuong bronze culture sites that have been dated by the carbon-14 method: Trang Kenh in Hai Phong province (3405 ± 100); Dong Dau in Vinh Phu province (3328 ± 100); Vinh Quang (3046 ± 120), Vuong Chuoi (3070 ± 100), and Chien Vay (2350 ± 100)—all in Ha-Son-Binh province; and Viet Khe in Hai Phong province (2480 ± 100). Although it is not clear how they identify a "Hung Vuong culture," their dating makes the bronze age in northern Vietnam older than had previously been thought.

In speculating about the origins of the Vietnamese, Coedès notes that information in early Chinese accounts describing the people of Nam Viet

25. Van Tan, "The Beginnings of Archeology in the Democratic Republic of Vietnam," *Vietnamese Studies* 2 (1964): 208.

26. Ibid., pp. 207–08; P. I. Boriskovskii, "Vietnam in Primeval Times (Part I)," *Soviet Anthropology and Archeology* 7, no. 2 (1968): 26–27.

27. Phạm Huy Thông, "Thêm một mùa gặt khảo cổ học" (Another Archeological Harvest), *Nhân Dân*, 7 July 1973; Nguyễn Lân Cường and Vũ Thế Long, "Định niên đại trong khảo cổ học" (Archeological Dating), *Nhân Dân*, 7 July 1973.

as wearing no clothes, blackening their teeth, chewing betel and areca, using poisoned arrows, and tilling with hoes of stone evinces the "traits characteristic of the Mon Khmer and Indonesian peoples of southern Indochina speaking non-tonal languages." [28] But, he adds, while the Nam Viet society was described as having a "hierarchical social organization of a feudal type" and this is alien to the southern highland groups, it is "identical with that of the T'ais and other ethnolinguistic groups of southern China speaking tonal languages." This suggests to Coedès two components in the pre-Chinese culture of northern Vietnam—southern elements contributed by the Lac and northern elements by the Viet—thus relating the ancient population of the region to the Mon Khmer and the Tai-speaking peoples.

While this would conform to Maspéro's theory that the Vietnamese language evolved from a fusion of Mon Khmer and Thai dialects (and a third unknown dialect), it is at variance with the position of Haudricourt, Thomas, and Headley that the Vietnamese language is of the Austroasiatic stock and very likely of the Mon Khmer family (see chap. 1).

It cannot be assumed that the ethnic groups now found in the central highlands existed in the distant past with the same ethnic identity they now possess. The highland groups, however, are culturally quite conservative, and it is interesting to note that some of the characteristics described for the people of Nam Viet resemble traits that are found among some of the highlanders, particularly those speaking Mon Khmer languages. Traditionally the highlanders were scantily dressed with the men wearing loincloths and the women going bare above the waist. Betel and areca are chewed by some groups, particularly those in the northern part of the central highlands—the Bru, Pacoh, Katu, Hre, and Cua. The Bru appear to be the only people among the highlanders who blacken their teeth, but most groups use bows and arrows (usually smeared with poison when hunting large game and, in the past, for warfare). All of the highlanders use hoes for tilling and, though the blades now are metal, they could easily have at one time been of polished stone.

Other characteristics of the Lac society also are found among the highlanders. (1) In marriage most of the groups have the levirate. (2) All of the highlanders have special deities associated with agriculture, and special offerings are made to them at planting time by both family groups and the

28. Coedès, *Making of South East Asia*, pp. 41–42.

village community. (3) Although they are removed from any tidal areas, the Mon Khmer-speaking Hre and Cua practice wet-rice agriculture, supplementing their food production by swidden farming. (4) While none of the highland groups has a structured hierarchy such as that found among the Tai-speaking people in northern Vietnam, it was pointed out in the previous chapter that those groups with unilineal descent tend to have locally entrenched elite families that provide the village leaders.

Finally, Coedès makes the point that the Vietnamese *dinh* or communal temple for the Guardian Spirit of the Village, which appears to be an indigenous, non-Chinese institution, usually is constructed on piling in northern Vietnam.[29] As indicated in the preceding chapters, this also is the case for the communal men's houses found among many of the Mon Khmer-speaking highlanders. Further, these upland communal houses, like the Vietnamese *dinh*, serve as ritual centers as well as gathering places for the village leaders. Both are focal institutions in village society.[30]

Funan and Chenla

In the first century A.D. a kingdom called Funan was established in the lower valley of the Mekong river (according to the Chinese accounts, which are the only written sources on this kingdom). Although it existed for six centuries, little is known about Funan. Coedès speculates that the name probably was a Chinese transcript of *bnam*, the word for "mountain" in most Khmer dialects.[31] He reasons that, since Funan was an Indian type of kingdom, a central feature would have been a natural or artificial mountain used as a place of worship for an Indian deity closely associated with the person of a king. Briggs, however, puts forth the view that the Funanese probably spoke a pre-Khmer Austroasiatic language, such as Pater Schmidt believes was spoken in most of Indochina.[32] Briggs notes that the three inscriptions attributed to the Funan period were in Sanskrit and the earliest Khmer language inscriptions found in the old Funan territory are dated 628–629, about the time Funan was annexed by

29. Ibid., p. 218.

30. For discussions about the functions of the dinh in northern and southern Vietnam, see Nguyen Van Khoan, "Essai sur le dinh et le culte du génie titulaire des villages au Tonkin," *BEFEO* 30 (1936): 107–39; and Gerald Cannon Hickey, *Village in Vietnam* (New Haven: Yale University Press, 1964), pp. 204–07, 225–30, 242.

31. Coedès, *Making of South East Asia*, p. 57.

32. Lawrence P. Briggs, *The Ancient Khmer Empire* (Philadelphia: American Philosophical Society, 1951), p. 15.

Chenla. More recently, after reexamining the Chinese sources, Wolters questions whether Funan and Chenla could properly be called "king-doms." He concludes that as of the seventh century the area that is today called Cambodia was comprised of "an unknown number of independent principalities, each of which was under the control of a ruling family." [33]

The origins of Funan remain a mystery, but according to a legend often cited it was established after an Indian Brahman named Kaundinya arrived in the area and took as his wife Soma, the daughter of the King of the Naga, that is, the local chief. It was this union that marked the beginning of what has come to be known as the Kaundinya dynasty. The kingdom at this time apparently consisted of some settlements located on the banks of the Mekong river between present Chau Doc in southwestern Vietnam and Phnom Penh. Each settlement had its own chief, and Kaundinya gave seven of these towns to his son as a royal fief. Drawing on Chinese accounts, Pelliot concludes that the dynasty actually began when the son of Kaundinya ascended the throne sometime in the latter part of the first century. [34] It continued until the beginning of the third century when a great general named Fan Man or Fan Shih-man became sovereign. At that time the kingdom appears to have been organized in the Indian manner with Fan Shih-man ruling a number of vassal principalities in the sur-rounding region. Soon after ascending the throne he began to expand his realm. Briggs notes that he probably first extended his authority over the lower valleys of the Mekong river and the Tonle Sap, and perhaps even parts of the Mekong river delta. [35] Subsequently he expanded his control over the coastal strip from the delta to Cam Ranh bay.

Coedès notes that his suzerainty may even have extended to the area of present-day Nhatrang, where the stele at Vo Canh, with the oldest Sanskrit inscription in Indochina, is located. [36] He points out that while in the past this was thought to be a Cham stele, it has come to be accepted as a relic of Funan, and he speculates that it may have been constructed by a descendant of Fan Shih-man, referred to in the epigraphy as Sri Mara. The Chinese accounts describe how Fan Shih-man constructed large ships and sent his armies overseas to conquer ten kingdoms.

33. O. W. Wolters, "North-western Cambodia in the Seventh Century," *Bulletin of the School of Oriental and African Studies* 37, pt. 2 (1974): 378–84.

34. M. P. Pelliot, "Le Fou-Nan," *BEFEO* 3, no. 2 (1903): 290.

35. Briggs, *Ancient Khmer Empire*, p. 19.

36. Coedès, *Making of South East Asia*, p. 58; idem, *Indianized States*, p. 40.

Fan Shih-man died during one of his overseas campaigns and his son Fan Chin-sheng succeeded him. However, a son of Fan Shih-man's sister usurped power and became the ruler under the name of Fan Chan. He established relations with India and China—more for economic than for political reasons, since Funan was in a favorable position close to the sea routes and profited from trade with these great kingdoms. Fan Chan's envoy to China in 243 carried products of his country and also included some musicians, for whom the Chinese established an institute near Nanking. The Chinese mission to Funan, sometime between 245 and 250, found a usurper named Fan Hsun on the throne and recorded that there were walled cities, palaces, and houses of wood. The Chinese described the people as "all ugly, black and frizzy-haired, going about naked and barefoot" and noted that they practiced agriculture. Their writing, the account said, was like that of the Hu, a general designation for the people of central Asia who use an Indian script. It also noted that there was trial by ordeal.[37]

At the end of the fourth century A.D. there was a revival of Indian influence through Southeast Asia, and according to Chinese records there appeared in Funan a second Kaundinya, who is said to have come from India via the Malay peninsula. Under his rule Indian traditions were revived, and during the reign of one of his successors, Jayavarman (who died in 514), Funan achieved a civilization of great brilliance. The capital at this time was Vyadhapura (The City of the Hunter), situated near the Ba Phnom hill close to the Mekong river, southeast of present Phnom Penh, some 120 miles from the sea. Coedès points out that this is approximately the distance between Ba Phnom and the archeological site of Oc Eo near the Gulf of Siam, which probably was the main part of Funan.[38] Research at this site by Louis Malleret has unearthed the foundations of buildings and objects such as Roman coins, which he feels indicate some trade relations with the west.

The Chinese history of the Southern Ch'i contains some fragments of information about the society of Funan. In the view of the Chinese visitors, the people of Funan were "malicious and cunning," and if their neighbors did not pay homage to the Funanese king they were enslaved. In the city the structures were of wood and the king's pavilion was a multistoried

---

37. Pelliot, "Le Fou-Nan," p. 254.
38. Coedès, *Making of South East Asia*, pp. 59–60.

building. The ordinary people constructed their houses on piling and used the large fronds from "great bamboo" that grew along the shore for their roofs. The Chinese noted that the Funanese constructed long boats with bow and stern like the head and tail of a fish. On ceremonial occasions the king rode on an elephant. The sons of the rich wore sarongs of brocade, while the poor were garbed in ordinary cloth. Many of the people were tattooed, and they amused themselves with cock fights and hog fights. There were no prisons, but there was trial by ordeal. (One such trial involved throwing the accused and accuser into deep water. The survivor was considered to be the one in the right.) The Chinese accounts also reported that the Funanese produced exquisite silver vessels, gold rings, and bracelets and that there was trade in silk as well as in gold and silver. The people venerated "spirits in the sky," and they represented these spirits with bronze images with two faces and many arms.[39]

In the thirteenth-century account by Ma Tuan-lin, the Funanese are described as "ugly and black" with fuzzy hair and as wearing no clothes and tattooing their bodies.[40] Ma also wrote that their towns were fortified.

According to the history of the Liang dynasty, when Jayavarman, the king of Funan, died in 514, Rudravarman, the son of a concubine, killed his younger brother, the son of the legitimate queen, and seized the throne. In Chenla, a vassal state to the north of Funan, Bhavavarman became king around 550, and it was about this time that Rudravarman died in Funan. His death apparently brought about a period of disorder during which Bhavavarman succeeded in making Funan a vassal of Chenla. Funan existed as a vassal, with its capital at Vyadhapura, probably under the descendants of its old line of kings. By 626, however, Funan was rarely mentioned in any of the accounts, and it appears to have been completely absorbed by Chenla.[41]

Coedès points out that the Chinese description of the Funanese as being black-skinned and frizzy-haired could also be applied to the mountain people, as well as to many Cambodians.[42] The Mon Khmer-speaking Stieng and Mnong groups along the Cambodian border are dark-skinned, and while their hair could not be described as "frizzy" they do have more hair whorl than the Chinese. Some of the traits reported earlier for the

39. Pelliot, "Le Fou-Nan," pp. 261–62, 269–70.
40. Ma Tuan-lin, *Wen-hsien t'ung-k'ao*, trans. Hervey de Saint-Denys, *Ethnographie des peuples étrangers à la Chine* (Geneva: H. Georg, 1883), pp. 436–43.
41. Briggs, *Ancient Khmer Empire*, pp. 29–32, 48.
42. Coedès, *Making of South East Asia*, pp. 62–63.

Funanese also are found among these as well as other highland groups. Most highlanders, for example, build their houses on piling (although Stieng houses are constructed on the ground). Slavery was widespread in the highlands and continues to exist among the Stieng and Mnong Gar. Trial by ordeal also is practiced among some groups. Gerber describes various forms of ordeal practiced by the Stieng, one of which involves plunging the accuser and the accused in water, the first to emerge being considered the loser.[43] (In the similar Funanese ordeal it was the survivor who won vindication.)

Briggs has found in the Sui-shu (A.D. 589–618) what appears to be the first written mention of the name Chenla in a record of an embassy sent to China in 616 or 617.[44] The original site of Chenla, Briggs believes, was in the region of southeastern Laos just below the mouth of the Mun river, and it was from there that the early kings expanded their territory southward. In the second half of the sixth century Bhavavarman, who had become king of Chenla around 550, conquered Funan with the help of his cousin Chitrasena. Around 600 Chitrasena succeeded Bhavavarman, taking the name Mahendravarman, and after his death around 611 his son Isana-varman ascended the throne.[45] The history of the Sui also notes that the men of Chenla were small in stature and dark of complexion while many of the women were fair. All rolled up their hair and wore ear pendants. When there was a marriage, the boy sent gifts to the girl, and after the girl's parents had selected a propitious day the bride, accompanied by an inter-mediary, went to the groom's house, where both families remained for eight days. Afterward the groom's parents gave him part of the family goods and he established his own household. There also were references to matrilineal descent; one text notes that in Chenla the offices in many great priestly families were transmitted through the female line, and this infor-mation was repeated in later texts of the Angkor period.[46]

Jayavarman I came to the throne of Chenla some time between 640 and 657. In his early years he expanded the territory, conquering central and upper Laos. Briggs notes that according to Chinese accounts the state of Sang Kao (in the vicinity of present Cammon) and several other little states (which had sent embassies to Isanavarman's court in 638) were con-

---

43. Gerber, "Coutumier Stieng," pp. 234–35.
44. Briggs, *Ancient Khmer Empire*, p. 37.
45. Coedès, *Indianized States*, pp. 68–70.
46. Briggs, *Ancient Khmer Empire*, pp. 39–51; Coedès, *Indianized States*, pp. 72–76.

quered.[47] These states extended into the highlands of Laos which were occupied by the upland groups (called "Kha" in most of the western sources), and eventually Chenla extended north to the Tai kingdom of Nan Chao. Coedès cites the T'ang histories as recording that around 706 the kingdom of Chenla became divided (after Jayavarman I died without a male heir) and anarchy ensued.[48] The northern half, a "land of mountains and valleys," was known as "Land Chenla." The southern half, bounded by the sea and containing many lakes, was called "Water Chenla." The division appears to have occurred when a prince of Anindatapura named Pushkara (or Pushkaraksha) became king of Sambhupura, a site represented by a group of ruins at Sambor on the Mekong river just north of the present city of Kratie.

Briggs points out that what little is known about Land Chenla is found in the Chinese accounts concerning embassies Chenla sent to the court.[49] The limits of Land Chenla appear to have extended to the present Chinese province of Yunnan. The first embassy from this country arrived at the Chinese court in 717. In 722 Land Chenla aided a revolt led by a native chief in present Nghe An province of Vietnam against Chinese rule. Le Thanh Khoi identifies this rebel chief as Mai Thuc Loan, a Muong chief, who received military aid from Land Chenla and Champa.[50] Maspéro notes that the Muong and other highland groups in that area had only been brought under Chinese domination some fifty years before, around 663, but that they nonetheless continued to be a source of trouble.[51] Relying on the chronicle of Kia Tan, written three-quarters of a century after the events of 722, Maspéro traces the land routes that could have been taken by the Cambodian troops from Land Chenla to Nghe An and concludes that there were two feasible routes: one to the northwest of present Vinh through Cua Rao and another to the east through Muong Borikhane. Both would lead to the Mekong river, where the troops could have been transported by pirogue.

Mai Thuc Loan and his allied armies were successful in capturing some thirty-two departments in Nghe An and the Red river delta. After the fall of Tong Binh, the capital of the protectorate, Mai Thuc Loan declared him-

47. Briggs, *Ancient Khmer Empire*, p. 54.
48. Coedès, *Indianized States*, pp. 85–86, 93–95.
49. Briggs, *Ancient Khmer Empire*, p. 59.
50. Le Thanh Khoi, *Le Viêt-Nam*, pp. 122–23.
51. Henri Maspéro, "Etudes d'histoire d'Annam," *BEFEO* 18, no. 3 (1918): 29–32.

self Hac-de (The Black Emperor). It was not long, however, before new armies began to arrive from China, and when it became apparent that he could not stand up to the reinforced Chinese forces "The Black Emperor" fled into the highlands. His Cambodian and Cham allies returned to their homelands.[52]

According to Coedès, Water Chenla was divided into several principalities.[53] In Anindatapura (in the south) the ruler was Baladitya, who gave his name to the city of Baladityapura, the true capital of Water Chenla. Two inscriptions dated 770 and 781 at Sambhupura (Sambor) refer to a king named Jayavarman. With the beginning of the reign of Jayavarman II in 802, the Chenla period of Cambodia ends and the Angkor period begins.

Lin Yi and Early Champa

There is not much known about the origins of Lin Yi, but it appears to have been founded around A.D. 192 in Hsiang-lin, the southernmost prefecture of Jih-nan—the commandery that incorporated the territory between Hoanh Son and Deo Hai Van (Col des Nuages) just above the present city of Danang. Stein cites various Chinese sources that describe harassment prior to 192 by "barbarians" (*K'iu-lien*) from "beyond the frontier" (*kiao-wai*) of the Chinese-controlled areas.[54] Stein concludes that the designation *K'iu-lien* refers to an ethnic group and that more than likely *K'iu* is the name of the leading clan of the group. The term *kiao-wai*, in his view, probably means "beyond the frontier of Jih-nan," that is, the upland area west of the coastal plain that had not been brought under Chinese control.

According to these Chinese accounts, in the year 100 some two thousand "barbarians" pillaged villages of Hsiang-lin and burned the administrative center, which prompted the Chinese government to name a military commission to provide protection for the prefecture. In 137 the "K'iu-lien barbarians" again attacked Hsiang-lin, reducing the administrative buildings to ashes and killing the prefect. When the governor of Kiao-Che (Tonkin) was unsuccessful in raising an army to send to the area, Chou Leang, the prefect of Kieu-chen (the area between present Thanh Hoa and Ha Tinh), managed to negotiate a peace with the K'iu-lien. The

52. Le Thanh Khoi, *Le Viêt-Nam*, p. 122.
53. Coedès, *Indianized States*, pp. 86–88.
54. Stein, "Le Lin-Yi," pp. 134–36, 142–46.

barbarians repeated their pillaging in 144. At this time they also formed an alliance with the barbarians of Kien-chen, and in 157 their combined forces rose in revolt against the Chinese authorities. Three years later Hia Fang, the new governor of Kiao-che, effected a peace with them, and it appears that the alliance between the barbarian groups continued. The Chinese accounts note that in 173 their "kingdoms" (Stein feels that this could also be interpreted as "principalities or chiefdoms") offered common tribute to the Chinese ruler and that this was repeated in 183.

In 192 a Hsiang-lin official's son (variously referred to as K'iu K'ouei, Kiu-lien, and Ch'u-lien) led a successful revolt and declared Hsiang-lin to be the independent kingdom of Lin Yi.[55] In 220 and 230 the government of Lin Yi sent embassies to Lu Tai, governor of Giao Chi. However, taking advantage of the political turmoil in China the ruler of Lin Yi sent his armies northward into the territory still under Chinese control in 248 to pillage the villages and occupy the area of Ch'iu-su up to Hoanh Son. The first king of this period to be mentioned in the Chinese records is Fan Hsiung, who ruled in 270.[56] Pelliot notes that T'ao Huang, who was governor of Kwangtung and Giao Chi, wrote in his biography in 280 that it would be unwise of the Chinese government to reduce the military garrison in the area because there were too many incursions by the armies of Fan Hsiung, whose control extended to the limits of Funan in the south. He added that "their tribes are very numerous" and indicated that these tribes lived in harmony with one another.[57]

Stein points out that sometime between 192 and 270 the name of the ruling family in Lin Yi had changed from K'iu to Fan, the same family name the Chinese reported for the ruling family of Funan, and he speculates whether there may have been intermarriage between them.[58] He cites such things as the account of T'ao Huang noted above as indicating that there probably was contact between the two kingdoms. At one point this would have involved Fan women from Funan going in marriage to Lin Yi and, given the Cham rule of descent through the female line, this would account for the change of the name of the ruling family.

According to Maspéro, matrilineal clans among the Cham survived the

---

55. The name of the official's son is given as K'iu K'ouei in Stein, pp. 241–42; as Kiu-lien in Ma Tuan-lin, *Wen-hsien t'ung-k'ao*, pp. 419–20; and as Ch'u-lien in Coedès, *Indianized States*, pp. 42–43.
56. Coedès, *Indianized States*, pp. 43–45.
57. Pelliot, "Le Fou-nan," p. 255.
58. Stein, "Le Lin-Yi," pp. 251–56.

Hindu colonization and the institution of the caste system. Each clan had a totem to distinguish it, and in the kingdom of Champa there were among the ruling families two elite clans, the Areca Nut (it was noted previously that an Areca Nut clan had existed among the Roglai) and the Coconut. The former, which boasted of having a "greater purity of race," dominated the northern part of the kingdom while the Coconut clan was in power in Pandurang (Phan Rang). Maspéro also notes that in the eleventh century the Cham ruler Harivarman III expressed pride at belonging to the Areca Nut clan, which was his mother's clan, but Maspéro adds that royal succession was in the male line in keeping with Hindu tradition.[59]

Around 270 Fan Hsiung, possibly with the assistance of Fan Hsun, the king of Funan, launched attacks against the commandery of Jih-han, and it took ten years for the Chinese governor T'ao Huang and his forces to push them back to the border of Lin Yi. In 284 Fan Yi, successor of Fan Hsiung, sent an official mission to China, but he also continued to harass southern Jih-nan. During the second half of his fifty-year reign, Fan Yi had an advisor named Wen, who in time became a legendary figure. Coedès reports that, according to some Chinese texts, Wen was a Chinese, a native of Yang-chou in Chiang-su who settled in Lin Yi.[60] Stein also found this information in Chinese accounts as well as a legend about Wen.[61] As a slave, Wen offended his master and fled into the mountains. There in a stream he caught two carp which were transformed into two "stones" that turned out to be iron. Wen forged the iron into two sabers and, holding them in the direction of the mountains, pronounced a supplication. If the carp had been changed into stones which were in turn changed into sabers, Wen reasoned, they must have magic powers that would enable them to split rock and divide the mountain. Should this be so, he went on, then he, Wen, would become ruler of the kingdom. If the sabers did not penetrate the rock, it would mean they had no special power. With this, Wen lunged at the mountain and the sabers split the rocks. As word of this feat spread, the people of the kingdom rallied to him and he became king. Examining legends reported for some of the ethnic groups in southern China and in Indochina, Stein sees a similarity in this theme and in some of those concerning the origin of the sacred saber of the King of Fire (see chap. 4).[62]

59. Georges Maspéro, *Champa*, pp. 16–19.
60. Coedès, *Indianized States*, p. 44.
61. Stein, "Le Lin-Yi," pp. 242–44.
62. Ibid., pp. 285–92.

According to Coedès, Wen traveled to China in 313 and 316 and there learned various military techniques such as construction of fortifications and production of offensive weapons.[63] Upon his return to Lin Yi he passed this information on to Fan Yi, the king. Pelliot notes that the Chinese accounts describe K'iu Su (sometimes transcribed Ch'u-su), the capital of Lin Yi which is thought to have been located in the vicinity of present Hue, as having impressive walls of brick with thirteen gates and containing some two thousand houses and public buildings that faced south. Speculating that these fortifications could not have gone back much beyond the first half of the fourth century, Pelliot feels that they probably can be attributed to Wen.[64] Grateful for his valuable assistance, Fan Yi made Wen a general, and when the old king died in 336 Wen ascended the throne with the royal name Fan Wen.

One of his achievements is supposed to have been the successful pacification of the barbarians. Stein cites a Chinese source that describes how Fan Wen became highly regarded by the "barbarians of the south," including those who "eat with the mouth but drink through the nose" and those who "etch their faces and bodies."[65] There also is mention of "the nude races" and the barbarian Lang-huang. Li Tao-yuan, a sixth century Chinese source, in describing a route through the highlands from Lin Yi to Funan, notes that the Lang-huang and Siu-lang occupy the upland river areas of Lin Yi, and if one continues south from their country "one arrives finally in Funan." He also records that the Lang-huang wear only loincloths of leaves and engage in silent nocturnal trade in gold, which they sniff to determine if it is good.[66]

Fan Wen sent an embassy to the Chinese court in 340, requesting that the northern border of Lin Yi be fixed at the Hoang Son mountain spur. When the emperor failed to respond, Fan Wen sent his armies to seize the area. Following his death during a military campaign in 349, his son Fan Fo succeeded to the throne and continued the policy of trying to expand the limits of Lin Yi northward. After two unsuccessful campaigns in 351 and 359, he relinquished control of the Jih-nan territory. Fan Fo was succeeded by Fan Hu-ta, who was either his son or grandson and who in 399, 405, and 407 launched new attacks on Jih-nan. In 413 he failed to return from

63. Coedès, *Indianized States*, pp. 44–45.
64. M. P. Pelliot, "Deux itinéraires de Chine en Inde," *BEFEO* 4, nos. 1–2 (1903): 191.
65. Stein, "Le Lin-Yi," p. 244.
66. Ibid., pp. 244–45; Pelliot, "Le Fou-nan," pp. 278–82.

an incursion into Jih-nan and was succeeded by his son Ti Chen, who abdicated soon after to travel to India. There is speculation that it is Ti Chen who is described in a seventh century inscription as Gangaraja—"the king who went to the Ganges."

In 420 a new dynasty appeared with a king called Yang Mah (Prince of Gold), who died the following year just after requesting investiture from the Chinese emperor. His son became king with the same name as his father and led raids against the coast of Jih-nan. This provoked a strong reaction from the Chinese, and in 446 T'an Ho-chih, the governor of Giao Chi, sent an army southward and seized the capital of Kiu-su. It was looted of a large number of gold statues (it never was determined what they represented) which were melted into ingots and shipped to China.[67]

Sometime during the second half of the fourth century there appeared a king with the Sanskrit name of Bhadravarman. Some scholars think this was a designation for Fan Hu-ta, although this never has been adequately proven. Stein disagrees with this view, believing that the name *Fan* cannot be equated with the terminal *varman* in a name such as Bhadravarman.[68] He suggests that the discrepancy between the Chinese and Sanskrit royal names at this time may have reflected a distinction between the rulers with their capital at K'iu-su near present-day Hue and the dynasty of kings farther south in present Quang Nam province.

With Bhadravarman there appears the first strong evidence of Indian influence. He founded the first sanctuary dedicated to Siva Bhadresvara at what was to become an elaborate temple complex near the village of My Son in Quang Nam–Da Nang province. To the east, near the village of Tra Kieu, he established his capital, and at this site there was found the oldest inscription in the Cham language. It is thought to date from the middle of the fourth century, thus providing convincing evidence that during that period Quang Nam was inhabited by Cham-speaking people.[69] Inscriptions at Tra Kieu also reveal that the dominant cult at the royal court honored Siva-Uma. At My Son the Bhadresvara was represented by a linga, the oldest known royal linga in Farther India.

Around 529 a new dynasty was founded and the center of the kingdom shifted from Thua Thien to the Quang Nam area. The first ruler of this

67. Coedès, *Indianized States*, pp. 56–57; Ma Tuan-lin, *Wen-hsien t'ung-k'ao*, pp. 429–30.
68. Stein, "Le Lin-Yi," pp. 71, 111, 251–57.
69. Georges Coedès, "La plus ancienne inscription en langue Cham," *New Indian Antiquary*, Extra Series, I, 1939, pp. 46–49.

dynasty was Rudravarman I, and as his predecessors had done before him the new king organized a raid against the north. However, he was defeated by a general of the Ly Bon who had just revolted against Chinese domination and made himself ruler of Tonkin. Rudravarman's successor was Sambhuvarman, and during his reign the Chinese invaded Champa, occupying Kiu-su and the capital farther south. Sambhuvarman's son took the name Kandarpadharma and had a peaceful rule during which he sent rich gifts to the emperor T'ai Tsung of the T'ang dynasty in 630 and 631. Around this period in the early seventh century, the name Champa first appears in inscriptions, although it is thought to have been in existence before that time. With the reign of Rudravarman II in the middle of the eighth century, the Chinese ceased to use the name Lin Yi and began to refer to the kingdom of Huan Wang.[70]

During this period the southern Cham provinces of Kauthara (Nhatrang) and Panduranga (Phan Rang) assumed new importance. At the Po Nagar temple in the latter province was found the oldest known written reference to the highlanders, an inscription on a stele dated 845. It relates how King Vikrantavarman, who was the sovereign at this time, dedicated to the deity Vikrantarudresvara a field called Rudraksetra, which was in an area inhabited by "savage" people referred to as Vrlas. This term has been interpreted as a general designation for the groups located in the upland area west of Phan Rang.[71]

Coedès reports that the account of the Chinese traveler Ma Tuan-lin describes the people of Champa as having "deep-set eyes, straight and prominent noses, and black frizzy hair."[72] He adjudged them to be a "cruel and bellicose people." Their weapons consisted of bows and arrows, crossbows of bamboo, sabers, and lances. Their houses were constructed of baked bricks coated with a layer of lime and mounted on a platform or terrace. When the king went out among the people he rode on an elephant and wore a high hat trimmed with gold flowers and a silk tassel. Corpses were cremated, the ashes of a king being placed in a gold jar and cast into the sea, the remains of mandarins being put in silver vases that were thrown into the mouths of rivers. He noted that all weddings took place in the

70. Coedès, *Indianized States*, pp. 70–72, 94–95.
71. Etienne Aymonier, "Première étude sur les inscriptions Tchames," *Journal Asiatique* 17 (1891): 24–25; Louis Finot, "Notes d'épigraphie," *BEFEO* 3, no. 2 (1903): 633; Georges Maspéro, *Champa*, pp. 6–7.
72. Coedès, *Indianized States*, pp. 49–50.

eighth lunar month and that it was the girls who asked for the boys in marriage. Also, intermarriage among people with the same family name was not prohibited.

In discussing the early population of Lin Yi, Coedès makes the observation that if the reference in Chinese accounts to "barbarians from beyond the frontier of Jih-nan" was not to the Cham then it surely was to "Indonesians who, if they were not already Indianized, soon became so."[73] Some of the information and observations already presented in the discussion of early Lin Yi, however, raise the question as to whether those who founded this kingdom were ancestral to the Cham, i.e. Austronesian-speaking people, or whether they might have been related to the Mon Khmer-speaking highlanders, particularly those in Binh-Tri-Thien province. Although he never states this as a hypothesis, Stein in his analysis of the origin of Lin Yi infers that this is a possibility. As indicated before, he concludes that the "barbarians from beyond the frontier of Jih-nan" who founded Lin Yi were from the area beyond the western frontier, i.e. the highlands west of Quang Tri and Hue. In attempting to trace the origin of the name *K'iu*, which he feels was the ethnic designation for the founders of Lin Yi, Stein looks to the present names of highland groups and some of the characteristics—dark skin, frizzy or wavy hair, and ironworking, particularly in association with shamanism—mentioned in Chinese accounts and in legends like the one cited above concerning Fan Wen.[74] In his discussion he considers two Mon Khmer-speaking groups—the Kuy, a group well known for their ironworking, in Cambodia and the Khmu in Laos. It is curious, however, that Stein neglected to consider the name *Vân Kiêu*, the Vietnamese designation for the Bru and Pacoh in upland southern Binh Tri Thien province. This is not to say that these groups existed in A.D. 132 with the same ethnic identity they have at the present time, but the possibility that Mon Khmer-speaking people lived in this area is strongly indicated by the findings of linguists that Muong and quite possibly Vietnamese are basically Mon Khmer languages. Further, as indicated previously, Stein concluded that the kings of Lin Yi who ruled in the vicinity of Hue and were described in the Chinese chronicles formed a separate dynasty from the kings with Sanskrit names farther south in Quang Nam. Boisselier speculates that by the middle of the fifth century

73. Ibid., p. 43.
74. Stein, "Le Lin-Yi," pp. 245–51.

the capital near the present site of Hue (which had been looted by the Chinese in 446) was still separate from that in Quang Nam.[75] By 491, however, an imperial Chinese decree described the "king of Lin Yi" as being of the southern coastal area, and Boisselier sees this as a unification of the coastal principalities—a "fusion" of Lin Yi and "Champa."

The foregoing discussion raises the possibility that Lin Yi may have been founded by Mon Khmer-speaking people who probably were strongly influenced by the Chinese culture that existed in the commandery of Jih-nan. Following the fusion of Lin Yi and Champa their ethnic identity underwent a transformation as they were in time absorbed into the Indianized culture of the Cham-speaking people farther south.

Highlander "Principalities"

Maitre puts forth the hypothesis that during this early period the Rhadé and Jarai had lived on the coastal plain and were among the "barbarians" conquered by Fan Wen.[76] As the Cham became civilized in the Indian great tradition, they looked with increasing disdain on their less advanced linguistic and racial kin and drove them from their land. Constantly retreating during the first millennium A.D., the Jarai and Rhadé finally settled in the remote fastness of the highlands. Maitre also feels that there were on the western side of the cordillera some Austronesian-speaking people who were isolated from their confreres on the eastern side by the expansion of Funan and subsequently of Chenla. As a consequence they were heavily influenced by the Mon Khmer groups around them. When they finally moved into the western highland to escape vassalage to the rulers of Chenla, they had already undergone great transformations in their language and culture.

Maitre also contends that the Maa had at one time been located on the plains "of lower Cochinchina," where they fell under the domination of expanding Funan. In order to escape this yoke they moved steadily northward, eventually settling in the relatively inhospitable area on the terrace zone between the Mekong river delta and the highlands. Maitre reports that once they were installed in these new surroundings, they formed a principality, the memory of which is still preserved in their oral tradition. The head of this was a "great chief, more or less a shaman," who func-

---

75. Jean Boisselier, *La statuaire du Champa* (Paris: Ecole Française d'Extrême-Orient, 1963), p. 9.
76. Maitre, *Les Jungles Moi*, pp. 429–34.

tioned as a potentate. Although the Maa at this time had tributary relations with the Cambodians, they enjoyed relative independence. Maitre also is of the opinion that a similar kind of principality existed among the Jarai, with the King of Fire and King of Water in positions of authority. They were, he thinks, among the "barbarian little kings" that are described in the Chinese annals as being brought under the domination of Fan Wen. Finally, Maitre notes that one or more of these principalities once were found among the Rhadé.

As will be discussed below, some historical evidence suggests that the highlanders at one time lived much closer to the coastal plain than they do at the present time. No highland groups, however, are identified. Moreover, it cannot be assumed, as Maitre does, that the present ethnic identities such as Rhadé and Jarai existed during the early historical period. No historical data supports Maitre's hypothesis that Austronesian-speaking people lived on the eastern side of the Annam Cordillera. Neither is there anything in the historical record or in Maa oral tradition indicating that the Maa ever lived on the plains of what later became Cochinchina. Finally, ethnographic information that has been and will be presented reveals that the Maa traditionally had elite patrilineages and in some areas the Rhadé and Jarai have clan-oriented elites, but there is no evidence that any of the three groups ever had principalities.

3 CHAM PRESENCE
IN THE HIGHLANDS

By the end of the first millennium A.D. the sweeping influence of the Chinese and Indian great traditions had vastly transformed the societies of the Vietnamese, Khmer, and Cham. Politically their chiefdoms and principalities had been welded into kingdoms, and by the tenth century they were on the threshold of becoming powerful states. In the Red river delta, the Vietnamese had just achieved independence from China and had established the kingdom of Dai Co Viet. Further south on the plains between the cordillera and the sea, Lin Yi had long since enlarged into the kingdom of Champa. To the west, Water Chenla and Land Chenla had been unified into the Khmer kingdom with its capital at Angkor.

In Champa the king ruled over a court that had achieved a certain splendor with its fabled treasure, its musicians and dancers, and lavish ceremonies. Cham architecture had reached a zenith with the completion of the great tower at the temple complex of My Son, and art flourished with exquisite sculptures. But the beginning of the second millennium A.D. also ushered in an era of seemingly endless wars among the Vietnamese, Cham, and Khmer. Great armies clashed, leaving many dead on the field of battle; capital cities were invaded, sacked, and burned; territories were won and lost. Surrounded as they were by these states, it was inevitable that the highlanders would be drawn into some of the struggles, and when this happened in the middle of the twelfth century, it marked the first time that they would be mentioned in the annals of history. It also marked the beginning of a Cham presence in the highlands.

There are two sources of information about this presence—material vestiges and legends. The vestiges consist of scattered towers containing sanctuaries, traces of a few settlements, and a variety of artifacts, including several which are described in the literature as "treasures." The remnants of Cham construction suggest the extent to which these more advanced lowlanders penetrated the highlands, and they also infer attempts at establishing Cham communities. Legends that reflect a great deal about Cham-highlander relations are found among both groups. A few of the Cham legends are recorded in the Cham language but those of the highlanders are purely of the oral tradition. Considering certain aspects of these legends in relation to ethnographic information already presented, some pertinent questions can be raised concerning the impact of the Cham presence on the societies of certain highland groups.

THE EVENTS OF HISTORY

An important turning point in Vietnamese and Cham history came in A.D. 939 when Ngo Quyen, who had just defeated the Chinese in the Red river delta, declared himself ruler of the independent kingdom of Nam Viet and established his capital at Co Loa, site of the capital of the early kingdom of Au Lac. The Red river delta at this time was fragmented into numerous principalities, each governed by a *sử quân* or lord, and Ngo Quyen spent the six years of his reign attempting unsuccessfully to rally their support. After his death, the Ngo dynasty ended when Dinh Bo Linh, the adoptive son and successor of one of the lords, won the support of the other *sử quân* and in 968 proclaimed himself emperor. He took the name Dinh Tien Hoang and established his capital at his native town of Hoa Lu. The kingdom was called Dai Co Viet, and in 970 Dinh Tien Hoang initiated tributary relations with China, which was being ruled by the newly founded Sung dynasty.[1]

To the south, in the kingdom of Champa, a new dynasty had been founded in 875 by Indravarman II at Indrapura in what is now Quang Nam-Danang province (see maps 1 and 3). In 972 a new king, whose name appears to have been Paramesvaravarman, ascended the throne of Champa, and during his reign there was the first struggle with the newly founded kingdom of Dai Co Viet. Dinh Tien Hoang was assassinated in 979, and a member of the Ngo family pleaded with the Cham king to assist

---

1. Le Thanh Khoi, *Le Viêt-Nam: histoire et civilisation* (Paris: Les Editions de Minuit, 1955), pp. 137–40.

him in regaining control of the throne that his family had occupied between 939 and 965. The Cham ruler agreed, and he sailed at the head of a fleet to attack Hoa Lu, but as the fleet was approaching the shore a sudden gale swept over the ships, destroying all of them except the ship of the king. That same year, the throne of Dai Co Viet was usurped by a minister named Le Hoan, who took the imperial title, Le Dai Hanh, and founded the dynasty that became known as the Former Le dynasty. He sent an envoy to Champa, only to have the envoy detained as a prisoner by King Paramesvaravarman. Angered at this affront, Le Dai Hanh dispatched an army to Champa and in 982 captured the capital city of Indrapura. During the fighting, the Cham king lost his life, the city was looted and burned, and the temples were destroyed. The Cham court fled to the south, where a member of the royal family declared himself the new emperor, taking the name Indravarman IV. At the same time, in the northern part of Champa, a usurper from Dai Co Viet named Luu Ky Tong seized power. Not long afterward, Indravarman IV died and Luu Ky Tong declared himself to be the ruler of all of Champa, asking for recognition from China in 986. Maspéro notes that the rule of the foreign usurper proved difficult for the Cham, and they began to leave the kingdom in great numbers, some seeking asylum on Hainan Island.[2] The Cham nobility rallied around a claimant of their own, enthroning him at Vijaya, inland from present Qui Nhon, and when Luu Ky Tong died in 869 the new king was given the name Harivarman II. Hostilities between Champa and Dai Co Viet continued, and in the year 1000 Yang Pu Ku Vijaya Sri, the successor of Harivarman II, moved the Cham capital from vulnerable Indrapura southward to Vijaya.

In 1009 a high mandarin named Ly Cong Uan became emperor of Dai Co Viet, taking the name Ly Thai To. To mark the beginning of his dynasty he moved the capital from Hoa Lu to Dai La in the Red river delta. His son led successful campaigns against Champa in 1021 and 1026, but after his ascension to the throne as Emperor Ly Thai Tong the Cham renewed the battle, pillaging the coast of Dai Co Viet in 1042. Ly Thai Tong retaliated by sending an army southward, where in present Binh-Tri-Thien province the Cham suffered a severe defeat. The Cham king Jaya Simhavarman II was decapitated on the battlefield, and Ly Thai Tong's forces pushed on to capture Vijaya. The city was sacked, and the

---

2. Georges Maspéro, *Le Royaume de Champa* (Paris and Brussels: G. Van Oest, 1928), p. 125.

royal harem and five thousand prisoners were taken back to Dai Co Viet.[3]

Ly Thai Tong's son took the name Ly Thanh Tong and changed the name of the kingdom to Dai Viet. Le Thanh Khoi points out that among Ly Thanh Tong's many achievements was a reorganization of the military forces, which included creation of some "batallions de Montagnards," although the historical annals did not specify the area of the highlands from which they came.[4] To the south, in Champa, Rudravarman III became king in 1062 and began to make plans for war against Dai Viet. In 1068 he launched his attack, but Ly Thanh Tong responded quickly, sending his fleet to the coast of Champa, where an army was put ashore. In the vicinity of Vijaya, the Vietnamese inflicted a defeat on the Cham armies. Seeing that the fall of the capital was inevitable, Rudravarman III fled. Soon after, the Vietnamese entered the city and Ly Thanh Tong ordered it to be burned. The Cham king was pursued and captured, and taken along with the royal family to Dai Viet. In exchange for their release, the Cham agreed to yield to the Vietnamese their three northern provinces, a territory that included present northern Binh-Tri-Thien.

Harivarman IV became king of Champa in 1074, and at the beginning of his reign he repulsed new incursions by the forces of Dai Viet. He also mounted a successful campaign against the Khmer, and his armies seized the city of Sambhupura (present Sambor on the Mekong river), destroying its sanctuaries. Then in 1076 the Cham and Khmer forces joined in a coalition with the Chinese to attack Dai Viet, but when the Chinese army was driven back by the Vietnamese the Cham and Khmer armies in Nghe An retreated. In 1103 the Cham ruler Jaya Indravarman II attempted to recapture the three lost Cham provinces, but he was able to maintain control over them only a few months before being driven out by the Vietnamese.[5]

Ly Thanh Tong ascended the throne of Dai Viet in 1127, and the following year he faced a new Khmer invasion. Khmer king Suryavarman II launched his attack by sea and land with a force of 20,000 men going overland into Nghe An, where they would be joined by a naval ex-

3. Le Thanh Khoi, *Le Viêt-Nam*, pp. 139–47; Georges Coedès, *The Indianized States of Southeast Asia*, ed. Walter F. Vella, trans. Susan Brown Cowing (Honolulu: East-West Center Press, 1968), pp. 122–25, 139–41; Maspéro, *Champa*, pp. 130–36.

4. Le Thanh Khoi, *Le Viêt-Nam*, pp. 147–48.

5. Ibid., pp. 158–67; Georges Coedès, *The Making of South East Asia*, trans. H. M. Wright (London: Routledge & Kegan Paul, 1966), pp. 85–86; Lawrence P. Briggs, *The Ancient Khmer Empire* (Philadelphia: American Philosophical Society, 1951), p. 190; Maspéro, *Champa*, pp. 137–55.

pedition. Maspéro traces the land invasion route through the mountain range via the Ha Trai pass west of present Thakhek on the Mekong river.[6] This path took them into the Pho Giang valley and present Huong Son district southwest of Vinh. There they were met by the Dai Viet forces led by General Ly Cong Binh, who defeated them and forced their retreat. The Khmer fleet of seven hundred ships arrived months later, pillaged the coast of Dai Viet, and returned to Cambodia. In 1132 a combined force of Cham and Khmer troops attacked Dai Viet. Maspéro feels that since the Khmer troops could pass through Cham territory, they probably crossed the mountains through the pass now followed by Route 9 (see map 5). When this attack was repulsed, the Cham and Khmer concluded a peace with Dai Viet. In 1138, however, the Khmer king Suryavarman II sent another army against Dai Viet. The Cham ruler Jaya Indravarman III refused to be an ally, and Maspéro believes that the Khmer force made its way into Nghe An through the Ha Trai pass and, more than likely, via the Mu Gia pass as well. This, as the other adventures, ended in defeat for the Khmer.

Furious at what he considered a betrayal by the Cham, Suryavarman II sent his armies into Champa, where they captured the city of Vijaya. In the course of the fighting, the Cham king Jaya Indravarman III disappeared, and it never was determined whether he had been taken prisoner or had died on the battlefield. With the Khmer occupying the northern portion of Champa in 1147, a new Cham king, Jaya Harivarman I, established himself at Panduranga in the vicinity of present Phan Rang, an area where there had always been ferment against the rulers farther north in Indrapura and Vijaya. Suryavarman II soon dispatched an army of Khmer and Cham troops southward, but on the plain of Rajupura the forces of Jaya Harivarman I won the day. The Khmer ruler persisted, sending another army "a thousand times stronger" than the first, but it too was defeated by the army of the Cham king. In the face of these setbacks, Suryavarman II attempted a new strategy, naming Harideva, the younger brother of his wife, as king of Champa. Harideva ascended the throne in Vijaya, and in 1149 Jaya Harivarman I marched on the city. On the plain of Mahisa, Harideva met Jaya Harivarman I in battle and the latter emerged victorious.

Jaya Harivarman I took possession of the throne in Vijaya, but he still

---

6. Henri Maspéro, "Etudes d'histoire d'Annam," *BEFEO* 18, no. 3 (1918): 33–35.

had to face the difficult task of unifying all of Champa under his rule. His first opponents were some of the highland groups. During the confused period when the kingdom was divided, bands of highlanders had invaded the coastal plain. Contemporary Cham inscriptions (see chap. 1) refer to the highlanders generically as *kiratas* (highland people) or *mlecchas* (savages) with some groups referred to explicitly as Randaiy (Rhadé) and Mada (probably Mdhur). Near the village of Slay, the king's forces engaged the "kiratas" and drove them back into the mountains. Aware of their weakness, the "kings of the kiratas" sought someone who could lead them. They chose Vamsaraja, the brother of Jaya Harivarman's wife, and in the city of Madhyamagrama proclaimed him their king. Led by Vamsaraja, the highlanders again engaged the Cham army, but a second time Jaya Harivarman I was victorious. Fleeing to Dai Viet, Vamsaraja appealed for assistance in regaining the throne of Champa. The Vietnamese ruler Ly Anh Tong put a large army at his disposal, but they were badly defeated by the Cham armies and Vamsaraja was left dead on the field of battle. An inscription on a stele in the temple complex at My Son proclaims Jaya Harivarman's victory over the Cambodians, Vietnamese, and the "kiratas." [7]

Following these successes, Jaya Harivarman I turned his attention to Cham lords who had recognized the usurper Harideva. First, he forced the submission of Amaravati, the northern portion of Champa in the area of present Quang Nam province, and then he sent his armies southward to Panduranga, which was brought completely under his control in 1160. With the coastal plains again under the authority of the throne, Jaya Harivarman I began a conquest of the area to the west—the highlands. An inscription at the Po Nagar temple in Nhatrang, dated 1170, describes the great victories of Jaya Harivarman I over the Cambodians, Vietnamese, "Randaiy, Mada," and other "mlecchas." [8] These victories also are proclaimed on an inscription at My Son but here the highlanders are referred to as "kiratas." [9]

Jaya Harivarman I died in either 1166 or 1167, and it is not clear whether his son Jaya Harivarman II ever actually reigned. If he did, however, he

---

7. Louis Finot, "Notes d'épigraphie," *BEFEO* 15, no. 2 (1915): 6, 50; Georges Maspéro, *Champa*, pp. 156–58.
8. Etienne Aymonier, "Première étude sur les inscriptions Tchames," *Journal Asiatique* 17 (1891): 41–44; A. Bergaigne, "L'Ancien royaume de Champa dans l'Indo-Chine d'après les inscriptions," *Journal Asiatique* 11 (1888): 86; Louis Finot, "Notes d'épigraphie," *BEFEO* 3, no. 2 (1903): 639–40; Georges Maspéro, *Champa*, pp. 159–60.
9. Finot, "Notes d'épigraphie" (1915), pp. 6, 50.

very soon was supplanted by Jaya Indravarman IV of Gramapura. This ruler sent a fleet up the Mekong river into the Great Lake where troops were landed to invade Angkor in 1177. The Khmer ruler Tribhuvanaditya, a usurper of the throne, was killed, and the city was sacked. While these events were taking place, Jayavarman, a descendant of the Khmer royal family through his mother's line, was conducting a military campaign in Champa, and when the news reached him that Angkor had fallen he returned to Cambodia to rid the country of the invaders. One of the naval battles that subsequently took place between the Cham and the Khmer is graphically depicted on the walls of the Bayon and Banteay Ch'mar. By 1181 peace was restored in Cambodia and Jayavarman VII was proclaimed king. During the reign of Jayavarman VII, Cambodia reached the height of its power. By 1203, as a result of his military successes, Jayavarman had reduced Champa to the status of a Khmer province, a situation that was to last until 1220. Jayavarman VII ruled Cambodia until 1218, which appears to have been the year he died, and by 1220 it was clear that his successors would have a difficult time maintaining the unity of such an extensive empire. An inscription at the Po Nagar temple in Phan Rang dated from 1220 relates that "the Khmer went to the sacred country, and the people of Champa came to Vijaya." Maspéro interprets this as meaning that the Khmer voluntarily evacuated Champa, and he notes that when the new Cham king Jaya Paramesvaravarman II was crowned in 1226, it marked the end of a century of wars between the Cham and Khmer.[10]

The new threat to the Vietnamese, the Cham, and the Khmer came from the north when in 1257 the Mongol armies led by General Uriyangadai moved through the Red river valley to attack the Vietnamese capital of Dai La. Emperor Tran Thai Tong rallied his forces and drove the invaders out. But the Mongol threat was not ended, for in 1260 Kublai became the Grand Khan, and even before completing his conquest of China set out to obtain the vassalage of those states to the south that had paid tribute to the Sung emperors. In 1278 and again in 1280 the Cham king Indravarman V was invited to present himself at the court in Peking, but he replied by sending embassies and gifts. Finally, in 1281 the Mongol general Sogatu and a Chinese named Liu-shen were sent to the Cham court to propose that Champa become a Mongol protectorate so as to "maintain the peace."

10. Georges Maspéro, *Champa*, pp. 162–69.

When the Cham king, strongly influenced by his son Harijit, refused to accept this kind of protection, the Mongols in 1282 launched an attack against Champa. King Indravarman V had maintained good relations with Dai Viet, and the Vietnamese emperor Tran Nhan Tong refused to allow the Mongol armies to pass through his territory. General Sogatu therefore had to move his forces by sea in a fleet of a thousand junks. They landed on the Cham coast. At the citadel protecting Vijaya, the Cham and Mongol forces engaged in a violent battle during which the citadel fell to the invading forces. Indravarman V fled his palace, leading his troops into the mountains where they were to remain for two years.

A group of Chinese seeking refuge in the Mongol camp reported that the Cham ruler and some two thousand troops were encamped on the Ya-heou mountain in the upland northwest zone of the province. Later some Mongol spies reported to Sogatu that Indravarman V had amassed 20,000 troops and had asked the rulers of Dai Viet, Cambodia, and Java for aid. Indravarman V sent a series of embassies to the Mongol general but he refused to meet with him personally. Despite increasing Cham guerrilla attacks against his forces, Sogatu continued to bring more Cham territory, including some areas occupied by highlanders, under his control.[11]

In 1282, General Sogatu sent a small expedition into Cambodia. Maspéro notes that it probably followed the route through Lao Bao of the present Route 9.[12] The expedition was a failure and its leaders were captured, but the Khmer king Jayavarman VIII nonetheless saw the wisdom of offering tribute to Kublai Khan in 1285. Early in 1284 Sogatu returned to China, and another expeditionary force replaced him. Kublai then decided to open the land route through Dai Viet by force. At the end of 1284 his armies, under the command of his son Prince Toghan, moved through Lang Son as well as down the Red river valley. It was then decided that Sogatu would land an army in Champa and attack Dai Viet from the south. Prince Tran Quoc Tuan, known as Tran Hung Dao, rallied the Vietnamese forces, however, and inflicted a defeat on Sogatu, who was killed (his head was presented to Emperor Tran Nhan Tong). Tran Hung Dao launched an offensive against Toghan's army, which was badly hampered by flooding rivers. Suffering heavy losses, the Mongols were forced to withdraw into China. In 1287 Toghan led another army

---

11. Ibid., pp. 171–81; Coedès, *Indianized States*, pp. 192–93.
12. Henri Maspéro, "Histoire d'Annam," pp. 35–36.

into Dai Viet, and although he succeeded in capturing the capital city of Thang Long he was dealt a devastating defeat by Tran Hung Dao in 1288. This ended the Mongol threat to Dai Viet and Champa.[13]

Coedès notes that the Cham ruler Indravarman V, already quite old at the time of the Mongol invasion, probably died soon after the visit of Marco Polo in 1285.[14] He was succeeded by his son Prince Harijit, who took the name Jaya Simhavarman III. In 1306 he sought the hand of the Vietnamese princess Huyen Tran in marriage, sending an envoy to the court of Dai Viet with magnificent gifts. The court hesitated, however, so the Cham ruler offered the districts of O and Ri north of the Deo Hai Van (Col des Nuages), and the Vietnamese emperor accepted.[15] Jaya Simhavarman III died the following year, but during his reign he erected the temple of Po Klaung Garai (in the vicinity of Phan Rang) and the tower of Yang Prong (located in a remote part of the highlands north of the town of Ban Don and close to the Cambodian border). Both contain similar inscriptions indicating that Jaya Simhavarman III generously donated "fields, slaves, and elephants" to these monuments.[16]

After Che Bong Nga ascended the throne of Champa in 1360, the struggles with Dai Viet intensified. In 1361 and in 1390 he led a series of successful expeditions against Dai Viet, and he also recovered the lost Cham territory north of the Deo Hai Van (Col des Nuages). After his death in 1390, however, the Vietnamese regained this territory from the new ruler whom they refer to as La Khat. This ruler's son succeeded him, taking the name Jaya Simhavarman V. His reign began badly when in 1402, in order to avoid war with Dai Viet, he had to yield Indrapura, the northern province of Amaravati where the hallowed sanctuary of Bhadresvara was located at My Son. The Vietnamese ruler Ho Quy Ly (who had abandoned the name Le in favor of Ho) launched a program of settling Vietnamese in the area taken from the Cham which prompted the indigenous Cham population to organize resistance against these outsiders.

In 1406 Chinese armies invaded Dai Viet, occupying and sacking the capital city of Thang Long. The Vietnamese ruler Ho Quy Ly died a prisoner in China, and the conquered country was renamed Giao Chi, the original name used during the Han period. The Chinese conducted a

13. Le Thanh Khoi, *Le Viêt-Nam*, pp. 179–89.
14. Coedès, *Indianized States*, p. 217.
15. Le Thanh Khoi, *Le Viêt-Nam*, p. 191.
16. Aymonier, "Les Inscriptions Tchames," pp. 67–81; Bergaigne, "Ancien royaume de Champa," pp. 101–02; Finot, "Notes d'épigraphie" (1903), pp. 635–36; Georges Maspéro, *Champa*, p. 191.

census that revealed a total population of 5.2 million, of which some 2,087,500 were "barbarians" (i.e., highland people).[17]

In 1418 General Le Loi, one of the most renowned heroes in the Vietnamese annals, began the long struggle to free Dai Viet of Chinese rule. Gradually the Chinese were forced to retreat into fortified strongholds, and by 1425 Le Loi's forces had captured Tay Do, the Ho capital. In 1427 the last of the Chinese troops sailed up the Red river. The following year Le Loi was proclaimed emperor, taking the name Le Thai To and establishing his capital at Dong Kinh. He died in 1433, and his son Le Thai Tong ascended the throne. This marked a period of peaceful relations between Dai Viet and Champa.

After the death of Jaya Simhavarman V in 1441, Champa was torn by dissension and went into a decline. In Dai Viet, Le Thai Tong was succeeded in 1442 by his son Le Nhan Tong, whose death the same year brought his son Le Thanh Tong to the throne. Eleven years later Le Thanh Tong's armies swept into Champa, overwhelming the city of Vijaya. Some 60,000 Cham died and 30,000 were taken prisoner, among them the king and fifty members of the royal family. The Cham general Bo Tri Tri assembled the remains of his army and fled southward to Panduranga, where he declared himself king of Champa. He also took an oath of vassalage to the Dai Viet ruler, Le Thanh Tong. Although the Cham still retained the territory south of the Cu Mong pass, the year 1471 marked the end of the kingdom of Champa. With these tragic events, great numbers of Cham fled into the highlands, most of them continuing westward into Cambodia.[18]

The provinces of Kauthara and Panduranga were now all that remained of Champa. Maitre describes Panduranga as having been a "turbulent province" which for a long time had probably functioned as a semi-independent entity.[19] Durand expresses the view that Panduranga was an independent or semi-independent state, and cites the Cham royal chronicles that list a succession of twenty-five rulers and five different capitals in Panduranga between 1000 and 1653.[20] This hypothesis, however, has not been accepted by other French scholars, who contend that the chronicles only describe the ruling dynasties of the kingdom of Champa.

17. Le Thanh Khoi, *Le Viêt-Nam*, pp. 204–06.
18. Georges Maspéro, *Champa*, pp. 219–41.
19. Henri Maitre, *Les Jungles Moi* (Paris: Larose, 1912), p. 444.
20. E. M. Durand, "Notes sur les Chams," *BEFEO* 5, nos. 3–4 (1905): 368–86.

After receiving the recognition of the Vietnamese ruler, General Bo Tri
Tri requested investiture by the Chinese emperor, but just as the Chinese
delegation arrived in 1478 to deliver the decree the Cham leader died. His
brother succeeded him and ruled until 1505, when for unknown reasons he
departed for Laos. His son, whose name in the Chinese annals is given as
Kou Pou-lo, was ruling in 1543, the year the last Cham embassy was
received in Peking. During this period, the Vietnamese were integrating
the newly conquered Cham territories. The northern part of Amaravati
(corresponding to present northern Quang Nam–Danang province) was
attached to the province of Thuan Hoa, which included the area north of
the Deo Hai Van. The area that today encompasses the province of Nghia-
Binh and the southern portion of what is now Quang Nam–Danang
became the new province of Quang Nam, and it was divided into three
prefectures. Schools, which admitted young Cham, were established by
the new administration, and đồn điền, military agricultural colonies (see
chap. 6), were organized throughout the area.[21] During the reign of Le Uy
Muc (1504–1509), the Cham in the newly occupied area rose up in
rebellion, and the Vietnamese reacted cruelly.[22] Troops were sent in to
force the Cham and highlanders off their land, which the Vietnamese then
occupied.

Political turmoil in northern Vietnam resulted in Emperor Trinh Kiem
appointing Nguyen Hoang governor of Thuan Hoa in 1558. The new
governor functioned with considerable autonomy and by 1570 had extended his authority over the province of Quang Nam to the south of
Thuan Hoa. Taking advantage of a Cham incursion into Quang Nam
during the year 1611, Nguyen Hoang sent his armies southward to occupy
the area north of Cape Varella. When Nguyen Hoang died two years later,
his son Nguyen Phuoc Nguyen succeeded him, and this initiated a period
of growing independence by the Nguyen from the Trinh rulers. Nguyen
Phuoc Nguyen increasingly ignored directions from the capital, and in
1626 he refused to send the expected taxes to the Trinh ruler. This was, in
effect, the final gesture of independence, and when Nguyen Phuoc
Nguyen assumed the title Sai Vuong or Chua Sai it marked the beginning
of the long dynasty of the Nguyen chúa or "lords" that eventually was to
become the ruling line that ended in 1955 with the departure of Emperor
Bao Dai from Vietnam.

21. Jean Boisselier, *La Statuaire du Champa* (Paris: Ecole Française d'Extrême-Orient, 1963),
pp. 372–73; Le Thanh Khoi, *Le Viêt-Nam*, pp. 230–31, 264–65.
22. Maitre, *Les Jungles Moi*, p. 447.

In order to secure the northern border of Thuan Hoa against possible invasion by the Trinh, Chua Sai had a wall constructed at Truong Duc in 1630 and another wall at Dong Hoi in 1631. Boisselier points out that this barrier to the north served to orient the expansionist bent of the Nguyen toward the south.[23] Although the Cham were in a weakened state, they did offer some resistance to the Vietnamese, and Father Alexandre de Rhodes, one of the first Catholic missionaries in Vietnam (see chap. 7), wrote that between 1620 and 1653 the Nguyen maintained continual concentrations of troops on the frontier of Champa to cope with the troubled situation there.[24]

Between 1627 and 1651 the ruler of Champa was Po Rome, who is considered the most renowned king in this last phase of the Cham state. Maitre, Aymonier, and Durand are in agreement that Po Rome had three wives, one of whom was a highlander.[25] The first wife, Po Bia Sucih, was the daughter of King Po Mo Taha (1622–1627), and Po Rome repudiated her when she declared that after his death she would refuse to follow him on his funeral pyre. His second wife, Po Bia Sancan, was from the highlands, and both Aymonier and Maitre claim that she was Rhadé, while Durand describes her as a "Moi Koho." Po Bia Ut, the third wife, was the daughter of a Vietnamese lord from Hue, and Durand reports that her treason led to a Vietnamese invasion of Champa. He also notes that after Po Rome was killed by the Vietnamese, Sancan, the highlander, threw herself on his flaming pyre.

The Royal Chronicles of the Cham indicate that each of the princely families that ruled Panduranga in succession had established its own *bal* (capital) that was located in the family village or on family land.[26] Also, given the repeated incursions by the Vietnamese and Khmer, Durand feels that they probably also had an alternate bal located in the highlands among the Koho-speaking people as a kind of redoubt.

In 1653 the Nguyen lord Hien Vuong defeated Po Nrop, the last of the rulers in the Panduranga dynasty, and the Vietnamese occupied Kauthara, which later became the province of Khanh Hoa.[27] Champa was now

23. Boisselier, *Statuaire du Champa*, p. 374.
24. Léopold Cadière, "Le mur de Dong Hoi: étude sur l'établissement des Nguyen en Cochinchine (XVIe–XVIIIe siècles)," *BEFEO* 6, nos. 1–2 (1906): 87–254.
25. Maitre, *Les Jungles Moi*, pp. 457–58; Etienne Aymonier, "Légendes historiques des Chames," *Excursions et Reconnaissances* 14, no. 32 (1890): 173–76; and E. M. Durand, "Le Temple de Po Rome à Phanrang," *BEFEO* 3, no. 3 (1903): 600–03.
26. Durand, "Les Chams," p. 385.
27. Ibid., p. 378.

reduced to the area south of the Phan Rang river. Boisselier points out that according to the *Atlas historique* of de Guedeville (1713–19) Cham territory extended southward to Cape Baké and as far west as the vicinity of present Bien Hoa (see map 3), which had been taken from the Khmer in the fifteenth century.[28] In 1697, when the Cham leader Ba Tranh refused to pay tribute to the Nguyen lord, he was taken to the capital at Phu Xuan, the site of present Hue, and put to death. The remaining Cham province of Panduranga became the Vietnamese province of Thuan Thanh (later Binh Thuan). By this time the only pockets of Cham autonomy were at Bal Chanar in the area of Phan Ri and around Cape Varella farther north. The Vietnamese ruler Nguyen Phuoc Chu allowed the Cham functionaries to remain in their positions, but they were obliged to wear Vietnamese garb. A Cham prince was allowed to rule at Bal Chanar, and when officers of the Compagnie Française des Indes ship *La Galatée* visited Phan Ri in 1720 this Cham prince granted them an audience.[29]

With the last Cham territory under their control, the Vietnamese began an expansion into the Khmer lands to the south and by 1780 had possession of all of the Mekong river delta. The last phase of this occupation took place during the Tay Son Rebellion (see chap. 6), and Boisselier expresses the view that as a result of this rebellion the last traces of Cham autonomy were suppressed.[30] The Tay Son swept over the Nguyen territories, forcing Nguyen Anh, heir to the throne, to flee to Siam. After he returned to Vietnam in 1787, Nguyen Anh succeeded in reestablishing his authority over the Mekong river delta, and by 1795 his forces had regained possession of the former Cham enclave at Panduranga. In order to consolidate his control, he deemed it necessary to suppress any remaining Cham autonomy. In a letter written in 1795, a French traveler named Lavoué related that the former Cham kingdom had become the Vietnamese province of Binh Thuan, the Cham ruler replaced by a Vietnamese governor.[31]

Citing Cham sources, Durand reports that in 1822 an "aged Cham princess," the daughter of Po Chon (also known as Po Cheun Chan) who was the last of the Cham princes, led a large exodus into the highlands (where she is remembered as Po Bia or "Queen") and then continued on to

28. Boisselier, *Statuaire du Champa*, p. 377.
29. Le Thanh Khoi, *Le Viêt-Nam*, pp. 264–65.
30. Boisselier, *Statuaire du Champa*, p. 378.
31. Léopold Cadière, "Documents relatifs à l'époque de Gia-Long," *BEFEO* 12, no. 7 (1912): 34.

Cambodia.[32] Although their leadership had vanished, a sizable Cham population still remained in what had been Panduranga. Between 1831 and 1834, however, the Vietnamese mandarin Nguyen Van Khoi led a revolt against Emperor Minh Mang, and the rebels, after accusing the Cham villagers of loyalty to the throne, ravaged their valley settlements. When Minh Mang succeeded in putting down the revolt, the Cham were accused of complicity with the rebels, and imperial troops devastated their villages. As a result, large numbers of Cham fled the coastal areas, making their way into the highlands, eventually settling in Cambodia.

Claeys, a member of the Ecole Française d'Extrême-Orient who made an extensive tour of the highlands in 1928, was informed by Cham personnel in the Garde Indigène in Danang that the last of the Cham princesses had died the year before.[33] After inquiries to a local Cham mandarin, Claeys was presented to a girl of from fifteen to eighteen years of age who the mandarin claimed was the daughter of that princess, a descendant of the former Cham rulers in Panduranga. Boisselier also mentions this Cham princess, adding that even in our time there are those who claim to be descendants of the last Cham dynasty.[34] They live in central Vietnam, where they have no authority except among some rare "subjects" and among various highland groups who long ago had been commissioned to guard the "royal treasures," several of which are described below.

CHAM VESTIGES IN THE HIGHLANDS

The Kon Klor Site

It was not until the late nineteenth century that Cham vestiges in the highlands began to be systematically reported and analyzed. Most of the initial finds were made by French Catholic missionaries. During his 1886 expedition in the highlands, Navelle, Administrator of Indigenous Affairs, discovered in Kontum an account written by Father Dourisboure, who had been a missionary in the area since 1850, concerning a statue of a man that he had come upon in the vicinity of Kon Klor, some four kilometers

---

32. Durand, "Les Chams," p. 385.
33. Y. L. Claeys, "Inspections et reconnaissances en Annam," *BEFEO* 28, nos. 3–4 (1928): 609.
34. Boisselier, *Statuaire du Champa*, p. 379.

away (see map 3). Although the account bore no date, it related that the statue, made of metal and one meter in height, had "very artistically modelled members." Standing at the base of a tree, it was surrounded by a circular trench, the circumference of which was lined with great trees. Navelle promptly went across the Bla river to Kon Klor but found the statue gone; all that remained were some relatively intact bricks and a stone slab that had served as a pedestal.[35] Dourisboure and Navelle's information about the Kon Klor site, as well as similar data provided by Father Jeannin of the Kontum Mission, were included in Parmentier's comprehensive 1909 inventory of Cham monuments.[36]

In 1918, Father Jeannin reported to the Ecole Française d'Extrême-Orient that the "table de sacrifice" at Kon Klor had been destroyed by local Vietnamese, who took the bricks and broke the slab. The following year, French scholar Henri Maspéro toured the highlands, visiting places where Cham vestiges had been found.[37] He described the Kon Klor site as having been located in a forested area called the "Chonang Bya" and reported that an excavation had revealed, at a depth of one meter, a circular paving two bricks thick.[38] The digging also had unearthed two vats for ritual ablutions, one carrying an inscription, and there were three stone pedestals that apparently had supported the vats. All of these objects, he added, had been removed to the house of the French résident where they had been duly catalogued.

Both Coedès and Finot determined that the inscription on the vat was dated A.D. 914, making it the oldest Cham vestige found in the highlands.[39] Finot reports that the inscription relates how the shrine had been constructed by a local chief named Mahindravarman and was dedicated to Mahindra-Lokesvara. More recently, Boisselier interprets this find as a "document mahayaniste," commenting that it appears to have been the last of its kind for centuries.[40]

When Claeys visited the Kontum area in 1928, he found at the Kon Klor

35. E. Navelle, "De Thi-Nai au Bla," *Excursions et Reconnaissances* 13, no. 30 (1887): 291–92.

36. Henri Parmentier, *Inventaire descriptif des monuments Cams de l'Annam*, 2 vols. (vol. 1, Paris: Imprimerie Nationale, 1909; vol. 2, Paris: Ecole Française d'Extrême-Orient, 1918), 1: 564–65.

37. Maspéro's report will be found in "Chronique," *BEFEO* 19, no. 3 (1919): 103–06.

38. In Etienne Aymonier and A. Cabaton, *Dictionnaire Čam-Français*, the Cham word *bia* is listed as meaning "reine" (queen), "dame" (lady), "princesse" (princess), or "déesse" (goddess).

39. Georges Coedès and Henri Parmentier, *Listes générales des inscriptions et des monuments du Champa et du Cambodge* (Hanoi: Imprimerie d'Extrême-Orient, 1923), pp. 36–37; Louis Finot, "Lokecvara en Indochine," in *Etudes Asiatiques* (Paris: Ecole Française d'Extrême-Orient, G. Van Oest), 1 (1924): 234.

40. Boisselier, *Statuaire du Champa*, p. 127.

site only "une vague terrasse" and some broken bricks surrounded by a small circular embankment.[41] In the garden of the French résident, he also came upon six fragments of pedestal and the two Kon Klor ablution vats.

On 3 November 1967, I visited this site in the company of Nghiem Tham and Tran Van Tot (both of the National Museum in Saigon), a local Bahnar leader named Hiup, and the Kon Klor village headman. Located under an old banyan tree in the midst of a thick bamboo grove, these vestiges consisted of some bricks, practically all of which were broken. One intact brick was about 30 cm long, 15 cm wide, and 13 cm thick. The headman said that according to village legend the Prum or Drang (both designations for the Cham) had come a long time ago and made the bricks and built an edifice. He related that it was for a highlander queen called Chonang Bia (apparently the same name Maspéro had reported in 1919), and the site had long been declared taboo by the *kra* (village elders). He added that the French had come there seeking gold but that they did not find any.

Another early find was made by Father Guerlach, head of the Kontum Mission, who in 1887 reported discovering in the Bahnar village of Kon Jodri an enormous rock that the local population called the "Tieunang Bia" (clearly a variation of Chonang Bia).[42] It had a flat polished surface, and the villagers claimed that at one time there also had been a stone slab named "the bed of Ia Bia" supported by four stone columns. Guerlach observed that the Bahnar made offerings on the rock. During a visit to Kon Jodri in the 1960s, Dournes found the rock as Guerlach had described it so many years before. Dournes also remarked that the rock was an object of veneration not only by the Bahnar but by local Vietnamese river fishermen too.

The Yang Mum Site

The first volume of the *Bulletin de l'Ecole Française d'Extrême-Orient*, published in 1901, contained several reports concerning two Cham towers located in the vicinity of the present town of Cheo Reo in Gia Lai-Cong Tum province.[43] One report was submitted by Adhémard Leclère, the French résident at Kratie in Cambodia, who had been informed by a Lao army lieutenant named Oum that there was a Cham ruin near Palai Chu

---

41. Claeys, "Inspections en Annam," p. 603.
42. Jacques Dournes, "Recherches sur le Haut Champa," *France-Asie* 24, no. 2 (1970): 144.
43. "Chronique," *BEFEO* 1, no. 1 (1901): 413.

(Plei or Buon Chu, the village that stood on the present location of Cheo Reo) in the valley of the Ja-Anhoun (Ayun river). A similar report came from Father Guerlach of the Kontum Mission, and his source was a Vietnamese who had visited the village of Bun-tiu (Buon Chu) where he found two relatively intact high towers. In one of them there were two statues of a "grandeur naturelle" and two stone elephants about 50 cm in height. There also were some inscriptions on the wall. When Guerlach himself visited the area, the local natives refused to accompany him to the towers because they were afraid of them. In his 1902 report to the governor general on the activities of the Ecole Française d'Extrême-Orient, Finot noted that Lavalle, Chief of the Post and Telegraph in Ban Muang in Laos, reported the existence of two Cham towers near the confluence of the Ayun and Ba rivers.[44]

Early in 1902 the *Bulletin de l'Ecole Française d'Extrême-Orient* recorded that Stenger, a French officer who had just established a military post at Cheo Reo, had found a Cham tower nearby that contained statues and inscriptions. The notice went on to say that this undoubtedly was one of the towers that had been previously reported. In June 1902 the French scholar Henri Parmentier visited Cheo Reo, and he found the tower in a nearby forest, obscured by a tangle of growth. It was constructed on a laterite stone terrace. There also was a stele containing legible inscriptions and a figure of Siva seated on a Nandin ("Delightful One," the name of the bull on which Siva rides) which also carried inscriptions. Inside the tower he came upon another statue of Siva sitting "Indian style." Parmentier noted in his report that there were smooth sandstone fragments lying about in the vicinity of the tower and, concluding that they were from the statues, recommended that they be preserved, since they represented a unique use of this type of stone by the Cham.[45]

In March 1904 the French scholar and administrator Prosper Odend'hal visited the tower, which by this time had come to be designated the Yang Mum,[46] but was slain shortly afterward by warriors of the King of Fire. In his obituary for Odend'hal, Finot referred to the entry in the scholar's diary in which Odend'hal wrote that the stele and the figure of Siva were

44. Louis Finot, "Rapport à M. le Gouverneur Général sur les travaux de l'Ecole Française d'Extrême-Orient pendant l'année 1900," *BEFEO* 2, no. 1 (1902): 116–17.

45. Henri Parmentier, "Nouvelles découvertes archéologiques en Annam," *BEFEO* 2, no. 3 (1902): 282.

46. According to Dournes, "Recherches sur le Haut Champa," pp. 150, 156–57, the Jarai name for this tower is Ya' H'Mum, derived from Rcom H'Mum, an ancestress of the Rcom clan.

originally located at another tower called the Drang Lai, situated four kilometers to the west near the village of Buon De, but on his visit to the site he had found only a laterite base and a pile of bricks where the tower had stood. Odend'hal also had made the observation that the inscriptions on the stele and the Siva were contemporary with similar inscriptions found in Bien Hoa dated from the fifteenth century.[47] Subsequently, Coedès established the date of the inscriptions on the stele as early fifteenth century, and the one on the Siva seated on Nandin as 1409.[48] The inscriptions belonged to the period when the Cham ruler Jaya Sim-havarman V was reoccupying the northern territory of Indrapura that had been yielded to the Vietnamese in 1402.

Parmentier's 1909 inventory includes detailed descriptions of both the Yang Mum and Drang Lai ruins and the statues associated with them. It also contains a relatively clear photograph of the Yang Mum.[49] His 1918 inventory, however, is considerably more extensive, and in it he compares numerous architectural features of the Yang Mum with other Cham towers.[50] He points out that the Drang Lai Siva is one of the few figures of that deity seated on a Nandin found in Cham art, and he also remarks on the unusual fact that Siva is wearing sandals attached to the feet with straps. In his analysis of the various phases of Cham art, Parmentier notes that the two sandstone Sivas are representative of a period during which the Cham used this material largely for pottery.[51] Finally, he sees the Siva found in the sanctuary—called the Yang Mum Siva—as a carving that characterizes the beginning of a new phase of truncated figures which ultimately led to a degenerate style of Cham art.

More recently, Boisselier, in his study of Cham statuary, devotes some attention to the Yang Mum Siva, which he adjudges to be of excellent quality and sufficiently unique to serve as a prototype for a particular style of Cham sculpture he calls "le style de Yang Mum," adding that it displays definite Khmer influence.[52] He concludes that although there is no real documentation on the sanctuary and its contents, the rare qualities of the Yang Mum Siva would seem to suggest the influence of some kind of local

47. Louis Finot, "Nécrologie, Prosper Odend'hal," *BEFEO* 4, no. 2 (1904): 534–35.
48. Georges Coedès, "Inventaire des inscriptions du Champa et du Cambodge," *BEFEO* 8, nos. 1–2 (1908): 43; Coedès and Parmentier, *Listes générales*, pp. 12–13.
49. Parmentier, *Inventaire descriptif*, 1: 559–63.
50. Ibid., 2: 24, 39, 110, 120, 163, 182.
51. Ibid., 2: 207, 291–92, 399, 472.
52. Boisselier, *Statuaire du Champa*, pp. 236, 288, 312, 341, 361–69, 384–86, 394, 422.

Siva of Cham origin, similar in style to the Yang Mum Siva, found in the vicinity of Kontum

tradition. Boisselier also briefly describes another Siva found in the vicinity of Kontum (now in the collection at the Musée Guimet in Paris) that resembles somewhat the Yang Mum Siva although it is not as well sculptured.

Visiting Cheo Reo in 1928, Claeys found the Yang Mum tower much reduced in size.[53] He photographed the tower, and a comparison of his photograph with that taken by Parmentier in 1909 reveals the deterioration: in 1909 the tower was more or less intact, but by 1918 the walls barely reached the top of the main entrance. The figures of Siva had been sent to the museums at Hanoi and Tourane (Danang). At Drang Lai the laterite foundation remained but the bricks were gone, apparently taken away around 1909 for construction of a *garde indigène* post. As Claeys continued his journey farther south, he encountered a quadrilateral earth embankment with a similar but small construction inside. There also were fragments of brick, laterite stone that had been cut, and broken glazed pottery, some of which was the color of green celadon. Dournes reports that around 1930 the commander of the French military post, a man the Jarai refer to as Oi Gula ("Mr. Gula"), had his soldiers and Jarai laborers dismantle the tower as he could use the bricks in the construction of buildings. The Jarai viewed this as a desecration and have continued to make offerings at the site of the tower. Dournes also reports that nothing remains of the Drang Lai tower; the stone base was removed to provide building material for construction of the road from the coast to Cheo Reo—"*la route de penetration chez les sauvages.*" When he last visited the site of the Yang Mum in 1970, Dournes found only a stone base remaining. Buon Chu village had been absorbed by the town of Cheo Reo (Hau Bon), and the forest in which the Yang Mum stood had given way to yam patches.[54]

Dournes writes that in 1961 he had heard the Jarai talk about an "elephant of stone" located near Plei Pa, a village close to the site of the Yang Mum.[55] He organized a party to search for it and near Mount Mo, not far from Cheo Reo, unearthed a stone elephant 50 by 50 by 20 centimeters, which they carried to Dournes' house. In April 1970 he brought it to the National Museum in Saigon, where it is now displayed. According to Jarai legend, the stone elephant had been on the slope of Mount Mo, and a band of Vietnamese tried to remove it. With the

53. Claeys, "Inspections en Annam," pp. 603–05.
54. Dournes, "Recherches sur le Haut Champa," pp. 150–51.
55. Ibid., pp. 152–55.

elephant lashed to a pole, they reached the base of the mountain when suddenly it was as if they were engulfed by water. They dropped the elephant and struggled to breathe. Moving as if they were swimming, they fell to the ground, tearing at their chests until they died. A man named Ama Khe from Plei Pa told Dournes how in 1920, as a boy, he and some friends were guarding buffalo when they came upon the half-buried stone elephant and dug it out. As a jest one of the boys jumped on its back; he immediately fell ill. Following this incident there was a wave of illness and a drought in the area. The Jarai associated these misfortunes with the stone elephant, so they buried it at the place where Dournes had found it.

Dournes also reports that in July 1966, when he was visiting the village of Plei Rongol, the Jarai commander of a local military post showed him two stone heads, probably of Cham origin, each of which was some 20 centimeters in height. They had been found by a Vietnamese patrol at Plei Wong Bong, some twenty kilometers away. The commander noted that the Jarai were outraged that the heads had been removed, fearing that this desecration would precipitate droughts. The Jarai called the heads "H'bia Pe" and "Pro Thai," which Dournes sees as a derivative of "Prum The," the Bahnar designation for the Cham. According to Jarai legend, H'bia Pe and Pro Thai were sister and brother. They committed incest and the Jarai judges decreed that H'bia Pe be dismembered. An elderly villager related to Dournes that he once saw the remains of a statue that everyone called "rup H'bia Pe" at the Yang Mum tower. He added that it was believed that the Yang Mum was the house of H'bia Pe and her brother Pro Thai. In spite of Dournes' pleas that the heads be put in a place where they would be safe from bombing and military operations, the post commander ordered that they be returned to Plei Wong Bong.

The Yang Prong Site and Other Darlac Finds

In 1901 the *Bulletin de l'Ecole Française d'Extrême-Orient* disclosed that the Lao army lieutenant named Oum, who as previously noted was one of the first to report the existence of the Cham towers near Cheo Reo, had found another temple.[56] It, too, was probably Cham and was located near the Hleo river in the vicinity of the Jarai village of Tali, north of the town of Ban Don and close to the Cambodian border. He brought the fragment of a sandstone acroterion containing the outline of a Nandin to Adhémard

---

56. "Chronique," *BEFEO* 1, no. 1 (1901): 409.

Prosper Odend'hal's 1904 sketch of the Yang Prong

Leclère, the résident in Kratie, and explained that the lintel in the tower contained an inscription but that he had not had time to make a stone-rubbing of it.

On 9 March 1904 Odend'hal had visited the tower, which he called Wat Cham, although it came to be known more commonly as Yang Prong (Great Spirit), the name used by the local villagers. He had had to wait for five days while the tower was cleared of bats. In the sanctuary he found a mukhalinga (a linga containing the head of Siva). He made a stone-rubbing of the inscription on the lintel and executed a sketch of the tower. The inscription, recorded by Finot in his obituary for Odend'hal, pro-claimed that the Yang Prong had been erected by King Jaya Simhavarman III.[57] Finot went on to say that this inscription, as well as the mukhalinga, are similar to those found at the Po Klaung Garai temple in the vicinity of Phan Rang which is attributed to the same ruler. As indicated previously, both epigraphs state that Jaya Simharvarman III, who died in 1307, had generously donated "fields, slaves, and elephants" to these monuments— which scholars feel were probably erected at the beginning of the four-teenth century.[58]

In July 1906 Maitre visited the Yang Prong in spite of an unwillingness on the part of any of the local residents to take him to the site. They feared the tower, and when they learned of Odend'hal's death these fears were reinforced. Maitre found the tower enveloped by a large tree, the roots of which looked like "enormous gray snakes" on the walls. The headman in the village of Tali informed Maitre that the tower was the abode of a "great spirit" (*yang prong*). A very long time ago, he added, Cham warriors had constructed the tower and a small walled settlement nearby in preparation for war on the King of Fire and King of Water. The Cham had been living in harmony with the Jarai, but a conflict had ensued over Cham claims to rice fields. After their defeat (presumably by the armies of the King of Fire and King of Water), the Cham abandoned the area. However, the village chief had no idea where they went because "his father did not tell him." Maitre found the mukhalinga in the sanctuary as Odend'hal had described it and also came upon foundations for "secondary structures."[59]

57. Finot, "Nécrologie, Prosper Odend'hal," p. 534.
58. Aymonier, "Les Inscriptions Tchames," pp. 67–81; Bergaigne, "Ancien royaume de Champa," pp. 101–02; Georges Maspéro, *Champa*, p. 191; Parmentier, *Inventaire descriptif*, 1: 557–59; 2: 16.
59. Henri Maitre, "Notes sur la tour Chame du Nam–Lien (Darlac Septentrional)," *BEFEO* 6, nos. 3–4 (1906): 342–44; idem, *Les Régions Moï du Sud Indo-Chinois* (Paris: Plon, 1909), pp. 217–23; idem, *Les Jungles Moï*, pp. 442–43.

In his 1909 inventory of Cham monuments, Parmentier includes descriptions of the Yang Prong tower and the mukhalinga based on the information and sketches supplied by Odend'hal and Maitre.[60] He also describes some features of the Nandin depicted on the fragment of the acroterion that Lieutenant Oum had carried to Kratie. The following year Maitre again visited the Yang Prong, and he informed the Ecole Française d'Extrême-Orient that the entrance of the tower had collapsed, leaving the two carved piers half buried in the debris. He also reported finding remains of what appears to have been a settlement near the tower. Amidst piles of bricks there were four laterite foundations, on one of which were fragments of four statues and a linga.[61]

In her 1952 account of travels in the highlands of Vietnam, Gabrielle Bertrand describes visiting the Yang Prong.[62] Reluctant to go near the tower, her Rhadé guides escorted her only as far as the nearby village. Making her way alone, she found the dark red brick tower in a tangle of forest. She noted, as had Maitre in 1906, that it was hidden by the growth of a large tree. She entered the sanctuary but found close inspection impossible because of the massive number of bats clinging to the vaulted ceiling. Horrified when at dusk the squealing bats suddenly began fluttering out of the tower, she returned to the village where her guides had remained.

Relating the form and other architectural features of the Yang Prong tower to other Cham monuments, Parmentier concludes that, because it dates from the early fourteenth century, it represents the last example of the Pyramidal Art phase in the sequences of the Second Period in the evolution of Cham art.[63] Boisselier expresses the view that the presence of a temple such as the Yang Prong in the remote fastness of the highlands suggests that, with the resistance against the Mongol invasion late in the thirteenth century, the Cham rulers realized the importance of the highlanders' role and sought to integrate them more closely into the kingdom.[64]

In 1904 Finot reported that a curious artifact of Cham manufacture had been deposited at the house of Adhémard Leclère, the résident in Kratie. It was an elongated stone block with a flat surface and rounded ends which

---

60. Parmentier, *Inventaire descriptif,* 1: 557–59.
61. Ibid., 2: 603; Maitre, *Les Jungles Moi,* p. 442.
62. Gabrielle Bertrand, *Le Peuple de la jungle* (Paris: Editions "Je Sers," 1952), pp. 86–92.
63. Parmentier, *Inventaire descriptif,* 2: 11, 20, 21, 120, 194.
64. Boisselier, *Statuaire du Champa,* p. 340.

tapered to a narrower base on which a Cham inscription read *Pu Vya* (Her Majesty the Queen).[65] It had been unearthed by an elderly Rhadé villager some forty kilometers north of Ban Don, and he had taken it to his longhouse. Afterward, however, fearing that it might have malevolent influences associated with it, he removed it to a place outside the village. A Lao visiting the village saw it and carried it to the local administrative headquarters. Subsequently, one of the civil servants had it delivered to Leclère. When Odend'hal was visiting the ruins at Yang Prong, he located the elderly villager who had discovered the stone and together they went to the place where it had been found, but there were no traces of any ruins or construction of any kind. Finot notes that the use of this stone, which was called the Rasung Batau, was a mystery until a similar stone block was found at a lowland Cham site. A stone roller was discovered with it, and he concludes that the stones were used to prepare a special paste, which in certain Cham rituals is applied to the faces of the statues of the deities. Parmentier includes a description of the Rasung Batau in his 1909 inventory, with the comment that Monsieur Besnard, the government commissioner for Darlac, had informed him that in 1904 a similar but simpler stone block had been discovered on a path washed out by water near the village of Ban Ma Truot, some ten kilometers west of Ban Me Thuot.[66]

The Kodo Ruins

In 1906 Father Jeannin of the Kontum Mission announced that he had discovered the remains of two monuments, which the local Bahnar Golar villagers called Sang Bia (House of the Queen), on the swampy plain of Kodo near the Motong river south of Kontum. One of the monuments, located on the west bank of the river, was described as consisting only of a pile of bricks six meters in height and hidden by growth. However, the monument on the east bank, located on a small hill, had a sanctuary containing the figure of a goddess but no inscriptions.[67] Parmentier's 1909 inventory includes a description of the "Kodo Ruins" and of the statue of the goddess, which had a broken arm and leg.[68] Father Jeannin had been informed by the local Bahnar that this damage had been done by a "great shaman" during a ritual aimed at ending a long drought.

65. Louis Finot, "Notes d'épigraphie," *BEFEO* 4, no. 3 (1904): 678–79.
66. Parmentier, *Inventaire descriptif,* 1: 556–57.
67. Henri Parmentier, "Nouvelles découvertes archéologiques en Annam," *BEFEO* 6, nos. 1–2 (1906): 344–45.
68. Parmentier, *Inventaire descriptif,* 1: 563–64.

Henri Maspéro visited Plei Wao, near the Kodo ruins, in 1919, and the villagers informed him that the tower east of the river was called Bomong Yang. He notes that in Cham *bamun yan* means "temple of the god" and that while the word *yang* in Jarai and Bahnar means "spirit," neither language has the word *bomong*, although the Jarai Arap, located farther north and west, use the term *bo-mong* to designate a temporary hut for making ritual offerings during a funeral. Maspéro found three small altars in the sanctuary of the tower. The statue that had stood on one of them had been taken to Kontum, and part of the wall had been removed to provide bricks for the construction of a militia post in Pleiku. Maspéro reported that the other tower, called the Rong Yang (*rong*, communal house; *yang*, spirit) was larger although the upper portion of it had collapsed. Inside this tower he found an ablution vat on which there was a bronze standing Buddha.[69] In 1928 Claeys visited the Cham sites at Kodo and found the Bomong Yang tower in much the same state as it had been described by Maspéro, except that the bricks had by then been removed, as had the fragments of the ablution vat.[70] The ruins had disappeared by the time Dournes visited the Motong valley in 1966, existing only in the memories of the local Bahnar.[71] One tower had been called Sang H'bia, which Dournes translates as "residence of the princess," or alternatively Bomong Yang (sanctuary). The other they referred to as either the Rong Yang (sacred house) or Rong Jung Jo (house of Jung and Jo)—Jung and Jo being renowned Jarai legendary warriors who had fought neighboring groups. The villagers explained that not long ago a door of one tower still stood. However, the French priest had dismantled it in order to use the bricks in building his new church. His successor, a Vietnamese priest, constructed a new chapel on the foundation of the tower. Stones and bricks from the towers also were used on Christian tombs. Some villagers recalled that there had been statues and inscriptions in the monuments, but Frenchmen from Kontum had carried everything away.

Less Important Discoveries

During his 1919 visit to Cham sites in the Kontum area, Maspéro reported finding some vestiges in the Vietnamese village of Phuong Hoa, located across the Bla river from the administrative center. There were fragments of an ablution vat (being used for sharpening knives) in the

69. "Chronique," *BEFEO* 19, no. 3 (1919): 104–05.
70. Claeys, "Inspections en Annam," p. 606.
71. Dournes, "Recherches sur le Haut Champa," pp. 149–50.

garden of the village chief. An excavation at this site revealed a circular paving of bricks 1 m 50 cm in diameter. At the western end of the village on a piece of land belonging to the Bahnar Tri Huyen, i.e., Judge in the Highlander Court, Maspéro was shown a place called *hapal bia* or "mortar of the queen," which was strewn with many broken bricks and tiles. Near the Bahnar village of Kon Hongo on the bank of the Bla river, he visited the remains of a Cham tower in the forest. A circular paving of bricks similar to that found in Kon Klor formed the base of the tower, which had a square sanctuary with three false doors. Most of the walls, however, had been pulled down some fifty years earlier to provide bricks for the stairway of the mission house that was being constructed in Kon Hongo.[72]

When Claeys visited Kontum in 1928, he reported that at Phuong Hoa the bricks described by Maspéro had all been gathered up by the inhabitants to use in their houses. At Kon Hongo he found the ruin of the Cham tower as Maspéro had described it, noting that it was not considered worth including in the lists of Cham vestiges. At the house of the French résident, Claeys came upon the fragments of the ablution vat with inscriptions that had been discovered at Kon Klor and sent them to the museum at Tourane (Danang). He also found the bronze figure that had been taken from one of the Kodo towers.[73] Dournes, on his 1966 visit, found that nothing remained of the Cham tower at Kon Hongo and that the local population claimed to know nothing about it. Also, at Phuong Hoa there was no trace of the vestiges Maspéro had seen. The Vietnamese priest informed Dournes that the French had dug out the site, removing everything.[74]

At the Chu Se pass, in the vicinity of Kontum town, Claeys happened upon a dozen stone blocks of irregular ovoid shapes some 60 cm in size containing carvings of simple symbols, most of which followed the form of the stones. Near the village of Plei Ya Pla in a place called Pxat Yan Glon (tomb of the great spirit), he found a flat stone measuring 1 m by 1 m 20 cm with similar but more complex engraving. The motif of the engraving suggested to Claeys a map with villages and roads indicated by small circles and gentle curves. Close by were similar stone blocks without engravings. In his report, Claeys also notes that Maulini, former commander of a military post at Dak To, showed him two stone axes that he had found in the Koki river some twenty kilometers to the west of Dak To. Maulini also

72. "Chronique," *BEFEO* 19, no. 3 (1919): 103.
73. Claeys, "Inspections en Annam," p. 606.
74. Dournes, "Recherches sur le Haut Champa," p. 149.

Rock engraving discovered in a Bahnar village near Kontum in November 1967

claimed that the Sedang in the area had two bronze axes that they jealously guarded as powerful talismans.[75] In November 1967 near the village of Plei Char some ten kilometers southwest of Kontum, I came upon a stone block about 30 cm thick with an engraving of curved lines. However, no information about it could be obtained locally.

Other less well identified vestiges were found on the eastern periphery of the highlands by Father Durand, a French missionary who lived at Kim Son, near Bong Son in Binh Dinh province. In 1899 he reported finding a stele measuring 1 m 70 cm in height and 90 cm in width close to the Ca Xom river where there are nine cascades called "the nine fringes" by the local population (who would appear to have been Bahnar). Durand thought the inscription on the stele was Khmer, and he made a stone-rubbing which he sent to Etienne Aymonier.[76] In a meeting of the Société Asiatique held on 8 December 1899, Aymonier reported on this find and identified the script of the inscription—an invocation to Siva—as vulgar Cham.[77] Subsequently the style of the script was established as one from the fourteenth century.[78] In addition to the stele, Durand also reported

75. Claeys, "Inspections en Annam," pp. 606–07.

76. E. M. Durand, "Les Mois du Son-Phong," *Bulletin de Géographie Historique et Descriptive*, 1900, nos. 1–2, p. 296.

77. "Séance du vendredi 8 Décembre 1899," *Journal Asiatique* 14 (1899): 544–45.

78. Parmentier, *Inventaire descriptif*, 1: 565; Coedès, "Inventaire des inscriptions," p. 44.

finding in the vicinity of Kon Tra a rock containing the very large imprint of a foot. The local highlanders would neither discuss it nor go near it.

Other Cham vestiges include various kinds of objects usually referred to in the literature as "treasures." Writing in 1890, Aymonier makes the observation that the Chru and "Koho" remained loyal to the Cham princes in Panduranga and that they faithfully continued to guard the "royal treasures" which consisted of ornaments associated with Cham deities and some cult objects.[79] Aymonier had reported in 1885 that Roglai villagers in the mountains west of Phan Rang were guardians of some ornaments that according to their legends were entrusted to them by Cham kings. At two annual rituals called Chabor and Katé, the villagers made offerings of bananas and betel to the deities associated with the ornaments and explained that failure to do so would bring on epidemics.[80]

In 1890 Aymonier reported that in the Roglai village of Glai Joboung west of Phan Rang the villagers venerated some Cham vestiges. These consisted of pieces of copper armament, a shield, some illegible manuscripts, and a human head that local lore held to be the head of the Cham king Po Bin No Svor (Po Binoethuor).[81] According to Durand, Po Bin No Svor was the ruler in Panduranga from 1328 until 1373 and also is identified in Cham oral tradition with King Che Bong Nga (1360–1390). Remembered as a warrior of great valor, legend has it that he was decapitated during a battle with the Vietnamese.[82]

Chru informants note that in several villages located in the Danhim valley there are "Cham treasures" which are venerated by the local population. In a complaint filed with the Tuyen Duc province authorities in July 1968, the elders of the Chru village of Plei Sop charged that when they returned to the settlement following an evacuation due to fighting in the area they found their temple destroyed and their "Cham treasures" stolen.[83] These treasures consisted of two carved gold guns, four swords, two antique knives, three pieces of ivory, five carved gold bowls, three

79. Etienne Aymonier, "Légendes historiques des Chames," *Excursions et Reconnaissances* 14, no. 32 (1890): 182.

80. Etienne Aymonier, "Notes sur l'Annam," *Excursions et Reconnaissances* 10, no. 24 (1885): 310–11.

81. Aymonier, "Légendes historiques," pp. 165–66.

82. Durand, "Notes sur les Chams," p. 377.

83. Chú-Tịch Ủy-Ban Bình-Định Xã Loan (The Chairman of the Loan Village Pacification Committee), *V/V báo cáo mất các bảo-vật cổ tích tại Đền Sop M'Drong Hai* (Report on the Loss of Precious Antiques at Sop M'Drong Hai Temple), Tuyen Duc Province, Republic of Vietnam, 25 July 1968.

gold cymbals, a gold platter weighing three kilos, an ivory stamp, seven antique vases, and some Cham silk.

CHAM AND HIGHLANDER LEGENDS

Aymonier found among the Cham in Cambodia some recorded poems about princes that mention the highlanders. One of these poems tells the story of Po Cheun Chan, the last Cham ruler in Panduranga, who according to Cham chronicles reigned between 1799 and 1822.[84] Po Cheun Chan, the poem relates, was named by the Vietnamese emperor (Gia Long) to command all of the troops of the Cham and of the "Koho" as far distant as the "Chorus Bala" (Ivory Chru). After a conflict with the Vietnamese mandarins, who at one point placed a cangue around his neck, the Cham leader took refuge among his own people and there organized an exodus of Muslim Cham into the highlands. At first the exiles were welcomed by the Koho, but soon after the highlanders turned against the Cham, and Po Cheun Chan spent four months subduing them. After the Cham had gathered the necessary buffaloes and food, they continued their exodus westward, still harassed by the Koho, and made their way into Cambodia, where they settled by the Mekong river.

Aymonier obtained from Po Ku, a descendant of Po Cheun Chan and Sneha Nores, three lists of the Cham leaders in Cambodia. Two of the lists include the name Po Phindisak.[85] A legend concerning this leader is preserved in a document called "The Poem of Phindisak," which Aymonier believes to be a mixture of the legends surrounding Po Binoethuor (1328–1373), whose head, as indicated above, is believed to have been an object of veneration by the Roglai, and Po Rome (1627–1651), the most renowned of the later Cham rulers. In the legend two Cham generals, Chei Nok (or Nong) and Chei Pok, are informed that a revolt has broken out among the "Chorus, Kahovs et Stiengs" (Chru, Koho, and Stieng), whereupon they ask the king for troops. He responds by sending General Nok five hundred men. The king also gives the generals special vestments and implores the divinities for a Cham victory. At noon on the day determined to be auspicious for their campaign, the two generals go forth at the head of

---

84. Aymonier, "Légendes historiques," pp. 152, 193–206.
85. Ibid., pp. 183–93.

an army resplendent with white, red, green, and violet standards and subjugate the rebellious highlanders.

In the oral tradition of the highlanders, the richest reported source of information on the kind of relations that existed between the Cham and some highland groups is a Cau Maa legend related by Boulbet.[86] The legend begins at a time when the kingdoms of the Khmer and Cham were on the decline, and there were great wars that inflicted death and slavery on entire populations. As the Vietnamese made increasing inroads on the northern part of Champa, the Cham rulers sought to assert greater authority over the highland people. When the groups located to the east of the Maa were brought under domination of the Prum (Cham) "uncles," the Maa were faced with the possibility that they too would lose their independence. Remaining free was essential to the Maa, for only as free men could they fulfill their responsibility as guardians of "the domain of the spirits."

This responsibility rested largely with the heads of the "great lineages" (see chap. 2) who functioned as an aristocratic elite in Maa society. One of the most prestigious of the lineage heads was K'Toong, the husband of Wil, both descended from the first ancestors of the Maa. K'Toong was a direct descendant in the male line of Rdeen, the celebrated hero, master of ironworking, and bastard son of the sun. According to the lineage myth, the deity associated with the sun became excited by the immodest beauty of K'Beeng, and a ray of the sun was injected into her vagina. After seven days of pregnancy she gave birth to Rdeen. As a descendant of this warrior-hero, it was K'Toong's responsibility to cope with the Cham threat, so he approached the chiefs of the neighboring Sre, the people to the east who farmed paddy fields and who already were vassals of the Cham, to have them arrange a meeting between him and the Cham king. The Sre chiefs told K'Toong that since there were numerous advantages to being vassals of the Cham it would be better for the Cau Maa not to resist their domination. K'Toong rejected this advice and told the Sre chiefs that, as guardian of the domain of the spirits, he would only talk to the Cham king as an equal. When the meeting was arranged, K'Toong and the Cham ruler agreed that the Maa would remain independent but that they would furnish troops to aid the Cham in arresting the advance of the Yuan

---

86. Jean Boulbet, *Pays des Maa domaine des génies Nggar Maa, Nggar Yaang* (Paris: Ecole Française d'Extrême-Orient, 1967), pp. 65–76.

(Vietnamese). For K'Toong, a scion of Rdeen's line, victory in battle was assured, and so for the first time Maa warriors, led by K'Toong and his son K'Bung and armed with their forged iron weapons, descended to Champa. Fighting with the Cham armies, they succeeded in stopping for a time the incursions of the Vietnamese, after which they returned to the domain of the spirits.

While K'Bung was among the Cham, he fell in love with a beautiful young Cham princess named He and took her back to the valley of the Rnga river on the plateau of Blao. K'Toong viewed this marriage as a compromise with the Cham, and so to counterbalance it he married his daughter Mhoo to the son of a chief of a great Maa lineage on the right bank of the river. There was a Kur (Cambodian) among the ancestors of this lineage, but K'Toong reasoned that the Cambodians, in principle, were allies of the Maa. Also, the Cambodians were no threat to the domain of the spirits, since they were quite far removed. Furthermore, to the southwest of the Maa country there were unpopulated marshy forests and to the northwest were the Bu Dinh and Bu Deh (subgroups of the Stieng), who were too warlike to allow any penetration of their territory. With the Cham, however, the situation was different, for they had much of the highlands under their control, particularly the valley of the Riam river, the access route to the Blao plateau.

With his initial passion somewhat diminished, K'Bung began to realize the drawbacks in having a Cham princess among the Maa. After his wife gave birth to their son K'Biom, numerous Cham "uncles" began to visit from the coast, and this increased his uneasiness. By this time the Vietnamese had pushed south of Cape Varella, and the Cham were searching for more highland territory into which they could expand. Several Cham expeditions already had been repulsed by the Maa in the area between the high Rnga river and the upstream area where the Coop, a subgroup of the Maa, were located. Although he was aware that it would not do to provoke the Cham, who were looking for an excuse to break their agreement with K'Toong, K'Bung nonetheless took a second wife, K'Ciet, member of a Maa great lineage.

When he grew to manhood, K'Biom, the son of K'Bung and the Cham princess, married K'Troe, a girl from a prestigious Maa lineage, and they had a daughter named Ngel. Later she married K'Cang Dam Boo, the scion of a great lineage who because of his handsome appearance and great courage was called "K'Cang the Magnificent." K'Cang led the continued resistance to the Cham expansion into the Maa country. Realizing that their armed pressure was not achieving any success, the Cham "uncles" settled on a new strategy; they kidnapped Ngel, who, as the granddaughter of a Cham princess, was considered to be of their royal line. K'Cang and his brother Krah, accompanied by the powerful shaman K'Wan, also known as "Mother Cicada," went to the court of the Cham king bringing a gift of two elephants with long tusks. K'Cang asked for the release of his wife, and the Cham ruler responded that he would grant this request if first the Maa would submit totally to Cham domination. After discussing the agreements that had been made long before by the ruling Cham king and the Maa chief K'Toong, K'Cang acceded to the Cham demands but pointed out that he could only speak for his own lineage and those allied with it. This did not include the great lineages descended from K'Toong and his wife Wil.

Leaving the shaman K'Wan with Ngel, who had given birth to a son, K'Dong, the two brothers returned to the highlands to confer with their kinsmen. Finally the agreement was concluded: Ngel would be returned to the Maa and K'Cang would become a vassal of the Cham ruler. The Cham authority would thus be extended to the country upstream from the high basin of the Da Rnga, which was occupied by the Cau Too and included the Maa lineages allied with K'Cang's lineage. But it would not extend farther west into the heart of the domain of the spirits. A Cham delegation accompanied Ngel, her son K'Dong, and K'Wan back to the highlands. At the village where they met with K'Cang there was a large celebration. A buffalo was sacrificed to proclaim the agreement between the Cham and K'Cang, and the delegation presented the Maa leader with a Cham saber and a copper seal to mark his investiture as a *Botao Prum*—a "Cham Lord." K'Cang's authority would now come from the Cham king to whom he would pay a periodic tribute. Giant bamboo trees were then planted around the clearing where the ceremony had taken place in order to mark the occasion.

Initially the tribute demanded by the Cham was modest—such things as tortoise shell, ivory, and Maa cloth. The Cham, for their part, were to protect the Cau Too. The Cau Too were now free to trade with the Cham, particularly for salt, a commodity highly prized by the highland people. After the departure of the Cham delegation, the new authority of K'Cang as Cham Lord was challenged when K'Pun Dam Dang, head of another great lineage, struck Ngel. This resulted in a duel between K'Pun and

K'Cang, who emerged victorious. The lineage of K'Pun was reduced to subservience to the lineage of K'Cang and eventually descended into slavery. K'Cang reorganized his fief, making each of his children heads of lineages and bestowing the title of Botao Prum on his son K'Raat, who eventually passed the Cham saber and seal to the chief of the K'Dat lineages. Subsequently the Cham made K'Coe, chief of Min Ndrong village, a Cham Lord as part of their attempt to extend their control farther west on the Blao plateau.

As the Cham lost more territory to the Vietnamese, their power waned and their "protection" became more illusory. At the same time their influence among the Cau Too had an increasingly baleful effect. The role of the Cham Lord with his saber and seal was an intrusive institution that disrupted the traditional pattern of authority transmitted through the great lineages with their carefully selected chiefs whose genealogies extended back to the first ancestors of the Maa. As guardians of the talismans and altars symbolizing the continuity of these lineages, these chiefs maintained the cohesiveness of Maa society. Now among the Cau Too, authority was vested in the Cham Lords, and titles were transmitted haphazardly, often being passed on to those who were nothing more than brigands. The traditional authority of the chiefs was shattered, and lineages fissioned. What authority remained in them was diffused, passed on through the male or female line without regard for tradition. But to the west, in the domain of the spirits, the Maa who remained free of Cham domination kept the traditional ways, and their leadership continued to function as it had in the past.

On the coastal plain, the Cham were reduced to their last enclave. Boulbet figures that, on the basis of information in the historical annals and number of generations in the Maa genealogies described in legend, this would have been around the middle of the eighteenth century. As noted previously, this was a period when the last Cham princes ruled with meager authority in the enclave at Bal Chanar in the vicinity of Phan Ri. However, the dwindling of their authority only strengthened the Cham resolve to establish their authority more solidly in the highlands so as to have a refuge. First, they established a Cham administration among the Sre—who for a long time had been vassals—and then they attempted to do the same thing among the Maa lineages which had been brought under their domination.

This provoked a gathering of the Maa chiefs on the Blao plateau at which they decided on a twofold solution: those lineages descended from K'Cang that wished to continue their vassalage to the Cham would remain in the area, while the free lineages would migrate downstream toward the west where there was a sparsely inhabited area. In addition to removing the Maa free lineages from the threat of Cham rule, this migration would relieve the population pressure on the Blao plateau, which was being farmed too intensely by the swidden method. K'Hek Dam Liong, leader of the free lineages, then met with a Cham chief on the summit of Mount Cirong Lae—a place where, in Maa legends, the giant Iut first cleared the forest to farm and where the "root of Lae" provided the wood for the first crossbow made by the giant K'Doong. The two leaders agreed to divide the territory; the Cham zone of influence would be to the east of the mountain and the Maa would have the area to the west. To mark their agreement, the Cham chief presented K'Hek with a saber, and the Maa leader reciprocated with a gift of some of the famous Maa cloth. K'Hek then led the migration of the free Maa lineages to the new land downstream.

Upstream, the Maa Too, under Cham rule, lost much of the Maa culture. The little weaving that they did was not in the elegant Maa tradition, and their great lineages disintegrated. Downstream, however, Maa traditions continued to thrive among the free lineages. The Cham did not attempt to expand their control downstream or in the direction of the country to the northwest of the Maa Too, where the Maa Huang and Maa Boloo lived, because they were reputed to be very warlike people. Farther north, some Cham armies moved along the Rtih river and Noong river in an effort to make their way into Cambodia. Any of them who ventured into the nearby country of the Maa Coop, however, were massacred.

Later, bands of Cham and Khmer soldiers, remnants of armies defeated by the Vietnamese in the Mekong river delta, moved up the Da (river) Huei, where they attempted to settle. All of them, however, were slaughtered by the indigenous Maa Krung. Boulbet notes that even in recent times there were traces of their paddy fields and terraces in the area.

The Cham also established tributary relations among the Chru but the pattern was quite different from that described in the Maa legends. The Cham were said to have entered the highlands from the present Phan Ri area, first settling in the vicinity of the villages of Tranang, Loang (Loan), Tukla (Tu Tra), and Linh Gia. From historical evidence already discussed, this would appear to have occurred sometime around the mid-seventeenth century. Interestingly enough, as was noted before, Durand expressed the view that it was during this era that elite Cham families established redoubts (*bal*) in the highlands.

Once settled in the highlands, Cham refugees intermarried with the Austronesian-speaking Roglai as well as with the Mon Khmer-speaking Koho. The new group which emerged were the Chru, speaking a language close to Cham. The elite clan among the Chru was the Bahnaria, and its chief, selected by its members, was a vassal of the Cham ruler, who bestowed on him the title *potao*. This chief also was given a Cham saber to symbolize his role. Traditionally, the Bahnaria chief was expected to send the Cham ruler an annual tribute consisting of rabbits, goats, horses, and various kinds of exotic birds, including peacocks, parakeets, and parrots. Also, every year the clan chief made a pilgrimage to the Po Nagar temple at Nhatrang to offer a horse, goat, and a rabbit in honor of the *potao Cham*, the deceased Cham kings.

The last great clan chief was Bahnaria Quang, who was recognized not only by the last Cham royalty but also by the Vietnamese and the French. His tenure lasted from the late nineteenth century until around 1930 when he died at well over the age of eighty years. According to Bahnaria clan history, Quang's maternal greatgrandmother married a Cham general, who recruited Chru to fight the Vietnamese. In the villages of Diom and Taniang there still are vestiges of forges that were used at that time to make weapons for the Cham army. Quang was guardian of the Cham general's ceremonial hat and robe, his medals, and his sabers. One saber was thought to have magical qualities, and it could not be removed from its sheath until a goat and a chicken had been offered to the spirits. In his role as arbiter of disputes, Quang made the parties in conflict take an oath on the saber.

Maitre recounts a legend passed on to him by the "northern Jarai" (probably the Jarai Arap) who described how in the distant past the Cham had come into their country in large numbers—such large numbers that, as one informant put it, "if one had a basket full of sesame seeds, one could not have given a seed to each of them."[87] The legend concerns three tragedies that befell the Cham troops in the area. The first took place at Lake Tenneung, a sacred body of water located between the present cities of Kontum and Pleiku, not far from Route 14. There the Cham blocked the water source with a large jar in order to divert the water from the nearby

87. Maitre, *Les Jungles Moi*, pp. 442–43.

swampy plain of Menam. When they removed the jar, the waters gushed forth, drowning all the Cham troops.

The second disaster occurred at Peto, between Lake Tenneung and the Jrai Li falls in the Sesan river. Here there was a sacred liana that grew very high in a tree. When the Cham troops came to this place, the spirits brought about a violent wind that stirred the branches of the trees. Hearing what they thought was the sound of rushing water in a subterranean rapids, the Cham began to dig a deep hole in the ground. Other Cham climbed the sacred liana but the spirits caused the liana to fall. Those clinging to it fell on the soldiers in the deep hole, and they all perished.

The third tragedy befell the Cham army at the Jrai Li falls in the Sesan river. At the thickly forested gorge, the Cham constructed a bridge of spears, but the foliage and mist obscured the passage. When the first soldier ventured onto the bridge, he fell into the abyss. The commander, unable to see him, shouted, "Have you arrived?" and his echo repeated the word "arrived." Thinking the bridge safe, the Cham soldiers filed onto it only to fall into the gorge. This continued through the night. In the morning, a father and son were about to step onto the bridge when an invisible force held them back. It was then that the remaining Cham troops, numbering about one hundred, perceived what had happened. They quickly dispersed, but the Jarai pursued them, killing all of them.

It was pointed out previously that when Maitre visited the Yang Prong tower near the Jarai village of Tali in 1906 he learned that according to local lore the Cham had constructed the tower and a small settlement in preparation for war on two powerful Jarai shamans, the King of Fire and the King of Water, and left the area after their defeat.[88] Conflict between the Cham and Jarai also is an element in one of the Jarai legends concerning the origin of the sacred saber of the King of Fire.[89] In this legend, Po The, the cunning hero, carries the sacred saber into battle with the Cham, inflicting on them a stunning defeat.

Bourotte, reporting on Roglai legends that relate how they fought at the side of the Cham, expresses the view that the Cham were able to survive in Panduranga for two hundred years because of the assistance given them by groups such as the Roglai, Chru, and Sre.[90] Bourotte also makes

88. Ibid.

89. Adhémard Leclère, "Légende Djarai sur l'origine du sabre sacré par le Roi du Feu," *Revue Indochinoise*, no. 6 (1904): 366–69.

90. Bernard Bourotte, "Essai d'histoire des populations Montagnardes du Sud-Indochinois jusqu'à 1945," *BSEI* 30, no. 1 (1955): 37.

reference to the "story of Tamrac," which he says can be traced back to that era. When the Cham chief Sunka called upon the highlanders to join his fight against the Vietnamese, the Roglai, Chil, and other groups responded by sending warriors armed with crossbows. Led by Tamrac, they battled on Mount Jodrung for seven days, but the Cham were defeated and Tamrac either was taken prisoner or committed suicide.

CHAM–HIGHLANDER RELATIONS

It seems logical to assume that the upland people played an important economic role in the kingdom of Champa, for the image of Champa as a rich country, *"merveilleuse et quasi fabuleuse"* in the eyes of other foreigners, particularly the Chinese, was largely due to the wealth that the Cham drew from the hinterland. Maitre feels that the highlanders must have "cooperated in hunting and capturing elephants and rhinoceros, in washing auriferous sands, and in gathering cardamom, wax, lacquer, and resins, in cutting wood and searching for eaglewood" and that probably most of the elephants used by the Cham for military campaigns as well as for royal processions came from the Rhadé and Jarai.[91] Maitre also notes that many of the tributary gifts sent by the Cham rulers to the Chinese court reflected an upland origin.

In A.D. 340, Fan Wen, one of the early rulers of Lin Yi, sent the Chinese court some domestic elephants as tribute. Scrutiny of the extant records of Cham tributes in later years shows these items presumably from the highlands: elephants, along with white quails and parrots, in 414 and 417; some splendidly arrayed elephants and parrots of variegated colors in 630; eleven rhinoceros horns in 642; elephants and elephant tusks in 686, 691, 695, 707, and 731; elephants and eaglewood in 731 and 742; rhinoceros horns, elephant tusks, camphor, and peacocks in 960; and elephants and live rhinoceros in 966. Then in 992 the size of the gifts increased considerably when ten rhinoceros horns, three hundred elephant tusks, and some sandalwood were dispatched. Tribute in 1018 included seventy-two elephant tusks, eighty-six rhinoceros horns, cardamom, eaglewood, areca nuts, and betel leaves. In 1050 the Cham king sent two hundred and one elephant tusks and seventy-nine rhinoceros horns.[92]

91. Maitre, *Les Jungles Moi*, pp. 434–35.
92. Ibid.; Georges Maspéro, *Champa*, pp. 57, 67, 87–88, 92, 120, 128, 133, 138.

The historical accounts, legends, and the inventory of Cham vestiges presented thus far support to some extent Maitre's hypothesis. Around the year 1000, the Cham clearly were being threatened by the Vietnamese at their northern border, and they surely were aware of the possibility of expanding their territory westward into the attractive areas of the uplands. The earliest Cham vestige in the highlands is the inscribed ablution vat dating A.D. 914 found at Kon Klor close to Kontum town. However, its significance is difficult to assess; it could attest to a Cham presence in the area at that date, but the vat could just as easily have been carried into the area at a later date. More substantive are the inscriptions at Nhatrang and My Son relating how Jaya Harivarman I brought the highlanders to the west of Panduranga under his control around 1160. The Ba river valley, which contains a number of Cham ruins, would have been a likely route of entry into the highlands, and it would have given the Cham access to the Darlac plateau and to the Ayun river area around present Cheo Reo as well.

None of the Cham vestiges found in the highlands date from the 1160 period, but the Yang Prong tower was constructed during the reign of Jaya Simhavarman III at the end of the thirteenth century. With the invasion of the Mongols in 1282, Jaya Simhavarman's father, Indravarman V, had fled into the highlands, where he remained for two years. As indicated previously, Boisselier puts forth the view that the presence of the Yang Prong in such a remote area of the highlands suggests that, with the Mongol threat, the Cham realized the importance of the highlanders, so they sought to better integrate them into the kingdom.[93] In this same vein, it is interesting that in 1402 Jaya Simhavarman V was forced to yield Indrapura in the northern province of Amaravati to Dai Viet, and vestiges in the Cheo Reo area date from this period: the Drang Lai Siva is dated 1409, the Drang Lai stele is early fifteenth century, and Yang Mum is fifteenth century. One might speculate that the presence of these towers also reflects an expansion of Cham authority into the Jarai country at this period.

Attempts by the Cham to establish tributary relations among the highlanders is a central theme in the Maa legend recorded by Boulbet.[94] Such a strategy would be in keeping with a similar pattern that characterized relations among the kingdoms, principalities, and chiefdoms of Southeast

93. Boisselier, *Statuaire du Champa*, p. 340.
94. Boulbet, *Pays des Maa*, pp. 65–76.

Asia from as early as the first century A.D. when the rulers in Funan and Chen La established their power by reducing neighboring chiefs to vassalage. By the same token, all of the states in Southeast Asia had, for centuries, tributary relations with China.

The Maa legend suggests that initially the Cham sought to establish tributary relations through negotiations rather than through force. The Cham had the advantage of great power, so that the highlanders would as vassals have had the protection of Champa. The legend also indicates that they would have had the right to trade with the Cham. The highlanders could have obtained such highly prized commodities as salt in exchange for locally produced items; for example, the Maa used their famous cloth both in trade and as tribute. Another highland product, eaglewood, was important in the Cham relations with the Roglai. When he visited Cochinchina early in the seventeenth century, Borri noted that the highly valued eaglewood came from the mountains of the Kemois (a designation for the highlanders), and Aymonier describes how in the late nineteenth century the Roglai still traded eaglewood with the Cham.[95] The Cham in the Phan Rang valley had a dignitary called *po-gahlao* (lord of eaglewood) whose function was to organize the search for eaglewood during every dry season. After making offerings to Po Klong Garai, Po Rome, Po Nagar, Po Klong Kashet, and Po Klong Garai Bhok—the "protectors of eaglewood"—the Cham proceeded to the villages of the Orang-Glai (Roglai) where the *po-va* or village headmen would assemble bands of men to assist the Cham in their search for the precious wood. Some of the other items traded and sent to the Cham as tribute by the highlanders were described previously.

The Maa legend also implies, however, that some highlanders, such as the Maa themselves, resisted Cham domination. In the case of the Maa, the Cham had to resort to kidnapping the wife of the head of a great lineage in order to have him accept the role of a Cham vassal. As a representative of the Cham ruler, this vassal was given a Cham saber and seal and the Cham title of *botao* or *potao*, which, as indicated previously, means "lord" or "master," and in some contexts was tantamount to "king." It is possible that Maitre, in reporting legends about an ancient "Maa principality" led by a chief who was "more or less a shaman," interpreted the accounts of

95. Cristoforo Borri, *Cochinchina: Containing Many Admirable Rarities and Singularities of That Countrey* (London: Robert Ashley for Richard Clutterbuck, 1633); Etienne Aymonier, *Les Tchames et leurs religions* (Paris: Ernest Leroux, 1891), pp. 72–77.

outstanding Maa lineage leaders, such as K'Toong and K'Cang, as referring to chiefs of a principality.[96] He also may have interpreted the lineage leaders' responsibilities as guardians of lineage talismans and altars, and their role as officiants at lineage rituals, as being shamanistic functions.

Both Cham and highlander legends indicate that, as the last traces of Cham power waned, conflict resulted from Cham attempts to establish themselves in the highlands. As noted above, the "Poem of Phindisak" reported by Aymonier describes a revolt by Chru, Koho, and Stieng against the Cham.[97] Aymonier also recounts a Cham poem about Po Cheun Chan, the last ruler of Panduranga, who reigned between 1799 and 1802. It describes how Po organized an exodus of Muslim Cham into the highlands. Initially the Koho welcomed them, but later they turned on the Cham, who fled to Cambodia. The Maa legend reported by Boulbet indicates that the Cham successfully established themselves among some highlanders, such as the Sre and Maa Cau Too, but they encountered hostility from other Maa groups.

Any discussion of relations between the Cham and the highlanders invariably raises the question of what impact the Cham presence had on the highland groups within their sphere of influence. Strong evidence would be borrowings by the highlanders from Cham language and culture, and Maitre sees the role of shamans called *pajao* (or a cognate word thereof) as such a borrowing.[98] The Cham had priestesses called *pajau*—or *paja*, pronounced padiao, according to Cabaton, who made a careful study of their role.[99] In the modern period shamans with cognate designations are found among the Jarai (*pojao*), Chru (*po-jau*), Mnong Gar (*njao*), Sre (*bijao*), Bahnar (*pojou*), Halang (*mjao*), and Jeh (*mojao*), the role now transformed in most of these cases to a male one.

Another apparent borrowing from the Cham is the Jarai custom of cremating the bodies of the King of Fire and King of Water, though the common practice in the highlands is to bury the dead.[100] This unique practice in the case of the King of Fire and King of Water, coupled with some of the information contained in the Maa legend, suggests that the roles of the King of Fire and King of Water may be of Cham origin. It is not

96. Maitre, *Les Jungles Moi*, pp. 431–32.
97. Aymonier, "Légendes historiques," pp. 184–93, 152, 193–206.
98. Maitre, *Les Jungles Moi*, p. 443.
99. Antoine Cabaton, *Nouvelles recherches sur les Chams* (Paris: Ernest Leroux, 1901), pp. 28–36.
100. Maitre, *Les Jungles Moi*, p. 443. This practice is also described in Cabaton, *Nouvelles recherches*, pp. 46–49.

inconceivable that the titles Potao Apui (King of Fire) and Potao Ea (King of Water) are derived from the Cham title potao given to vassals. To this day, the Rcom clan in the vicinity of Cheo Reo, and the Siu clan generally, are considered elite. At some time in the distant past their clan leaders, like the lineage chief K'Cang in the Maa legend, may have become vassals of the Cham, after which the title potao was bestowed upon them. The sacred saber of the King of Fire could well have been presented to the original Potao Apui when he became a Cham vassal. One can speculate that when the chiefs of the Siu and Rcom clans were invested as Cham Lords their authority was divided territorially, with the King of Fire ruling the eastern area of the mountains and the King of Water holding sway over the western portion.

From the Maa legend also it is possible to infer that the Cham influence had a negative influence on the Maa who accepted their domination. The role of the Cham Lord conflicted with that of the lineage chiefs who had traditionally maintained the fabric of Maa society. With their old leadership destroyed, the Maa Too experienced a breakdown in their traditional ways and at the end of the legend have become culturally impoverished, incapable of producing the elegant weaving for which they were famous.

Another question worth exploring is whether the Cham may have influenced the subsistence activities of some of the highland groups. In the past the Cham had wet-rice agriculture with extensive paddy fields along the coastal plain and in adjacent valleys. In addition, they had smaller paddy fields in terraces arranged on the hillsides. Aymonier describes a sophisticated irrigation system which, according to Cham belief, was the invention of the divinized ruler Po Klong Garai, who Durand notes is listed in the Royal Chronicles as having ruled in Bal Hanav between 1151 and 1209.[101] Wet-rice farming is still found among some of the highlanders and, interestingly enough, exists not only where the physical ecology is amenable but also in areas where, according to available evidence, there was some Cham presence. This would include areas adjacent to the coastal plain (where groups such as the Hre, Cua, and Chru have paddy fields on bottom land as well as on terraces with relatively sophisticated irrigation systems) and the more remote interior region, within the limits marked by Cham vestiges (where some Jarai, Bahnar, Monom, Rhadé, Mnong, Sre, and Lat have paddy fields). The local lore surround-

101. Aymonier, *Les Tchames et leurs religions*, pp. 66–72; Durand, "Notes sur les Chams," p. 377.

ing the far-removed Yang Prong tower described the Cham there as having rice fields.[102] Also, in the Maa legend, the Maa, who were not under Cham domination, practiced shifting agriculture, while the neighboring Sre, who for a long time were Cham vassals, had paddy farming.

Finally, given the kind of relationships that the Cham had with some highland groups over a long period of time, it is curious that they did not have a greater impact on these highland cultures. While the Chru, who claim some Cham ancestry, had a Cham script, there is nothing to indicate that the Cham attempted to implant the Indian great tradition among the highlanders. Significantly, although a few honorific Cham titles such as potao and bia made their way into some of the highland people's vocabularies, there do not appear to be any cognate words for the Hindu deities venerated in the sanctuaries. One might respond that since the Brahman religion among the Cham was elitist, their disdain for the less advanced "kiratas" prevented their attempting any conversion of these "savages" to the cult. But on the other hand, the Cham seemed prepared to bestow prestigious titles on some highland leaders and in some instances to intermarry with them. In many respects the Cham presence in the highlands seems to have been as ephemeral as the morning fog, but perhaps more extensive research on the Kingdom of Champa and its role in the highlands will reveal deeply rooted Cham influence among the highlanders.

102. Maitre, *Les Jungles Moi*, pp. 442–43.

4 THE KHMER RULERS AND THE KINGS OF FIRE AND WATER

After an arduous journey I suddenly found myself out of the forest near a beautiful causeway paved with large slabs of stone. The entrance was guarded by lions sculptured in a somewhat fantastic fashion. This causeway crossed extensive ditches transformed into swamps where troops of buffalo grazed and bathed. On either side of the causeway I saw small pavilions partly in ruins but retaining some of their former elegance. I then entered the first gallery, where three half-collapsed towers broke the long architectural line. After this came the second interior gallery. These two immense rectangular cloisters with their walls covered with bas-reliefs of the finest carving, surrounded the shrine itself. When I entered the shrine I found it the depository of Buddhist and Brahman divinities in more or less good condition. It also was the abode of countless bats that did not leave an agreeable fragrance. In the center of the two galleries, but much more elevated than they, rose a fortress of stone, and this, according to some documents, is Angkor Wat. At each corner of this gigantic and splendid edifice stood a beautiful tower, and each one had the shape of an immense tiara. Much higher than the rest was the central tower, measuring fifty-six meters from the ground to the summit. Connecting these towers were galleries, the walls of which were decorated with carvings. The shrine was reached by four monumental stairways. This edifice was constructed almost entirely of sandstone admirably carved by the Khmer artists. It must be said, however, that these adept workers did not understand anything about depicting the human figure: their portrayals were nearly always grotesque.[1]

Thus did Father Bouillevaux, a French missionary, describe his first impressions of the ruins of Angkor Wat in 1850, ten years before their

1. C. E. Bouillevaux, *L'Annam et le Cambodge* (Paris: Victor Palme, 1874), pp. 131–32. The quotation is my translation.

"discovery" by Henri Mouhot. Actually the existence of the ruins always was known to the Cambodians, and in the late sixteenth century they had been visited by some Portuguese missionaries.

After his visit to Angkor Wat, Bouillevaux traveled into northeastern Cambodia and in September 1851 went into the country of the Penongs (a Cambodian designation for the highlanders) east of Sambok, a town on the Mekong river near present-day Kratie. There informants told him that further north among the Charai (Jarai) was a man called the King of Fire and Water who did not have any real authority but who nonetheless commanded considerable respect because he was the keeper of a sword and other objects to which the Jarai attached *"une importance superstitieuse."* Bouillevaux's informants added that the kings of Cambodia and Cochin- china sent gifts to the King of Fire and Water every three years.

Although the information that Bouillevaux reported was inaccurate in describing one rather than two kings, it was the first western account of tributary relations between the Khmer rulers and the Kings of Fire and Water. Subsequently, other French investigators also reported the ex- istence of the King of Fire and the King of Water and some describe their relations with the Cambodian kings. Much of their information, however, must be seen in the context of post-Angkorian Khmer history, particularly some of the events that took place in the late sixteenth and early seven- teenth centuries.

HISTORICAL SUMMARY

For a variety of reasons, one of the most important of which was repeated invasions by the Thai, the Cambodians decided sometime around 1432 that Angkor Thom must be abandoned as the capital city. As Briggs puts it, "First the king and the surviving notables, and then the people fled from the 'great and glorious capital' of Khmer civilization as if it were ridden with plague."[2] This event also marked the end of epigraphic information on the succession of Khmer rulers. The post-Angkorian genealogies and historical dates are based on the less reliable chronicles of the Cambodians, Thai, and Chinese. Some valuable historical data, however, are found in

2. Lawrence P. Briggs, *The Ancient Khmer Empire* (Philadelphia: American Philosophical Society, 1951), p. 261.

the Spanish and Portuguese accounts of the sixteenth and early seventeenth centuries, such as those used by Groslier.[3]

Coedès places the royal court at Basan in 1433.[4] The following year it was moved to the present site of Phnom Penh, where in 1441 Ponhea Yat was crowned King Suryavarman. After he abdicated in 1459, the throne went to his first son and then to his second son, who was captured by the Thai during a 1473 campaign in which the Khmer lost the provinces of Korat, Chandapuri, and Angkor. Ponhea Yat's third son led a successful campaign to drive the Thai from the country and was crowned king with the name Dhammaraja. He died in 1504, and a usurper named Kan seized the throne. Dhammaraja's nephew Ang Chan successfully toppled Kan and established a new capital at Lovek. After repelling another attack by the Thai in 1540, he had a palace built in the new capital and there in 1553 ascended the throne. Ang Chan, who died in 1566, is remembered as one of the greatest of the post-Angkor Khmer rulers.

Ang Chan's successor was his son Paramaraja, who became King Barom Reachea I. According to Moura this took place in 1567, but Garnier reports the date as 1576 (illustrating the variation in dating according to the different chronicles).[5] Both authors describe Reachea's struggles with the Thai and his recapture of the province of Korat. Garnier reports that he died in 1576, while Moura tells us that it was in the year 1567. Reachea was succeeded by his son Satha, who took the name Chetta I and established his court near the site of Angkor Wat. It was at this time that the Portuguese and Spaniards began to visit Cambodia, and some of them were the first Europeans to see Angkor. Groslier states that Nareshvara came to power in 1590 in Ayudhya and the following year attacked Lovek, which fell in January 1594.[6] Satha and his two elder sons fled to Laos. In his absence a usurper named Reamea Chung Prei seized the throne with the aid of Cham and Malay troops that Satha had recruited to fight the Thai.

Among the westerners who appeared in Cambodia during Satha's reign were two soldiers of fortune, a Portuguese named Diogo Veloso (whose

3. Bernard-Philippe Groslier, *Angkor et le Cambodge au XVIe siècle d'après les sources Portugaises et Espagnoles* (Paris: Presses Universitaires de France, 1958).

4. Georges Coedès, *The Making of South East Asia*, trans. H. M. Wright (London: Routledge & Kegan Paul, 1966), pp. 196–97; idem, *The Indianized States of Southeast Asia*, ed. Walter F. Vella, trans. Susan Brown Cowing (Honolulu: East-West Center Press, 1968), p. 237.

5. J. Moura, *Le Royaume du Cambodge*, 2 vols. (Paris: Leroux, 1888), 2: 45–50; Francis Garnier, "Chronique royale de Cambodge," *Journal Asiatique*, October-December 1871, pp. 351–53.

6. Groslier, *Angkor et le Cambodge*, pp. 17–19; Coedès, *Making of South East Asia*, p. 197.

name is spelled in various ways in the European and Cambodian accounts) and Blas Ruiz, a Spaniard. Veloso arrived in Cambodia around 1580–81 and, after learning the language, developed very friendly relations with King Satha, who arranged a marriage between Veloso and his cousin. After Satha's defeat by Nareshvara, Veloso and Ruiz successfully obtained the intervention of the Spanish, resulting in expeditions from Manila in 1596 and 1598. The 1596 fleet was dispersed by a storm, and the ship carrying Veloso and Ruiz struck the coast of the Mekong river delta. Making their way to Phnom Penh, they found the usurper Reamea Chung Prei in power and accepted his invitation to join him in Basan. However, upon learning that he planned their murder, they organized a raid on the royal palace and assassinated him. They then sought Satha in Laos but, finding that he and his eldest son had died, took the second son, Chau Ponhea Ton, back to Cambodia, where he became King Barom Reachea II.[7]

Leclère notes that the Cambodian chronicles describe this as a time of great disquietude in Cambodia, with dire signs of impending catastrophes.[8] It was said that the sacred spring at Banon in Battambang province had ceased to run, and blood was seen on the chest of a statue of Buddha in the Preah Vihear Suor temple. Worst of all, rust had appeared on the blade of the Prah Khan—a sacred sword of the "ancient Varmans" which, according to legend, had been found in the hollow of an almond tree—and the Baku, the Brahman priests who guard the royal treasure, were unable to remove the spots.[9]

By 1598 the situation in Cambodia had improved somewhat, and in gratitude for their aid King Barom Reachea II gave Veloso and Ruiz governorships over the provinces of Babhnom and Treang. Their attempts to negotiate a treaty of protectorate between Cambodia and Spain, however, generated a great deal of resentment among those around the king. While Veloso and Ruiz were in Basan with the king, a force of Malays led by their chief, Laksamana, attacked the Spanish enclave in Phnom Penh. Hearing of the attack, Veloso and Ruiz hurried to assist their colleagues and were killed with the others. This massacre marked the end of Spanish influence in Cambodia. Toward the close of 1599, King Barom Reachea II was assassinated on the orders of Laksamana.[10]

7. Groslier, *Angkor et le Cambodge*, pp. 34–35.

8. Adhémard Leclère, *Histoire du Cambodge* (Paris: Librairie Paul Geuthner, 1914), p. 185.

9. The same bad omen was reported in Phnom Penh in April 1970 just after Prince Sihanouk was deposed.

10. Groslier, *Angkor et le Cambodge*, pp. 51–55.

The new king was Ponhea An, half-brother of Satha and Soryopor (who still was a prisoner of the Thai). Ponhea An took the name Barom Reachea III and renounced any Spanish support. He also forced the Cham and Malay troops, along with their leader Laksamana, to withdraw into Champa. At the end of 1600, however, he was assassinated. Ponhea Nhom, Satha's third son, was named regent while the Queen Mother, the widow of Barom Reachea I and an influential political figure, requested the Thai ruler Nareshvara to release Soryopor. After being set free, the Cambodian prince took the throne with Thai assistance. There is some discrepancy as to the year he became king. Coedès and Groslier give the date 1603, but Leclère holds that it was 1600.[11] A chronicle included in a special issue of *France-Asie* on Cambodia lists Soryopor as king from 1601 until 1618.[12]

According to Leclère, Soryopor founded a Buddhist monastery in 1601 at Sambok, a town on the Mekong river near present-day Kratie, which at the time was an important trading center. He also donated a plot of land to the monastery. To mark this occasion, the king issued a charter, the text of which Leclère reported on to the Commission des Inscriptions et Belles Lettres in Paris in 1903 (see below).[13] This charter explicitly made the governor of Sambok responsible for receiving the ambassadors who came from the north and east as well as accepting letters from foreign countries in those directions. It also stated that he would have particular reponsibility for transmitting to the Sdach Phloeung (King of Fire) and Sdach Tuk (King of Water) the gifts that the Cambodian kings "since antiquity" had sent every three years with the wish that these two highland kings would continue to guard well the routes and forests which the enemies might attempt to invade.

Soryopor ruled with the name Barom Reachea IV, abdicating in 1618 in favor of his son, who became King Chetta II. The new king established his court at Oudong and in 1620 married the daughter of Nguyen Phuoc Nguyen, who ruled as Sai Vuong in the Vietnamese Nguyen dynasty. Through his wife's intervention, Chetta authorized a Vietnamese customs house at Prei Kor, the site of present Saigon. This represented an important step in the subsequent Vietnamese settlement of the Mekong river delta. Chetta II was succeeded in 1628 by his son Ponhea To, who in turn was

11. Coedès, *Making of South East Asia*, pp. 197–98; Groslier, *Angkor et le Cambodge*, pp. 55–58; Leclère, *Histoire du Cambodge*, pp. 334–38.

12. "Chronologie des rois du Cambodge," *France-Asie*, nos. 114–15 (1955), p. 335.

13. Adhémard Leclère, "La charte de fondation du Monastère de Sambok (1601)," in *Compte Rendu de l'Académie des Inscriptions et Belles Lettres* (Paris, 1903), pp. 376–77.

replaced in 1630 by his brother Ponhea Nu. In 1640, Ang Non I, son of the earlier ruler Barom Reachea IV, ascended the throne.

One of the western visitors to Cambodia at this time was the Dutchman, Gerrit Van Wusthoff, whose account has been annotated by Francis Garnier.[14]. On 5 August 1641, Van Wusthoff reached the town of Sambok, which he described as a sizeable settlement inhabited by Cambodians and Chinese. Some of the latter were merchants who traded with an upland place Van Wusthoff called Phnough. Garnier interprets this as a deformation of *phnong*, a Cambodian designation for the highland people, and notes that this term would refer to the "Bnong, Cedar, Banar, etc." (probably Mnong, Sedang, and Bahnar). A journey into the interior required three months, and the Chinese traded in Phnough. Van Wusthoff noted that part of the land of Phnough had tributary relations with Cambodia, while another part extended geographically to the kingdom of Champa.

A palace revolt in 1642 brought Chan, the son of Chetta II, to the throne as King Chan Reameathipedey. He married a Cham princess and converted to Islam, taking the name Ibrahim. This put the Muslim community—the Cham, Malay, and Javanese—in favor with the court but angered the Cambodian nobility, who considered him an apostate. Particularly rankled was Chetta's widow, the Vietnamese princess, and opposition to the king rallied around her two sons. She appealed to her kinsman, the Nguyen ruler Hien Vuong, who responded by sending an army that toppled the regime of Chan. The deposed king was taken in an iron cage to Vietnam, where he died. The grandson of Chetta II became king in 1659 with the name Batom Reachea, and he ruled from the capital at Oudong until 1672. There followed a period of fratricidal civil wars that left Cambodia weak and gave the Vietnamese the opportunity to settle the Mekong river delta by a slow process of infiltration, as they had settled the territory that once had belonged to the Cham.[15]

THE KINGS OF FIRE AND WATER AND THE SACRED SABER

It was noted above that the Cambodian chronicles recorded the rusting of the Prah Khan, the fabled sacred sword of the "Varman" kings, during the

14. Francis Garnier, "Voyage lointain aux royaumes de Cambodge et Laouwen par les Néerlandais et ce qui s'y est passé jusqu'en 1644," *Bulletin de la Société de Géographie*, September–October 1871, pp. 253–55.
15. Coedès, *Making of South East Asia*, pp. 193–203; D. G. E. Hall, *A History of South-East Asia* (New York: St. Martin's Press, 1970), pp. 925–26.

troubled period at the end of the sixteenth century as a particularly dire sign. The Prah Khan is mentioned in most historical sources on Cambodia, and some of them relate this fabled sword to the sacred saber of the King of Fire. Moura, who wrote some of the earliest French works on Khmer culture, reports that the Prah Khan has always played an important role in the investiture of Khmer kings, and Leclère cites chronicles describing how in 1613 Soryopor, who already had been ruling for thirteen years, "took the sacred sword and sat under the sacred parasol" to take the oath of his royal office.[16]

Noting that the sacred sword is a palladium of the Khmer kingdom and the most important item in the royal treasury, Guy Porée and Eveline Maspéro cite the account of Chinese envoy Chou Ta-kuan in which he commented that at the end of the thirteenth century Srindravarman obtained power because his wife, the daughter of reigning King Jayavarman VIII, stole the golden sword from her father and gave it to her husband, who ruled as Indravarman III.[17]

There are numerous accounts concerning the origin of the sacred sword. In an 1883 publication, Aymonier reports that according to Norodom, the Cambodian monarch at the time, the Prah Khan was made for King Prah Ket Mealea.[18] Norodom added that if it should rust it would be a bad omen for the kingdom. Aymonier also was told that the hilt of the Prah Khan was in the hands of the Sdach Phloeung (King of Fire) while the sheath was held by the Sdach Toeuk (King of Water). The Prah Khan blade, however, was kept in the care of the Baku at the royal palace with some other sacred arms—the two crossbows of Prah Ket Mealea, the saber of King Prah Ream, and the spear of King Trasak Phaem.[19] King Prah

16. Moura, *Royaume du Cambodge*, 1: 240; Leclère, *Histoire du Cambodge*; p. 337.

17. Guy Porée and Eveline Maspéro, *Moeurs et coutumes des Khmèrs* (Paris: Payot, 1938), pp. 134–35.

18. Etienne Aymonier, "Notes sur les coutumes et croyances superstitieuses des Cambodgiens," *Excursions et Reconnaissances*, no. 16 (1883), pp. 172–73.

19. All of the scholars who have written about the Prah Khan note that it is in the care of the Baku, Brahmans who guard the royal treasure. In Briggs, *Ancient Khmer Empire*, pp. 25, 81, they are described as "members of a clan said to be descended from the royal chaplains of the ancient Angkorean kings, whose hereditary task it is to keep the Sacred Sword and to preserve the ancient customs." Briggs adds that they are responsible for certain Brahman rites and ceremonies and that they also traditionally assisted in the selection of a king in the event of a disputed succession. According to Moura, *Royaume du Cambodge*, 1: 213–14, Baku informants describe themselves as being descended from Brahmans who came to Cambodia from Romvisay, which Moura notes some writers locate in northern India. During the reign of King Prea Ket Mealea, when the king became ill and trouble befell the kingdom, Siva and Vishnu directed a holy man named Eysey Srey Reac, whom Moura identifies as the great Brahman ascetic Asita, and a group of his followers to go to Angkor. The holy man cured the king of his malady and restored peace to Cambodia. When he was about to leave, Prea Ket Mealea implored him to remain and assist him by advising on matters of health and in directing the affairs of the country. The holy man declined but agreed to leave seven of his disciples. They were the original Baku.

Ream and King Trasak Phaem, like King Prah Ket Mealea, are generally considered legendary figures.[20]

In 1971 the French scholar Martine Piat was informed by the Baku that the crossbow of King Prah Ket Mealea had been among the royal treasures until its loss in a fire.[21] They did show her the arrows that had been with the crossbow, and she noted that the arrowheads were of bronze and appeared to be very old. The Baku also pointed out the spear of King Trasak Phaem, which still is displayed in the royal treasure.

Georges Maspéro reports that according to Cambodian legend King Prah Ket Mealea, with the assistance of the divine architect Prah Visvakarman, constructed a splendid palace and bequeathed to the Khmer kings the Prah Khan, a sacred sword.[22] Maspéro points out that in popular Cambodian beliefs Prah Ket Mealea is identified with the early ruler Jayavarman II, who constructed a great palace on Mount Mahendra. However, Maspéro himself expresses the view that Prah Ket Mealea is a legendary figure who more or less embodies all the achievements of the early Khmer kings.

The Prah Khan is still displayed among the royal treasures in the palace located in Phnom Penh, and the guardians continue to be the Baku. Piat reports that the Baku have no idea concerning the origin of the Prah Khan, and they informed her that there are four sacred swords associated with the *Sdach Kran*, the vassals that protect the kingdom at the four cardinal points.[23] One of these swords is the Prah Khan, which is kept in the royal palace, while the other three are at Wat Baray. Piat cites two documents from the Royal Chronicles, one dated 1932 and the other 1944, which

20. In Eng Sut, "Akkasar Mahaboros Khmaer" (Documents on Cambodian Heroes), trans. Im Proum (Phnom Penh, 1969), pp. 1–4, a document contained in the chronicles from Wat Kompong Tralach Krom, there is a legend that Trasak Phaem had been a simple farmer named Ponia Chey who specialized in raising cucumbers in the Praset Mountain area. He also was a musician in the orchestra at the court of King Senakkeriec. Each time Ponia Chey went to play at the palace he brought some cucumbers to the king, who savored them because they were unusually sweet. The king informed the farmer that he desired to have all of the cucumbers that were grown, and he ordered Ponia Chey to take special precaution in guarding the patch lest some thieves steal some of the precious cucumbers. One dark night the king decided to test the farmer's security, so he stole into the cucumber patch. Alert to any intrusion, Ponia Chey attacked the shadowy figure with his spear, killing him. It was decided that since Ponia Chey had had no idea of the intruder's identity and was rightly protecting his property, no punishment would be meted out to him. It was also decided that since the king's only son, Prince Sihak, had died in Laos, Ponia Chey should be crowned king. So he became King Trasak Phaem and ruled from 998 to 1048.

21. Martine Piat, personal correspondence, 16 October 1971.

22. Georges Maspéro, *L'Empire Khmer* (Phnom Penh: Imprimerie du Protectorat, 1904), p. 31.

23. Martine Piat, personal correspondence, 16 October 1971.

describe how one of the swords came to be possessed by the Khmer kings.[24] The 1932 document relates that in 1644 King Ponhea Chan, because of his great love for a Cham princess named Fati (or Vati), converted to Islam. Before the conversion ceremony, the girl's family plotted with Tuan Chai, the great Cham-Javanese priest, to intensify the king's love for Fati. When the ceremony began, Tuan Chai presented the ancient sword to the king, asking permission to bathe it with lustral water. After the king agreed, Tuan Chai secretly put a love potion in the lustral water, and it further inflamed the heart of the monarch. The 1944 document recounts that during the conversion ritual of King Ponhea Chan four great Cham priests came forward and presented to the king an ancient sword with a hilt and sheath of gold. It was accepted and put in the care of the Baku, who took it to the temple of Panchaksitre.

In the archives of the Commission des Mocurs et Coutumes in the Buddhist Institute in Phnom Penh, Piat found a document describing two sacred swords made in the distant past by Prah Pisnukar.[25] Each had an ivory hilt on which the face of Brahma was carved, and on the sheaths were cabalistic formulae and designs. The swords were used by the elephant hunters to foretell the future of the kingdom. Eventually the sheaths came to be possessed by the Pnongs (highlanders) while the Khmer retained the blades and hilts and replaced the lost sheaths with wooden ones. According to the document, one of these swords, called the Prah Kambet, is kept at Pursat, where it plays an important role in a divination ceremony attended by all of the elephants and mahouts in Cambodia. While the soft music of conch shells plays, the elephants are lined up in a row and the sacred sword is removed from a reliquary for examination. Rust on the sword is an omen of epidemics. Spots that resemble blood are a sign of future war. If the blade has become detached from the hilt or if the face of Brahma is damaged in any way, it presages troubled times for the kingdom.

In the first detailed western account of the King of Fire and the King of Water, Moura mentions that the Cambodians and Cham believe that the talismans held by the two kings, including the sacred saber, once belonged to the Khmer and Cham rulers.[26] Expressing the view that the two

24. Chroniques Royales Cambodgiennes, 1932, Fascicule 6, Bureau des Douanes (trans. Martine Piat); Chroniques Royales Cambodgiennes, 1944, Fascicule 32, Bureau des Douanes (trans. Martine Piat).

25. Non Meas, "Sur le cornacs chasseurs d'éléphant," Document no. 99007, Commission des Moeurs et Coutumes, Institut Bouddhique, Phnom Penh, 13 June 1934 (trans. Martine Piat).

26. Moura, *Royaume du Cambodge*, 1: 432–36.

highland figures were "good peasants" without any real political authority who lived by their labor and the gifts of followers, Moura concedes that nonetheless their supernatural powers are unquestioningly acknowledged by the people. Their reputations, he notes, are widespread throughout southern Indochina. On the occasion of marriages and rituals honoring the spirits, the people summon the King of Fire. A special place is prepared for him, white cloth is placed on the ground, and his path is strewn with ribbons of cloth. The faithful press behind him, holding the train of his loincloth and shouting with joy. When the Kings of Fire and Water appear in public, everyone must bow, for if this homage is not rendered terrible storms will ensue.

The Jarai, he writes, fear above all three power talismans that the Kings of Fire and Water possess. One of these is the fruit of a liana called *cui* which had been cut from the vine centuries ago but has remained fresh and green through the years. Another is a rattan that also is ancient but has not withered and died. The third talisman is the sacred saber, which embodies a spirit that has brought miracles to the King of Fire. Illustrating the fame of the sacred saber, Moura notes that the kings of Siam and Cambodia as well as Pu Kombo, the well-known Cambodian rebel at the time, all had attempted to gain possession of this weapon because it would have enhanced their prestige and guaranteed them success in battle. The spirit in the saber did not permit this, and the Jarai retained ownership of the famous talisman, which they keep wrapped in exquisite silk further protected by cotton cloth.

Moura also expresses the view that since there has been a profound Indian influence in southern Indochina, it is conceivable that the King of Fire represents the Brahman deity Agni, the god of fire, while the King of Water represents Varuna, the god of water. He adds that the deity Agni usually is depicted with a spear in his hand, corresponding to the saber of the King of Fire.

French investigators have reported various highlander legends concerning the sacred saber of the King of Fire. The following Jarai legend is recounted by Leclère and also by Besnard.

> Long ago there lived on an island an old king named M'ta Olah (The Lazy One) whose name was derived from the fact that he spent the greater part of his time lying under the *na-ra*, a type of fig tree, waiting for the ripened fruit to fall into his mouth.
>
> One day a shipwreck occurred close to the island, and the sole survivor, a

man named Po The, swam to the shore. He crawled up on the beach near the place where the king reposed under the fruit tree. Po The approached the old man and asked if there was some way of getting to the continent. The king told him that if he gathered enough fruit to satisfy his appetite, he would tell Po The the secret. Po The gorged him with the exotic fruit, and when the king was satisfied, he confided that "every night a thousand wild boars come to the island to eat the fruit of the na-ra tree, and thanks to a magic stone they possess, they can walk on the water." "This stone," the old king went on, "is held in the mouth of an old boar who leads the others, and when they are eating, the old boar places the stone on the ground." Leaning close to Po The, the king whispered, "If you hide nearby, you can snatch the stone. With it you can walk on the water to the mainland."

Night came, and Po The watched as the thousand wild boars walked on the sea, moving in a single file, each holding in his mouth the tail of the one in front of him so as to transmit the magic from the stone held in the mouth of the old boar at the head of the file. Arriving at the na-ra tree, the leader put the stone on the ground, and they all began to eat the fruit. It was clear to Po The, however, that it would not be possible to slip into the herd and grab the stone.

The next day, on the advice of the old king, Po The dispersed the fallen fruit, placing some near the shore and some back in the forest. As usual, the wild boars arrived that evening and began eating the fruit closest to the shore. They ate their way into the forest, leaving the stone unguarded. Po The swiftly took the stone and hid in a tree. When the wild boars were ready to leave, they returned to the place where the leader had placed the stone. Discovering that the stone was gone, they became greatly agitated and dashed into the sea, where they all disappeared.

Clutching the magic stone, Po The set out on the surface of the sea and reached the mainland. Watching him approach the shore was a man who owned the *po kuoy*, a magic fruit which if thrown to the ground would produce great wind and rain. When Po The explained that his magic stone permitted him to walk on the water, the man proposed that they exchange talismans. Po The agreed. As the man walked away, Po The threw the fruit in his direction, causing a fearful storm that tossed the man about, leaving him dead.

Po The retrieved the magic stone and the fruit, and after traveling a long way he came upon a man who possessed the *kley-ka-achan*, a cord capable of tying itself, and the *l'akay-tha*, a baton with the power to strike by itself. Po The offered to exchange magic objects, and, after the man agreed, Po The ordered the cord and baton to take vengeance on their former owner. The cord bound the man, and the baton beat him to death. Po The gathered up all four talismans and went on his way.

Later, Po The encountered a man who owned a handful of precious stones called the *pol-r'tanpol r'ho*, which, at the command of their owner, could transform themselves into a thousand bees, a thousand ants, or a thousand warriors. This man also had the *quay chan atre nhon*, a rattan that could bring on darkness. The man proposed to Po The that they travel together, and Po The agreed. Eventually they came to the bank of a great river, and there they found the kings of all the people—the Cham, Cambodians, Vietnamese, Lao, Rhadé, Jarai, and so forth. These kings were plunging into the river trying to retrieve a sacred saber that had fallen from the sky and lay glimmering at the river bottom. The Cham king was successful but Po The got the saber away from him and fled into the Jarai country. At the same time the Cambodians managed to get the scabbard, which they took back to their homeland.

Furious at the loss of the saber, the Cham launched a war against the Jarai. Thanks to his talismans, Po The was able to lead a successful resistance to the Cham, but after the Cham began to employ some magical powers the outcome of the struggle became uncertain. Po The addressed the saber, saying, "If you really are from heaven prove your power by taking the side of the Jarai or the Cham." Then taking the saber, Po The charged into the Cham army. Immediately the saber produced vast quantities of fire and water, either burning or drowning all of the Cham. Po The also invoked the rattan, and it produced darkness that prevented the Cham soldiers from escaping, and all were slaughtered.

After this victory, Po The advised the Jarai to live in harmony with the Cambodians because in giving the scabbard to the Cambodians and the saber to the Jarai, heaven decreed that the two should be allies. But in giving the Cambodians the scabbard, which is of less significance than the saber, heaven has indicated that in their gift exchanges the Cambodian king should give things of greater value. He should give elephants, ornate cages, and excellent cloth while the Jarai would respond with slaves, ivory, and rhinoceros horns.

Finally, Po The consigned the saber to the Ly Pa-tao, the King of Fire, after which he disappeared without leaving a trace.[27]

Father Guerlach of the Kontum Mission and the French explorer Lavallée report a different legend. It was told to Guerlach by Pim, the well-known Bahnar Golar chief of the late nineteenth century.

> A very long time ago there lived in the Jarai country a man named Xep who possessed many slaves and many goods, among them two ingots of iron, one small and one large. Xep's destiny was tied to the smaller ingot so that his soul (being) felt any changes that might take place in this piece of metal.
>
> Xep's son wanted to forge a sword, and he asked his father for one of the ingots. "Take the larger one," Xep said, "but don't touch the other one or it will bring great misfortune." The young man, however, found the larger ingot too big for his purpose so, ignoring his father's warning, he forged the

27. Adhémard Leclère, "Légende Djarai sur l'origine du sabre sacré par le Roi du Feu," *Revue Indochinoise*, no. 6 (1904): 366–69; H. Besnard, "Les Populations Moi du Darlac," *BEFEO* 7, no. 1 (1907): 80–83. The quotation is my translation.

smaller ingot, and in doing so he "forged the soul of his father." Even though the blade was rough and unfinished it continued to burn with a white heat, melting the stone serving as an anvil. Water touching it burst into flame. The young man was startled, and he did not know which spirit to implore.

Meanwhile a slave named Pang was busy preparing rattan for a sheath to enclose this extraordinary sword, and as he stretched the strands of rattan over the edge of his knife he cut his finger deeply and blood flowed. Holding his wound, he said to Xep's son, "What is this iron that burns and consumes all that it touches? Let me water it and see," whereupon he let five or six drops of blood fall on the sword. This produced a tremendous effervescence. "Ah!" shouted the slave, "It wants to devour me! It wants to devour me!"

Soon after, all of the heads of the village households came to see Pang. Each brought a jar of alcohol and a chicken. The slave drank with the chiefs, after which he ate the heart, liver, and a leg of a chicken. Then squatting near the sword, he suddenly seized the incandescent blade and bit it. A ball of flame enveloped his body, and Pang penetrated the iron, where he joined Xep. Immediately the iron cooled, and since that day a "divinity" resides in the sword. It must be kept in a bamboo basket covered wih red cloth. The rattan also is stored along with a pot cover and bamboo tube filled with salt and red peppers, all of which belonged to Xep. The sword must never be taken from its storage place or it would cause the end of the world.[28]

Maitre reports a Mnong legend about the sacred sword which he feels may actually be of Cambodian origin.

There were two Mnong brothers named Prang and Iyang. One day Iyang, the younger of the two, found a wondrous stone which, if it were thrown at a person, could enter his body and kill him. After a series of adventures, Prang abandoned Iyang, leaving him in the current of a river that carried him to China. There he was welcomed into the house of an elderly couple who adopted him.

At the royal court of China, the king had decided to give his beautiful daughter Neang Pou to a monstrous dragon, a Naga. Determined to save the girl, Iyang went among the Yeak, a race of ogres, who sometimes were benevolent, and he implored the king of the Yeak to forge a saber out of the magic stone. The king agreed, and the stone was forged into a saber that was capable of cutting the strongest trees in the forest.

Iyang hastened back to the palace, and when the dragon appeared he cut off its head. After obtaining Neang Pou's promise not to tell the king who had killed the dragon, Iyang returned to the house of his adoptive parents. After seven days the king learned of the dragon's death, and he questioned the

28. J. B. Guerlach, "Quelques notes sur les Sadet," *Revue Indochinoise*, no. 1 (1905), pp. 184–88; M. A. Lavallée, "Notes ethnographiques sur diverses tribus de Sud-Est de l'Indo-Chine," *BEFEO* 1, no. 4 (1901): 303. The quotation is my translation.

princess. Faithful to her promise, she feigned ignorance, but she gave her father the sheath for the magic saber and the fringe of the sash that Iyang had left with her. The king then organized a search for the dragon slayer. First he assembled all of the Mnong, Jarai, Stieng, and Samre [an ethnic group in Cambodia], but he could not find anyone without a sheath or without fringe on their sashes. A similar search among the Cambodians, Indians, and Lao proved fruitless. When he learned of a Mnong living at the house of an elderly couple in the kingdom, he dispatched some envoys to accompany the Mnong to the royal court. Iyang, however, refused to go with them, and even when the king sent ten, then fifty, and finally two hundred men to the house, Iyang still refused.

Finally, Iyang made it known to the king that it was he who slew the dragon. The king honored him as a hero and gave him Neang Pou in marriage. After some new adventures, Iyang succeeded his brother-in-law as king. There followed a series of wars, and in one of them Iyang's forces were defeated, so he was forced to flee the kingdom. He went to Cambodia, where he left the sheath of his sacred saber, and then he went to Siam, where he left the hilt. Finally he carried the blade to the Jarai country, where it remained.[29]

Recently, Dournes mentioned three types of Jarai myths with interweaving motifs, one of them involving the "sacred sword."[30] The first type concerns the deeds of the strong and powerful *kotang*, those who are born possessing a saber and shield and who from their infancy strike terror into every heart. In the legend they make war on the potao, i.e., the local lord, who is equally strong but who is plundered of his authority, his wife, his followers, and his possessions by the kotang. The second type of myth has as its hero the unexpected figure of Rit, the poor little orphan, who is the intended victim of the potao. Through the miraculous intercession of "the inhabitants of the forest," Rit has come to acquire not only some possessions but also the beautiful H'bia, the embodiment of Jarai womanhood and Jarai culture. The tyrannical local potao covets all that Rit has, but when he attempts to seize his belongings he is thwarted by the wily Rit, who, in the end, wins over the tyrant. But unlike the powerful kotang, he does not seize the authority of the local lord. The possession of power is not his goal; he prefers to remain the simple, unencumbered man.

The third category of myth centers around the *ddau*, the blade of the sacred saber. In some versions it is Rit, and in other versions it is the powerful kotang, who discovers a remarkable piece of iron that reddens in

29. Henri Maitre, *Les Jungles Moi* (Paris: Larose, 1912), pp. 438–39.
30. Jacques Dournes, "Potao, les maîtres des états," *Asie du Sud-Est et Monde Insulindien*, 4 (1973): xx–xxi.

the forge with an undying brilliance. It absorbs a human being and gains ascendancy over fire, water, and air. Desiring its possession, great states struggle with one another, but the saber remains in the hands of the Jarai as a guarantee of peace so long as it remains hidden (the symbol of a power that is not exercised). Dournes adds that it is guarded by "les *Potao* actuels," but it is not clear whether he is referring to the present Potao Apui (Fire Master) alone or to the Potao Ia (Water Master) and Potao Angin (Air Master) as well.

In addition to the common theme of a saber with magical qualities that becomes the responsibility of the King of Fire, the legends reported by Guerlach, Lavallée, and Dournes have the same theme of a burning blade forged from mystical iron that absorbs a human. There is also the recurring figure of the simple man of no particular prestige—the clever Po The, the Mnong Iyang, the slave Pang, and the orphan Rit—and in all cases he achieves the status of hero. Similarly, in the legend of Wen reported by Stein (see chap. 2), it is a simple man, Wen, the slave, who finds two carp that are transformed into iron and forged by Wen into two magic sabers. When he splits the mountain with them, he is acclaimed king. Stein points out that this resembles the motifs in legends concerning the saber of the King of Fire as well as some themes found in legends among Chinese and mountain people in southern China and northern Indochina.[31]

In November 1970, Ksor Wol, a Jarai elder and assistant to the King of Fire, told me a quite different legend concerning the saber of the King of Fire in which a Jarai man and his wife who had no children went to invoke the help of Ding Buol, the powerful spirit at his longhouse. After the couple had explained their problem, Ding Buol consulted Oi Adei, the supreme deity, who gave him a very small amount of a powerful medicine. Ding Buol relayed the supreme deity's instruction that the wife was to eat only a speck of it each year for seven years, and she would have a child each year. On the way back to their village the couple expressed doubt about the medicine and decided that, since it was so small, the wife should consume it all in one dose. She did, and before they reached their longhouse she had given birth to seven children, which they named Yung, Yor, Hmeng, Kleng, Drit, Prong Pha, and Abiaring Knhi. The seven children grew very fast, consuming ever increasing amounts of food and drinking the river

---

31. Rolf A. Stein, "Le Lin-Yi," *Han Hiue: Bulletin du Centre d'Etudes Sinologiques de Pékin* 2 (1947): 242–44, 285–92.

dry. All but Prong Pha and Abiaring Knhi died, and the former became possessed of the sacred saber. Eventually a man named Thih came to own it.

TRIBUTARY RELATIONS

Although Bouillevaux, Leclère, and several other early observers referred to tributary relations between the Khmer rulers and the Kings of Fire and Water, Moura was the first westerner to give any details on this relationship.[32] He writes that, until Norodom ascended the throne in 1859, the Khmer sovereigns sent annual gifts consisting of a richly harnessed young male elephant, some brass wire, glassware, iron, cotton cloth, and elegant silk cloth to wrap the sacred saber. These gifts were taken upriver to the governor of Kratie, who was responsible for transmitting them to the highland kings. Moura was unable during his visit to the Cambodian provinces nearest the highlands to locate anyone who had been in the land of the King of Fire and King of Water. The Cambodians expressed fear of the dreaded "forest fever" in the highlands and claimed that there were no routes or means of transport as well as an absence of any authority to whom one might turn in case of trouble. The Khmer king's gifts were therefore passed from one highland group to another until they reached their destination.

The Kings of Fire and Water, on their part, reciprocated by sending "their august Khmer brother" a large loaf of wax bearing the thumbprint of the King of Fire, and two large calabashes, one filled with rice and the other with sesame seeds. Sometimes they also sent ivory and rhinoceros horns. Upon arrival in the Khmer capital, these presents were put in the care of the Baku, and Moura notes that when he visited the royal treasure, it still contained one of the rhinoceros horns sent by the Kings of Fire and Water. The wax was used to make candles for ceremonies at the palace. During times of distress such as epidemics, floods, or war, some of the sesame and/or the rice was cast on the ground to appease the evil spirits.

Moura also reports that when King Ang Duong (1841 or 1845 to 1859) was warring with the Vietnamese the Kings of Fire and Water sent him nine elephants to aid in his struggle. They were driven by Jarai mahouts to the capital at Oudong, and there was a celebration to welcome them.

---

32. Moura, *Royaume du Cambodge*, 1: 432–36.

When they set out, laden with gifts, for the return journey to the highlands, some of the mahouts fell victim to smallpox and died. The following dry season, the King of Fire sent a request to the Khmer king to have the mahouts' bodies returned to the highlands. Unfortunately their remains could not be found, so Ang Duong arranged to have special gifts sent to the King of Fire as compensation. Moura adds that Norodom in 1859 ceased sending the traditional gifts to the Kings of Fire and Water, and only a few years before Moura's arrival in Cambodia some Jarai notables approached the governor of Kratie to inquire why no more gifts were being sent. Norodom did not respond, so the Jarai returned to the highlands. This marked an end to these tributary relations.

Leclère, who as noted above also pursued the matter of tributary relations between the Khmer kings and the Kings of Fire and Water, observes that these relations had existed "since antiquity," citing as evidence the text of a charter marking the 1601 founding of a Buddhist monastery at Sambok. In 1903 Leclère presented his findings to the Académie des Inscriptions et Belles Lettres in Paris.[33] According to his report, the monastery was founded by the ruling king, Soryopor, at a time when the town of Sambok was an important trading center, a "gate of the kingdom" on the east bank of the Mekong river. The governor of Sambok was responsible for receiving ambassadors and messages from Laos and for transmitting to the King of Fire and the King of Water the gifts sent by the Khmer ruler every three years.

Leclère describes the charter—he apparently had seen a copy of the text and not the original document—as being divided into two parts. The first part declared that half of the taxes collected from the town merchants who dealt in betel leaves, wooden platters, trunks, plates and dishes, and fabrics would be donated to the monastery. The other half would go to the governor so he could continue delivery of the royal letters and the gifts to the Kings of Fire and Water. He also was given a royal palanquin on which the gifts would be conveyed, and two parasols to protect them. Finally, the governor would receive annually two measures of white rice, three measures of salt, three hundred areca nuts, three hundred packets of betel leaves, two pots of lime for chewing betel and areca, and four pounds of tobacco.

The second part enumerated the array of gifts to be sent to the Kings of

33. Leclère, "Fondation du Monastère de Sambok," pp. 376–77.

Fire and Water every three years. Two each were specified for many of these gifts, including male elephants, red palanquins for riding them, loincloths with fringe, loincloths for ceremonies, striped vestments, red garments, *lomton* cloth, silk for the dancers, silk for the Prah Khan and the Prah Rompat, turbans of red silk, red skullcaps, parasols with long handles, paper fans, combs, sleeping mats, pillows, and cushions. Also to be sent in duplicate were Pursat mats, *chi-chuot* mats, curtains, service sets for rice and water, trays to hold the water during the oath ritual, trays of wood with instruments for preparing areca nuts and betel leaves, areca nut trays, areca nut cutters, and copper pots containing the chewing lime. Other items on the list were two tambourines, large and small flutes, monochords, guitars, bowls of five colors, small copper bowls, bamboo bowls with lids set on trays, *kombet prea* knives, knives for shaving rattan, and machetes. In addition there were one hundred rice bowls and an equal number of soup bowls, two hundred small porcelain bowls, one hundred napkins, four carts of salt, four wooden scissors, two hundred needles, two hundred fish hooks, five hundred ingots of iron, twenty ingots of lead, two hundred copper rings, ten pounds of areca nuts, and ten pounds of tobacco.

The charter also specifies that should either the King of Fire or the King of Water die, the Khmer monarch would send a royal catafalque (*prasada*) transported by a male elephant and a female elephant to carry the corpse in the funeral procession. Three dignitaries would accompany the catafalque and the gifts. Leclère notes that it would require a large convoy to get the gifts to the Jarai country, which in the charter was referred to as the Srok Ayonapar (*Srok* is the Cambodian designation for "country" and *Ayonapar* combines Ayun and Ea Pa, the names of the rivers that converge near present Cheo Reo, the heart of the Jarai area where both the King of Fire and King of Water live).

According to Leclère, the charter outlined very explicitly the ritual presentation of the gifts. First the three dignitaries had to purify themselves by rubbing their bodies with the fruit of the *sambuor* tree (a variety of resinous cassia, *acacia rupota*). After this was done, they were to place the gifts in two rows, in the middle of which one of the dignitaries, the spokesman for the Khmer king, would sit. Then, while the flutes played softly in keeping with Jarai custom, the spokesman would present the letter of the Cambodian ruler (*Prah Chau Longvek Krung Kambubujadhipati Sirisirin Indipat*), after which he would enumerate each gift that had been sent to Ayonapar. Addressing the King of Fire and the King of Water as "nephews" of their "uncle" the Cambodian sovereign, the spokesman would express the hope that they would continue to prosper and to retain their titles and that they would continue to guard the Prah Khan and to live on the summit of Mount Oudam Prakath. The "uncle" also would be most desirous that his "nephews" remain the sovereigns (*ang mchas*) of all the land of the Rhadé, Jarai, and Phnong as they had since antiquity and that they guard well the routes and forests against the enemies and those with evil intentions. Finally, the "uncle" would pray that the "spirits of the forest" (*tepreakh*) and the "spirits of the villages" (*arakh*) would bring his "nephews" long life, abundance, and continuing authority.

Leclère points out that in its uncle–nephew phraseology this invocation expresses a superior status for the Cambodian monarch in relation to the two highland kings which would appear to be some kind of alliance, probably originating with some great service that the Kings of Fire and Water at one time rendered the Khmer king. To support this view, Leclère cites another document that describes a ritual held in the royal court of Cambodia to bring rain in times of drought. In the ritual, the king addresses the "five protectors of the kingdom" (*kshatriyas*)—Narayana, Siva, Ganesa, Kajjayana, and Prah Khan. Then, taking a piece of ivory, the horn of a rhinoceros, and a vestment sent by the King of Fire and the King of Water, he sprinkles them with lustral water while the four Mahachay (Mahajaya) squat and imitate the croak of frogs. This, to Leclère, is a manifestation of the great value placed on the gifts sent by the two highland potao as well as a recognition of the King of Fire's power to unleash lightning, stop the sun, and produce fire and of the King of Water's ability to control water and bring about inundations.

There are several versions of the Sambok Charter. Recently, Meyer found one (also dated 1601) in the archives of the Baku.[34] In comparing this document (translated by Maing Mory) with that of Leclère, Meyer finds considerable variation, which he attributes to translation errors. First of all, Meyer points out, the gifts reported by Leclère were not presented every three years but only on the installation of the new King of Fire and King of Water. This ritual involved bathing with lustral water and anointing with oil and powder. After this the Chau Ponha Thuk Chrya proclaimed that the potao was elevated to the status of "nephew" of his

---

34. Charles Meyer, "Les mystérieuses relations entre les rois du Cambodge et le 'Potâo' des Jarai," *Etudes Cambodgiennes*, no. 4 (1965), pp. 18–26.

"uncle" the Khmer sovereign. The "nephew" was given the responsibility of guarding the sacred saber, of governing the Jarai and Phnong according to their own traditions, and in maintaining the forest trails, keeping them clear of enemies. Meyer's version of the charter specifies that the Khmer king would receive news of the Kings of Fire and Water every three years. Meyer adds that it is unlikely that the king's envoys presented themselves to the two potao with empty hands.

Meyer also notes that his document states that among the gifts there would be seven elephants to symbolize union (four of the elephants represent the female while three represent the male). Also included is *kolao*, a resinous concretion that is a power talisman for success. Meyer sees in the tributary relations an alliance between the "spiritual majesties" committed to mutual protection. The Sambok Charter is to him a codification of a relationship that is of ancient origin.

In the archives of the Commission des Moeurs et Coutumes at the Buddhist Institute in Phnom Penh, there is a document written by Keo-Han, a retired Cambodian magistrate from Kampong Cham province, who claims to have seen a document written on palm leaf in the pagoda at Sambok.[35] According to Keo-Han, this document relates that there was a king named Botom, a resident of the Khum of Sambok, who ordered the construction of the pagoda with a large stupa in the compound. This would appear to be a reference to King Botom Reachea, whom Coedès describes as ruling in Oudong from 1659 until 1672 and Leclère dates as having begun his reign in 1641.[36] The document states that King Botom decreed that forty families of Nak-Na and Pol Prah were to settle in the vicinity of the pagoda and be responsible for its upkeep.[37] Keo-Han noted that "today the descendants of these slaves continue their work in the pagoda," and they told him that when the stupa was being repaired they saw some ancient vessels called *can bancaran*—bowls of five colors. (It was noted above that bowls of five colors were included with the gifts sent to the two potao.) This document also refers to a King of Fire and a King of Water who annually sent tribute to King Prah Bat Botom. The gifts

35. Keo-Han, "Les étrangers dans le Cambodge," Document no. 89004, Commission des Moeurs et Coutumes, Institut Bouddhique, Phnom Penh, 10 May 1951 (trans. Mme. Pich Sal from Khmer).
36. Coedès, *Making of South East Asia*, pp. 198–99; Leclère, *Histoire du Cambodge*, pp. 343–45.
37. According to Martine Piat, the Nak-Na and Pol Prah were two types of slaves. The Nak-Na were descended from condemned persons and were subject to corvée for the king. The Pol Prah also were descended from the condemned but labored for the pagodas; they were literally "slaves of Buddha."

offered by these "Phon" kings consisted of elephant tusks, soldiers, bowls of five colors, jars for rice alcohol, and highland gongs (*khmoh*) with circular indentations in the center. Prah Bat Botom reciprocated with gifts of salt, red cloth, and copper wire.

Another document in the archives of the Commission des Moeurs et Coutumes, written by Nun Suon in 1944, contains some information on the Kings of Fire and Water and also describes a ritual still held in recent times at Sambok to reenact the gift exchange between the Khmer king and the two potao.[38] Noting that the King of Fire is keeper of a sacred saber and that the King of Water is guardian of a sacred rattan whip, the author points out that in the past these two guardians were powerful enough for the Khmer king to proclaim them chiefs or kings of their tribes. He adds that all that remains of the saber is the blade, which is wrapped in cloth and kept on a tray in a hidden cave separate from the sacred rattan whip. The King of Cambodia sent gifts every three years to the Kings of Fire and Water. Included among the gifts were cotton and calico, and the highland leaders reciprocated with rhinoceros horns, ivory, wax, beans, and sesame seeds. Afterward there was a large feast. This exchange of presents took place at Sambok in a stable specifically constructed to shelter the elephants of the "Phnon" kings. In 1944, when he wrote his report, Nun Suon noted that there still was a site near Sambok that was referred to variously as "The Spirit of the Prah Khan Sacred Sword" (*Neak Ta Preah Ang Preah Khanh*), "The Spirit of the Elephant Stable" (*Neak Ta Rong Damrei*), and "The Spirit of the King of Water and King of Fire" (*Neak Ta Sdach Tuk Sdach Ploeung*). The elephant stable was located some two and a half kilometers northeast of the Sambok pagoda, which traditionally was called "The Gate of the Capital" (*Tvea Phreah Nakor*) and which marked the frontier between the Cambodian kingdom and the highlands.

According to Nun Suon, after the tributary relations ended, the people of Sambok continued to maintain the elephant stable and observe the ritual feasting that marked the exchange of gifts. He was informed by elderly residents of Kratie and Sambok that the "sacrifice and offerings" to the Spirit of the Elephant Stable took place once a year. A man from Sambok was designated "assistant to the spirit" and had responsibility for collecting from each household the prescribed offerings of roast chicken, boiled

---

38. Nun Suon, "Le roi de l'eau et le roi de feu," Document no. 63003, Commission des Moeurs et Coutumes, Institut Buddhique, Phnom Penh, 15 June 1944.

chicken, glutinous rice, cotton, Chinese rice alcohol, another special kind of rice alcohol called *sra ek*, and *sra phnon*, jar alcohol made in the highlander manner and an indispensable item because the spirit associated with the Elephant Stable was believed to be of phnon origin.

Two men were selected to represent the King of Fire and King of Water, and on the day of the ritual all of the offerings were brought to the site of the stable. After a ritual presentation of the gifts to the Spirit of the Elephant Stable, cotton bracelets were put on the children's wrists to bring them good fortune. This was followed by feasting and drinking. Every three years a particularly elaborate ceremony was held, and among the offerings were pigs' heads. Around 1924 the stable representing the Spirit of the Elephant Stable was removed and placed at the entrance of Sambok village, where, at the time of Nun Suon's visit, offerings and feasting took place every three years. He was told by his informants that the people of the vicinity continue to regard the site of the Elephant Stable with reverence, and each year some offerings are placed there. Also, anyone who passes the place puts some leaves on it, as a gesture of respect.

KHMER-HIGHLANDER RELATIONS

Information in this and previous chapters indicates that, unlike the Cham, the Khmer never established any kind of presence in the highlands. It also would appear that relations between the Khmer and highlanders were more consistently amiable than those between some of the highland groups and the Cham.

Maitre's hypothesis (see chap. 3) is that at a very early period the Maa, who then were located on the "plains of lower Cochinchina," were under the domination of Funan and Chen La and, after their migration to the highlands in their quest for independence, continued their tributary relations with the Cambodians.[39] The Maa legend reported by Boulbet (chap. 6) does not, however, indicate any such tributary relations.[40] In fact it suggests that, although there was some intermarriage between the Khmer and Maa, there was relatively little contact.

More substantive is the evidence in this chapter regarding the tributary

39. Maitre, *Les Jungles Moi*, pp. 429–34.
40. Jean Boulbet, *Pays des Maa domaine des génies Nggar Maa, Nggar Yaang* (Paris: Ecole Française d'Extrême-Orient, 1967), pp. 65–76.

relations that clearly did exist between the Khmer rulers and the Jarai Kings of Fire and Water. Although at the present time these potao both have predominantly shamanistic functions, the historical information, particularly that contained in the Sambok Charter, would indicate that in the past they had considerable stature as political leaders, not only among the Jarai but also among some of the other highland groups such as the Rhadé and Mnong. Leclère and Meyer would seem justified in their conclusion that this charter is evidence of some kind of military and political alliance between the Cambodian monarch and the Kings of Fire and Water, who were regarded as the guardians of the mountains northwest of the Khmer kingdom.

Most investigators agree that this tributary relationship was more than likely of ancient origin, but the 1601 Sambok Charter is the earliest historical source that describes the relationship. This raises the question as to whether this formalized exchange of gifts between these leaders goes back further than the sixteenth or seventeenth century. Dournes points out that by 1611 Vietnamese control had extended below Cape Varella, thus putting the Cham south of the Jarai country.[41] He speculates that the Jarai, always faithful to the Indianized states, turned to the Khmer, and that the 1601 Sambok Charter represents merely a codification of the diplomatic exchanges between the Cambodian ruler and the Kings of Fire and Water.

41. Jacques Dournes, "Recherches sur le Haut Champa," *France-Asie* 24, no. 2 (1970): 160.

5 PRE-TWENTIETH CENTURY VIETNAMESE-HIGHLANDER RELATIONS

A central and pervading theme in the drama of Vietnamese history is the *nam tiến* or "advance southward," the designation for the historical expansion of the Vietnamese from their original abode in the Red river delta, along the coastal plains southward, eventually into the Mekong river delta (see map 4). When the Vietnamese gained their independence from the Chinese in A.D. 939, their southern border was marked by the Hoanh Son mountain spur that juts into the sea forming a natural boundary with Champa to the south. By 1069, however, the Vietnamese had taken over from the Cham the coastal plain north of the present city of Hue, and in 1306 Vietnamese control was extended over the area to the Deo Hai Van (Col des Nuages) just above Danang. Following the crushing defeat of the Cham in 1471, the Vietnamese swept southward into the coastal plain to a point south of Qui Nhon. Between 1611 and 1697 the remaining Cham lands, reaching almost to Vung Tau (Cape St. Jacques) and Bien Hoa, fell under Vietnamese domination. Continuing the advance southward, Vietnamese settlers began moving into the Mekong river delta, which had been part of the Khmer empire, and by 1757 were south of the Bassac river. With these developments the advance southward was shifting into an "advance westward," as the Vietnamese annexed additional Khmer territory. Finally, by 1780, the remainder of the Mekong river delta from Ha Tien to the tip of the Ca Mau peninsula came under Vietnamese control.

In his map depicting these phases of the "advance southward," Vietnamese historian Le Thanh Khoi shows Vietnamese domination extending westward to the present borders with Laos and Cambodia.[1] However, these frontiers were not fixed until the French colonial administration was organized in the highlands in the late nineteenth century/early twentieth century period (there continue to be disputed border areas to this day). Also, as will be discussed below, at no point did the Vietnamese in the pre-twentieth century establish hegemony over the highland area reaching to these borders. Some Vietnamese settlements were established in the upland trade areas adjacent to the coastal plain, as well as in the An Khe valley, and some military forces penetrated into Laos, occupying for a time a stretch of the Mekong river. Also, at some point, tributary relations were established between the court of Hue and the Kings of Fire and Water among the Jarai. None of these, however, amounted to a Vietnamese presence in the highlands comparable to that of the Cham at an earlier era. By and large the advance southward was a historical event that was restricted to the lowlands.

THE ADVANCE SOUTHWARD

In order to understand the type of relations that developed historically between the Vietnamese and the highlanders, it is important to examine certain aspects of the advance southward. It was a phenomenon that occurred over the centuries, and in many respects it reflected some Vietnamese social, economic, and political values that are found in village society to this day. At the same time, since it involved a constant expansion of the Vietnamese population, it wrought many changes in Vietnamese institutions.

Given the character of the southward advance, Vietnamese contact with highlanders took place for the most part on two levels. First, there was the level of the Vietnamese settlers and traders who, as new areas to the south opened, penetrated the valleys and in certain cases the higher elevations adjacent to the coastal plain where the highlanders lived. Then there was the level of the Vietnamese civil-military administration that was always organized in newly gained territories and had as one of its goals strict control over any contact between Vietnamese and highlanders.

1. Le Thanh Khoi, *Le Viêt-Nam: histoire et civilisation* (Paris: Les Editions de Minuit, 1955), p. 530 (map 16).

In discussing the reasons for the Vietnamese expansion southward, Le Thanh Khoi focuses on the economic factors involved.[2] He notes that by the tenth century Vietnamese society had become very village oriented. A strong central administration that had successfully struggled against the raging waters of the unruly Red river through a system of dikes and drainage canals also had developed. Effective irrigation permitted the emergence of a thriving subsistence pattern based on wet-rice agriculture, which in turn gave rise to a continual population increase. This increase led to a decision to expand beyond the confines of the Red river delta, but the highlands to the north and the west of the delta did not lure any Vietnamese settlers. For one thing, the uplands lacked sufficient level land and water sources to permit paddy farming on a scale suited to the Vietnamese. Also, the Vietnamese believed that the mountains were the abode of evil spirits and that through the upland streams ran the dreaded *nước độc* (poisoned water) which caused fever (malaria). In contrast, the flat, well-watered plains to the south of the delta lent themselves to wet-rice farming, and so in the tenth century it was in that direction that the Vietnamese began to expand.

Chesneaux, while in agreement with Le Thanh Khoi that the southward expansion of the Vietnamese was due primarily to the development of paddy cultivation and the concomitant increase in population, feels that this expansion began prior to the tenth century, and he visualizes it as a peaceful infiltration of Vietnamese into an area occupied by a semi-sedentary population that sustained itself largely through hunting and fishing.[3] He neglects to specify whether or not this population was Cham, but he does note that there was, in this coastal plain, some land abandoned by the Cham. Protected by imperial troops, Vietnamese settlers cleared and cultivated, establishing farmsteads and villages. As the population increased, pioneers moved farther south to repeat the process.

From the historical evidence reviewed earlier (see chap. 3) it seems probable that, while much of the coastal plain immediately south of the Red river delta may have been uninhabited, some of it more than likely was being farmed by Cham. Le Thanh Khoi believes that when the Chinese general Ma Yuan brought Chiu-chen (*Viet.*, Cuu Chan), the low-

2. Ibid., pp. 32–33.
3. Jean Chesneaux, *Contribution à l'histoire de la nation Vietnamienne* (Paris: Editions Sociales, 1955), p. 31.

lying coastal strip south of the delta, under his control toward the end of A.D. 43 it was a wild place of swamps and forests whose inhabitants lived by hunting and farming small swiddens.[4] Around the administrative centers that were established, the Chinese colonists arranged paddy fields. In A.D. 192, Lin Yi was founded south of the Hoanh Son spur, and subsequently it became part of the kingdom of Champa. Chesneaux observes that the small Cham aristocracy thrived primarily on slave trade and pillaging the neighboring Vietnamese coastal areas. He also notes that Cham farmers cultivated paddy fields using relatively sophisticated iron plowshares and *norias* (large water wheels for irrigation).[5]

While these ecological, economic, and demographic factors undoubtedly were important in the advance southward, the phenomenon also reflected cultural values and numerous historical events, particularly sociopolitical developments. There are among the Vietnamese certain cultural values, some of them religious in character, that surround the ownership of land, and they tell us a great deal about why the peasant was willing to leave his natal place and migrate. For the villager, possession of land is important not only for the well-being of his family but also for the perpetuation of his line. In addition, it is a guarantee that he will know happiness in the afterlife. Descent among the Vietnamese is reckoned through the male line, and traditionally all of those related through the male line and descended from a common ancestor in the fifth ascending generation are members of the same patrilineage (*tôc*). Immortality lies in having an undying lineage, so it is important to have sons and to provide them with land so that the family may remain together in the same location.

However, bliss in the afterlife can only be attained through a properly maintained cult of the ancestors, with its prescribed gathering of lineage members to honor their deceased kin and make ritual offerings for the happiness of their souls. In this regard it is important for a Vietnamese peasant to have a substantially constructed house that will endure for generations and become the ancestral house, the central sanctuary for altars honoring the ancestors of the patrilineage and the place where cult rituals and feasting can be held. Similar sentiment is attached to stone tombs that

4. Le Thanh Khoi, *Le Viêt-Nam*, pp. 102–03.
5. Chesneaux, *Contribution à l'histoire*, pp. 31–32.

will stand through the years as mute reminders of past generations. If no such cult is offered, the deceased is doomed to become a malevolent errant spirit (*cô hồn các đẳng*) that wanders ceaselessly in search of offerings.

Financial support for the cult of the ancestors is derived from *hương-hỏa* (family patrimony), the income of which by Vietnamese custom and law must be used to defray the cost of rituals and feasting—a cost which can be quite high for large lineages. Cult land is owned collectively by the adult members of the patrilineage, and guardianship is vested in the head of the kin group, usually the eldest male.[6] For the peasant, therefore, land has social, economic, and religious functions, and those without it have been and still are willing to become pioneers in order to acquire it.

There also are recorded in Vietnamese history some sociopolitical developments that gave impetus to the southward expansion. Following their independence from the Chinese in the tenth century, the Vietnamese retained the cultural and political institutions of their Sinitic heritage.[7] Chesneaux observes that this allowed the Vietnamese rulers of the Ly dynasty (1010–1225) to consolidate their authority, enabling them to sponsor more effectively the advance southward.[8] The Ly rulers also sought to provide a Confucianist moral tone to the society, thus reinforcing the values noted above surrounding family, land, and the cult of the ancestors. Everyone was encouraged to conform to Confucian tradition and not to disturb the "heavenly ordained order" (*thiên-mệnh*), which included the right of the emperor to rule by virtue of his heavenly mandate. Filial piety was extolled. The study of science was disdained, but the pursuit of agricultural activities was exalted.

In 1048, Ly Thai Tong (1028–1054) instituted the Chinese-style cult of agriculture, wherein the sovereign was the highest officiant. It was he who

6. Gerald Cannon Hickey, *Village in Vietnam* (New Haven: Yale University Press, 1964), pp. 82, 88–91; Pierre Huard and Maurice Durand, *Connaissance du Viet-Nam* (Hanoi: Ecole Française d'Extrême-Orient, 1954), pp. 91–105; Đào Duy Anh, *Việt-Nam Văn-Hóa Sử-Cương* (Hue: Quan-Hải Tùng-Thư, 1938), pp. 73–84; Alfred Schreiner, *Les Institutions Annamites en Basse-Cochinchine avant la conquête Française*, 3 vols. (Saigon: Claude & Cie., 1901), 1: 181–89.

7. Le Thanh Khoi, *Le Việt-Nam*, pp. 146–47, describes the postindependence Vietnamese administration as continuing to have the *phủ* and *huyện*, equivalent to province and district respectively, and below them the *xã*, the villages or communes in which the bulk of the population lived. Each commune was administered by a functionary, *xã-quan*, appointed by the central government who kept the registry of male residents. All male citizens in the kingdom were categorized. The princes and mandarins ranked highest, and next came the military. There was a category of diverse professions including monks, medical practitioners, and actors. Another category grouped ordinary citizens between the ages of eighteen and sixty, and finally there were the elderly and infirm.

8. Chesneaux, *Contribution à l'histoire*, pp. 30–32.

performed the springtime rite (*tịch-điền*) in plowing the first furrows, and he also assisted in gathering the rice at harvest. Ly Thai Tong constructed the *Xã-tắc-đàn*, The Esplanade of the Gods of the Soil and Harvest, at the south gate of the capital, and offerings were made there to bring rain and abundant crops.

In 1044, Ly Thai Tong undertook a road construction program which linked the capital at Thang Long with every provincial administrative seat. Couriers, traveling on foot or horseback depending on the urgency, carried dispatches from the king to his provincial authorities and military commanders along the roads and vastly improved communications.[9]

The long series of wars between the Vietnamese and the Cham described previously provided most of the impetus for the advance southward. In response to the recurring Cham raids on the Vietnamese coast, Ly Thai Tong in 1042 sent his armies into Champa, where they defeated Jaya Simhavarman's forces and burned the capital of Vijaya. The Cham king perished, but the queen, the royal harem, and five thousand soldiers were taken prisoner. Subsequently Ly Thai Tong ordered the Cham soldiers to be given land and settled in the underpopulated areas of Hung Hoa province, and he allowed them to name their new settlements after their native villages in Champa.[10]

Ly Thai Tong's successor, Ly Thanh Tong (1054–1072), erected a monumental temple dedicated to Confucius at Thang Long. He also instituted the examinations for civil and military mandarins based, as they were in Peking, on the Confucian classics. Chinese calligraphy was retained, although in time it developed into a specifically Vietnamese script (*chữ nôm*).[11] Another Ly Thanh Tong achievement was the reorganization of the army. The royal guard was comprised of sixteen *quan*, each with 3,200 men, while the regular army was composed of one hundred battalions, one of which (as noted in chap. 4) was made up of highland people.[12]

During the reign of Ly Thanh Tong, the first territorial concessions by the Cham to the Vietnamese took place. In 1068 the Cham king Rudravarman III launched an attack against the Vietnamese, and the

---

9. Le Thanh Khoi, *Le Viêt-Nam*, pp. 146–48.

10. Ibid., p. 164; A Launay, *Histoire ancienne et moderne de l'Annam* (Paris: Challamel, 1884), pp. 48–49.

11. Chesneaux, *Contribution à l'histoire*, pp. 30–31.

12. Le Thanh Khoi, *Le Viêt-Nam*, pp. 146–48.

following year Ly Thanh Tong sent his army into Champa, where they captured Vijaya. The Cham king and his royal entourage were taken prisoner, and for their release the Cham yielded to the Vietnamese their three northern provinces, a territory that embraced present northern Binh-Tri-Thien province. General Ly Thuong Kiet was sent into the area to organize the provincial administration and prepare maps. In 1076 the emperor issued an invitation for Vietnamese to settle the newly acquired lands, and, although the northern portion attracted few settlers, the southern part filled quite rapidly.[13]

Chesneaux observes that as the settlers moved into the new territories the Vietnamese monarchy established there the same "feudal" social organization as then existed in the Red river delta. Lands were distributed to royal princes and mandarins but the peasants were the ones who bore the burden of military duty, taxes, and corvée.[14] In his discussion of the traditional Vietnamese communal village society, Briffaut sees the marginal members of the society as the pioneers in the advance southward.[15] To Briffaut the Vietnamese village was not simply an administrative unit or commune, it was a *cité* (city or town) in the sense of having its own political life, gods, patricians, priests, territory, public order, interests, and past. In his view, the pre-French (i.e., preurban) Vietnamese society had two categories of ordinary citizens: those who were sedentary and part of the cité and those who were apart from it, the wanderers he specifically calls *les errants*. But in spite of its sedentary character, it was the village society that produced the pioneers who ventured forth to clear new fields and organize new villages. These pioneers came for the most part from among the errants, i.e., those without land, house, ancestral altars or family tombs (somewhat akin in concept to the errant spirits noted above). They included people from weakened clans without resources as well as those who had been forced to flee from their natal villages because of war, natural disasters, injustice, or unpaid debts or taxes. Numbered among them also were criminals—those guilty of antisocial behavior such as spying, provoking disturbances, indulging in the slave trade, and swindling. In addition there were individuals with certain nonagricultural pursuits such as

---

13. Léopold Cadière, "Géographie historique du Quang Binh," *BEFEO* 2, no. 1 (1902): 59–60.

14. Chesneaux, *Contribution à l'histoire*, p. 32.

15. Camille Briffaut, *La Cité Annamite*, 3 vols. (Paris: Librairie Coloniale & Orientaliste, Emile Larose, 1912). The first volume has a preface by Justin Godart, the second a preface by Maurice Violette, and the third a preface by Felix Chautemps.

porters, woodcutters, and sorcerers. Going forth as pioneers, they were protected by the chiefs of powerful and rich clans (patrilineages) who paid their taxes and fended off any bandits. Some new settlements, however, were independently established by rebels, convicts, and malefactors.[16]

Briffaut points out that this pattern of new settlements being founded by clients of a powerful local chief or by rebels and criminals was not looked upon with favor by the central government because the loyalties of the inhabitants were not directed to the throne.[17] To some extent this probably was the case, but nonetheless there were some village institutions that, regardless of how the village had been founded, tended to create bonds between the new settlement and the emperor. When a new community was established, it was given a name selected by the inhabitants with the consent of the emperor, who in recognition of the settlement becoming a proper village (*xã*) appointed a guardian spirit or spirits to watch over the village and bring it peace and prosperity. On its part, the village was expected to construct a *đình* or communal temple as a repository for the imperial document naming the guardian spirit. Each village also traditionally had communal lands (*công điền* and *công thổ*) which provided some income to support the Cult of the Guardian Spirit of the village. These communal lands also were subject to regulation by the central government.[18]

There was a significant change in this pattern of founding new settlements following the decree in 1266 of Emperor Tran Thanh Tong authorizing the nobles to press vagabonds and those without work into serfdom to have them clear and farm unused land. This marked the beginning of the Vietnamese great estates (*tráng-điền*) which allowed the aristocracy to dominate the expansion southward until the fifteenth century.[19]

During the fourteenth and fifteenth centuries, the acquisition of Cham territories continued, as occurred in 1306 when the Cham ruler Jaya Simhavarman III, to win the hand of the Vietnamese princess Huyen Tran, yielded to the Vietnamese emperor the northern Cham districts of O and Ri. This extended the southern border of Dai Viet to the Deo Hai Van, the pass just north of Danang. In 1402, in order to avoid a war with Dai Viet,

16. Ibid., 3: 10–23, 30.

17. Ibid., 1: 24–25.

18. Vu Quoc Thuc, *L'Economie communaliste du Viet-Nam* (Hanoi: Presses Universitaires du Viet-Nam, 1951), pp. 34–37, 135–36.

19. Le Thanh Khoi, *Le Viêt-Nam*, p. 173.

the Cham ruler Jaya Simhavarman V conceded to Emperor Quy Ly the northern province of Amaravati, where the hallowed Cham sanctuary of Bhadresvara was located in present Quang Nam–Danang province. The newly acquired territory was divided into four administrative units. Subsequently, Vietnamese settlers, supported by the army, began to move into the area, but there was considerable resistance to them by the indigenous Cham population, and this marked the beginning of a period of conflict between the two ethnic groups at the local level.[20]

Le Thai To (1428–1433) also brought about socioeconomic reforms, some of which encouraged the exploitation of new lands by individuals. There was, for example, provision for a general redistribution of land. Everyone from high ranking mandarins to ordinary citizens, including the elderly, orphans, "isolated persons" (widows and widowers), and youths, received a share. The formation of large landholdings was forbidden, and communal lands, which would be periodically redistributed according to social rank, were rendered inalienable. For the purpose of a more effective tax system, a census of all registered citizens was taken, and it revealed that the population totaled 700,940, of which 390,000 were located in the six provinces of the Red river delta.[21]

A passage in the royal annals for 1460—the year Le Thanh Tong's (1460–1497), the most powerful ruler of the Le dynasty ascended the throne—tells of his decree that those who had been convicted of crimes were to be sent into the more remote parts of Quang Binh province to organized agricultural communities.[22] This signaled Le Thanh Tong's concern with bringing unused land under cultivation, and it also presaged a new period of Vietnamese expansion southward.

Recognizing that agriculture produced the basic wealth of Dai Viet, Le Thanh Tong launched a program for agricultural development. The state reiterated its ban on large landholdings while it encouraged the establishment of *công điền*, the communal lands noted above. There continued to be private landholdings, and the emperor rewarded deserving army officers with plots of land that did not revert to the state after the officers' deaths. In every province, bureaus were created to organize dike surveillance and the

20. Ibid., p. 202.
21. Ibid., p. 218; Vu Van Hien, *La Propriété communale au Tonkin* (Paris: Les Presses Modernes, 1939), pp. 24–30.
22. Cadière, "Géographie historique," pp. 65–66.

digging of new canals. These bureaus also disseminated information to improve animal husbandry and cultivation of mulberry trees.

An imperial decree forbade letting farm land be wasted, and a plan to bring virgin lands systematically under cultivation was launched. The primary device for achieving this goal was the establishment of *đồn điền* (*đồn*, fort; *điền*, field or paddy) for soldiers and their families. Some forty-two such military colonies were founded in the rugged western country of Nghe An and Ha Tinh provinces in 1487. Troops and their dependents were sent into the area to build their settlements along the roads and clear the surrounding fields for farming. The following year mandarins were dispatched to these military colonies to set taxes for the fields already under cultivation. Subsequently, those sent to the military colonies included laborers and nonregistered people, and when the Nguyen lords settled lands taken from the Cham and Khmer, they sent prisoners and criminals to the đồn-điền.[23]

Like the earlier Ly rulers, Le Thanh Tong sought to create a Confucianist moral tone in Vietnamese society. He forbade the construction of any new non-Confucianist temples, and a new Confucianist moral code promulgated by the king was to be read in all villages on ceremonial occasions. This code praised ideals related to the family, particularly those concerned with marriage and death, and it extolled the model of uncorrupt, just leadership for the state. In discussing this, Lê explicitly points out that this moral code decried the levirate and like practices of the "tribus montagnardes."[24]

Administrative reforms under Le Thanh Tong resulted in a well-structured hierarchy of civil and military functionaries. Ministries of Rites, Interior, Finance, Armed Forces, Justice, and Public Works were formed, the kingdom was redivided into twelve provinces, and the emperor commissioned the preparation of a new administrative map. Finally, Le Thanh Tong made sweeping changes in the army. By 1467 it numbered 170,000, and in 1471 the Vietnamese army crushed the Cham, opening vast new territories to the south for future expansion.

23. Đào Duy Anh, *Việt-Nam Văn-Hóa*, pp. 224–25; E. Deschaseaux, "Notes sur les ancien *don dien* Annamites dans la Basse-Cochinchine," *Excursions et Reconnaissances*, no. 14 (1889), pp. 133–36; Le Thanh Khoi, *Le Việt-Nam*, pp. 224–25; Schreiner, *Les Institutions Annamites*, 1: 99–100; Trần Trọng Kim, *Việt-Nam sử-lược* (Saigon: Tân Việt, 1964), p. 243.

24. Le Thanh Khoi, *Le Việt-Nam*, pp. 225–26.

EARLY VIETNAMESE CONTACT WITH THE HIGHLANDERS

Long before the advance southward brought their first contact with the people of the central highlands, the Vietnamese had been imbued with a pejorative attitude toward the ethnic groups in the mountains. Briffaut observes that, while all non-Vietnamese were regarded with suspicion and some disdain, the inhabitants of the mountains surrounding the Red river delta were viewed as *mọi* (savages).[25] The Tai-speaking Tho, because they were strongly influenced by the Vietnamese, were considered superior to the other highland groups, but still beyond the pale. Even the Cham with their advanced civilization were thought of as little better than the highlanders, and a royal ordinance in 1449 forbade intermarriage between Vietnamese and Cham.

It generally was believed that familiarity with the highland barbarians held the danger of polluting superior Vietnamese ways. The goverment, therefore, sought to control as much as possible contacts between the settlers moving into new areas and the inhabitants of the mountains. In the case of officials and military personnel this could be done to a great extent through regulations; for example, article 333 in Le Code, the famous set of laws written between 1470 and 1497, held that any government functionaries or employees who contracted marriages with indigenous highland chiefs would be punished. Restricting individual settlers and traders, however, was a different matter, although Briffaut notes that, in spite of the fact that most of them were rootless errants, they shared this deprecating view of the highlanders. Still, Briffaut adds, it was they who had contact with the highlanders. They were the hardy pioneers who preceded the military colonies in the mountain valleys to "pacify" the local mountain people and bring them some "social education."[26]

As the Vietnamese pursued their policy of settling territories taken from the Cham, it was inevitable that there would be further conflicts between the newcomers and the indigenous Cham farmers. Some accounts of these conflicts indicate that people considered "highlanders" were settled in lowland Cham areas. Following the Cham defeat in 1471, military colonies were established in Quang Nam, and during the reign of Le Uy Muc (1504–1509) the Cham rose in revolt. The emperor dispatched an army

---

25. Briffaut, *La Cité Annamite*, 3: 10–16.
26. Ibid., 3: 10–30.

into the area with instructions to cut down the rebellion by any means and to slay all prisoners. It is recorded that the Cham and the "highland people" were forced to take refuge in the mountains while Vietnamese occupied their abandoned farms.[27]

Not long after the repression of this Cham uprising, the Vietnamese adopted a scheme for coping with the various problems that had arisen in settling areas adjacent to the uplands, such as protection for the new communities from the hostility of the mountain people, the control of contacts between highlanders and Vietnamese, and, related to this, regulation of trade between highlands and lowlands. This scheme is described in a document written in 1871 by Nguyen On Khe, the pen name for Nguyen Tan, a mandarin who served as head of the Son Phong pacification program in Quang Ngai (see below).[28] The document begins by explaining that Quang Ngai had been part of the kingdom of Champa but that after 1471 Le Thanh Tong had commenced to settle the coastal plain with Vietnamese from farther north. The first governor, Tran Quan Cong, known more commonly as Bui Ta Han, was appointed in 1540, and it was he who devised the special provisions of the scheme.[29] He created four *nguyen* or subdistricts in the mountainous interior: Da Bong and Cu Ba in Binh Son district, Phu Ba in Chuong Nghia district, and Ba To in Mo Duc (see map 6). An indigenous chief with the title Giao-Dich was placed at the head of all these subdistricts, and minor Vietnamese mandarins were assigned to each subdistrict, primarily to regulate commerce with the highlanders. The intermediaries in this trade were the commercial agents, who dealt with certain highlanders holding a license to trade. These highlanders paid taxes to the agents, who in turn passed a specified amount on to the mandarins. The taxes were quoted in Vietnamese money, but the highlanders paid with local products.

According to the author of this document, the aboriginal highland population at this time was very small, and "pressed by their misery" they worked as domestics for the Vietnamese settlers. Nonetheless, forts were constructed along the mountainous frontier on the edge of the highlander country to protect the settlers. When Bui Ta Han died in 1568, his

---

27. Ibid., 3: 15; Le Thanh Khoi, *Le Viêt-Nam*, pp. 230–31; Launay, *Histoire ancienne*, p. 121; Henri Maitre, *Les Jungles Moi* (Paris: Larose, 1912), p. 447.

28. Nguyen On Khe, "*Phu man tap luc* ou notes diverses sur la pacification de la region des Moi," *Revue Indochinoise* (1904), no. 7, pp. 445–69; no. 8, pp. 641–48; no. 9, pp. 706–16; no. 10, pp. 789–96.

29. According to this document the appointment took place in the Le Chanh Hoa period, but this would have been during the later portion of the Le Hi Tong reign (1676–1705), which clearly is in error.

administrative organization was adjudged a success, and as the advance southward continued his system was extended to newly acquired areas.[30]

Political struggles during this period in the Red river delta farther north were to have a deep effect on the situation in central Vietnam and on relations between the Vietnamese and the highlanders. Following the death of Le Thanh Tong in 1497, the dynasty fell into a period of decline. However, with the beginning of Le Chieu Tong's reign in 1516, a struggle for power arose among three families—the Mac, the Nguyen, and the Trinh. General Mac Dang Dung, having put down a revolt during which Le Chieu Tong had fled the capital, seized power in 1524 and three years later received the recognition of China. Nguyen Kim, a high ranking officer who had remained loyal to the Le ruler, had escaped to Laos and there raised an army. In 1532 he proclaimed Le Trang Tong, son of Le Chieu Tong, to be the rightful king. Nguyen Kim led the struggle against the Mac until his assassination in 1545. He was succeeded by his brother-in-law Trinh Kiem, who had as his ally Nguyen Hoang, the second son of Nguyen Kim. By this time the country was divided, with the Le forces in control of the area south from Thanh Hoa and the Mac controlling from Son Nam north.

As the struggle continued, Nguyen Hoang became distrustful of Trinh Hiem's motives and requested that he be appointed governor of Thuan Hoa, the province south of Hoanh Son. Anxious to have his kinsman far from the political center, Trinh Kiem agreed, and in 1558 Nguyen Hoang assumed his new post. The Trinh struggle with the Mac ended in 1591 when Trinh Tung, son of Trinh Kiem, emerged victorious and restored the Le in the capital of Thang Long. The Mac fled into the northern highlands, where they maintained a redoubt in the vicinity of Cao Bang until their final defeat in 1677.

After assuming his governorship, Nguyen Hoang consolidated his power, eventually extending his control over Quang Nam province to the south, while at the same time assuming greater autonomy from the rulers in Thang Long. Meanwhile, the Trinh acquired all of the important posts in the royal court, as they professed themselves to be restoring the rightful rule of the Le. Nguyen Phuoc Nguyen's refusal in 1626 to send the expected taxes to the capital led to an open conflict between the Trinh and

---

30. Nguyen On Khe, "*Phu man tap luc,*" no. 9, pp. 706–08; no. 10, p. 794.

the Nguyen. To secure the northern border of Thuan Hoa, Nguyen Phuoc Nguyen had walls constructed in 1630 and 1631, thus physically dividing the kingdom in two. In the territory from the Gianh river to Cape Varella, the Nguyen now in effect ruled as a separate dynasty.[31]

In 1687 Nguyen Phuoc Tran moved his residence to Phu Xuan, which later became the city of Hue. Still, as Le Thanh Khoi points out, at the beginning of the eighteenth century the Nguyen had not achieved complete autonomy.[32] They continued to recognize the Trinh sovereignty and received their titles from Thanh Long. In 1702 Nguyen Phuoc Chu sent an ambassador to Peking to seek investiture from the Chinese court but was refused. Nonetheless, in 1744 Nguyen Phuoc Khoat (1738–1765) assumed the royal title of *vương*. Known in history as Vo Vuong, he established his court at Phu Xuan and divided his domain into twelve provinces—Quang Binh, Vo Xa, Bo Chanh, Quang Nam, Phy Yen, Binh Khang (Khang Hoa), Binh Thuan, Tran Bien, Phien Tran, and Long Ho (Bien Hoa, Gia Dinh, and Vinh Long).

In the Official Biographies of Dai Nam (part of the annals in Hue) it is recorded that in the thirteenth year of Vo Vuong's reign (1751) *Thủy Xá* and *Hỏa Xá* (references to the King of Water and the King of Fire respectively) sent an emissary bearing tribute.[33] The two upland leaders were rewarded by the emperor, and until the Tay Son Revolt became intense in 1773 tribute was sent regularly.

This is the first actual mention of tribute being delivered by the upland shamans to the court of Hue. Nonetheless, Vietnamese and French scholars in the past and at the present time contend that these tributary relations date to 1558, when Nguyen Hoang became governor of Thuan Hoa. In a letter to the French governor general dated 6 November 1888, Vietnamese scholar Truong Vinh Ky, better known as Petrus Ky, wrote that the

31. Léopold Cadière, "Le mur de Dong-Hoi, étude sur l'établissement des Nguyen en Cochinchine (XVIᵉ-XVIIIᵉ siècles)," *BEFEO*, vol. 6, nos. 1–2 (1906): 87–236; Georges Coedès, *The Making of South East Asia*, trans. H. M. Wright (London: Routledge & Kegan Paul, 1966), pp. 208–10; Le Thanh Khoi, *Le Viêt-Nam*, pp. 232–42.

32. Le Thanh Khoi, *Le Viêt-Nam*, pp. 272–73.

33. Nghiêm Thẩm, "Tìm hiểu đồng bào thượng" (Understanding the Highland Compatriots), *Quê Hương*, no. 31 (1962), p. 137. An English translation of this article by Donald E. Voth can be found in *SA* 1, no. 4 (1971): 335–65. Literally translated, *thủy* is "water" and *hỏa* is "fire"; *xá* could be translated as "abode" or "haven." The references therefore are to places rather than to persons, but since there is consensus among investigators that they were intended to identify the King of Water and the King of Fire these designations will be used.

principalities of Thủy-xá and Hỏa-xá had since 1558 paid tribute to the Nguyen.[34] The same information was contained in a May 1889 report by Captain Luce, a French military officer who in 1888 had been commissioned by Governor General Constans to conduct research in the archives of the court of Hue in an attempt to determine the extent of Vietnamese suzerainty in the highlands (see chap. 8).[35]

In his 1912 work, Maitre cites the Luce report, speculating that after the defeat of the Cham in 1471 the Vietnamese continued their expansion southward and that when they reached the Ba river valley they, like the Cham earlier, probably sent small army units into the Jarai country. Then around 1558 the Jarai would have recognized the suzerainty of the Nguyen, thus initiating the tributary relations.[36]

Similar views were reiterated by Bourotte and also by Nghiem Tham, who writes that when Bui Ta Han assumed the governorship of Quang Nam in 1540 he succeeded in bringing the highlanders in present Quang Nam–Danang, Nghia Binh, and northern Phu Khanh under his authority.[37] In 1558 the Kings of Fire and Water began paying tribute to the Nguyen lords, although it was not until 1611 that the Vietnamese actually entered the Jarai country via the Song Ba valley. His conclusion is based on a passage from the Official Biographies of Vietnam, which he notes was the same source used by Luce.[38] It relates that "the Nguyen court at the beginning saw that the two countries of Thuy Xa and Hoa Xa bordered on Phu Yen province." It then goes on to describe how every five years the Nguyen sent the King of Water and the King of Fire gifts that included brocade garments and hats, bronze pots, iron pans, rice bowls, plates, and other kinds of china. The two highland leaders reciprocated with local products such as deer horns, beeswax, bear bile, and male elephants.

On the basis of available historical evidence, the 1558 date for the beginning of tributary relations between the Nguyen and the highland kings would appear to be too early. That was the year Nguyen Hoang became governor of Thuan Hoa, and it is unlikely that he would have

---

34. Trương Vĩnh Ký to Monsieur le Gouverneur General, 6 November 1888, "Mission du Capitaine Luce au sujet de la délimitation de frontière de l'Annam dans la vallée du Mékong," Section Outre-Mer, Siam 32/Carton 2, Archives Nationales, Paris. This document was provided by John Murdoch.

35. L. De Reinach, Le Laos, 2 vols. (Paris: A. Charles, 1901), 2: 30–32.

36. Maitre, Les Jungles Moi, pp. 448–49.

37. Bernard Bourotte, "Essai d'histoire des populations Montagnardes du Sud-Indochinois jusqu'à 1945," BSEI 30, no. 1 (1955): 39; Nghiem Tham, "Tìm hiểu," pp. 133, 137.

38. Nghiêm Thẩm, "Tìm hiểu," pp. 136–37.

established tributary relations with the highland leaders, who at that time were very far removed from the Vietnamese administration. There is nothing in the historical record to indicate that the Vietnamese had any contact with the Jarai at this early date. Also, the passage from the annals indicates that the relations were established with "the Nguyen court," and in 1558 no such court existed. In fact, as is noted above, the Nguyen continued to recognize the sovereignty of the Trinh court until the beginning of the eighteenth century, and it was not until after Vo Vuong assumed power in 1744 that a court definitely was established at Phu Xuan. Interestingly enough, the earliest recorded date for any actual payment of tribute by the Kings of Fire and Water was in 1751, during the reign of Vo Vuong.

In addition, while some of the European accounts from the seventeenth century make references to the highlands, they do not indicate that the Vietnamese had any suzerainty over the area. In his 1629 work on Cochinchina, the domain of the Nguyen, Borri recounted that the mountainous interior was inhabited by Kemoi or "savages," and he explicitly remarked that "they will not acknowledge the king nor obey him in anything, cantoning and fortifying themselves in those mountains almost inaccessible." [39] This implies not only lack of Vietnamese suzerainty in the highlands but a hostile attitude on the part of the upland people. Also, in his 1666 account of his travels through Laos and Tonkin, Marini reported that there were in the mountains of the Rumoi two kings—the King of Fire and the King of Water—whom the "savages" followed, but he makes no mention of their being vassals to the Vietnamese rulers. [40]

It also is significant that during the reign of Vo Vuong there was for the first time an extension of Vietnamese authority into the highlands of present Savannakhet province in Laos, west of the Ai Lao pass. Prior to Vo Vuong's rule that area had been occupied by an ethnic group known as the Pheng My (who appear to have been a Mon Khmer-speaking people), and for a long time they had paid tribute to the Nguyen lords. At some indeterminate time around the beginning of the eighteenth century they were invaded by Tai-speaking Phuthai (who had originated in northeastern Laos) and the Sue (a group that resulted from intermarriage

39. Cristoforo Borri, *Cochinchina: Containing Many Admirable Rarities and Singularities of That Countrey* (London: Robert Ashley for Richard Clutterbuck, 1633), pp. B1, B2.
40. G. F. Marini, *Relation nouvelle et curieuse des royaumes de Tunquin et de Lao* (Paris: Gervais Clouzier, 1666), pp. 34–35.

between the Phuthai and the Mon Khmer-speaking So). As the newcomers arrived, the Pheng My dispersed, many of them settling in the vicinity of Cam Lo. The Phuthai and Sue divided the former Pheng My territory into the principalities (*muong*) of Vang, Champone, Tchepone, and Phong. All recognized the authority of Vientiane. Seeking to assert Vietnamese authority in the Tchepone area, Vo Vuong notified the court of Vientiane that the former tribute of one elephant annually would be paid by the leaders in the four new principalities. The King of Vientiane acquiesced, and Vo Vuong attained effective control over the strategic Ai Lao pass (see map 2).[41]

Taking all of this evidence into consideration, it would seem that the most likely period during which tributary relations between the rulers in Hue and the Kings of Fire and Water were initiated was sometime after the Vietnamese occupation of Phu Yen in 1611 and the appearance of a Nguyen court with the beginning of Vo Vuong's reign in 1744. My own feeling is that it occurred at a time around the latter date.

As they made contact with the highlanders, the Vietnamese, like the Cham before them, established trade relations. There are indications that the Chinese and possibly the Japanese participated in this trade, and some Europeans may have become involved under the Nguyen lords. The Chinese and Japanese had been using the port of Faifoo (Hoi An) for a long time when in 1540 the Portuguese commenced trade with Cochinchina (their designation for the territory under Nguyen rule). The first Catholic mission was founded in Faifoo soon after the first missionaries arrived in 1615. In his 1629 work, Italian Jesuit Borri described one of the most important export items of Cochinchina to be eaglewood, which he noted came from the mountains of the Kemois (highlanders).[42] Similarly, in his 1666 account Father Marini reports that eaglewood was one of the primary products of the country.[43] Also important were cinnamon, ebony, and other precious woods. In 1637 the Dutch were authorized to found a factory at Pho Hien in Tonkin (the European designation for the domain of the Trinh farther north) as were the English and French in 1680. Toward the end of the seventeenth century, however, European commerce in

---

41. Maitre, *Les Jungles Moi*, pp. 465–67; Bourotte, "Essai des populations Montagnardes," p. 42; M. Damprun, "Monographie de la province de Savannakhet (Laos Française)," *BSEI*, 1904, pp. 23–71.

42. Borri, *Cochinchina*, pp. D-D2, O-O2.

43. Marini, *Relation nouvelle*, pp. 35–36, 46–48.

Vietnam began to decline; the English closed their factory in 1697, and three years later the Dutch terminated their trade relations.[44]

During the latter part of the seventeenth century the Vietnamese steadily expanded into the northern portion of the Mekong river delta. One major step toward this movement was the authorization by the Cambodian ruler Chetta II for the establishment of a Vietnamese customs house at Prei Kho (the present site of Saigon). In 1699 Nguyen Phuoc Chu founded the new provinces of Tran Bien (Bien Hoa) and Phien Tran (Gia Dinh) and 40,000 families numbering some 200,000 individuals, most of them landless peasants and vagabonds, were rounded up in the area from Quang Binh to Binh Thuan to be transported to the new territory, where they were settled in military colonies (*đồn điền*) as well as civilian colonies (*đinh điền*).[45]

Maitre speculates that the route from Tri An to the Maa country at the confluence of the Da Houei and Dong Nai rivers, whose traces the French explorer Gautier discovered in 1882, probably was constructed by the Vietnamese as they occupied the terrace region north of the Mekong river delta. This event, at the end of the seventeenth century, led to the "downfall of the Maa principality" and plunged the Maa into a state of anarchy.[46] Maitre also cites the "annales" (he fails to specify which annals) in describing how the Maa and "Traos" (probably Chrau) became involved in the Vietnamese campaign against the Cambodians in 1755. This also is related in the account by Trinh Hoai Duc written during the reign of Minh Mang (1820–1841).[47] Both tell how, during a military operation in Gia Dinh province, a Vietnamese unit commanded by Captain Chan and comprised of highland troops—highlanders who had left their native mountains in Binh Thuan to settle farther south in Khmer country—turned the tide of battle against the Cambodians. With the onset of the rainy season there was a lull in the fighting. Then, during the dry season of 1756, Vietnamese general Thien ordered ten thousand of the highlanders to gather at Go Vap, where they were attacked by a large Cambodian force. About five thousand were rescued by General Nguyen Cu Trinh, and subsequently some of these highlanders were settled in the vicinity of Nui Ba

44. Le Thanh Khoi, *Le Viêt-Nam*, pp. 285–88; Vu Quoc Thuc, *L'Economie communaliste*, pp. 137–44; Joseph Buttinger, *The Smaller Dragon: A Political History of Vietnam* (New York: Frederick A. Praeger, 1958), pp. 198–209.

45. Le Thanh Khoi, *Le Viêt-Nam*, pp. 268–69; Trinh Hoai Duc, *Histoire et description de la Basse Cochinchine*, trans. G. Aubaret (Paris: Imprimerie Impériale, 1863), pp. 8–9.

46. Maitre, *Les Jungles Moi*, pp. 461–65.

47. Trinh Hoai Duc, *Histoire*, pp. 12–15.

Den (Black Lady Mountain) near Tay Ninh. Many others, however, were recruited for General Trinh's forces, and they formed the advance guard of the army that entered Phnom Penh.

In the middle of the eighteenth century, the two hundred years of peace that had been attained in the highlands of present Quang Ngai province under Bui Ta Han was broken when the highlanders rose in rebellion. Vietnamese settlers abandoned their villages and farms as the highlanders attacked from the mountains. Around 1770, Tran Ngoc Thu was sent into the troubled area with an armed force to subjugate the rebels and repopulate the empty settlements. Initially the troops farmed the fields, using the income to help defray the cost of the military occupation. Then, just as the villagers began to return, the Tay Son Revolt broke out farther south at An Khe, a valley in the highlands of Binh Dinh province.[48]

Vo Vuong had died in 1765, after secretly arranging for the throne to pass to Dinh Vuong, a son by a favorite concubine, rather than to Chuong Vo, the legitimate heir. According to Le, the seething discontent with this new ruler was the principal cause of the Tay Son Revolt.[49] This uprising broke out in the An Khe valley where Route 19 now runs from coastal Qui Nhon into the highlands to Pleiku (see map 6). The leaders were three brothers named Nhac, Lu, and Hue, grandsons of Ho Phi Khang, a native of Nghe An province who during one of the wars between the Trinh and Nguyen was taken prisoner and sent to the military colony of Tay Son in the An Khe valley. There the Nguyen had established new settlements to group war prisoners, vagabonds, exiles, and other undesirables. Ho Phi Khang apparently was a man of learning, and his son Ho Phi Phuc was named head of the Tay Son camp. Vietnamese historian Van Tan reports that Nhac, Lu, and Hue changed their family name from Ho to Nguyen, the surname of their mother, to take advantage of the prophecy proclaiming that "he who supports the Nguyen shall govern."[50] The three brothers became students of Professor Hien, a political refugee who opposed the Nguyen lords, and Van Tan expresses the view that the decision by Nhac and his brothers to organize a struggle against the Nguyen rule was largely due to Hien's influence.

After completing his studies, Nhac became involved in trade with the highlanders in the vicinity, exchanging lowland products for betel leaves

48. Nguyen On Khe, "*Phu man tap luc*," p. 462; Maitre, *Les Jungles Moi*, pp. 467–68.
49. Le Thanh Khoi, *Le Viêt-Nam*, pp. 296–99.
50. Văn Tân, *Cách mạng Tây Sơn* (Hanoi: Nhà Xuât Bản Văn Sử Địa, 1958), pp. 34–35.

and areca nuts. He also was named chief of the camp and tax collector and, according to Le Thanh Khoi, fled to Tay Son in 1771 after losing a considerable amount of the tax money on gambling.[51] There he gathered a group of malefactors, discontented peasants, and army deserters into what would become a dissident movement. Van Tan disagrees with this version, claiming that the reports about Nhac gambling away the tax money were lies perpetuated by the Nguyen dynasty to deprecate Nhac and his movement. Van Tan sees Nhac as being motivated by the revolutionary spirit kindled by Professor Hien and feels that he sought his mountain retreat to organize a resistance movement against the Nguyen regime. Van Tan also notes that Nhac successfully rallied support among the local highlanders.[52]

The Tay Son rebels captured the port town of Qui Nhon in 1773, and soon thereafter the Trinh moved against the Nguyen court, now in a state of disarray. When Phu Xuan was captured by the Trinh, Dinh Vuong and the royal family, including his nephew Nguyen Phuoc Anh, son of Chuong Vo and the rightful heir to the throne, fled to Quang Nam and from there to Saigon. The Tay Son, however, had reached the vicinity of Saigon, and they pursued the royal refugees, capturing the king and his small son, both of whom were beheaded. The royal nephew, Nguyen Anh, and his group made their way to safety with the aid of a French Catholic missionary, Father Pigneau de Béhaine. Nguyen Anh rallied loyal forces and renewed the struggle against the Tay Son, and as part of his effort to enlist aid from foreign governments he sent Father Pigneau to seek assistance from the court of Louis XVI. Pigneau successfully stirred up interest in supporting Nguyen Anh's cause through his articulate arguments that Cochinchina, with its strategic islands and deepwater harbors, would provide an ideal base for expanding French political and commercial interests in the Far East. The result was the Versailles Treaty of 28 November 1787 granting France sovereignty over several offshore islands and the right to establish settlements on the mainland of Cochinchina in return for French military assistance.

Pigneau de Béhaine arrived back in Saigon in July 1789 to learn that the rule of Louis XVI was crumbling in France, rendering his treaty invalid. Since he had enlisted considerable aid from the French in Pondicherry and the Mascarene Islands, and also had recruited some capable young French

51. Le Thanh Khoi, *Le Viêt-Nam*, pp. 297–98.
52. Văn Tân, *Cách mạng Tây Sơn*, pp. 36–37.

officers while en route back to Saigon, Pigneau went ahead with his plan to help Nguyen Anh regain the throne. The war raged on until 1802 when the last Tay Son troops surrendered. On 1 June 1802, Nguyen Anh officiated at a ritual offering to Heaven and Earth in the family temple in Phu Xuan. He sent an envoy to Peking to obtain recognition of his mandate by the Chinese emperor, who responded by acknowledging Nguyen Anh as the rightful ruler with the name Gia Long. The domain from the border of China to the Gulf of Siam was united for the first time, and Emperor Gia Long gave it the name Vietnam, locating his capital at Hue.[53]

According to Maitre, after their final defeat by Nguyen Anh's force, the surviving Tay Son troops fled into the highlands.[54] Bourotte, however, reports that although the Tay Son remnants did escape into the mountains they were pursued by generals Le Van Duyet and Le Chat, who forced their surrender.[55]

HIGHLANDER–VIETNAMESE RELATIONS DURING THE NINETEENTH CENTURY

With the new century and the reign of Gia Long, the Vietnamese renewed their efforts to bring more of the highland groups under their administrative authority so as to control trade with the uplands and continue the program of settling Vietnamese in the interior valleys. Also, tributary relations between the court of Hue and the Kings of Fire and Water were reestablished. Soon after he assumed the throne, Gia Long set about rebuilding the kingdom, which had been badly disrupted by the long years of war, and he also embarked on a plan of expansion into the mountainous interior. The kingdom was redivided into twenty-three provinces with a special zone around the new capital at Hue, and in 1802 and 1803 the former tax on the trade with the highlanders was revived.[56]

In 1804 a special province called the Tran Man (lit., barbarian province) was created in the highland area from Quang Nam to Binh Dinh. It was placed under the authority of Nguyen Cong Toan, a military mandarin who had won a reputation during the Tay Son Revolt for his rout of a

---

53. Le Thanh Khoi, *Le Viêt-Nam*, pp. 288–322; Georges Taboulet, *La Geste française en Indochine*, 2 vols. (Paris: Adrien-Maisonneuve, 1955), 1: 163–279.
54. Maitre, *Les Jungles Moi*, p. 468.
55. Bourotte, "Essai des populations Montagnardes," pp. 48–49.
56. Nguyen On Khe, *"Phu man tap luc,"* p. 707.

band of highlanders caught raiding a Vietnamese settlement. The previous administration with its four subdistricts and with trade carried on through commercial agents was restored, though there were changes in the military organization. The whole area was redivided into six military zones, each with four hundred troops distributed among posts strategically placed along the mountainous frontier. Military colonies were then organized in the valleys to bring security and to allow cultivation of abandoned fields. As areas became secure, the Vietnamese settlers began to return, and eventually a communal temple (*đình*) was constructed in each settlement, after which a tribunal or prefecture (*nha*) was organized in the local area.[57]

The Vietnamese administration drew a distinction between those highlanders who accepted Vietnamese authority and those who did not.[58] The former were referred to as *mọi thuộc* (savages who know) or sometimes, in the case of highlanders engaged in trade with the Vietnamese, *mọi buôn* (commercial savages). The latter were called *mọi hoang* (degraded savages) or *mọi cao* (high savages), a reference to the high elevations at which they lived.

As was the case with prior regimes, that of Gia Long discouraged any contact between the Vietnamese and highland people. The only exceptions were the military personnel who provided security for the frontier and the commercial agents who carried on trade with the highlanders. This interdiction was formally articulated in the Gia Long Code, promulgated in 1812 to supercede the Le Code as the law of the land. This code, which was composed of 22 books and 398 articles, was not an original work but was based on the Chinese code of Ts'ing.[59] Briffaut detects in the Gia Long Code an attitude even more disdainful of the highlanders than that found in the Le Code.[60] Article 204, for example, states that the Mang (or Man, the Chinese designation for "barbarians") and Moi (Vietnamese for "savage") "do not have any family in the legal sense, being people who live in bands, encampments, clans, and tribes." Also, while it was permissible for a Vietnamese to enter the frontier areas and settle in one of the military colonies, it was forbidden for him to remain in the milieu of the

57. Bourotte, "Essai des populations Montagnardes," pp. 48–49; E. M. Durand, "Les Moi du Son-Phong," *Bulletin de Géographie Historique et Descriptive*, 1900, nos. 1–2, pp. 285–87; Le Thanh Khoi, *Le Viêt-Nam*, pp. 325–26; Maitre, *Les Jungles Moi*, pp. 468–70; Nguyen On Khe, *"Phu man tap luc,"* p. 714.

58. Durand, "Les Moi du Son-Phong," pp. 285, 290–91.

59. Le Thanh Khoi, *Le Viêt-Nam*, p. 330.

60. Briffaut, *La Cité Annamite*, 3: 8–16.

highlanders, for in doing so he would contaminate himself. Article 109 of
the Gia Long Code specified that any Vietnamese who contracted marriage with a person "of barbarous races" would be subject to one hundred
blows with a rod.

In spite of this dim view of the highlanders, Gia Long was anxious to
reestablish the tributary relations with the King of Fire and the King of
Water which had been disrupted by the Tay Son Revolt. A brief passage in
the Official Biographies of Dai Nam mentions that at the beginning of Gia
Long's reign an ambassador from the King of Fire and the King of Water
appeared in Phu Yen province and offered gifts to the sovereign. This
envoy was amply rewarded and allowed to return to the highlands.[61]
Then, according to Woodside, in 1815, Gia Long published a list of
thirteen countries with which he had tributary relations. Included along
with such countries as France, England, Luang Prabang, Vientiane,
Burma, and Tran Ninh (a plateau principality in eastern Laos) were Thủy
Xá Quốc and Hỏa Xá Quốc, i.e., the Land of the King of Water and the
Land of the King of Fire.[62]

Gia Long claimed that these vassal states conceded the legitimacy of
Sino-Vietnamese diplomatic laws, which were an "important theoretical
complex" borrowed from China. The Nguyen called these laws "the
harmonious management of distant peoples" (*nhu viễn*, lit., accommodate
the distant). The laws governed the presentation of tribute by these vassals
and participation of their ambassadors in ceremonies at Hue marking the
New Year and the emperor's birthday. In 1965 the annals concerning these
foreign relations were published in modern Vietnamese.[63]

Woodside observes that one consequence of this emulation of the
Chinese system of vassalage was the "magnification of the Vietnamese
court's tendency to isolate minority peoples, while Sinicizing them, and to
erect barriers between different peoples within Vietnam itself." The court
of Hue thus applied the Chinese system to a much smaller world, and a
highland group like the Jarai took on the significance that whole nations

61. Nghiêm Thẩm, "Tìm hiểu," p. 137.
62. Alexander Woodside, *Vietnam and the Chinese Model* (Cambridge: Harvard University Press,
1971), p. 237.
63. *Nhu viễn trong Khâm-định Đại Nam Hội-điển sự-lệ* (Foreign relations in the collection of official
administrative regulations of Dai Nam), 2 vols., trans. Tạ Quang Phát into modern Vietnamese, rev.
and ed. Bủ u Cẩm (Saigon: Bộ Văn-Hóa Giáo-Dục, 1965). Pertinent parts of this work were translated
into French by Do Van Anh of the Institute of Historical Research in Saigon specifically for the present
study.

did in the Chinese sphere. In addition, the Jarai-occupied areas "were important to Hue because, as potential cultural transition zones, they could be used to filter Vietnamese influence into Cambodia."[64]

It should be noted also that since the middle of the eighteenth century, the central highlands had assumed an important place in the court of Hue's general strategy. By that time the advance southward had become an "advance westward" as the Vietnamese occupied increasing amounts of Khmer territory. The Vietnamese also had asserted their authority in the Tchepone region of central Laos by maintaining tributary relations with the leaders there. Since the Khmer rulers already had tributary relations— bearing military overtones—with the Jarai Kings of Fire and Water, a Vietnamese sovereign like Vo Vuong would have seen numerous advantages in establishing similar relations. In the nineteenth century, as Khmer power crumbled in the face of Siamese expansion eastward, good relations between Hue and the Jarai took on new urgency, for it was increasingly clear that the central highlands would become a zone of Siamese- Vietnamese competition.

By the time Gia Long assumed the throne, the farthest that Vietnamese influence had penetrated the highlands was in the Phuthai muongs west of the Ai Lao pass (see map 2) where Vo Vuong had established tributary relations with their leaders. Maitre describes how Gia Long not only maintained these tributary relations but also expanded his control (he gives no dates) over the Ai Lao pass and westward to the Mekong river, with his troops occupying the east bank from the 16th to the 17th parallel in the basin of the Bang Hien river—a much-frequented river trade route from Quang Tri to Khemmarat on the Mekong river.[65] The muongs paying tribute to the Hue court were reorganized, and new administrative seats were established at Na Bon (Tchepone), Lao Bao (in the Ai Lao pass), and Lang Co. The highlanders in the area were subject to annual tribute to the Vietnamese throne, and small military posts were constructed throughout to supervise the timber trade.

At the same time, there was a steady expansion of Lao authority to the east and south of the Mekong river valley. Vientiane had gained control of Attopeu on the Boloven plateau in the sixteenth century and had asserted its authority in the Tchepone area sometime in the eighteenth century.

64. Woodside, *Vietnam and the Chinese Model*, pp. 237–38, 243–44.
65. Maitre, *Les Jungles Moi*, pp. 470–71.

Now, during Gia Long's reign, the Lao were infiltrating the Halang country in the western highlands, and Maitre notes that French accounts from the late nineteenth century describe the *peng*, a Halang gold measure established by a Lao chief who had ruled the area for use in the sale of buffalo.[66]

Continuing in the same southeasterly direction, the Lao moved along the Poko river and the Bla river into the area where Kontum now stands. During his 1894 visit to Kontum, Odend'hal was informed by local Bahnar that in the past there had been Lao settlements across the river, the site of Kontum.[67] Some elderly informants reported having seen Lao in the vicinity when they were young, and local Vietnamese continued to refer to some paddies as "Lao fields" because they were alleged to have been cleared by the Lao. Maitre also writes that some Sedang claimed that they had learned their ironworking from the Lao who had lived in the vicinity.[68]

By 1814 the Thai occupied Stung Treng in Cambodia, forcing a Lao migration into present Ratanakiri province in northeastern Cambodia and what is now western Dac Lac province in Vietnam. Following the Srepok river, Lao settlers installed themselves in Ban Don on the edge of the area occupied by the Rhadé and Mnong. According to Maitre, there also were some Khmer settled nearby, and intermarriage with the Lao produced a Lao-Khmer local population.[69]

Meanwhile in the Tran Man, the "barbarian province" embracing the uplands from Quang Nam to Binh Dinh provinces, harassment of Viet-namese settlements by hostile highlanders began to cause some concern in Hue, prompting Gia Long in 1819 to send his trusted general Le Van Duyet into the mountains to organize a more effective system of security. The general concluded that containment of these hostile groups was the only means of attaining this goal, so he obtained permission to construct a defense wall called the Truong Luy along the entire frontier. Ninety kilometers in length, this wall had ditches and hedgegrowths along the outer perimeter. Some 115 guard posts, each with a ten-man garrison, were spaced along the wall, and at each post the personnel maintained their own paddy fields and gardens to sustain themselves.[70]

66. Ibid., pp. 475–76.
67. Prosper Odend'hal, "Itinéraires d'Attopeu à la Mer," *Revue Indochinoise* 9, no. 82 (1908): 751.
68. Maitre, *Les Jungles Moi*, p. 476.
69. Ibid., pp. 478–79.
70. Nguyen On Khe, "*Phu man tap luc*," pp. 714, 790.

All of the royal annals mentioned thus far contain considerably more about tributary relations between the Kings of Fire and Water and the court of Hue during the reigns of Minh Mang, Thieu Tri, and Tu Duc than for any previous period. With the rule of Minh Mang these relations became more formalized, and for the first time there were written Vietnamese accounts of visits to the Jarai country.

It is recorded in the Official Biographies of Dai Nam that in 1820, the first year of Minh Mang's reign, an emissary of the Land of the King of Water arrived in Phu Yen with gifts that included a candleholder and wax of high quality, and he requested a tribute ceremony.[71] The court of Hue agreed to it. Two years later Hue was informed that the King of Water, Ma At (probably derived from Ama At or "Father of At," the teknonymous usage in keeping with Jarai custom), had died. The following year it was learned that "the people of the Land of the King of Water" had selected Ma Moi (Ama Moi or "Father of Moi") as successor. However, he only agreed to be king for a limited time. He expressed his desire to send tribute to the royal court but died before his emissary departed. His son Ma Lam became the King of Water and continued to send tribute to Hue.

When in 1829 no tribute arrived from the highlands, Minh Mang dispatched a military officer named Nguyen Van Quyen to determine the reason. This envoy was warmly greeted by Ma Lam who directed two assistants, Ma Dien and Ma Xuan, to take an elephant tusk and accompany Nguyen Van Quyen to Phu Yen in order to make the proper tribute. When news that the tribute had been paid reached Hue, the emperor ordered that the highland emissary Ma Dien be given high quality muslin, silk vestments, a royal blue foulard, and one *lượng* (a tael weighing 37 grams 783) of silver. The emperor then inquired of Ma Dien whether Thuy Xa and Hoa Xa were one or two countries, and Ma Dien replied, "There is the Land of the King of Fire, and I have never heard of the Land of the King of Water. It was called the Land of the King of Water because of an interpreter's mistake." The designation was then changed to read "Land of the King of Fire," though later it was discovered that "Land of the King of Water" was indeed the correct title.

According to the aforementioned Foreign Relations in the Collection of Official Administrative Regulations of Dai Nam, with the 1831 tribute Minh Mang decreed very explicit protocol for the highland delegation.[72]

71. Nghiêm Thẩm, "Tìm hiểu," pp. 137–38.
72. *Như viễn*, 1: 31, 55–57; 2: 109, 203, 219.

This delegation, as described in various parts of these annals, consisted of a principal ambassador and an entourage of nine—a deputy ambassador, three attachés, an interpreter, and four other attendants. The officials in Phu Yen province were directed by Hue to receive the highlanders at the Phuc Son fort in the foothills and accompany them to the province capital, where they were to remain until an auspicious date for their arrival at the court was determined. A royal edict specified that the Phu Yen officials give the highland delegation some silver, a pig, five chickens, and five ducks, two *phương* (a rectangular container measuring 40 by 60 by 60 cm and holding about 33.54 kilograms) of glutinous rice, five phuong of white rice, some fish sauce, white alcohol, betel leaves, and areca nuts. It also specified that, as the delegation was escorted through Binh Dinh, Quang Nghia (Quang Ngai), and Quang Nam, the officials in each place would provide them with money, two chickens, two ducks, and a jar of fish sauce.

In the capital city the delegation was treated to a banquet with special dishes and a theater performance. They also were presented with money, glutinous rice, white rice, fish sauce, chickens, ducks, a pig, alcohol, fermented shrimp, betel leaves, areca nuts, oil, wax, and fruit. On the day determined for the presentation of tribute, the Palace of Civilization was decorated, and officials in their mandarin robes accompanied the Jarai ambassador to the reception room where a special table had been placed to receive the tribute. After five prosternations before the sovereign, the ambassador presented the gifts while a mandarin in ceremonial garb read the official letter. After the emperor accepted the tribute, the highland ambassador expressed gratitude.

The emperor then addressed the envoy, asking whether his leader paid tribute to the court because of his faithfulness or because his people desired it. The envoy replied that his leader much admired the virtues of the emperor, but that the elderly highlanders also advised payment of tribute in the belief that if the highland people were respectful and faithful to the Vietnamese ruler they would enjoy abundant crops and happiness. Minh Mang concluded the ceremony by declaring that the Land of the King of Water would pay a tribute of two elephant tusks and two rhinoceros horns every three years.[73]

The Royal Geography of Vietnam, prepared in 1833, contains some descriptions of the highlands, particularly the lands of the King of Fire and

73. Nghiêm Thẩm, "Tìm hiểu," p. 138.

The sacred Hodrung mountain of the Jarai

the King of Water.[74] It locates these lands to the west of Hoai Nhan (the name of which was changed to Quy Nhon during Minh Mang's time), which is described as a rich area where highland products such as eagle-wood, rhinoceros horns, horses, gold, silver, beeswax, honey, and betel leaves were traded. The highest peak in the mountainous interior was Nam Ban, to the west of which reigned the King of Fire and to the east the King of Water. Both lived in thatched houses attended by several hundred servants. It was specifically noted that, in their farming, the people of these remote lands burned trees and grass, and used knives to loosen the soil in order to plant their crops. "Since they do not know how to harvest, they pluck the kernels of rice from the stalks" was the description of the harvesting techniques (still used today).

The Kings of Fire and Water were described as "black and ugly," whereas their wives were "beautiful and dressed in colorful clothes." When the kings went forth on elephants to collect taxes, they were accompanied by soldiers and, as they approached a village, gongs were struck three times. The villagers prepared for such a visit by constructing a house for the king outside the village because to have either king enter the village itself would bring misfortune. The visiting king was honored with cooking pots, white cloth, sugar cane, and bunches of bananas.

According to this source, while the two kings were alive there was a star called Duong brightly manifest over the Nam Ban mountain. At times it flashed heavenward "like a piece of very white silk." When one of the kings died, the highlanders watched to see over which house the star

74. Ibid., pp. 135–36.

settled, for that was the sign that the head of that household had been divinely ordained to be the new king. In the Land of the King of Fire there was a citadel of white stone called the White Stone City (Bach Thach Thanh) which covered an area of four *mẫu* (a northern Vietnamese *mẫu* is 0.36 hectare) and had four entrances. Inside was a stone elephant and a reclining stone horse.[75] Normally the White Stone City was forbidden to the Kings of Fire and Water, but when a new king was selected he entered the citadel to place a mat ceremoniously over the two stone figures as part of his inauguration. The forty or fifty chiefs of the "barbarian people" came to pay homage to the new king. Afterward the king returned to his abode below the Nam Ban mountain.

Information in both the Official Biographies of Dai Nam and Foreign Relations annals indicates that with the presentation of the 1834 tribute the court of Hue sought to elevate the King of Water to the level of a proper chief of state.[76] In a royal decree of that year, the emperor speculated about the possibility of bringing the highlanders into the sphere of Vietnamese civilization by means of the elegant protocol surrounding the presentation of tribute, inasmuch as the Land of the King of Water was a distant place where the customs were "honest and pure," where the people tied knots in strings in order to keep records (quipu), and where they planted and harvested rice. Moreover, these people had never revolted against the Vietnamese court. "Why then," the emperor mused, "since their heads have hair, their mouths have teeth, and they have been endowed by nature with knowledge," could they not learn to do "virtuous things?" He concluded that this could be done by their observing the protocol involved in presenting tribute. They would, for example, wear the prescribed tunics instead of appearing in "bare skin," and their participation in the royal rituals would have a civilizing effect upon them.

Soon after, a royal edict specified that when the highland delegation arrived in Phu Yen it should be presented with ten phuong of white rice. Two officials, Dan Duc Thiem and Nguyen Van Hao, were directed to arrange for a ship and an escort of ten soldiers to convey the highlanders to Hue by sea.[77] The annals relate that when the ambassador and his deputy

75. Nghiêm Thẩm speculates that this White Stone City might have been the Yang Prong. It would seem to me more likely to have been the Yang Mum and Drang Lai, both of which were located closer to the present villages of the King of Fire and the King of Water. Interestingly enough, the stone elephant found by Dournes was in the vicinity of these ruins.

76. Nghiêm Thẩm, "Tìm hiểu," p. 138; *Nhu viễn*, 1: 187.

77. *Nhu viễn*, 1: 59; 2: 69, 171.

arrived in Hue they were presented with robes for mandarins of the second class of the seventh degree in the civil service. The ritual protocol for presenting the tribute was the same as that in 1831. Following the presentation of tribute, Minh Mang rewarded the ambassador with an occidental porcelain tea service, a crystal wine service, a decorated crystal box with matching plate, and two red agate figures. The deputy ambassador received some special silk, a jacket of green silk, and pantaloons of local scarlet silk. The interpreter was presented with a short jacket of royal blue muslin and pantaloons of local scarlet silk, while the others in the entourage each received a piece of local muslin.

Soon after the ceremony the emperor wrote, "Today, enthroned in the royal palace so as to receive tribute from these envoys, I saw with my own eyes that they were properly garbed, and they bowed in the prescribed ceremonial manner. I greeted them warmly." The sovereign then decreed that the King of the Land of Water, whose name was Ma Lam, be given the Vinh and the personal name Bao, and the two envoys Ma Duyen and Ma Tai be given the Vietnamese names Linh and Kieu respectively. The Ministry of Rites was also directed to use the designation "king of state" (*quốc vương*) when referring to the King of Water. In the same vein a royal edict specified that in all reports of orders concerning the King of Water, the character *ma* would be replaced by the character *lung*, which designates an official personage.[78]

Woodside interprets the bestowal of the Sino-Vietnamese name Vinh Bao on the King of Water as an attempt by Minh Mang to sinicize the Jarai leader.[79] Also, his upgrading of the highland leader to the rank of "king of state," the same status accorded Minh Mang by the Chinese court, is seen by Woodside as an artificial inflation of the shaman's importance to meet political ends. Minh Mang's treatment of the King of Water satisfied his need to have numerous envoys so he could regard himself as the Southeast Asian version of the Chinese emperor. Thus, the highlanders were categorized, along with the neighboring Southeast Asian states and European merchants, as vassals of the court of Hue, and so, Woodside notes, "all of them played a part, whether they were aware of it or not, in the construction of this Sino-Vietnamese dream fabric."

In 1837, on the occasion of the seventieth birthday of Thuan Thien Cao

78. Ibid., 1: 31; 2: 17; Nghiêm Thẩm, "Tìm hiểu," p. 138.
79. Woodside, *Vietnam and the Chinese Model*, p. 238.

Hoang Hau, Minh Mang's mother and second wife of Gia Long, the King of Water sent local highland products to the royal court. In the twelfth month of that year, the court was informed that Vinh Bao, the King of Water, had died, and in keeping with Jarai custom a nephew (in the female line) named Liet had assumed the role. Emperor Minh Mang sent gifts and a letter of recognition in which he advised the new king that he could use the surname Vinh but he should retain his own given name Liet.[80]

The year 1840 marked the fiftieth birthday of Minh Mang, and the King of Water sent a delegation bearing a message of congratulations and gifts. The emperor, in gratitude, sent the King of Water presents of brocade, cloth (some of it European), handkerchiefs, garments, and silver. The envoys also were rewarded with cloth and silver.[81] There is a passage in the Official Biographies of Dai Nam about a letter which Truong Minh Giang, a military mandarin who had defeated a Thai army invading the Mekong river delta and who subsequently organized Cambodia as the Vietnamese Tran Tay or "Western Province," sent to Emperor Minh Mang in 1840 concerning the King of Water.[82] The letter tells of a tribal chief, called Thúy Xá (King of Water), who had appeared among the Cambodian tribes in Son Tinh accompanied by two servants and two elephants. This chief had sent a letter to Liet, the district chief, indicating his desire to visit, and Liet had in turn informed Truong Minh Giang that in the past the King of Water had known the emperor and sent him tributary gifts every three years. Liet added that this upland chief was reputed to be possessed of great magic, and wherever he went the people acclaimed him, presenting him with gifts.

Upon seeing the letter from Truong Minh Giang, Minh Mang issued a decree stating that "from the time of our childhood" the two lands of Fire and Water were known and that magnanimity should be shown the King of the Land of Water. The emperor wanted to know whether this country had cities and borders like a proper state (*quốc*) or whether the population lived in caves "like the Lao tribes." By the time Truong Minh Giang received the emperor's decree, however, the King of Water had departed, so the emperor ordered Truong Minh Giang to select an "industrious mandarin" to visit the Land of the King of Water. In the emperor's order it was specified that this mandarin be accompanied by a man named Mat,

80. Nghiêm Thẩm, "Tìm hiểu," p. 138.
81. *Như viễn*, 1: 191–93.
82. Nghiêm Thẩm, "Tìm hiểu," pp. 139–42.

who was reputed to know the route into the highlands, and that they carry gifts to the King of Water and the King of Fire.

In response to this order from the sovereign, Truong Minh Giang sent a report that Mat and a companion named Ke had prepared for the Cambodian ruler as a result of a trip into the highlands the previous year (1839) for the Khmer court. Mat and Ke had carried gifts to the two highland shamans from the Khmer ruler, who sought the help of their powerful spirits. Mat and Ke had entered the highlands via a road running eastward from the Cambodian district of Son Boc (probably Sambok) and after fifteen days of travel had reached the village of the King of Water, which they described as having around one hundred dwellings surrounded on three sides by mountains and by vast fields on the fourth side. The King of Water lived in a thatched house with seven rooms, one of which contained two altars for the spirits. There were fifteen kinsmen and servants in the house but "there was no fortress" in the village. The village of the King of Fire, a three-day walk to the east, was located on a plain with "no dangerous mountains or streams." His house and attendants were much the same as those of the King of Water, but the envoys noted that he had a "pagoda" for worshiping the spirits. The two observers then detailed various Jarai practices.

When Mat and Ke made their presentation of gifts from the Khmer ruler to the Kings of Fire and Water, some twenty people gathered for a buffalo sacrifice—which the two outsiders were not allowed to attend. The buffalo was slaughtered and offered to the spirits to enlist their aid for the Cambodian ruler. Afterward, Mat and Ke were offered bowls of buffalo flesh with the warning that their refusal to eat of the buffalo would make them fall ill. Then the Jarai "mixed alcohol with clear water, poured it in a vase, and used bamboo tubes to draw it up and drink it." Regarding other aspects of Jarai society, the envoys noted that the people had no plows or harrows but simply cut trees and dug up the earth to plant. They also recorded that "the people are illiterate, and when they make a loan they use a string tied in knots to keep a record of it" (quipu).

Matrilocal residence among the Jarai drew this comment: "When a boy and girl love one another, the family of the boy takes betel and alcohol to the girl's house, and they invite neighbors to eat and drink as they proclaim the marriage. Most of the boys remain at the houses of their wives, and only seldom do the girls go to the houses of their husbands." The two lowlanders also observed that at funerals the Jarai stuff cooked rice into the mouth of the deceased and that "in happiness and sadness the highland people use large and small brass gongs, a cymbal, and a drum" to provide music.

Mat and Ke were informed that the King of Fire had a knife and the King of Water a rattan whip and two large stones, all of which were powerful talismans. They were told that, should these kings meet, both would die. Neither king would ever be succeeded by his own son because "this would not be beneficial." The two envoys recorded that they found little among the Jarai that resembled their idea of a state, pointing out that there were no taxes, mandarins, or organized armies. The king demanded nothing of his subjects, and when he went among them on an elephant he shaded his head with a leaf hat because "they have no parasols."

When the lowlanders declared that they wished to return to their homeland, the Kings of Fire and Water sent them two gourds of glutinous rice, two gourds of sesame seeds, and a piece of wax bearing the imprint of their hands. These gifts were intended for the emperor, with a message advising him that in the event of calamities such as fierce winds, heavy rains, drought, or epidemics, he should burn the wax and sprinkle a handful of the rice and sesame on the ground while praying to the two kings for help—the same instructions the Khmer kings were given. In addition, each king sent the Vietnamese sovereign a servant, an elephant tusk, and an ox horn.

Liet, the Vietnamese district official mentioned earlier, reported to Truong Minh Giang that he had himself traveled in the Land of the King of Water and seen some of the same things Mat and Ke had. Liet observed in his report that the King of Water farmed like everyone else, and he too remarked that the role of this leader was linked to a sacred rattan whip left by the ancestors. After seeing these reports, the emperor ordered Truong Minh Giang to send Mat and a party to the highlands—a plan that had to be abandoned because of a revolt in the Tran Tay (Cambodia).

Later that same year (1840) a decree issued by the Ministry of Rites directed authorities in Phu Yen province to send someone into the Land of the King of Fire to discuss the matter of tribute that had not been sent to Hue and also to determine the best land routes into that domain. Months later the court received a report from Le Van Quyen, an administrative official who had undertaken the mission.[83] Traveling ostensibly as a silk

83. Ibid., pp. 142–43.

and garment merchant, he had presented some of his goods along with salt and candle holders to both the King of Fire and the King of Water. In his report, he noted that the Land of the King of Water had been mistakenly referred to previously as the Land of the King of Fire. The Land of the King of Water, he explained, was bordered on both the west and the south by the Land of the King of Fire, on the east by the Phuc Son fortress in Phu Yen and the Bach Thach Thanh (White Stone City), and on the north by the Hoang tribe of Binh Dinh province.[84] With a hired guide, Quyen had first visited the Land of the King of Fire, which he described as having mountains on three sides and a large plain with a hundred dwellings (the same description Mat and Ke had given for the village of the King of Water). Outside of the house of the King of Fire he encountered two local chiefs and twenty men, all clutching knives, and they advised Quyen that in order to be presented to the King of Fire he would first have to offer a pig, a jar of alcohol, and three baskets of white salt. After providing these things, Quyen entered the house. There was a center room in the middle of which stood a bamboo platform, with gongs and drums hung to one side of it. In a room to the left there was a large cooking pot, an earthenware vase, several lacquered trays, and a lacquered box inlaid with mother-of-pearl. Several of the men slaughtered the pig Quyen had provided and placed some of the meat above and below the bamboo platform. The King of Fire appeared wearing a turban and loincloth of white material. Quyen judged him to be about seventy years of age and observed that he had mottled hands. The king proceeded to pray softly in front of the platform and then sat upon it. After eating some of the raw pork, he drew alcohol from one of the jars through a tube while attendants played the gong and drums and several men performed a dance. When he had finished eating and drinking, the King of Fire summoned Quyen to his side. "This is the Land of the King of Fire," he explained, and went on to describe how in the past he had cooperated with the King of Water in sending tribute to the court of Hue. Gesturing toward the cooking pot and lacquerware in the adjacent room, he said that these were treasured gifts from the Vietnamese ruler and that it was his wish to reestablish a tributary relationship with the court of Hue. Quyen promised to relay his proposal to the emperor.

From there Quyen traveled to the Land of the King of Water. In his

---

84. This reference is not clear, and it will be pointed out below that the designation *hoang* was used during this period to refer to those upland ethnic groups that were not under Vietnamese authority, i.e., the uncontrolled "savages."

meeting with Vinh Liet, the king, he took the opportunity to inquire why, when the tribute was brought to Phu Yen the previous year, the King of Water pretended to be the King of Fire. Vinh Liet responded that it was the fault of his emissary Ma Sanh, who upon questioning pleaded that his illiteracy had made him become confused and use the wrong designation.

In his report Quyen observed that the two highland kings farmed rice fields and wove cloth like other highlanders and that the only reason they were honored as kings was because they were guardians of some sacred objects. When there was too much rain, the people implored the King of Fire for clear skies, and in times of drought they looked to the King of Water for rain. Although there seemed to be considerable conflict among the local chiefs, neither king involved himself in these struggles.

During the reign of Minh Mang, relations with the highlanders improved in the cinnamon trading areas in central Vietnam. Despite the elaborate fortifications that had been constructed in the Tran Man, the "Barbarian Province," during the reign of Gia Long, conflict between the Vietnamese and the highlanders had persisted, one cause being the cinnamon trade. Maitre writes that under Gia Long this trade was open to all but was dominated by the Chinese, with most of the cinnamon being shipped to China.[85] One effect of the open trade was to increase the migration of Vietnamese into the highlands of Quang Ngai, and trade settlements were established at Tra My and Phuoc Son, both of which also became centers of conflict between highlanders and dishonest lowland merchants. Minh Mang, upon ascending the throne in 1820, made the cinnamon trade a royal monopoly, putting it in the hands of his brother Prince Kien An, who issued ordinances designed to control the flow of cinnamon to markets. Under the new system the administrators who dealt in the cinnamon trade were selected from among village notables of good reputation in the areas where the commerce thrived. These administrators served for one year and were directly responsible to Prince Kien An. An immediate consequence was a sharp decline in further Vietnamese settlement in the Quang Ngai highlands with a resultant improvement in Vietnamese–highlander relations.

Farther south in the region of An Khe a more commercial type of liaison was established with one of the Bahnar chiefs. Sometime around the end of Minh Mang's reign in 1840 the mandarins of the court of Hue obtained a

85. Maitre, *Les Jungles Moi*, pp. 513–14.

certificate naming Kiom, a Bahnar Bonom chief, as "leader of the high-landers" in the vicinity of An Khe in Binh Dinh province.[86] This distinction was bestowed on Kiom (1.1), to whom many later Bahnar leaders trace their ancestry, because he functioned as intermediary between the Vietnamese officials and merchants and the highlanders with whom they traded. The arrangement permitted the Vietnamese to benefit from a trade network that already existed among the highlanders in the An Khe-Kontum region. Dourisboure, who arrived at the highland mission in January 1851, reports that the Bahnar and other ethnic groups around Kontum obtained their iron tools and weapons from the Sedang, who had access to iron deposits in their area. The Rengao and "western Bahnar" wove cotton for cloth which they traded, and the Bahnar Alakong (Kiom is identified in this source as a Bahnar Alakong, although he was a Bahnar Bonom), who had neither iron nor good cloth, traded salt which they received from the Vietnamese.

During the reign of Minh Mang there also was a military expansion of the Thai into the area of Laos where Vietnamese control had been es-tablished during Gia Long's rule. After their capture of Vientiane in 1827, the Thai armies began moving into some of the valleys east of the Mekong river. In their initial clash with the Vietnamese in the vicinity of the Hien river southwest of the Ai Lao pass—the ancient invasion route (see maps 2 and 4)—the Thai were repulsed, but they mounted a new offensive, and the Vietnamese abandoned the area. The local population, including offi-cials, fled and many made their way to the Vietnamese town of Cam Lo on the coastal plain, where they remained until 1830.[87]

Not long after, in 1836, the Vietnamese reasserted their authority in the Ai Lao pass when in the wake of the Le Van Khoi revolt Minh Mang embarked on a program to establish military posts along the frontiers of the kingdom. One such post was the Ai Lao fort. This was a time of Christian persecution by Minh Mang (see chap. 6) and many of the Christians were exiled to the pass, where they were pressed into military service.[88]

In 1841, the first year of the reign of Thieu Tri, the Ministry of Rites issued a decree stating that in all previous texts any references to the Land of

---

86. Pierre Dourisboure and Christian Simmonet, *Vietnam: Mission on the Grand Plateaus*, trans. Albert J. LaMothe, Jr. (New York: Maryknoll Publications, 1967), pp. 13, 67.

87. Maitre, *Les Jungles Moi*, pp. 470–71.

88. M. Silvestre, "Rapport sur l'esclavage," *Excursions et Reconnaissances*, no. 14 (1880), p. 114; Schreiner, *Institutions Annamites*, 1: 244.

the King of Fire be changed to the Land of the King of Water. When the new ruler ascended the throne, the two highland kings sent an emissary to the court with a message of congratulations and expressions of respect. Thieu Tri issued an edict intended for Vinh Liet, the King of Water, stating that "your country has kept its duty as a vassal in a respectful manner and has for a long time enjoyed the benefits of His Majesty, my late father." Then, after noting the day of Minh Mang's death and the day of his own succession, Thieu Tri added, "I mount the throne to lead my people and to appease and advise inferior countries, and knowing that your land is one of those tributary nations I have accorded you a royal letter for your elucidation." Later in the edict the emperor declared, "Your country has customs that are simple and you have come to value the dress of the great country," whereupon he bestowed upon the King of Water a splendid robe brocaded with a flowered serpent motif. Thieu Tri concluded by approving a joint presentation of tribute by the King of Water and the King of Fire. Shortly after, the emperor issued a decree giving Ma That, the King of Fire, the name Cuu Lai, and in the text it was noted that this signified "reliance on long-term assistance." It also was specified that the triannual tribute to be sent by the King of Water would be two elephant tusks and two rhinoceros horns while the King of Fire would be responsible for two of the former and only one of the latter. In addition, both were to send eaglewood.[89]

In a later edict, Thieu Tri authorized the envoys of the Kings of Fire and Water to present themselves before the throne in the Palace of Civilization and to follow the prescribed protocol in proffering gifts and homage. This passage in the annals also notes that at this time native chiefs from nine districts in the Cam Lo area were authorized to render homage before the sovereign, and all were to follow the same protocol observed by the King of Fire and the King of Water.[90]

With the presentation of the required tribute in 1841, Thieu Tri lavished upon the Jarai leaders as well as upon the ambassadors and those in the entourage such gifts as mandarin garments, vases, faience boxes containing betel leaves and areca nuts, silk, various kinds of cloth, crystal bottles and bowls, silver, and coins issued by Minh Mang and Thieu Tri. An envoy sent to the court of Hue in 1843 reported that famine and disease were plaguing the lands of the highland kings. Taking pity, the emperor allowed

89. Nghiêm Thẩm, "Tìm hiểu," pp. 143–44; *Nhu viễn*, 2: 25–29, 75, 109, 175.
90. *Nhu viễn*, 1: 35.

the emissary to present his tribute and return immediately to the mountains.

A royal decree in 1845 granted the Kings of Fire and Water the privilege of offering congratulations and presenting gifts to Thieu Tri the following year, the year of his fortieth birthday. It also specified that when the next period of regular tribute came at the end of 1846, the highland envoy could make the presentation in Phu Yen rather than at the capital city. Upon the Great Festival to celebrate the birthday, the King of Fire sent one elephant tusk and one rhinoceros horn while the King of Water sent two tusks and three horns. In appreciation, the sovereign sent the Jarai leaders an array of gifts similar to those bestowed in 1841.

In the first year of the reign of Tu Duc (1848), the Kings of Water and Fire requested permission to send a delegation to Hue to express their fidelity to the new ruler. Tu Duc issued an edict declaring that the two upland leaders had for a long time been respectful, obedient, and faithful in their payment of tribute, and he granted their request. In appreciation, the two kings sent two elephant tusks, two rhinoceros horns, and some eagle-wood to the royal court.[91]

Neither the Official Biographies of Dai Nam nor the Collection of Official Administrative Regulations (including those books on Foreign Relations) contain any references to the King of Fire or the King of Water after 1848. Nghiem Tham reports, however, that the Official Summary of the Royal Court (*Triều chính biên toát yêu*), published in modern Vietnamese at Hue in 1925, has some information on the post-1848 period.[92] It relates that in 1868, on the occasion of the fortieth birthday of Tu Duc, the King of Water and the King of Fire sent an envoy with gifts, and the emperor directed officials in Phu Yen to receive this tribute. One passage notes that the following year the upland leaders sent two elephant tusks to Emperor Tu Duc, and this constitutes the last entry concerning these tributary relations. Nghiem Tham points out that with the end of the reign of Tu Duc in 1883 Vietnam lost its independence and the French replaced the court of Hue in dealing with the highlanders.

During the reign of Thieu Tri the unrest that had been chronic in the uplands of Quang Ngai erupted into armed clashes that forced many of the Vietnamese villagers to flee as they had done in the middle of the eigh-

91. Ibid., 1: 35, 63; 2: 75, 113, 183; 3: 203–10; Nghiêm Thẩm, "Tìm hiểu," pp. 144, 147–48.
92. Nghiêm Thẩm, "Tìm hiểu," p. 148.

teenth century. In 1842, when a group of thirty-three highland notables appeared at the administrative headquarters to offer their submission, they were put to death. As a result the highlanders in the vicinity refused to pay their taxes and commercial dealings came to a halt. Vietnamese villages were harassed, but several military operations in 1844 finally restored some semblance of normality. Then in 1853, with Tu Duc now on the throne, a new insurrection broke out. When a lowering of taxes failed to quell the unrest, eighty new military posts were constructed to reinforce the seventy-one already in operation. In 1855 five hundred Vietnamese from the frontier area were recruited for military operations in the disturbed area. After attacking the highlanders at Minh Long, the Vietnamese troops took to the forest path at night and in the darkness the murmur of the wind and the cries of swans sent a wave of fear through their columns. The fear gave way to panic, resulting in many of the troops being killed by their own comrades. In another encounter at Nuoc To in 1859, many soldiers and weapons were lost during a surprise attack by the highlanders.[93]

On 1 September 1858 French naval forces attacked Tourane, but their campaign to reach the capital city of Hue never succeeded. In February 1859, however, the French captured Saigon, a victory which marked the beginning of the long French colonial presence in Vietnam. When he signed a treaty with the French in 1862 recognizing their control of the eastern provinces of Cochinchina, Tu Duc became determined to consolidate his rule over the territories remaining under the throne. This led to a new pacification scheme for the upland areas of Quang Ngai and Binh Dinh provinces called the Ngìa-Ðinh Sơn-Phòng (Quang Ngia or Ngai-Binh Dinh Mountain Defense), better known in the French literature as the Son Phong. In 1863 Nguyen Tan, a mandarin from a landed family and direct descendant of Nguyen Cong Toan, the outstanding administrator of the earlier Tran Man pacification effort, was named by the royal court to head the Son Phong. In his own account of his role (the 1871 *Phu man tap lục* written under the pen name Nguyen On Khe) Nguyen Tan describes how he was serving as a provincial judge at Thai Nguyen in the northern highlands when he decided to request that the throne name him head of the Son Phong. Since Quang Ngai was the land of his ancestors, he felt he could not leave it at the mercy of the "savages" and saw it his duty to pacify the area.

93. Nguyen On Khe, "*Phu man tap luc*," pp. 708–09, 791–92; Maitre, *Les Jungles Moi*, pp. 507–08; Bourotte, "Essai des populations Montagnardes," pp. 59–60.

When the emperor granted his request, Nguyen Tan assiduously gleaned all of the information he could find, particularly studying the geography of the area. The initial phase of his strategy involved the construction of a line of fortifications from Tra My, the cinnamon trading center in southern Quang Nam, to Chi Doc in Binh Dinh and the manning of this line by 3,600 troops recruited locally and supported by local partisans. The area was divided into two military commands with headquarters at Mo Duc in Quang Ngai. Nguyen Tan's account reflects great care in planning. He gave explicit instructions to his field commanders and provided detailed geographic information on the remote uplands they were to penetrate and pacify. The commanders were advised to take into consideration the variation in terrain when deciding which access routes to use and were cautioned to make sure they had good intelligence on enemy hideouts. Nguyen Tan even explained to his commanders that javelin spears, cannons, arquebuses, and rattan shields were suitable weapons for the terrain whereas clubs, sabers, and lances were not.

Another aspect of his strategy was to ensure that the field commanders had ample ethnographic information on such things as house types, clothing, artifacts, food, marriage and funeral practices, law, and village leadership to enable them to deal efficaciously with the local populations. In his account, Nguyen Tan named the ethnic groups in the area as the Thanh-Bong, La-Thu, and Thanh-Cu, although these designations do not seem to be used for any of the ethnic groups in the area at the present time. He also included a sampling of seven words from their languages. Oliver Trebilco, who has done considerable research on the Hre language, claims that the words in the list for the "Thanh-Cu" are transliterations of Hre.[94] The word list combining words of the Thanh-Bong and La Thu is less clear. Jacqueline Maier, an authority on the Cua language, finds among the seven transliterations four cognates of Cua, one cognate of Hre, and two words that cannot be identified.[95]

The field commanders were instructed to obtain an interpreter immediately after occupying an area for better communication with the local leaders, and Nguyen Tan supplied the names of some of these chiefs. Every one on this list bore the surname Dinh, the name mandated for all Cua and Hre by the Vietnamese authorities. These chiefs were to be treated with

94. Oliver Trebilco, personal correspondence, 23 February 1976.
95. Jacqueline Maier, personal correspondence, 23 January and 3 August 1976.

politeness and firmness, and Nguyen Tan gave specific instructions on how the commanders should greet the chiefs. The local populations were to be assisted with such things as rice and medicines but severe punishments were prescribed for failure to cooperate with the authorities. Nguyen Tan suggested to the commanders that they establish military posts in the occupied areas to demonstrate their resolve to remain there. Finally, the collection of taxes, a responsibility of the local highlander officials (giao dịch) since the sixteenth century, was taken over by Vietnamese administrators.[96]

Nguyen Tan's strategy proved successful, and by 1869 the upland area of Quang Ngai was quiet. He was succeeded by his son Nguyen Do, who in turn was followed by his son Nguyen Thanh, brother-in-law of Emperor Dong Khanh (1886–1889). Also known as Van-Minh, Nguyen Thanh served as minister of war and was one of the high-ranking members of the Cơ Mật, the "Secret Council" that advised the emperor. In 1887 Nguyen Thanh reorganized the Son Phong, diminishing its military character in favor of an administrative structure to foster and control commercial activities. He created five districts—Ha Tinh, Tra My, Nghia Hanh, Duc Pho, Bong Son. The head of each district was assisted by five officials, some of whom (at the lower levels) were highlanders. Markets for trade with the highland people were opened in certain lowland locations but most of the trading took place outside the markets under the direction of the Son Phong agents. In the cinnamon trading areas these agents were the lãnh mại, descendants of the representatives of Prince Kien An. Over a period of time, these representatives had sublet the right to collect taxes and control commerce in cinnamon to subagents, variously known as tổng-dịch, thứ ngũ, or thừa biện. With the Son Phong, these subagents came to be called tổng nguồn, although in some areas the former designations persisted. South of the cinnamon area in Binh Thuan and Khanh Hoa provinces, these tax collectors had unbridled control over trade with the highlanders—the Roglai, Chru, and Koho-speaking groups—and they realized great profits through fixing prices on salt and other commodities. With no law to protect them in their commerce with the Vietnamese and Cham, the highlanders were sadly exploited.[97]

According to Aymonier, in the 1870s and 1880s the three Vietnamese

96. Nguyen On Khe, "Phu man tap luc," pp. 459–69, 641–48, 711–14.
97. Durand, "Les Moi du Son-Phong," pp. 288–90, 297–99; Etienne Aymonier, "Notes sur l'Annam," Excursions et Reconnaissances, no. 24 (1885), pp. 324–33.

subagents in Binh Thuan province not only exploited the highlanders under their control but permitted banditry from which they profited.[98] It was common for them to take pigs, cattle, and goats from highlanders when they pleased, and they exacted excessive annual tributes from the Roglai, Koho, and Chru villagers. Roglai residents of one canton, for example, were required to pay the mandarin at the Mang Ri citadel a pair of elephant tusks, a rhinoceros horn, a goat, a buffalo, thirty deer pelts, thirty pair of deer antlers, and some turtle shells. Similar tribute was expected of Roglai in the vicinity of Phan Rang, but in 1877 the subagent increased the amount, forcing many Roglai villagers to relocate in the more remote interior close to the independent Rhadé. There also were instances where, in order to provide elephant tusks, Roglai villagers had to purchase them with buffalo or silver bars, and some were forced to sell their children into slavery to do so. In May and June the highlanders were required to go to Parik with their tribute. Those who brought the proper amount were congratulated and given brass neckpieces. Those who defaulted were beaten or put in cangues, and sometimes their wives and children were sold to provide the compensation.

Another form of exploitation of the highlanders by local Vietnamese officials was the annual *hóa-mại* or purchase of valuable products for the court of Hue. Each year the court sent out a list of products that it required for fetes, personal needs of the royal family, or palace repairs. These included such things as eaglewood, precious hardwoods, rhinoceros horns and pelts, resinous torches, rattan, thatching, special mats, and certain oils. The provincial authorities were responsible for obtaining these products and paying a price fixed in Hue. Brière reports, however, that in the late 1880s all of the Cham and highlanders he encountered who were expected to furnish some of these products complained that they were never compensated for doing so.[99]

In the highland-lowland trade, most of the actual buying and selling was carried out by roving Vietnamese traders (*các lái* or *lái buôn*). One of the important market centers in Khanh Hoa province was located some fifteen kilometers northwest of Ninh Hoa, and Brière reports that it was a focal point for a floating population of Vietnamese "parasites" who carried out trade in the upland villages, sometimes with the authorization of the

98. Aymonier, "Notes sur l'Annam," pp. 318–24.
99. M. Brière, "Notice sur les Moi du Binh Thuan et du Khanh Hoa," *Excursions et Reconnaissances*, no. 32 (1890), pp. 248–50.

canton chief and sometimes clandestinely at the behest of Chinese merchants.[100] They were an undisciplined lot, given to heavy opium smoking and other excesses that lent an air of anarchy to the place. There also were some highlanders (*mọi thuộc*) who served as intermediaries for trade between the lowlanders and unpacified upland groups (*mọi hoang*). One particular category of such intermediaries was the *mọi trân*, who specialized in obtaining products from the remote highlands for the mandarins and officials in the Khanh Hoa citadel, but with the insurrection of 1885 (see chap. 7) this group disappeared. Finally, there were some highlanders from the mountains to the west who brought their products directly to this market center, arriving after a six or seven day trip with packsaddle horses or elephants loaded with products for sale.

According to Durand, the most remunerative trade in the highlands was the sale of slaves, and he points out that some of the Bahnar Bonom chiefs (such as the aforementioned Kiom) were engaged in it on a grand scale.[101] During his 1877 expedition from Bassac on the Mekong river to Hue, French naval doctor Harmand observed how the Lao organized annual slave hunts, raiding the villages of the highlanders.[102] The children were kept and the adults sold to buyers from Cambodia, Bangkok, and even Burma. Slaves also were provided by highlanders who conducted raids on other highland villages as well as Lao and Vietnamese settlements. Harmand saw some Vietnamese slaves who had been captured by highlanders some ten years before in Quang Binh province. Later, when Odend'hal was traveling through the Boloven Plateau in 1894, he came upon a Vietnamese slave who had been a soldier in the Son Phong area.[103] This slave and some other Vietnamese slaves from the area of Tra My and Tra Bong in Quang Ngai province had been captured by highlanders and subsequently sold to Lao traders.

Most Vietnamese traders, however, sold such items as knives, hatchets, axes, several kinds of sabers, copper bowls, brass bracelets and bells, silver earrings, jars for alcohol, salt, lime for garnishing betel areca, chickens, pigs, buffalo, cattle, and goats. They also sold English cotton cloth from Singapore and Canton, and perhaps the most important items sold were gongs of varying sizes and quality. Most highly valued were the Chinese

---

100. Ibid., pp. 236–37, 240.
101. Durand, "Les Moi du Son-Phong," p. 308.
102. Jules Harmand, "De Bassac à Hué (Avril-Août 1877)," *Bulletin de la Société de Géographie,* January 1879, pp. 86–89.
103. Odend'hal, "Itinéraires," no. 79, p. 504; no. 83, p. 838.

gongs and those from the foundries of Hanoi and Nam Dinh. Among the highland groups in Binh Thuan and Khanh Hoa provinces, the Chinese gongs (called *mala*) and Tonkinese gongs (called *cồng*) were sold in sets of three—a large, a medium, and a small gong—with the value determined by size and resonance.

From the highlanders these merchants purchased tobacco, betel leaves, areca nuts, sesame, wax, indigo, honey, cotton, cardamom, upland rice, maize, castor beans, ground nuts, bananas, yams, cinnamon, stag antlers, rhinoceros horns, resin torches, pigs, goats, buffalo, chickens, ducks, deer pelts, and turtle shells.[104] As indicated previously, eaglewood was a highly prized commodity in the Binh Thuan-Khanh Hoa area, as was ivory, and Brière reported that in spite of strict controls imposed by the court of Hue both commodities were traded clandestinely to the Chinese, who shipped them to China.[105]

Some of this commerce was carried on through barter and the rest through the exchange of Vietnamese money. Prior to the arrival of the French, Vietnamese money produced in Hue for the court and the mandarins consisted of ingots of gold or silver in varying sizes. There were coins of copper, bronze, or zinc for the ordinary folk. Imitative of Chinese money pieces, the coins were called *đồng tiền* by the Vietnamese and *sapèques* by the French. A hole in the center permitted them to be strung, and a string of six hundred coins was called a *quan tiền* by the Vietnamese and a *ligature* by the French.[106] During the reign of Gia Long, a ligature of copper coins was worth six of zinc coins. Minh Mang ordered copper coins of two sizes, and a ligature of the smaller coins became worth only four times a ligature of zinc coins. Emperors Thieu Tri and Tu Duc maintained the same relative value until the latter fixed the value of the copper coin at six times that of the zinc coin. Aymonier states that sometime between 1872 and 1874, at the instigation of a Chinese-Vietnamese named Tran Chuyen Thanh, the Hue court sold the right to manufacture the coins to the Chinese, who immediately began to diminish their weight while maintaining the same value.[107] Soon thereafter Chinese in Saigon and

104. Aymonier, "Notes sur l'Annam," pp. 318–33; Brière, "Notice sur les Moi," pp. 230–37; Durand, "Les Moi du Son-Phong," pp. 308–12; H. Haguet, "Notice ethnique sur les Moi de la région de Quang-Ngai," *Revue Indochinoise* 1 (1905): 1423–24.

105. Brière, "Notice sur les Moi," pp. 241–42.

106. E. Langlet, *Le Peuple Annamite*, with a preface by Albert de Pouvourville (Paris and Nancy: Berger-Levrault, 1913), pp. 277–78.

107. Aymonier, "Notes sur l'Annam," pp. 255–56.

Cholon started counterfeiting coins and flooded the area from Quang Nam to Binh Thuan with them.

Within the jurisdiction of the Son Phong, a local medium of exchange was the Vietnamese *mat*, equivalent to one ligature of copper coins. Ten mat amounted to one *rong* (or *run*) while one hundred mat equaled one *vang* (or *van*). One mat purchased an iron hatchet or a small iron hoe or a pair of small cups or ten rice cups of salt. It also bought ten packages of betel leaves (each package containing two hundred leaves) or ten packages of tobacco (each containing one hundred leaves). A buffalo was worth ten rong.[108]

Aymonier points out that, since the Hindu Cham viewed the buffalo as a sacred animal, there were relatively few in Binh Thuan prior to the arrival of the Vietnamese.[109] By the latter part of the nineteenth century, however, buffalo were a common medium of exchange in highland-lowland trade. A buffalo could be traded, for example, for a very large boiling pot, or two faience Chinese alcohol jars, or a high-quality gong of medium size, or six copper trays, or two sabers, or two spears. A rhinoceros horn was worth eight buffalo, and a pair of large elephant tusks could be exchanged for six buffalo. Other things of value could be bartered. Two sets of gongs, one Chinese and one Tonkinese, were worth a kilo of eaglewood and a rhinoceros horn could be traded for fourteen kilos of ivory.[110]

By the late nineteenth century the Son Phong subagents descended from the representatives for Prince Kien An in his cinnamon trade monopoly, had come to enjoy, as Brière observes, complete autonomy in dealing with the highlanders under government control.[111] They also had become content to remain in their own villages and leave the commerce in cinnamon to the roving traders (*lái buôn*) who were familiar with the ways of the highland people and spoke their languages. Many of the roving traders, however, fell into debt to the Chinese cinnamon buyers and in effect became the creditors' agents in the highlands. In their attempts to extract themselves from debt, the traders often were guilty of abuses that led to serious conflict between the highlanders and lowlanders in places such as the Vietnamese settlements at Tra My and Phuoc Son. Brière cites incidents where traders stole cinnamon bark from highland villagers. In

108. Durand, "Les Moi du Son-Phong," p. 299.
109. Aymonier, "Notes sur l'Annam," p. 233.
110. Durand, "Les Moi du Son-Phong," pp. 312–17.
111. M. Brière, "Culture et commerce de la cannelle," *Bulletin Economique de l'Indochine* 6, no. 33 (1904): 935–50.

one such incident a few traders, accompanied by a group of coolies, made the five-day trip on foot into the Quang Ngai uplands during the favorable weather of the second and third lunar months. There, having installed themselves in the small guest houses the highland people constructed at the entrances to their villages, they went out with the village leaders to survey the cinnamon trees, marking some of the bark for purchase. The traders arranged for a large celebration to accompany the price negotiations. Buffalo were slaughtered and many jars of alcohol were provided. While all ate and drank, the Vietnamese traders discussed with the villagers payment for the cinnamon bark on the marked trees. But when the highlanders proceeded to get drunk, the traders' coolies stealthily stripped both marked and unmarked trees. The deed done, the traders slipped away from the merriment and with their coolies took to the path leading down to the coast. Upon discovering they had been plundered, the highlanders rose in anger, attacking nearby Vietnamese settlements to slaughter villagers or carry them off to be sold into slavery.

Trinh-The was the last head of the Son Phong, which the French began to dismantle at the end of the nineteenth century. The first official manifestation of this effort was the report sent by Boulloche, the résident supérieur of Annam, to the French résidents of the four southern provinces. It announced that on 28 July 1898 the Cơ Mật, or Secret Council, had advised Emperor Thanh Thai that reforms would have to be made in the Son Phong in order to develop commerce between the highlands and the lowlands. In essence, it stated that the Vietnamese agents who had been serving as intermediaries in the existing trade were obstacles to further development because they "abuse the credulity" of the highlanders. Among the reforms recommended was the abolishment of the agent's role, explicitly the Tan Thu in Binh Dinh, and the Thu Ngu, Thua Bien, and Thong Dich of Binh Thuan. Where necessary, they would remain as interpreters. The highlanders would deal directly with the provincial officials and the résidents. The system of highlanders making tax payments in kind also was to be changed; varying cash tax rates were fixed for particular areas for males between the ages of eighteen and sixty, but the Rhadé in Khanh Hoa still were to pay their taxes in yellow wax. The report stated that the highlanders would be responsible for assuring that roads into the mountains were constructed and maintained—the beginning of the corvée imposed by the French on the highland people.[112]

112. Trinquet, "Le Poste administratif du Lang-Ri (Quang Ngai)," *Revue Indochinoise* 10 (1908): 346–48.

6 ARRIVAL OF THE FRENCH

In the world beyond the central highlands during the seventeenth and eighteenth centuries, a series of interrelated events was taking place that would culminate in the French conquest of Indochina—a dramatic turning point in the history of Southeast Asia. Even before French rule became a reality, however, an equally important development for the highlanders had occurred with the establishment of a French presence in their midst. Initially this took the form of a small mission in the remote interior set up by French priests hoping to elude the Vietnamese persecutions of Christians. These priests, the first Europeans to penetrate the highlands, founded the Kontum Mission.

In many respects the sequence of events that led to the French presence in the highlands began on 18 January 1615 when Father Buzomi, an Italian, and Father Carvalho, a Portuguese, both from the Jesuit mission in Macao, landed at Tourane in its magnificent setting of mountains meeting the sea. At this time, following Portuguese precedents, the Europeans knew the land of the Nguyen as Cochinchina and the land of the Trinh farther north as Tonkin. Eager to introduce Christianity among the Vietnamese, the two priests selected a site at Faifoo (Hoi An), south of Tourane, and there established the Cochinchina Mission.[1]

In 1624 the two priests were joined by Father Alexandre de Rhodes, a scholar from Avignon who had a remarkable gift for languages. The mission thrived, encouraging the Jesuits to extend their activities to Tonkin, and Father de Rhodes was chosen for this task. Granted an audience with Trinh Trang in 1627, Father de Rhodes presented to the emperor a lavishly gilded book on mathematics along with other gifts and

---

1. The first Catholic priest to reach Vietnam was the Spanish Dominican Diego Adverte, who arrived in 1596, but the army of Nguyen Hoang forced him and his escort of Portuguese troops to leave almost immediately.

received from the emperor permission to open a mission. By the end of 1629 Father de Rhodes had baptized some 6,700 converts. But his conversion of several princesses of the royal court alarmed the emperor, who ordered Father de Rhodes expelled. The priest returned to Macao and, after several brief trips to Cochinchina, sailed for Rome. There he presented to the papal authorities a plan for a new mission to Cochinchina independent of Portuguese patronage. He also began publishing the results of linguistic research he had done during his mission years. In the course of his research, he had devised a Latin script for the tonal Vietnamese language which would later form the basis for modern Vietnamese orthography. In 1650 he published a catechism in the new script and Latin and the following year produced a Vietnamese-Latin dictionary.

Portuguese opposition to his new mission plan, combined with the normal lengthy deliberation process in church decisions, caused a seemingly interminable delay and Father de Rhodes became impatient. He journeyed to Paris in the hope of recruiting French missionaries for Cochinchina and Tonkin. Fortuitously, there was at this time in Parisian government and mercantile circles a heightened interest in overseas commercial ventures, and the articulate priest's vivid descriptions of the natural wealth and beauty of distant Cochinchina won an attentive audience. In addition, Father de Rhodes found that his friend Father Bagot was in charge of the Auberge de la Rose Blanche, where laymen and clerics of the nobility and the bourgoisie, all members of the powerful and pious secret Compagnie du Saint Sacrement, were gathered. Father de Rhodes stirred great interest among them in the possibility of an evangelization mission in Cochinchina and Tonkin, only to have his role in these events cut off when he was sent to Persia to launch a new mission. He died in Ispahan in 1660.

Alexandre de Rhodes' efforts had not been in vain. In 1658 Rome named Francois Pallu and Lambert de la Motte, two of the "Rose Blanche" group, as apostolic vicars with the rank of bishop. They and some other members of the group formulated a plan for a Far East company that would have the dual function of propagating the faith and expanding French commercial interests. Fermanel de Favery, a well-to-do Rouen merchant, agreed to purchase and equip a frigate to transport missionaries to the Far East, and on 27 November 1660 Bishop de la Motte and Fathers de Bourges and Deydier embarked for their new mission venture. Subsequently they were followed by Bishop Pallu. In order to assure the recruitment of new missionaries, the Seminaire des Missions

Etrangères was founded in 1664 with headquarters on Rue de Bac in the heart of Paris. That same year Colbert organized the Compagnie des Indes Orientales—the commercial East Indies Company.

The French missionaries began to work among the Vietnamese who had been converted by the Jesuits, and Bishop Pallu kept Colbert well supplied with political and commercial intelligence on Cochinchina and Tonkin. As before, the Vietnamese emperor became restive over the missionaries' activities, and in 1662 Trinh Tac promulgated his "Instructions for the Reform of Mores" which among other things condemned the "false doctrine," i.e., Christianity. Father Deydier was imprisoned for a period, but the missionaries were undaunted, and in 1668 Lambert de la Motte ordained the first two Vietnamese priests. In 1680 the French commercial mission was established in Tonkin. Although by the end of the century European commerce with Vietnam had diminished considerably, the French missionaries remained active in both Tonkin and Cochinchina.[2]

Anti-Catholic sentiment among the Vietnamese rulers continued through the eighteenth century, periodically erupting into verbal denunciations and, at times, overt persecution. Trinh Cuong in 1712, Trinh Doanh in 1754, and the Nguyen at various times, forbade any preaching by the priests, hounding them and burning their Christian books. Nonetheless, the missionaries carried on their work and, paradoxically, some Jesuits gained positions close to several of the Nguyen rulers. During the Tay Son Revolt, Father Pigneau de Béhaine saved the life of Nguyen Anh, heir to the throne, and subsequently served as his advisor. Nguyen Anh's reign as Emperor Gia Long brought a respite in the harassment of the missionaries, but as the Europeans swept into Burma, Malaya, and the Chinese coast the Vietnamese sovereign became increasingly uneasy. With the English occupation of Singapore in 1819, Gia Long recommended to his son Minh Mang (who succeeded him in 1820) that he treat the Europeans, particularly the French, well but never allow them any preponderant place in Vietnam.[3]

Minh Mang, like his father, viewed the west with suspicion, and when in

2. Le Thanh Khoi, *Le Viêt-Nam: histoire et civilisation* (Paris: Les Editions de Minuit, 1955), pp. 290–94; A. Launay, *Histoire ancienne et moderne de l'Annam* (Paris: Challamel, 1884), pp. 152–54; Christian Simmonet, "Les Missions Etrangères de Paris en Indochine," *Indochine*, no. 112 (1942), pp. 11–14; Georges Taboulet, *La Geste française en Indochine*, 2 vols. (Paris: Adrien-Maisonneuve, 1955), 1: 10–22, 80–90.

3. Le Thanh Khoi, *Le Viêt-Nam*, pp. 293–94, 338–43; Joseph Buttinger, *Vietnam: A Political History* (New York: Frederick A. Praeger, 1968), pp. 73–74.

1821 Jean-Baptiste Chaigneau, one of Pigneau de Béhaine's associates and an advisor to Gia Long, returned to Vietnam as French consul with instructions to negotiate a treaty of commerce the emperor refused the offer. He also assumed a very strong antimissionary position, issuing an edict in 1825 charging the "perverse religion of the European" with "corrupting the hearts of men." General Le Van Duyet defended the Christians until his death, but afterward Minh Mang unleashed a wave of persecution against the missionaries and the Vietnamese Catholics. In 1830 some 24,000 Christians abandoned their homes and fields to take refuge in remote areas. The situation for the Christians worsened with the 1833–1835 revolt led by Le Van Khoi, adoptive son of Le Van Duyet. Convinced that the French priests and native Catholics supported the revolt, Minh Mang ordered retribution, and numerous Catholics— among them seven European priests—were executed. Also it was during this period that large numbers of Christians were pressed into military servitude and sent to the Ai Lao fort in the mountains west of Quang Tri.[4]

In France the missionaries had the support of the large Catholic population as well as the sympathy of the French navy. Many naval officers had acquaintances among the missionaries, who usually were the only fellow Frenchmen they encountered in the Far East. In 1838 a French naval officer named Fourichon conceived of a plan for an assault on Tourane as a graphic warning to the Vietnamese ruler. The plan was formally proposed to the French government, but in Paris the regime of Louis Philippe was anticlerical and Foreign Minister Guizot was more interested in restoring France's place of power in Europe than in engaging in Asian ventures. Consequently the missionaries were left to their own devices. In January 1841 Minh Mang died, and his successor Thieu Tri, although at first conciliatory toward the missionaries, soon reverted to the same policy pursued by his father.[5]

The missionaries faced the new reign of Thieu Tri with foreboding, particularly in view of the lack of support from France. In this uncertain setting Bishop Etienne Cuenot, Apostolic Vicar of Eastern Cochinchina, made a decision that would have a profound effect on the French presence in the highlands. Should the position of the missionaries become more

---

4. Launay, *Histoire ancienne*, pp. 214–17; Alfred Schreiner, *Les Institutions Annamites en Basse-Cochinchine avant la conquête Française*, 3 vols. (Saigon: Claude & Cie., 1901), 1: 244.

5. Buttinger, *Vietnam*, pp. 73–76; Le Thanh Khoi, *Le Viêt-Nam*, pp. 338–43; Launay, *Histoire ancienne*, pp. 217–21.

precarious, he reasoned, it would be well to have a place of refuge well beyond the reach of the forces of persecution. The solution would be to establish a new mission somewhere in the mountainous interior, west of the Vietnamese settlements of the An Khe valley, in Binh Dinh province. This would be the first attempt at evangelization among the highland people of that region, although earlier efforts among the Stieng people farther south had taken place in the eighteenth century. In 1765 Monsignor Pigues, Apostolic Vicar of Cochinchina, reported that there were "montagnards" between Cambodia, Laos, and Cochinchina who were amenable to conversion. He identified them as Stieng and "others, Proue, Queraie, Penong, etc." Noting that the Penong (a general Khmer term for the highlanders of northeastern Cambodia) were "simple, sincere, and charitable," he declared that he had already baptized several who had been brought in as captives by the Cambodians.[6] In 1770 Father Juget attempted to start a mission among the Stieng in the Prek Chlong area of eastern Cambodia, but he died in 1774 and his efforts were not continued. Subsequently another priest, Father Faulet, spent a brief time among the Stieng, and a third priest, Father Grillet, is reported to have traveled on foot some sixty kilometers into the Stieng country.[7]

The two priests selected to establish this new mission among the highlanders were Fathers Pierre Duclos and Jean Claude Miche. On 10 February 1842 they set out from Phu Yen to follow the Ba river, the ancient route into the highlands followed by the Cham and Vietnamese. They were the first westerners to penetrate the highlands, but six days after their departure they fell into the hands of soldiers sent by the Phu Yen mandarins to capture them. According to their own account, the two priests were "in the territory of the King of Fire" when they were apprehended in the village of Buon Vang.[8] The soldiers took their belongings, put cangues around their necks, and brought them before the governor and the criminal judge of Phu Yen province. The priests pleaded that since they were within the boundaries of the land of the King of Fire the Vietnamese had no jurisdiction over them. They added that the subjects of

6. A. Launay, *Histoire de la mission de Cochinchine, 1658–1823*, 3 vols. (Paris: Anciennes Maison Charles Douniol et Retaux, 1924), 2: 433–34.

7. Bernard Bourotte, "Essai d'histoire des populations Montagnardes du Sud-Indochinois jusqu'à 1945," *BSEI* 30, no. 1 (1955): 57; *Nécrologe de la Société des Missions Etrangères de Paris, 1659–1930* (Hong Kong: Imprimerie de Nazareth, 1932), pp. 18, 77, 220.

8. Taboulet, *Geste française*, 1: 334–35.

the King of Fire and the King of Water could not encroach upon the territory of the Vietnamese, because as outsiders they would be punished with death. This argument fell on deaf ears, and in May the prisoners were taken to Hue, where they were beaten, put in cages, and condemned to death along with several other French missionaries. The threat of death hung over them until May 1843, when the French corvette *l'Heroine* appeared at the mouth of the Song Giang (River of Perfumes) in nearby Hue, at which point Thieu Tri agreed to release the captives.

This incident raised a fresh clamor among Catholic circles in France, and Guizot was forced to grant the French navy permission to protect missionaries in personal danger, though his permission carried the qualification that such protection could be extended only if it did not involve the French flag in a clash with the Vietnamese. In addition, by 1843 there were winds of change in Paris regarding political and commercial expansion in the Far East. With the English occupation of Hong Kong in 1841 following the Opium War, a new era of Western expansion had been launched, and Guizot knew all too well that France could not remain aloof from the competition. In 1841 he sent a mission to explore the possibility of trade with China, and two years later it was decided to dispatch a naval unit to protect French political and commercial interests in the Far East. The small French fleet arrived in Macao in August 1844 under the command of Admiral Cécille, who saw the coast of Vietnam as an ideal place for France to establish a naval base. Furthermore, his missionary friends assured him that a pretender of the Le dynasty retained considerable following among the Vietnamese and that French intervention to restore him to the throne would bring royal favor for the naval base and for missionary activity.

Early in 1845 Monsignor Lefèbvre was condemned to death by the Vietnamese and in May Admiral Cécille sent the warship *Alcmène* to Tourane, forcing Thieu Tri to release the prisoner. The following year Monsignor Lefèbvre attempted to reenter the country and was captured again and sentenced to death. Early in 1847 Cécille ordered Captains Lapierre and Rigault de Genouilly to Tourane. Although Lefèbvre was again released, the two officers attempted to force acceptance of a letter of protest Cécille had written to the emperor. Irked by the mandarins' refusal to accept the letter, the French stripped the sails from the Vietnamese ships in the harbor and, after waiting two weeks, shelled the port, causing many deaths. This unauthorized action was defended by the promissionary groups in Paris, and on his return to France in 1847 Cécille demanded that henceforth the French talk to the Vietnamese "only with guns." [9]

There were two important political changes in 1848: in France the July Monarchy of Louis Philippe was overthrown and in Vietnam Thieu Tri was succeeded by his son, who took the name Tu Duc. Also in 1848, Bishop Cuenot, now in hiding in rural Binh Dinh, concluded that the situation for the missionaries was not likely to improve and so revived his plan for a mission in the mountains, though this time with better preliminary research. Since intelligence on a route into the highlands and an efficiacious location for the mission was badly needed, a Vietnamese deacon named Dzo was sent into western Binh Dinh. Hiding his identity as a Christian cleric, he traveled on foot to An Son in the An Khe area and there took employment as a domestic in the house of a Vietnamese itinerant merchant. He soon began to accompany his employer on trading trips into the back country, using the opportunity to became familiar with the geography as well as with some of the local highlander customs and languages. When he decided he had acquired enough information, he returned to the lowlands to report to the bishop.

To achieve the second phase of the reconnaissance, Dzo disguised himself as a merchant and with four Vietnamese seminarians traveled farther west into the country of the Jarai Hodrung, the area of present Pleiku. This trip was cut short, however, when Dzo found out that the Jarai were plotting to rob him of his merchandise and to sell him and his assistants as slaves in Laos. Dzo and his companions fled back to the coast. Dzo and Bishop Cuenot decided that Fathers Combes and Fontaine should accompany Dzo back into the highlands. They would avoid the Vietnamese merchants by taking back trails to the north of An Khe, and Dzo cautioned that they should remain clear of certain highland chiefs, notably the notorious Bahnar Bonom leader Kiom (1.1). As court-designated "chief of the highlanders" in the region of An Khe, Kiom served as go-between in the highland-Vietnamese trade as well as arbitrator of any conflicts the roving merchants might have with local villagers.

Dzo and the two priests took a route north by northwest from Binh Dinh but after being attacked by a herd of elephants they returned to the lowlands. The bishop was furious at their lack of courage, so after a short rest they took to the footpaths again. As they continued into the rugged

9. Buttinger, *Vietnam*, pp. 75–81; Taboulet, *Geste française*, 1: 342–77.

green interior, they reached the village of another feared Bahnar chief named Ba Ham, who forced them to remain with him for a month. Once free to leave, the mission group walked westward, finally coming to the village of Kon Phar, where much to their horror they happened upon Kiom, who had come there to retrieve a runaway slave. The dreaded chief was as surprised as they, for the two priests with their long beards were the first westerners he had ever seen. Much to the relief of the missionaries he greeted them warmly and, speaking in Vietnamese to Dzo, promised to protect them, even proposing an alliance ritual—which Dzo immediately accepted. A chicken was roasted as a jar of rice alcohol was prepared. Then Kiom muttered some incantations while he and Dzo let a few drops of their blood mix with the alcohol. After a wild boar tusk, a spear, and some arrowheads had been plunged into the jar, both drank from it through bamboo tubes to seal their alliance.

Taking advantage of the new alliance, the French priests asked Kiom to accompany them farther west where they could establish a mission beyond the range of the Vietnamese merchants. Kiom agreed, and after one day of walking they arrived at the village of Kon Kolang, where Bliou, the chief, greeted them. The priests decided to remain there so Kiom and his warriors departed. In a secluded part of the forest near the village, the missionaries built a hut: the very beginning of the highland mission. In January 1851 they were joined by Fathers Dourisboure and Desgouts, and later that year the mission was relocated to Kon Koxam on the banks of the Bla river. Eventually small branches were founded in the villages of Kon Trang, Plei Chu, and Kon Rohai, where the present city of Kontum is located.[10]

By 1852 the pro-Catholic Second Empire regime of Louis-Napoleon was receptive to any suggestion of intervention in Vietnam on behalf of the missionaries. Moreover, with the end of the Crimean War and the convening of the Congress of Paris in early 1856 there was renewed interest in new commercial and political efforts in the Far East. It was decided to send the diplomat Charles de Montigny to negotiate a treaty of friendship, commerce, and religion with Emperor Tu Duc. To prepare for the Montigny Mission two naval ships, the *Catinat* and *Capricieuse*, sailed into Tourane harbor with a letter to the emperor announcing the impending arrival of de Montigny. When the mandarins refused to accept the

10. Pierre Dourisboure, *Les Sauvages Bah-Nars (Cochinchine orientale): souvenirs d'un missionnaire* (Paris: Pierre Téqui, 1922), pp. 1–63; Pierre Dourisboure and Christian Simmonet, *Vietnam: Mission on the Grand Plateaus* (Maryknoll, New York: Maryknoll Publications, 1967), pp. 7–69.

letter, the commander of the *Catinat* ordered a shelling of the harbor forts, after which he put ashore a landing party. Lack of supplies forced the French force to withdraw, and when de Montigny arrived in January 1857 he was greeted coldly by the Vietnamese ruler, who refused even to discuss the treaty. His mission a failure, the diplomat departed.

The Montigny Mission had enraged Tu Duc and also convinced him that the French threats of intervention were hollow. As a result, he embarked on a new series of persecutions against the Christians, and this in turn produced fresh outcries among the Catholics in France. Early in 1857 Napoleon III met with Father Huc, a French missionary from China and friend of Count Bourboulon, an advocate of intervention in Vietnam. Father Huc held that Pigneau de Béhaine's Versailles Treaty of 1787 gave France an incontestable right to occupy certain points in Vietnam, notably Tourane. He further argued that Le dynasty descendants in Tonkin were politically active, had the support of many oppressed Vietnamese Christians, and were prepared to support any French moves against the Nguyen rulers in Hue, usurpers of the mandate of heaven. Moved by these arguments, the French ruler ordered the formation of a Commission on Cochinchina. Its final report, submitted in May 1857, stated that French policy in Cochinchina would have to be revised drastically if France were not to become a second-rate power without Asian possessions. The Versailles Treaty, it concluded, did not provide a strong basis for intervention but something could be made of it. Napoleon accepted these views, and the course was set for France to become involved in Vietnam and eventually in all of Indochina.

In August 1858, Admiral Rigault de Genouilly, accompanied by Monsignor Pellerin, set sail for Vietnam, and on 1 September the French fleet began bombarding Tourane. The town was occupied the following day, but there was no sign of any uprising by the Christians; in fact the whole population had fled. Lacking indigenous labor, debilitated by tropical maladies, and bogged down by the heavy rains, the French troops were unable to move overland to Hue. In Paris the admirals, dismayed at the news, blamed the missionaries for what they considered to be a complete misrepresentation of the situation. The missionaries for their part retorted that it was the admirals' fault for not attacking in Tonkin where they would have received such support. However, Admiral Genouilly had no intention of moving north; leaving a small garrison in Tourane, he headed for the city of Saigon, which was captured in February 1859.

In April 1859 France went to war with Austria, shattering any hope Rigault de Genouilly might have had for reinforcements, and so the Tourane garrison was evacuated in March 1860. A great cloud of doubt about the efficacy of the Far East policy descended on government circles in Paris, but there were also fresh outcries for military operations to support the Saigon garrison. This time the loudest voices were not those of the missionaries and their supporters but those of politicians, military officers, merchants, and manufacturers who feared that France was in danger of losing out in its competition with the English, then making gains in Burma and China. Should the French abandon their efforts in Saigon, the English might move in to replace them. Moreover, there appeared at this time an increasingly vocal group of nationalists who espoused a new kind of "mission" for France—bringing its superior civilization to the backward yellow and black races of the world. In the Far East, so their argument ran, France with its high culture had the humane responsibility of educating and guiding people like the Vietnamese, and in order to attain this noble goal France would first have to bring these people under its benign control.

One of the most ardent advocates of this *mission civilisatrice* was the Marquis de Chasseloup-Laubat, who was named minister of the navy in mid-1860. In October of that year a large flotilla under Admiral Charner was ordered to Saigon for military operations against the Vietnamese. By June the following year the three major provinces between Saigon and the Cambodian border were in French hands. In spite of these defeats, Tu Duc was not ready to capitulate. The court mandarins advised the emperor that he could not afford to concede the loss of the three important rice-producing provinces, and that if he continued to resist the French might be forced to withdraw. There was, they pointed out, considerable grumbling in Paris over the "Cochinchina adventure," and the thinly spread French troops were suffering from physical ailments as well as harassment by guerrillas. But in November 1861 Charner was replaced by Admiral Bonard, who pushed the military campaign, capturing Bien Hoa in December and Vinh Long in March 1862. At the same time, an uprising led by Le Phung, a pretender of the Le dynasty, erupted in the Red river delta, forcing Tu Duc to deploy a portion of his forces to the north.

Both Admiral Bonard and Tu Duc were ready for negotiations and a treaty was signed in Saigon on 5 June 1862. The terms gave Christians freedom of worship throughout Vietnam. The French gained possession of Gia Dinh, Bien Hoa, and Dinh Tuong provinces, and three ports, including Tourane, were opened for French and Spanish commerce. The Vietnamese granted the French free passage up the Mekong river to the Cambodian border and agreed to pay a large indemnity for French losses in the war.[11]

Although the treaty was duly ratified in Hue, the Vietnamese struggle against the French in Cochinchina was far from over. On 16 December 1862 a revolt led by the mandarin Truong Cong Dinh burst forth in the eastern region around Go Cong, and there also were attacks on French posts close to Saigon. As the unrest spread, the forested areas to the north and east of Saigon became refuges for the insurgents. Bourotte reported that some of the Stieng north of Thu Dau Mot (Phu Cuong), as well as groups of Chrau east of Baria (Phuoc Le), joined in the struggle against the French, who reacted by mounting military campaigns in both areas.[12] Not all of the Chrau cooperated with the Vietnamese; one insurgent leader named Su was turned over to the French authorities by the highlanders only to be executed at Baria on 9 May 1863.

In western Cochinchina during this period some of the Stieng and Mnong became engulfed in dissidence originating in neighboring Cambodia. In 1861 a revolt led by Cambodian prince Sivotha broke out and lasted several years. In 1864 Assoa, a former slave who claimed to be Prince Ang Phim, son of Prince Ang Em, a rival of King Ang Chang, mounted a rebellion that came to an end in 1866. That same year there was another uprising led by a Buddhist monk named Pu Kombo who claimed to be the son of King Ang Chang. Both Moura and Maitre describe him as having been a Kui, one of the ethnic groups found in Cambodia.[13] When Pu Kombo attracted attention with his claim, he was invited to Saigon where the French kept him under surveillance, but in May 1866 he escaped to Tay Ninh in western Cochinchina. There he gathered some of the former followers of Prince Sivotha and Assoa, as well as some Vietnamese, Cham, and Stieng, and unleashed an uprising which spread along the frontier and into the neighboring Cambodian province of Baphnom. As the fighting intensified, many Khmer villagers of Kapong Siem and Baphnom provinces fled eastward into the Chhlong river area, displacing

---

11. Buttinger, *Vietnam*, pp. 79–89; Launay, *Histoire ancienne*, pp. 222–27; Le Thanh Khoi, *Le Viêt-Nam*, pp. 365–72; Taboulet, *Geste française*, 1: 378–417; 2: 431–90.

12. Bourotte, "Essai des populations Montagnardes," pp. 68–70.

13. J. Moura, *Le Royaume du Cambodge*, 2 vols. (Paris: Leroux, 1888), 2: 159; Henri Maitre, *Les Jungles Moi* (Paris: Larose, 1912), p. 492.

some Stieng and Mnong who moved farther east into higher elevations.[14] Many of the Stieng and Mnong also joined the forces of Pu Kombo. As the revolt swept into the Stieng country, Father Azémar, the French priest who in 1861 had founded a mission in Brolam near present Budop in Phuoc Long province, was forced to flee and the rebels destroyed the settlement.[15] As related earlier, Pu Kombo attempted to gain possession of the famed sacred saber of the King of Fire to enhance his prestige and guarantee him success in battle.[16]

Initial French and Cambodian efforts to crush the movement failed, but finally the tide turned against Pu Kombo. He was killed in December 1867. Two of his lieutenants, A-Nong and A-Chreng, took refuge among the Stieng, and later that year A-Chreng sent a drum and two elephant tusks to King Norodom along with a letter asking pardon for himself and his two thousand rebel followers. The Khmer ruler agreed, and A-Chreng came out of hiding. A-Nong remained a dissident until 1875, when he requested amnesty and agreed to pay Norodom an annual tribute. In accepting the offer, the king gave A-Nong the right to settle in the Stieng country.[17]

In addition to coping with dissidence in their newly won territories, the French continued to expand their sphere of control, particularly after Admiral de la Grandière became governor of Cochinchina in May 1863. With only scant support or direction from Paris, de la Grandière embarked on his own course of action and in August 1863 reached an agreement with King Norodom to place Cambodia under French protection. The agreement required the approval of the king of Siam, who had for some time determined Cambodian policy. It took four years to accomplish the feat, but a treaty was signed on 15 July 1867 in which Siam recognized a French protectorate over Cambodia and France approved Siamese annexation of the two provinces of Battambang and Siem Reap.[18]

From the beginning of the French occupation of Cochinchina, some of the younger and more adventurous French naval officers wanted to explore the remote and mysterious interior. All that was known about the Mekong river was that it originated in China, and even the native Vietnamese had no knowledge about the green, heavily forested back

14. Maitre, *Les Jungles Moi*, p. 492.
15. H. Azémar, "Les Stiengs de Brolam," *Excursions et Reconnaissances* 12, no. 27 (1886): 147–48.
16. Moura, *Royaume du Cambodge*, 1: 432–36.
17. Maitre, *Les Jungles Moi*, p. 492; Taboulet, *Geste française*, 2: 644–52.
18. Buttinger, *Vietnam*, pp. 89–90; Taboulet, *Geste française*, 2: 621–22, 653–54.

country. A group of these young naval officers began to hold informal discussions in the evenings at Cholon. One of the organizers was Francis Garnier, who had played a brief but important role in the French expansion into other areas of Indochina. A subject of particular interest to the group was the Mekong river, and in 1864 Garnier and two other officers submitted to de la Grandière a project for exploring this vast river. The plan made its way to Admiral Bonard in Paris, who forwarded it to Minister of the Navy Chasseloup-Laubat with a note pointing out the possibility of opening the Mekong to commerce, thereby making Saigon an entrepôt in trade with China and Tibet.

Approval of the plan came in 1865 and the following year an expedition led by Doudart de Lagrée with Francis Garnier as assistant departed from Kratie in Cambodia, following the river northward into Laos and into southern China. To their disappointment they found the Mekong too segmented by rapids for shipping, but they also ascertained that the Red river provided a southern access route from Tonkin into China.[19]

Although this discovery placed Tonkin in a new strategic light, nothing was done about it until 1873, when a series of dramatic events involving three diverse figures—Admiral Dupré, Francis Garnier, and Jean Depuis—took place on the Red river. In 1868 at Hankow, Depuis had met Garnier, then fresh from his adventure with the Doudart de Lagrée expedition, and Garnier had spoken fervently of bringing French glory and civilization to this part of the world. Although their meeting was brief, Garnier's account of the exploratory trip appears to have had a profound effect on Depuis, who decided to unravel the mystery of the Red river. After several journeys into the interior of China, Depuis sailed a ship full of arms and ammunition up the treacherous Red river from Hanoi into Yunnan in March 1873. There he sold his cargo at a great profit, purchasing a shipment of tin which he sold in Hanoi in May. Barred from making a second voyage, he had a group of 150 mercenaries he had recruited in China set up a headquarters in a compound of houses in Hanoi. This soon became an armed enclave.

In June 1873 some of Depuis' party raised the tricolor and fighting broke out with some Vietnamese troops. The following month Depuis appealed to Admiral Dupré, the governor of Cochinchina and a strong advocate of French control of the river. Dupré sent Francis Garnier to Hanoi with a

19. Taboulet, *Geste française*, 2: 552–55.

military force and explicit instructions to take whatever course of action he saw fit to open the Red river. Garnier joined Depuis, and on 20 November 1873 Garnier's forces captured the Hanoi citadel, subsequently conquering much of the Red river delta. On 21 December 1873, however, Garnier was killed outside Hanoi at the Paper Bridge.

A treaty was signed on 15 March 1874. The French withdrew their military force and Depuis was ousted from Tonkin. The Vietnamese recognized French control over areas they occupied in the south and also agreed to open the Red river and the ports of Hanoi, Haiphong, and Qui Nhon to commerce.[20]

It was only a question of time before France would extend control over all Vietnam. In Europe the politics of imperialism had taken hold. Moreover, following its disastrous war with Prussia, France was experiencing a period of intensive industrial development. With the demise of the Second Empire, the power of the Church gave way to the forces of commercialism, and in 1878 the German ambassador wrote that "the world of high finance rules Paris." Business and commercial circles clamored for new markets and new sources of raw materials. Under these pressures, the Third Republic, which in its earlier phase had been dominated by political groups opposed to overseas ventures, now was rapidly becoming the regime that would build France's greatest colonial empire.

Reports reaching Paris that the area was rich in coal and possibly other minerals stirred a sudden new interest in Tonkin as well as apprehension over potential inroads by other foreign powers. In 1878 England and Germany announced that they were accrediting commercial agents to deal with the Vietnamese authorities in Haiphong. In this setting, Le Myre de Vilers, a former naval officer, was named governor of Cochinchina, a post he assumed in May 1879. Soon after, commercial interests in Paris formed the Société des Mines de l'Indochine, which in the fall of 1881 sent a group of French engineers to research the anthracite coal mines at Hon Gay in Tonkin. Not long after, it was learned that the court of Hue was favorably disposed to the proposition of a Sino–British corporation for the exploitation of these mines. In March 1882, Le Myre de Vilers dispatched Captain Henri Rivière and a 233-man force to Tonkin. The events that followed were curiously similar to those earlier. On 25 April, Rivière

20. Buttinger, *Vietnam*, pp. 92–97; Le Thanh Khoi, *Le Viêt-Nam*, pp. 372–75; H. McAleavy, *Black Flags in Vietnam* (New York: Macmillan, 1968), pp. 113–46; A. Thomazi, *La Conquête de l'Indochine* (Paris: Payot, 1934), pp. 116–32.

attacked and captured the Hanoi citadel, and in the midst of the flaming city the governor Hoang Dieu hung himself. Rivière's forces set up a defense in the city but received only small reinforcements. The situation remained stable, and in February 1883 Jules Ferry, the foremost advocate of French colonial expansion, assumed the role of minister of foreign affairs. This amounted to a guarantee that Rivière's Tonkin campaign would be supported in Paris, and a month later Rivière captured the Vietnamese strongholds at Nam Dinh and Hon Gay. The royal court in Hue, mustering all the support it could get, enlisted the aid of the Black Flags, a largely Chinese band under the chieftainship of Liu Yung-fu, which swept down from the mountains to encircle Hanoi. Rivière, like Garnier, led a force out of the west gate on 19 May 1883 and, ironically, fell under the hostile gunfire of the Black Flags at Paper Bridge.

Ten days before the news of Rivière's death arrived in Paris the Chamber of Deputies voted approval of a proposition, introduced by Ferry, for funds to support a military expedition in Tonkin. In June the French government sent Jules Harmand from Saigon to Hanoi. Harmand was well qualified for the task, having participated in the Delaporte mission in Cambodia in 1873, been a companion of Francis Garnier during the 1873 events in Tonkin, and in 1876 led one of the first expeditions among the highlanders in northeastern Cochinchina.[21] Harmand's instructions were to temper the ardor of the French military in Tonkin but his presence had the opposite effect. Gloom engulfed Hue when it became apparent that the French intended to pursue their conquest. Disheartened and exhausted, Emperor Tu Duc died on 17 July 1883 after cursing the invaders who had devastated his land. French naval vessels began to shell Thuan An at the mouth of the Perfume river on 18 August, and with this threat to Hue the Vietnamese government capitulated.[22]

The convention that had been prepared by Harmand was signed in Hue on 25 August 1883. The first article declared that the government of Annam recognized the protectorate of the French, the second that the province of Binh Thuan was to be annexed to the French colony of Cochinchina. Taboulet speculates that the latter provision was the result of

21. His private papers are available in the Harmand Collection, Olin Library, Cornell University, Ithaca, New York.
22. Alfred Cobban, *A History of Modern France*, 3 vols. (Baltimore: Penguin Books, 1965), 1: 9–40; Le Thanh Khoi, *Le Viêt-Nam*, pp. 375–79; McAleavy, *Black Flags*, pp. 189–218; Taboulet, *Geste française*, 2: 755–97; Thomazi, *Conquête*, pp. 132–57.

Harmand's conviction that French control of Binh Thuan would provide a better opportunity to develop good relations with the highlanders.[23] Highlander support would enable the French to extend their control to the Mekong river. The Harmand convention was not approved by Paris. Peking protested that any treaty with Vietnam would require the approval of the Chinese ruler, and the acquisition of new territory was not viewed favorably by the French Chamber of Deputies. A revised treaty of protectorate leaving Binh Thuan part of Annam was signed on 6 June 1884 and ratified by the Chamber of Deputies on 7 May 1885.

While the events surrounding the French conquest were taking place in the lowlands, the Catholic Mission in Kontum continued to function, although at times with great difficulty. When the persecution of Christians reached a peak in the early 1850s, the mandarin at An Son in the An Khe valley made several attempts to capture the French missionaries, but they were protected by their friend Kiom, the Bahnar Bonom chief. From the time of the 1857 attack on Tourane until peace was more or less restored in 1863, the mission was very isolated, and during this period several of the priests died.[24]

The account of the mission by Dourisboure reflects something about the general situation and also about leadership among the Bahnar Jolong and neighboring groups in the mid-nineteenth century.[25] There apparently was considerable intervillage warfare as well as periodic conflict between elements of different ethnic groups. The priests found the Bahnar Jolong to be "gentle, polite, and hard-working" as compared with the neighboring Sedang who were "rough and less tractable." Sedang incursions against the Bahnar Jolong were not uncommon, and the priests helped the Bahnar villagers to organize defenses against the Sedang as well as the Jarai. There were powerful chiefs, such as Kiom and Ba Ham, who commanded considerable following in local areas. Outside such areas, the villages functioned independently of one another and there was a good deal of intervillage quarreling, often for reasons the priests viewed as insignificant. Nonetheless, there were strong kin bonds among villages, and they often entered into alliances with one another.

Writing at a much later period, Guilleminet, résident at Kontum during the late 1930s and early 1940s, speculates that prior to 1850 Bahnar society

23. Taboulet, *Geste française*, 2: 807–11.
24. Dourisboure, *Sauvages Bah-Nars*, pp. 161–71.
25. Dourisboure and Simmonet, *Vietnam*, pp. 19–51.

was in a state of "regression." The subgroups to the east were being pushed back into the remote higher elevations by the advance of the Vietnamese into places like An Khe. To the west and southwest, the Jarai were constantly attacking the Bahnar, as were the Sedang to the north and northwest. The Bahnar, Guilleminet concludes, were at this time doomed either to extinction or complete subservience to their more aggressive neighbors.[26]

The traditional *toring*, a territory shared by several villages, was an important social, economic, and political unit among the Bahnar Jolong. There also were some outstanding chiefs, and Guilleminet lists some of those reported to him by Mohr (1.6), the grandson of Kiom (1.1). Kiom himself was the recognized leader of the northern Bahnar Bonom and Bahnar Alakong. Among the Bahnar Golar, the chiefs were two brothers, Sam and San. Farther south, the Bahnar Ayun followed a leader named Duon, who was assisted by Han, the husband of his younger sister.[27] Finally, the chief of the Bahnar Bonom of the south and the Bahnar Tolo was Yom, who died around 1860 without a successor. Mohr informed Guilleminet that these chiefs were independent of one another but because of their constant quarrels and destructive conflicts their authority eroded, much to the advantage of the village chiefs whose power increased.

26. Paul Guilleminet, *Coutumier de la tribu Bahnar des Sedang et des Jarai de la Province de Kontum*, 2 vols. (Paris: Ecole Française d'Extrême-Orient, 1952), 1: 17–27.

27. This must be a reference to the Bahnar Kon Kodeh, who are located in the vicinity of the Ayun river.

7 FRENCH EXPLORATION OF THE HIGHLANDS, 1876–1895

The opening of the Kontum Mission had shed some light on the mountainous interior of Annam, but generally there was little known about the heavily forested upland expanse between the Mekong river and the coast of the South China Sea. Although Fathers Juget, Faulet, and Grillet had penetrated the southwestern portion of the highlands occupied by the Stieng, they left no accounts. This also was the case with Father Vuillaume, who fled the anti-Christian persecutions at Phan Rang in 1865 to take refuge on the Djiring plateau where the Maa and Sre live.[1]

Following the Tonkin events of 1873, there was an upsurge of interest in exploring the uplands. Jules Harmand, Néis and Septans, Lieutenant Amédée Gautier, Paul Nouet, Naval Ensign Humann, and the French administrator Navelle all led expeditions. The most bizarre of the explorers was Charles David, better known as Mayréna, whose adventurous exploits—not the least of which was his founding the Kingdom of the Sedang with himself as its ruler—contributed to the extension of French control over the highlands. Others who went to the highlands in this early period included Captain Cupet, a member of the Pavie Mission, and Dr. Alexandre Yersin, a pioneer in establishing western medicine in Vietnam. By the end of the nineteenth century, the beginning of a French administration had been organized in parts of the highlands, ushering in a new era for many of the mountain people as they experienced for the first time the ways of the modern world.

---

1. Msgr. Cassaigne, "Les Mois de la région de Djiring," *Indochine*, no. 131 (1943), p. 11.

JULES HARMAND

The first official expedition into upland Cochinchina was conducted in 1876 by Jules Harmand, a navy doctor and naturalist who had participated in the Tonkin events and, as noted above, had also been involved in the politics of the French conquest. This expedition, sanctioned by the governor of Cochinchina, traveled up the Dong Nai river in the area northeast of Saigon to obtain information on the geography, flora, fauna, and ethnic groups (generally referred to collectively in French reports and accounts as "les sauvages" or "les Mois"). Accompanying Harmand was another French naval doctor named Vergnians, whose account of the journey contains some perceptive observations about the organization of such expeditions.[2]

Harmand obtained a large junk owned by the director of the Saigon Botanical Garden for the first phase of the journey. He also engaged a Chinese assistant named A-Hoi who was "calm, intelligent, and an adept hunter," a Vietnamese cook who was "a brave man but an inferior scrounger," and an interpreter named Tay who was "very sharp but lazy." An escort of Cambodian soldiers occupied the spacious cabin, and eight rowers guided the junk as it moved with the strong incoming tide upstream to Bien Hoa on 5 November 1876. There Harmand obtained some oxen and carts, and the provincial administrator provided him with a large sheet of paper covered with "Chinese characters" (probably old Vietnamese *chữ nôm*) and many seals and stamps. Vergnians observed that the writing was not important since most village chiefs were unable to read it, but that it was the stamps and seals that impressed the rural population. Harmand carried a seal with him on all of his journeys, so that when he encountered opposition to such things as requisitioning quarters, he immediately produced a paper copiously stamped. Invariably, all opposition crumbled.

With the tide in their favor, the junk sailed from Bien Hoa on 8 November 1876, and Vergnians noted that the banks of the Dong Nai river were lined with sugar cane plantations. They passed a large abandoned sugar mill that had been constructed by the French with European equipment at great expense only to have the Vietnamese planters

2. H. Vergnians, "Souvenirs d'un médecin de Marine en Cochinchine: une excursion chez les Mois en 1876 (extraits des lettres du Dr. H. Vergnians à sa famille)," Harmand Collection, Olin Library, Cornell University, Ithaca, New York.

refuse to bring their cane to what they considered to be a strange, forbidding establishment. The machinery had been sold to a Dutch company in Batavia. Farther along the river they passed the property of a Frenchman named Blanchy who had introduced coffee trees in Cochinchina but after pests destroyed his crop had shifted to pepper production.[3] At six o'clock in the evening the junk stopped at a small potters' village, and after Harmand made a few purchases they continued up the river.

On 11 November they reached the confluence of the Dong Nai and Song Be, where they disembarked to study the flora and fauna, hunt small game, and investigate local streams in pirogues. The junk was docked, and the expedition moved on in oxcarts. After a day of travel they came upon a curious house in a forest clearing. Its owner proved to be an elderly, very hostile Vietnamese who refused to be impressed by Harmand's stamped paper. Nonetheless, they camped on his property and as the cook prepared their evening meal (cold sausage, curried chicken, rice, and a chocolate dessert) they learned from their unwilling host that they would have to walk the narrow forest paths to the nearest highlander villages. Following this advice, the next day they reached a village of "half civilized" highlanders. The chief, whom Vergnians describes as "an authentic Moi" (because he was garbed in a loincloth and carried a crossbow), informed them that he and his people called themselves "Khero"—probably a variation of "Chrau," which means "highlander" in the language of the Chrau-speaking people now found in the area this expedition had reached.

The chief agreed to be their guide. Several days later they found themselves on the edge of another village where men in loincloths, carrying spears, greeted them. Harmand presented gifts of knives, glass beads, and other cheap jewelry, obtaining in return some cloth and artifacts. After several days of getting samples of plants, taking physical measurements of the villagers, and recording ethnographic information, the party made its way back to the junk and by the end of November they were in Saigon. On 10 December 1876, Harmand departed for Laos, where he undertook another expedition.

With the goal of reaching Hue from the Mekong river, Harmand set out in April 1877 from the river town of Bassac, continuing to Khemmerat by boat. Then more or less following the Bang Hien river, he made his

---

3. This was Paul Blanchy, who later became a celebrated champion of French businessmen in Cochinchina.

way into the mountains, carefully taking notes on geography, flora and fauna, and the highlander villages encountered. He described one group called Tao-oi, who still are found on the Laotian side of the Ai Lao pass, and he also came upon some Bru villages, although they would appear to have been located farther west than they have been in recent times.[4]

In the vicinity of Muong Phine, Harmand found a number of Phuthai villages. As noted earlier, at some indeterminate period around the end of the seventeenth century, this area had been invaded by Phuthai and Sue, who divided the territory into the muongs of Vang, Champone, Tchepone, and Phong. Initially under the kingdom of Vientiane, these muongs subsequently had tributary relations with the court of Hue.[5] Harmand found that the muong of Tchepone continued to pay tribute of silver, wax, resins, and ivory to the Vietnamese court. In order to maintain good relations with the Lao, however, the chief of Tchepone periodically sent the Chau muong of Khemmerat a bronze cooking pot. The Phuthai also served as trade intermediaries between the Lao and Vietnamese. The Vietnamese merchants brought fish sauce, salted fish, bronze cooking pots, sabers, and spearheads into the Phuthai country to trade for buffalos, cattle, elephants, and forest products.

Crossing the Ai Lao pass, Harmand descended to Cam Lo on the coastal plain, noting the market there attracted highlanders and Phuthai, who purchased bronze cooking pots and arms which they carried to their mountain villages on their backs. Harmand continued to Quang Tri and ended his expedition in Hue on 14 August 1877.[6]

In the course of this expedition, Harmand had come upon examples of slavery, finding both Vietnamese and highlanders who had been captured and sold to Lao slave traders.[7] No doubt as a result of this experience, Harmand in 1879 wrote a treatise deploring slavery in Indochina.[8] In it he concluded that the slave trade consisted primarily of lowlanders hunting down the "savage" populations of the interior, selling them into slavery.

4. Jules Harmand, "Rapport sur une mission en Indo-Chine de Bassac à Hué (16 Avril-14 Août, 1877)," *Archives des Missions Scientifiques et Littéraires* 5 (1879): 247–62.

5. M. Damprun, "Monographie de la province de Savannakhet (Laos Française)," *BSEI*, 1904, pp. 23–71.; Henri Maitre, *Les Jungles Moi* (Paris: Larose, 1912), pp. 465–67.

6. Harmand, "Rapport sur une mission," pp. 272–81; Jules Harmand, "De Bassac à Hué (Avril-Août 1877)," *Bulletin de la Société de Géographie*, January 1879, pp. 97–104.

7. Harmand, "De Bassac à Hué," pp. 86–89.

8. Jules Harmand, "Conference sur la traîte des sauvages Indo-Chinois et les moyens de la supprimer," February 1879, Harmand Collection, Olin Library, Cornell University, Ithaca, New York.

He recommended that the slave markets in Bangkok and Phnom Penh be closed, pointing out that Admiral Dupiere had received assurances from King Norodom that slavery in Cambodia would be abolished. Harmand also recommended that there be surveillance to guarantee that commerce in slaves not be continued.

The slave trade in the highlands at this time also received attention from some French administrators. In May 1880 Silvestre, chief of indigenous justice, submitted a report on slavery to the governor of Cochinchina.[9] In it he described how Vietnamese and Chinese merchants trading with villagers in the mountainous zone from Quang Nam to Binh Thuan also purchased slaves which were then sold in Annam. Silvestre cited several French sources which described trade in slaves in other parts of Cochinchina, particularly in the area north and northeast of Saigon.

NÉIS AND SEPTANS

Prompted more by economic motives than a concern for slavery, Le Myre de Vilers developed a great interest in exploration of the remote northeastern regions of the colony after becoming governor of Cochinchina in 1879. This led to the expedition of French naval doctor Néis and Lieutenant Septans, who departed from Bien Hoa on 11 February 1880 hoping to find the source of the Dong Nai river. The party proceeded upriver to the confluence with the Song Be, as did Harmand in 1876, but Néis and Septans continued deeper into the uplands, following first the La Nga river and then the Houei. Although they never did succeed in finding the source of the Dong Nai, they did collect information on the geography of the area—particularly the hydrography of the rivers—and Néis collected physical measurements of the highland people they met. The most important group they found was described in their account as the Traos Tioma—probably a variation of "Chrau Cau Maa," meaning the highlander Cau Maa since *chrau* simply means "highlander"—a group found in the vicinity of Bao Loc (Blao).[10] This is substantiated by Boubet's observation that Néis and Septans, as well as other French explorers, reached the southern Maa country occupied by the Drung and Cau Maa. In

9. M. Silvestre, "Rapport sur l'esclavage," *Excursions et Reconnaissances*, no. 14 (1880), pp. 95–144.
10. Paul Néis and Lt. Septans, "Rapport sur un voyage d'exploration aux sources du Dong-Nai," *Excursions et Reconnaissances*, no. 10 (1881): 15–80.

some cases, the French penetrated the western area where the Maa Too live.[11]

Néis and Septans also mention the Traos Baria, apparently a reference to highlanders in the vicinity of Baria (Phuoc Le), and the Traos Lays. Conceivably the term *Lays* might be derived from *palay*, a component of some of the designations like Palay Jro and Palay Vajieng for some of the Chrau-speaking people. The explorers were informed that farther north there were the Late, more than likely the Lat people in the area of present Dalat, and the Rde, probably a variation of Rhadé. At the confluence of the Dong Nai and Houei, they came upon groups called the Traos Lacang-dong and the Chop, neither of which can be identified with any present groups.

Between 15 May and 15 June 1880 Dr. Néis conducted anthropological research among the highlanders in Baria province at the behest of the governor of Cochinchina. The result was some detailed information on physical types found among the "moi" in the northern part of the province as well as some ethnographic data. Also, Néis reported that there were twenty-one highlander villages under French authority and that they paid a "light tribute" to the colonial government, as they had previously to the court of Hue.[12]

A communication from a member of the governor's cabinet to Dr. Harmand dated 16 April 1880 relates that as of 16 February Néis and Septans had reached the area just north of the La Nga river at the frontier of the "Mois of Bien Hoa" and the "Mois of the king Patao," and it noted that the Patao appears to be some kind of undisputed leader of the region.[13] As it turned out, Néis and Septans had passed through the area ruled by the chief called Patao, although they never actually met him. After their return to Saigon, Le Myre de Vilers was informed that a "king" of the Tioma (Cau Maa) country intended to visit him and discuss possible commercial relations with the French. The governor assigned Néis and Septans the

11. Jean Boulbet, *Pays des Maa domaine des génies Nggar Maa, Nggar Yaang* (Paris: Ecole Française d'Extrême-Orient, 1967), p. 78.

12. Paul Néis, "Rapport sur une excursion scientifique chez le Mois de l'Arrondissement de Baria du 15 Mai au 15 Juin 1880," in *Variétés sur le pays Mois* (Saigon: Gouvernement de la Cochinchine, 1935), pp. 1–30.

13. Cabinet de Gouverneur, Gouvernement de la Cochinchine à Dr. Jules Harmand, Saigon, 16 April 1880, Harmand Collection, Olin Library, Cornell University, Ithaca, New York. It was noted previously that *potao*—and cognates thereof in Cham and several highland languages—means "king," "lord," or "master." In a primer of the Chrau language, Bô Quốc-Gia Giáo-Dục (Ministry of Education), *Chrau* (Saigon, 1964), p. 59, *patau* is listed as meaning *vua* (king) in Vietnamese.

responsibility of meeting this "king," who soon identified himself as Patao. He was accompanied by twelve highland chiefs, several of whom Néis and Septans recognized as chiefs of villages they had visited, as well as by a Chinese merchant interested in trade with the highlanders. The two explorers noted that Patao was taller than the others and clearly exercised considerable authority over them. He told the two Frenchmen that when they came through his domain he remained in hiding, although he had ordered his chiefs to assist them in their journey to Binh Thuan.[14]

AMÉDÉE GAUTIER

Le Myre de Vilers then sponsored three more expeditions, all of which began in 1882. One was conducted by Lieutenant Amédée Gautier, and there are several relatively detailed accounts of his venture. Less well documented is the expedition of civil administrator Nouet, and the third expedition leader, another civil servant named Carrau, wrote only a short article on commerce and agriculture among highlanders (although he never specified which highlanders).[15]

The governor selected thirty-one-year-old Amédée Gautier, a lieutenant in the Infanterie de Marine, to conduct an expedition into the area surveyed by Néis and Septans. In a letter to Gautier dated 3 February 1881 Le Myre de Vilers specified that he would like the expedition to travel northward from Bien Hoa to the east of the Dong Nai, as Néis and Septans had done, and, if possible, to push as far north as Hue. He also alerted the lieutenant to the possibility that he would meet a "Moi chief" of Laotian origin (the Patao) who had visited Saigon the previous year. The governor considered this chief an intelligent man whom Gautier would find useful and he promised to send a photograph for identification. The governor particularly wanted Gautier to find out about the origin of the populations of the area—"the Stiengs, Benons, Banards, Mois, etc." (*Benons* may be a reference to Mnong while *Banards* probably means Bahnar.) Although the highlanders were quite gentle, the governor continued, he recommended great prudence in approaching them because they had been tracked down like beasts by Lao, Vietnamese, and Cambodian slave hunters and con-

14. Néis and Septans, "Rapport sur un voyage," p. 15.
15. P. Carrau, "Du Commerce et de l'agriculture chez les Mois," in *Variétés sur le pays Mois* (Saigon: Gouvernement de la Cochinchine, 1935), pp. 60–83.

sequently were apt to be unduly suspicious: "at the least act of brutality they flee, leaving one abandoned without necessities and transport." The letter ended with the advice that Gautier take along proper medicines regardless of the confidence he might have in his own health.

Gautier purchased medicines, firearms, tools, and cloth to exchange with the highlanders for food and also obtained a sampan with a roof. With his two assistants (one of whom was Mani, a young man of mixed Chinese, Cambodian, Javanese, and Indian parentage), his dog, and a map prepared by Dutreuil de Rhins, he set out from Bien Hoa on 5 February 1882. Going northwest on the Dong Nai, they reached the confluence of the Song Be, where they came upon the establishment of Tong Hen, a Vietnamese-Chinese of some seventy-five years who seemed to function as the canton chief. He came forward with both hands extended to greet Gautier, inviting him into his house which was set in a lush plantation. The guest was given a room and copious meals. But after three days Gautier realized that Tong Hen was successfully keeping from him all of the information he desired concerning the source of the Dong Nai river.

The young explorer also became aware that Tong Hen's authority derived from the fact that he had a great many of the highlanders in the vicinity indentured to him. He bought rice from the poor villagers and then in lean times sold it back to them at exorbitant prices, plunging them into debt. Some worked in his extensive gardens, and villagers provided him with pirogues and ox carts. In return, Tong Hen kept them supplied with salt, tools, and adornments and provided security against famine and bandits. His wives maintained his household and he took many of the attractive local girls as concubines. Gautier noted that throughout the country of the Tioma (Cau Maa) and on the right bank of the Dong Nai, Tong Hen's sons looked after his interests.

Tong Hen tried unsuccessfully to dissuade Gautier from following his plan to continue northward on the Dong Nai into the country of the "grands Mois" (probably a reference to the larger ethnic groups such as the Rhadé and Jarai). The lieutenant did agree, however, to accept Tong Hen's two nephews as guides. As they set out on foot, the two guides, following the secret orders of their wily uncle, led Gautier to the northeast rather than to the north. When he realized this deception and accused them of it, they steadfastly refused to change directions. Then the highlanders in the escort voiced their refusal to go northward saying they feared tigers and evil spirits. When Gautier sought to reassure them by claiming to have powerful talismans to counteract the spirits, they retorted that, even if that were true, it was now the dry season and in the forests to the north there would be no water sources. Leaving most of the party in place, Gautier took a small band of highlanders to investigate the country immediately to the north but found that there were no paths and indeed no water sources. Plagued by leeches, wood ticks, and scorpions, he finally elected to return to Tong Hen's plantation.

On 22 February 1882 Gautier set out again, attaining the confluence of the Houei river. Left at camp while his escort returned to Tong Hen's plantation for additional supplies, he explored the vicinity and along the Dong Nai came upon the remains of a "military road" as well as traces of what he thought must have been an encampment. From these vestiges Gautier estimated that the encampment could have contained at least twelve thousand men and concluded that it had probably been constructed by the armies of Gia Long as they moved from central Vietnam into the Mekong river delta.[16] Visiting the site a few years later, Maitre saw in these remains evidence of the Vietnamese military expansion southward, bypassing the Cham enclave at Panduranga, to destroy what still existed of the "Ma Confederation" (see chap. 3).[17]

Gautier returned to Tri An and soon afterward left on yet another expedition toward the northwest, this time carrying only a small supply of rice and taking with him only a highlander guide, his servant Mani, and a dog named Bismark. But he found himself blocked by impenetrable forests and had to return to Tong Hen's establishment. Not discouraged by these failures, Gautier wrote in his account that he now felt sufficiently conditioned to perform his role as an explorer very well and that Tong Hen was wickedly testing his constitution by plying him with heavy pastries in the vain hope of making him ill. The lieutenant's next goal was to locate the source of the Houei river, so he set off anew with a guide, Mani, the dog Bismark, and an oxcart containing some supplies. Misfortune overtook the explorer, first when hostile highlanders (he fails to identify them) refused to provide him with food and then when his guide abandoned him. He constructed a shelter by a small river, but his supplies of rice, tinned sardines, and

16. Maurice Dubourg, "Une tentative de colonisation en pays Moi: la mission d'Amédée Gautier," *Revue d'Histoire des Colonies* 37 (1950): 101–06; Amédée Gautier, "Voyage au pays des Mois," *Excursions et Reconnaissances*, no. 14 (1882), pp. 219–24; idem, "Voyage au pays des Mois accompli en Février, Avril, Mai et Juin 1882," in *Variétés sur le pays Mois* (Saigon: Gouvernement de la Cochinchine, 1935), pp. 31–59.

17. Maitre, *Les Jungles Moi*, pp. 463–64.

Dutch cheese ran out and he had to subsist by hunting wild hares, monkeys, and iguanas until Mani could get to Saigon and back with supplies. All the while Gautier staunchly conducted explorations into the surrounding country, recording information on geography and local highlanders. Le Myre de Vilers sent the explorer a message dated 26 May 1882 advising him to take care of himself. He also noted that the administration was very interested in maintaining good relations with the "savage populations" because one day they all would be grouped under a French protectorate encompassing the territory from the Red river in the north to the Dong Nai river in the south.

When Gautier returned to Saigon on 26 June, he found that although the governor was occupied with "the Tonkin question" he was interested in having Gautier continue his expeditions, primarily to find out more about the activities of the court of Hue in the frontier zone between Binh Thuan province and the French colonial province of Baria. In his "ordre de mission" the governor directed Gautier to proceed to the frontier of Cochinchina to ascertain the boundary of the colony and also to visit Patao, the self-proclaimed "king of the Moi," to see what information could be gotten from him. Proceeding into the La Nga river region, Gautier met Patao at Tra Cu and found him to be unusually tall, thin, and quickwitted. On his left arm he bore a curious tattoo depicting a crowned figure of an Indian-style warrior clutching a scepter or rod. Patao, who appeared to be of Lao origin, had been in the area some ten years and had established himself at the base of Mount Ong in present Binh Tuy province.

The Frenchman built himself a small house on the banks of the La Nga river and obtained some livestock and chickens. He learned that, although Patao was a recognized leader, his brigandage had lost him many followers who had rallied to a Vietnamese competitor named Huong Pho. A band of highlanders had attacked Patao, forcing him to retreat to the summit of Mount Ong. It was at this point that Néis and Septans had visited the area. Subsequently, when Patao was welcomed in Saigon by Le Myre de Vilers, his prestige was more or less restored.

On instructions from the governor, Gautier began a series of explorations northwest of Mount Ong, reaching the territory occupied by the Benons (this could be a variation of Mnong) and Beleus (possibly a reference to the Bulo, a subgroup of the Stieng).[18] Boulbet lists Gautier as

18. Dubourg, "Tentative de colonisation," pp. 106–28; Gautier, "Voyage," *Excursions et Reconnaissances*, pp. 224–49.

one of the French explorers who got to the country of the Krung, Cau Too, and Cau Maa (all subgroups of the Maa) and to the Stieng area.[19]

The governor also instructed the lieutenant to keep an eye on Patao, since he might be of service to the French, but it was Patao who saw the possibility of Gautier being of service to Patao. He proposed to the Frenchman that he join him in some of his raids on nearby rich villages. The clever Lao pointed out that it would lend Gautier, who had neither wives nor slaves, the prestige he badly needed. In raiding the villages they would not only realize enough rice to fill their granaries for three years but also net some beautiful girls and strong buffalo. Gautier rejected the proposal, and soon Patao announced that he had to go to his fifth wife's mother's funeral. When he returned several days later, he had large quantities of paddy, a group of young women, and a small herd of buffalo. All of these, he explained, were part of his inheritance from his late mother-in-law. Not long after, envoys of the mandarins of Binh Thuan came to Patao to contract an alliance and offered him women and buffalo. Patao smiled graciously and replied that he would gladly accept the buffalo but not the women because they were ugly. He advised the envoys to take the women back to Binh Thuan, warning that if they returned their heads would be chopped off. Patao explained to Gautier that the women were prostitutes, who would betray him. Besides, he added, if he wanted Vietnamese women, he did not have to rely on the Binh Thuan mandarins to obtain them.

In January 1883, while Gautier was still conducting his expeditions, Le Myre de Vilers was recalled to France and replaced by Charles Thompson. The new governor was not enthusiastic about Gautier's expeditions. The Director of the Interior, however, helped to alter his attitude by pointing out that Gautier was providing useful intelligence on the strategic region along the Binh Thuan frontier. On 16 April 1883 Gautier submitted a report to Governor Thompson in which he described a deteriorating situation in the region. Chinese bandits had been stealing livestock and Vietnamese insurgents had installed themselves in the mountains and in the Dong Nai river basin. They could, he warned, move on Bien Hoa and take the French by surprise. He requested that a French sergeant and three or four men patrol the area, but the governor refused and suggested that he return to Saigon. When Gautier was informed that he would have to go back to France, he paid a last visit to Patao. Among the possessions he

19. Boulbet, *Pays des Maa*, p. 78.

divided among the highlanders and Patao were eighty bottles of wine. Putting some quinine into each bottle, Gautier advised them to drink small quantities of the mixture to ward off fevers. The explorer then reported to Saigon, where he was promoted to captain before departing for France.[20]

PAUL NOUET

Another expedition commissioned by Governor Le Myre de Vilers in 1882 was led by Paul Nouet, an administrator for the civil services. The primary purpose of this effort was to examine the frontier zone so as to define the border between Cochinchina and Annam. Nouet was also instructed to investigate a charge of buffalo theft which had been brought by Patao. Riding a horse and escorted by a French lieutenant and thirty Vietnamese riflemen, he left Bien Hoa on 22 April 1882. The party proceeded to Tri An and then followed the La Nga river to reach Patao's installation at the base of Mount Ong. According to Nouet, Patao had been placed under French protection, and no settlements were permitted in a zone between fifteen to twenty kilometers along the La Nga river.

In his report Nouet includes considerable information on the geography, particularly those features that figured in the four different border lines he presents. His observations regarding the local highlanders reflect the evaluations of a French civil servant. For example, he observes that they had no idea of the future and lived from day to day. They also had no law or religion. He found their houses to be miserable hovels, and he disapprovingly noted that there was much swidden farming in spite of its having been forbidden by a decree dated 15 September 1875. He also found Patao to be an unsavory figure who drank a good deal of the time and was given to sudden outbursts of temper.

Nouet also pointed out that although the French had been in Cochinchina over twenty years a "frontier policy" had never been artic-

20. Dubourg, "Tentative de colonisation," pp. 128–38. This source reports that Gautier subsequently returned to Tonkin to participate in military operations there and also spent some time in Annam. In 1901 he retired in the Charente-Inférieure, and in 1933 he was reported to have left the hospital of Jonzac and disappeared. Curiously, in Bernard Bourotte, "Essai d'histoire des populations Montagnardes du Sud-Indochinois jusqu'à 1945," *BSEI* 30, no. 1 (1955): 71, Gautier is described as having participated in the topographic mission to determine the route for the trans-Indochina railroad, later leaving the army to become a colonist, at which point he died of malaria. In Henri Lamagat, *Souvenirs d'un vieux journaliste Indochinois*, 3 vols. (Saigon: SILI, 1942), 3: 10, it is reported that Gautier returned to the highlands while still a military officer and was fatally attacked by a leopard.

ulated. During that time small Vietnamese colonies had sprung up east of Bien Hoa in the midst of the forest area inhabited by highlanders. The Vietnamese traded copper drums for animal pelts, wax, and honey. Although he felt that contact with the Vietnamese was for the most part harmful to the highlanders, Nouet felt that their complete isolation would only result in their eventual disappearance.[21]

M. R. HUMANN

On 4 February 1884 Naval Ensign M. R. Humann set out from Baria to explore the La Nga river, proceeding first to Dat Do and from there up to Trinh Ba and Thanh Ta. Reaching Tanh Linh, Humann moved on to the base of Mount Ong, where he found the village of Tra Cu and the establishment of Patao. The explorer also came upon the ruins of the hut that Gautier had lived in until mid-1883. The highlander houses around it were abandoned; the only people living in the vicinity were four or five "sick, dirty, and rapacious" Chinese. Humann also met Patao, who supplied him with horses and agreed to accompany him as a guide. On 20 February they departed in a northeasterly direction into the area where the La Nga is known as the Rgna river. Although primarily concerned with geography, particularly the hydrography of the La Nga river and its tributaries, Humann nonetheless gathered information on the physical appearance and costumes of the highlanders, although he failed to report any names for them.[22] According to Boulbet, Humann was one of the French explorers who reached the Maa country.[23]

On 28 February 1884 Humann arrived at the Yang Yut mountain to find what he considered to be the source of the La Nga river. Turning south, he came upon the route to Binh Thuan used by Néis and Septans. At one point Humann and Patao stopped at a poverty-stricken highlander village that had recently been raided by Vietnamese. Many of the inhabitants still bore marks on their backs from rattan rod blows administered by the raiders in an attempt to get the inhabitants to disclose where they had

21. P. Nouet, "Excursion chez les Mois de la frontière nord-est," *Excursions et Reconnaissances*, no. 19 (1884), pp. 5–26.

22. M. R. Humann, "Excursion chez les Moi Indépendants," *Excursions et Reconnaissances*, no. 19 (1884), pp. 27–37.

23. Boulbet, *Pays des Maa*, p. 78.

hidden their cattle, horses, and elephant tusks. Afterward Humann and his party made their way back to Patao's village. From there the Frenchman followed the trails to Baria, arriving on 6 March 1884.[24]

NAVELLE

On 14 December 1884 Navelle, the administrator for indigenous affairs, departed on a journey that would take him from Qui Nhon to Kontum and then back to the coast. Riding on horseback, he was accompanied by a sizable military escort with porters and packhorses carrying supplies. They ascended into the highlands, passing through the An Khe valley. As they continued westward, they entered the area west of present Pleiku town. It had been arranged that Navelle would meet Father Vialleton, Superior of the Kontum Mission at the village of Pim, the son of the Bahnar Bonom chief Kiom (1.1 and 1.5). According to Navelle, Kiom had been forced by some of his enemies to leave the Bonom area and move northeast into the Golar country to settle in a village close to the residence of Ba Ham, the Golar chief with whom the priests had stayed on their journey to set up the Kontum Mission. Although Kiom died before he could gain revenge on his enemies, he imbued his son Pim with the resolve to do so.

Accompanied by his loyal kinsmen, Pim returned to his native country but encountered no opposition from any of his father's remaining enemies. Then, in spite of longstanding enmity between the Bahnar and Jarai, Pim befriended a young Jarai Hodrung chief, whom he persuaded to join in an alliance which developed into a kind of confederation. Navelle found Pim to be an impressive leader, "young, handsome, brave, eloquent, and confident in the future." He observed, however, that Pim's young Jarai ally was less gifted and was susceptible to jealousy, although Pim displayed great tact in dealing with him. Navelle considered it curious that in spite of his great prestige, Pim wore nothing to distinguish him from other Bahnar males. He was garbed in a loincloth with the traditional toga-like loose wrap draped over his shoulder. His house was longer than any other in the village but this was because of the large number of occupants. Six compartments were occupied by various kin and slaves, and there was one large

24. Humann, "Les Moi Indépendants," pp. 37–42.

room where on 17 December 1884 Navelle and Father Vialleton were received by Pim.

They sat by an open hearth as smoke billowed through the rooms from the preparations being made for a celebration in their honor. Pim shot with his crossbow one of the many chickens scampering around by the house, then called for musical instruments. Gongs were removed from their rattan containers and struck as Pim beat a large drum suspended from the rafters, filling the air with resonant music. While some of the men performed a dance depicting war, more logs were put on the fire, roasted chickens were brought in, and alcohol jars were readied. Bamboo tubes were inserted into the jars and Pim invited the two visitors to drink, after which they were proffered pieces of chicken. The following day Pim took the Frenchmen around the village, walking through newly cleared fields of dry rice, maize, tobacco, and millet. The chief put a dried leaf on a tree trunk to use as a target and invited Navelle to demonstrate his firearms. The Bahnar leader, duly impressed with the force and accuracy of the weapons, declared, "You are not the sons of men, you are the sons of gods."

Navelle and his party continued to Kontum and the nearby village of Kon Klor where there was reported to be an elegantly worked bronze statue but found the figure gone (see chap. 3). On 28 December 1884 Navelle visited the village of Kon Dia, located on the site of the present Kontum market, to meet a local Bahnar leader named Up (1.2). He was welcomed to Up's elaborate house with a jar of alcohol and a meal.[25] Hiar, an elderly informant and leader in the Kontum area (1.7), called Up the most renowned chief in the vicinity of Kontum during the late nineteenth century. He was the eldest of three brothers—the other two were Hma and Ye, Hiar's paternal grandfather (1.2, 1.3, 1.4). Up was known for his courage and his remarkable ability to organize the Bahnar Jolong chiefs into a cooperative defense network to ward off attacks by the neighboring Sedang and Jarai. His wealth included land, cattle, and slaves.

Leaving Kontum, Navelle entered the Jarai country. Attacked there by warriors from Plei Tio, the party suffered one dead and nine wounded. Finally on 16 January 1885 they reached Qui Nhon.[26]

25. E. Navelle, "De Thi-Nai au Bla," *Excursions et Reconnaissances* 13, no. 30 (1887): 218–39, 291–95.

26. J. B. Guerlach, *"L'Oeuvre néfaste," réplique du Père J. B. Guerlach, missionnaire apostolique au F. Camille Paris, colon en Annam* (Saigon: Imprimerie Commerciale, 1905), pp. 94–95.

MAYRÉNA

By far the most bizarre mission into the mountains was led by a Frenchman named Charles David who called himself Baron de Mayréna and is referred to in the literature simply as Mayréna. He had served in the French army in Cochinchina in 1862 as well as in the Franco-Prussian war of 1870–71. In May 1885 at the age of forty-three he arrived in Saigon ostensibly en route to Atjeh, the sultanate in northern Sumatra, to search for gutta percha, then much in demand in Europe. Once in Saigon, Mayréna informed French officials that his "scientific expedition" to Sumatra was really a secret mission to pass arms to the Atjehnese rebels engaged in a struggle against the Dutch.

Mayréna proposed that while in Cochinchina he would be willing to investigate the restless Binh Thuan-Baria border area. Gaining official approval, he set out from Bien Hoa in June 1885, returning in July. His report related that in a small village near the frontier he had learned that a mandarin held sway with an armed force of fifty men. Mayréna had hired two Vietnamese bandits to spy on the mandarin and his activities. Just as Mayréna was ending his trip, the Revolt of the Literati broke out in Annam.

It all began on 3 July when General de Courcy arrived in Hue to take command of the French expeditionary force, asserting his authority in a manner the Vietnamese considered brutal and arrogant. Anger, mixed with fear, spread among the mandarins at the royal court with their realization that the French might usurp what remained of their prerogatives. On the night of 5 July, Ton That Thuyet, regent for Emperor Ham Nghi, ordered imperial troops to attack the French concession. De Courcy's forces routed the attackers and occupied the royal palace. But Ham Nghi and the court had fled to Quang Tri, and from there they hurried into the highlands as Ham Nghi called for a general uprising. This triggered the Revolt of the Literati, so called because it was led by the mandarins. Vietnamese Christians as well as the French were the targets of the uprising and between July and October 1885 some 24,000 Christians, including French and Vietnamese clergymen, were tortured and slaughtered. In September the French replaced Ham Nghi with Dong Khanh, but the former continued to lead the resistance from his highland redoubt among the Mnong people.[27]

27. Jean Marquet, "Un aventurier du XIXe siècle: Marie Ier, Roi des Sédangs (1888–1890)," *Bulletin des Amis du Vieux Hué* 14, nos. 1–2 (1927): 1–18; Marcel Ner, "Review of Jean Marquet, 'Un aventurier du XIXe siècle: Marie Ier, Roi des Sédangs (1888–1890),' *Bulletin des Amis du Vieux Hué*,

Mayréna succeeded in gaining approval for another trip into northern Baria in October 1885. He visited the same area as before and reported additional evidence of local support for the insurgents, this time even among the highlanders (probably Chrau-speaking people). For example, he came upon a communal house that was furnished with beds, tables, and chairs, which he interpreted as evidence that they were housing rebels. In his report, Mayréna recommended that the troubled area be secured by placing it in the hands of a civil administration led by someone experienced with the problem. He also suggested the creation of agricultural colonies along the northern zone of Cochinchina. He noted that past expeditions into the "moi country," such as that conducted by Gautier, were unsuccessful at winning the support of the highlanders because these populations were more primitive than at present. He also noted that Patao had asked for French protection, an indication that some of the leaders were favorable to the French. In a second report dated 18 November 1885 Mayréna summarized the relations that had existed between the highlanders and the French, concluding that by and large the administration had ignored this segment of the population. He felt that if more were known about them they could be won over to the French side and that this would bring better security to the border area. Mayréna's views were given some recognition by the officials in Saigon, but nothing came of them.

Mayréna's next project was the establishment of a "plantation" at Thuan Bien on the coast in Baria province, not far from the Binh Thuan border where he claimed to be experimenting with gutta percha trees while keeping an eye on border activities. Conflict with the French province chief led to an investigation of Mayréna's plantation that revealed a large cache of arms, but no charges were brought. Mayréna abandoned the project and went to Cambodia, where he unsuccessfully tried to interest King Norodom in forming a Royal River Navigation Company.

Mayréna returned to Saigon and in November 1887 sent to Constans, the first governor general of the newly formed Indochinese Union, a proposal to conduct an expedition among the "independent moi." He described the highlanders living in the territory of western Binh Dinh between the coastal plain and the Mekong river as being "exploited by the Siamese and Lao." [28]

1927, and Maurice Soulié, *Marie Ier, Roi des Sédangs, 1888–1890*, Paris, Marpon et Cie., 1927," *BEFEO* 27 (1928): 308–17; Le Thanh Khoi, *Le Viêt-Nam: histoire et civilisation* (Paris: Les Editions de Minuit, 1955), pp. 382–83; Guerlach, *L'Oeuvre néfaste*, pp. 59–60.

28. Marquet, "Aventurier du XIXe siècle," pp. 18–22; Ner, "Review of Marquet," pp. 317–23.

Mayréna's proposal came at a time when the French were becoming particularly interested in the highlands of western Annam, primarily because of increased Siamese expansion eastward in Laos, a development they attributed to English influence. In October 1885, with the French busy coping with the Revolt of the Literati, the Siamese sent forces into the Plain of Jars and installed two emissaries in Luang Prabang to supervise the affairs of the kingdom. The Quai d'Orsay dispatched a note to Bangkok stating that the court of Hue claimed sovereignty over Xieng Khouang and Luang Prabang and suggesting that Siam agree to join a commission to examine the boundaries of Luang Prabang. In May 1886 Siam granted France the right to post a vice consul in Luang Prabang. The man named to this position was Auguste Pavie, who later would be instrumental in bringing about the creation of the French protectorate of Laos.[29]

Meanwhile there were related developments farther south. Using Saravan as their base, the Siamese began pushing eastward along the Khong river, and in 1886 they occupied the area of the Tchepone and Bang Hien rivers, preventing the muong leaders from paying their tribute to Hue. Later, a Siamese officer supported by a force of twenty soldiers established a permanent post at Attopeu.[30] In the western zone of present Dac Lac province, Lao influence had been increasing, and around 1887 a somewhat strange event took place. According to Maitre, a band of fifty Burmese led by a chief named Kham Leu arrived at Ban Don. Uniting with some twenty Lao and one hundred Mnong, they invaded the territory of the Bih to the southeast. A Bih chief named Ngeuh (later he is identified as Ama Trang Guh) mustered a force of between 700 and 800 warriors which inflicted a serious defeat on the invaders, leaving many, including Kham Leu, dead on the field. Fearing the vengeance of the Bih, most of the Mnong villagers fled the Srepok river area to take refuge in the mountains to the southwest.[31]

In addition, there were disturbing reports that Ham Nghi and his partisans had taken refuge among the Siamese in Tchepone, where it was said he was seeking aid from other countries. Actually he had hidden among the Muong, an ethnic group in Ha Tinh province; he was captured there in November 1888 and exiled to Algeria. On 30 January 1888 the

---

29. Ner, "Review of Marquet," pp. 325–26; D. G. E. Hall, *A History of South-East Asia*, 3d ed. (New York: St. Martin's Press, 1970), pp. 679–86.
    30. Ner, "Review of Marquet," pp. 326–27; Maitre, *Les Jungles Moi*, pp. 522–23.
    31. Maitre, *Les Jungles Moi*, p. 489.

résident of Binh Dinh announced that three Vietnamese who had been sent by Ham Nghi to the king of Siam with gifts and letters had been captured in a Bahnar village near Kontum. This report stirred fears among French officials of collusion between the rebels and Siamese and the possibility of their recruiting highlanders to fight on their side.

Another reason for the sudden French interest in the central highlands was a series of reports from missionaries and visitors to Kontum that there were minerals to be found in the region north of the town. The Sedang were said to mine iron, which they used to make their weapons and tools, and it was known that the Halang panned for gold in the rivers.[32]

Soon after assuming his post as governor general, Constans formulated a plan to secure French interests in the region east of the Mekong river. In the initial phase, information would be gathered about this vast area, particularly intelligence on Siamese incursions. The next step would be to block further Siamese moves while making it known among the population that Siamese occupation had no legal basis. Visits to these areas by French nationals and the establishment of French military posts would attest to the administration's intention to counteract Siamese incursions. Constans also felt that it was necessary to search for documents that might shed light on the status of this highland region. On 8 February 1888 General Begin, commander of the French forces in Indochina and résident general of Annam and Tonkin, sent to the governor general a packet of documents concerning the frontiers of Annam, Laos, and Cambodia indicating that the western limit of Annam was not the mountain range but the Mekong river. In March, Constans ordered Captain Luce, an officer in his personal guard, to find documents that would clarify the rights of Annam in this territory.[33]

The first assertion of French authority in the mountains took place early in 1888. A series of events involving a Siamese military commander named Vai Voronat and the French vice consul Auguste Pavie resulted in the latter settling on a scheme to bring under French control the Sib Song Chu Thai, the twelve Tai cantons that straddled the present northern borders of Laos and Vietnam. Late in March, after returning to Luang Prabang, Pavie informed Vai Voronat of this plan, and soon after Pavie was sent to Hanoi, where General Begin entrusted him with the task of organizing the

32. Ner, "Review of Marquet," pp. 325–26.
33. Ibid., pp. 326–28.

annexed area. This resulted in Pavie's first "mission" or expedition, which was led by Captain Cupet, who later would head another mission into the central highlands of Vietnam. The exploration began on 3 April and took the party from Luang Prabang to Tak Khoa and Xieng Khouang on the Tran Ninh plateau before terminating in July. In August 1888 another party went from Luang Prabang to Dien Bien Phu. A subsequent exploration which lasted from 8 November 1888 until 2 January 1889 took some of Pavie's men to the Tran Ninh plateau and eastward into the Hua Phan Thang Hok where Sam Neua is now located. Finally, between 12 January and 7 April 1889, Luce and his colleagues traveled from Luang Prabang to the Vietnamese city of Vinh on the Gulf of Tonkin.[34]

While these events were unfolding in Laos, Mayréna was making progress in his scheme to conduct an expedition into the central highlands. On 5 January 1888 he resubmitted to Governor General Constans his request for permission to carry out his proposed exploration. The heightened enthusiasm to assert French authority in that region overshadowed some doubts about Mayréna's character that had lingered in the minds of some of the officials and they agreed to his plan. Secretary General Kloboukowski wrote a letter of recommendation for Mayréna, who sailed for Qui Nhon early in March accompanied by his friend Alphonse Mercurol, a former soldier with a sordid reputation. Lemire, the résident at Qui Nhon, read the letter, which said in part, "Monsieur de Mayréna, who disembarks today, proposes to explore the region that extends westward from Binh Dinh to investigate the natural communications that might exist between this country and our colony of Cochinchina." Lemire encouraged Mayréna to research the routes from Qui Nhon to Kratie and Attopeu and to examine the flora, fauna, and any traces of mineral deposits. He also informed the explorer that Pim, the Bahnar Bonom chief and son of Kiom (1.1, 1.5), was striving to form a confederation of all of the Bahnar, Rengao, and Jarai Hodrung.

Mayréna confided in Lemire that he was in agreement with the view of Governor General Constans that the highland groups in the region were independent of any outside authority and if he, Mayréna, could win their support and become their chief and protector it would render them susceptible to French influence. The French would therefore have access to

---

34. Hall, *History*, pp. 685–86; Auguste Pavie, *Mission Pavie en Indochine*, 11 vols. (Paris, 1879–1895), 3, *Voyages au Laos et chez les sauvages de sud-est de l'Indo-Chine* by Captain Cupet, introduction by Auguste Pavie (Paris: Ernest Leroux, 1900), pp. 38–175.

this vast territory with its mineral deposits without having to get the approval of Annam or Siam. Lemire, however, was hesitant. The missionaries in Kontum also held that the highland groups of the interior were independent, but Lemire reasoned that if this were the case it might invite others to move into the region east of the Mekong river. In addition, he suspected that Mayréna might intend to secure for himself a mineral concession, a move that would surely cause chagrin among the missionaries and perhaps stir up unrest among the highlanders.

Ner points out that the policy of the French administration was not clear, and quite possibly Governor General Constans was entertaining several alternatives.[35] There was, first of all, the view that the highlanders were independent. Also, some held the opinion that they were under the hegemony of the court of Hue. De Kergaradec, the French consul general in Bangkok, felt that from a diplomatic point of view the latter was the more efficacious position to assume. Furthermore, De Kergaradec was strongly influenced by Truong Vinh Ky (better known as Petrus Ky), a pro-French Vietnamese scholar who had written a history of Vietnam in French. In a letter dated 12 May 1888 to Navelle, now secretary general and lieutenant governor, Petrus Ky stated that formation of a commission to discuss with the Siamese the matter of borders was unnecessary.[36] All the French had to do was to pressure the court of Hue into asserting its sovereignty over "its tributaries; Luang Prabang, Vientiane, Thúy Xá, etc." The reference to Thúy Xá, Land of the King of Water, clearly is to the tributary relations between Hue and the two Jarai leaders, the King of Water and the King of Fire. For Petrus Ky, the assertion of this claim could be achieved by reoccupying former garrisons in these areas to present the Siamese with a fait accompli based on legitimate claims. As Ner pointed out, Constans' ambivalence was largely due to the indecision of the court of Hue, which left unresolved the question of whether the highlanders were independent or under its hegemony.[37]

For Mayréna, however, there was no question about his course of action: he would penetrate the remote highlands, endeavor to establish his authority among the ethnic groups, and pass on to the French administration the right to exploit the riches. In addition, once these areas were under

35. Ner, "Review of Marquet," pp. 329–32.

36. Jean Bouchot, *Pétrus J.-B. Truong-Vĩnh-Ký, érudit Cochinchinois (1837–1898)* (Saigon: Editions Nguyen-Van-Cua, 1927), pp. 93–94.

37. Ner, "Review of Marquet," pp. 329–32.

French authority, there would be no danger of a new revolt in Annam because the rebels would be deprived of any upland redoubt. Furthermore, the mountains would provide the French with a military base area in which they could recruit highlanders for their militia. Before leaving Qui Nhon, Mayréna succeeded in gaining the confidence of Bishop Van Camelbeke, who gave him a letter of introduction for the priests in Kontum. Noting that Mayréna was a representative of the French government, the bishop asked the priests to lend what assistance they could. At the end of the letter he expressed hope that the "famous affair of the Jarai," still unresolved, would have a favorable ending.[38]

The Jarai affair to which the bishop referred occurred early in December 1885 and was the culmination of a long period of trouble between the Bahnar and the Jarai. Missionary Father Guerlach wrote that upon his arrival at the Kontum Mission in January 1883 one of the most pressing problems was harassment by the neighboring Sedang and Jarai, particularly the latter.[39] Periodically they would swoop down on the Bahnar fields, carrying off women and children, killing all who resisted. They also would ambush the mission's elephant convoys coming from Qui Nhon with supplies.

In December 1887 the Jarai ambushed a large convoy in which Guerlach was riding. When he protested their looting of supplies, the leader replied, "When you catch the frogs and fish in the rivers, why do you do it?" Once in Kontum, Guerlach asked Lieutenant Metz, a French army officer who had been sent into the highlands months before to do topographic research, if he would lead his escort of militiamen and some Bahnar warriors in a campaign against the bellicose Jarai. Metz, however, firmly informed the priest that he was in the highlands to study the topography and nothing more. Efforts to obtain assistance from the French authorities in Qui Nhon brought no results. Guerlach decided to cope with the situation his own way. In mid-February 1888 he called for all the Bahnar and Rengao who had suffered from the Jarai raids to send their hardiest warriors to Kontum. Some twelve hundred responded, but since no Bahnar or Rengao had ever defeated the Jarai, some of the local chiefs were skeptical of Guerlach's effort. A Rengao chief named Thu predicted that "Father Guerlach will depart on a horse but they will carry him back." Guerlach issued his army

38. Ibid., pp. 331–32.
39. Guerlach, *L'Oeuvre néfaste*, pp. 94–97.

two orders: first, regardless of good or bad omens they must continue to obey orders and keep marching and, second, they were to attack only the men, avoiding the women and children. The campaign proved a success: the Jarai were sent into a disorderly retreat and shortly thereafter sued for peace. When the news of the priest's victory became known, it was said that a powerful spirit had taken possession of him, rendering him immune to arrows and spears.[40]

Mayréna, riding an Arabian horse, led his expedition westward out of Qui Nhon into the mountains on 21 April 1888. Included in the group were Mercurol, their two Vietnamese mistresses, a cook named Paoli, eighteen armed guards, eighty porters, an interpreter, and four Chinese who were interested in the possibility of finding gold. The party reached the village of Kon Jaritul, where they were greeted by Pim, the son of Kiom. Pim, like his father, had been a friend of the French priests, and during the 1885 revolt, when Vietnamese forces tried to penetrate the highlands and destroy the Kontum Mission, Pim had blocked them. This chief was prepared to welcome Mayréna as he had earlier welcomed Navelle. He was immediately impressed by his visitor's striking physical appearance—Mayréna was six feet tall, husky, and had a trimmed black beard—and his claim to shamanistic powers. The Bahnar chief was particularly taken with a music box Mayréna brought out to display his magic, as well as with the Frenchman's skill with his firearms. Mayréna succeeded in concluding a treaty with Pim, who already had formed his own alliances with some of the Rengao and Bahnar leaders. Mayréna explained all of this in a letter to the governor general written eight days after leaving Qui Nhon. He also reported in this letter that the Vietnamese had constructed a road behind the frontier of Annam, running the entire length of the kingdom, to serve as a route for Vietnamese troops.[41]

Mayréna's initial success in arranging this treaty, however, was marred by the flight of all his Vietnamese porters, who apparently were frightened by the strange surroundings, particularly the sight of Pim and his warriors. In response to Mayréna's appeal for assistance, Father Guerlach of the Kontum Mission appeared at Pim's village with elephants, packhorses, and porters. The priest was surprised to find that Mayréna was flying a flag with three white clovers emblazoned on a blue background. The explorer

40. Maitre, *Les Jungles Moi*, p. 523.
41. Ner, "Review of Marquet," pp. 332–35.

explained that he used this flag to avoid any diplomatic rumblings from European powers that might result if his mission were known. The party continued to Kontum, arriving on 23 May, and the following day Mayréna was taken to Kon Trang, where he was welcomed by Father Irigoyen. This priest accompanied Mayréna to Polei Tobau and Kon Trang Money, where in a communal house they met with leaders from both villages. The leaders signed a treaty with Mayréna. This process was repeated again at Kon Gung Tih and Kon Gung Je.[42]

On 3 June 1888 Mayréna promulgated the Constitution of the Sedang Kingdom. Among other things it stipulated that he, Mayréna, would be the king (with the name of Marie I) and that his authority would be absolute. The national flag would have a white cross with a red star in the center against a blue background. Human sacrifices were to be forbidden, and all religions would be free. Soon after, with Guerlach's help, Mayréna signed a treaty of alliance with a Kayong chief named Khen who had received the honorific title Phia Keo from the Siamese. Mayréna obtained

42. Guerlach, *L'Oeuvre néfaste*, pp. 129–36.

A Sedang communal men's house

approval of a chief named Sui to grant Mercurol, now styled Marquis of Henui, a gold mining concession in the vicinity of the Henui river. On 10 June Mayréna and the priests of the Kontum Mission signed a treaty, after which he and Guerlach went northwest to Kon Homong to meet with a gathering of local chiefs, some of whom were Sedang, to sign the constitution.

At this point Mercurol was sent to Qui Nhon to obtain fresh supplies and inform the administration of the new developments. He was also instructed to ascertain whether the governor general desired to meet with the highland chiefs from the Sedang Kingdom in Saigon. On 1 July Mayréna and Father Irigoyen met with the chiefs of Kon Jeri to have them agree to revisions in the constitution; there was a new article forbidding the sale of any Sedang slaves to other groups, and the article declaring that all religions would be free was amended to make Catholicism the official religion of the kingdom.

While these events had been taking place, Father Vialleton, head of the Kontum Mission, had been contacting all of the Bahnar and Rengao chiefs in the area to gather them at Kontum. There they agreed on a Bahnar-Rengao Confederation, electing as president a Bahnar chief named Krui (whose sons Father Vialleton had taught to read and write the Bahnar script introduced to the Kontum area by the priests around 1870).[43] On 4 July 1888 an alliance between the Bahnar-Rengao Confederation and the Kingdom of the Sedang was agreed upon by Krui and Marie I (Mayréna).[44]

Even before Mercurol reached Qui Nhon, a trickle of news concerning events in the highlands was causing some consternation in the French administration. In mid-May, Lemire, the résident in Qui Nhon, had transmitted his misgivings about Mayréna's intentions in the highlands and raised questions about the explorer's authorization. The matter of Mayréna's authorization proved difficult to determine, since on 21 April, the very day Mayréna had left the coast for the highlands, Governor General Constans, who had authorized his venture, had sailed for France. Richaud, his replacement, expressed his support for Mayrena's mission so as not to appear to be in opposition to his predecessor. But in none of his

---

43. Paul Guilleminet, "Langages spéciaux utilisés dans la tribu Bahnar du Kontum," *BEFEO* 50 (1960): 119. This script was based on the modern Vietnamese orthography and used some of the same diacritical marks.

44. Guerlach, *L'Oeuvre néfaste*, p. 98; Ner, "Review of Marquet," p. 339.

communications did Mayréna mention anything about his having assumed a royal title, so Mercurol's arrival with messages from the "King of the Sedang" produced shock in Qui Nhon and Saigon.

Once he had assumed his royal title in June, Mayréna lost no time in exercising royal authority. In addition to making Mercurol a marquis, he created a postal service, customs office, an army, and three decorations— the Royal Order of the Sedang, the Royal Order of Saint Marguerite, and the Royal Order of Sedang Merit (the slogans written on the stamps and medals were in Bahnar, not Sedang). The battle cry of the kingdom was "God! France! Sedang!" From his "palace" (a thatched Bahnar house) in his "capital" at Maria Polei (a Bahnar village), Mayréna sent reports to his "ministers" and outlined the protocol that would be observed at his "court." He also repudiated his French citizenship and dissolved his marriage to his French wife.

Early in September 1888 Mayréna returned to Qui Nhon, where Résident Lemire, despite his skepticism, warmly greeted the explorer and honored him with a formal dinner. It soon became clear, however, that Mayréna had no intention of turning over his rule to the French administration as originally planned. In a letter to Lemire dated 19 September 1888 Mayréna pointed out that he was authorized by Krui, president of the Bahnar-Rengao Confederation, to deal with the French authorities. He warned that should the French refuse to deal with him he was prepared to turn to the English. After meeting with Mayréna, Lemire forwarded the letter to the résident general of Annam, adding in an accompanying note that the "king of the Sedang," if recognized by the French, would accept a consul in his capital. Otherwise he would have no scruples about dealing with the English, Germans, Siamese, or Chinese.

When no response to his proposal was forthcoming, Mayréna made his case public in a long letter dated 8 October 1888 to the director of the *Courrier d'Haiphong*. After describing his expedition into the mountains and his selection as "war chief" by all of the village headmen north of Kontum, Mayréna went on to claim that this had resulted in the retreat of some Germans who had been seen in the territory farther west. At the request of the chiefs he had waged a successful war against the Jarai, after which the Sedang leaders had implored him to be their king. The highland people were independent of any outside authority, Mayréna maintained, and the Vietnamese ruler in Hue was not aware of the extent of Mayréna's suzerainty in the uplands, even though Captain Luce was busy compiling documents to determine the limits of royal authority in the western Annam. Indeed, the independent status of the highlanders was reflected in the fact that the noted Vietnamese scholar and historian Petrus Ky (Truong Vinh Ky) had never mentioned them in any of his works.

In Qui Nhon the initial flush of glory was fading fast. Mayréna found himself without funds and was dismayed to receive news that his Vietnamese "queen" had died in the highlands and his friend Mercurol had absconded, making off with much of the "mission equipment." On 29 October 1888 Mayréna departed for Haiphong with the intention of seeing the résident general of Tonkin-Annam. While awaiting an appointment, he arranged with a printer to produce numerous certificates of the Order of Saint Marguerite and placed an order with a Chinese tailor for a thousand uniforms for his Sedang troops. By this time an increasing number of his compatriots were dismissing him as a reckless adventurer and the résident general refused to give him an appointment. Enraged, Mayréna wrote a letter dated 4 November to the president of the French Republic reiterating many of the points that had been made in his adjuration in the *Courrier d'Haiphong*. The letter was signed "Marie de Mayréna, Roi des Sedangs." There was no answer.

Mayréna sailed for Hong Kong and was initially welcomed by the French consul as well as the French missionaries, who had a house there. Resplendent in ceremonial garb, he was received by the governor of the colony. At the gentlemen's clubs he aroused particular interest among members of the French and English business community, who felt they had been ignored by the colonial authorities in Indochina and saw in Mayréna the prospect of gaining a foothold in this new kingdom so rich in minerals. It was not long, however, before word reached Hong Kong from the governor general of Indochina about Mayréna's duplicity in his venture. Mayréna attempted unsuccessfully to cash a bogus letter of credit for 200,000 francs, purportedly signed by Bishop Van Camelbeke of the Missions Etrangères de Paris. Becoming even more desperate, he turned to the German consul to seek his support, also without success. On 20 January 1889 Mayréna left for France on a Danish ship, flying his Sedang flag. The arrival of the dashing Marie I, King of the Sedangs, produced excitement on the Paris boulevards but, other than being sought after by the fashionable crowd at the Café Riche, Mayréna was disappointed at his reception: the financial circles were not interested in his proposals.

He had more success in Belgium, where a financier provided 200,000 francs for an expedition to Indochina to regain his lost kingdom. Five Belgians, all endowed with noble titles by Mayréna, joined the expedition which sailed for the Far East on 13 January 1890. But it was doomed to failure. When Mayréna and his party were refused permission to enter Indochina, they remained in Singapore, where the English authorities seized cases of arms consigned to one of the Belgians, now a "general" in the army of the Sedang kingdom. Mayréna took a Malay wife and embraced Islam. It soon became clear, however, that they could not remain in Singapore, so Mayréna, his wife, two of the Belgians, and two Egyptian servants went to the island of Sirbua. It was a particularly inhospitable place, and before long Mayréna was abandoned by his whole entourage. Undaunted, he proceeded to the island of Tioman in the South China Sea north of Singapore. Mayréna died there on 11 November 1890. The death certificate listed the cause of death as snakebite. Other sources claimed that he was killed in a duel.[45]

The Mayréna affair effectively resolved the French administration's ambivalence concerning the status of the highland groups. The view of Mayréna and the missionaries now gave way to the argument that the court of Hue historically had hegemony over the ethnic groups of western Annam between the coastal plain and the Mekong river. This position accorded with documents sent by General Begin, the résident general of Tonkin and Annam, to Governor General Constans in February 1888 and was also suggested in a letter dated 12 May 1888 from the Vietnamese scholar Petrus Ky (Truong Vinh Ky) to Navelle, then secretary general and lieutenant governor.[46] On 6 December 1888, in a long letter to Governor General Richaud describing tributary relations between the court of Hue and the Kings of Fire and Water, Petrus Ky wrote:

> I am taking advantage of this occasion to call your attention to the lower valley of the Mekong [left bank] where there are located the two small states or principalities of Thúy-xá and Hóa-xá [names by which they are known to the Vietnamese], tributaries and vassals of Annam, paying regularly triannual and annual [1883, 1884, 1885] tribute since 1558 under the Nguyen lords and from 1802, 1821, and 1885 under the Nguyen kings [official document of the Ministry of Rites].[47]

---

45. Marquet, "Aventurier du XIXe siècle," pp. 37–105; Ner, "Review of Marquet," pp. 338–50; Pierre Dourisbourne and Christian Simmonnet, *Vietnam: Mission on the Grand Plateau* (Maryknoll, New York: Maryknoll Publications, 1967), pp. 265–78; Maitre, *Les Jungles Moi*, pp. 523–26.

46. Ner, "Review of Marquet," p. 326; Bouchot, *Pétrus J.-B. Trương-Vĩnh-Ký*, pp. 75–76.

47. Trương Vĩnh Ký to Monsieur le Gouverneur Général, 6 December 1888.

He went on to give some of the previously mentioned geography and the early history of these two states from the Royal Geography of Vietnam. This included information on the "white stone city," the deaths of the two kings, the selection of their replacements, and their installation rituals, as well as descriptions of them as being "black and ugly." Stressing that "since the time of the founding of the present Nguyen dynasty in 1558, these two states have been tributaries of Annam," Petrus Ky described the payment of tribute by the Jarai leaders, explicitly noting that for his homage the King of Fire was rewarded with the honorific name Vinh Bao. After some details on the tribute paid to Thieu Tri, the letter ended with the note that this information was supplied by the official documents, which would serve as an excellent point of departure for research being conducted by those who were commissioned by the governor general to study this question.

More than likely this was a reference to Captain Luce, who in March 1888 had begun a search of the Hue archives for documents that would define the rights of Annam in the mountain regions.[48] His report, published in May 1889, concluded that the maps, geographies, and historical works all seemed to indicate that the southern provinces of Annam— Quang Nam, Quang Ngai, Binh Dinh, Phu Yen, Khanh Hoa, and Binh Thuan—extended westward to the Mekong river but that their western portions were occupied by "savage Moi tribes" and Laotians who had no administrative relations with the provincial authorities. The annals of the Ministry of Rites, however, mentioned the two states of Thủy-Xá and Hỏa-Xá, tributaries and vassals to Annam since 1558, and Luce noted that "they seem to be in the country presently known as the country of the Sedangs, Bahnars, and Djarais." They regularly sent tribute to Hue through Phu Yen, and in 1841 Emperor Thieu Tri had bestowed upon them the title of third degree military mandarins.

In addition, Luce found that following the Siamese invasion of Vientiane between 1825 and 1827 Minh Mang had annexed the hinterlands of Quang Tri, Ha Tinh, and Nghe An provinces, all of which extended to the Mekong river, and that since that time most leaders in these areas had been paying tribute to Hue. The Phu of Cam Lo in Quang Tri had three cantons which paid tribute, three were exempt from payment, and three on the right bank of the Mekong river were prevented from

48. L. de Reinach, *Le Laos*, 2 vols. (Paris: A. Charles, 1901), 2: 30–32.

paying by the Siamese. Also, the Phu of Tran Ninh, bordered on the north by Luang Prabang and the south by the Mekong river, was described as having paid tribute since the fifteenth century. However, for three years prior to the report it had been occupied by Siamese who collected taxes there. Muong Lu, encircled by Burma to the west, Yunnan to the north, and Luang Prabang to the south, was another area that paid tribute to Hue.

The Mayréna affair produced recriminations between the missionaries and the French administration. Guimar, the new résident in Binh Dinh, charged that Mayréna could not have achieved what he did without the collaboration of the priests and that Krui, the Bahnar president of the Bahnar-Rengao Confederation, was nothing more than a front man for the Kontum Mission. In some administrative circles it was intimated that the priests sought to organize a theocratic state in the highlands so as to be able to proselytize among the highlanders without restraint. On their part, the priests contended that Mayréna had come to them on an official mission with a letter from the résident of Binh Dinh and that therefore as loyal French citizens they had considered it their duty to protect this envoy and lend him whatever assistance they could.[49] Eventually the controversy subsided, although in 1906 Father Guerlach felt the need to publish a strong defense of the missionaries' position in the Mayréna affair.[50]

Bourotte and Ner both observe that, while Mayréna may not be remembered as a hero, his activities contributed a great deal to giving the French control of the Kontum area, a development which turned out to be vital in preventing the expansion of the Siamese into the central highlands.[51] Mayréna's adventure stirred considerable interest in this rather unknown region and, despite the conflict noted above, in the long run brought about an effective collaboration between the Kontum Mission and the French administration. On 23 February 1889 Rheinart, the résident general of Annam, wrote a letter to Krui, the president of the Bahnar-Rengao Confederation, informing him that Résident Guiomar of Binh Dinh would visit Kontum to resolve the Mayréna affair. When Rheinart himself arrived in March with his assistant Simoni and six Vietnamese militiamen, he found that the missionaries had gathered all of the chiefs, including Krui. Rheinart, after stressing that Mayréna did not represent France, assured the gathering that the French administration had no desire

49. Ner, "Review of Marquet," pp. 336, 346.
50. Guerlach, *L'Oeuvre néfaste,* pp. 129–49.
51. Bourotte, "Essai des populations Montagnardes," p. 77; Ner, "Review of Marquet," p. 347.

to occupy the country but would exercise its influence through the missionaries.

THE PAVIE MISSION

Meanwhile in Laos, Pavie was continuing his efforts to assert further French influence and arrest Siamese expansion. After being prevented in February 1889 from traveling through the uplands of the Khammouane area between Thakhet and Savannakhet, Pavie returned to France, where he tried to convince the Quai d'Orsay to adopt the policy that the western borders of Tonkin and Annam extended to the Mekong river. He also planned a series of scientific expeditions to study the geography, flora, fauna, and natural products of the Mekong river basin and to gather information on existing commercial procedures in the area. A Syndicat Français du Haut-Laos was formed to support this project and put fifteen tons of merchandise at the disposal of the mission. The Pavie Mission ultimately produced volumes of valuable information on remote regions of Cambodia, Laos, and Vietnam, and it also brought about the annexation of additional territory for the French empire.[52]

Pavie's new effort, which he considered his "second mission," began in January 1890. He established his headquarters at Luang Prabang and organized a division of the mission explorers, composed of military officers and civil servants, into two groups. One, under Pavie, would study the Black river area while the other, under Captain Cupet, would conduct reconnaissance in the region between the Tran Ninh plateau and Cambodia. Cupet's party included lieutenants Cogniard, Dugast, Rivière, and Malgalive as well as two civilians—a functionary named Lugan and a naturalist named Counillon. The explorers met in Hanoi and from there, after dividing up, took varying routes into Laos. Eventually all of the explorers converged on Luang Prabang, conferring with Pavie until 5 July 1890. Again separating, they continued their exploration of the area, and on 14 November 1890 Cupet's party met at Bassac, where they planned further trips into the region of the San river, Khong river, and Srepok. One of their goals was to reach the country of the "sauvages indépendants," i.e., the highlanders not under Lao, Vietnamese, or French authority. While in

---

52. Hall, *History*, pp. 686–87.

Bassac, Cupet received a letter from Father Guerlach of the Kontum Mission, who offered whatever assistance the explorer needed with the wry comment that the Mayréna situation demonstrated the priests' willingness to be of service to France. Guerlach reassured Cupet that the Jarai of the Bla river area, with the exception of the one village that attacked the Navelle party in 1885, would offer no trouble to the explorers. He also advised Cupet to bring such things as laminated tin sheets, cloth, flints, scissors, and needles to use as exchange items with the highlanders. The region was rife with fevers, Guerlach added, so it would be well to bring a good supply of quinine.

On 27 November 1890 Cupet and his party headed south into Cambodia from Bassac, separating at Siempang. In northeastern Cambodia on 9 December, while "seated in a melancholy mood on the trunk of a tree" awaiting his convoy in Voeune Sai (Virachey), Cupet was approached by a Lao medical practitioner who explained that he had made a sojourn into the Rhadé country. He said that if the Frenchman wished to go there he first must have the approval of a great chief called the "sadete," which Cupet at the time took to be a deformation of the Lao word *somdet* (king) and only later learned was a designation for the King of Fire.[53] The Lao went on to point out to Cupet that if he offered the appropriate gifts, such as one or two elephants, he could obtain the favor of the sadete. When Cupet gasped at hearing the cost of such favor, the Lao quickly responded, "But he is the king of all the savages." At that point the convoy arrived and Cupet continued his exploration, which finally terminated in Stung Treng. From there they traveled to Saigon to make plans for their expedition into the country of the independent highlanders.[54]

According to their plan, Cupet would journey from Kratie to Kontum, while Dugast and Cogniard would go by sea to central Vietnam and then into the mountains, the former from Qui Nhon, the latter from Tourane. Garnier, Inspector of the Militia, would travel through the Sayan pass into the highlands. All would rendezvous in Kontum on 20 February 1891. From his account, it appears that Cupet took advantage of his stay in Saigon to gain some additional information about the sadete, in particular, reading the report on the Kings of Fire and Water by Moura.[55] He noted

53. The terms Sadet of Fire and Sadet of Water became widely used in French literature on the two kings.

54. *Mission Pavie en Indochine*, 3: 121–260.

55. J. Moura, *Le Royaume du Cambodge*, 2 vols. (Paris: Leroux, 1888), 1: 432–36.

Khunjanob and his wife in an 1891 sketch by a member of the Cupet expedition

in planning his expedition that he would traverse the region between the Mekong river and the "village du Sadete des Djarais." The sadete had had friendly relations with the Khmer ruler and received gifts from him, Cupet observed, and although these relations ceased to exist they must have left fond remembrances among the highland people.

On 21 January 1891 Cupet left Kratie at the head of a convoy consisting of ten Cambodian militiamen, six elephants, and a dozen oxcarts. As they made their way into the highlands to the east, the trail narrowed to the point where they had to abandon the oxcarts, but on 6 February they reached Ban Don, a small settlement that, according to Rhadé informants, had been founded by the Lao in the mid-nineteenth century with the sanction of a powerful chief named Ama Bloi ("Father of Bloi"). In 1891 Ban Don was ruled by a Mnong-Lao named Khunjanob (also variously known as Koun-Iounop, Khun-Snoup, and Khun Senote), who derived his authority and wealth from his control of the elephant trade. These precious animals were bought—or taken—from the highlanders and most were sold to the Cambodians, Siamese, and Lao. This leader had received the honorific Lao-Siamese title *Khun* after he had sent a rare white elephant to the King of Siam in Bangkok.

Khunjanob did not greet Cupet warmly and refused to lend any assistance, such as guides or boats to cross the Srepok river, saying that the Rhadé did not allow anyone, even the Lao, to enter their territory. Should he assist Cupet, it would incur their wrath and soon ten thousand Rhadé warriors would swoop down on Ban Don to carry everyone into slavery. While in Ban Don, Cupet talked with some elderly residents who recalled seeing, in times past, Cambodian elephant caravans on their way into the country of the sadetes.

Fortunately a Lao trader offered to get the party across the river downstream from Ban Don and, ignoring Khunjanob's warnings, Cupet accepted. As he proceeded in a northeastern direction, he found the influence of the Kings of Fire and Water to be quite strong. Several times he was advised to obtain their protection. At one village the chief claimed to be a kinsman of the King of Water and surprised Cupet by stating that, foreigners were in the highlands to block further attempts by the Siamese to penetrate the region. He inquired if Cupet had gifts for the Kings of Fire and Water, noting that "if you wish to enter their houses you must make an offering of buffalo, pigs, chickens, iron, and copper bracelets to the spirits."

On 13 February the party reached the village of Ban Khasom, a sizable community of 150 houses on the Nam Kieou river ninety-three kilometers northeast of Ban Don. Cupet was informed that the previous evening the King of Fire had arrived at the village to visit a kinsman and would receive the Frenchman. Cupet was escorted to a longhouse where in a large room he found some thirty people huddled around numerous alcohol jars. In spite of the fact that he was followed by a large crowd of villagers, no one stirred, and he observed that "the libations must have been copious judging from the number of dead drunk natives lying along the wall." The King of Fire was sitting on a kind of bamboo bed in front of a box containing some tobacco leaves. Cupet was disappointed. The famous shaman whose reputation spread as far as Phnom Penh did not have an impressive air. Other than his height—he was taller than the average European—there was nothing to distinguish him from the other highlanders. No particular deference was being paid to him by those present, and he sat smoking a long copper pipe "like a simple mortal."

In response to a sign by the King of Fire, a large gong was struck and silence fell on the assemblage. The shaman then informed Cupet that before they could talk they would have to make offerings to the spirits and drink from the same jar. Cupet brought out ten ingots of iron to pay for a jar of alcohol and a piece of red cloth for a chicken. Stirring the alcohol, the King of Fire muttered invocations and invited Cupet to drink through a bamboo tube. A one-eyed man who had been pestering Cupet since he arrived in the village squatted beside him and inquired why he had come into the mountains. "You do not resemble the Cambodians nor any of our neighbors nor us, so from where do you come?" He told Cupet that prior to his arrival it had rained, an extraordinary event for this time of the year, and the sun had darkened, both inauspicious omens. It was suspected that Cupet had come to steal the sacred saber of the King of Fire. He added, "The foreigners are already in Annam and Cambodia, and they stopped the gifts that had been sent by their rulers to the Kings of Fire and Water for centuries." Cupet became angered and retorted that if it had rained and the sun had darkened, it was because the foreigners' talismans were more powerful than those of the Kings of Fire and Water. And, as for the gifts, they had ceased years before the foreigners arrived.

A discussion ensued among the group gathered around the King of Fire, who finally addressed Cupet, asking to see the powerful talisman. The Frenchman produced his compass, which the one-eyed man took and set on the floor. The needle moved rapidly and then stopped. The one-eyed man attempted to touch it but was prevented by the glass, something the highlanders had never seen before. The assemblage was astonished, and they concluded that it was this talisman that had darkened the sun.

But the one-eyed man was not finished with his interrogation. He wanted to know what gifts Cupet had brought to the King of Fire. Had the King of Cambodia given him anything for the shaman? Cupet had five elephants, surely one could be presented as a gift. Cupet responded that before he proffered anything, he wanted to know if the King of Fire would be his friend and supply him with guides. Furthermore, his presents would not include an elephant because all the elephants were needed to transport baggage and supplies. There was another discussion among those around the King of Fire, after which one of the group informed Cupet that he had the friendship of the shaman and guides would be provided. The Frenchman then spread out on a mat an array of offerings including cloth of all colors, articles of clothing, mirrors, iron, copper, and tin. The one-eyed man scrutinized the display, saying to Cupet, "The kings of Cambodia sent silk. Don't you have any?" Cupet ignored the question, but the man persisted, asking the cost of these items and inquiring whether Cupet had any silver. Meanwhile the King of Fire donned a knit vest and coat he had found among the clothing and wrapped a piece of red cloth around his head. The drinking from the jars began again. As Cupet prepared to leave, the King of Fire gave him a brass bracelet and a measure of rice, explaining that the bracelet would be a sign to all the highlanders on the eastern slope of the chain that Cupet was a friend of his. If a village should refuse aid, the King of Fire advised, Cupet was to thrust some of the rice on the ground while invoking his name and it would render the soil infertile.

On 15 February 1891 Cupet and his party continued toward their destination, Kontum, which they reached on 21 February. Dugast had already arrived there after a journey filled with frustrations. He was supposed to have left Qui Nhon in January, but the Vietnamese mandarins refused to provide him with guides, saying that they all had died. Delayed until 5 February, he reached An Khe and proceeded in the direction of the King of Fire's village to the south where he hoped to find Cupet. However, en route his porters fled, abandoning all the baggage. Then the local Jarai villagers refused to take him to the shaman's village, so he returned to An

Khe, going directly from there to Kontum. Cogniard had reached Tra My but was stopped by the rains, and when he fell ill with fever he returned to Tourane. There was no news of Garnier.[56]

As Cupet and his colleague investigated the Kontum area, particularly the Bla river plain, they became aware of its strategic importance. It commanded the access route to Attopeu on the Boloven plateau as well as the Jarai country to the south, and they concluded it would make an ideal base of operations for blocking the Siamese expansion into the central highlands. At this point, the missionaries received a report that a column of Siamese troops had been spotted in the lower San river moving in the direction of the hinterlands. This was followed by intelligence that bands of Lao were moving east in an area only three days' walk from Kontum. As a result, some of the local population began filtering into the settlement seeking protection. Cupet, Dugast, and their escort set out for Attopeu on 2 March but had not gone far when they learned that a Siamese force of four hundred men commanded by the Luong Sakhon—a commander Cupet had dealt with previously in Bassac—had departed from Stung Treng on 23 February, going in the direction of Ban Don. Leaving Dugast at the San river, Cupet and six militiamen swung south. They reached the point where the San river crosses the present Cambodian border to find that a Siamese column from Attopeu had been seen at a place three days' march away. Cupet moved on to Bokkham (Bo Kheo), but when it became apparent that the Siamese thrust would be against Ban Don he changed his strategy. He sent word to Dugast and other colleagues to harass the Siamese troops moving eastward and requested the governor general for sixty more militiamen. Cupet and his escort of four Cambodians then set out through the Jarai country to reach Ban Don ahead of the Siamese.[57]

On 18 March, Cupet passed close to the village of the King of Water, and the shaman sent a Lao who had lived a long time in the village to see the Frenchman. Cupet explained the situation, offering his friendship and suggesting that he visit the shaman. The King of Water proposed that Cupet first send him some pigs, buffalo, and a jar of rice alcohol as offerings for the spirits. When Cupet complied, also sending some gongs and other gifts, the King of Water performed a brief ritual with a chicken to determine the will of the spirits. The results were favorable so he accepted

56. *Mission Pavie en Indochine*, 3: 294–324.
57. Maitre, *Les Jungles Moi*, p. 528; *Mission Pavie*, 3: 360–69.

Cupet's offer of friendship, sending him a brass bracelet. Then, at the Frenchman's request, he provided him with guides and porters. When Cupet reached Ban Don on 22 March, he found the Luong Sakhon and his force (370 Lao and 22 Siamese soldiers) already camped outside the settlement. Cupet met with the Luong Sakhon and took a firm stand, declaring that he had gained the support of all the highlanders who did not wish to pay tribute to the Siamese. He emphasized that he had succeeded in winning over the Kings of Fire and Water, showing his bracelets as evidence of their alliances. The Luong Sakhon deliberated and then, much to everyone's surprise, ordered his troops to retreat.

This produced considerable excitement among the highlanders in the area of Ban Don. It was the first attempt by the Siamese and Laotians to invade the country, and they had been turned back by Cupet, who only had four militiamen with him. News spread that the Frenchman had a powerful spirit in his stomach. Khunjanob celebrated with a large feast and many jars of alcohol. During the celebration, Khunjanob informed Cupet that a Vietnamese rebel, a follower of Ham Nghi, had recently been in hiding among the Rhadé. The rebel had sent his assistant and thirty men to Khunjanob asking that he arrange for them to get to Bassac because they had gifts, including cinnamon, a box encrusted in gold, and a beautiful girl for the King of Siam. Khunjanob had refused to give them guides so they had disappeared.

On 6 April 1891 Cupet set out for the coastal city of Nhatrang. Moving down the trail that more or less traced present Route 21, he reached the village he called "Buon Me Sao" after its chief "Me Sao" (this is a Vietnamese designation found in French sources, but the Rhadé remember him as Ama Jhao). Cupet was lodged in the chief's longhouse and recorded that this chief gave him some rice. He also noted that the chief was a man of great wealth, possessing around one hundred slaves and two hundred head of cattle.

The Cupet mission ended on 15 April 1891 in Nhatrang. In the summary of his findings Cupet noted that the "independent" highlanders had succeeded in maintaining their "racial purity" and their indigenous cultures while those under the rule of the Vietnamese, Cambodians, and Lao had degenerated due to exploitation by these more advanced peoples. He observed that in Annam the French were dealing with the highlanders through the Vietnamese mandarins, who allowed the uplands to be used by the rebels. The only solution in Cupet's view was for the French to bring the highlands into their political sphere, extend commerce into the area, and colonize it.[58]

While Cupet was making his way from Ban Don to the coast, the other members of the expedition were coping with the Siamese. Dugast encountered a Siamese force at Semet in the vicinity of the San river south of Kontum, and the Siamese retreated. At Dak Rode he joined Garnier, who had arrived at Kontum on 29 March 1891 after a long, arduous journey from Tra My with Delingette. Dugast and Garnier returned to Kontum, leaving Delingette at Dak Rode, where he sought the support of the local Halang to block the Siamese. Meanwhile, Cogniard and Bricourt moved through the region of the King of Fire's village, but, encountering no Siamese, they returned to Kontum, where they found Odend'hal (whose travels in the highlands were discussed earlier) and Breugnot with the sixty militiamen Cupet had requested from the governor general. On 26 April it was learned that a Siamese column under the Luong Sakhon was moving on Dak Rode, prompting Cogniard, Odend'hal, Breugnot, and Father Guerlach to join Delingette there. Some two hundred Halang warriors rallied, but when Cogniard met with the Luong Sakhon he elected to retreat. Three days later while en route to Attopeu the Luong Sakhon died in the forest and his troops dispersed in disarray. This ended the Siamese threat to the highlands, so the French officers departed, going their separate ways.[59]

ALEXANDRE YERSIN

The next expedition into the highlands was led by Dr. Alexandre Yersin, one of the pioneers in the introduction of western medicine in Indochina. In July 1890, at the age of twenty-seven, he was ship doctor on the Messageries Maritime vessel *Saigon*, plying up and down the coast of Vietnam. He landed at Nhatrang with the idea of journeying into the mountains to trace an overland route from Saigon to that coastal city. The French résident Lenormand, who lived in a thatched house on the splendid beach, gave Yersin advice for his venture. Finally, finding a guide in Phan Rang, Yersin set out for the mountains with only a musette bag containing five cans of corned beef. The journey proved arduous over tortuous trails

58. *Mission Pavie*, 3: 399–424.
59. Maitre, *Les Jungles Moi*, pp. 529–32.

in the downpour of the rainy season. By the time they reached the plateau of Djiring, Yersin's white linen shoes were worn out and his clothes were in tatters. So the party returned to coastal Phan Thiet.[60]

For his second effort, an expedition from the coast to the Mekong river, Yersin sought the approval of the French administration. He contacted Captain Cupet, who had just completed his last exploration, and this veteran advised the doctor to search for the source of the Bang Khan river, a tributary of the Mekong, and also, if possible, the source of the Dong Nai river. Approving of the Yersin expedition, the administration requested that he gather information on geography (particularly hydrography) and the highland people in the area, and he also was asked to assess the economic potential of the region.[61]

Yersin spent more time and effort planning this new expedition, and his supplies required a great deal more than a musette bag. Included were several compasses, a pocket barometer, two chronometers, two thermometers, and a camera. In addition, there were items for exchange, such as eleven pieces of cloth, twelve blankets, ten colored handkerchiefs, ten kilos of glass pearls, twenty-four small nickel knives, twelve watch chains, some small mirror boxes, seven rolls of copper wire, thirteen small brass gongs, and "rings of various kinds." His weapons included several rifles (one of which was an 1873 Winchester), a revolver, and quantities of ammunition. Food supplies consisted of cheese, sausage, boxes of powdered milk, potatoes, coffee, three bottles of cooking fat, and three bottles of cognac. In addition to two Vietnamese servants, Yersin had forty porters, and he envisaged renting elephants in villages along the way.[62]

On 29 March 1892 Yersin set out on an elephant at the head of his expedition. When he entered the mountains, he followed the trade route from Ninh Hoa and came upon the village of M'Siao (the chief Cupet called Me Sao). After agreeing to make a return visit, Yersin continued to the village of chiefs named Kheung and M'Houe, whom he describes as being the first "independent" leaders he met, i.e., they did not pay tribute to the Vietnamese or to other highland chiefs. En route to the village of another chief named Ai Roui, Yersin encountered some of his warriors,

60. Noël Bernard, *Yersin: pionnier, savant, explorateur (1863–1943)*, with preface by Pasteur Valléry-Radot (Paris: La Colombe, 1955), pp. 47–50; A. Yersin, "Premier contact avec les pays Mois de l'Annam," *Indochine*, no. 99 (1942), pp. 1–3.

61. "Itinéraire de la côte d'Annam au Mé-Kong," procès-verbal, séance de 4 Novembre 1892, *Bulletin de la Société de Géographie*, nos. 15–16 (1892), p. 399.

62. Bernard, *Yersin*, pp. 50–52.

armed with spears and crossbows, on their way to harass the village of Kheung in the hope of some booty or prisoners. Ai Roui explained that for twenty years he had been in conflict with Kheung because a resident of his village had purchased a horse from a subject of Kheung without ever making full payment. Although the horse and both parties were now dead, the conflict had been rekindled when some fifteen of Ai Roui's cattle wandered into the territory of Kheung, who seized them. Another cause for the quarrel was Ai Roui's detaining of a messenger who had been sent by Kheung. Yersin attempted to bring about peace between the two chiefs. But when Ai Roui declared that although he would return the prisoner for eight of the cattle the conflict would continue, the Frenchman departed.

After visiting several more independent chiefs, Yersin reached the area of the Beuongs (probably Mnong) along the Krong Ana river. Continuing in a northwesterly direction, he reached Ban Don on 24 May and was greeted by "Thou" (another name for Khunjanob). From there he followed the Ban Khan river and Srepok to the Mekong. After reaching Stung Treng, he worked on his field notes before going on to Saigon and Bangkok, where he conferred with Pavie, the French representative in Siam.[63]

With the support of Louis Pasteur, his teacher, Yersin was able to organize another expedition into the highlands early in 1893. Again the goal was to gather a wide range of information on the mountain regions of South Annam. After arriving in Saigon from France early in 1893, Yersin met with Governor General de Lanessan. The governor general wanted to construct communication routes into mountainous regions—as he had begun to do in Tonkin—with the dual aim of opening the area for commercial development and establishing some French presence. He asked Yersin to study the possibility of establishing routes from Saigon through the hinterlands terminating at some point along the coast of Annam. The governor general also expressed an interest in the potential for exploitation of forest products and minerals as well as the development of animal husbandry.

At Bien Hoa, Yersin joined Wetzel, one of the *garde-forestiers* and a well-known hunter, and on 26 February they arrived at Tri An, where some French colonists already had a few coffee plantations.[64] From there they

63. Ibid., pp. 53–55; A. Yersin, "Voyage de Nhatrang à Stung-Treng par les pays Mois," *Indochine*, no. 103 (1942), pp. 4–7; no. 104 (1942), pp. 3–7.

64. The *garde-forestiers* were somewhat comparable to American forest rangers. In the region of Bien Hoa one of their responsibilities was to prevent the highlanders from practicing swidden farming.

traveled by oxcart to Tra Cu, visiting a Cham village whose residents were eager to be attached to Cochinchina in order to escape the excessive taxes demanded by the Vietnamese mandarins of Binh Thuan.[65]

In his second report to Governor General de Lanneson, Yersin pointed out that in the vicinity of Tra Cu and Tan Linh there was a route that passed through some Vietnamese and highlander villages that probably would serve well as a line of communication to the coast of Annam.[66] He also noted that a man named Mercier had been the first French settler in Tan Linh. Mercier had died some five years before and his house was in ruins. From Tan Linh, Wetzel returned to Bien Hoa, but Yersin continued to Phan Thiet, ending the journey in mid-March.

Determined to examine the inland route from the coast to Tan Linh, Yersin set out on 8 April 1893 with a party consisting of eight porters, an elephant, and six packhorses to trace the route used by Cham and Vietnamese traders. Before leaving Nhatrang Yersin got a request from the French résident to detain any Vietnamese he encountered who did not have the proper permit to trade with the highlanders; he found fourteen such violators. His route took him into the area occupied by the Roglai where he claimed to have located some tin deposits. Later he reached the Danhim valley, occupied by the Chru. From there he went into the Maa country to the southwest before descending into the La Nga valley to Tan Linh.

Rather than take a direct route back to Phan Rang, Yersin elected to return to the Maa country, following the La Nga river along the same trail followed earlier by Néis, Septans, and Humann. On 9 June he arrived at the banks of the Riam river, a branch of the Dong Nai. Then he swung northward to investigate the Lang Bian mountain, the highest peak in the region. Emerging from a pine forest on 21 June 1893, he was overwhelmed by the sight of a grassy plateau that swept upward like an undulating green sea to a summit. This was the Lang Bian peak and the future site of the city of Dalat. Yersin rested at the Lat village and Dankia (which is still located on the side of the mountain) and then descended to

65. A. Yersin, "Sept mois chez les Mois," in *Variétés sur les pays Mois* (Saigon: Gouvernement de la Cochinchine, 1935), pp. 166–70; idem, "Ier Rapport: le Docteur Yersin en mission à Monsieur le Gouverneur Général de l'Indo-Chine, Tanh Uyen, 25 Fevrier 1893," Harmand Collection, Olin Library, Cornell University, Ithaca, New York.

66. A. Yersin, "2e Rapport: le Docteur Yersin en mission à Monsieur le Gouverneur Général de l'Indo-Chine, Tan Linh, 15 Mars 1893," Harmand Collection, Olin Library, Cornell University, Ithaca, New York.

the Danhim valley to visit Diom and other Chru villages before continuing to the coast. As he neared the coastal plain, he was savagely attacked by a band of Vietnamese brigands; yet in spite of being badly wounded he succeeded in dispersing them. On 26 June he reached his destination at Phan Rang.[67]

In a report to the minister of public education, Yersin briefly described the geography of the Lang Bian region, noting that there were tin and iron sulfide deposits, wild tea plants, and vast pasture lands resembling those in the mountains of France.[68] He also included information on the inhabitants (the Maa were different from the Bih and Rhadé who are "bellicose and greedy"), many of whom were exploited by the Vietnamese tax collectors in collaboration with the traders. There was little that could be done to remedy this situation, Yersin felt, as long as there was no French résident in the highlands. In a letter to Captain Cupet dated 10 July 1893, Yersin described his exploration route, pointing out some errors he had found in the map prepared by Néis.[69] He also reiterated his enthusiasm for the Maa, expressing the view that they were "the most peaceful people in the world."

Yersin was not long in Nhatrang before he began to organize another expedition into the Rhadé country. On a previous trip he had promised M'Siao, the Rhadé chief he and Cupet (who called him Me Sao) had previously visited, that he would return to his village for a stay. This became one goal of the expedition.

This chief is remembered as Y Yen Ayun or Ama Jhao ("Father of Jhao"), and four people willingly supplied information about him: his great-grandson (his son's daughter's son); Y Yen Ayun (named for his ancestor); a retired schoolmaster living in Buon Ea Kmat near Ban Me Thuot; and Y Dhuat Nie Kdam, a Rhadé civil servant. Ama Jhao was born in the Rhadé Ktul village of Buon Ea Yong in the Cadé area east of Ban Me Thuot. As a newborn infant, he cried incessantly until he received the name of his ancestor, Y Yen Ayun. (Among the Rhadé, it is a common practice to name a child after a deceased member of an older generation.)

67. A Yersin, "Premières reconnaissances du plateau du Lang-Bian," *Indochine*, no. 101 (1942), pp. 4–6; idem, "Rencontre avec des pirates sur le plateau Moi," *Indochine*, no. 100 (1942), pp. 9–10.

68. A. Yersin, "3e Rapport: le Docteur Yersin en mission à Monsieur le Ministre de l'Instruction Publique, Nhatrang, 4 Juillet 1893," Harmand Collection, Olin Library, Cornell University, Ithaca, New York.

69. "Extraits d'une lettre du Dr. Yersin au Capitaine Cupet, Nhatrang, 10 Juillet 1893," *Bulletin de la Société de Géographie*, November 1893, pp. 353–55.

Ama Jhao (Me Sao) and his family in an 1891 sketch by a member of the Cupet expedition

Ama Jhao became head of a band that levied "taxes" on caravans passing through the Cadé area, a major route in the highland-lowland trade. He also is credited by the Rhadé for keeping the Vietnamese out of the highlands, and for this he is remembered as a hero.

Many of the French sources, however, describe Ama Jhao as a debauched despot. Such is the view of Maitre, who reports that he was born of a poor family and married the daughter of a chief for whom he led raids on villages to loot and obtain captives to be sold into slavery.[70] When this chief died, the widow remarried, and the new husband, jealous of Ama Jhao, chased him from the village. Ama Jhao and a band of followers installed themselves in the vicinity of Cadé, along the trade route from Ban Don to the coast, and from there they conducted raids on the convoys. After his wife died, Ama Jhao married Ha Gai, who had poisoned her husband in order to wed the bandit leader.

Around 1880 Ama Jhao worked out an arrangement with the Vietnamese mandarins and merchants in Khanh Hoa and Phu Yen by which he began to function more or less as their agent in the highlands. He permitted their convoys to pass unharmed but raided other convoys, trading the ivory, rhinoceros horns, animal skins, and wax with his lowland contacts for trinkets and other merchandise. Maitre also claims that Ama Jhao dealt in the slave trade, and as his fortunes increased he was given to numerous excesses. Some of his victims were put to death with spears or decapitated; others had their hands plunged into boiling resin. He learned to smoke opium and drank vast quantities of alcohol. His wife used poison on anyone whose property she coveted. Between them they were alleged to have committed more than two hundred murders.

Cupet, whose sojourn in Ama Jhao's village was brief, did not report anything unusual about the chief. Nor did Yersin on his first visit to Ama Jhao's longhouse. However, his next stay revealed the chief to be more brigand than hero. Ama Jhao seemed anxious to have Yersin as his guest. When the chief's servants made their periodic trips to purchase salt in Ninh Hoa, they inquired if their leader should send elephants to get Yersin. Finally on 15 July 1893 the Frenchman sent Ama Jhao three metal bracelets, asking for six elephants to transport him and his supplies to the highlands. When no elephants had arrived at Ninh Hoa by 24 July, Yersin took to the upland trail only to meet the convoy of elephants en route to get

70. Maitre, *Les Jungles Moi,* pp. 542–43.

him. They reached Ama Jhao's village on 28 July. Garbed in his red ceremonial trousers, the highland chief greeted the French doctor. Yersin estimated that Ama Jhao was around sixty-five years of age, and he described him as being of medium height, obese, with a thick face that did not reflect "brilliant intelligence." It soon became clear that the chief had somehow concluded that Yersin was to have been accompanied by a large force of soldiers prepared to assist him in his feud with nine neighboring chiefs. When Yersin registered surprise, Ama Jhao explained that a man from Nhatrang had told him that this was the case. Yersin responded that the résident would never agree to having his troops used by someone like Ama Jhao in his "little quarrels." This angered the chief and his wife (who is described as constantly smoking a pipe and chewing areca and betel).

Yersin retreated into the room he had been given in the longhouse, but around eleven o'clock in the evening he was awakened by a loud noise. It was Ama Jhao, lugging a large, heavy saber, which the Frenchman immediately assumed to be an ominous sign. The chief's wife, who had accompanied him, explained that they had settled on a plan to raid a neighboring rich village. The attack would be led by Yersin firing his rifle, and in the surprise they would slaughter all the inhabitants and burn their houses to the ground. In return for his role in this venture, he would be given an elephant. Yersin told them to "go to the devil" and went back to sleep. The following day Ama Jhao sent his servant O-O Fi to Nhatrang to determine if the résident might send troops to aid him. While awaiting a response, he detained Yersin, who had planned to go to Ban Don and obtain elephants from Khunjanob. The doctor retaliated by refusing to drink from the jar or to allow any sacrificial pig blood to be put on his feet.

Finally on 1 August Yersin was told he was free to leave the village, so he went southward to Buon Knieng, a village with several chiefs. At one chief's house he found a Vietnamese tax collector and his family. He observed that while near the coast such officials were regarded with awe, but here they were not considered important and were even held prisoner sometimes by the Rhadé chiefs. This collector lamented that one of the chiefs had taken his horse on the pretext that he would let it graze and then demanded twice the horse's value for its return. Leaving this village, the Frenchman continued to the village of a chief named Kheune, whom he had visited previously. This leader was gravely ill, and several neighboring chiefs had gathered for a buffalo sacrifice to placate the spirits and restore the victim's health. One of the visitors was named M'Brang. He was at war with Ama Jhao because one of his servants had taken a woman from Ama

Jhao's house as a wife without observing the prescribed customs. M'Brang agreed to accompany Yersin farther west into the "Bih country." They met another chief, M'Bleng, who also was having a feud with Ama Jhao. Ama Jhao had stolen two of M'Bleng's elephants, and he in turn had responded by stealing one of Ama Jhao's elephants. M'Bleng also informed the doctor that prior to his arrival in the highlands, Ama Jhao had spread the news that the Frenchman was coming to aid him with many troops.

M'Bleng told Yersin that in order to reach the "valley of Darlac" (Darlac is a deformation of the Rhadé term Dak Lak) with its beautiful lake he would have to pass through the village of a chief named M'Seu. It would be necessary to notify M'Seu in advance because his territory was sown with hunting traps and sharpened bamboo stakes. M'Seu was notified, and when Yersin arrived at his village he found that the chiefs of the vicinity had been gathered. They informed him that if he and his soldiers would refrain from making war on them they would present him with an elephant. Yersin explained that he had no troops and no intention of making war on anyone. He added that if they had been told otherwise by Ama Jhao, it was a lie. Somewhat placated, the chiefs invited Yersin to kill a buffalo for a sacrifice with his rifle. He agreed, and standing thirty steps away he fired an eight-caliber round that felled the beast, much to the amazement of the assembled chiefs.

The following day, with some porters from the village, Yersin walked southward into the Dak Lak valley with its splendid lake surrounded by paddy fields. He thought the inhabitants were the handsomest highlanders he had yet seen. He also noted that they were not familiar with salt, using ashes to garnish their rice. Returning to M'Seu's village, Yersin learned that the chiefs gathered there still believed he had warlike intentions. This time they offered him an elephant tusk. Declining their offer, the Frenchman made his way on foot to the village of Keune, who had just died. His village was in the midst of mourning with rows of rice alcohol jars and endless gong and drum music. On 10 August 1893 Yersin arrived back at Ama Jhao's village to find a group of boxes that had been brought from the coast for him. One contained a variety of alcoholic beverages, a gift from the résident for Ama Jhao. Yersin presented the chief with a bottle of absinthe and one of peppermint liqueur. An hour later, having drunk both bottles, the chief came back asking for more. When the doctor refused, telling him he should rest rather than drink, Ama Jhao stalked away to drink from one of his own rice alcohol jars.

The following morning Yersin tried to impress upon Ama Jhao—who was suffering from a raging hangover—that the chiefs with whom he was in conflict were prepared to resolve their differences. All of the neighboring leaders, including those who were neutral, put the blame on Ama Jhao. If he agreed to return M'Bleng's elephants, peace between them could be restored. Ama Jhao was not moved by any of this and refused to consider any such gesture. Ama Jhao's wife was more conciliatory and, with Yersin, worked out a plan for a gathering at Knieng of all the chiefs over which the French doctor would preside.

On 16 August Ama Jhao invited Yersin to accompany him to the village of Moué, a chief he alleged had stolen three of his horses and nine servants. If Yersin could get this chief to repay the loss, Ama Jhao would supply elephants for Yersin's return to Ban Don. The Frenchman agreed. At his village, Moué promised to return the stolen horses and prisoners. In the course of their discussion, Moué mentioned that he paid tribute to the King of Fire. Several days later Ama Jhao asked Yersin to go to the village of another chief named Dang, an old enemy, to propose that he return seven prisoners. In exchange Ama Jhao would give back one of the elephants he had taken. Again Yersin agreed, but when they arrived at Dang's village the chief retreated into his house, emerging later clutching a spear and saber. Finally, talking to the French doctor, he explained that his quarrel with Ama Jhao resulted from a series of incidents. Only a year before, Ama Jhao had become sick and had accused Dang of causing him to do so. "You understand," Dang observed, "if I had the power to make him ill, I would have arranged for him to have a fatal illness!" Disdaining peace with Ama Jhao, the chief declared he would rather retain the prisoners than see his elephants. As their discussion continued, Dang called for jars of rice alcohol. Then, suddenly leaving Yersin by the fire, he absented himself to discuss the matter with his confreres. Soon small groups of warriors carrying spears, crossbows, and sabers began filtering into the room. When some two hundred had assembled, Yersin grew nervous and put his revolver on his lap. Finally, Dang returned and announced that he would accept the conditions for peace. After Yersin gave him a bracelet, the warriors set aside their weapons to take up gongs and drums.

Ama Jhao was not stirred by the news, and he indifferently offered Yersin a tired-looking horse to go to Ban Don. He also stated that if Yersin would impose similar conditions for peace on seven more of his adversaries, he would provide the elephants the Frenchman needed. His patience was tried, Yersin berated Ama Jhao, threatening to walk to the coast. He added that the spirits would surely punish the chief for his lies. This had its desired effect, and Ama Jhao provided the doctor with elephants. On 24 August 1893 Yersin departed for Ninh Hoa, noting in his diary that the chief "had the effrontery to invite me to return and visit him soon." Shortly after, at the request of the governor general, Yersin made another expedition from Nhatrang into the highlands through the Danhim valley and south to Tanh Linh terminating at Bien Hoa on 5 September 1893.[71]

In a letter to the president of the Société de Geographie Commerciale, Yersin recounted that a major objective of his expeditions was to determine a feasible route from Saigon to the coast at Khanh Hoa or Binh Thuan provinces.[72] But, he lamented, while he was engaged in his research a young administrator named Outrey, who had been commissioned to study the possibility of a route from Saigon to Kratie, had captured the imagination of the administration with a grand scheme for a railway through the interior to serve Stung Treng, Attopeu, and Tourane. This overshadowed Yersin's plan for a road through the Tri An sector, and his efforts to interest Governor General de Lanessan had been of no avail. Yersin expressed the view that this was due to the governor general's "politique annamitophile," which blinded him to the dangers of a new uprising in Annam. He cited the attack on him by a Vietnamese band during his recent expedition and enclosed in the letter a "proclamation of the Rebels of Binh Thuan for June 1893" purportedly written by a mandarin.[73] It contained orders from a "great general" for a coming uprising in which all villagers would play a role. Unfortunately, Yersin noted, de Lanessan did not take heed. Neither would he consider enlisting the aid of the "former auxiliaries of Monsieur Pavie" because of his opposition to the military.

Yersin's remarks that de Lanessan followed a "politique annamitophile" clearly was a reference to the leader's view that the French in Tonkin and Annam should rule through a collaboration with the mandarins, who, he

71. A. Yersin, "Un Mois chez M'Siao (Juillet-Aout 1893)," *Indochine*, no. 117 (1942), pp. 3–8.

72. A. Yersin, "Dr. Yersin to Monsieur le Président de la Société de Géographie Commerciale, 15 Decembre 1893," Harmand Collection, Olin Library, Cornell University, Ithaca, New York.

73. In this document (which was dated according to the reign of Ham Nghi in spite of his already having been deposed and exiled) the author, a mandarin of the Bo Thanh Su rank, was transmitting orders received from a "great general" of the Ton That family. These orders instructed every villager to store food, water, arms, wood, and other essentials so they could assist the Great Army in the coming revolt. This document also described an attack on the Phan Ri fortress that resulted in the death of a rebel mandarin.

felt, could maintain effective control of the administrations as they had historically.[74] He noted that the mandarins exercised a great deal of influence over the population "like the bourgeoisie in France." In putting down the Revolt of the Literati, which largely was led by the mandarins, the French attempted to tighten their control when, in de Lanessan's view, the colonial administration should have attempted to achieve "benevolent but effective control" through the indigenous structure of authority, while at the same time engaging in economic development.

In the final report on his expeditions, Yersin briefly summarized some of his findings and assessments.[75] He was particularly struck with the Maa, whom he found to be very attractive people. He did not have the same opinion of the Rhadé Bih ("they take after the Vietnamese in their deceitfulness and the Siamese in their laziness"). He considered the Maa plateau to have an enormous potential for economic development. His comment that "it is there that one will establish the future *résidence* among the Mois of South Annam" was in effect an echo of that made earlier by Cupet that the highlands should be brought into the French political sphere. This clearly was a view held by a wide circle of Frenchmen with experience in the region. Yersin advocated direct rule of the highlands by the French: this would permit the French to exploit the economic potential through colonization, thereby eliminating the Vietnamese traders and mandarins whose influence in the highlands most French investigators— such as Aymonier, Brière, and others already noted—considered deleterious. A French presence in the mountains also would render it very difficult for the Vietnamese rebels to use the area as a redoubt. Finally, the primitive highlanders, unlike the Vietnamese, would accept French rule as a permanent condition.

A series of events took place in Laos during 1893 that would have considerable bearing on the French decision to organize their colonial administration in the highlands. At the beginning of the year the French military efforts at blocking Siamese expansion into the region east of the Mekong culminated in a confrontation between the two powers as a result of two incidents. First, two French agents were expelled from Oudene by Siamese authorities. Second, the French agent in Luang Prabang was

74. J. L. de Lanessan, *Principes de colonisation* (Paris: Félix Alcan, 1897), pp. 112–35.
75. A. Yersin, "4e Rapport: le Docteur Yersin en mission à Monsieur le Ministre de l'Instruction Publique, Saigon, 20 Décembre 1893," Harmand Collection, Olin Library, Cornell University, Ithaca, New York.

reported to have been murdered. (It later was revealed that he had died of natural causes.) Pavie, under instructions from Paris, reiterated the assertion that all the territory east of the Mekong belonged to Vietnam, and he called for a Siamese evacuation. In April 1893 three French columns moved into Laos and northern Cambodia from Annam. One seized Stung Treng and the island of Khong in the Mekong, the second advanced toward Muong Phine, and a third occupied the Cammon area. Tensions mounted as French warships moved into the Chao Phraya below Bangkok and on 25 July blockaded the river. Soon thereafter the Siamese capitulated to French demands and in the Treaty of Bangkok, signed on 3 October 1893, relinquished all claims to any territory in Laos on the east bank of the Mekong. As protectors of the Vietnamese emperor's suzerainty over this territory, the French were now in control.[76]

Revived interest in a route from Saigon to Annam led to a new expedition by Yersin early in 1894. In a letter to Dr. Calmette, another pioneer in bringing western medicine to Vietnam, Yersin complained of being under the "dépendance despotique de Monsieur de Lanessan," whose support he nonetheless accepted for an expedition to trace a route from Nhatrang to Tourane through the mountains.[77] Departing in February, he returned to the Danhim valley and the Lang Bian peak before turning northward into the rugged country that lay between this peak and the Dak Lak valley. He encountered hostility from the Mnong in the area, and on 1 March one of the Vietnamese soldiers in his escort was wounded by the Mnong. When other soldiers opened fire, the villagers shouted and ran about burning down their own houses. Yersin and his party were forced to abandon many of their supplies as they hastily departed. On 4 March their encampment was attacked by a force of several hundred Mnong warriors. Arrows fell like rainfall, but when the soldiers fired into the air the attackers fled in panic. Finally, Yersin and his party reached the Krong Ana river and the village of M'Bleng, one of the chiefs the Frenchman had visited the previous year.

Stopping briefly at the village of Ama Jhao, the expedition continued northward into the Jarai country. At Kontum, Yersin visited for twelve days with the missionaries. In the company of Father Guerlach he visited Sedang villages, concluding that they were "the most bellicose of the

76. Hall, *History*, pp. 686–96.
77. "Dr. Yersin to Dr. Calmette, Saigon, 12 Janvier 1894," Harmand Collection, Olin Library, Cornell University, Ithaca, New York.

Moi." Leaving Kontum, he proceeded in a northwestern direction to the
Halang village of Dak Rode, where he arranged for the release of a
Vietnamese who had been captured at Tra My by highlanders and sold into
slavery. From there the party continued to Attopeu, where a French
administrator had just been assigned (one also was posted in Khong).
Following a somewhat winding route through the rugged, heavily
forested mountains, Yersin and his group reached the coastal city of Faifoo (Hoi An) on 5 May 1894. After a visit with Boulloche, the résident
superior of Annam in Tourane, Yersin returned to Saigon by ship.[78]

In a letter to Dr. Harmand, Yersin reported that de Lanessan was about
to return to France and pointedly inquired, "Do you think he will
return?"[79] De Lanessan did not return. He was replaced by Paul-Armand
Rousseau. Apparently the new governor general did not share de
Lanessan's suspicions of Pavie's military associates, for late in 1894
Odend'hal, one of Pavie's officers who had participated in an earlier
mission led by Cupet, conducted an expedition that took him from Hue to
Saravan, then to Attopeu and Kontum, finally terminating at Faifoo on the
coast. Departing from Hue in November, Odend'hal reached Saravan on 5
December and proceeded southward to the Boloven plateau town of
Attopeu. His findings, some of which were noted earlier, included information on geography, geology, ethnology, and slavery. He also carefully
recorded possible routes for future road construction, and he included his
assessment of the possibilities for economic development of the region.
Going southeast from Attopeu, Odend'hal visited Dak Rode, where he
was still remembered from his 1891 visit (the villagers continued to address
him as *quan*, the Vietnamese term for "mandarin" the highlanders used to
address French officers and officials). On 27 December he arrived in
Kontum, and from there he made his way back to Attopeu, then across the
rugged mountain country to the northeast, finally reaching Faifoo in mid-
February 1895.[80]

The year 1895 was a pivotal one for the future of the highlands. The
treaty of 1893 had given France control of the territory between the

---

78. Bernard, *Yersin*, pp. 60–69; A. Yersin, "De Nhatrang à Tourane par les plateaux Moi,"
Indochine, no. 137 (1943), pp. 3–9; no. 146 (1943), pp. 5–9; no. 150 (1943), pp. 4–8.

79. "Dr. A. Yersin to Dr. Harmand, Nhatrang, 20 Septembre 1894," Harmand Collection, Olin
Library, Cornell University, Ithaca, New York.

80. Prosper Odend'hal, "Itinéraires d'Attopeu à la mer," *Revue Indochinoise* 9 (1908): no. 78,
pp. 399–413; no. 79, pp. 499–513; no. 80, pp. 575–89; no. 81, pp. 684–88; no. 82, pp. 742–58; no.
83, pp. 835–48.

Mekong river and the coast of Annam, and in January 1894 the first French administrative posts were established at Khong and Attopeu. On 1 June 1895 a decree promulgated by Résident Superior Boulloche divided the new territory into two zones, Upper Laos and Lower Laos. Each was to be administered by a commandant superior, one residing in Luang Prabang and the other in Khong. Lower Laos encompassed the region east of the Mekong, including the central highlands, and there were three résidences—one at Stung Treng, one at Attopeu, and one at Saravane. At the same time that these changes were announced, the Bahnar-Rengao Confederation, the only indigenous political entity, was abolished. The highlanders now were nominally under the authority of the French.

8 BEGINNINGS OF THE FRENCH ADMINISTRATION, 1895–1914

As the nineteenth century drew to a close, much of the mystery that had veiled the green mountainous hinterlands of Indochina was being slowly dissipated by French explorations. Now, many of the principal rivers with their rich, brown-colored waters were being charted, and a great deal of the varied, sometimes spectacular, topography was being described in prosaic geographic terms. Explorers' journals imparted a new awareness of the ethnic variation that existed among the highlanders together with considerable information on the social traits of the mountain people—particularly their leadership—and their physical appearance. As a result, even the somewhat majestic aura that had surrounded the Kings of Fire and Water diminished as they were found at first view to differ little from other highland chiefs who wore loincloths and lived in ordinary houses.

The explorations also revealed the potential for economic exploitation of the natural resources that abounded in the highlands. As the new century dawned, it became readily apparent to the French authorities that they would have to move from the nominal control they had gained in 1895 to some form of real control. A French military and administrative presence would have to be established, and the highlanders would have to accept French rule—which meant, among other things, accepting taxation and corvée duty. When this was accomplished, the mountain region could be opened for colonization. In the early years of the twentieth century, military posts were transformed into administrative posts, footpaths that the explorers had followed became rudimentary roads, and the first towns began to grow at Kontum, Ban Me Thuot, and Dalat.

In order to rule the highland populations under their control, the French officials sent to the highlands followed the example of the earlier explorers, relying on the local chiefs—who submitted to French authority voluntarily or as the result of military "pacification." The strategy of using these chiefs as intermediaries in the newly established administration resulted in drastic changes in their traditional roles. They took on numerous new functions, such as collecting taxes and organizing corvées; their mandates of authority now were derived from an alien source, the French administration; and for the first time their roles were stipendiary. Although they were from widely separate places in the highlands, these chiefs were brought together periodically by the French administration for various types of ceremonies. As a result, the social distance that had previously existed began to diminish as did their parochial view of the world around them. This signaled the increased contact that the highlanders within and between ethnic groups would have as a result of the French presence. It was an important development for spreading awareness of not only individual group affiliation but also highlander ethnic identity.

THE DOUMER ADMINISTRATION

Two related events in December 1896 were to have long-range effects on French policy toward the highland people. On the tenth, Governor General Rousseau died at his post in Hanoi, and, on the twenty-seventh, Paul Doumer was named to replace him. Doumer arrived in Vietnam on 13 February 1897, determined to end the administrative chaos that plagued the colony and turn it into an economic asset for France. A dynamic and capable man, still under the age of forty, Doumer realized that France would do well to focus its efforts at economic development on Vietnam. In order to transform it into a rich colony, it would be necessary to develop a strong central government under French control. This could only be achieved by eliminating all remnants of Vietnamese political authority, so in addition to other administrative innovations, Doumer in September 1897 dissolved the Cơ Mật (or Secret Council), a ministerial cabinet through which the emperor had performed those functions he retained after the protectorate of Annam had been established. While the name Cơ Mật remained, it now became a new council of ministers in which every Vietnamese member had a French counterpart. Rather than being headed by the emperor, it was under the French résident superior of Annam, who was subject only to the orders of Doumer.

Another thrust of Doumer's administration was the "economic development" of the colony, particularly Tonkin and Annam, which thus far had produced only debts but which held the potential for economic projects that would ultimately enrich France. "Economic development" would mean a more systematic exploitation of such things as mines as well as vast public works projects—including road, bridge, and railroad construction—to transform the colonies into modern productive states. On 14 September 1898 Doumer's scheme for a trans-Indochinese railroad linking Hanoi and Saigon was approved, and soon he began construction of a section from Saigon to Qui Nhon. A rail line from Qui Nhon over the mountains of Binh Dinh to Attopeu in Laos, however, was not approved. Doumer also favored road construction into the mountains ("penetration routes" they would be called) to open this region for French colonization. In 1897 a number of new taxes were levied to increase revenues for the colonial budgets. Among these were levies on cinnamon, salt, and wood, all important commodities in highland-lowland commerce. Doumer also is remembered for having founded the Ecole Française d'Extrême-Orient, intended "to develop knowledge of the old civilization of the East and to protect historical monuments." Finally, he organized a medical school in Hanoi and administrative services to deal with geography, geology, meteorology, and statistics.[1]

With political power in Annam now more or less held by the French, it became necessary to establish some kind of administration in the highlands so as to consolidate control and begin opening the region for colonization. Among the highlanders already under control of the Vietnamese administration, i.e., those groups adjacent to the coastal plain who traded with the lowlanders and paid taxes to the court of Hue, it was essentially a matter of reorganizing the existing administrative apparatus and replacing Vietnamese with French authority. But organizing French rule among the "independent" highland groups in the more remote uplands was to prove a more complicated task. At this time, many of the groups were scarcely accessible, and they had little or no experience in dealing with outsiders. Furthermore, some of them were apt to be hostile, as the attacks on Odend'hal by the Cua and on Yersin by the Mnong indicated.

---

1. Joseph Buttinger, *Vietnam: A Dragon Embattled*, 2 vols. (New York: Frederick A. Praeger, 1967), 1: 7–35.

The strategy established by the explorers provided a pattern for the French in dealing with the independent highland groups. The first step was to make contact with the local leaders and one way or another gain their cooperation. These leaders would then serve as intermediaries between the French and the local populations. This had been the case with the Bahnar Bonom chief Kiom, who aided the missionaries in founding the first Catholic mission in the highlands. It also was true in the case of Kiom's son, Pim, as well as the Bahnar, Rengao, Sedang, and Jarai chiefs who had participated in the Bahnar-Rengao Confederation and the ill-fated Kingdom of the Sedang. The Rhadé chief Ama Jhao also had lent considerable assistance to Yersin. In all of these examples, however, the chiefs had already had some experiences in dealing with outsiders (notably the lowland traders) and were prepared to make some accommodation with the French. But, as the explorers' accounts indicated, many other chiefs had no intention of being cooperative. If a chief could not be won over through peaceful means, however, the French were ready to use force, a strategy they referred to as "pacification."

HIGHLAND CHIEFS AT THE TURN OF THE CENTURY

Although Cupet's encounter with the King of Fire did not result in a description of him as any kind of a great chief, at that time the King of Fire and his confrere the King of Water were still the most prominent of the highland leaders.[2] Their tributary relations with the Khmer and Vietnamese rulers lent them a certain air of majesty, and they also enjoyed widespread reputations as powerful shamans. Cupet was perhaps expecting more of the grandeur and trappings associated with powerful figures among more advanced people. Such is not the case with the highlanders, and to the outsider the great are indistinguishable from the ordinary folk.

Around the turn of the century, additional information on the Kings of Fire and Water began to appear. Following his travels through the central highlands, Lavallée, in 1901, published some information on the two kings that he had received in Kontum from Father Guerlach (who subsequently published almost the same data).[3] Both observed that the King of Fire was

---

2. Auguste Pavie, *Mission Pavie en Indochine*, 11 vols. (Paris, 1879–1895), 3: 294–324.

3. M. A. Lavallée, "Notes ethnographiques sur diverses tribus du sud-est de l'Indo-Chine," *BEFEO* 1, no. 4 (1901): 291–311; J. B. Guerlach, "Quelques notes sur les Sadet," *Revue Indochinoise*, no. 1 (1905), pp. 184–88.

held in particular awe by the Bahnar and Jarai, who regarded him as a kind of demigod because of the sacred saber he possessed. The Bahnar Bonom chief Pim had told Guerlach a legend surrounding this talisman (see chap. 4) and also supplied one version of how the new king is selected. Guerlach claimed that this version was incorrect and presented what he asserted was the true selection process, as told by Jarai informants. After the King of Fire or Water died, the dignitaries who formed his entourage gathered to drink from alcohol jars and to discuss who would be the successor. The King of Fire must be of the Xeu (Siu) clan while the King of Water must be a member of the Rocham (Rcom) clan. Therefore either successor usually is a younger brother of the king or a son of the king's sister (in keeping with the Jarai regulation for matrilineal descent). For the investiture, the new king wore a white loincloth, and a member of the Koxor (Ksor) clan tied a cotton bracelet around his wrist. Afterward the new king selected his "officers," a group of male and female assistants. The highest ranking of the males was the assistant who poured water into the alcohol jar when the king made his ritual libation. Next was the one who cooked the king's rice, and below him were the basket maker who wove the small stool on which the king sat, a smith who made the knife used to cut the string bracelets (which were worn for seven years and then burned), and the assistant who put new string bracelets on the king's wrist. There were four female assistants: one who grew cotton for the string bracelets, another who wove a bracelet, a third who made his clothes, and a fourth who sewed the small cloth packet in which the king kept his tobacco.

During the first year the new king made a tour of all the Jarai country as well as the area occupied by the Bahnar Golar. This tour was repeated two years later and again five years after that. Following this, he made the ritual visit whenever he pleased. The inhabitants of the villages he visited were expected to provide a buffalo and a pig to offer the spirits in a ritual sacrifice, after which a large feast was held. Each village also was expected to present the king with a large copper pot, a pig, and one head of cattle, and each household offered him either a small hand ax or a bit of wax.

Following the installation of a new king, envoys were sent to Phu Yen to carry the news to the court of Hue, and traditionally they were presented with a brilliant white metal urn by the Vietnamese emperor. The highlanders told Guerlach that the gift was of silver, but he expressed doubt that the Vietnamese ruler would be so generous, speculating that it undoubtedly contained a good deal of tin.

Guerlach was informed by the Jarai that when the king fell ill, and it appeared that death was near, his family and assistants gathered. As he was drawing his last breath, a spear was plunged into his abdomen. As the news of the death spread through the countryside, villages sent representatives bearing jars of wine, and pigs or chickens. For several days the king's village mourned, with everyone weeping and wailing while drinking and eating as gongs and drums sounded continually. A pyre of special woods was constructed, and, in an atmosphere of pomp, the body was placed on it and burned. When the fire had subsided, the charred heart, teeth, and bones were placed in the metal urn sent by the Vietnamese emperor after the king had been invested. The other remains were gathered up and put in a coffin which was buried. Over the grave a provisory shelter was constructed in which the urn was placed. The king's widow came to weep and then, taking the urn on her back with a sling, walked around the grave sweeping it. The urn was returned to the shelter, and the widow placed before it a cup of water and a leaf containing rice, marking the end of the burial. At the beginning of each lunar month there was the Glom Porr ceremony wherein the widow and other mourners gathered to drink from the jars all night while she carried the urn around the grave. This was repeated for five years, after which an impressive tomb was constructed. At the Mut Bru ritual the urn and coffin were placed in the tomb, which was then abandoned.

Although the initial contact that Cupet had with the King of Water and King of Fire was relatively amiable, it would appear that their attitude toward the French subsequently changed. According to Maitre, in December 1894 the commissioner of Stung Treng went with an escort of soldiers into the Jarai country where they were attacked by the forces of the *Patau Ia*, the King of Water, and forced to retreat.[4] However, the commissioner was determined to bring the area under control. In January 1897, leading a column of troops, he returned and routed the King of Water and his warriors. When the French troops reached the shaman's village, they put it to the torch, but the King of Water had fled to take refuge in the vicinity of the King of Fire's village.

Twelve years after this incident, Besnard, the résident of Darlac, was told by Jarai informants that it was the King of Fire, not the King of Water, who had attacked the French troops.[5] They went on to say that, when the French punitive expedition returned, the local population looked to the

4. Henri Maitre, *Les Jungles Moi* (Paris: Larose, 1912), p. 537.
5. H. Besnard, "Les Populations Moi du Darlac," *BEFEO* 7, no. 1 (1907): 80–86.

King of Fire to exterminate the French with his sacred saber. This did not occur, and as the troops burned the village a large ball of fire was seen ascending into the sky from the hut where the sacred saber was kept. It was taken as a sign that the King of Fire's power had gone.

Another version of this incident was related in May 1964 by a very elderly Jarai chief named Nay Nui (2.11), usually referred to by his teknonymous designation Ama H'bu. At the time of the interviews, this chief was alleged by his kinsfolk to be around one hundred and twenty years of age.[6] He lived in the splendid longhouse of his youngest daughter Rcom H'blon and her husband Siu Banh (2.15) in Buon Broai, across the Apa river from Cheo Reo. Nay Nui was by then blind, and he sat on a mat in the large main room of the house weaving fish nets. Wearing only a traditional loincloth, he appeared very wrinkled and thin, but he quickly pointed out that he still had all of his teeth. He was indeed very old but he had about him the air of one who in the past had commanded respect. Here was someone who had been a great chief.

Nay Nui was born sometime in the latter half of the nineteenth century in the village of Bon Mpuh (in an area south of Cheo Reo) where his father, Sa Gam, was a well-known local leader. Family legend has it that at the time of his birth, a large white toad with unusually broad legs appeared near the house. His father grabbed it and put it in the river but it returned the following day. Again it was placed in the river only to come back the next day. After this happened a third time, Nay Nui's father offered a pig and three jars of rice alcohol to the spirits, and the toad disappeared. The incident was interpreted as a sign that the newborn child was favored by the spirits and was destined to be a leader among the Jarai.

As a youth, Nay Nui displayed remarkable physical prowess, a manifestation of *kdruh* (the favoritism of the spirits) that predestined him to a role as a leader. He recalled how he was able to leap from the ground up to the high platforms (usually six to eight feet in height in the Cheo Reo area) in the front of the longhouses. His daughter Rcom H'ban (2.18) told an oft-repeated story of his feat in jumping over a row of seven water buffaloes.

Nay Nui remembered the first Frenchmen who appeared in the Cheo Reo area and described them as "big men with large stomachs and red faces." He also recalled how they tried to assert their authority over the Jarai. However, he joined forces with Oi At, the King of Fire, and they

---

6. These interviews were conducted through Nay Luett (2.26), husband of Rcom H'om (a descendant of Nay Nui).

drove the French away. He claimed to have killed one Frenchman during the fighting. Several years later, however, the French returned with more troops. He lamented that the Jarai with their crossbows, sabers, and spears were no match for the guns of the outsiders, so they had had to accept French rule.

Nay Nui's status as a leader in the Ayun-Apa rivers area was enhanced to a great extent by his marriage to Rcom H'lion, a member of the prestigious Rcom clan. A family history and genealogy (see charts 2 and 3) of the segment of the clan that settled in this area was supplied by some clan members.[7] They reveal a great deal about how the Ayun-Apa rivers area was settled by the Jarai and how some of the villages were founded by members of the Rcom clan. They also tell about the origins of the name Cheo Reo.

The common ancestress of the segment of the Rcom clan now found in the vicinity of Cheo Reo was Rcom H'it (2.1), and she had two daughters, Rcom H'wik (2.2) and Rcom H'ko (3.1). H'wik had two daughters, Rcom H'bem (2.3) and Rcom H'lok (2.4), who, in keeping with the Jarai tradition remained in H'wik's house following their marriage. After a smallpox epidemic forced them to separate, they settled around one kilometer apart. H'bem had three children, the eldest of whom was Rcom H'leo (2.5), who married a local chief named Nay Jak.

Rcom H'leo's younger brothers were Rcom Chu (2.8) and Rcom Reo (2.9).[8] According to clan legend, the two brothers differed physically: whereas Chu was small in stature and tended to be "lazy," his brother Reo was robust and dynamic. Indeed, Reo was exceptionally strong and was alleged to be capable of clearing a large field for farming in much less time than anyone else. Atypically, neither brother married, but both had the reputation of being great lovers who carried on many affairs with girls from neighboring families as well as with female slaves. Rcom Reo usually employed the same strategy: he would take kindling wood to the longhouse of a beautiful girl, saying he had come to help with the cooking, and this initiated many love affairs.

---

7. The data for the family history and genealogy were provided during interviews conducted between 1957 and 1971 with Rcom Ko (3.9), Rcom H'areng (3.3), Rcom H'nher (3.4), and Rcom H'ban (2.18). In his work on the Jarai, *Coordonnées structures Jörai familiales et sociales* (Paris: Travaux et Mémoires de l'Institut d'Ethnologie, 1972), Jacques Dournes reports similar data but with some variations.

8. In Dournes, *Coordonnées structures Jörai*, pp. 77–78, it is reported that Cu and Coreo were cousins, sons of two sisters of the Rcom clan.

At that time the country around the confluence of the Ayun and Apa rivers was covered with forests in which wild animals such as tigers, rhinoceros, deer, and gaurs roamed, and it became a favorite hunting place for Chu and Reo. It was the two brothers who led their mother and the family into the vicinity at the time of the epidemic, and a banyan tree which H'leo planted there stands to this day. The village that grew on the site became known as Buon Chu-Reo, a name which the French, arriving at the end of the nineteenth century to build their military post, took over as Cheo Reo.

According to elderly Rcom ladies H'areng and H'ner, Nay Jak arranged the marriage of his daughter H'lion (2.10) to Nay Nui. They settled in the longhouse now occupied by their eldest daughter Rcom H'bu and her husband in Bon Chu Ama Bu (Village of the Father of H'bu) named for Nay Nui. This village was subsequently engulfed by the town of Cheo Reo. The marriage proved to be an auspicious one, and Nay Nui recalled during the interview that he came to possess a great many valuable alcohol jars, some two hundred head of cattle, three hundred head of buffalo, and many houses, including the massive longhouse next to the banyan tree. He also became the recognized chief among the Jarai in the area of the Ayun and Apa rivers and formed alliances with some of the neighboring chiefs— Ama Tuao, Ama Dep, and Ama Rin among the Bahnar and Ama Pia and Ama H'nhao among the Krung. He also had close relations with Oi At, the King of Fire, and pointed out that in the Jarai country every village or group of villages had a "representative" of the King of Fire. In the vicinity of Cheo Reo, he had this role. He related that when the King of Fire visited he would be responsible for providing shelter and food and making arrangements for any rituals. Oi At died and was succeeded by Oi Tu. When Nay Nui himself became too elderly to be representative he turned over the role to Ksor Seng, husband of Rcom H'areng (3.3). Reflecting further about the King of Fire, Nay Nui added that he is the guardian of a sacred saber, which according to Jarai legend was found at the bottom of a river. The Khmer took possession of the sheath, while the Jarai retained the saber itself. Nay Nui then noted that the Khmer were friends of the Jarai and that their ruler used to send elephants to the King of Fire. He also observed that the Lao too were friendly with the Jarai but that the Vietnamese were not. Nay Nui then pointed out that he had been a friend of Oi Kteo ("Grandfather of Kteo"), the King of the Wind, who had been replaced by Oi Coba. After his death Oi Coba was in turn succeeded by Tung Re, who died in 1964.

In spite of his having opposed them, the French sought Nay Nui's support in dealing with the local Jarai population. During the interview the old chief produced a box filled with various medals attesting to the French administration's appreciation for his service. He recalled that in carrying out his duty to organize corvée among the villagers he had traveled on horse and elephant throughout the Jarai country. One of the large projects for which he mustered labor was the construction of Route 7 which runs from Pleiku in a southeasterly direction through Cheo Reo and then follows the Apa river into coastal Phu Khanh. Also, as a representative of the Jarai he was summoned by the French to go to Ban Me Thuot and Kontum for various celebrations, and twice he was a member of a delegation of highland chiefs that journeyed to Hue to assist at gatherings held in the royal court. He described being in the presence of emperors Khai Dinh (1916–1925) and Bao Dai (1925–54). One of his most memorable experiences, however, was a ride in the steam train down the coast.

Some of the other highland chiefs of the late nineteenth century have been described previously. One of these was Pim (1.5), son of the renowned Bahnar Bonom chief Kiom. Pim became involved in the Mayréna affair (see chap. 7) but was scarcely mentioned in the literature thereafter. It is apparent, however, that his ambitions to establish a Bahnar-Jarai-Rengao Confederation never were realized. His authority remained limited to a group of Bahnar Bonom villages. Krui, the Bahnar chief who had risen to the role of president of the Bahnar-Rengao Confederation at the time of the Kingdom of Sedang in 1888, retained his authority until the confederation was dismantled in 1895. According to informants he then retired to his village and faded as a leader in the Kontum area. Also, despite their having been among the first Bahnar to attain literacy, Krui's sons never assumed any kind of leadership role.

Another leader mentioned previously was Up, the outstanding leader of the Kontum area when Navelle visited there in 1884.[9] Hiar, an elderly Bahnar Jolong informant, said that Up had two brothers, Hma and Ye (Hiar's paternal grandfather, 1.3). Up is remembered for having organized an effective defense of the local villages against incursions by the bellicose neighboring Sedang, and he and his brother Hma were the wealthiest men in the area, possessing numerous slaves, cattle, gongs, and jars, as well as large landholdings. Ye, the youngest brother, was less affluent, but he was respected for his great courage.

9. E. Navelle, "De Thi-Nai au Bla," *Excursions et Reconnaissances* 13, no. 30 (1887): 291–95.

Some of the Rhadé and Mnong chiefs have already been mentioned. Additional information on them, as well as on other leaders, was obtained from various oral and written sources in the vicinity of Ban Me Thuot.[10] At Ban Don, the leader was Khunjanob, who had been described by Cupet. Rhadé informants noted that he was a Mnong–Lao, and he is remembered as the "Ivory King" because of his monopoly on the elephant trade. Among the Rhadé Kpa, in the vicinity of present Ban Me Thuot, the noted chief was Ama Bloi. It was indicated in the previous chapter that he had allowed the Lao to establish the trading post at Ban Don in the mid-nineteenth century. After his death late in the century, his brother Ama Thuot, for whom the town was named, succeeded him.[11]

Northwest of Ban Me Thuot the local chief among the Rhadé Adham was Ama Ual. The present Mewal village and French-owned Mewal coffee estate are named for him. Northeast of Ban Me Thuot in the area of present Buon Ho district the leader of the Krung was Ama Hjik, and to the east in the Cadé area the Rhadé Ktul chief was Ama Jhao, described in Yersin's accounts. Ama Jhao also is known among the Rhadé by another teknonymous name, Ae Wiegn ("Grandfather of Wiegn"), as well as by his real name, Y Yen Ayun. Still farther east, Ae Bung ("Grandfather of Bung") and M'drak (for whom the M'drak area is named) were the foremost leaders among the Rhadé Mdhur, Rhadé Blo, and Rhadé Epan.

South of Ban Me Thuot among the Rhadé Bih the leader of wide repute was Ama Trang Guh, who in a previous chapter was described as the chief who fought an incursion of Burmese, Lao, and Siamese in 1887.[12] The foremost chief in the area occupied by the Mnong Rlam, Mnong Gar, and Mnong Kuenh was Bak, known as the "Paddy King" because of the extensive paddy fields he owned in the Dak Lak area. According to Y Puk Buon Ya, his mother's father, Ae Dak ("Grandfather of Dak"), was recognized as chief by six Rhadé Bih villages and had wealth in cattle, jars, and gongs. Among the Mnong Nong and Mnong Preh, the most mem-

10. Oral sources include Y Char Hdok, a Mnong Rlam who was the second highlander to receive a bachelor's degree from an American university, and numerous elderly Rhadé villagers. Written materials include Y Dhuat Nie Kdam, "Customs of the Rhadé Highlanders in Darlac Province" (typewritten translation by Y Thih Eban, Ban Me Thuot, 1966), and Y Bham Enuol, "Extraits de l'histoire des Hauts-Plateaux du Centre Viet-Nam (Pays Montagnards du Sud-Indochinois)" (mimeographed, Zone d'Organisation, 1965). The author of the former was a civil servant in Ban Me Thuot. The latter was written by the head of a highland dissident movement that became active in the 1950s and 1960s.

11. Ban Me Thuot is a Lao version of the Rhadé name Buon Ama Thuot, i.e., "Village of the Father of Thuot."

12. Maitre, *Les Jungles Moi*, p. 489.

orable leader was Pu Trang Lung, who resisted French rule (and, as will be discussed below, was responsible for the death of Henri Maitre, the French explorer).

Unlike the groups such as the Bahnar, Jarai, Mnong and Rhadé that were considered "independent," the Chru had for centuries been under the domination of the Cham and subsequently of the Vietnamese. Under the Cham, authority was vested in the head of the Banahria clan who held the title *potao* and possessed the saber, the symbol of his authority presented by the Cham monarch. According to Touneh Han Tho, the Banahria line of authority endured until the end of the nineteenth century when Banahria Quang, the head of the clan, was the prominent Chru leader in the Danhim valley. He functioned under the authority of the Cham mandarins appointed by the court of Hue. In addition, he possessed extensive landholdings, many cattle, jars, and gongs, as well as some valuable, prestigious family heirlooms of Cham origin.

In the Maa oral tradition, as recorded by Boulbet (see chap. 3), it is related that only part of the Maa accepted Cham rule when K'Cang, the leader of the Cau Too elite lineage, became the Cham potao.[13] Although his followers remained on the Maa plateau, his own lineage splintered and lost its traditional functions. Boulbet also reports that at the end of the nineteenth century the title potao was still vested in one elder, a descendant of K'Cang, but the traditional symbols of authority that had at one time been kept by the lineage head had become dispersed.

The Maa oral tradition also described how the Cau Maa, who had not accepted Cham rule, had moved downstream under their leader K'Hek. He had received a Cham saber after making an agreement with a Cham chief concerning the division of the territory. According to Boulbet, five generations later the Cau Maa leadership was still in the hands of a direct descendant of K'Hek and this descendant still retained possession of the saber, a symbol of independence.

PACIFICATION AND EARLY ADMINISTRATION

In writing about the French effort to establish a presence in Quang Ngai at the very beginning of the twentieth century, French military officer Trinquet noted that Governor General Paul Doumer made it known that

13. Jean Boulbet, *Pays des Maa domaine des génies Nggar Maa, Nggar Yaang* (Paris: Ecole Française d'Extrême-Orient, 1967), pp. 65–78.

he wanted to hear no more about "independent savages," and he gave the order for an effective "penetration" of the highlands.[14] This ended the relative indifference with which the colonial administration previously had regarded the mountainous interior. The decree of 1 June 1895 placing the central highlands under the administration in Lower Laos had provided a legal basis for establishing a French administration in the region, and under the Doumer regime implementation began in earnest.

The strategy was one of first establishing military-administrative posts where some cooperation from local leaders already had been attained. Where this was not the case, military pressure through "pacification" would be employed to force cooperation. Since French priests had been installed in Kontum since the middle of the century, it was the logical place for an administrative foothold. This was achieved with some ease by naming Father Vialleton, the superior of the Kontum Mission, as the representative of France in that particular region. The official document stating the priest's prerogatives and responsibilities was issued on 7 March 1898 by Tournier, the commandant superior of Lower Laos. It began by pointing out that "civilization" had been brought to that region by the French missionaries but that the remainder of the highlands still had to be brought under French control through pacification. Only through the priests could the Kontum area be administered, so the decision had been made to put all religious, civil, military, and judicial powers in the hands of Father Vialleton. The military aspect, Tournier emphasized, would be purely defensive, mainly to protect Christians. Should the priests require arms, he was prepared to send them thirty-five carbines (1874 models) and two hundred rounds of ammunition. Regarding justice, one of the principal duties would be to see that slavery (which had been abolished in Laos by the French) would not be practiced. Father Vialleton also would see that taxes were collected, and he was to give some attention to economic development, particularly in animal husbandry and cultivation of cardamom.[15]

At the same time, the French administration set out to reorganize the Son Phong, the Vietnamese "pacification" program originally organized

<hr/>

14. Trinquet, "Le Poste administratif du Lang-Ri (Quang Ngai)," *Revue Indochinoise* 10 (1908): 347.

15. J. B. Guerlach, *"L'Oeuvre néfaste," réplique du Père J. B. Guerlach, missionnaire apostolique au F. Camille Paris, colon en Annam* (Saigon: Imprimerie Commerciale, 1905), pp. 110–13; R. Le Jarriel, "Comment la Mission Catholique à servi la France en pays Moi," *Bulletin des Amis du Vieux Hué* 29, no. 1 (1942): 49–50.

in 1863 as a means of consolidating Vietnamese control over the uplands of Quang Ngai and Binh Dinh. The Son Phong had become almost exclusively commercial by the end of the nineteenth century, and Trinquet observes that it had also become the veritable fief of Nguyen Tan's descendants, who were enriching themselves on it.[16] As a result the system was rife with abuses, not the least of which was the exploitation of the highlanders by Vietnamese traders and mandarins. In addition, the Son Phong supported slavery, victimizing not only highlanders but Vietnamese as well. These practices had led to decades of conflict between the highlanders living close to the coastal plain and the lowland Vietnamese. As recently as 1896 and 1897, bands of highlanders had raided villages in the Hoai An and Nghia Anh districts in Quang Ngai. It was the French-commanded Garde Indigène, a militia of locally recruited men organized in Annam in 1886, that had had to cope with these disturbances.[17]

The reorganization of the Son Phong, which would lead ultimately to its demise, came about as the result of a report issued on 9 October 1889 by Boulloche, the résident superior of Annam. In it he informed the French résidents of the southern provinces of Annam that the Co Mat had advised Emperor Thanh Thai that reforms in the Son Phong were essential to any future development of commerce between the highlands and lowlands. The Vietnamese agents who served as intermediaries in the existing trade were obstacles to such development because they "abused the credulity" of the highland people. The report recommended, therefore, that the agents' roles be abolished. The highlanders would deal directly with province officials, including the résidents, and the Vietnamese agents would only be retained where they were needed as interpreters. Also, the report recommended that markets be established in certain areas to allow trade to take place under the surveillance of the representative of the provincial résident. Payment of taxes in kind would in most instances be replaced by new annual taxes to be imposed on all highlanders between the ages of eighteen and sixty in the areas where trade was conducted. In Binh Dinh and Phu Yen, this tax was set at 1.00$ (1 piaster) while in Khanh Hoa and Binh Thuan it was 1.50$. Only the Rhadé in Khanh Hoa, who were considered less accustomed to handling cash, were allowed to pay their tax with

16. Trinquet, "Poste administratif," p. 347.
17. E. Daufès, *La Garde Indigène de l'Indochine de sa création à nos jours*, 2 vols. (Avignon: Imprimerie D. Serguin, 1934), 2: 113–118.

yellow wax. This marked the beginning of a French tax on highlanders that eventually would be extended throughout most of the uplands. Finally, the report recommended that the labor needed for construction and maintenance of routes into the mountains be the responsibility of the local highland villagers. This was the beginning of the corvée system that in time would be imposed on all of the highlanders under French rule.[18]

This reorganization of the Son Phong came at a time when new French investments in plantations were being made in some of the areas affected. A royal ordinance dated 27 September 1897 made it possible for French citizens and "protégé Français," i.e., foreigners in Annam with permanent residence status, to receive clear title with no payment or only a token payment for land concessions on the public domain. A subsequent royal ordinance issued on 28 April 1899 granted the governor general the right to devise a method for simplifying the granting of such titles.[19]

Some of these French estates were described by Pierre Sauvaire, Marquis de Barthélémy, who with his companion the Viscount de Marsay made a journey beginning in January 1899 through the highland areas of central Vietnam adjacent to the coast.[20] At An Diem, near the confluence of the Cai and Buong rivers, they visited the estate of Richardson and Borel, who had received their concession in 1897 but were delayed in exploiting it because of obstacles raised by the local mandarins. When Barthélémy saw the estate, there were sixty hectares of paddy fields and five hectares of sugar cane seedlings. At Tra My, the center for the cinnamon trade, Barthélémy and his companion found a rice estate being organized by two French brothers on land that had been paddy fields farmed by inmates of a penal colony once located there.

After traveling through the "Davach" (Hre) and Sedang countries, the two Frenchmen reached Kontum in March 1899. From there they journeyed southeast to An Khe, where they visited the Delignon-Paris coffee and rubber estates. En route back to Qui Nhon they came upon a Frenchman who had received a concession for a rice and tobacco estate. He informed them that he found upland rice farmed by the highlanders was best suited to the local soil and weather conditions.

The mandarins of central Vietnam took a dim view of the proposed

18. Trinquet, "Poste administratif," pp. 347–48.
19. Paul Doumer, *Situation de l'Indochine (1887–1901)* (Hanoi: F. H. Schneider, 1902), pp. 430–31.
20. Marquis de Barthélémy, *Au Pays Moi* (Paris: Plon-Nourrit et Cie., 1904), pp. 56–57, 78–81, 158–68.

changes in the Son Phong, and Trinquet observes that the passing of authority into the hands of the French administrators not only lessened the power of the mandarins but also seriously diminished the profits realized in their collusion with the trade agents.[21] The mandarins' strategy for retaliation was to foment trouble among the highlanders in the hope that the French would realize that only through the intercession of the mandarins could order be restored. Much to their chagrin, the French ignored them and instead launched an effort to occupy militarily the troubled areas. In April 1900 that portion of the Son Phong located in Binh Dinh was put under the French résident, and shortly thereafter most of the forts along the wall protecting the frontier of the highlands were abolished. In January 1901 the former Son Phong forts at Ba To and Mang Ta became French outposts, and by 1905 French militia posts had been established at Lang Ri, Minh Long, Hoanh Son, Nuoc Van, Duc Pho, Liet Son, and Gia Vuc. This gave the French military control over most of the Son Phong area and, combined with the administrative changes, altered the Son Phong to the point that it no longer continued to function.

While these transformations in the Son Phong were taking place in Quang Ngai province, the French began a military "penetration" of upland Quang Nam province, particularly the area inland from the port of Faifoo. The highlanders dwelling there—later to be called the "Katu"—were regarded as particularly warlike. For a long time they had been conducting raids on Vietnamese valley settlements. In an effort to stabilize the situation and establish a French presence, in 1904 a military post was built at An Diem on high ground above the Song Buong close to some Vietnamese villages. This brought peace to the valley but, as will be discussed below, it was only a temporary solution.[22]

Meanwhile the French "penetration" also was taking place farther south in the Rhadé country. It was recounted earlier that, in spite of initial hostility, French explorer Cupet was able eventually to win the cooperation of Khunjanob, the "Ivory King," at Ban Don. When the French decided to extend their authority into the Rhadé country, Khunjanob expressed willingness to cooperate. On 31 January 1899 a small military-administrative post was established at Ban Don. Bourgeois was placed in charge and the post was put under the authority of the commissioner at Stung Treng. According to the oral history related by Y Thih Eban, the

21. Trinquet, "Poste administratif," pp. 349–50.
22. J. Le Pichon, "Les Chasseurs de sang," *Bulletin des Amis du Vieux Hué* 25 (1938): 357–60.

respected Rhadé Kpa chief Ama Thuot at first opposed the French occupation but was swayed by his friend Khunjanob. As a result, on 2 November 1899 the French created the autonomous "montagnard" province of Darlac (a deformation of the Rhadé name Dak Lak) under the administration in Laos. On the advice of Khunjanob the administration center was shifted to the large Rhadé Kpa village Buon Ama Thuot, named after the chief but later Laoized to Ban Me Thuot. Khunjanob claimed that the climate there was healthier, and it was also more the geographic center of the Rhadé country.

While some other Rhadé chiefs such as Ama Ual submitted to the French, a few resisted. Notable among those defying the French was Ama Jhao (the chief described in Yersin's account), who according to Monfleur was assisted in his opposition by Vietnamese trade agents.[23] Another was the Rhadé Bih chief Ama Trang Guh, who had successfully turned back the 1887 incursion by a force of Burmese, Siamese, and Lao. When Bourgeois led his pacification force consisting of Vietnamese, Cambodians, and Lao militiamen into southern Darlac on 1 March 1900, he was met near Buon Tour by some five hundred warriors under the leadership of Ama Trang Guh. Although armed with their traditional spears and crossbows as well as ten flintlock rifles, they proved no match for the French force. The village was captured and burned to the ground. Then the French captured neighboring Buon Trap, also razing it, but when they moved on Ama Trang Guh's village of Buon Tieuah they encountered a hail of arrows that wounded many of the militiamen. Nonetheless, the French forced Ama Trang Guh and his followers to retreat southward into the mountains, where they were joined by some 250 families who had carried their belongings and the bones of their ancestors, From his redoubt, Ama Trang Guh conducted some relatively small raids on the French posted at Buon Tour until his death in 1903.

To the southeast of Darlac in the region of present Dalat, the establishment of a French administration was linked with two Doumer projects— the creation of a hill station and construction of the Saigon-Hanoi railway. In 1897 Doumer met with Dr. Yersin, whose explorations in the highlands rendered him an expert on the region, to discuss the possibility of founding a hill station and sanitarium in an upland location where the cool climate would provide a balm for the French colonials living in the sultry low-

23. A. Monfleur, *Monographie de la province de Darlac* (Hanoi: Imprimerie d'Extrême-Orient, 1931), pp. 10–11.

lands. Yersin recommended the Lang Bian peak. Shortly afterward Doumer ordered the formation of a military mission to research a possible route from the coast to Lang Bian.

The mission was put under the command of Artillery Captain Thouard, and one of the party was a topographer named Cunhac, who later would be the first administrator for Dalat city. Leaving Nhatrang in October 1897, the mission wound its way into the mountains, carefully recording the geographical features. At last they reached the Prenn Falls and walked into the present site of Dalat. Where Dankia now stands, one of the soldiers, a Pomeranian named Missigbrod, arranged a small kitchen garden to provide fresh vegetables for his comrades, Eventually it was to develop into the Dankia Farm, the first agricultural station in the highlands. The Thouard Mission ended its work in September 1898 and returned to Saigon.

A second mission was organized to construct an access road along the route selected by Thouard and his colleagues. The first section would be unpaved but suitable for all vehicles from Phan Rang to the foot of the mountains. From there it would be a mule trail up the slopes to the soaring Lang Bian peak. The mission set out in 1898 under the command of cavalry Captain Guynet, and the route was completed late in November 1899. A decree on 1 November 1899 created the "montagnard" province of Haut Donnai with administrative posts at Dalat and Tan Linh, the small Vietnamese town on the old trading trail through the forested coastal plain that Yersin had recommended as the path for a route from Saigon to central Vietnam. The French administrator for the new province, Ernest Outrey, took up his post at Djiring, a Sre village southwest of Dalat. His primary responsibility was to organize corvée among the highlanders to assist the various French missions led by Odéra, Garnier, Bernard, and Genin who were searching for a feasible route for the projected railway between Saigon and central Vietnam. Some missions were making their way from Saigon into the Maa country and Djiring, while others were surveying a possible route along the coast through Tan Linh. In 1900 Outrey constructed a wooden house with a sheet metal roof in Dalat, the very beginning of the hill station envisaged by Doumer. The following year, however, it was decided that the mountains were too formidable a barrier to any rail construction, so the coastal route was chosen. The new province of Haut Donnai was abolished, and Djiring was placed under the administration of Phan Thiet, while Dalat was put under Phan Rang. Cunhac, a member of the earlier Thouard Mission, was named *délégué* in

Dalat. But Doumer left Indochina in 1902 and his ambitious plans for a hill station came to an abrupt halt. Cunhac stayed on as the sole French administrator, and in 1903 he was transferred to Djiring, remaining there until 1915.[24]

Although the hill station scheme was abortive, some French entrepreneurs were nonetheless lured into the Dalat area. Taking advantage of the concession decrees cited above, on 18 April 1900 a Frenchman named Grosieux requested 885 hectares in Haut Donnai and on 18 October 1901 was awarded clear title. On 28 August 1901 another Frenchman named Armavon received title to 3,000 hectares in Dalat.[25]

Dalat was not Doumer's only hill station project. In 1901 he had commissioned Captain Debay of the Infanterie de Marine, a veteran of several highland expeditions, to survey the uplands of Quang Ngai and Quang Nam for a likely location for a hill station and sanitarium to serve the French population of central Vietnam. Debay selected the summit of a mountain he called Bana, a name derived from the highland village at its base. Located inland from Tourane (Danang), Bana was relatively accessible and its higher elevation was cool. Doumer was scheduled to visit the site in November 1901, but his trip was delayed and ultimately had to be abandoned when the following year he left for France. As a result, this project, like the Dalat scheme, was shelved.[26]

There were at this time some indications of how the French conceived of the highlanders' role in this new era of upland economic exploitation. In his report published soon after returning to France, Doumer wrote that, until the French began their program of "economic development" of the highlands, the "primitive populations" there had had no contact with Europeans and were not benefiting from any of the economic movements of the period. Now, however, with the construction of "penetration routes," the establishing of Haut Donnai and Darlac provinces, and the arrival of French commercial interests, the highland people were living in peace and beginning to realize the benefits of these changes. He also noted that "the Mois more and more furnish us regularly with strong and honest labor" and that since they now had become familiar with handling cash the

24. A. Baudrit, "La Naissance de Dalat," *Indochine*, no. 180 (1944), pp. 23–24; P. Munier, "Dalat," *Indochine*, no. 29 (1941), pp. 6–7; Nyo, "Pénétration française dans les pays Mois," *BSEI* 12, no. 2 (1937): 60; Maitre, *Les Jungles Moi*, pp. 540–41.

25. Doumer, *Situation de l'Indochine*, pp. 435–36.

26. L. S., "Bana," *Indochine*, no. 160 (1943), p. 12; Trinquet, "Poste administratif," p. 364; Le Pichon, "Chasseurs de sang," p. 360.

French-supervised markets—that had been proposed in the 9 October 1898 report discussed above—were attracting many outside merchants. The only use of highlander labor mentioned in his report was the notation that two decrees dated 23 January and 20 August 1901 authorized French planters to recruit *gardes champêtre* among the French or "*indigènes assermenté*," i.e., highlanders who had taken an oath of loyalty to the French.[27]

Resistance against the French, such as that encountered in Darlac, began to take place in other highland areas. In March 1900 a French *délégation* was established at Cung Son on the Ba river in Phu Yen province to administer the highlanders in the area to the borders of Khanh Hoa and Darlac. A month later, a revolt led by a man named Le Vo Tru (his name would indicate that he was Vietnamese) erupted north of Cung Son. Known as "king of the Moi," Tru was reported variously to be a monk or a sorcerer, with a following of some nine hundred troops, two hundred of which were highlanders. Tru and his army moved out of their base in the Dong Xuan massif with the goal of attacking coastal Song Cau and slaughtering the French résident and his wife. Since most of the Garde Indigène were in Cung Son, Tru hoped to surprise the remaining garrison of fifty men at Song Cau. His troops got to within a kilometer of the town when the small garrison routed them. Two weeks later Tru was captured and fined a "war tax." The delegation at Cung Son continued to function until January 1904 when a new post was established at M'drak, inland from Ninh Hoa (along present Route 21) to deal with the highlanders in eastern Darlac and upland Khanh Hoa.[28]

At the same time there was unrest among the highlanders in the region north of Kontum. Bands of Sedang based in the Psi river area and led by a chief called Thang Mau (apparently a Vietnamese designation for the Sedang leader) were conducting raids on Vietnamese settlements. In 1900 the Garde Indigène mounted a successful military operation during which Thang Mau was reported to have been killed.[29] The following year, however, a wave of new troubles plagued the area. At the beginning of 1901 the résident of Attopeu established a military post on the Psi river, and its Vietnamese garrison was put under the command of a French officer named Robert who was responsible for assuring the collection of taxes and

---

27. Doumer, *Situation de l'Indochine*, pp. 291–92, 435–36.
28. Maitre, *Les Jungles Moi*, pp. 546–47; Daufés, *Garde Indigène*, 2: 121–22.
29. Daufés, *Garde Indigène*, 2: 122.

preventing the Sedang traffic in Vietnamese slaves who were being sold to
the Halang and Jarai. French military regulations in the region called for all
posts in normal times to open their main gates at seven in the morning and
for all personnel to clean their weapons daily during the morning hours.
Although the surrounding Sedang were known to be particularly bellicose, their usual pattern was to mount attacks at night, so Robert gave the
order to observe the normal regulations. On the morning of 29 May the
gates of the post were duly opened, and soon a large force of Sedang rushed
in and fell upon the defenders with their spears and knives. Caught in his
quarters cleaning his revolver, Robert was knocked to the floor by the
Sedang but managed to scramble to his feet and bolt out the door shouting,
"Ralliement, pas gymnastique!" The Sedang pursued him, inflicting
twenty-four wounds, and he lost consciousness. When he awoke, the
attackers had already left, after causing heavy casualties and pillaging some
of the buildings. Bleeding profusely, Robert insisted that the militiamen
take him to Kontum. They bandaged him as best they could, put him on a
litter, and set out for Kontum, but when they stopped for the night the
scent of his blood attracted an army of black ants that swarmed over the
wounded man until the militiamen could fend them off. At Kontum the
priests dressed his wounds and kept him there in spite of his determination
to return to the post. Meanwhile the Sedang attacked the post again,
burning it to the ground. In Kontum, Robert's strength declined, and
despite all efforts by the priests he died at the end of June 1901.

The Sedang turned their fury on the French missionaries. On 10 June
1901 Father Kemlin learned that Dak Drei, the village where he lived, was
about to be attacked by the Sedang. All of the women and children were
evacuated to the other side of the Poko river, and the men prepared a
defense of the village. No attack materialized, but the tense situation
continued until the night of 24 November when a force of some 450
Sedang poured from the forest. The village defenses held against the
assault, and as the Sedang retreated one of their number was captured and
proved a valuable source of information on which Sedang chiefs had been
involved in the attacks. On the basis of this, the commissioner of Attopeu
launched military operations in the Sedang area in April 1902 and succeeded in gaining the submission of the rebellious chiefs. The military post
on the Psi river, renamed Poste Robert, was reestablished, and by the end
of the year peace was restored to the area.

There were, however, disturbances in other parts of the highlands. In

1901 the Garde Indigène in Quang Ngai was called upon twice to go to the rescue of Vietnamese villages being attacked by highlanders. In response to a series of conflicts involving Chil and Lat north of Dalat, Inspector Canivey led a column into the area, but at the village of Tre Luong Pe they encountered sharpened bamboo stakes hidden on the path and a sudden rain of arrows that wounded some of the militiamen, including Canivey. In the ensuing fighting a number of the highlanders were wounded or killed, and two weeks later the chief of Tre Luong Pe village surrendered. In 1904 trouble again erupted among the Sedang, resulting in the wounding and death of some Vietnamese militiamen, and in Quang Ngai a convoy of militiamen suffered casualties when they were attacked by highlanders. At An Khe there was a series of conflicts between Bahnar and Vietnamese at the Delignon-Paris estate, prompting the résident superior to send a Garde Indigène unit under Vincilioni to intervene and hear the highlanders' complaints.[30]

For the French administration, the most shocking incident in the highlands during this disturbed period was the assassination of Prosper Odend'hal, a respected member of the French community, who had participated in some of the Pavie missions. A recognized scholar and member of the Ecole Française d'Extrême-Orient, he had contributed valuable information on Cham ruins in the mountains. On 12 February 1904 Odend'hal wrote to Father Guerlach of the Kontum Mission that he intended making a tour through the central highlands to gather what ethnographic, linguistic, or archeological data he could find that might shed some light on the origins of the highland people. He was particularly interested in some of the ruins that had been discovered in various places and, noting that there was now a new French military post at Cheo Reo, expressed his intent to go there and see the Cham towers at Plei Chu with the hope of making stone-rubbings of the inscriptions. Following that, he wanted to visit the "sadetes," i.e., the King of Fire and the King of Water, after which he would make his way to Kontum. Guerlach wrote back strongly urging Odend'hal to abandon his plan to visit the Kings of Fire and Water because there was too much unrest in the region. Furthermore, previous expeditions had stirred up considerable hostility toward the French among many of the chiefs.[31]

Odend'hal did not heed Guerlach's warnings, and after visiting some

30. Ibid., 2: 117–30; Maitre, *Les Jungles Moi*, pp. 544–47.
31. Guerlach, *L'Oeuvre néfaste*, pp. 124–27.

ruins in western Darlac he proceeded to Cheo Reo, where he stayed with Stenger, commander of the French military post. He visited the Cham ruins, taking notes and making a stone-rubbing of the inscriptions. In discussions with Stenger, however, Odend'hal confided that his mission had additional goals; he intended to gain the King of Fire's submisson to French authority and to see the fabled sacred saber. Stenger had misgivings about these objectives. To begin with, it was taboo for anyone to gaze upon the saber. In addition, since the incursion by Vincilioni and his Garde Indigène force in March, the Jarai had become very restive and suspicious of French intentions. Odend'hal was not to be deterred from following his plan and even refused Stenger's offer of an armed escort. Leaving Cheo Reo, he proceeded to Plei Kueng, a village several kilometers from the abode of the King of Fire.[32] He was welcomed by Miong, the chief of the village, and according to Dournes it was Nay Nui (2.11), the aforementioned Jarai chief, who served as intermediary between Odend'hal and Oi At, the King of Fire.[33]

The King of Fire notified the Frenchman that he would come to Plei Kueng to see him, and Odend'hal describes in his diary the arrival of the shaman and his entourage at the village. Dressed in a tunic with a red and yellow floral pattern and supporting himself on a stick, the King of Fire walked at the head of a long procession. Behind him was a woman garbed in clothes the Jarai traditionally wear at ceremonies. Following these two personages came the King of Fire's various assistants. A file of some 250 unarmed robust young Jarai warriors made up the rest of the entourage. Odend'hal judged the shaman to be about fifty-five years of age and noted that he was slightly deaf and without teeth. The overall impression was one of a nice but somewhat simpleminded child. His assistants selected a clearing at the edge of the village and carefully placed a mat for the King of Fire. Odend'hal was invited to sit on some leaves spread on the ground, and he lost no time informing the shaman that France only wanted peace and liberty for the highland people. The French would leave the Jarai spirits undisturbed. The King of Fire responded that he was glad the fighting between the Jarai and French was over but that he wanted the Jarai to be free of taxes and corvée and to have the right to circulate freely throughout the region. Odend'hal then presented the King of Fire with some gifts,

32. Bernard Bourotte, "Essai d'histoire des populations Montagnardes du Sud-Indochinois jusqu'à 1945," *BSEI* 30, no. 1 (1955): 88–89.
33. Dournes, *Coordonnées structures Jörai*, p. 78.

among them a music box whose operation he explained in great detail. But when he stated that he intended offering the shaman a buffalo he drew a dark look, which Odend'hal interpreted as apprehension that gifts of such magnitude would require reciprocation. He therefore reassured the King of Fire that no reciprocal gifts were expected.

During the presentation of gifts, some of the Jarai constructed a small shelter over which they placed a red cloth. When it stood ready, the King of Fire sat within it facing east. His first assistant set about preparing a jar of rice alcohol, staking it to the ground in front of the shaman and thrusting a long bamboo tube into it. At the same time, other assistants roasted a chicken (one of Odend'hal's gifts). The King of Fire rose and took the place of his first assistant by the jar, into which he poured water while he muttered a chant. He then took some of the cooked chicken, split it with his knife, and placed the pieces on a copper plate. Taking some bits of the flesh and innards, he threw them first to the right and then to the left, after which he split a large piece of chicken in half and offered Odend'hal one part, telling the Frenchman that their sharing the chicken symbolized peace and friendship. Odend'hal took the chicken but instead of eating it passed it to his Vietnamese assistant. Following this, the King of Fire began drinking from the jar through the tube. When he had consumed the prescribed amount, he passed the tube to Odend'hal but the guest declined, saying that he only drank water. The shaman and his Jarai attendants exchanged comments in surprised tones, and they continued drinking. When Odend'hal asked to see the sacred saber, the King of Fire drew back in anger. At this point the Frenchman left the gathering to return to Plei Kueng.

The following day, 1 April, Odend'hal went again to the King of Fire's village, and in his diary he remarked on the cold reception he got; still he claimed to have had "a good meeting" with the shaman. Odend'hal had sent messengers to Kontum to request elephants to transport him and his gear to the mission there. On 2 April news reached him that the elephants were on their way to Cheo Reo. The next few days were uneventful, and then on 5 April a strange thing occurred. Odend'hal went to the King of Fire's village to find it completely deserted. The inhabitants had left the night before, and when the Frenchman sent some of his assistants to find them he learned that the King of Fire had conducted a ritual to decide whether or not he should comply with Odend'hal's proposals (although it is not mentioned explicitly in the diary, they presumably concerned the shaman's submission to French authority) and the omens were all inauspicious.

On 6 April the villagers returned to their homes, and Odend'hal decided he would visit the King of Fire the following day. The last entry in his diary, dated 7 April, read, "Miong and Luang ask me not to . . . ," a reference to Miong, the chief of Plei Kueng, and Luang, one of his Vietnamese assistants. Odend'hal may have been interrupted by the arrival of the elephants he had requested from Kontum, for he used these elephants to visit the King of Fire's village that afternoon. Accompanied by Miong, a Vietnamese interpreter, two Vietnamese merchants, and a Lao, Odend'hal arrived at the shaman's village to find the main gate closed. Although he was informed that the King of Fire was not present, he insisted that the village notables San, Yeng, and M'nop allow him to enter and offer more gifts, including a buffalo. They proceeded to Yeng's house, where Odend'hal insisted that a ceremony be organized to mark a presentation of his gifts. Suddenly a group of Jarai warriors entered the house and, with spears and the heavy pestles used for husking rice, attacked Odend'hal and his party. Miong was wounded but managed to escape. The others were less fortunate. The Jarai warriors took their bodies to a thatched hut, which was then set afire. Later, a Jarai woman of the village claimed that she had heard the Frenchman's screams issuing from the burning hut.

The tragedy was reported by Stenger, and soon Vincilioni arrived with a detachment of Garde Indigène. About the same time Bardin, the résident of Darlac, also appeared with some troops. They found the King of Fire's village empty. The population had dispersed and the shaman had fled with a group of followers into the forest. Odend'hal's remains were taken to Song Cau on the coast, where they were buried.[34]

The French administration was shocked by the Odend'hal assassination and, after the King of Fire was captured, formal legal proceedings began. Since the King of Fire himself was not present at the time of the Frenchman's death, no charge could be brought against him. He nonetheless was put under the surveillance of the post commander at Plei Tour.[35] The Jarai notables Yeng and San were brought to trial in Hanoi during March 1907. Initially, the question was raised by the defense whether the court in Hanoi had valid jurisdiction over any case involving highlanders because they were not located "in French territory nor in the protec-

34. Louis Finot, "Nécrologie, Prosper Odend'hal," *BEFEO* 4, nos. 1–2 (1904): 529–37.
35. Henri Maitre, *Les Régions Moi du Sud Indo-Chinois* (Paris: Plon, 1909), p. 309.

torate," but the court decided that, since the highlands were under the suzerainty of the court of Hue, the French did have a legal authority over them. The two were found guilty and sentenced to five years in jail. When the judge asked the prisoners if they had anything to say, one of them responded, "Five years is a long time. We have some buffalo in our village if you want to take them instead." [36]

The Odend'hal affair made it clear to the French administration that a reorganization of the hinterland was necessary in order to carry out an effective pacification of the highlands. A decree dated 22 November 1904 attached Darlac to Annam and reintegrated Stung Treng into Cambodia. Soon after, Besnard, the new résident in Darlac, launched a new pacification and his first target was the troublesome Rhadé chief Ama Jhao, operating from his base east of Ban Me Thuot. When Besnard's forces moved into his area, Ama Jhao and his followers fled into the forest and proclaimed an armed resistance against the French. But in January 1905 some of Ama Jhao's followers turned against him, delivering him to the French authorities, who put him in jail, where two months later he died. [37]

Pacification efforts also were extended to the Pleiku area, where there had been further disturbances among the highlanders. In January 1905 a column of 150 militiamen led by Renard, a French officer, left the Cho Don post in An Khe and moved westward until they came upon a recently established Vietnamese settlement completely abandoned. The body of a Vietnamese merchant attested to some kind of violence which had caused the population to flee. As the column continued toward the west, they came upon refugees who described a Jarai attack on the village that had left seven of the Vietnamese dead. Some of the Vietnamese had subsequently obtained weapons from the Kontum Mission and had attacked Jarai villages, burning them to the ground. As unrest spread, Renard arranged a meeting with Khoun, chief of eight Jarai villages, who in turn served as intermediary with Tai, a chief whose authority was recognized by twenty-one villages in the Pleiku area. Tai, however, let it be known that he would not make any agreements with the French without the authorization of Oi At, the King of Fire.

With no prospects for negotiations, Renard ordered his unit back to An Khe, a five-day walk. On the way they were attacked by Tai's warriors. Repulsing the assault, Renard managed to capture Tai, who finally agreed

36. "Chronique Tonkin," *BEFEO* 7, no. 1 (1907): 175–78.

37. Maitre, *Les Jungles Moi*, p. 544; Le Jarriel, "Comment la Mission Catholique," pp. 51–53.

to accept French authority. Following this, three groups of Bahnar villages submitted to the French and provided building materials for a new French post at Tai's village (Plei Tai). On 23 May 1905 some forty-six chiefs accompanied by more than two hundred warriors gathered at An Khe to offer their submission to French rule.[38]

In a move to consolidate colonial authority over this newly pacified region, the governor general issued a decree on 4 July 1905 declaring that the territory occupied by the Sedang, Halang, Rengao, Bahnar, and Jarai would be reintegrated into the protectorate of Annam as the autonomous province of Plei Ku-Der (a name taken from a village near the site of present Pleiku). Soon after its creation, however, this new province was plagued with unrest that was not being coped with effectively for two reasons. First, the French résident insisted on remaining in Tuy Hoa on the coast and, second, the militia sent into the area to deal with any disturbances was French-commanded and consisted of Vietnamese soldiers, so it was an alien force.[39]

The worst incident took place early in 1907 at the Bahnar Bonom village of Kon Klott. On 23 January Paris, director of the Delignon-Paris estate at An Khe, accompanied by Barreaud, an employee, several highlander guides, and a militia unit under Inspector Fort, set out in search of wild rubber plants. Two days later they arrived at Kon Klott to find the village in the midst of a drunken feast to celebrate the capture of a Vietnamese child. When Paris asked for hospitality the village chief refused, so the party camped nearby on a hill. Paris put his militiamen on alert and the village chief reacted by posting guards. The following morning Paris and his group found the path back to the village blocked with traps and sharpened bamboo stakes. Nonetheless they made their way to the village gate only to be met by a shower of arrows suddenly let loose by warriors hidden in nearby trees. Six militiamen and eight porters were wounded. At Fort's command the militiamen opened fire on the trees, killing the village chief, but under continued Bahnar resistance the French force retreated. Paris was struck in the abdomen by an arrow and died as the rest of the party fled to a Vietnamese settlement and then on to the post at Cho Don. There they gathered a larger force and returned to retrieve Paris' body— but found the village of Kon Klott completely abandoned.[40]

    38. Daufés, *Garde Indigène*, 2: 133–34.
    39. Paul Guilleminet, *Coutumier de la tribu Bahnar des Sedang et des Jarai de la Province de Kontum*, 2 vols. (Paris: Ecole Française d'Extrême-Orient, 1952), 1: 67.
    40. Daufés, *Garde Indigène*, 2: 145–47.

Following this incident it was decided that Plei Ku-Der would have to be divided into two zones, one administered by a new delegation in Kontum under the authority of Binh Dinh and the other, with its delegation at Cheo Reo, under Phu Yen.[41]

At the beginning of the twentieth century there were in the colony of Cochinchina similar efforts at "penetrating" the uplands north of Saigon through the same pattern of exploration first, followed by military occupation and establishment of a French administration, after which the area would be opened by creating new lines of communication. There also were the familiar attempts at gaining the support of the local chiefs. At the beginning of 1900, soon after he returned from central Vietnam, the Marquis de Barthélémy and his colleague the Viscount de Marsay were given a mission to explore the Stieng country with the goal of finding a suitable route for a railroad from Tay Ninh to Darlac. Going into the area through Tay Ninh, by 22 February they were well into the Stieng country, but it was becoming increasingly difficult to find trails, and the local villagers were uncooperative, sometimes hostile. Fevers and other ailments were sapping their Vietnamese armed escorts, who also were becoming demoralized. On 25 February they decided to end the search and go back to Thu Dau Mot.[42] Finished with his explorations de Barthélémy turned his attention to Cam Ranh bay, where he established a copra estate, a lumber business, and other enterprises.[43]

Early in 1904 another expedition attempted to penetrate the inhospitable Stieng country. Officially sanctioned by the colonial administration, it was led by Paul Patté, who hoped to make contact with the chiefs of the "independent" Stieng and win their acceptance of French authority. Patté was accompanied by Le Groignec, a doctor interested in gathering data on the physical anthropology of the natives, and Pierre Baron, a young Eurasian who wanted to study the languages so as to become an interpreter. A French sergeant was in charge of the Vietnamese military escort. On 28 January Patté went to Thu Dau Mot to meet the escort, and the party traveled to Hon Quan, the gate to the Stieng region. Moving eastward, they visited numerous villages, establishing a small military post at Mount Bara where the present town of Song Be is located. They continued to the Dong Nai river and the southern part of the Maa country. After a month,

41. Guilleminet, *Coutumier de la tribu Bahnar*, 1: 67.
42. Barthélémy, *Au Pays Moi*, pp. 212–54.
43. S. Jourdan, "Pierre Sauvaire, Marquis de Barthélémy, colon de la baie de Camranh," *Indochine*, no. 108 (1942), pp. 9–10.

however, Dr. Le Groignec was forced to return to Saigon for reasons of health, and Baron subsequently died under mysterious circumstances that triggered many rumors in Saigon. The expedition ended on 21 June 1904. Although Patté published a detailed journal on the expedition, he failed to include any kind of appraisal of his efforts to win over the Stieng chiefs.[44]

In the early years of the new century an ever-increasing number of travelers crossed the mountain chain from the Mekong to the coast of Annam. In 1901 Prince Henri d'Orleans, the great grandson of Louis Philippe, went from Kratie to Nhatrang but apparently contracted some illness during the trip and in August 1901, at the age of thirty-three, died in Saigon.[45] Tournier, the résident superior of Laos, followed a similar route the same year. In 1903 Captain Cottes, a French military officer, made this journey as did some of the French civil servants in the Darlac administration.[46] Four years later the Duke of Montpensier, son of the Count of Paris and first cousin of the unfortunate Prince Henri d'Orleans, made several hunting expeditions between Djiring and Phan Thiet, after which he drove his Lorraine-Dietrich automobile from Saigon (the city boasted some forty automobiles at the time) to Angkor Wat in twenty-nine days.[47]

Still, much of the region remained unexplored, and between 1905 and 1908 Henri Maitre, whose works on the highlands have been cited extensively in this volume, conducted a series of expeditions in the Darlac and Lang Bian areas. Leaving Nhatrang on 4 September 1905 with a convoy of elephants, the twenty-three-year-old Maitre began the first of numerous explorations that were to take him throughout the Darlac plateau, the area round Dalat, and into the Jarai country. He traveled as far west as Kratie and in July 1906 visited the Cham tower called the Yang Prong in western Darlac. Also, in February 1908, he accepted the hospitality of the French commandant of the post at Plei Tour, who was responsible for keeping the King of Fire under surveillance. They visited the shaman, whom Maitre afterward described as bent with age, his hair completely white, and his skin as dried and shriveled as old bark.[48] Maitre's explorations ended in

44. Paul Patté, *Hinterland Moi* (Paris: Librairie Plon, 1906), pp. 14–258; Henri Lamagat, *Souvenirs d'un vieux journaliste Indochinois*, 3 vols. (Saigon: SILI, 1942), 3: 67–91.
45. A. Baudrit, "Henri d'Orleans mort à Saigon le 9 Août 1901," *Indochine*, no. 210 (1944), pp. 20–24.
46. Maitre, *Les Régions Moi*, p. 268.
47. S. de Saint-Exupéry, "S.A.R. Monseigneur le Duc de Montpensier," *Indochine*, no. 116 (1942), pp. 11–15.
48. Maitre, *Les Régions Moi*, p. 309.

May 1909. He summarized his findings in a volume entitled *Les régions Moi du Sud Indo-Chinois* published that same year.

After taking leave in France, Maitre returned to Indochina and was given the task of establishing a French presence in the turbulent "three frontiers" area where the borders of Annam, Cochinchina, and Cambodia met. This resulted in further explorations and his major work, *Les jungles Moi*. At the end of this book Maitre lamented that although Frenchmen of good intent had lost their lives in the highlands the things they and others had achieved were being wasted because the region was ignored by the colonial administration. He explicitly noted that the Stieng and Mnong areas were seething with unrest and the situation could only be ameliorated through effective administration.[49]

In 1912, the very year he completed his book, Maitre was stationed in Djiring when reports began to circulate of serious unrest in the Mnong country to the west. According to most sources, it was being stirred up by a well-known and much-feared Mnong chief called Pu Trang Lung ("Father of Trang Lung"), a man of small stature with a resounding voice and an enormous head he claimed he could transform into a stag's head. While this chief was absent from his village, two Cambodian militiamen had kidnapped his wife and daughter. Pu Trang Lung and his warriors pursued them, slaying the kidnappers and attacking the military post from which they came. When news of these events reached Maitre, he ordered a unit to Pu Trang Lung's village where they killed his wife and daughter, slaughtered his buffalos, smashed his collection of jars, and then burned the entire village. The chief had fled into the forest and, when no further disturbances occurred, Maitre sailed for France to be married. On his return in 1914 he set about establishing additional military posts in the Mnong country and also formed an alliance with R'ding, a celebrated Mnong chief. At Maitre's behest, R'ding convoked a gathering of Mnong chiefs at the village of Bunor to offer their submission to the French. Maitre arrived there on 5 August 1914 with his Vietnamese cook and ten militiamen. Unbeknownst to the Frenchman, R'ding had made a secret agreement with Pu Trang Lung, who had arrived at Bunor earlier and was hiding. Before the ceremony, R'ding and the Mnong chiefs piled their weapons on the ground and invited Maitre and his escort to do the same. Maitre complied and had just sat to begin drinking from one of the jars when Pu Trang Lung emerged and slew him. Maitre and his cook were

49. Maitre, *Les Jungles Moi*, pp. 548–59.

buried in a shallow grave in the nearby forest; the French tried to locate it but never succeeded. A French military post that later was established in the vicinity was named for Maitre, and when Route 14 was constructed in the three frontiers area a monument was dedicated to him.[50]

After killing Maitre, Pu Trang Lung led his forces in overrunning the post at Mera, capturing 40 carbines and 2,000 rounds of ammunition. With the outbreak of World War I in August 1914, French efforts at further pacification in the highlands came to a halt. The following year Truffot, French governor of Kratie, was ambushed and killed by Pu Trang Lung's men at Sre Khtum, and the post there was abandoned, leaving the Stieng and Mnong areas without a French presence.[51]

50. Bourotte, "Essai des populations Montagnardes," pp. 90–91; J. Y. Claeys, "Un pionnier français des pays Mois," *Indochine*, no. 110 (1942), pp. 16–18; M. Gerber, "A la recherche de la tombe de Henri Maitre et de ses miliciens, assassinés en Août 1914 près de Bu-nor," *Indochine*, no. 129 (1943), pp. 8–10.

51. Paul Lechesne, "Les Mois du Centre Indochinois," *Revue Indochinoise*, no. 10 (1924), p. 181.

9 HIGHLANDERS IN THE FRENCH ADMINISTRATION, 1914–1930

By the beginning of World War I the "penetration" that had been desired by Doumer had been achieved in certain regions of the highlands. Pacification had been effective, provincial administrations had been organized, centers such as Kontum, Ban Me Thuot, and Dalat were growing into towns with market functions, and some French economic ventures had been launched. From the time of the first explorations by the French in the highlands, importance had been placed on making contact with the local chiefs, and this pattern continued as the new administrators took up their posts in remote places like Ban Don, Ban Me Thuot, Kontum, and Dalat. It was the local leaders who would serve as intermediaries between the administrators and the indigenous populations. It was they who would explain to the villagers what the French wanted of them.

Previously, it was noted that highlanders who had been taxed by the Vietnamese were by the end of the nineteenth century being taxed by the French, and now for the first time highland villagers in the more remote interior found themselves subject to taxation. They also were expected by the French to provide corvée for road construction and other public works projects related to the economic exploitation of the highlands, and in some instances this included labor for privately owned French plantations. The responsibility for all of this rested with the local chiefs, and some of them also began to function as judges in the new highlander law courts organized by the French. Whereas in the past their mandates had been derived from traditional concepts of leadership, these new leaders' authority now was vested in them by the French administration.

The changes during this period were even more drastic among younger highlanders (many of them descended from the earlier chiefs) who benefited from the establishment of schools in Ban Me Thuot and Kontum. Also, since the families of the leaders lived in proximity to the towns, they were more exposed to the modern influences of the French, Chinese, and Vietnamese. Towns like Kontum and Ban Me Thuot became, in effect, windows to the outside world. As they left school, these young highlanders were given positions in the administration either as civil servants or as teachers. They spoke French and became competent in certain aspects of French culture, even to cutting their hair as the French did and wearing western clothes in town. Nonetheless, they retained their ethnic identity. They spoke their mother tongues among themselves and in the villages, lived in traditional style houses, ate traditional food, wore traditional clothes, and observed the customs of their own groups. They moved with apparent ease between the village-oriented world of the highlanders and the rural French colonial milieu.

HIGHLANDER LAW COURTS AND PRIMARY SCHOOLS

In 1907, at the time the province of Plei Du-Der was divided, Jules Guenot was named *delégué* in Kontum and he immediately began to rely on Hma, the aforementioned Bahnar chief (1.4), in dealing with the local population, particularly in the matter of justice. Guilleminet observes that, although Hma had considerable authority, it did not extend beyond his *toring*, i.e., the traditional Bahnar village territory.[1] Since the French felt the need to recognize to some extent the suzerainty of the court of Hue in the highlands, they bestowed upon the local leaders cooperating with their administration some Vietnamese mandarin titles, although such titles did not have the same significance they did in the lowland provinces. Thus Hma was given the title Quan Huyen, a designation that did not have any relation to official status in the Vietnamese administration (wherein *quan* usually was used to indicate a mandarin or person of status and *huyện* was a Vietnamese administrative unit of which at the time none existed in the highlands).[2] Hma's responsibilities included collecting taxes, organizing

1. Paul Guilleminet, *Coutumier de la tribu Bahnar des Sedang et des Jarai de la Province de Kontum*, 2 vols. (Paris: Ecole Française d'Extrême-Orient, 1952), 1: 68–70.
2. The Vietnamese *tỉnh* was equivalent to a province, and ordinary tinh were divided into *huyện*. Large tinh were divided into *phủ* which in turn were made up of huyen.

corvée for public works projects, and serving as judge in arbitrating conflicts among highlanders. To lend an official aura to his role, Guenot presented Hma with a seal containing an elephant motif.[3]

In a letter to the résident at Qui Nhon, Guenot described the problem of justice among the highlanders, emphasizing that while Hma performed his role as judge very well there was need for recognition of other native chiefs who could do the same thing.[4] In noting how difficult it was to cope with crime among the highlanders under his authority, he cited the criminal act of the Potao Apui, the King of Fire, an obvious reference to the Odend'hal affair. The priests of the mission were not qualified to act as arbiters in conflicts among highland people, and Guenot noted that he himself did the best he could, traveling throughout the territory, personally intervening whenever possible.

Guenot felt that one solution would be to name Pim, son of the renowned Bahnar Bonom chief Kiom, as a kind of general intermediary for the territory occupied by the Bahnar Bonom and Bahnar Alakong, with the title Huyen Thua (which like Quan Huyen did not have any significance in the Vietnamese system). Guenot then provided some interesting information on Pim. He was at the time sixty-five years of age but still extremely vigorous and highly regarded as an honest and brave man. Plei Bong, his village, had for a long time been a place of refuge for highlanders fleeing war or famine, and it had become an important trade center where salt from the coast was exchanged for white honey and wax. Although the Bahnar-Rengao Republic which Pim had formed at the behest of the priests "only existed on paper," he had established some effective alliances with neighboring chiefs; for example, one of his many daughters married Lul (1.9), son of Tham, chief of the large village of Kon Gang, and another daughter married Piu (1.8), son of Nom, chief of the important village of Plei Phion. Although Pim had supported Mayréna, he had done so in the honest belief that it would bring peace to the region, a goal he had sought all of his life. Guenot stressed that Pim was known to be in favor with the French and had been credited with blocking the Vietnamese forces which moved up from the coast during the 1885 insurrection to destroy the Kontum Mission. Finally, Guenot put forth the

3. "La France en pays Moi: les insignes des chefs de secteur et de canton Moi," *Indochine*, no. 116 (1942), p. 5.
4. L'Administrateur Délégué à Kontum à Monsieur le Résident de France à Qui-Nhon, An-Khe, 24 Mai 1910, no. 159, Archives du Gouverneur Général de l'Indochine, Aix-en-Provence, France. This document was provided by Nancy Volk.

opinion that if Pim had had more authority such lamentable incidents as the murder of Paris at Kon Klott in 1907 would not have occurred.

No decision naming Pim as Huyen Thua was forthcoming, however, and Guenot went on leave to France, replaced in his absence by Sabatier. A decree issued 9 February 1913 made Kontum a province and named Guenot the résident. Another royal decree dated 7 July 1913 outlined the organization of a new juridical system of Kontum based on three courts. One would have jurisdiction over cases involving only Vietnamese and would be presided over by a Vietnamese Tri Huyen selected by the Ministry of the Interior. Another court would be for litigation involving only highlanders and would be presided over by a highlander Tri Huyen, Hma, who would judge cases on the basis of customs of the ethnic group or groups involved. The third tribunal would be for mixed cases, i.e., those involving Vietnamese and highlanders. Arbitration would be by the résident in conjunction with the Vietnamese and highlander judges drawing upon both legal systems.

On 13 July 1913 Résident Superior Albert Sarraut issued an order stating that the French administration approved of the royal decree, and this, in effect, gave for the first time official sanction to a system wherein highlanders would be judged by their own leaders drawing upon indigenous laws.[5] The Bahnar leader Hiar (1.7) recalled during an interview in 1971 the celebration marking the investiture as Tri Huyen of his paternal uncle Hma. Although he was a child of nine, Hiar was struck by the great crowd, the large number of buffalos slaughtered for the occasion, the rows upon rows of alcohol jars, and the resounding drum and gong music.

The legal system remained unchanged until 1925 when, on the recommendation of Résident Fournier, a royal ordinance dated 8 July outlined a new structure. Whereas previously the résident had controlled the highlander court through Hma as the judge, control now was shared by the résident, a highlander judge, and ten village chiefs acting as *assesseurs* (or assistant judges). Hma was retained as judge, a position he held until his death in 1930.[6]

While these administrative changes were taking place, another significant development was occurring in Kontum province—the appearance of primary education. Sometime around 1870 the French priests at Kontum had devised a Bahnar script based on the type of orthography used

5. Guilleminet, *Coutumier de la tribu Bahnar*, 1: 69–73.
6. Ibid., 1: 81–86.

for modern Vietnamese with some of the same diacritical marks. Formal instruction in the Bahnar language, however, did not come until 1892 when Father Vialleton returned from France determined to organize primary schools. The beginnings were modest, and among the first pupils were several sons of Krui, president of the Bahnar-Rengao Confederation (1888–1895). In 1908 the Cuenot School, named after the bishop who devised the plan for a mission in the highlands, was opened in Kontum. It offered three years of training in reading and writing Bahnar and in catechism. By 1912 there were several literacy courses being offered in the mission territory and the pupils included three or four Bahnar girls. In 1923 Father Kemlin expanded the Cuenot School curriculum and extended it to six years, and a similar primary level education program was begun for "les petites Moiesses," i.e., young highland girls.[7]

In his report of 1912, Guenot outlined a proposal to organize primary schools to train secretaries, interpreters, and medical service personnel. But it was not until 1919 that several classes for Bahnar were added to the small Vietnamese school that already had been functioning.[8] Among the first pupils was Nguyen Huu Phu, from one of the oldest Vietnamese families in Kontum. He was born in 1906, and his mother, who died in 1971, had been born in Kontum in 1887 of parents who several years before had come to the mission from Bong Son in Binh Dinh to escape anti-Catholic persecutions. During a series of discussions between 1971 and 1973, Phu recalled that the first schoolmaster was a Vietnamese from Hue and that there were seven pupils, five of them Vietnamese and two highlanders. One of the latter was Yim, son of a local leader, who later drowned in the Bla river. The other was Nay Der (2.12), a Jarai who would become a Viet Minh and National Liberation Front leader. Phu remembered Der as being "very light in color, almost white," and of medium height but very husky. He also was a very adept linguist who spoke, in addition to his own Jarai language, Rhadé, Vietnamese, French, and Lao, a language he taught Phu to speak.

In 1922 the seven students completed the available courses—a complete primary school curriculum was not yet available in Kontum—and Nay Der went for further study at the Collège de Qui Nhon in that coastal city.

---

7. J. B. Guerlach, *"L'Oeuvre néfaste," réplique du Père J. B. Guerlach, missionnaire apostolique au F. Camille Paris, colon en Annam* (Saigon: Imprimerie Commerciale, 1905), p. 104; Paul Guilleminet, "Langages spéciaux utilisés dans la tribu Bahnar du Kontum," *BEFEO* 50 (1960): 119; Marcel Ner, "Humbles constructeurs de l'empire," *Indochine*, no. 143 (1943), pp. 7–9.

8. Ner, "Humbles constructeurs," *Indochine*, no. 144 (1943), pp. 13–14.

After several years of training, Der returned to Cheo Reo. A one-year school program with a Vietnamese instructor had been established there in 1913, and Nay Der became the first highland schoolmaster (see below). Since there was no secondary school in Kontum, Phu continued to study at the Franco-Bahnar School, where he was in the same group as Hiar, nephew of Hma. Phu left school in 1925 to become Chief of the Post, Telephone, and Telegraph in Pleiku, and in 1927 he assumed the same role in Kontum, keeping that position until 1945. He also recalled that in 1927 he, a Bahnar leader named Mohr (1.6) who was the nephew of Pim, and a Jarai chief named My went to Hue for a conference at the Chambre des Représentants du Peuple (Chamber of the Peoples' Representatives).

Hiar related that he began his formal education at the Cuenot School in June 1919, subsequently transferring to the Franco-Vietnamese School, where he received his Primary School Certificate in June 1924. The following year he was appointed an instructor in the school, a position he held until he was elected to the 1955 National Assembly during the administration of Ngo Dinh Diem.

According to Hiar, the first highlander in the Kontum area to gain a position in the cadre of the French colonial service was Hma's eldest son Ber (1.10), who was born at Plei Roloi in the late nineteenth century. He learned to read and write Bahnar and to speak French. In 1914 he organized a two-year literacy course in Bahnar, using a local communal house to hold classes for his five pupils. Two years later he had to close the school so he took a position as interpreter for the French officials in Kontum. He became adept at reading and writing French and in 1920 was appointed secretary to the résident. Later he was sent to Mytho in the Mekong river delta for formal training in the civil service. When he returned to Kontum he was assigned to the provincial public works, where he assisted in planning roads until his death in 1957.

During this time there were similar developments taking place farther south in Darlac province. According to some elderly Rhadé informants, shortly after Bourgeois founded the French administrative post at Ban Don in 1899 a very small school offering the "preparatory" (*préparatoire*) three-year cycle of primary school education was opened. In 1904 this school was moved to Ban Me Thuot, and the first teacher was a Cambodian named Keng Kmau. Among the initial group of pupils were Y Say Ktla and Y Ut Nie Buon Rit, sons of local elite families. A retired schoolmaster, Y Toeh Mlo Duon Du (5.1), recalled that by 1912 Y Ut had begun to instruct in the school, probably the first highlander to serve as a teacher.

THE SABATIER ERA IN DARLAC

With the outbreak of war in Europe in 1914 the French government could not concern itself with new programs in its colonies, but nevertheless that year marked a time of great changes in Darlac province due to the dynamic leadership of Léopold Sabatier, one of the best known of all the French administrators in the highlands. Between 1899, when the "autonomous province" of Darlac was created, and the arrival of Sabatier in 1914, conditions had remained much the same. The primary source of revenue for the province was taxes levied on the lucrative elephant trade conducted by Khunjanob. In 1908 two hundred elephants were registered by the administration, their value ranging from 300$ to 600$ depending on age and the condition of their tusks. Most of the buyers were Lao, who often made their purchases with gongs and jars. There also were Burmese traders who brought excellent gongs made in Mandalay and exquisite Burmese swords to trade for elephants. The buyers were obliged to pay a tax before leaving Annam, which until 1905 was fixed at 250$ per elephant. Between 1899 and 1908 the number of sales varied. For example, in 1899 eight elephants were sold. This figure rose to thirteen in 1904, jumped to fifty-six in 1907, then fell to twenty-four in 1908. Maitre points out that the total tax revenue during this period was 34,279 piasters.[9]

At this time Ban Me Thuot was a small post with only four Frenchmen, one of whom was a trader. The residence and other administrative structures were built on piling and had thatched roofs like the longhouses in nearby Buon Kram. They were hidden in a profusion of palm, mango, guava, and yew trees and colorful hibiscus. Near the residence was a tennis court and close by were quarters for the militia, which was composed of Vietnamese, Lao, and Cambodians. There was also a small school. Rudimentary roads had been built to Ninh Hoa and Ban Don.[10]

After serving temporarily in Kontum, Sabatier was assigned to Darlac in 1914. Bourotte did not see Sabatier as an impressive figure.[11] A small man, he had a dry manner that was accentuated by his mustache and severe curving pince-nez that framed cold piercing eyes. Nonetheless, his accomplishments were many. In 1915 the Franco-Rhadé School opened

9. Henri Maitre, *Les Régions Moi du Sud Indo-Chinois* (Paris: Plon, 1909), pp. 149–51.
10. A. Monfleur, *Monographie de la province de Darlac* (Hanoi: Imprimerie d'Extrême-Orient, 1931), pp. 16–17.
11. Bernard Bourotte, "Essai d'histoire des populations Montagnardes du Sud-Indochinois jusqu'à 1945," *BSEI* 30, no. 1 (1955): 94.

with an enrollment of thirty students, all of them Rhadé from Ban Me Thuot and nearby Buon Kosier. According to Y Toeh Mlo Duon Du (who had been one of the first pupils), Keng Kmau, the Cambodian schoolmaster at Ban Don, was also an instructor at the Franco-Rhadé School as was Y Ut Nie Buon Rit. When Keng Kmau died in 1917, Sabatier, in spite of his anti-Vietnamese sentiments, brought in Nguyen That Bon as head instructor. The curriculum included training in the French languages, history, and geography with some instruction on Rhadé customs. In 1922 the first examinations for the Certificat d'etudes primaires to be held in the highlands took place at Ban Me Thuot, and three of the four candidates passed.[12] One of those who succeeded was Y Toeh Mlo Duon Du (5.1), who joined the staff as an instructor.

Sabatier also encouraged Y Ut, another teacher Y Jut Hwing, and his secretary Y Say Ktla to devise a Rhadé alphabet with the assistance of some of the advanced students. Around 1918 Y Ut went for one year of secondary-level training at the Collège de Qui Nhon and then spent two years in advanced studies at Hue. In 1922 he returned to teach in Ban Me Thuot. By 1926 there were some five hundred students, many of them boarders, and the curriculum had been expanded to include literacy in Rhadé, some technical training, and physical education.

According to Antomarchi, who later became a well-remembered school director, a few years after arriving at his Darlac post Sabatier became aware of the Rhadé legal procedure, which involved having a hearing presided over by an elderly male steeped in the traditional customs.[13] After the plaintiff and defendant presented their cases, the judge intoned the relevant customs in a soft chant and this provided a basis for decision acceptable to both parties. When Sabatier suddenly realized that these judges knew by heart all of the Rhadé customs, he encouraged Y Say to begin writing down all of the chants in Rhadé. In 1923 a highlander law court similar to that in Kontum was established in Ban Me Thuot. The first judge, a Lao, was soon replaced by Khunjanob, who was assisted by two elderly Rhadé. The court proceedings were oral, though in 1927 the customs recorded by Y Say and Y Ut were published in the Rhadé language and later compiled into a formal code in Rhadé and French.[14]

12. F. P. Antoine, "L'Ecole Montagnarde," *Indochine Sud Est Asiatique*, no. 29 (1954), pp. 33–37.
13. Dominique Antomarchi, "Le 'Bi Due': recueil des coutumes Rhadées," *Indochine*, no. 25 (1941), pp. 5–10.
14. Dominique Antomarchi, *Recueil de coutumes Rhadées du Darlac* (Hanoi: Imprimerie d'Extrême-Orient, 1940), pp. 24–280.

Sabatier undertook a program for improving communications within Darlac and with the outside world. In 1916 construction was begun on a road, Colonial Route 21, from Ban Me Thuot to the coast via Ninh Hoa. During the season when school was not in session, Y Ut served as interpreter and supervisor. Rhadé village men between the ages of eighteen and fifty-five provided ten days of corvée per year at a daily pay rate of 10 centimes per day. Penal labor also was used. Other roads were built to Ban Don and Dak Lak (Poste du Lac). By 1926 there were some 608 kilometers of roads and trails with wooden bridges throughout the province. A post office with telegraph service to Nhatrang was opened, and telephone lines were strung to Nhatrang and Ban Don, primarily so that Sabatier could maintain close contact with Khunjanob. Electricity for the residence and other public buildings was supplied by a hydroelectric plant tapping the waters of the Ea Sir stream that coursed through Ban Me Thuot. In addition, a medical service with a resident French doctor and a maternity center with a training program for male Rhadé nurses was founded. An agricultural service was organized which included training Rhadé in the use of the plow, better gardening techniques, and cultivation of mangoes, cinnamon (this was not successful due to soil and climate), and coffee. Some Rhadé mechanics were given formal training, and Y Ghao Buon Ya was sent to Saigon for a special course, returning to Ban Me Thuot to be chief mechanic for the French administration. Finally, Sabatier organized a theater-cinema to be a center of art and have as one of its functions the preservation of Rhadé folk art.[15]

Also during his tenure as province chief, Sabatier organized the first Garde Indigène composed of highlander militiamen. The initial group, recruited in 1921 from among the students at the Franco-Rhadé School, were called "les clairons" (the buglers). One of them was Y Sok Eban, who now lives in retirement in his natal village of Buon Ko Tam. In his written biography, Y Sok gave his birthdate as 20 December 1900.[16] His boyhood included the usual responsibilities of tending the pigs, chickens, and cattle. He also learned to play the gongs and at ceremonies would fetch water to pour into the jars while the adults drank. In addition to attending school he helped in the fields during the planting season. He also helped hew coffins out of hardwood logs. On 8 August 1921 he joined the Garde Indigène as

15. Monfleur, *Monographie*, pp. 17–19; P. Boudet, "Léopold Sabatier, Apôtre des Rhadés," *Indochine*, no. 113 (1942), pp. 1–7.

16. Y Sok Eban, "Autobiography of Y Sok Eban" (typescript trans. Y Thih Eban, Buon Kmrong Prong, 1964), pp. 1–5.

an 11th class militiaman and the following year was assigned to an operation that involved relocating some "isolated" Mnong so they could be
better kept under the watchful eye of the French authorities.

As the number of projects increased, Sabatier sought more taxes from
the highlanders and, whereas in 1912 before he became résident the annual
tax revenue amounted to only three or four thousand piasters, by 1923 it
had increased to 30,000$.[17]

On 2 July 1923 Darlac became an official province and Sabatier was
appointed résident. On 30 July Pierre Pasquier, the résident superior of
Annam, issued an important circular concerning a general policy for the
highlands.[18] According to Bourotte and also Boudet, Pasquier was
strongly influenced by Sabatier, who felt that with the threat of a land rush
into the highlands by French business interests the time had come to state
clearly the administration's position on colonization.[19] The circular reflects not only some ideas similar to those manifest in Sabatier's Darlac
administration but also the curious mixture of empathy with the highlanders with strains of paternalism and flashes of authoritarianism that
appear to have been characteristic of Sabatier.

Pasquier began the circular by pointing out that there was considerable
social and linguistic variation in the highlands, adding that the population
had retained only a "vague recollection of their history" and that they had
suffered centuries of exploitation by the neighboring Cambodians, Lao,
and Vietnamese who regarded them as backward "savages." The French,
as Pasquier saw it, had the moral responsibility of rescuing the highlanders
from the low state to which they had descended. The first step would be to
provide order and peace. It would be an error to push them farther into the
remote areas as the Vietnamese had done or to follow "the American
formula" of segregating them in delimited zones. Education would provide the best means to prepare the "mois" to defend themselves against the
inroads of the more advanced people. The fruitful results of such a policy
could be seen in the way the Rhadé and Jarai dealt successfully with
outsiders.[20] It also was true of the groups in the vicinity of Kontum where

17. Boudet, "Léopold Sabatier," p. 3.
18. Bourotte, "Essai des populations Montagnardes," pp. 96–97; Boudet, "Léopold Sabatier,"
p. v.
19. Ibid.
20. The first systematic population statistics for Indochina were published in Gouvernement
Général de l'Indochine, Direction des Affaires Economiques, *Annuaire statistique de l'Indochine: recueil de
statistiques relatives aux années 1913 à 1922* (Hanoi: Imprimerie d'Extrême-Orient, 1927), vol. 1, p. 42.
There were reported to be 20 Vietnamese in Darlac, 500 in Haut Donnai, and 7,000 in Kontum (see
appendix A for highlander population).

the Catholic mission had long been installed, but it was not so in the Lang Bian (Dalat) area where Vietnamese had been brought in to meet the needs of the Europeans while the local highlanders were neglected.

At this point Pasquier interjected some comments about the groups that had not accepted French authority, saying that they were hostile because of fear engendered by the exploitations of the Cambodians, Lao, and Vietnamese. But such defiance cannot be tolerated, because it is a barrier to the spread of "French civilization." He then declared, "I have therefore decided to pacify and open these regions that still escape our administrative influence." The kind of administration envisaged was one that would place most responsibilities in the hands of each chief who would be guided by his own laws and customs. It was essential therefore, Pasquier noted, that the résidents have the laws of the highland groups under their authority codified.

In the realm of economic affairs, Pasquier expressed the view that swidden farming was deleterious for the soil and caused destruction of forests. The solution as he saw it was to force highlanders to adopt permanent paddy fields in areas where the physical ecology was amenable and irrigation systems could be provided. Furthermore, encouraging the cultivation of kitchen gardens would help stabilize the "nomadic" highlanders. Commerce in salt was another important consideration. This commodity was one of the most prized trade items in the highlands but it was only obtainable through the lowlanders who "abused the credulity" of the highland people. For Pasquier, the solution was to organize markets at set places controlled by French agents, who also would license the vendors.

Pasquier then turned his attention to the matter of colonization of the highlands. For him, the most important thing was the determination of zones where the colonists might settle without coming into conflict with the highlanders. The résidents would have to work this out themselves but there were some factors that they would do well to consider. For example, where land was claimed by the indigenous population, such as where the "matriarchy functioned," i.e., where the matrilineal descent system obtained, land tenure was well defined and should be respected. It was important that the highlanders realize that it was not French policy that they be pushed off their land but rather that the indigenous villagers and the colonists live side by side, mutually benefiting from the economic development of the rich highlands. Another matter was that of bringing Vietnamese labor into the highlands for the new estates, but Pasquier simply pointed out that there were existing regulations governing Vietnamese migration into the mountain areas.

Pasquier felt that roads were "the great instrument of civilization and pacification." He noted that trails with drainage ditches, open in the dry season to light motor traffic, already formed a network linking Kontum, An Khe, and Ban Me Thuot with Poste du Lac and M'drak. In time, however, these trails should be paved and bridges built over the waterways. In areas not controlled by the French, military posts and the first trails were the symbols of the initial phase of pacification. In conjunction with road construction there was the need for airstrips and fuel dumps to accommodate aircraft conducting aerial surveys.

The résidents were also advised to conduct surveys to determine the potential for economic exploitation of resources not yet discovered. Then too, experimentation in agriculture would be another means of tapping potentialities. Also, big game abounded in the highlands, and it would be a lure for tourists. Finally, in the economic sphere, Pasquier pointed out that another goal of pacification was to levy taxes on the populations for maintaining local budgets.

Pasquier moved on to review the state of the Garde Indigène Moi, the militia recruited from among the local highland villagers. It was important that they be commanded by men from their own ethnic group, and in addition to performing military duties they were also to provide labor for road construction. After their terms of recruitment had been met, the militiamen were released from duty to return to their villages with the status of "partisans," still maintaining ties with the French, and as such they served "as the best means for propaganda for the administration." To reinforce these ties, from time to time they were called to the province capital or to a military post to remain there briefly. For this they received an indemnity.

Regarding education, the résident superior encouraged the résidents to organize schools of the "Franco-Moi" variety already functioning in Ban Me Thuot and Kontum, with indigenous teachers and instruction in the local languages. Transcriptions should be devised for these languages as they had for Bahnar and Rhadé, and the primary school curriculum should include instruction in the native customs along with simple mathematics, principles of modern agriculture, and some physical fitness training. Literacy courses should be organized for the militia. Pasquier recommended that brighter pupils be given instruction in French so that they could return to their villages and be the literate liaison with the provincial officials as they already were in Darlac.

Other recommendations dealt with such things as the need to develop medical facilities and the advisability of résidents gathering ethnographic data, particularly photographs of people, house types, and so forth. He also encouraged the résidents to further the native arts. The final recommendation was that the résidents organize an annual gathering of all the highland chiefs in their province each year during the slack season immediately following the harvest. Such a meeting would be a "fête du serment de fidélité à la France"—a swearing of loyalty to France. He noted that on his first visit to Darlac he had been the guest of honor at such a fete, during which the chiefs touched the symbolic ring of the résident and swore, "If France tells us to die, we die. If France tells us to live, we live."

The circular contained an interesting postscript in which Pasquier ordered the administrators to avoid using the terms *moi*, *kha*, or *phnong*, all of which were pejorative designations meaning "savage." Rather, they were to use the exact designations for each group, e.g., Rhadé, Jarai, Bahnar, Sedang. This directive, the first official attempt to have the administrators use proper ethnic designations, was clearly due to Sabatier's influence. According to Boudet, he always referred to the highlanders as *montagnards* rather than *Moi* or *sauvages*, the usual designations used by the French.[21]

Sabatier had strong feelings about keeping Darlac free from intrusions by outsiders, particularly French business interests and Vietnamese of any kind. The relative isolation of Darlac was breaking down rapidly. Colonial Route 21, which ran from Ban Me Thuot to Ninh Hoa where it connected with Colonial Route 1, was being improved and soon would be an all-weather road. In addition, a decree dated 19 June 1918 approved construction of a new road, Colonial Route 14, that would run from Saigon to Tourane via Loc Ninh and Darlac. Surveys already were being conducted prior to construction.[22] Informant Y Thih Eban related how older Rhadé described Sabatier in 1923 ordering some of the wooden bridges on the road to Ninh Hoa burned so as to prevent people from Saigon reaching Ban Me Thuot. Also, he refused to have any Vietnamese in the administration or to employ Vietnamese or Chinese as domestics in his house.

Keeping French colonists out of Darlac was, however, a different matter since legislation allowing colonization already existed. It was noted previously that the royal orders dated 27 September 1897 and 28 April 1899

21. Boudet, "Léopold Sabatier," p. ii.
22. J. H., "La Route Coloniale No. 14 reliera Saigon à Tourane par les plateaux Mois," *Indochine*, no. 129 (1943), pp. 11–12.

made it possible for French citizens and "protégés Français" to receive titles for land concessions on the public domain and that estates had been established in parts of the highlands. Another decree dated 13 April 1909 held that the territory encompassing the provinces of Kontum, Haut Donnai, and Darlac as well as the highland areas of neighboring provinces would be divided into three types of zones determined by the résident superior of Annam. The first was the "reserved zone" (*zône réservée*) into which no one could penetrate without special permission. The second type was the "supervised zone" (*zône surveillée*), access to which could be obtained under certain conditions. The third was the "free zone" (*zône libre*), open to commerce and colonization. In this zone any of the colonists, be they French or native, who desired to have Vietnamese labor could obtain permission from the résident to have up to twenty Vietnamese families enter the area to settle in their own community. These families would be registered and exempt from taxes for three years.[23]

Two decrees dated 30 July 1923, the same date as the above circular, issued by résident superior Pasquier dealt with matters of colonization and immigration. One decree held that in highland zones opened by the résident superior for colonization Vietnamese settlers would have to be grouped in villages of twenty families, and it repeated the 1909 regulation that they would have to be registered.[24] The area that they would be free to exploit would be determined by the chief of the administrative unit in which they were located. The other decree stated that in any territory claimed by highland families or villages, with the exception of the autonomous circumscription of Lang Bian (Dalat), no contract for exploitation of less than five hundred hectares could be made without the approval of the head of the local administration.[25] Any contract involving more than five hundred hectares would have to be approved by the résident superior. One article in this decree stated explicitly that this legislation was intended to safeguard the rights, customs, and interests of the "mois" and insure the peaceful "penetration" and economic development of the highlands.

Additional legislation by Pasquier outlined changes in the corveé and

23. J. de Galembert, *Les Administrations et les services publics Indochinois* (Hanoi: Imprimerie Mac-Dinh-Tu, 1931), pp. 922–23.

24. Pierre Pasquier, "Arrêté fixant le régime des terres de l'hinterland Annamite, No. 1885, 30 Juillet 1923," in *Variétés sur le pays Mois* (Saigon: Gouvernement de la Cochinchine, 1935), pp. 257–58.

25. Pierre Pasquier, "Arrêté règlementant la colonisation Annamite dans l'hinterland, 30 Juillet 1923," in *Variétés sur le pays Mois* (Saigon: Gouvernement de la Cochinchine, 1935), pp. 259–60.

personal taxes for Darlac province. One decree dated 6 October 1923 declared that all natives, Vietnamese, Laotians, and registered "assimilated Asians" between the ages of eighteen and sixty and residing in Darlac province would be subject to corvée amounting to ten days annually.[26] It stipulated, however, that those responsible for corvée could buy their way out of it by compensating the administration at a fixed cash rate per day. This meant in effect that the outsiders, most of whom were traders, would be relieved of the corvée while the highlanders, who at that time rarely used cash, would be subject to it. A companion decree set an annual personal tax of 2 piasters 20 centimes for every Vietnamese, Laotian, and Cambodian between the ages of eighteen and sixty living in Darlac province with the exception of those in public service or in the militia.[27]

With its reputation as an area with rich soil amenable to cultivation of coffee, tea, and rubber, it was inevitable that French business circles would seek land concessions in Darlac province. A decree dated 12 February 1925 created in Darlac province the three types of zones outlined in the 1909 law.[28] Soon after, bids for land totaling 92,000 hectares were received by the administration. The bidders ranged from individuals interested in establishing a small or modest estate to representatives of large French corporations seeking very large concessions. Sabatier quickly issued two reports, the first of which concerned land tenure systems among the highlanders in the province.[29] It pointed out that while some land was unclaimed there were territories carefully apportioned by individuals, families, clans, or villages.

The second report contained some suggestions regarding land policy. Unclaimed land (*res nullius*) should be made available for colonization. Where land was claimed by highlanders, however, the bidder would need not only the approval of the administration but also that of the highlander or group of highlanders who claimed the land, and then would only be entitled to a 99-year lease (*bail emphythéotique*). Sabatier cited as an example the territories among the Rhadé claimed by clans with their *po lan* and the

26. Pierre Pasquier, "Arrêté No. 1125 du Résident Supérieur en Annam, 6 Octobre 1923," in *Variétés sur le pays Mois* (Saigon: Gouvernement de la Cochinchine, 1935), pp. 241–42.

27. Pierre Pasquier, "Arrêté No. 1126 du Résident Supérieur en Annam du 6 Octobre 1923," in *Variétés sur le pays Mois* (Saigon: Gouvernement de la Cochinchine, 1935), pp. 243–44.

28. Galembert, *Administrations*, p. 922.

29. Léopold Sabatier, "Documents de colonisation française en territoires non soumis à la jurisdiction et l'administration annamites," manuscript in two parts, 1925, Ecole Française d'Extrême-Orient, Paris.

local village headman as well. Finally, Sabatier recommended that only local highlanders be recruited as laborers on the new estates and that no Vietnamese be brought into the highlands.

On 1 January 1926 Sabatier presided over a large gathering of highland chiefs who had come together to swear an oath of allegiance to the French. Held in the Ban Me Thuot gymnasium, it included leaders from the Rhadé Kpa, Rhadé Adham (among them the chief Ama Ual), and the Rhadé Bih as well as the Krung, the Jarai (Sabatier described them as being from "the rocky land of the King of Water"), the Mnong Rlam, Mnong Gar, and a group he called the Mnong Lach. Résident Superior Pasquier dedicated the celebration to H'ni. Sabatier's daughter H'ni had been born of a Rhadé woman and was called "the soul of my mother" by Khunjanob, who believed her to be a reincarnation of his mother.[30] Sabatier noted that the honored guests included Louis Finot, director of the Ecole Française d'Extrême-Orient; Dereymez, an inspector of the Garde Indigène; Halot, an agricultural engineer and planter; and several French military officers.[31] He also made the point that two months after this celebration Darlac province was opened for colonization.

The celebration was a mixture of French drama and highland tradition. There were the usual rows of jars and music from gongs and drums. A number of elephants were gathered for the occasion, and at one point they came forward to kneel before the résident superior and the guests as a salute. There also was the traditional buffalo sacrifice, but before that Sabatier officiated at the oath-taking in a long speech that was sprinkled with allegorical references taken from Rhadé lore.

In his speech Sabatier exhorted the chiefs to preserve their laws, and the chiefs replied affirmatively as they touched his bracelet, a gesture of promise. This was repeated when he asked them to eschew slavery and to bring under control those acting outside the law. Sabatier extolled the advantages of using the medical facilities provided by the French and he proclaimed the need to maintain the roads. At this point he cried, "O chiefs believe me! The spirits do not frequent the neglected roads, and it is along such roads that misfortune comes." Touching his bracelet, the chiefs promised to maintain the roads. Then came the matter of recruiting for the Garde Indigène. "Give me robust, honest young men to assure the security

30. Boudet, "Léopold Sabatier," p. vi.
31. Léopold Sabatier, *Palabre du serment du Darlac* (Hanoi: Imprimerie d'Extrême-Orient, 1930), pp. 11–15.

of your villages, the tranquillity of your villages, the tranquillity of the great country of Darlac." Again the chiefs agreed and touched the bracelet, after which they also agreed to promote attendance in the schools Sabatier had built. Finally the résident urged the chiefs to guard well their lands, never selling any of it but treasuring it as their ancestors had done. They should arrange paddy fields on the swampy terrain and plant coffee trees to become rich. He remarked that two years previously he had distributed seeds of Cambodian cotton and that two years hence he would punish those villages having no cotton to sell.

Sabatier then signaled for the drums and gongs to be played and alcohol jars to be brought out, exclaiming that the blood of the sacrificed buffalo and the rice alcohol would be offered to the spirits who would witness the oath. He pointed to the honored guests who had been sent by the governor general to witness the oath-taking and who had arrived by "flying pi-rogues" (aircraft). They too would touch the bracelet and drink from the jars. Sabatier concluded by declaring that the "news of an alliance between the great country of Darlac and the great country of France would be carried on the winds to the lands of the Vietnamese, Laotians, Siamese, and Cambodians." [32]

In a report dated 16 January 1926 Pasquier informed the governor general that it now would be possible to open the "rich province of Kontum" as well as the mountainous regions of central Vietnam in general to colonization. Darlac province, he pointed out, should be dealt with in another way because the Rhadé, who were more educated, were capable of conducting economic development if "led by us in modern-izations without imposing on them any contact with the sometimes brutal western ideas." [33] In a letter to Pasquier dated 5 February 1926 Sabatier lamented that the Jarai lands in Kontum were being taken and divided by prospectors, and, calling attention to some of the sentiments about land that had been expressed during the Ban Me Thuot oath ceremony, he declared his concern as to whether the "red lands of montagnards" would remain untouched. [34] He also voiced the hope that the land tax scheduled to be imposed on the *po lan* (guardians of Rhadé clan lands) in 1927 would have the effect of rendering their lands indisputable. Whether or not Sabatier's evaluation of the situation in Kontum had any effect on Pasquier

32. Ibid., pp. 17–94.
33. Monfleur, *Monographie*, pp. 19–20.
34. Sabatier, *Palabre*, p. 95.

is not clear, but a decree dated 5 April 1927 created a reserved zone in Kontum closed to colonization.[35]

In spite of his achievements in Darlac province, Sabatier was not hailed as a hero by everyone. He was criticized in Saigon and Paris commercial circles for his policy of keeping colonists out of the province. He also had a bad reputation among the Catholic missionaries. This is amply reflected in Simonnet's observation that Sabatier was a "dyed-in-the-wool Freemason" who sought to maintain Darlac as his "fief."[36] The priest also deprecatingly likened Sabatier to Mayréna, but "a Mayréna without dash, without the gift of gab, without fantasy, a Mayréna who would have been content with a satrapy instead of a kingdom." Also among the critics were some of the Rhadé, particularly Y Ut Buon Rit, who, according to Y Thih Eban, came into conflict with Sabatier in 1925 as the result of Y Ut defending some Rhadé students who had gone back to their villages without the permission of the authorities. Y Ut also came to the defense of some Rhadé villagers who had started a forest fire when they set a beehive ablaze in their effort to get the honey. Sabatier accused Y Ut and some other Rhadé civil servants of having goaded the villagers to disobedience, and Y Ut retorted that Sabatier treated the Rhadé like slaves. The résident then ordered some of the Rhadé civil servants arrested and put in stocks. At the insistence of Y Ut and Khunjanob, a French representative in Hue named d'Elloy went to Ban Me Thuot to arbitrate the dispute.

Some elderly Rhadé informants complained that Sabatier slept with too many Rhadé girls, and in 1923, as a result of one liaison, he had the aforementioned daughter H'ni. There also was some resentment among Rhadé chiefs over the compulsory attendance of the children at the Ban Me Thuot school. One chief stated, "Ask of us what you will, put us in jail, but do not expect us to give up our children," and there was muttering about the "corvée d'école."[37]

The powerful financial forces won the day, and in April 1926 Sabatier was relieved of his position as résident. He became an inspector, but he was discontented and in 1929 requested permission to return to France with his daughter. They sailed for France and not long afterward Sabatier died.[38]

---

35. de Galembert, *Administrations*, p. 922.
36. Pierre Dourisboure and Christian Simonnet, *Vietnam: Mission on the Grand Plateaus* (Maryknoll, New York: Maryknoll Publications, 1967), pp. 229–30.
37. Ner, "Humbles constructeurs," *Indochine*, no. 144 (1943), pp. 15–16.
38. Boudet, "Léopold Sabatier," pp. iii–iv.

COLONIZATION COMES TO THE HIGHLANDS

Sabatier was replaced by Giran, who expressed the opinion that "a handful of Frenchmen living in the midst of the population would do more for their evolution than all the most eloquent official palavers." On 23 July 1926 Giran wrote a report elaborating this theme and as a result Darlac province was opened to colonists. The administration was immediately inundated with twenty-seven demands for a total of 167,845 hectares of land, almost the entire province. Since no provision had been made for declaring village lands inalienable, there was fear among some French officials that the highlanders might react negatively to the invasion of colonists. There also was the sudden realization that the planters would have difficulty finding sufficient labor among the local villagers. The administration therefore decided to grant concessions to eight select bidders, all of them affiliated with important financial groups, but this did not take place until 1929.

A decree dated 27 March 1929 outlined the zones reserved for indigenous populations in Darlac province, and 99-year leases were subsequently granted to some bidders. The Compagnie Agricole d'Annam formed by French business interests (that already had large investments in Java) received a lease on 8,000 hectares, and the Compagnie des Hauts Plateaux Indochinois (formed by the Compagnie de Navigation et de Commerce d'Extrême-Orient) received 13,200 hectares. The Société Indochinoise got 975, while the Group de la Société Indochinoise de Commerce, d'Agriculture et de Finance was awarded a lease for 8,000. Labor for the new estates was recruited among the Rhadé and also among Vietnamese in the coastal provinces.

Giran also launched some public works projects in Ban Me Thuot and throughout the province. The road to the coast was improved, and a new official residence was built along with new houses for the assistant résident and the director of the Franco-Rhadé School. A decree issued on 29 September 1929 created the new Franco-Rhadé Group Scholaire in Ban Me Thuot with elementary level courses organized in a four-year cycle and primary school level in a two-year cycle. The director was a French professor who also served as Inspector of Education for the highlands. New quarters for the Garde Indigène were constructed. In 1927 a plan was formulated for a regular military unit of highlanders, part of the French army, but it was not implemented until 1930.

In 1929 Giran suddenly departed from Darlac and Thiebaut was named the new résident. He immediately reorganized the province administration, bringing for the first time a French administrative structure to the outlying areas. Up to this point the traditional system of having a village headman deal with most problems had continued to function, and since 1923 any conflicts that could not be resolved within the confines of the village were brought before the highlander law court. With the new administration, however, 22 sectors or cantons, embracing some 418 Rhadé and Mnong villages, were organized. All of the village headmen were brought together to select the 22 canton chiefs, who were to be assisted by Rhadé secretaries trained at the Franco-Rhadé School. Through these canton chiefs the résident transmitted orders, and the canton chiefs reported on their agricultural production, public health problems, deaths, epidemics, and any crimes.[39]

The sight of colonists arriving and clearing land in their midst rankled the highlanders in Kontum and Darlac provinces. According to Ner, their resentment was most patently manifest in the flight of students from the schools.[40] Between 1926 and 1930 the enrollment in Ban Me Thuot fell from 560 to 180, and in 1928, during one night, 75 out of 150 students fled the school. In Kontum an estimated 30 percent of the students returned to their villages.

In 1929 the first American missionaries arrived in the central highlands. The Christian and Missionary Alliance, sponsored by American Protestant congregations, had set a goal in 1887 of doing missionary work in Vietnam, but opposition by the French administration prevented it until 1911 when the Reverend Robert Jaffray was given permission to organize a mission in Tourane. Three years later the first Christian and Missionary Alliance church began to function, and in 1919 a new mission was established in Saigon. One of the first missionaries there was the Reverend Herbert Jackson. During a visit to Dalat in the early 1920s he had become determined to organize a missionary effort among the highlanders. When Jackson's son fell ill in 1929, a doctor advised the cool climate of Dalat, so the mission authorities approved his moving there, marking the beginning of an American presence in the highlands.[41]

---

39. Monfleur, *Monographie*, pp. 20–22, 45–47.
40. Ner, "Humbles constructeurs," *Indochine*, no. 144 (1943), pp. 14–16.
41. Winton T. Thomas, "The Evangelical Church in French Indo-China," *Occasional Bulletin of the Missionary Research Library* 5, no. 6 (1954): 6; D. I. Jeffrey, "The Word of the Christian and Missionary Alliance," *Occasional Bulletin of the Missionary Research Library* 4, no. 15 (1953): 8; Homer E. Dowdy, *The Bamboo Cross* (London: Hodder and Stoughton, 1964), pp. 11, 41.

In the vicinity of Cheo Reo through the first decades of the twentieth century, Nay Nui (2.11), the renowned Jarai chief, continued to function as intermediary between the French administration and the local population. Unlike his confreres Khunjanob in Darlac and Hma in Kontum, Nay Nui never assumed any official role as judge. The Rcom clan also continued to be recognized as the elite family in the Cheo Reo area, and, since the marriage of Nay Nui to Rcom H'lion had proven so auspicious, it set a precedent for marriages between Nay males and Rcom females in this branch of the Rcom clan. Around 1924 Nay Nui arranged a marriage between his third child Rcom H'but (2.13) and Nay Der (2.12), who, it was noted above, had studied in Kontum and Qui Nhon, after which he returned to Cheo Reo to become its first schoolmaster. Nay Der was born around 1900 in the village of Buon Oi Nu, now a hamlet of Le Bac village south of Cheo Reo. As the schoolmaster, Nay Der rapidly gained a reputation of being an honest and capable leader as well as the most intelligent man in the area. His sister-in-law Rcom H'ban (2.18) echoed the view of Nguyen Huu Phu that Der was very light in color—"like a Frenchman," she exclaimed. He is also remembered as being a very gentle man who dealt with everyone in a kindly manner.

In the late 1920s another leader in the Cheo Reo area was R'mah Dok (3.7), who, like Nay Nui, gained considerable status through his marriage into the Rcom clan. According to several Rcom informants, Nay Nui's mother-in-law Rcom H'bem (2.3) and her sister Rcom H'lok (2.4) shared their maternal longhouse. As mentioned earlier, when a smallpox epidemic struck, they thought it best to separate their families and so built new houses about one kilometer apart. H'lok's daughter Rcom H'kuet (3.2) married Ksor Plol, who became a local leader. They had a son named Djong, and as a village grew around their longhouse it became known as Buon Ama Djong (Village of the Father of Djong) in honor of Plol. One of their daughters, Rcom H'areng (3.3), married Ksor Seng, who also became a local chief, eventually replacing the aging Nay Nui as the representative of the King of Fire in the area. Their eldest daughter Rcom H'nher (3.4) married Ksor Wol (3.5), who also attained status as a Jarai notable and in time succeeded Ksor Seng as representative of the King of Fire. Another daughter, Rcom H'kra (3.6), married R'mah Dok (3.7), who was selected by the French to be intermediary between the administration and the Pleiku, Cheo Reo, An Khe, and highland populations. Later Dok let it be known that he wanted a second wife, so H'areng arranged for him to marry a younger daughter, Rcom H'dla (3.8). Essentially, Dok was a leader more in the pattern of Nay Nui, functioning as intermediary for the French and seeing that taxes were collected and corveés organized. There was little opportunity for him to expand his role as had Khunjanob and Hma because Cheo Reo, unlike Ban Me Thuot and Kontum, remained a minor administrative center with no law courts.

Farther south in the vicinity of Dalat, no great change took place until around 1920. When Doumer departed in 1902, his plans for a Dalat hill station came to a halt, and by 1908 the administrative center consisted of several brick buildings, one of which housed the French representative Champoudry, locally known as "the mayor." Nearby was a small wooden guest house built on piling, a marketplace around a small fountain, and ten thatched houses occupied by Vietnamese and Chinese who had come to engage in commerce with the highlanders. Some Vietnamese and Chinese traders also had settled in Djiring which they reached from Phan Thiet by the road built in 1910. Their appearance in both places marked the beginning of an immigration of lowlanders into this region of the highlands.[42]

A new effort to transform Dalat into a hill station was launched in 1912 when Governor General Albert Sarraut made funds available for construction of new roads into the area and for new buildings in Dalat. Soon after, construction began on an automobile service road, Colonial Route 11, from the coast to Krongpha and Dalat via the Danhim valley and Bellevue. During 1914 and 1915 a route between Dalat and Djiring was completed. Early in 1916 the province of Lang Bian was created with Dalat as administrative center, and Cunhac, who had participated in the 1897 Thouard Mission, was named résident. Now more accessible to the outside, Dalat began to attract French visitors, most of them interested in big game hunting. Also in 1916, the first Langbian Palace Hotel, a wooden structure on piling with a long veranda and sheet metal roof, was completed. When in 1920 Lang Bian became the province of Haut Donnai with its administrative seat at Djiring, Dalat became an autonomous administrative unit under Commissioner General Garnier. However, Cunhac retained his role as résident. His administrative offices were on the ground floor of his chalet and his primary responsibility was taking care of the big game hunters.[43]

In 1922 implementation began on the Dalat city plan worked out by the

42. P. Duclaux, "Le Dalat de 1908," *Indochine*, no. 39 (1941), pp. 2–5; no. 40 (1941), pp. 7–11.
43. A. Baudrit, "La Naissance de Dalat," *Indochine*, no. 180 (1944), pp. 23–24.

Chru leader Touneh Han Dang (in hat) and on his right his sons Han Tho (slightly to the rear) and Han Din, together with other members of the family in front of their house in Diom (1966)

French urbanist Hébard. It envisaged a city of 300,000 inhabitants that would be a "corner of France" in the mountains of Vietnam. There would be an artificial lake, government buildings, widely scattered villas and chalets as well as a modern central market. Dalat was to be a garden city with parks, many trees, and flowers everywhere.[44] By 1925 there were around a dozen French-style chalets dispersed in the woods and in 1928 an English visitor laid out a nine-hole golf course. In 1925 the Public Works Service proposed a plan to furnish the city with electricity generated from the Ankroat falls, but no financing was available. In 1929, however, O'Neil, one of the first planters to settle in Dalat, arranged a generator powered by Cam Ly falls and produced the first electricity in Dalat.[45]

Dalat also began to attract educational institutions. The Petit Lycée de Dalat for children of French families (and a small number of Vietnamese and Cambodian children from among the well-to-do) was founded in 1927. At the same time, the Sisters of Saint Paul opened the Crèche de Nazareth for small children.[46]

During this period of change the most influential highland leaders in the

44. P. Munier, "Dalat," *Indochine*, no. 28 (1941), pp. 7–8.

45. R. Planté, "Les aménagements hydroélectriques du Sud-Annam," *Indochine*, no. 111 (1942), p. 13.

46. Direction Générale de l'Instruction Publique, *Le Service de l'instruction publique en Indochine en 1930* (Hanoi: Imprimerie d'Extrême-Orient, 1930), pp. 27–28; A. Morval, "Dalat: cité de la jeunesse," *Indochine*, no. 133 (1943), pp. ix–xi.

Dalat area were from among the Chru, who are located in the Danhim valley between Dalat and the coastal plain. Although they are a relatively small ethnic group (around 15,000), the Chru are the most advanced of the highlanders because of their historical relationship to the Cham. The Banahria clan had traditionally been the elite among the Chru, and at the end of the nineteenth century Banahria Quang functioned as the Chru chief in dealing with the Vietnamese and French. According to Touneh Han Tho (4.2), another member of this clan, Banahria Ya Gut, served as leader of the Chru during the early decades of the twentieth century. Born around 1870, he married a kinswoman of Touneh Han Tho's father's mother's sister. They had one daughter, Ame Mabo, who in 1975 was still living in Diom. They also had a son who became a lieutenant in the French army. In addition to being a noted leader among the Chru (a street in Dalat was named for him), Ya Gut is remembered as having been a gifted composer of epic chants, a talent he is said to have inherited from his ancestors. These chants were about contemporary events, and Han Tho recalls that some were about the Japanese occupation and the Indochina War.

When the French administrative post at Dran was established in 1909, Ya Gut was named Tri Huyen, a role similar to that of Hma in Kontum and Khunjanob in Ban Me Thuot. He was intermediary between the administration and the local populations, and he served as judge in arbitrating conflicts among highlanders. It is noted in an account written by Touneh Han Din (4.3), half-brother of Touneh Han Tho, that one of Ya Gut's primary responsibilities was organizing corvée (the French called the highlanders recruited for corvées "coolies Moi") for road construction and transporting goods.[47] They also had to carry the open palanquins favored by the Frenchmen and their Vietnamese "wives," whom the villagers jokingly called "Bà đầm tẹt mũi" ("flat-nosed French ladies"). Each male villager between the ages of sixteen and sixty was expected to work from fifteen to twenty days a year without pay or food. The work was arduous, and often the French or Vietnamese supervisor would strike the laborers with green rattan boughs. The corvée was detested, and some villagers fled into the forest rather than submit to it. According to Han Din, most of the one hundred families living in a village near the post of Dran

---

47. Touneh Han Din, "Dran-Canrang-Don Duong hay cánh đồng Danhim trước chương-trình tân-thiết" (Dran-Canrang-Don Duong or the Dran Valley in the Process of Development), *Địa phương chí tỉnh Tuyên Đức* (Tuyen Duc Province Bulletin), 1962, pp. 1–5.

moved to a more remote area in the mountains rather than perform the corvée. A popular Chru song at the time expressed their sentiments:

> I wept under the heavy burden I carried
> I removed my head cloth to wipe my tears
> After I passed three stations
> My heart perspired
> I used my garment to wipe my heart.

In reviewing some of the history of this period, Monseigneur Cassaigne notes that the construction in 1910 of the route from coastal Phan Thiet to the administrative post at Djiring cost the lives of "numerous coolies" and two French engineers.[48]

Another Chru leader during this period was Touneh Han Dang, whose son Touneh Han Tho compiled an account of his life for this study from oral sources, memoranda, and documents.[49] Born around 1880 in Diom village, Han Dang was one of seven children, and his parents were reasonably well off (his mother was related to the Banahria clan). Like other village boys, Han Dang helped his father in the fields and spent his free time hunting and fishing. When he reached the age of fifteen he began accompanying some of the Chru men on their trips down to coastal Phan Rang where they traded betel leaves, areca nuts, and other forest products for salt, fish sauce, and clothes. Being a robust youth of independent spirit, within a few years Han Dang began to organize his own monthly trade trips. Near Phan Rang was the Cham village of An Phuoc, a place noted for having produced many leaders. It had a primary school of good reputation so Han Dang enrolled for training in Cham script, Vietnamese, and French. Absorbed with his studies, he spent more and more time in An Phuoc. But his parents became distressed that he might be drifting away from them and arranged to have two elderly Cham and Vietnamese teachers instruct him at home in Diom. After finishing his daily chores, Han Dang met with his teachers for two hours, and in the evening his Vietnamese instructor taught him *võ Việt Nam*, a Vietnamese version of Chinese boxing.

When in 1905 the French began construction on a dirt road from Phan Rang to Dalat, Han Dang and his father were subject to corvée. Since his

48. Msgr. Cassaigne, "Les Mois de la région de Djiring," *Indochine*, no. 131 (1943), p. 11.
49. Normally among the matrilineal Chru the children take the clan name of the mother, but since Han Tho's mother is Cham-Vietnamese his parents elected to have their children assume their father's clan name, Touneh.

father was quite elderly, Han Dang assumed the corvée responsibility for both, although he openly refused to carry any of the Frenchmen or their "wives" on their palanquins. The loads the highlanders bore were often very heavy and Han Dang recalled that going uphill they could only attain a maximum of fifteen kilometers per day. Nonetheless he and other porters had their compensations; some of the cargo consisted of large casks of wine for the French colony in Dalat, and the porters would make small holes to pour themselves cups of refreshment, replenishing the loss with water.

With some money saved, Han Dang expanded his trading activities, going into the back country to purchase valuable elephant tusks and wild honey from the Roglai for sale in Phan Rang. By this time he had gained considerable stature among the valley people as a young man of ability and good character. Around 1907 he began directing some economic innovations he felt would improve the lives of the Chru villagers. First, he arranged for some Cham women to go to the Danhim valley and teach better weaving techniques to the Chru. Second, he sent his cousin, a lady named Ba Cam, to Phan Rang to learn the Cham methods for making clay pots. She returned to start a whole new pottery style in her village. Han Dang is also credited with having introduced a stronger and more efficient Cham plow among the Chru. Less successful was his campaign to get Chru males, who customarily wore loincloths, to adopt trousers.

In 1910 Han Dang was selected to be village chief (they used the Vietnamese designation Ly Truong) of Diom. Two years later, in keeping with their policy of establishing an administrative structure more or less in conformity with that existing in Annam, the French established the *huyện* of Tan Khai, an administrative unit similar to those already established in Kontum and Ban Me Thuot and later to be created at Djiring.[50] This made Ya Gut's position as Tri Huyen for highlander law cases an official role in the Vietnamese administrative structure.[51] Han Dang was named Tru Dich (interpreter). When Ya Gut retired as Tri Huyen in 1919, he was replaced by the Sre leader K'brai (see below), who retained the role until 1922. Han Dang was named to this position, but at the time the official title was Tri Huyen Moi and Han Dang objected to the pejorative term "moi." (On his French identity card at this time he was described as being of the *Race Moi*.) The administration in Hue relented and an elegant document

---

50. In Annam the *tỉnh* was the equivalent of a province and was divided into *huyện*, which in turn were composed of *tổng* (canton) and then of *xã* (villages), which were made up of *làng* (hamlets).

51. According to Touneh Han Tho, a Tri Huyen was paid 50 percent by the province and 50 percent by the court of Hue. The government also paid a retirement pension.

issued by the Minister of the Interior of the "Grand Empire d'Annam" declared that on 22 February 1922 Touneh Han Dang was named Tho Tri Huyn of Tan Khai—*thô* being a more literary designation for "those who live in the remote hinterlands." [52]

As a continuation of his earlier efforts at improving life in the Danhim valley, Han Dang proposed to the French administration in 1919 that an elementary school be established at the village of M'lon. Résident Cunhac and Tran Van Ly, the Quan Dao, opposed the project on the grounds that the "backward Moi" did not need any schools since they were only capable of working as unskilled laborers. Han Dang did not give up, however, and in 1922 when the construction of the Saigon-Dalat road brought about a need for local labor he struck a bargain—the highlanders would provide the labor if the school were built. The result was a small thatched school-house and seventeen students, all from the Lat, Chil, and Chru ethnic groups. Among them were such future leaders as K'Kre (4.5), Touprong Hiou (4.4), and Banahria Ya Don (4.6), who joined the Viet Cong in 1959. No funds for purchasing food were available, however, so for the first three years Han Dang paid the cost himself.

Until his departure from Dalat in 1927, Tran Van Ly, the Quan Dao, was in constant conflict with Han Dang and succeeded in blocking any new programs for the highlanders. After his departure, Han Dang got the provincial administration to authorize a food budget for the school and to extend the curriculum to four years and increase enrollment to forty pupils. Provision also was made for qualified pupils to continue their primary education in Dalat, where they were lodged at Han Dang's house. He then obtained approval for some of the students who had completed their primary education to continue studies at the Collège de Qui Nhon.

Among other things, the French rewarded highlanders who served in the administration with medals. A decree issued 2 September 1925 by the governor general of Indochina awarded Han Dang a silver Medal of Honor, second class, for his services as Tri Huyen. According to Touneh Han Tho, on 14 February 1927 with the opening of the Krongpha-Bellevue section of the railway the résident of Haut Donnai presented him with the Kim-Tien medal, third class. The Chevalier du Dragon d'Annam decoration was awarded in 1929, and in 1933 he received the Kim-Khanh medal, third class.

52. Ministère de l'Intérieur, Grand Empire d'Annam, 23 Février 1922, personal papers of Touneh Han Dang, Saigon, Vietnam.

Among the Sre people southwest of Dalat, the prominent leader at this time was K'Brai (4.7), head of an elite family in the village of Djiring which in 1899 had become the administrative seat for the "montagnard" province of Haut Donnai. In 1901 this province was abolished and Djiring was placed under Phan Thiet. According to Touneh Han Tho, it was around 1914 that the French named K'Brai a Tri Phu, a role similar to canton chief. He was responsible for collecting taxes and organizing corvée as well as arbitrating any conflicts among the Sre. As indicated above, when Ya Gut retired as Tri Huyen in 1919, K'Brai replaced him, keeping this role for several years. Because of his corvée demands and other practices, K'Brai was not popular among many of the Sre villagers, and in the mid-1920s he was slain. The French authorities eventually apprehended seven Sre men for the crime.

Father Cassaigne arrived in Djiring in 1927 to organize the first Catholic mission there and two years later began construction of some thatched huts for a leprosarium. During that period he also learned the Sre language and eventually produced the first primer in the Koho language.[53]

Farther north in Quang Nam province there was at this time an effort to develop a hill station similar to Dalat on Bana, a mountain inland from Tourane. A site for a hill station to serve Annam had been selected in 1901 by Captain Debay at the behest of Governor General Doumer, but when Doumer departed in 1902 the plan was shelved. Because the highlanders of interior Quang Nam were considered particularly hostile, a military post had been established in 1904 at An Diem inland from Faifoo to protect Vietnamese settlements along the Boung river. In 1912 the Bana massif was designated a forest preserve, and Sogny, the commandant at An Diem, began a survey of the highland people in the region. The following year Sogny completed a census of 250 villages, estimating the population to be around 10,000. He concluded that they were of one "race" with a common language and gave them the name "Katu." Soon after, however, Sogny left his post, and interest in the Katu faded.[54]

After World War I ended in 1918, there was revived interest in building a mountain retreat on Bana away from the stifling heat of the coastal plain. At the beginning of 1919, Galtier, the résident in Tourane, ordered the construction of an access route to the base of Bana mountain. A decree dated 27 May 1919 approved setting aside part of the forest preserve for

53. P. A., "La Léproserie de Djiring," *Indochine*, no. 54 (1941), p. 8.
54. J. Le Pichon, "Les Chasseurs de sang," *Bulletin des Amis du Vieux Hué* 25 (1938): 359–60.

construction of a hill station. By the end of the year construction had begun on five chalets on the peak of the mountain, and in 1923 the owners of the Hotel Morin in Tourane finished building a small hotel with twenty-two rooms at Bana. The new resort still was difficult to reach; an auto route ended at the base of the mountain, and ascent required a four-hour trip on an open palanquin followed by three hours on foot. Nonetheless, by 1928 some twenty-five additional structures had been built on Bana.[55]

Aerial reconnaissance was conducted in 1925 in western Quang Nam as part of a survey to determine the most efficacious route to follow in constructing a section of Colonial Route 14 from Kontum to Tourane. As a result of the survey, it was decided that the best route would be north from Kontum to Dak Sut, then in a northeasterly direction through various passes in the rugged, heavily forested mountains to Phuoc Son. A portion of Route 14 had already been built from Phuoc Son to Faifoo on the coast where it linked with Colonial Route 1, the Route Mandarine. Between 29 November and 6 December 1929 a French reconnaissance party from Phuoc Son conducted a ground survey of the proposed route, carefully mapping the topography in the region. By the end of 1930, work on Route 14 north of Kontum had begun.[56]

The influx of colonists in Kontum in the late 1920s provoked a strong reaction among the highlanders in the area. In addition to the drastic reduction in school attendance noted above, there were such violent manifestations as ambushes of automobiles, cutting of roads, and attacks on Vietnamese colonists' settlements. Telegraph poles were chopped down and the wires removed. In March 1929 the Garde Indigène launched a "pacification" effort, directing it at Kon Bar northeast of Kontum, one of the main centers of dissidence. A military aircraft was called in to bomb the village, the first known aerial attack in the highlands. Terrorized by the "fire from the sky," the dissidents and all of the villagers in the vicinity fled into the forest.[57]

However, the dissidence had not ended. In fact, it spread to the An Khe area, and between July and September 1929 some twenty-seven

55. L. S., "Bana," *Indochine*, no. 160 (1943), pp. 14–15.

56. F. Enjorlras, "Reconnaissance de la région de Moi-Xe et du trace de la route coloniale no. 14 entre Tan-An et le Dak-Main," *BSEI*, no. 4 (1932), pp. 411–41.

57. E. Daufés, *La Garde Indigène de l'Indochine de sa création à nos jours*, 2 vols. (Avignon: Imprimerie D. Serguin, 1934), 2: 180; Officiers l'Etat-Major du Général de Division Aubert, *Histoire Militaire de l'Indochine Française des débuts à nos jours (Juillet 1930)*, 2 vols. (Hanoi-Haiphong: Imprimerie d'Extrême-Orient, 1930), 2: 289.

Vietnamese were killed in various attacks. At the Delignon estate, numerous rubber trees were destroyed. To cope with the situation, Garde Indigène commander Condominas organized an operation and succeeded in gaining the submission of the dissidents centered in Plei Xu. Subsequently he mounted a similar operation north of Kontum in the Sedang country where violence had accompanied the appearance of teams surveying the proposed extension of Route 14. Condominas and his troops encountered numerous ambushes and paths filled with traps and sharpened bamboo stakes. By the beginning of 1930, however, most of the Sedang villages had submitted to French authority.[58]

The mid-1920s rush for land on which plantations could be established affected the remote areas of Thudaumot and Bien Hoa provinces in Cochinchina, where the red soils were found amenable for cultivation of rubber trees. These areas, to the north and east of Saigon, had generally been ignored, and in 1925 there was pressure from business interests to bring them more effectively under French control. Between 1925 and 1927, Thiebaut, a Bien Hoa official, and Odéra, who previously had conducted an expedition to search for the railway route, established the French administration in part of the Maa country. In the Stieng area around Nui Bara, three new cantons were formed. In 1927 Commandant Carrier conducted a mapping expedition (financed by a private firm) in the thick forests of the Stieng country west of Nui Bara. The following year Gerber became the administrator at Bu Dop and began a systematic study of Stieng language and customs that were later published. That same year, Odéra was named administrator at Vo Dat. By 1930 trails had penetrated the hitherto inaccessible areas, small military posts were established in various places, and plans for rubber estates in the region were being implemented. Interestingly, however, although the French appear to have dealt with the indigenous population as they did in Annam, no leaders of any note appeared in Thudaumot or Bien Hoa.[59]

58. Daufés, *Garde Indigène*, 2: 180–85.

59. Pagès, "Rapport sur la pénétration en pays Moi au cours des cinq dernières années," in *Variétés sur le pays Mois* (Saigon: Gouvernement de la Cochinchine, 1935), pp. 207–12.

10 EROSION OF FRENCH RULE IN THE HIGHLANDS, 1930–1945

By 1930 the presence of towns such as Dalat, Ban Me Thuot, and Kontum; the proliferating estates where wild forests gave way to neat rows of coffee, tea, and rubber seedlings; and the network of roads running through the valleys, across the plateaus, and over the mountain passes attested to the success of the French "penetration" that Doumer had envisaged at the turn of the century. Although "pacification" operations continued in the more remote hinterlands, there already was much to give the impression of a permanent French presence. In any of the towns or estates, a colonist at this time might easily have looked from his veranda at the striking highland scenery with a feeling that his future in this region was secure.

During the 1930–1945 period, however, a series of events unfolded that increasingly rendered the impression of a permanent French presence an illusion. Some manifestations of discontent with French rule in the areas around Ban Me Thuot, Kontum, and Dalat during the 1920s were noted in the preceding chapter. A more striking reflection of this discontent came in 1937 when belief in a diety called the "Python God" swept large parts of the highlands. French officials were puzzled at first by what they considered bizarre behavior, such as refusal to perform corvée, by many highland villagers. But puzzlement gave way to deep concern when the officials learned that this "new religion" promised a golden age for the highlanders, a time when they would be rid of all outsiders, including the French.

During the 1930s another threat to French rule not only in the highlands but throughout Vietnam appeared with the rise of nationalist movements among the Vietnamese. During World War II one of these movements, the Viet Minh, emerged as a powerful force in the lowlands and northern highlands as it gained support in its struggle against "Japanese fascism and French imperialism." Culmination came with the Viet Minh takeover of the administration in Vietnam following the August 1945 surrender of the Japanese. In the highlands, many of the educated—teachers, civil servants, and military personnel—rallied to the Viet Minh call for a struggle to bring an end to French rule in the highlands.

Both the Python God and the Viet Minh movements, each in its own way, placed emphasis on the collective highlander identity. One belief associated with the former was that only the highlanders had the potential power (due to favor by the Python God) to survive a predicted catastrophe that would destroy the French, Vietnamese, and Lao. For the Viet Minh, the highlanders were "the southern highland ethnic minority," who would enjoy autonomy when the French were expelled.

The effect of these two movements on highland leadership varied. By and large, the Python God movement did not seem to have made any significant changes in the existing leadership. Those propagating the Python God beliefs were not of the group of educated highlanders already described. Rather, they were shamans and they did not form any kind of hierarchy. Moreover, their roles do not appear to have ever taken on a political tone—which may have been due to their having been arrested by the French when the movement was still new. The Viet Minh, however, recruited members of the existing leadership group. In doing so, it transformed these leaders' roles as teachers and functionaries into new roles as revolutionaries. Among other things, this resulted in a long-lasting dichotomy between those who remained in the Viet Minh and those who never joined or who dropped out.

Another important development during this period was the increasing number of young highlanders beginning to receive secondary education. In addition to the training available at Hue and Qui Nhon, there now were secondary level courses taught at Kontum and Ban Me Thuot. These centers attracted students from different ethnic groups. Bonds of friendship that would be important in the years to come were created among them. This experience also broadened the horizons of these young highland men: those in Qui Nhon became familiar with Vietnamese ways and the language, those in Kontum learned to speak Bahnar, and those in Ban Me Thuot used Rhadé as their lingua franca, along with French.

THE PRE–WORLD WAR II PERIOD

The bright promise of economic gain that had precipitated the land rush in the mid-1920s suffered a setback with the world economic crisis of 1930. The major exports from Indochina were rice and maize, both highly susceptible to price fluctuations. When prices began to tumble in 1930, the effect was felt throughout the colony. Larger corporations already invested in highland plantations began to limit their plans for future expansion, concentrating on lands under cultivation, while some of the medium and small business corporations ceased operations altogether.[1] In Darlac, by 1930, the Compagnie Agricole d'Annam had cleared 1,800 hectares, 800 of which were in tea, the remainder in coffee. This estate had some 1,200 laborers, of which 400 were Rhadé and the remaining 800, separately lodged, were Vietnamese. The Compagnie des Hauts Plateaux Indochinois had 668 hectares of rubber trees, some of which by 1930 had attained the height of 1 m 40, in addition to 135 hectares of coffee seedlings and 40 hectares of tea plants. There were 950 Vietnamese and 450 Rhadé working on the estate. The Société Indochinoise had 125 hectares of coffee and had cleared an additional 250 for coffee production. Individual holdings only amounted to 30 hectares.[2]

By 1932 in Kontum province there were 300 hectares of privately owned land and 2,350 hectares of corporation-owned land under cultivation. Farther south, in Haut Donnai, private holdings totaled 500 hectares; corporations owned 2,000 hectares. In this province there was, in addition to coffee production, considerable truck gardening. The opening in July 1932 of Colonial Route 20 linking Saigon with Dalat made this area particularly accessible to the lowland markets. In other parts of the highlands, however, there was less success not only because of the economic crisis but also due to poor soils. At An Khe, for example, an attempt to establish an extensive rubber estate on grey soils proved a failure, as had another effort to cultivate coffee in the same area.[3]

As the economic crisis continued, the planters began to group into

1. Le Thanh Khoi, *Le Viêt-Nam: histoire et civilisation* (Paris: Les Editions de Minuit, 1955), pp. 412–13.

2. A. Monfleur, *Monographie de la province de Darlac* (Hanoi: Imprimerie d'Extrême-Orient, 1931), pp. 45–47.

3. Eugéne Teston and Maurice Percheron, *L'Indochine moderne: encyclopédie administrative, touristique, artistique et économique* (Paris: Librairie de France, 1932), pp. 876–77.

associations so as to coordinate their operations and give them unity in
dealing with the administration. In 1933, the Société des Plantations Indochinoises de Thé (The Society of Indochinese Tea Plantations) was formed,
and two years later the Société Indochinoise des Plantations d'Hévéas (The
Indochinese Society of Rubber Plantations) was organized.[4]

The effects of the economic crisis began to subside by 1936, and by 1939
some of the estates were producing cash crops. Five tea estates totaling
2,000 hectares were producing annually some 9,000 *quintaux* (a quintal or
100 kilograms) of dried tea. At Pleiku, the Catecka plantation had 800
hectares with an annual crop of 4,000 quintals. There were 1,400 laborers
on the estate and an additional unreported number of highlanders
performing corvée at the rate of twenty to thirty days a year each. The
proprietors of Catecka shipped some 600 metric tons of rice each year from
the coast to feed the workers. There also were in the highlands a total of
2,800 hectares of coffee trees producing annually some 9,150 quintals of
beans. In addition, around Kontum town and Djiring there were small
Vietnamese concessions totaling 275 hectares producing 1,000 quintals of
coffee annually.[5]

In his 1935 report, Governor of Cochinchina Pagès conceded that some
of the unrest among the highlanders plaguing the administration in
Thudaumot and Bien Hoa provinces (which will be discussed below) was
due to the abuses of the corvée system by the rubber planters.[6] They had
been operating without restraints, and Pagès reasoned that their excesses
were creating the impression among the highlanders that the French
presence meant quasi-servitude. In noting that greater control would be
forthcoming, the governor reiterated that the local highland chiefs, acting
as intermediaries for the administration, would be responsible for mustering corvée among males from eighteen to fifty-five years of age.
Each would have to labor fifteen days per year.

According to Touneh Han Din, highlanders not only performed corvée
in the new plantations, they were also expected to work in the gardens
belonging to French military and administrative officials.[7] He reports that

4. Le Thanh Khoi, *Le Viêt-Nam*, p. 413.

5. "Les hauts plateaux du Sud-Annam," *Indochine*, no. 20 (1941), pp. 10–11.

6. Pagès, "Rapport sur la pénétration en pays Moi au cours des cinq dernières années," in *Variétés sur le pays Mois* (Saigon: Gouvernement de la Cochinchine, 1935), pp. 216–17.

7. Touneh Han Din, "Dran-Canrang-Don Duong hay cánh đồng Danhim trước chương-trình tân-thiết" (Dran-Canrang-Don Duong or the Dran Valley in the Process of Development), *Địa phương chí tỉnh Tuyên Đức* (Tuyen Duc Province Bulletin), 1962, p. 2.

this was common in Dalat, and a popular Chru song of the time went:

> Stay with the junior lieutenant
> Must work all the days planting flowers
> Be a coolie for the captain
> Must plant three rows of greens.

During this period there was a vast increase in the lines of communication between the highlands and the outside world. In October 1936 the first trains completed the voyage on the Transindochina Railroad from Saigon to the Chinese border, and a spur line ran from Tour Cham (on the main line near Phan Rang) to Dalat. The plan for the system had been adopted in December 1897, and Governor General Doumer had obtained funds to begin the initial construction. In 1905 the line from Hanoi to Vinh opened, and three years later trains began running on the track from Tourane to Dong Ha via Hue. In 1913 the Saigon-Nhatrang section was completed, and in 1927 the Vinh-Dong Ha line opened. In 1931 funds were approved to complete the final 532 kilometers of track, including that from Tour Cham to Dalat which was opened in 1933. A ceremony to mark the completion of the system was held at the border of China on 1 October 1936 by French and Chinese officials. The following day the first train to complete the trip from that site arrived at the Saigon station. During his long address at the Saigon ceremony, Gassier, Inspector General of Public Works, extolled the many virtues of the new railroad, which he saw as one means of opening the interior to colonization. Then he added prophetically, "We will see, probably in the near future, populations from the deltas spread throughout the empty spaces of the Annamite Chaine." [8]

Construction of new roads into the highlands also was begun during this period, as the French plan, devised by Doumer at the beginning of the century, continued to be implemented. It was noted above that Route 20 between Saigon and Dalat opened in July 1932, and an incident related to this project reported by Touneh Han Dang symbolizes to some extent the impact of this modern development on the traditional world of the highland people. One of the Chru leaders, Banahria Ya Hau (4.8), the Tri Huyen of Tan Khai, was responsible for mustering corvée for the section from Djiring to Dalat. While clearing forest along the route, the laborers

---

8. Inspection Générale des Travaux Publics, *Inauguration du chemin de fer Indochinois* (Hanoi: Imprimerie G. Taupin, 1936), pp. 11–25.

came upon a very large old tree known locally as "the tree of the snake spirit" (*kieu yang ala*), so called because it was the abode of countless snakes of all sizes and colors. The French engineers insisted that the tree be removed, but the highland laborers, who viewed it as a sacred place, refused to continue working unless the tree was left unharmed. Ya Hau sought the advice of Han Dang, who went to the résident in Dalat and requested that they be allowed to leave the tree standing and build the road around it. The résident refused to consider this proposal, pointing out that the engineers had said that the tree blocked the only possible route. The French, he assured Han Dang, would remove the tree. The French engineers saturated the grass around the tree with gasoline, and when they lit it the mass of snakes sought refuge in the tree. As flames engulfed the tree, the snakes' cries filled the air—or so claims Han Dang—and writhing snakes shot out from the branches like water spraying out of a fountain. The highlanders interpreted this as a sign that the *yang* was leaving the tree, and all quickly departed to their villages, refusing to work even when the French threatened them with jail. Finally the résident relented and a tortuous curve was constructed around the charred tree. Touneh Han Tho recounted that in 1972 the engineers of an American road construction company busy improving Route 20 used a bulldozer to remove the remains of the tree, all the while making sarcastic remarks about the "dumb French road builders and their hairpin curves."

Since some of the new routes passed through regions where the highlanders remained hostile toward the French, pacification preceded construction. This was the case with the southern portion of Route 14 from Saigon to Tourane via the highlands. In 1930 the portion from Ban Me Thuot to Kontum was opened, although it was only a dirt road scarcely usable during the rainy season. In 1929 it was decided to construct the stretch from Saigon to Ban Me Thuot by way of Budop in the Stieng country, following a route into Cambodia through Palkei and Sre Khtum, then swinging back northeast through the area occupied by the Mnong to Ban Me Thuot. The problem, however, was that the ethnic groups in this region were still hostile. Although a French military post had been established at Bu Dop in 1913, the following year Henri Maitre had been assassinated in the Mnong country just to the north, and in 1915 a French official, Truffot, was killed at Sre Chi inside the Cambodian border. As unrest spread among the Mnong and Stieng, further French efforts at bringing the region under control ceased. By 1929, however, business interests were eager to establish rubber estates in the area, so it was decided that a new pacification campaign would have to be organized.[9]

The pacification mission was put under command of Gatille, district chief of Snoul, who began to muster corvée among the highlanders for construction of the road between Palkei and Sre Khtum. Since there was unrest in that area, a heavy militia guard was provided, and work began in 1930. In May 1931, however, Gatille was killed in an ambush laid by local highlanders and construction ceased. The governor general called for a new pacification effort that would draw upon the military forces in Cochinchina, Annam, and Cambodia. The posts at Ban Me Thuot, Djiring, Sre Khtum, Bu Dop, Nui Bara, and Vo Dat were informed of a plan to converge military units in the troubled area from the north and the south.

On 3 February 1932 a Rhadé company arrived at Bu Djeng Drom on the Dam river which forms the border between Annam and Cambodia southwest of Ban Me Thuot. There they established a base for military operations farther south where the borders of Cambodia, Cochinchina, and Annam met—a place that became known as Trois Frontières. Meanwhile a Cambodian unit had departed from Sre Khtum but had been slowed when malaria struck, disabling two hundred men, twenty of whom died. Despite this the unit moved on and in October 1932 established Poste Le Rolland, which became the administrative seat for the new Haut Chhlong sector. On 6 January 1933 a force of Mnong from the vicinity attacked the post but were repelled. Determined to continue with the road construction, the French authorities ordered units of sixty men each dispatched from Bu Djeng Drom, Le Rolland, and Bu Dop into the country of the Mnong Biat and Mnong Bunor. They were to provide security so that the portion of the road south to Trois Frontières could be constructed. As part of this operation, Poste Maitre was established at Trois Frontières in April 1933. The delegation at Dak Dam was relocated there.

The situation seemed well in hand and construction on Route 14 moved ahead. New trouble erupted, however, when on 29 October 1933 Morère, the administrative representative at Nui Bara, was assassinated on a backwoods trail. This triggered another wave of unrest.[10] In his 1935 report on

9. Bernard Bourotte, "Essai d'histoire des populations Montagnardes du Sud-Indochinois jusqu'à 1945," *BSEI* 30, no. 1 (1955): 97–98; J. H., "La Route Coloniale No. 14 reliera Saigon à Tourane par les plateaux Mois," *Indochine*, no. 129 (1943), pp. 11–12.

10. Nyo, "Pénétration française dans les pays Mois," *BSEI* 12, no. 2 (1937): 62–65.

the progress of the French penetration during the previous five years, Pagès, the governor of Cochinchina, emphasized that such acts of murder against colonial officials undermined French authority and could not be tolerated.[11] At his order the four villages from which the attackers were alleged to have come were burned to the ground, whereupon the inhabitants fled into the forests. Their mature rice crops also were burned, but as the soldiers lit the fires they were subject to a hail of arrows. Upon leaving the villages, they found the paths filled with sharpened bamboo stakes and traps.

On 1 January 1934 the French military administrator at Haut Chhlong learned that a force of four to five hundred Mnong were massed in the forest, preparing to mount an attack on Camp Le Rolland which would signal a more general uprising by the Mnong Biat. The following day the attack came, but not where it was expected. Instead, it occurred southeast of Nui Bara, where some three hundred Stieng attacked the post at Bu Coh. They were repelled, but they cut several hundred trees to block the auto route, thus isolating the post. The ensuing unrest in the region west of the Dong Nai river prompted the French to undertake a reorganization of their defenses. As a result Poste Deshayes was established in Haut Chhlong district (in Cambodia) on 4 March 1935.

During the particularly dark night of 5 March a guard at Camp Le Rolland was slain, alerting the garrison to an attack by several hundred Mnong. The defenders lost five dead and eight wounded. The post was reduced to rubble. This attack set off a wave of rebellion led by Pu Trang Lung, the Mnong chief who in 1914 was reported to have slain Henri Maitre. Now over fifty years of age, he was determined to drive the French from the region and more than fifty villages had sent five hundred warriors in answer to his call. On 30 March there was an abortive attack on Le Rolland, and a 24 April nocturnal assault on Poste Gatille was repulsed. Five days later Gatille was attacked again. Before the defenders could fend off the Mnong warriors, some of them succeeded in entering the post. The French responded by gathering Cambodian troops and elements of the Highlander Riflemen Battalion of South Annam in addition to some Garde Indochinoise units to sweep the region between April and June 1935. This operation was acclaimed a success and the French reported that Pu Trang Lung had been killed.[12]

11. Pagès, "Rapport sur la pénétration en pays Moi," p. 213.
12. Bourotte, "Essai des populations Montagnardes," pp. 98–99; Nyo, "Pénétration française," pp. 65–66; Le Commandant, "Les tirailleurs montagnards du Sud-Annam," *Indochine*, no. 1 (1940), p. 12.

In 1937 the French administration renewed its efforts to complete the Saigon-Ban Me Thuot portion of Route 14. Surveys were conducted to find a route that would avoid the troubled areas in Cambodia. A new route from Dong Xoai to Ban Me Thuot via Poste Maitre and Camp Le Rolland was settled upon in February 1938. The following year the section from Camp Le Rolland to Ban Me Thuot was opened.[13]

Farther north in Quang Nam province, construction of Route 14 between Kontum and Tourane was proceeding slowly. The route had been planned to pass from Kontum through Dak Sut over the heavily forested mountains to Phuoc Son, terminating at the coastal town of Faifoo, where it would connect with Route 1 that continued northward to Tourane. The area west of Phuoc Son was the Katu country, where trouble in 1904 had prompted the French to establish a post at An Diem. Military operations had continued until 1913, after which the area remained quiet. A French survey for the road construction was conducted in 1929 and by the early 1930s work was progressing north of Kontum.

According to Nguyen Huu Phu, around 1932 the French established a political prison at isolated Dak Pek in the Jeh country north of Kontum. It held some four hundred prisoners of varying political affiliation. Among its more famous inmates were Le Van Hien, who later became minister of labor in the Viet Minh government and subsequently served for a long time as North Vietnamese ambassador to Laos; Ha The Hanh, one-time Viet Minh minister of information; and Nguyen Duy Trinh, who became minister of foreign affairs for the Socialist Republic of Vietnam after having held the same position in North Vietnam. The prisoners were used as laborers on the road construction, and Phu related that they once brought about the death of a disliked French supervisor by felling a tree on him.

As the road construction edged northward in 1935, the French built an outpost at Ben Giang in the Katu country above Dak Pek, the area through which the road was to pass. The following year the long period of quiet in the area ended when the Katu mounted a series of attacks on Vietnamese settlements near An Diem. The French officials in Quang Nam (including Le Pichon, author of the previously cited work on the Katu) decided that they would have to establish a French military presence in the heart of the Katu country in order to prevent the unrest from spreading. In January 1937 a unit of the province militia penetrated as far as A Tep, close to the

13. J. H., "Route Coloniale No. 14," pp. 11–12.

Laotian border, while another unit moved southward to Kontum. The post at An Diem was replaced by one at Ben Hien, farther west on strategic high ground near the confluence of the Con and Ka Lam rivers and near the Vietnamese trade routes into the interior. At the same time Poste 6, located on a plateau commanding a view of the Song Gian, Song Cai, and Song Buong valleys, replaced the fort at Ben Giang. By 1938 relative calm had returned to the area and automobiles were able to reach Ben Hien over a dirt spur road from the portion of Route 14 running inland from Faifoo.[14] With the outbreak of World War II in 1939 and the fall of France in 1940, plans for bridges and other construction projects on Route 14 north of Kontum came to a halt.[15] The war also prevented the construction of proposed Route 23, the "Interior Route," which as its name implies would have run from coastal Dong Ha through the Annam Cordillera through southern Laos, crossing Routes 12 and 9, finally terminating at Route 19 midway between Pleiku and Stung Treng. In effect, it would have traced the same course later followed by the Ho Chi Minh Trail.[16]

During this period there was an increase in the number of students from different ethnic groups going to Qui Nhon and Hue for advanced training. This was a significant development both in terms of future highland leadership and in the emergence of a highlander ethnic identity. First of all it brought together young men, generally of elite families, from widely separated parts of the highlands, and many lasting friendships were established. Some of those who were part of this program were convinced that in the alien lowland surroundings their highlander identity intensified. Regardless of their different ethnic affiliations, they felt closer to one another than to the French and Vietnamese with whom they had daily contact. They also were treated as a separate group by the French and Vietnamese. Moreover, they constituted the first group of highlanders to spend any time in a lowland Vietnamese milieu and it later became important that they were familiar with the ways and language of the Vietnamese.

Among these students were some future leaders in the highlands. The

14. J. Le Pichon, "Les Chasseurs de sang," *Bulletin des Amis du Vieux Hué* 25 (1938): 357–61.

15. J. H., "Route Coloniale No. 14," p. 12.

16. "XXX," "Construction de la route des plateaux Moix, dite Route intérieure," *Indochine*, no. 98 (1942), pp. 3–9; "X," "Le Développement du réseau routier en Indochine," *Indochine*, no. 137 (1943), pp. 14–15.

Rhadé included Y Ngong Nie Kdam (currently a Communist leader), Y Soay Kbuor (1.11), Y Dhuat Nie Kdam (later a civil servant), Y Blieng Hmok, and Y Bham Enuol (who became a dissident leader). From among the Chru were Touprong Hiou (4.4), Touneh Han Din (4.3), and K'Kre (4.5), who is from a village whose population is actually a mixture of Chru and Sre. Others were Ksor Glai (3.10), a Jarai, and two Bahnar, Pierre Yuk (1.12) and Paul Nur (1.13), the latter the first Minister for Development of Ethnic Minorities.

In 1930 opportunities for advanced training were expanded to include courses at the Collège Quoc-Hoc in Hue, where in September two Rhadé students were enrolled in the normal school section. Also, when the scholastic year began in 1930, twenty highland students began training at the Ecole Pratique d'Industrie in Hue, where the training included driving and care of motor vehicles, electricity, and carpentry. Among those in this program were future highland leaders Rcom Rock (3.11) of the elite Jarai Rcom clan in Cheo Reo and a Rhadé, Y Pem Knoul, who became an army officer.[17]

Around 1930 small one-grade schools opened in various places. For example, one such school was begun for Sedang children in Dak To north of Kontum and another for the Jarai in Pleiku.[18] According to retired Bahnar schoolmaster Hiar, in 1935 the number of Vietnamese students in the Kontum school had increased to the point where the French decided to establish a Franco-Bahnar School exclusively for highland children.

The most notable changes in education for highlanders during this period took place in Darlac province following the 1930 arrival of Dominique Antomarchi as the new director of the Franco-Rhadé School. In the previous chapter it was noted that Rhadé discontent with the French expropriation of land was most graphically manifest in their hostility toward the education system. Antomarchi arrived to find that two-thirds of the students had fled back to their villages. Undaunted by his dismal situation, the new director met the challenge by learning to speak Rhadé and revising the texts for instruction in the Rhadé language. He also codified the indigenous laws that had been published by Sabatier, and his

17. Direction Générale de l'Instruction Publique, *Le Service de l'instruction publique en Indochine en 1930* (Hanoi: Imprimerie d'Extrême-Orient, 1930), p. 91; Exposition Coloniale Internationale, *Indochine Française* (Hanoi: Imprimerie d'Extrême-Orient, 1931), pp. 5–20; F. P. Antoine, "L'Ecole Montagnarde," *Indochine Sud Est Asiatique*, no. 29 (1954), pp. 35–36.

18. Antoine, "L'Ecole Montagnarde," p. 36.

revised code was published in 1940.[19] At the same time he undertook a program to change the school curriculum, adding courses that would have some practical appeal to village children. Instruction in animal husbandry and kitchen gardening were emphasized. The school garden provided food for the students, and the school cows supplied the students as well as the town of Ban Me Thuot with fresh milk. Antomarchi met with success, and the number of students rose from 132 in 1930 to over 500 in 1935. In 1938 there were 634 and by 1942 the figure had jumped to 1,119 (75 of whom were girls).

Antomarchi also launched a program for village schools so that the Rhadé would not feel that their children were being taken from them. This also proved a success and became the model for village school programs in other parts of the highlands. Indigenous languages were taught in addition to French, and study of local customs also became part of the curriculum. Nonetheless, many highlanders continued to harbor negative feelings about the schools, and in 1937 when the governor of Cochinchina was visiting the province a village chief remarked to him, "Better a crossbow than a pen for our sons." Antomarchi departed in 1941 to return to France where he died not long after. In his memory the vastly improved school at Ban Me Thuot was renamed the Groupe Scholaire Antomarchi.[20]

In 1937, as a result of Antomarchi's program in Darlac, a standard curriculum explicitly for highland students was formulated. There were two cycles each of three-year duration. The first cycle, the "primaires élémentaires," emphasized instruction in the maternal language, using orthographies devised under the sponsorship of the Ecole Française d'Extrême-Orient, and the French language also was taught. This led to a Certificat d'études élémentaires. The second was the "cycle primaire complémentaire," offering continued training in the indigenous language and in French along with instruction on local customs. This terminated with a Certificat d'études primaires complémentaires. In addition there were new "écoles de pénétration" of one or two grades established in the more remote areas.[21]

Between 1930 and 1935 the first schools for highlanders were opened

19. Antomarchi, "Le 'Bi Due': recueil des coutumes Rhadées," *Indochine*, no. 25 (1941): 5–10.

20. Marcel Ner, "Humbles constructeurs de l'empire," *Indochine*, no. 144 (1943), pp. 14–18.

21. Antoine, "L'Ecole Montagnarde," pp. 36–37; "L'Enseignement chez les populations Montagnardes du Sud Indochinois," *Education* (Rectorat d'Académie, Bureau des Affaires Culturelles, Saigon), 1950, pp. 131–32.

in the colony of Cochinchina. At Hon Quan in Thudaumot province, two young highlanders from another area (unspecified) began teaching twenty-eight Stieng pupils, and in Bien Hoa province elementary schools were begun at Vo Dat, Bu Dop, and Nui Bara.[22]

Dalat continued to develop as an education center, but initially most of the facilities were for the French and Vietnamese rather than the highlanders. In 1932 the Grand Lycée de Dalat, with a curriculum leading to a baccalauréat, was opened, and in June 1935 the name was changed to the Lycée Yersin to honor the noted medical pioneer. Also in 1932, the Christian Brothers opened the College d'Adran for boys. In 1935 the sisters of the Congrégation of Notre-Dame began a secondary school called Notre-Dame du Lang-Bian, usually known as the Couvent des Oiseaux, for French and Vietnamese girls of well-to-do families.[23] A decree dated 27 June 1939 created the Ecole d'Enfants de Troupe, a school for the Eurasian sons of French military personnel. The students, most of whom had been abandoned by their parents, were boys between the ages of twelve and twenty, and after receiving military training along with their regular primary school curriculum those who qualified were admitted to the Lycée de Dalat, perhaps to continue studies subsequently in a French military school. By September 1941 there were 150 boys in this school.[24]

Dalat also continued to grow as a tourist resort, attracting numerous French and Vietnamese from the steamy lowlands. The city's beauty was enhanced in 1935 when a lake was created by the damming of a stream that coursed through the town. Dalat also was becoming a research center. In 1936, having already established Pasteur Institutes in Saigon, Hanoi, and Nhatrang, Doctor Yersin opened a new branch in Dalat, where the climate lent itself to the preparation of certain vaccines.[25]

According to Touneh Han Tho, his father Han Dang made great efforts at this time to improve the educational facilities for the highlanders in the Dalat area. He also sought to obtain higher pay for highlanders laboring on the French-owned estates. When his appeals to the résident and the higher officials in the colonial administration proved of no avail, Han Dang wrote to Emperor Bao Dai and Léon Blum, then president of France. Nothing

22. Pagès, "Rapport sur la pénétration en pays Moi," pp. 128–29.

23. P. Munier, "Dalat," *Indochine*, no. 29 (1941), p. 8; Noël Bernard, "Le Docteur Alexandre Yersin (1861–1943)," *France Indochine*, no. 76 (1951), p. 99; I. C., "Le Couvent des 'Oiseaux'," *Indochine*, no. 119 (1942), pp. 14–18.

24. "A Dalat l'Ecole d'Enfants de Troupe," *Indochine*, no. 57 (1941), pp. 17–18.

25. "Les Instituts Pasteur d'Indochine," *Indochine*, no. 99 (1942), pp. 12–14.

came of these efforts and finally, during a heated discussion over these matters, Han Dang struck the résident. Shortly thereafter the Frenchman was removed from office. In 1937 Han Dang resigned in protest against the continued abuses of the administration and returned to Diom, where he functioned unofficially as a leader in the Danhim valley.

During this period the development of hill stations in central Vietnam also continued. The upland resort on the summit of Bana mountain, inland from Tourane, had been started in the early decades of the century, but between 1925 and 1937 little development took place. Then, with the beginning of new road construction in 1937, new chalets appeared everywhere on the slopes in Bana. While in 1925 there were some 120 annual visitors, by 1943 this figure had increased to 450.[26]

In 1932 Girard, an engineer in the French public works, launched a search for a new hill station convenient to the city of Hue. For the French residents of that city, Dalat was too far away, and to reach the resort at Bana one had to cross the difficult Col des Nuages (Deo Hai Van). On 29 July Girard arrived at the summit of Bach-Ma mountain, located just north of the pass, and decided this would be the ideal site. The following year a wood chalet was built, and in 1934 a trail permitting the use of open palanquins was cleared. By 1936 there were 17 chalets at Bach-Ma, and following completion of an auto route two years later 40 additional chalets were constructed. With World War II the resort gained in popularity and by 1943 the number of chalets totaled 130. In addition, there were two small hotels as well as a children's swimming pool and tennis courts.[27]

During the 1930s the French continually increased recruitment of highlanders into military forces. Some of those who joined were later to become leaders. By 1930 the Garde Indigène included 131 Rhadé dispersed in posts at Ban Me Thuot, M'drak, Poste du Lac (Lac Thien), and Ban Don and, as was noted above, later in the decade they became involved in pacification operations in the Mnong country.[28] According to retired Rhadé teacher Y Toeh Mlo Duon Du, one of those who joined the Garde Indigène during the late 1920s was Y Bih Aleo, who would become a major leader in the Viet Cong movement among the highlanders.

As early as 1928 the French had begun to form regular army units composed of highlanders, and in 1931 the special Bataillon Montagnard

---

26. L. S., "Bana," *Indochine*, no. 160 (1943), pp. 15–16.
27. X, "Bach-Ma," *Indochine*, no. 159 (1943), pp. 14–17.
28. Monfleur, *Monographie*, pp. 26–27.

du Sud-Annam (Highlander Battalion of South Annam) was created. Among those who joined was a young Jarai named Nay Moul (2.17), later to be known as an important leader in Cheo Reo. He had been born around 1913 in Plei Rongol Ama Drung near the Apa river. He had no formal education. The French were looking for able-bodied highlanders, and husky, alert Nay Moul was well qualified. During the training period at Ban Me Thuot, Moul and another Jarai, Nay Ble—whose son Roo Bleo (5.3) became a leader—distinguished themselves with their physical feats; Moul was particularly adept at pole vaulting.

In 1932 Nay Nui, the famous Jarai chief, arranged a marriage between his daughter Rcom H'lion and Nay Moul (in keeping with the pattern of Rcom women marrying men of the Nay clan). Although he was to remain in the French army for eighteen years, Moul, because of his unusual physical strength and other manifestations of charisma (*kdruh*) as well as his marriage into the prestigious Rcom clan, attained the role of a local leader. As Nay Nui aged, Moul assumed a greater role as intermediary for the French administration.[29]

According to Bahnar informant Hiar (1.7), the French in 1930 officially banned any form of slavery or indentured servitude in Kontum. His father Jom, who since 1913 had been chief of Kon Robang, had a group of indentured servants (because of unpaid debts) who lived as members of the family. They and others were released in a large celebration called Chung Roh ("to cut the root") marked with the slaughter of many buffalos, pigs, and chickens. Hiar recalled that the gongs and drums played as everyone drank from the many rows of jars.

Between 1930 and 1940 the highlander law courts received considerable attention from the French administration. In 1930 Khunjanob, the judge in the highlander law court in Ban Me Thuot, retired and was replaced by his sister's son Y Keo Khue, also known teknonymously as Ama Kham Suk. That same year, due to the large influx of Vietnamese workers for the new plantations, a Vietnamese Quan Dao (a mandarin with juridical functions) who would also represent the court of Hue, was appointed for Darlac province. An additional responsibility of this mandarin was liaison for the new political prison the French established in Ban Me Thuot in the wake of the 1930 Yen Bay revolt (see below).

In Kontum the noted Bahnar chief Hma, who had served as judge in the

29. This information was supplied by Nay Moul's wife Rcom H'lion and his son-in-law Nay Luett.

Y Keo Khue (nephew of Khunjanob) and his wife in front of their house in Ban Don (1956)

highlander law court, died in 1930 and his juridical role was taken by Mohr (1.6), another well-known Bahnar leader. Guilleminet describes Mohr as the grandson of Kiom, the Bahnar chief who aided the first French priests in the highlands.[30] A genealogy (part of chart 1) obtained from Mohr's daughter Rou (1.14) reveals that this was indeed the case. Mohr was the son of Kiom's daughter Tok, the sister of Pim (1.5), who got involved in the Mayréna affair. Tok had married a Bahnar named Djo, and Mohr was their son. Mohr took a Bahnar wife named Bech, and their children were Ring (who was killed by the Viet Cong in 1965) and two daughters, Mek and Rou. By his second wife Hmem, Mohr had another son Mo (1.15).

When Rou was interviewed—Mo served as interpreter—in a dismal refugee settlement on the edge of Pleiku in July 1972, she was a small woman with bright eyes and pleasant smile. With her grey-streaked hair pulled back in a bun, she looked like a highland woman one might see in any village. Her family, she noted, considered Plei Bong, a settlement north of Route 19 east of Pleiku, as their home. She also identified herself and the family as being of the Bahnar Bonom ethnic group. She re-

30. Paul Guilleminet, *Coutumier de la tribu Bahnar des Sedang et des Jarai de la Province de Kontum*, 2 vols. (Paris: Ecole Française d'Extrême-Orient, 1952), 1: 71.

membered that Mohr's father Pim was chief of Plei Bong and a man of "medium height with a full beard." Her father had told her the story of her ancestor Kiom who had "kept the priests alive." The priests had come from the coast against the will of the Vietnamese, who did not want any French or Vietnamese Catholics to enter the highlands. Kiom hid the Frenchmen and later took them to Kontum. When the Vietnamese tried to assassinate Kiom, a Vietnamese Catholic woman warned him and he escaped. For this the Vietnamese killed the woman and other Catholics in the An Khe area.

Rou then produced an old photograph of Mohr, who had a very thin face and high forehead. He was dressed in a French-style long-sleeve jacket on which many medals were pinned. He also was wearing a ceremonial Bahnar loincloth and, somewhat incongruously, long socks and white tennis shoes. Next to him stood his son Mo, dressed in a loincloth and wearing a red French beret. They were posed at the foot of a long stairway leading up to the veranda of Mohr's house in Kontum. Rou recalled that her father had been judge for all the highlanders in the Kontum area and was recognized as a leader not only by the Bahnar but by the Jarai, Rengao, Sedang, Halang, and Jeh as well. He often went to Hue to represent these highland groups at the court. From time to time she accompanied Mohr on visits to other highland leaders, and periodically these leaders would come to Kontum for ceremonies and celebrations (such as when Emperor Bao Dai visited in 1932). She recalled events that brought together such leaders as Hma (1.4) and his son Ber (1.10), both Bahnar notables, the Rhadé leaders Y Ut Nie Buon Rit and Y Say Ktla, and the noted Jarai chief Nay Nui (2.11) and his son-in-law Nay Moul (2.17). In 1940 a marriage was arranged between Rou and Phem (1.17), son of Ber. This, in effect, linked the two elite kin groups in the Kontum area. The marriage, however, lasted only two years.

In the early 1930s Guilleminet was named résident of Kontum. One of his major projects was the codifying of Bahnar, Jarai, and Sedang customs for use in the highlander law court. Nguyen Huu Phu recalled how Guilleminet went every morning to the house of Father Alberty of the Kontum Mission to study the Bahnar language as part of his effort to produce a Bahnar dictionary and a codified set of laws. Phu also described how Guilleminet and the Vietnamese Quan Dao, Ton That Toai, son of the well-known regent, and Ton That Han (see below) greeted Emperor Bao Dai when he visited Kontum in 1932.

A decree dated 24 May 1932 created the new province of Pleiku, and its administration included a highlander law court similar to those already functioning in other highland provinces.[31] During this period additional codes of indigenous customs were being prepared in other parts of the highlands. Various administrators in the Dalat-Djiring area had collected customs of local groups, and these unpublished reports were kept in the provincial archives. While he was an administrator in Dalat in 1911, Canivey wrote a report on Lat laws, and in 1921 Cunhac did likewise. Some customs also were recorded in 1932 by Adelé, an official in the Garde Indigène.[32] In 1936 all of the information contained in these reports was compiled into an unpublished code of "Koho" customs by Monseigneur Cassaigne, who also produced a Koho dictionary.[33]

In Quang Ngai province, the French official Vuillame produced an unpublished report on the customs of the Hre in 1937.[34] In Cochinchina, Gerber, the administrator in the French post at Bu Dop, was collecting Stieng words, which he compiled into a dictionary, and Stieng customs which later were organized as a legal code.[35]

Several decrees issued in December 1938 authorized the résident superior of Annam to reorganize the highlander law courts, and at a 1939 meeting of the résidents of highland provinces it was agreed that there would be a uniform organization of the law courts and that the additional codes would be used in these courts as they were made available.[36]

Throughout the 1930s the missionary efforts of the French Catholics and American Protestants continued in the highlands. In 1932 the first three Bahnar priests were ordained. Three years later the role of the Kontum Mission expanded considerably when Bishop Jannin opened a seminary, which he described as an "apostolic school" for producing missionaries to

31. Ibid., 1: 85–86.
32. Jules Canivey, "Notice sur les moeurs et coutumes des Moi de la région de Dalat," Archives du Résident, Dalat, 1911; Cunhac, "Rapport sur les Moi de Dalat," Archives du Résident, Dalat, 1921; Cunhac, "Notice précisant certaines bases du droit coutumier en région Moi (circonscription du Haut-Donnai, plateaux des Ma)," Archives du Résident, Haut Donnai, 1921; Adelé, "Renseignments recueillis sur les Ma B'sre," Archives du Résident, Djiring, 1932.
33. Msgr. Cassaigne, "Le Coutumier Koho," Archives du Résident, Haut Donnai, 1936; idem, *Dictionnaire Koho* (Saigon: Imprimerie de l'Union, 1936).
34. Vuillame, "Rapport sur les coutumes des Hre," Archives du Résident, Quang Ngai, 1937.
35. T. Gerber, *Lexique Française-Stieng* (Saigon: Imprimerie du Théatre, 1937); idem, "Coutumier Stieng," *BEFEO* 45 (1951): 228–69.
36. Guilleminet, *Coutumier de la tribu Bahnar*, 1: 86–88. In Paul Guilleminet, "Coutumes juridiques contemporaines du pays des Bahnars et de leurs voisins, et quelques autres," *Education* (Rectorat d'Académie, Bureau des Affaires Culturelles, Saigon), 1949, pp. 127–47, there is a discussion of all the available sources on highlander customs of this time.

work in the highlands. It was to attract young men not only from the highland groups but also from among the several thousand Vietnamese already settled in the mountains as well as some lowland Vietnamese.[37]

Five years after the Reverend Herbert Jackson of the Christian and Missionary Alliance arrived in Dalat in 1929 to establish the first American Protestant mission in the highlands, he had a Vietnamese pastor named Nam working among the Koho-speaking groups. That same year the Reverend Gordon Smith and his wife Laura arrived in Ban Me Thuot to launch a new missionary effort among the Rhadé.

In numerous discussions about their work, Gordon Smith supplied many details of the experiences he and his wife had had, beginning with their arrival in Saigon by ship in October 1929 after nine months of French language instruction in France and Switzerland. They first went to Cambodia where the Christian and Missionary Alliance had been established in 1922 and began a new mission at Kratie. In the spring of 1934 the Smiths moved to Ban Me Thuot where they stayed at the Auberge du Grand Cerf, a favorite place of the big game hunters who visited the highlands. It was a large building, built on piling with a thatched roof and spacious veranda. In 1936 the Smiths returned to the United States on leave, going back to Vietnam later the same year. This time they rented a house that belonged to a Frenchman named Bourgery who had earlier lived in Tientsin where he had installed a streetcar system. In 1935 Bourgery had constructed a dam and electrical plant at Ban Me Thuot. Smith recalled that at that time there were few Vietnamese in Ban Me Thuot and only a few Chinese shops near the market. Khunjanob was still considered the great leader of the province and would appear at public events wearing a white coat covered with medals. He usually also had a special sword at his side. Another influential leader was Y Say Ktla, who had helped devise the Rhadé script and compile Rhadé laws for Sabatier. Smith said that Y Say always wore a white shirt under his traditional Rhadé shirt.

Smith recalled that one of the achievements during this period was the 1937 drainage of the swamps in the vicinity of Ban Me Thuot, which had lessened the danger of malaria, a major problem in the area. Also in 1937 Smith received authorization to build a chapel in Buon Ale-A, just south

---

37. Pierre Dourisboure and Christian Simonnet, *Vietnam: Mission on the Grand Plateaus* (Maryknoll, New York: Maryknoll Publications, 1967), pp. 234–35.

of Ban Me Thuot on Route 14. The French officials granting this authorization pointed out that they could not risk having a situation like that in Kontum, where the missionaries had more power than the civil administration, and forbade any proselytizing by Smith. But there was nothing to prevent him from leaving the chapel door open during services, and people from Buon Ale-A wandered in out of curiosity. Some of the first converts were from that village. Smith noted that one of those in Ban Me Thuot who most opposed him was Dominique Antomarchi. A major point of contention was the transcription of the Rhadé alphabet; Smith's version did not agree with that of Antomarchi.

In 1938 Smith was allowed to begin formal instruction. One of his most adept students was Y Ham Nie Hrah (5.4), son of the respected school principal Y Toeh Mlo Duon Du (5.1). Both lived in Buon Ale-A. As back country roads were opened, Smith began to preach in the more remote villages. He noted that French officials were able to obtain the corvée needed for such road construction because they threatened to bring in Vietnamese laborers if the Rhadé chiefs did not supply local workers.

By the middle of the 1930s French control in the highlands had consolidated to the point where the provincial résidents began to feel the need for better coordination of their administrative policies. Auger, the résident of Haut Donnai, suggested to the résident superior of Annam that officials from the provinces along the border of Annam and Cochinchina hold a meeting to discuss some legal questions concerning villages in this area. The résident superior liked the idea and passed it on to the governor general, who also approved. The resultant conference in Dalat on 8 July 1935 brought together officials from Haut Donnai province in Annam and the Cochinchinese provinces of Bien Hoa and Thudaumot. In addition, the inspector of political and administrative affairs from Saigon and the administrator from Song Be were invited. As the meeting progressed, the agenda was expanded to include discussion of banditry and police action along the border, taxes, mapping, hunting preserves, medical programs, and local highland leadership.

Since this conference was adjudged to have been successful, a second meeting was called for 18 January 1936 at Dalat. The same participants from Cochinchina attended, but the invitation list for Annam was expanded to include the résidents of Darlac and Binh Thuan in addition to the administrator from Djiring, the commander of the Garde Indochinoise at Dalat, and Adelé, the chief of the B'sre post who had produced a report on local highlander customs. Presided over by Résident Auger of Haut Donnai, the gathering again discussed border problems, taxation, and hunting preserves in addition to the problem of transcribing "Moi" languages, slavery, and the "politics of salt" (see below).

The third conference was held in Dalat on 24 May 1937, and the guest list again was expanded to include the administrators from Nui Bara and Ta Lai in Bien Hoa province and two representatives from Cambodia—Le Bon, résident of Kratie, and Captain de Crèvecoeur, commander of the Haut Chhlong post. Most of the same topics were discussed. First, there was the question of the demarcation of borders. Rocher, the administrator from Nui Bara, commented that the "Mois" paid little heed to borders, often farming their swiddens across the border from their villages. This led to a discussion about the need to mark borders more clearly on the ground. Next came the matter of "penetration trails," and it was noted that such trails were needed to improve communication between Haut Chhlong and Ban Me Thuot as well as between Bien Hoa and Binh Thuan provinces. A more complete network of these trails also was important to develop communication between military outposts. Subsequently, the problem of policing the frontiers was focused upon. Finally, the participants talked about taxes and corvées imposed on the highlanders. Lebon, the résident of Darlac, suggested that corvée requirements be made uniform throughout the highlands, and it was agreed that fifteen days per year would be the standard corvée period.

Esquivillon, inspector of political and administrative affairs for Cochinchina (functioning as chairman of the conference), explained that the "politics of salt" was an expression that reflected the administration's strategy of providing badly needed salt to the highlanders at low prices in order to attain "the happy consequences that this can have from the political point of view." Discussion centered on the matter of standard salt prices in the upland areas. Regarding indigenous justice, the participants agreed that the best approach was to judge criminal cases in the places where the crimes occurred and to hear civil matters in the locale of the defendant.

The next topic concerned providing food for highlanders performing corvée. The delegates from Cambodia pointed out that they did not feed the laborers, and it was revealed that in Annam it no longer was the policy to provide meals. Two representatives from Cochinchina noted that a 1935 decree made it obligatory to supply nourishment although the amount was not stipulated; for example, at Nui Bara the laborers received 750 grams of rice, while at Bu Dop it was 900 grams of rice and 50 grams of salt. When the chairman suggested a decree requiring meals for all corvée laborers, it was pointed out that the ruling heads of state in Annam and Cambodia would have to produce their own texts on this. Nothing therefore was concluded regarding this matter.

Next on the agenda was discussion about languages in the highlands, and the chairman noted that a special conference organized by Georges Coedès, an eminent scholar of Asian history and culture, had recommended the adoption of a uniform transcription for all highland languages. Guerrini, administrator of Bu Dop, noted that his successor, Gerber, had written a Stieng manuscript that he soon would have published. After some additional observations had been made, it was concluded that a special linguistic commission study the matter of selecting in each province a language that could be the vehicle of communication for the area to the exclusion of "less important languages." Also, the study of French would be developed throughout the highlands.

Commerce in the mountain regions was the next subject discussed. Du Bois, résident of Darlac, advocated widespread use of the system employed by Guilleminet in Kontum wherein only traders approved by the résident could function. After some brief comments by several participants about controlling outside traders, the subject shifted to the problem of setting prices (particularly for rice) in places under the surveillance of the administration. It was agreed that fairs and markets be organized where supervision was possible and that prices fixed by the administration would have to be disseminated throughout the region.

With all of the subjects on the agenda exhausted, the chairman called for any additional matters that any of the officials might like to discuss. The question of hunting preserves was brought up and the chairman noted that it was under study. Bonnemain, province chief of Thudaumot, called to everyone's attention that the sale of alcohol was forbidden in the highlands and that they must be on their guard to prevent any licenses being issued and cancel those now in use. Questions concerning health programs emphasized the need for malaria control and mobile health teams.

There was some discussion about the type of antimalaria medicines that should be employed, and Du Bois suggested that a massive inoculation program be undertaken. Auger noted that the former provincial doctor in Haut Chhlong traveled 10,000 kilometers a year in his automobile in order to give shots to villagers and the results were impressive.

Le Bon, résident of Kratie, brought up "crimes of sorcery," noting that there were "two categories of sorcerers: good sorcerers and wicked sorcerers, whose influence can cause one person to kill another." What, he asked, would be the guilt of a person who came under the influence of a wicked sorcerer? The chairman expressed the view that such an individual would certainly bear some responsibility, but he would have the right to claim extenuating circumstances. At the end of the conference it was agreed that the next meeting would be held in January 1938 at Phnom Penh.[38]

THE PYTHON GOD MOVEMENT

It is ironic that the May 1937 conference ended with a minor mention of the problem of sorcery, because the participants had no sooner dispersed than the French administration found itself faced with a serious threat to its authority by actions of what it described as "sorcerers" (the sources used *sorciers* without the distinction among sorcerers, witches, and shamans made earlier in this volume). The whole affair was centered on belief in a deity called the Python God which was spreading over a large area of the central highlands, much to the consternation of the administration. Among other things it cast some doubt on the effectiveness of French control in the highlands and also brought out the important role the Kontum Mission had in highland affairs.

At the beginning of June 1937 French officials in the highlands began to report on what they considered to be bizarre behavior on the part of highland villagers in Phu Yen, Pleiku, and Darlac provinces. Many had stopped work in their fields and there was an inordinate number of animals sacrificed. Some highlanders barricaded themselves behind their stockades and were hostile to anyone who sought entry. There also were widespread refusals to do corvée. In addition, there was a sudden rush for one-cent (from *centime*, also called a *sou*) bronze coins. Their value quickly inflated, and in some places the Vietnamese were exchanging twenty silver coins for a one-cent bronze piece.

Receiving information on these occurrences from missionaries and

38. Esquivillon, "Procès-verbal de la conférence inter-pays pour les régions moi (réunie conformément aux instructions de Monsieur le Gouverneur de la Cochinchine et de M. M. les Résidents Supérieurs de l'Annam et du Cambodge)," *La Question Moi* Collection, Department of Manuscripts and University Archives, Cornell University, Ithaca, New York.

Vietnamese Christians, Bishop Jannin, head of the Kontum Mission, informed the officials in the highlands and in Hue that the incidents were due to a belief spreading through the region that a new "king" would soon appear among the mountain people. When he did, there would be no further need for them to work their fields and care for their livestock. The bishop had heard that these beliefs were part of a "new religion" launched by an elderly bearded man of "unknown race" (he later was identified as a Hroy or Hroai, a subgroup of the Jarai) from the village of Ea Luy in upland western Phu Yen. He dressed in Vietnamese garb and lived in a Vietnamese style house of plank boards. With the threat of "ill effects" for all who did not heed him, he obliged every village within one hundred kilometers to send a delegation of five men bearing offerings of silver, pigs, and alcohol, in exchange for which he recited some incantations and presented the pilgrims with bottles of "magic water." No one possessing this water could be harmed by another, and it was specified that should the holder refuse to do corvée he would be immune to punishment by the French. This man also predicted that there would soon be a great calamity that would rid the highlands of the outsiders—notably the French, Lao, and Vietnamese—while those with the magic water would survive.

Soon after, the résident of Pleiku reported that this man was known in the locale of his village as Ma Cham (from Ama Cham or "Father of Cham") but that he was more widely known as Sam Bram (other names reported later were Sam Bam, Dam Bam, and Mang Lo). He also was widely known as a sorcerer.[39]

A later report prepared by the Kontum Mission and submitted to the French authorities provided considerably more information on this "new religion" sweeping the central highlands.[40] It declared that a legend was spreading that one beautiful day a Jarai woman living in the Ayun river valley gave birth to a python that could "talk like men." This was the god Dam Klan (*dam* in Jarai means "handsome young man" and *klan* is "python"), who at times appeared in human form as a dashing young man with bronze skin and large round eyes. It took up its abode in the forest, returning to the village from time to time in order to make pronounce-

39. Msgr. Jeannin, "Extrait du rapport politique de mois de Septembre 1937: affaire du sorcier Sam-Bram dit Sam-Bam, Mang Lo, Ma Cham, et Dam Bam," *La Question Moi* Papers, Department of Manuscripts and University Archives, Cornell University, Ithaca, New York.

40. "Dieu nouveau-religion nouvelle: supplément au compte rendu de la Mission de Kontum," 1937, *La Question Moi* Papers, Department of Manuscripts and University Archives, Cornell University, Ithaca, New York.

ments. On one such visit it ordered the villagers to construct three communal houses for its use. Subsequently, it went to live in the depths of the sea by the Ngur rocks on the Phu Yen coast. From there, however, it visited distant places, moving through the air "like the wind."

While the Python God was in the forest it elaborated a set of prescriptions and taboos that the Kontum report referred to as "commandments." The first ordered the highlanders to obey the authority of the French and Vietnamese but promised a day when the Python God would hold sway. The second concerned proper comportment, specifying that fornication and rough behavior be avoided. Anyone violating a taboo should make the prescribed offering of a pig or buffalo. At the same time Dam Klan forbade some of the traditional rituals, such as the nocturnal ceremony that is part of funeral observations, and any animal sacrifices except those related to taboos or associated with construction of new houses or granaries. The fourth rule was against eating any spoiled meat or flesh of animals that had died, and it interdicted consumption of any aquatic birds, snakes (particularly pythons), and crustaceans. These food taboos, however, were only to be observed until after the predicted calamity had ended. The fifth "commandment" forbade the highlanders to own any white animals whether chickens, ducks, goats, pigs, or buffalos. Such animals already possessed must be slain and the meat sold at any price. Finally, the Python God decreed that the highlanders work six days in succession and rest on the seventh and on days of the full and new moons.

According to this report, the Python God had only one representative, a man named Dam Bam (another name for Sam Bram), who was empowered to work miracles and spoke all highland languages. It also was asserted that Dam Bam disliked Christians and would say to them, "You depend on the missionaries, but the others depend on me." When the French claimed to have put Dam Bam in jail, the highlanders replied that he who was imprisoned was only a slave or underling of Dam Bam.

Regarding the magic water, the report noted that the highland people believed that the Python God had infused it with the power to heal the sick, protect against catastrophes, and resurrect the dead. To obtain this water, a village had to express sorrow for the past sins of its inhabitants and collect some one-cent bronze coins—which were difficult to come by in the remote areas. Then an even-numbered delegation would visit the village of Dam Bam, present the coins, and make proper offerings, after which they would receive the water. Should anyone in the village violate the Python

God's rules, the water in the bottle would begin to diminish. Only propitiation to the Python God could replenish it.

Dam Klan let it be known that during the seventh month in a future year there would be a great calamity that would eliminate all nonbelievers. On that day there would be an unusually beautiful sunrise, and this would be a sign that the village elders should place the bottle of water in a central place. Over the horizon would come a fierce typhoon that would uproot all trees in the forest, split mountains, and shatter all countries. All foreigners in the highlands—French, Vietnamese, and Lao—would be destroyed. Only the villages with the magic water would remain, and the survivors would divide the goods of the foreigners. From that day on they would be free of outside controls, with no more corvées or taxes. The typhoon would occur just at the beginning of the planting season, and afterward Dam Bam would announce in the name of the Python God that all would receive five grains of rice. Putting a grain at each corner of the field and one in the middle, the villagers would wake the following morning to find a green and magnificent field of plants heavy with rice ready to harvest.

Writing in 1941, Guilleminet, the résident of Kontum and scholar of Bahnar customs, reported that the name Sam Bram or the synonyms Sam Bam and Dam Bam mean "beard."[41] These terms are associated with the legendary Bahnar hero Set, son of the thunder god Bok Glaih. The Bahnar believe that Bok Glaih's magic saber came to be possessed by the King of Fire. Guilleminet also points out that pythons figure prominently in the oral traditions of the Bahnar, Jarai, Rhadé, and Sedang. In some of their legends, the Bahnar associated the python with Set or one of his sons, Biong.

Soon after the Kontum Mission's reports were circulated, Salomon, the résident of Darlac, raised the question of whether Sam Bram was only a sorcerer or also an agitator capable of causing more harm in the highlands. He then requested permission to arrest Sam Bram. This provoked Jeannin to call a meeting of the résidents of Phu Yen, Pleiku, and Darlac to discuss some course of action. They decided against the arrest and their report noted that Sam Bram had long been a man of stature in highland Phu Yen, where the Garde Indigène commanders and sector chiefs had used his influence to administer the population. Furthermore, Sam Bram had made no attempt to flee since the affair began.

---

41. Paul Guilleminet, "Recherches sur les croyances des tribus du Haut-Pays d'Annam, les Bahnar du Kontum et leurs voisins les magiciens," *IIEH* 4 (1941): 26–33.

At this time Padovani, commander of a Garde Indigène post near Sam Bram's village, passed on the information that the whole affair began when Sam Bram, a respected leader and shaman, demolished his old house with the intention of building a new one in the grand style of a highland chief. It would be not only an abode but also a kind of communal gathering place where he would receive his followers and "vassals," thus vastly enhancing his prestige. Following an "ancestral custom," Sam Bram asked the small contribution of one cent a head from his immediate tenants. In addition he requested a small pig and jar of alcohol from each group of houses in the vicinity. These offerings would be used for the prescribed house building ritual, to which all would be invited. While officiating at this ritual, Sam Bram presented each of those present with small bottles of "magic water" and some grains of "sacred rice," which, if planted in the middle of a newly sown field, would guarantee an abundant harvest.

Reflecting on this report Jeannin was prompted to speculate that the funds collected more than likely were insufficient, so Sam Bram sent out emissaries to gather additional contributions (one of these might well have been the Huyen Thu of Ma-Bo, a kinsman of Sam Bram with a sordid reputation). Jeannin concluded that as long as this affair was within the framework of sorcery it would be well for the French to demonstrate that their powers exceeded those of Sam Bram. He therefore recommended to the résident of Phu Yen that Padovani take Sam Bram into custody, putting him in a village other than his own in order to isolate him from outside contact. On 25 June 1937 Sam Bram was delivered to the résident of Pleiku, who put him under surveillance. The résident instructed Corso, commander of the militia, to make frequent tours of the area where Sam Bram's village was located in order to ascertain that none of his kinfolk were still selling the magic water. Despite these precautions, however, Sam Bram's relatives continued to vend the water to pilgrims coming to the sorcerer's village.

While making a tour of southern Annam at this time with the governor general, Bishop Jeannin saw signs that belief in the Python God was gaining more and more adherents. He noted that there even were manifestations of it among the Highlander Riflemen Battalion personnel stationed in Ban Me Thuot. Rhadé informant Y Bling Buon Krong Pang, who was a student at the Franco-Rhadé school in Ban Me Thuot during this period, reports that he and his fellow students heard about Sam Bram and the Python God. News of the coming catastrophe struck fear in the hearts of many students, prompting them to return to their villages.

Disturbed by the spread of the Python God beliefs, Jeannin met on 6 July with the résident of Pleiku, and it was decided to take stronger measures against Sam Bram. Three days later he was jailed in Ban Me Thuot, and the administration made a special effort to disseminate the news throughout the highlands. This strategy had more or less its desired effect. By the end of August fields were again being cultivated and highlanders returned to do corvée. But the inordinate sacrifice of animals continued, as did the quest for bronze coins even though their circulation was now banned.

In September 1937 Jeannin learned that highlanders in Quang Nam and Quang Ngai provinces were seeking the one-cent bronze coins, a sign that news of the Python God had traveled northward.[42] This was corroborated in a confidential official report that indicated there had been armed conflict between highlanders and a detachment of Vietnamese militiamen from the Garde Indigène in the mountainous interior of Quang Ngai, where there was unrest in the Ba To and Son Ha areas. Two of the militiamen had been killed, and the attackers had escaped into the forest. The report attributed the unrest to news of the Python God, and it also noted that this news had spread as far south as Lagna and as far north as Dong Ha, where the magic water was being sold.[43] A month later in northeastern Kontum Garde Indigène parties from Gia Vuc and Kon Plong made contact with some three hundred highland "dissidents" and suffered the wounding of four guards.[44]

Beginning in September 1937, equally disturbing reports began to indicate that the cult of the Python God had found new adherents in southwestern Annam and adjacent provinces in Cambodia. On 30 September the résident at Ban Me Thuot, Salomon, sent a secret communication to the résident superior of Annam saying he had just been informed that an elephant hunter from Ban Don had come upon a sorcerer in Kratie province who called himself the "younger brother of Sam Bram."[45] This sorcerer had several Mnong Biat villages under his influence and had

42. Jeannin, "Extrait du rapport politique," pp. 3–5.

43. Le Chef Adjoint de Cabinet, "L'Agitation au pays Moi et arrestation du Dieu Serpent: extrait du rapport politique du mois de Novembre 1937," *La Question Moi* Papers, Department of Manuscripts and University Archives, Cornell University, Ithaca, New York.

44. Graffeuil, "Bulletin politique du mois de Décembre 1937: extrait des évènements en pays Mois," *La Question Moi* Papers, Department of Manuscripts and University Archives, Cornell University, Ithaca, New York.

45. Salomon, le Résident de France au Ban Me Thuot à Monsieur le Résident Supérieur en Annam, 30 Septembre 1937, *La Question Moi* Papers, Department of Manuscripts and University Archives, Cornell University, Ithaca, New York.

advised the inhabitants to "continue to obey the administration, pay your taxes, and go to work when summoned." But the sorcerer also warned, "I have nothing more to say, however. If one day I want to move against the administration, it will be done rapidly."

An investigation immediately was launched in Kratie province, and on 31 October 1937 Captain de Crèvecoeur, the administrator at the remote Haut Chhlong post in northeastern Cambodia, filed a report on the situation.[46] The most telling sign that the Python God cult had spread into the region, he noted, was the shortage in recent months of one-cent bronze coins despite their being constantly brought in by traders and French officials. Another incident that had aroused his suspicions was the visit to the post of a young Mnong named N'Krok, a former "partisan" (local men hired for military duty on a temporary basis) whom the French distrusted, to change ten piasters into one-cent bronze coins.

On 19 October Captain de Crèvecoeur and some of his officers had begun field investigations in the territory marked by Bu Plok (or Ban Phlok), Palkei, Poste Gatille, Poste Deshayes, and Camp Le Rolland. They found nothing unusual. Harvests were good, there were many white animals to be seen, and no one seemed to be preparing for any disasters. In fact, one party was welcomed into N'Krok's village. On 21 October, however, de Crèvecoeur was informed that in the Nam Phum massif between Poste Deshayes and Bu Plok there was a sorcerer who was receiving pigs and rice from villagers in the vicinity. He promised them good health and abundant harvests if they gave him "offerings" but death if they did not. De Crèvecoeur and his officers again set out to conduct field expeditions in the heavily forested area, even using aircraft from the escadrille at Bien Hoa for aerial reconnaissance, but they found nothing.

More concrete information was received by de Crèvecoeur on 28 October when he was notified by the captain in charge of the Dak Dan administrative post that a sorceress from Bu Jen Dram named Me Deng and her husband M'Blao had been taken into custody. This action resulted from an investigation conducted by Lieutenant Castella, commander of the Bu Jem Dram outpost, who on 23 October had come upon a convoy of six elephants from Bu Ropet carrying pigs and alcohol jars. Suspecting that these things were destined for a sacrificial ritual, he interrogated the

46. Le Capitaine de Crèvecoeur, Délégué Administratif du Haut-Chhlong à Monsieur le Résident de France à Kratie, 31 Octobre 1937, *La Question Moi* Papers, Department of Manuscripts and University Archives, Cornell University, Ithaca, New York.

mahouts and learned that the pigs and jars were tribute intended for a sorceress who already had been receiving gifts from the villagers in the Poste Deshayes, Poste Maitre, and Camp Le Rolland areas. She was a woman named Me Deng, and according to Castella there was a belief that she had been pregnant for five years. She had a dream that she would give birth to two children, both of whom would be great sorcerers. In March 1937, during a violent storm, she bore a son named Tamla and a daughter, Pia Ragni. They told their mother that they would depart for a period and meanwhile she should gather as many offerings as she could. Tamla went in the direction of the rising sun to join his uncle, the great sorcerer Sam Bram. Ragni went in the direction of the setting sun into the Nam Phum mountain area. Both had the power to heal, and after they had effected a great many cures Tamla joined Pia Ragni in the Nam Phum mountains, where they established a village. Afterward, both of them went to visit Me Deng to see how many gifts she had gathered.

Castella was told that Me Deng had fixed prices for her services. To attain wealth and good health, it cost two cents for a man, one cent for a woman, and the same price for a household, but an additional two cents for each nuclear family (it was specified as one cent per cooking pot and one cent per water vat). Pursuing his investigation, Castella went to Me Deng's house and found a group of twenty-two pilgrims (he called them "coolies"), most of whom were from the Poste Maitre and Camp Le Rolland sectors. He also learned that the suspect N'Krok had departed the evening before.

On 15 November 1937 de Crèvecoeur reported to the résident in Kratie and a commander in the French military forces in Phnom Penh that N'Krok and eight of the "Buneurs" (Mnong Bunor) who had been at Me Deng's house had been taken into custody and interrogated.[47] They claimed that Me Deng's reputation had spread among the Mnong after Khunjanob, the famous "Ivory King," had gone with his family to present Me Deng with two buffalos and a box of silver. She gave him magic water, announcing that there would soon be a disaster marked by several weeks of darkness. Subsequently, in September 1937, some three hundred Lao died

47. Le Capitaine de Crèvecoeur, Délégué Administratif du Haut-Chhlong à Monsieur le Résident de France à Kratie, Monsieur le Chef de Bataillon, Commandant la Division Militaire du Cambodge à Phnompenh, Novembre 1937, *La Question Moi* Papers, Department of Manuscripts and University Archives, Cornell University, Ithaca, New York.

in a Stung Treng flood, which was taken as a sign that the catastrophe was imminent. The news had disseminated in all directions, and the pilgrims flocked to Me Deng's village to obtain the magic water.

The detained highlanders also described large sacrificial rituals organized by some sorcerers in the Nam Phum mountains. Investigation revealed that these sorcerers were two brothers known as Tiong and Bong, and de Crèvecoeur recalled that the Haut Chhlong archives contained a 1935 dossier on both of them. Described there as "sorcerers and healers," they had been accused of killing a Cambodian secretary in 1935 during an attack on Camp Le Rolland. They had been tracked down and, after a fight during which Bong was wounded, captured. But on 25 November 1935 they broke their chains with the hammers they had been given to smash rocks, slipped through a small opening in the stockade, and made their way into the forest. Now they threatened villagers with death if they did not bring rice, buffalos, and jars of alcohol for secret sacrifices in the mountains. Bong declared that he soon would become "King of the Phnongs." De Crèvecoeur remarked that in all likelihood the brothers had heard of the "Sam Bram doctrine" and were trying to emulate Sam Bram.

On 30 November 1937 de Crèvecoeur submitted another report on the situation in Haut Chhlong, listing four troublesome sorcerers: the two brothers Tiong and Bong (who, he noted, claimed to be possessed by the spirit of Me Deng); another named Be Muth N'Dot; and Be Dak Nglong (said to be possessed by two spirits, Hi Hap and Menoun, sisters of Du Cong Ka, the fish spirit of the Mekong river, a figure in a Mnong Biat legend).[48] Be Dak Nglong's brother had been killed in April 1935 while leading an attack of some one hundred Mnong against Poste Gatille and Nglong had sworn revenge against the French. De Crèvecoeur speculated that both Nglong and the two brothers probably had heard of the Python God and decided to use the ferment caused by it for their own ends.

The Mnong who had been at Me Deng's house were released after a promise to aid the French in capturing the four sorcerers. On 12 December 1937 some of them sent a message to Poste Deshayes asking for a detachment to aid them in capturing Nglong. At midnight a French lieutenant reached the rendezvous in the Bu Xa forest to find the sorcerer bound to a

---

48. Le Capitaine de Crèvecoeur, Délégué Administratif du Haut Chhlong à Monsieur le Chef de Bataillon Commandant la Subdivision Militaire du Cambodge et à Monsieur le Résident de France à Kratie, 30 Novembre 1937, *La Question Moi* Papers.

tree. But on the way back to Poste Deshayes the captive Nglong allegedly fell to his death from the top of the elephant on which he was riding.[49]

On 4 January 1938 Bong was reported dead, although the circumstances of his death were not clear. On 24 January his brother Tiong turned himself in to the French at Camp Le Rolland. A secret intelligence report dated 7 March 1938 declared that Tiong's surrender marked the end of the "Nam Phum dissidence."[50]

From the time the initial reports concerning the Python God "religion" were received there had been considerable discussion among the French about its origin and dissemination through the central highlands. Bishop Jeannin thought that the movement appeared to have an organization which should be examined.[51] He also recommended to the Service de la Sûreté that an inquiry be made to determine whether there might be Vietnamese agents involved. The Python God cult, he added, might have political goals. A report by the Kontum Mission noted that the movement had "unimagined success" and raised some questions about the "real cause."[52] One such question concerned the possibility that the wave of unrest might be rooted in the highlanders' reaction against perceived excesses of the French administration. These would be such things as the head tax and corvées. The report recalled that in 1904 there had been strong resistance by the Jarai against the French, and it also made a reference to "recent trouble among the Alakong" (Bahnar Alakong). Could there, the report queried, be something symbolic in the slaughter of white animals? Might they be associated with the detested whites? In addition, the report speculated about the significance of massing bronze coins in the highlands and mentioned the formation of special councils of notables in the villages to oppose the *chủ làng* (Vietnamese term for village chiefs) created by the French. The report concluded that the agitation stemmed from political and xenophobic sentiments.

In a secret report dated 8 November 1938 General Deslaurens, commander of the Brigade d'Annam in Hue, suggested that the Python God movement might have originated outside the highlands and have to do

49. Général de Division Martin, Information No. 3, Secret, Origine: Capitaine-Délégué Administratif du Haut Chhlong, Saigon, 5 Janvier 1938, *La Question Moi* Papers.

50. Général de Division Martin, Information No. 100, Origine: Rapport en date du 20 Février 1938 du Captaine Délégué Administratif du Haut Chhlong, Saigon, 7 Mars 1938, *La Question Moi* Papers.

51. Jeannin, "Extrait du rapport politique," pp. 4–5.

52. "Dieu nouveau-religion nouvelle," p. 6.

with agents foreign to the "Moi country" seeking to create difficulties for the French administration.[53] He doubted that the arrests of Sam Bram and others would prevent the continuation of unrest among the "credulous and impressionable population" in the highlands. His solution would be to send into the highlands a sufficient number of military units to "pacify" the entire region.

A December 1937 dispatch from the assistant chief of the cabinet's office reported that a Garde Indigène officer in the highlands of Phu Yen had received information that Sam Bram had been the tool of a Vietnamese from Song Cau who paid him with silver and other gifts to launch the Python God movement.[54] This dispatch, too, intimated that the movement was part of a plot by a "foreign power" to discredit the French in Indochina.

In December 1937 Jardin, inspector of administrative affairs in Annam, accompanied by the résident of Phu Yen and a military officer, made a tour on horseback through the Hroy country along the Phu Yen–Pleiku border area where Sam Bram's village was located. In his report Jardin related that prior to his departure Padovani, the Garde Principale, informed him that he had been given a "miraculous pearl" by the brother-in-law of Sam Bram, but it turned out to be nothing more than a small ball of copper.[55] It had been transmitted from one highland village to another under a threat that, should any village retain it, dire consequences would result. An investigation was launched, and the résident of Pleiku revealed that on 29 November he had found out that a highlander named Tam, who had been arrested, claimed that Sam Bram was the originator of the "pearl." Jardin speculated that Sam Bram may have done it to revive the fading Python God movement. Then too, he added, it might have been the work of Mang Nhang, an "enemy and imitator of Sam Bram."

As his party rode through the vicinity of Sam Bram's village, Jardin was struck by the large number of Vietnamese living there and found many manifestations of a strong Vietnamese influence. Most of the highlanders, for example, spoke some Vietnamese, and most of the important highland chiefs, such as Sam Bram, wore Vietnamese clothes. As to Sam Bram himself, Jardin heard his tenants describe him variously as bright, half-mad,

53. Général de Brigade Deslaurens, Compte-rendu, Secret, 8 Novembre 1937, *La Question Moi* Papers.
54. Le Chef Adjoint de Cabinet, "L'Agitation au pays Moi."
55. Jardin, Note au sujet de l'affaire dite de sorcier Sam Bram (dit Ma-Cham, etc.), Décembre 1937, *La Question Moi* Papers.

and "more or less a sorcerer." Jardin noted that Sam Bram's family did not appear to have reaped great profits from the Python God affair and that Sam Bram was highly regarded as a local leader. In 1932 and 1933 Sam Bram had visited Hue to register complaints about raids conducted by bellicose highlanders from across the Apa river, and this had enhanced his reputation. Jardin felt that if the Python God incidents had not occurred Sam Bram would more than likely have been named official representative of all the Phu Yen highlanders.

Jardin concluded from his investigation that Sam Bram was the unwitting dupe of unscrupulous Vietnamese who sought to use his reputation to perpetrate "the Python God swindle." He noted that the authors of this affair had concentrated their initial efforts at impressing upon the highlanders Sam Bram's magic powers. They succeeded in creating a Sam Bram mystique, and though Sam Bram himself benefited it was the Vietnamese, exchanging bronze coins at vastly inflated rates, who gained the most. Jardin felt that the spread of this mystique even to the remote parts of the highlands was the doing of the Vietnamese traders—the *các lái* so omnipresent in the back country of Annam. They knew how to play upon the gullibility of the highlanders and had long harbored resentment against the supervision exercised by the French résidents. Since the whole affair was well organized, however, it might easily have included other agents, such as Vietnamese Communist revolutionaries. Finally, Jardin noted that, although the Python God mystique might well have been exaggerated, it nonetheless could not be suppressed by the French. It would have to fade away in its own good time. Meanwhile the administration would do well to improve security in the uplands, particularly where there had been resistance to French rule.

By the end of 1937 the ferment that had begun in June was subsiding, but now there began a wave of criticism in some of the lowland newspapers against the methods employed by the French in the highlands. A confidential communication from Governor General Brevié to Governor Pagès dated 4 January 1938 began, "Various newspapers in Annam, Cambodia, and Tonkin have recently published articles concerning incidents that have taken place in the Moi country, and the reality of the facts has been profoundly distorted." [56] Brevié advised Pagès to put the press in Cochinchina on guard against the allegations in these newspapers.

---

56. Le Gouverneur Général de l'Indochine à Monsieur le Gouverneur de la Cochinchine, Objet: Incidents en pays Moi, 4 Janvier 1938, *La Question Moi* Papers.

On 26 February 1938 the newspaper *Le Populaire d'Indochine* reported that the correspondent of the Vietnamese newspaper *Tân-Tiên* in Qui Nhon filed a story about a revolt among the highlanders in Kontum and An Lao.[57] It claimed that on 19 and 23 February detachments of 120 militiamen had been sent to the troubled areas. In order to protect them from poisoned arrows, 1,000 zinc shields had been ordered from a French company. The article made the observation that "one suspects that the eye of Moscow is on it." On 1 March 1938 *Le Peuple* published an article recalling that in the 1932–1935 period units of Vietnamese and Cambodian militiamen burned dozens of "Moi Phnong" villages in "Haut Darlac" for what the article said was the "crime" of opposing those outsiders who would disrupt their "vie naturelle." It also cited the "atrocities" in Quang Ngai and Binh Dinh in 1933 that resulted in many villages destroyed, many highlanders killed, and one hundred condemned to forced labor. It repeated the news of shields being provided for troops being sent to the highlands and asked, "Would one want to see in the Moi provinces another edition of the tragic events at Nghe An and Yen Bay of 1930–31?" Such repressive measures, the article said, were an indignity to the Popular Front government in France, and it called on the government to restore to the highlanders lands that had been expropriated, to diminish the financial burdens imposed on the population, and to improve the living standards of the highland people.[58]

A communique from Governor Pagès to the résident superior of Annam dated 5 March 1938 called attention to the two articles.[59] Regarding the article in *Le Populaire d'Indochine*, Pagès asked for particulars about the alleged incidents that could be sent to the newspaper. In a much stronger reaction to the article in *Le Peuple*, Pagès called it "erroneous and calumnious" and recommended that action be taken against the newspaper.

Soon after, Pagès sent to the résident superior of Annam a copy of a second article in *Le Peuple*, dated 8 March 1938, in which the administration was accused of falsely blaming the Communists for the unrest in the highlands when the real cause was the "shameful regime of ferocious exploitation and oppression."[60] It stated that lands of the highlanders had been expropriated for the profit of the colonists, whose efforts have been

---

57. *Le Populaire d'Indochine*, 26 Février 1938, *La Question Moi* Papers.
58. *Le Peuple*, 1 Mars 1938, *La Question Moi* Papers.
59. Le Gouverneur de la Cochinchine à Monsieur le Résident Supérieur en Annam, Saigon, 5 Mars 1938, *La Question Moi* Papers.
60. *Le Peuple*, 8 Mars 1938, *La Question Moi* Papers.

supported by well-armed troops against which the highlanders' crossbows and spears were of little use. The article then accused the administration of employing a divide-and-rule strategy in attempting to use indigenous ethnic groups to fight one another, and it claimed as an example the use of "Mois, Muong, Tho, and Man" against the Vietnamese rebels in 1930–1931 (see below). The article concluded by calling on the administration to withdraw its Vietnamese militia from the highlands, give the "Mois" back their lands, abolish personal taxes imposed on the highland people, allow free movement in the highlands, and punish the colonists, whose tyranny caused the unrest.

A confidential letter from the résident superior of Annam to the governor of Cochinchina documented rebuttals to the accusations made in the *Le Peuple* article but noted that there would be nothing gained by entering into a public dispute with the newspaper.[61] Should *Le Peuple* continue such attacks, however, the résident superior recommended that "exemplary sanctions" be brought to bear.

According to Bourotte, Sam Bram was brought to trial and was cleared of responsibility.[62] Rhadé informant Y Bling Buon Krong Pang, however, reports that he was sent from the Ban Me Thuot jail to serve a life sentence at Lao Bao, a political prison in the Ai Lao pass near Khe Sanh. He was released by the Japanese in 1945, and some Rhadé military personnel returning from Hanoi reported seeing Sam Bram riding in a mail truck on his way back to the highlands.

On the basis of available information (notably *La Question Mọi* Papers), it appears that by June 1938 the French administration considered the Python God affair to have subsided sufficiently so as not to be a matter of major concern. It also appears that the administration never adequately determined whether the movement was purely of highlander origin, i.e., Sam Bram acting alone or in league with other highlanders, or due to outside agitation, more than likely Vietnamese. It is conceivable that there might have been anti-French Vietnamese elements involved—nationalists, Communists, or traders (who also may have been interested in making a profit from the sale of bronze coins). It is equally conceivable that the affair might have been launched by Sam Bram in his effort to finance a new house and that subsequently, although unintended by Sam Bram, it spread for a variety of reasons, one being discontent with French rule in the

61. Le Résident Supérieur en Annam à Monsieur le Gouverneur de la Cochinchine, Hue, 21 Mars 1938, *La Question Moi* Papers.
62. Bourotte, "Essai des populations Montagnardes," pp. 100–01.

highlands—as was suggested by the previously mentioned Kontum Mission report.

French contact with the highlanders, which began in the mid-nineteenth century, had by the 1930s become very widespread as more "penetration routes" opened new territories, leading to the inevitable pattern of military posts, then administrative centers, and in a few places colonization. Some groups, such as the Mnong, Sedang, and Hre, met the French incursion into their territories with hostility, while among other highlanders, such as the Rhadé around Ban Me Thuot and the Bahnar and Jarai near Kontum, there was manifest resentment at the expropriation of lands for plantations. At least one leader, Touneh Han Dang, expressed his frustration at the French administration's attitude toward the highlanders by retreating to his natal village.

In this setting the Python God affair had many characteristics of what Linton calls a "magical nativistic movement." [63] Such movements, he notes, "usually originate with some individual who assumed the role of prophet and is accepted by the people because they wish to believe." In addition, such movements "always lean heavily on the supernatural and usually embody apocalyptic and millennial aspects." Linton also points out that this type of movement often arises in a contact situation between two ethnic groups wherein "a dominated group feels itself inferior, a condition common among societies of low culture which have recently been brought under European domination."

Throughout most of the central highlands the French were dominant, while in more restricted areas adjacent to the coastal plain the Vietnamese dominated. Both groups regarded the highlanders as inferior, an attitude graphically reflected in their common use of the reference term *moi*. Sam Bram was the proclaimed prophet of Dam Klam, the Python God, and the apocalypse was the predicted typhoon which would rid the highlands of the French, Vietnamese, and Lao and lead to a millennium, a period of bliss for the highlanders. Some aspects of the movement were innovative; for example, a standard set of taboos and prescriptions for all highlanders. Essentially, though, it exalted traditional highlander ways and idealized precontact times. In addition, such important symbols as the python spirit and "magic water" were symbols of the traditional Jarai belief system, e.g., "magic water" is associated with the King of Fire.

Additional information on the Python God movement would permit

63. Ralph Linton, "Nativistic Movements," *American Anthropologist*, n.s. 45, no. 2 (1943): 230–40.

an interesting and undoubtedly fruitful comparison with the Ghost Dance nativistic movement among the western American Indians toward the end of the nineteenth century as described by Mooney.[64] Both the Indians and the highlanders were being encroached upon by the dominant whites and envisaged a better time in the future for not just one group but a whole people—all the Indians and all the highlanders—when the alien intruders were gone and their goods would be divided. Neither movement sought to engender antiwhite attitudes or behavior, and both movements were explicitly nonviolent. Wovoka, the messiah of the Ghost Dance religion, and Sam Bram were believed to have supernatural powers and attained considerable charisma in the eyes of their followers. Both were known by a variety of names, and neither dressed in the garb of his own people. Both movements spread among different ethnic groups and underwent changes accordingly. Finally, both movements emphasized ethnic identity. For the highlanders, it was the first movement in their history that made its appeal to the highlanders in general and expressed their common ethnic identity.

EVENTS BEYOND THE HIGHLANDS

A number of historical events taking place outside their mountainous homeland during the 1930s would eventually envelop the highland people in the turmoil of international conflicts. Among the Vietnamese there had been some form of resistance against French rule since the conquest, and by the 1930s new waves of nationalism had begun to sweep the lowlands. In June 1925 three Vietnamese revolutionaries, Nguyen Ai Quoc (better known as Ho Chi Minh), Ho Tung Mau, and Le Hong Phong, all of whom had taken refuge in China, organized the Thanh Niên Cách Mạng Đồng Chí Hội (Association of Vietnamese Revolutionary Youth), which had as its goal mass action against the colonial regime. In October 1930 Ho Chi Minh and a group of revolutionaries formed the Đông Dương Cộng Sản Đảng (Indochina Communist Party). In addition to being dedicated to the overthrow of French imperialism, it advocated confiscation of "plantations and property belonging to the imperialists and the Vietnamese reactionary capitalist class" in order to distribute them to poor peasants.[65]

---

64. James Mooney, *The Ghost-Dance Religion and Wounded Knee* (New York: Dover Publications, 1937), pp. 657–62, 764–91.

65. Jean Lacouture, *Ho Chi Minh: A Political Biography* (New York: Vintage Books, 1968), pp. 48–50.

In 1927 a group of non-Communist Vietnamese led by members of the intelligentsia had formed the Việt Nam Quôc Dân Đảng (Vietnamese Nationalist Party), usually called the VNQDD, with an independent Vietnam as its goal. Early in February 1930 the Yen Bay garrison in northern Vietnam, which had been infiltrated by the VNQDD, mounted a revolt. The French reacted swiftly, dispatching Légionnaires to the town and the air force to bomb the post. The rebel soldiers were condemned to death, and some VNQDD leaders were captured and beheaded. Those who survived fled to China.

On 1 May 1930 the Communists mounted demonstrations in northern Annam, where there was dire poverty and in some places famine. The French reacted again with force, resulting in hundreds of deaths. Six months later peasants of Nghe An, Ha Tinh, and Quang Ngai set up their own "soviets," replacing the French administration in some areas. The French repression of the soviets lasted through 1931, and nationalist sources claimed that some ten thousand Vietnamese died and fifty thousand were deported. By 1932 the French continued to hold more than ten thousand political prisoners in jails, including those at Dak Pek, Ban Me Thuot, and Lao Bao, site of the old Vietnamese prison. On 17 December 1932 Governor General Pasquier declared, "Communism has disappeared."

Pasquier had succeeded Varenne as governor general in August 1928 and held this post until his death in an airplane accident in January 1934. It was during his administration, on 8 September 1932, that Bao Dai, the son and heir to Emperor Khai Dinh (who died in 1925), returned to Vietnam. Although only eighteen years of age, Bao Dai sought to gain the support of the people and announced that he intended to exercise constitutionality and gain what powers he could through concessions by the colonial government. Seizing his prerogative, on 3 May 1933 he named some nationalists to posts in his cabinet. Pham Quynh became chief of cabinet, and a thirty-two-year-old mandarin named Ngo Dinh Diem was named minister of the interior.[66]

In neighboring Siam, a coup d'état in 1932 brought the military party of Luang Pibul Songgram to power, resulting in a constitutional monarchy, a new national spirit, modernization of the army, and closer ties with Japan. On 23 June 1939 the name Thailand replaced Siam as the designation for

66. Joseph Buttinger, *Vietnam: A Political History* (New York: Frederick A. Praeger, 1968), pp. 146–47, 179–80.

the country, part of a strategy to rally under the flag of Thailand all of the Tai-speaking groups of the Indochinese peninsula.[67] This took place as the political horizons of Europe and Asia began darkening with the clouds of war. In 1931 Japan had occupied Manchuria, and in July 1937 it had launched an undeclared war against China. The following month the Japanese protested to the French Ministry of Foreign Affairs against arms shipments reaching China through Tonkin. In the face of such an ultimatum, it was clear that the French had little choice but to capitulate or fight. Georges Mendel, minister for the colonies in the Daladier cabinet, together with Governor General Jules Brevié formulated a political, economic, and military program to strengthen Indochina against the growing threat. In 1939 a loan of 400 million francs was made available for the defense of Indochina, and there was a call for an additional 20,000 native recruits.[68] According to General Marchand, the ground forces at that time consisted of two divisions and an autonomous brigade—the Autonomous Brigade of Annam which included the Battalion of Highlander Riflemen of South Annam that had been formed at Ban Me Thuot during the early 1930s.[69]

The new defense plan was never implemented, and in August 1939 Brevié was replaced by retired General Catroux, marking the first time in fifty years that a military man was named to that post. The following month war broke out in Europe, and at the same time France found itself in conflict with Thailand. On 15 September 1939 Marshall Pibul demanded the "retrocession" of the right bank of the Mekong river. By October, incidents along the frontier heralded a small-scale border war that would continue for some time.[70] According to Y Ue Nie Buon Kriek (5.5), a Rhadé retired from the army, the Highlander Battalion of South Annam was involved in some of the fighting. The unit was sent to the Pakse sector in 1940, the first time that it had been in combat. Y Ue served as paymaster at the headquarters in Nhatrang but periodically would go to Pakse. He recalled that the Thai employed military aircraft and that aerial bombardment was a new experience for the highlander troops.

Paris fell to Hitler's armies in June 1940 and shortly thereafter France surrendered. Indochina came under the control of the new Petain-Darlan

---

67. Le Thanh Khoi, *Le Viêt-Nam*, pp. 451–52.
68. Ibid., pp. 185–87.
69. Jean Marchand, *L'Indochine en Guerre* (Paris: Les Presses Modernes, 1954), pp. 32–33.
70. Le Thanh Khoi, *Le Viêt-Nam*, p. 452.

government centered in Vichy. The Japanese, who early in 1939 had taken Hainan Island and the Sprately Islands, lost no time in taking advantage of the French defeat. On 19 June they sent Catroux an ultimatum demanding the closing of the Tonkin-China border. They also proposed sending a Japanese military mission to supervise the termination of all aid to China. Catroux, no sympathizer of the Axis, had unsuccessfully sought to obtain Anglo-American support and knew he had to accede to Japanese demands. Although this was the desire of the Vichy government, when Catroux did accept the Japanese ultimatum he was relieved of his post (after which he joined the Free French forces). He was replaced by Vice Admiral Jean Decoux, commander of the French fleet in the Far East, who was considered by Vichy to be more reliable politically.[71]

THE DECOUX ADMINISTRATION

Admiral Decoux became governor general on 20 July 1940 and soon found himself coping with the problem of keeping the Japanese out of Indochina. By September, however, he had no choice but to conclude an agreement with General Nishihara permitting the Japanese to station 6,000 men north of the Red river and 25,000 throughout the rest of Indochina. The Japanese also were to have the use of Haiphong harbor and three airfields in Tonkin.

This was the beginning of a series of concessions to the Japanese that would continue to erode French sovereignty in Indochina. Early in 1941, for example, the Japanese, who needed Thai cooperation for their future strategy in Southeast Asia, forced the French to cede to Thailand three Cambodian provinces and some Laotian territory on the right bank of the Mekong river. Following this, in May 1941, the first of a series of Franco-Japanese commercial agreements integrated Indochina further into the Japanese Greater East Asia Co-Prosperity Sphere. Indochina was to furnish the Japanese 80 percent of its export, including rice, rubber, maize, coal, and various minerals.

Nonetheless, Decoux attempted to consolidate what control the French retained, launching a number of programs that he thought would win the support of the indigenous populations. In November 1940 he suspended all

71. Buttinger, *Vietnam*, pp. 187–88.

elected bodies in the Indochinese states, replacing them with one "federal council" of thirty natives and twenty-three French, all selected by Decoux. This actually had the effect of centralizing power, giving the French—particularly Decoux—greater control. Along with this he sought to develop what he called the "Indochinese mystique," which he believed would tie the native population closer to France. This involved a wide range of social and economic programs. Particular emphasis was put on winning more support among the youth. A new Commissariate for Youth and Sports was organized, and a Youth of the Empire movement was launched. New rural schools were constructed, resulting in a rise in the number of students between 1939 and 1944 from 450,000 to 700,000. In Hanoi the university was expanded with a new school of science and a new dormitory-student center.

Decoux also began a program of giving Vietnamese a greater role in the administration. In an interview in July 1972 Nguyen Ngoc Tho, who had been vice president under Ngo Dinh Diem and prime minister in the Duong Van Minh government, pointed out that this program reflected the view of French naval officers who tended to be more liberal than the officials from the Ecole Nationale d'Administration. The plan, Tho noted, was to send selected Vietnamese to Paris for a year of study and practical training in civil administration. The worsening international situation, however, prevented overseas travel, so the training program was organized in Hanoi. Tho was in the first group of trainees and in 1943 became the first Vietnamese to be appointed to a cabinet position in the colonial administration, serving as an "attaché" to represent the Vietnamese point of view in cabinet discussions concerning administrative programs and policies.

According to Tho, in September 1943 the court of Hue made a formal claim of sovereignty over the Tran Ninh plateau in Laos. The claim was submitted to Decoux's cabinet in the form of a letter signed by Pham Quynh in the name of Emperor Bao Dai. It cited documentary evidence from the Royal Annals in Hue that described the chiefs of the ethnic groups on the Tran Ninh plateau and in the central highlands as vassals of the court of Hue. Tho laughed, declaring that the mandarins were indeed very crafty in citing historical sources that the French themselves had evoked in the late nineteenth century as a justification to extend their control over the area east of the Mekong river as protectors of the court of Annam's hegemony. Decoux and the cabinet, however, rejected the claim. In the course of the discussion, several members of the cabinet expressed concern over what they considered to be displays of Vietnamese imperialistic tendencies. As the meeting ended, Aurillac, the director of cabinet, "half-jokingly" observed to Tho that, as dynamic as they were, the Vietnamese might one day invade neighboring territories and eventually control everything to the Thai border.

Buttinger points out that, regardless of any good will that may have motivated Decoux, Vietnamese intellectuals and nationalists saw in his programs only selfish French schemes.[72] In their view the French colonials were only interested in improving the university because their own children could not now go back to France for advanced studies. Similarly, a program to train native administrators was essential for the continuance of the colonial regime because new civil servants could not be brought from France. Buttinger also observes that the main instrument of French rule remained in the Sûreté Générale, directed by the notorious Louis Arnoux. He organized a "legion of combatants" to hunt down not only Vietnamese nationalists but also Frenchmen suspected of being sympathetic to de Gaulle. On a provocation as slight as an anonymous accusation, one might be sent to any of the already bursting prisons or concentration camps.

According to the American missionary Gordon Smith, the facilities of the Ban Me Thuot political prison were hopelessly overtaxed. From time to time there would be organized demonstrations and, passing by, Smith could hear the din and shouting of the inmates. When he departed in October 1941, Smith felt that the prison situation had become serious.

In 1940 Ton That Hoi was named Quan Dao at Ban Me Thuot. It was noted previously that his brother, Ton That Toai, had served as Quan Dao in Kontum. Both Hoi and Toai were sons of the well-known mandarin Ton That Han, who had been born in 1854 into a branch of the royal family in Hue. A strong advocate of collaboration with the French, Ton That Han served under eight monarchs and was regent during the reigns of Duy Tan (1907–1915) and Bao Dai (1925–1955). In April 1943, when he celebrated his 90th birthday (according to the lunar calendar), some 200 descendants gathered. He died the following year.[73]

In an interview in Ban Me Thuot on 2 November 1972, Ton That Hoi

72. Ibid., pp. 191–92.
73. Tran Dang, "Le 90e anniversaire de son altesse Ton That Han, ancien régent du royaume d'Annam," *Indochine*, no. 137 (1943), pp. 13–14; idem, "In memoriam, S. A. l'Ex-Régent Ton That Han n'est plus," *Indochine*, no. 212 (1944), pp. 26–27.

pointed out that, since his major responsibilities were legal, he had certain responsibilities for the Vietnamese prisoners. The jail had been established in 1930 to hold several hundred political prisoners but by 1940 there were over a thousand inmates. Ton That Hoi found the conditions woefully inadequate, justifying the frequent protest demonstrations. Since bad food was the worst complaint, late in 1941 Hoi began a program to establish prison gardens worked by the inmates. From these gardens came not only better food for the inmates but also a cash crop of vegetables and fruits for the Ban Me Thuot market. He also began a workshop where prisoners could practice or learn a métier, and medical facilities in the prison were improved.

In his efforts to consolidate his authority, Decoux also attempted to gain control of the press in Indochina. Between 1940 and 1943 seventeen newspapers and periodicals were suppressed.[74] The voice of the administration was the weekly journal *Indochine*, which began publication in September 1940 and continued until the end of the Decoux government in March 1945. Its relatively short articles were nonpolitical and reflected the isolation of Indochina from the Metropole in their focus on a wide range of local subjects, including many aspects of the people and history of the highlands. The articles were prepared by popular writers as well as scholars— some were well-known members of the Ecole Française d'Extrême-Orient. In addition to feature articles, there was news of events in Indochina with many photographs of Admiral Decoux (always dressed in a white naval uniform) and his wife Suzanne (always stylishly dressed, wearing a hat as French ladies were expected to do). News of the world was brief, and most issues of the journal were sprinkled with sayings of Marshall Pétain.

With revenues flowing into Indochina as a result of Japanese purchase of exports, and with most of France under German rule, there were funds available for public works projects—and Decoux undertook a number of them. He was particularly interested in developing Colonial Route 14, intended to link Saigon and Tourane via the highlands, because it made the lowland accessible to the areas of colonization on the *"moi plateaux."*[75] Work was renewed, and by 1943 the section from Trois Frontières to

74. Joseph Buttinger, *Vietnam: A Dragon Embattled*, 2 vols. (New York: Frederick A. Praeger, 1967), 1: 245.

75. Jean Decoux, *A la barre de l'Indochine: histoire de mon Gouvernement Général (1940–1945)* (Paris: Librairie Plon, 1949), p. 454.

Kontum was completed and only one section in the Mnong country remained unfinished in the new route from Saigon to Kontum. In February 1943 Decoux, using the dedication of a large monument to Henri Maitre at Trois Frontières as the occasion, announced the progress of road construction in the highlands. Work on the section of Route 14 from Kontum to the coast was progressing—it was near completion in March 1945 when the Decoux administration ended—and Route 19 from Qui Nhon to Stung Treng in Cambodia via Pleiku was scheduled to be finished in 1944.[76]

There also were several hydroelectric projects in the highlands. In 1942 a hydroelectric plant was constructed at the sprawling Catecka tea estate near Pleiku and another one was built near the town. At Dalat the existing plants were improved. New ones were constructed at Danhim and Krongpha.[77]

During the years of the Decoux administration, Dalat underwent more sweeping changes than any other place in the highlands. Unable to leave Indochina, the French began to spend their vacations in Dalat. Already an education and research center, there now was talk that Decoux would establish a new capital in Dalat. (It did become the "summer capital" from May until October 1942.) In 1941 the Geographic Service was moved from Gia Dinh to Dalat. Near the Lycée Yersin the administration constructed an attractive Cercle-Hotel in Mediterranean style to house it.[78]

On 31 January 1942 Admiral Decoux presided over a conference on the "moi country" in Dalat attended by the chief administrators of Cochinchina, Annam, Tonkin, Laos, and Cambodia and by some specialists on the highlands. Official estimates at the time placed the entire upland population at 1,000,000 of which some 700,000 were living on the "high plateaus" of Annam. The overall goal of the conference, outlined by Decoux in the first session, was to examine the problem of securing for the highland populations sufficient space to carry on their way of life and protect them against abuses arising from continued colonization. There also was the matter of improving their living standards, particularly with

76. Jean Decoux, "L'Inauguration du monument Henri Maitre 'aux Trois Frontières'," *Indochine*, no. 128 (1943), pp. 3–5.

77. R. Planté, "Les Aménagements hydroélectriques du Sud-Annam," *Indochine*, no. 111 (1942), pp. 13–19.

78. L, "Le Service Géographique de l'Indochine s'installe à Dalat," *Indochine*, no. 143 (1943), p. 19.

health programs. Finally, there was the need to improve the highland people's communication with the outside world, a task Decoux felt could be made easier by drawing on the long experience of the missionaries.

The first subject discussed was the problem of village administration, and it was agreed that each village should select its own headman. The villages would then be grouped into districts according to ethnic affiliation, and the inhabitants themselves would choose the district leaders. Village headmen would be compensated by the administration, thereby freeing them from the need to farm full-time and so enabling them to devote more attention to village affairs.[79] Then the matter of justice came under discussion. An order by Decoux dated 24 November 1941 had called for a semiannual convening of a commission composed of the administrative heads of Cochinchina, Annam, Cambodia, and Laos to study needs related to legal organization among the highland people.[80] Now the participants advocated more codified laws as the greatest need in the legal system.

Education also received considerable attention. It was pointed out that while there was a continued need for primary school teachers, the new Normal School at Ban Me Thuot would soon be producing more instructors. Also new teachers would be coming from a recently established Normal program organized in Kontum. The final subject dealt with health programs, and it was agreed that the administration would organize a new program to train nurses from the highlands.[81]

There were several direct results of the Dalat conference. First, a new special seal with an elephant head on it, modeled on the one Guenot, the first résident of Kontum, had presented to Bahnar chief Hma in 1909, was given to the new highland sector and canton chiefs.[82] Second, highland people from various parts of Indochina were selected in 1942 for special medical training at the Ecole de Médicine Sociale. This school was located in a colonial style building, later to house the Ministry of Health, set in a green park behind the Norodom Palace in Saigon. The group from the central highlands included five Rhadé—Y Tlam K'buor, Y Djac Ayun, Y Puk Mlo, Y Nue Buon Krong, and Y Ngong Nie Kdam (who later became a highland Communist leader, see below), and one Chru, Tou-

---

79. R. Vannel, "La Conférence des Pays Moi," *Indochine*, no. 79 (1942), pp. 1–3.
80. Guilleminet, *Coutumier de la tribu Bahnar*, 1: 88.
81. Vannel, "Conférence des Pays Moi," pp. 1–3.
82. "La France en pays Moi: les insignes des chefs de secteur et de canton Moi," *Indochine*, no. 116 (1942), p. 5.

prong Hiou (4.4). Hiou gave his birthdate as 1917—although he often claims it was 1902 in order to give himself seniority—and his birthplace as the Danhim valley village of Labouille. His early education was in the first Chru elementary school, the one begun at Mlon by Touneh Han Dang, who also arranged for Hiou and other Chru to receive further training at Qui Nhon. Subsequent to his Qui Nhon schooling he received nursing training between 1936 and 1938 at the Ecole des Infermiers in Nhatrang. Hiou began nursing in 1938 at the Djiring leprosarium, founded in 1929 by Father Cassaigne. Also in 1938, Father Chauvel became director of the facility and was joined by Sisters Emilie and Agathe of the St. Vincent de Paul order. By 1941 there were 129 lepers at the hospital (some 285 had been treated since 1929) and the hospital served as a center for the 600 Christians, half of whom were highlanders, at Djiring.[83]

During this period Dalat also became a favorite place for Emperor Bao Dai, the Empress Nam Phuong (a Catholic from Cochinchina), and their children. They were installed in a modern imperial residence, the children were enrolled in the Dalat schools, and Bao Dai spent considerable time in big game hunting. A symbol of the ever-growing Vietnamese presence in Dalat was the inauguration on 10 September 1941 of an imperial style Vietnamese tomb for Pierre Nguyen Huu Hao, Duke of Long My and father of Empress Nam Phuong and her sister Baroness Didelot. The ceremony, held in the Church of Saint Nicolas, was attended by the two daughters, Emperor Bao Dai, and a group of French dignitaries which included Admiral Decoux and his wife Suzanne; Bishop Cassaigne; résident superior Grandjean of Annam; and Bishop Drapier, the Apostolic Delegate.[84]

The need for services by the many French residents of Dalat was one reason for the increase in the Vietnamese population. Another was the expanding Vietnamese-operated truck gardening industry in Dalat. An example of this development is the evolution of the Vietnamese hamlet of Ha Dong, inhabited by truck gardeners and their families. In 1938 seven families composed of forty persons arrived from Tonkin to organize a truck gardening enterprise under the sponsorship of a local mandarin and with a loan from the Central Mutual Aid and Assistance Committee.

83. P. A., "La leproserie de Djiring," *Indochine*, 54 (1941), p. 8; Msgr. Cassaigne, "La Lèpre en pays Mois," *Indochine*, no. 148 (1943), pp. ix–xi.

84. Nguyen Tien Lang, "Le premier monument historique Annamite à Dalat," *Indochine*, no. 58 (1941), pp. 9–10.

Naming their cluster of houses Ha Dong hamlet, they began gardening on vacant unforested land. But before the first harvest some of the residents became discouraged and returned to Tonkin. It took until the end of 1941 for those who remained to repay their loan with profits from the sale of vegetables, which now included lettuce, carrots, leeks, artichokes, onions, cabbages, and green beans. As of the end of 1942, however, the hamlet had twenty-eight families numbering more than two hundred people.[85]

Animal husbandry in Dalat also developed greatly during the war years. Dairy products required by the European population now had to be supplied locally. In October 1942 there were 180 milk cows in Dalat; a year later the figure had risen to 250. In August 1942 the cows were producing 160 liters of milk a day; by October 1943 production had increased to between 250 and 300 liters per day.[86]

Admiral Decoux made special efforts to make Dalat a resort town "open to all," i.e., all French. On 19 December 1942 he opened the Saigon Exposition and among the many exhibits, including a highlander tomb with its carved wood figures, was a model of a proposed Cité Jardin Amiral Jean Decoux (Admiral Jean Decoux Garden City) to be built in Dalat on the former Borel concession. The garden city would be a community of new Alpine-style chalets of varying elegance for rent at equally varying prices. They would be available not just to French civil servants and military personnel but also to French employees of private business firms, and planters as well. There would be a lake, market, stadium, and swimming pool. In 1942 construction began on the garden city, and by February 1943 the first of 30 chalets were ready for habitation. As of March 1945 there were estimated to be 6,000 Europeans (most of them French) living in Dalat, and the number of villas had increased from 400 to 800 including 60 in Admiral Jean Decoux Garden City.[87]

On 23 July 1943 "by virtue of his heavenly mandate" Emperor Bao Dai in a colorful imperial ceremony in Dalat conferred on Admiral Decoux the title Prince Protector of the Empire, the highest honor of the court of Annam. Files of mandarins in elegant traditional robes accompanied the emperor and formal royal protocol was followed.[88] In his memoirs,

85. Dinh Am, "Une Visite aux maraîchers de Dalat," *Indochine*, no. 122 (1942), pp. 22–23.

86. Roussel, "Elevage à Dalat," *Indochine*, no. 163 (1943), pp. 11–12.

87. Decoux, *A la barre de l'Indochine*, p. 461; M. Brun-Buisson, "Précisions su la cité-jardin Amiral Jean Decoux," *Indochine*, no. 134 (1943), pp. vi–ix; J. Sauveplane, "La Cité 'Amiral-Jean-Decoux'," *Indochine*, no. 94 (1942), pp. 9–11.

88. Nguyen Tien Lang, "Investiture solennelle à Dalat," *Indochine*, no. 154 (1944), pp. i–v.

Decoux recalled that it was his decision to have the ritual in Dalat since he was in summer residence at the time.[89]

According to Touprong Hiou, Bao Dai was a notorious womanizer (he used the French expression *coureur*), and from time to time this caused rifts with the empress, who sought the advice of Madame Decoux. On 6 January 1944 while en route to Dalat for a meeting with the empress, Madame Decoux was involved in an auto accident and died that same day in a Dalat hospital.[90]

The Decoux administration had a special impact in the region the French called the "high plateau," the heart of which was Darlac. At Ban Me Thuot on 1 January 1941 Admiral Decoux and Emperor Bao Dai officiated at the Oath Ceremony in keeping with the tradition that had been started by Sabatier in 1926. American missionary Gordon Smith recalls that the emperor wore a robe of gold cloth and the traditional tightly wound Vietnamese turban. Jouin reports that Ae Bo, the King of Water, also attended, and a special hut was built for him.[91] When, however, two longhouses burned and two highly prized elephants died, the Rhadé thought that these disasters were due to the powerful spirits surrounding the King of Water, so he was not invited for any more ceremonies.

According to Antomarchi, preparations for the Oath Ceremony began two days in advance as chiefs leading delegations—some from villages a hundred kilometers distant—converged on the outskirts of Ban Me Thuot.[92] Members of the delegations carried their spears and crossbows, and many were weighed down by heavy alcohol jars. The ceremony was held in an open field at the entrance to the town, and the résident, dressed in white uniform laden with medals, accompanied Emperor Bao Dai and Admiral Decoux to the reviewing stand. In front of it was a large chair that in the past had been occupied by Khunjanob, the "Ivory King," but now was the place of his nephew Y Keo, who had succeeded him as judge in the highlander law court. In the field before the reviewing stand were five hundred chiefs, each squatting before a bowl of rice on which an egg had been placed, the symbols of tribute. Around the fringes of the gathering were townspeople and some French tourists from Saigon.

89. Decoux, *A la barre de l'Indochine*, p. 280.
90. "Madame Jean Decoux," *Indochine*, no. 178 (1944), pp. 7–10.
91. B. Y. Jouin, "Histoire légendaire du Sadet du Feu," *BSEI* 26, no. 1 (1951): 83.
92. Dominique Antomarchi, "La fête du serment à Banmethuot," *Indochine*, no. 20 (1941), pp. 23–26.

A parade of three hundred elephants began the celebration. The résident rose and addressed the chiefs in Rhadé, after which all of them filed past to touch his bracelet and swear an oath of loyalty to France. Afterward the résident sat before an alcohol jar and a platter of ritual food offerings was placed at his feet. An elderly Rhadé officiant named Ma Diam squatted before him and chanted an invocation while the résident sipped through the tube inserted into the jar. Then Ma Diam squeezed the résident's bracelet between two fingers, and at that moment the gongs began to play loudly. Ma Diam invoked the "spirits of the east and west" and those "above and below" to come and partake of the offerings—jars of alcohol and buffalos. He asked them to protect the résident and others from sickness: "May their heads not be sick, their stomachs not heavy, and their limbs not paralyzed." A "salute" by the elephants to the honored guests marked the end of the ceremony.

Mandarin Ton That Hoi recalled that he was present at the 1941 ceremony along with various highland leaders, including Nay Nui, Y Ut Nie Buon Rit, Touneh Han Dang, and Mohr and his son Ber. Hoi noted that they often gathered for such events, and from time to time he accompanied these leaders to Hue for state occasions.

The notable changes in the "high plateau" were the influx of outsiders and the increase in production on the plantations. The first official census in the highlands, conducted in 1943, reported that there were 1,000,000 highlanders.[93] Of these, 494,000 were living in the provinces of Darlac (77,000), Kontum (150,000), Pleiku (130,000), Haut Donnai (27,000), and Phan Rang (10,000). The 1943 census also revealed that there were 42,267 Vietnamese living in Darlac (4,000), Haut Donnai (10,000), Kontum (7,000), Pleiku (21,000), and Dalat (267). The French population totaled 5,090, with 219 in Darlac (75 percent of them military personnel assigned to the Highlander Rifle Battalion of South Annam), 199 in Haut Donnai, 141 in Kontum, 70 in Pleiku, and 4,461 in Dalat.[94]

Most of the Vietnamese in Darlac were laborers on the plantations. Some were engaged in commerce, although commerce was dominated by the Chinese, some 200 of them, and the French. Of the 250 "Indochinese" civil servants, 120 were highlanders (particularly numerous in the teaching

---

93. *Annuaire des Etats-Associés, Cambodge, Laos, Vietnam, 1953* (Paris: Editions Diloutremer et Havas, 1953), pp. 66–67.

94. Ministère de l'Economie Nationale, *Annuaire Statisque du Vietnam* (Saigon: Institut de la Statistique et des Etudes Economiques, 1951–   ), vol. 1 (1949–1950), p. 24.

staffs as well as in the medical, forestry, public works and veterinary service) while the remaining 130 were Vietnamese. There were 400 highlanders in the Garde Indochinoise.

Production in the plantations during this period increased. In 1943 Darlac produced 800 metric tons (800,000 kilos) of coffee, compared to the total 9,145 quintals (914,500 kilos) in 1939 for the entire highlands. The province also produced 100 metric tons of tea and 600 of rubber.[95]

Kontum was less affected by the colonization than by the efforts of the Kontum Mission, which was expanding rapidly. By 1944 there were over 22,000 Christians in the mission. Of these, 4,500 were Bahnar Jolong; 6,000 Sedang; 5,800 Rengao; and 6,300 Vietnamese. Bishop Sion presided over 24 districts with 165 highlander and 37 Vietnamese congregations that gathered in 26 churches and 135 chapels. Among the clergy there were 16 French, 13 Vietnamese, and 3 Bahnar priests.[96]

As of 1944 the Mnong country, the scene of turbulence in the 1930s, still was not considered pacified by the French administration. With the intention of rallying more support among the Mnong, a series of five "oath ceremonies" were held in Dak Mil (formerly Dak Dam) district during February and March 1944. Two companies of the Highlander Riflemen Battalion of South Annam bivouacked by the memorial to Henri Maitre at Trois Frontières while Mnong chiefs gathered at Dak Mil. Among the guests were Gerbinis, résident of Darlac, the French district chief, and Ton That Hoi. In the usual manner, the résident addressed the chiefs, calling for their renewed loyalty to France and their "strong arms" to complete Colonial Route 14. He also asked that they sell more crops to pay for the local schools and military posts. Then the chiefs came forward to touch his bracelet.[97]

In Tonkin during the years of the Decoux administration, the Communists were making considerable progress organizing among the various highland groups, particularly among the Tai-speaking people such as the Tay (Thổ) and Nung. One of the leaders in this effort was a Nung named Chu Van Tan, who had been born in 1909 in Thai Nguyen province. His father had fought with the partisans of De Tham, a Vietnamese who had led resistance against the French conquest of the

95. G.-M. Proux, "Le Darlac," *Indochine*, no. 211 (1944), pp. 6–13.
96. J. L., "Visite à la mission de Kontum," *Indochine*, no. 192 (1944), pp. 26–30.
97. Lt. Tibault, "Aperçu sur la question Moi," *Indochine*, no. 221 (1944), pp. 23–24; "Aux Trois-Frontières les Mnongs prétent serment à la France," *Indochine*, no. 191 (1944), pp. 24–27.

Tonkin highlands in the late nineteenth century. In keeping with family revolutionary tradition, Chu Van Tan joined the Indochinese Communist party in 1934 and was assigned to organizing the movement in the upland Vu Nhai area of Thai Nguyen province.

For a long time there had been considerable ferment against the French in the northern highlands. Among other things, there had been the same discontent with heavy taxes and corvée that existed in the central highlands. When the Japanese attacked the French at Lang Son on 22 September 1940, causing them to retreat, it precipitated an uprising at Bac Son. On 27 September some six hundred Tay (Thổ), Nung, Yao (Mien), and Vietnamese stormed the administrative center and some French troops in the vicinity were ambushed. As a result, in October 1940 a Communist war zone was organized in the Vu Nhai–Bai Son area with Chu Van Tan as commander.[98]

On 8 February 1941 Ho Chi Minh returned to Vietnam from China and organized his headquarters at Pac Bo in the isolated mountains of Cao Bang province. In May he convened and presided over the eighth plenum of the Central Committee of the Indochinese Communist party, and during this gathering the League for Vietnamese Independence (Vietnam Độc Lập–Dồng Minh), better known as the Viet Minh, came into being. Its program called for the overthrow of Japanese fascism and French imperialism and it outlined a strategy for achieving this. One aspect of the strategy was "to expand the organizations into the provinces where the movement is still weak and into ethnic minorities." In private, Ho said to Chu Van Tan, "The ethnic minorities are alike wherever they live. Once they have put their trust in someone, they remain loyal to the end. You come from an ethnic minority, and it must be easy for you to understand the minorities, but you must always be careful in your work."[99]

In September 1941 the Army for National Salvation was formed, and Chu Van Tan became one of its commanders. As the Viet Minh movement spread through Cao Bang province, the French sent troops to counteract it.

98. Mai Elliott, Translator's Introduction to General Chu Van Tan, *Reminiscences on the Army for National Salvation*, Department of Asian Studies, Cornell University, Southeast Asia Program Data Paper no. 97 (Ithaca, New York, 1974), pp. 1–2.

99. Chu Van Tan, *Reminiscences on the Army for National Salvation*, pp. 52–53. An excellent description of the role of the northern highland minority groups in the Indochina War is contained in John T. McAlister, Jr., "Mountain Minorities and the Viet Minh: A Key to the Indochina War," in Peter Kunstadter, ed., *Southeast Asian Tribes, Minorities and Nations*, 2 vols. (Princeton: Princeton University Press, 1967), 2: 771–844.

Chu Van Tan in his memoirs notes that the presence among the French troops of units from the central highlands rendered it more difficult to devise propaganda, since the highlander languages were unknown to the Communist cadre.[100] By 1943 the Viet Minh controlled more of Thai Nguyen and Bac Can provinces than the French, and as of June 1945 six provinces between Hanoi and the Chinese border were in the hands of the Viet Minh.[101]

While most of the French in Indochina supported the Decoux government, a small resistance movement against the Japanese led by Mario Bocquet, a French planter in Cochinchina, was begun early in 1941. He and his group established relations with the Americans in China, passing them information on Japanese activities and occasionally aiding downed Allied airmen. In 1942 the U.S. 14th Air Force under General Claire Chennault established the Air Ground Air Service at Kunming-Kweilin in southern China. When the American landing in North Africa provoked the complete occupation of France by the Germans, some of the French officers in Hanoi established radio contact with the Chinese wartime capital of Chungking. In 1943, Force 136 was organized by the British to carry out clandestine activities against the Japanese in Southeast Asia, and in November the French section began to function. Major Langlade, an agent of the Free French, was put in charge. On 6 June 1944 he parachuted into the Lang Son area in the Tonkin highlands and made his way to Hanoi where he met with General Mordant, the pro-de Gaulle commander of the French forces in Indochina. Beginning in October 1944, the Royal Air Force began dropping agents, arms, and equipment into the remote areas of Indochina, including the central highlands. As these operations increased, their clandestine character diminished.

Well aware of what was going on, the Japanese first reacted by increasing their troop strength in Tonkin. Their next move was to assume complete control of Indochina. On 9 March 1945 Ambassador Matsumoto went to see Admiral Decoux at the governor's palace in Saigon and presented him with an ultimatum demanding that all French troops in Indochina be placed under Japanese command. When the French did not accept within hours, the Japanese took it as a refusal and ordered all French units disarmed. There was resistance and bloodshed in some areas and

100. Chu Van Tan, *Reminiscences*, pp. 81, 86.
101. Buttinger, *Vietnam: A Political History*, p. 203.

general disorientation among the French population when they realized that their rule had come to an end.[102]

THE JAPANESE OCCUPATION OF THE HIGHLANDS

The Japanese moved on 9 March 1945 with rapidity, taking the French by surprise. In the cities, the French garrisons were quickly neutralized, but in some of the more remote rural posts, such as An Khe, French units put up some resistance. However it was to no avail. Admiral Decoux and some of the high-level French civil servants were interned in one of the Loc Ninh rubber plantations. Thereupon the Japanese ambassador informed Emperor Bao Dai that on 10 March the Vietnamese could celebrate national independence.[103]

Touprong Hiou in a conversation told of the fate that befell him and other highlanders then in nursing training in Saigon when the Japanese took over the governor general's palace near their school. All were imprisoned, as was Y Pem Knuol, a Rhadé who in 1943 had joined the French navy and was in Saigon.

At Ban Me Thuot, Touprong Hiou's younger brother, Touprong Ya Ba (4.9), who had joined the French army in 1941, fled into the forest when the Japanese attempted to disarm his unit. Making his way on foot for several weeks over the rugged mountains, he finally arrived in the Danhim valley and his home village of Labouille, only to be apprehended there by the Japanese. He and other highlanders from the French military service were sent to Djiring for forced labor in the tea plantation of Boulandry, which had been taken over by the Japanese. His brother, Touprong Y Mouc, who had worked for the French, was ordered beheaded by the Japanese commander at Dran.

Retired school teachers Y Yut Nie Hra and Y Toeh Mlo Duon Du (5.1) related how the Japanese troops in Ban Me Thuot rounded up the French administrators, military personnel, and planters, sending them to Nhatrang. They also rifled the administrative offices, destroying all the records, archives, and other papers. The plantations were taken over by the

102. Philippe Devillers, *Histoire du Viet-Nam de 1940 à 1952* (Paris: Editions du Seuil, 1952), pp. 114–31.
103. Marchand, *L'Indochine en Guerre*, pp. 75–86; Buttinger, *Vietnam: A Political History*, pp. 205–06.

Japanese troops. Ton That Hoi was named province chief. The Japanese commander announced that anyone bringing in Frenchmen who escaped into the forest would be amply rewarded. Heeding this call, Y Som Eban (son of a Cambodian father and Rhadé mother who became the second wife of the local leader, Y Say Ktla) rounded up some of the French and informed where others were hiding. His reward was several bags of salt. According to Y Tuic Mlo Duon Du (5.6), who had been in the army since 1937, many of the Rhadé military personnel melted into the forest. Those like Y Tuic who remained were formed into Japanese-Rhadé units. Y Tuic himself was named a battalion commander.

Some highlanders studying in Pleiku and Ban Me Thuot became frightened and tried to make their way back to their home villages. Y Thih Eban (5.2) was at the Franco-Jarai school in Pleiku and he joined a group of Rhadé boys who walked over the back trails to Darlac. Hiu (1.16) and three other Bahnar students, accompanied by a Sedang and a Jarai, Rcom Yonh (who later joined the Viet Minh), attempted to go northward from Ban Me Thuot along Route 14. They were stopped by Japanese troops who, because the boys were wearing school uniforms, thought they were military personnel. Phem (1.17), son of Bahnar leader Ber (and former husband of Rou), was a sector chief in Darlac and interceded for the youths, who were allowed to continue on their way. It took them two weeks to reach Kontum. Again, however, near the town they were stopped by Japanese who inspected their school books, thinking the boys might be spies. Hiu added that just before he fled Ban Me Thuot the Americans began bombing the airstrip near the town.

In some areas the Japanese move brought about a halt in new school programs. At Djiring, for example, Touneh Han Din (4.3), son of Chru leader Touneh Han Dang, and Ya Yu Sahau (both of whom had studied at Ban Me Thuot) had just opened a new school. It was a simple, one-room building of wood with a thatched roof and dirt floor, and the two young instructors collaborated with the Catholic missionaries to devise an alphabet for the Koho languages spoken by the Sre, Maa, Lat, Tring, Nop, Rdaa, Koyon, Jroo, and Dalaa. Han Din also worked with the priests on a roman alphabet for the Chru language; the Chru already had an Indian-type script borrowed from the Cham. When the Japanese approached Djiring, the two teachers fled into the forest to make their way back to their natal villages in the Danhim valley.

According to Nguyen Huu Phu, the Japanese occupation of Kontum was achieved without a struggle. When Morell, the résident, was told that the Japanese troops were moving toward the town on Route 14, he and the Vietnamese Quan Dao, carrying white flags, went to greet them just south of the bridge over the Dak Bla. French civilians and the missionaries gathered at the bishop's rooms in the rambling Norman-style mission headquarters. The French military garrison dispersed into the surrounding highland villages.

All of the French were taken into custody, and the Quan Dao was named province chief. The Japanese troops systematically destroyed the province records and archives. Soldiers also looted the homes of the French, selling much of what they took (Phu purchased a ten caliber French rifle). The Japanese commander then issued an order declaring that rewards, such as several bags of salt or some clothes, would be given to anyone who brought in French military personnel. By this time some of the French already were beginning to straggle back into Kontum, but there were highlanders who responded to the Japanese call and brought others in as prisoners. Some, Phu recalled, were unable to walk because their boots had worn out, and they were carried in on makeshift palanquins. Phu also noted that Cesarini, the French commander of the Garde Indigène, was the only one who did not return.

At the same time, the Japanese began a search for some downed American pilots who were reported to be hiding in the vicinity of Dak Ha in the Toumarong valley north of Dak To. Phu remembered that there was a report that some French priests in remote villages had hidden pilots, giving them Vietnamese conical hats to wear while they led them into the mountains. When one party of Japanese soldiers returned, they had two American pilots, but they also carried six dead Japanese, an indication to the Kontum townspeople that there must have been stiff resistance by the Americans. Hiu recalled seeing one American pilot who had been captured at Dak Gley north of Dak Pek. Hiu edged as close as he could to hear the American speak English, a language he had been studying on his own. While visiting a village north of Dak To in 1957, the French priest residing there told how he had hidden three American flyers. One day, however, he saw the Japanese soldiers coming in the front gate of his compound and warned the Americans, who fled into the forest. The priest later learned that one had been captured and beheaded, but the other two made good their escape.

The Japanese move also precipitated a curious odyssey for some of the highlanders serving in the French army. One version of such an experience was related by Rcom Hin, a Jarai who later became a lieutenant colonel in the South Vietnamese army. Hin was born in 1927 in the village of Buon Choma, three kilometers from Cheo Reo. After completing primary school in Pleiku, he joined the French army on 29 July 1942 and was assigned to the 4eme Bataillon Montagnard du Sud Annam, which at the time was attached to the 6eme Régiment de l'Infanterie Coloniale stationed in Kontum. On 24 December 1944 the unit proceeded by foot for four days to Qui Nhon where they boarded the train for Hanoi.

Most of the personnel in the battalion were Jarai and Rhadé, with some Sedang and Bahnar. From Hanoi the three companies were dispersed in the upland "Tai country" north of the Red river delta, and Hin's unit went to Cho Chu in Thai Nguyen province. When the Japanese struck on 9 March 1945, the French officers ordered all the units to scatter in the mountains and rejoin at Cho Chu to move northward. On 4 April they crossed the border of China, and Hin reports that they were immediately attacked by Chinese armed bands who left two highlanders dead. After a burial ceremony they continued northward, drenched by heavy rains, to a small post where a Vietnamese doctor tended the sick. After staying the night, they continued on the trail only to be attacked again, losing another highlander. Subsequently stopping at several small posts, they finally reached Ta Li Foo (this might have been Tali, also called Dali, in Yunnan province) where they remained one month. From there the troops walked to Tetsopa (possibly the local dialect name for Te-Ch'ang between Tali and Chungking in Szechwan province) where they stayed five months. Hin noted that they were well treated and given food by the Chinese garrison. The highlanders also were paid with Chinese money. During this period an assortment of other French military units, including some Legionnaires, straggled into the town. When all the French troops were rested and rearmed, they were reorganized in a new force called the Groupement Quiliquini for the French colonel who became commander.

Hin recalled that they had only vague news of the events taking place in Indochina. They had heard that the Japanese had surrendered and that French troops had reentered Saigon, but there were no details. Once the new unit was ready to move, they were ordered back to Indochina and crossed the border on 31 January 1946 at Phong Tho in the "White Tai country." After remaining there one week—Hin remarked that the high-landers were glad to be in Indochina, even if still a long way from their homes—they moved down the Da river to Li Chau. Then they turned southwest into the valley of Dien Bien Phu and made their way over the mountains to Luang Prabang on foot. Cholera struck the troops, leaving two highlanders dead. After a brief rest in Luang Prabang they were transported down the Mekong river on large pirogues to Vientiane. They continued by boat southward to Pakse and then to Stung Treng in Cambodia. From there they walked overland to Tay Ninh. Finally, they were provided with vehicles, and the highland troops reached Ban Me Thuot on 15 July 1946. There they were given back pay and three months leave. Hin reached Cheo Reo and his own village in August to be welcomed with "many sacrifices and rows of alcohol jars."

After their leave had expired, the highlanders converged on Ban Me Thuot to be reassigned. Hin and twenty-three highland officers and non-commissioned officers were sent to Bien Hoa to join the 3eme Bataillon, 22eme Régiment de l'Infanterie Coloniale under Commandant Rivet, a French officer fluent in Jarai. They were now ready for their participation in the Indochina War.

The end of the Decoux regime and the formation of the Japanese-sponsored government of Tran Trong Kim provided the Viet Minh with a situation favorable for expanding their activities and propaganda throughout Vietnam. The Viet Minh had by this time gained the reputation of being the leader in the anti-Japanese struggle and it also was thought of as the only organized nationalist movement, despite the existence of such others as the VNQDD and Dai Viets. In addition, the Viet Minh had succeeded in rallying support from non-Communist nationalist elements and anti-French factions. It was apparent in mid-1945 that the Japanese were heading for defeat, and Ho Chi Minh realized that when this occurred he would have only a brief time to take over the government before Allied troops landed in Vietnam. Viet Minh leaders and cadres prepared themselves for this event. On 7 August 1945 the city of Hiroshima was destroyed by the atom bomb and by 10 August the war in the Pacific was over: 16 August was proclaimed V-J Day.[104]

THE VIET MINH REGIME IN THE HIGHLANDS

On 16 August 1945 in Tuyen Quang province north of Hanoi a People's Congress led by Ho Chi Minh gathered sixty delegates of "all

104. Buttinger, *Vietnam: A Political History*, pp. 207–08.

nationalities"—meaning representatives of the ethnic minorities—and also of varying political elements. This Congress created the "National Liberation Government of Vietnam," intended as the nucleus of a provisional government, and the Viet Minh guerrillas were transformed into the "Army of Liberation." That same day the first Viet Minh guerrilla units were entering Hanoi. On 2 September 1945, before an enormous rally in Hanoi, Ho Chi Minh proclaimed the independence of Vietnam under a new regime called the Democratic Republic of Vietnam.[105]

Viet Minh troops also moved into Hue and Saigon, winning widespread support from the urban populations. Touprong Hiou related that he and the other highland students in the medical program who had been jailed by the Japanese were immediately released by the Viet Minh and that they returned to the highlands.

On the available evidence, it does not appear that the Viet Minh had at the time of the "August Revolution" organized any armed guerrillas among the highlanders. The centers of Viet Minh activities in the highlands were the political prisons. It appears that it was from these prisons that a certain amount of Viet Minh propaganda was disseminated, particularly among the highlanders in the Garde Indigène assigned to the jails. According to numerous informants, some of the Rhadé guards learned to speak Vietnamese and a few of the Vietnamese prisoners learned to speak Rhadé. One guard converted to the Viet Minh cause as a result was Y Bih Aleo, later a leader in the Viet Cong movement in the highlands. Born in 1901 in the Rhadé village of Buon Dray H'ling, ten kilometers from Ban Me Thuot, Y Bih received his Primary School Certificate from the Franco-Rhadé School and secured a position in the Geographic Service. In 1928 he joined the Garde Indigène, and during the 1930s he was assigned to the Ban Me Thuot prison, where he had considerable contact with the political detainees from the Viet Minh.

Following the August Revolution the Japanese opened the doors of the highland prisons. Most of the inmates immediately made their way to the lowlands, but some remained to begin organizing the Viet Minh among the highlanders. At Ban Me Thuot they were joined by Vietnamese cadre from the coastal provinces and set up a new administration, at the same time launching an intense anti-French propaganda campaign. According to all highland informants, the main theme was that, with the Viet Minh in

---

105. Ibid., pp. 208–10; Le Thanh Khoi, *Le Viêt-Nam*, pp. 464–66; Ellen Hammer, *The Struggle for Indochina* (Stanford: Stanford University Press, 1954), pp. 98–105.

power, "French suppression of the highland minority" was ended. The Viet Minh promised freedom and autonomy if the highlanders would support their cause.

According to Garde Indigène Sergeant Y Sok Eban (who was jailed for sixteen days by the Viet Minh), a political prisoner known only as "Mr. Tuan" designated himself "military commander" and organized a Temporary Administrative Committee (*Ủy-Ban Hành-Chánh Lâm Thời*). Initially, Y Ut Nie Buon Rit, the Rhadé leader who was the first highland schoolmaster, was named Chief (Chủ-Tịch) of the committee, but he soon was replaced by Y Plo Eban. Y Sok Eban and retired school teacher Y Toeh Mlo Duon Du both related how Y Plo Eban was a Rhadé Mdhur (a sub-group located in a remote area northeast of Ban Me Thuot). Y Plo had been kidnapped from his village as a small child by two brigands known only as Y Cu and Y Ri. Both had been followers of the famous Ama Jhao, after whose death in 1905 Y Cu and Y Ri carried on his practice of raiding villages to loot and carry off inhabitants who were later sold into slavery. Y Plo was taken to the village of Buon Emap, and in July 1924 the French résident Sabatier sent the militia into the area to capture the bandits. In the fighting that ensued, Y Cu was killed and Y Plo was carried back to Ban Me Thuot with other captives. He was put in the care of Y Tuop Nie, who brought him up as a son.

At an early age Y Plo Eban began to manifest unusual capabilities. At the primary school he excelled in mathematics and was sent for advanced education to the Collège de Qui Nhon, where he rose to the top of his class. He was the first highlander to be accepted at the Lycée Yersin in Dalat, where he received the first baccalaureate. Y Plo returned to Ban Me Thuot to teach at the Groupe Scholaire Antomarchi, soon gaining the reputation of being one of the most respected of the Rhadé leaders. Y Toeh and Protestant Pastor Y Ngueh Buon Dap recalled that he was a very tall man with quite dark skin, and they emphasized that Y Plo was the "most erudite" and "most intellectual" of the Rhadé. He devised a new Rhadé alphabet and carefully rewrote all the customs that had been recorded in the old script.

Y Thih Eban (5.2) recalled that when he was a boy Y Plo was the hero of the younger Rhadé, for whom he organized theater performances of tradi-tional music and dancing. Y Thih spent a good deal of time with Y Plo, whom he addressed by the kin term for "mother's brother." Since Y Plo was an older man of the Eban clan, he played the same role as that expected of the mother's brother, i.e., teaching young Y Thih how to hunt and fish. Y Thih noted that Y Plo, although very respectful of Rhadé customs, was against the shamans and what he considered their baleful influence.

The Viet Minh organized a committee of Rhadé to recruit and spread propaganda for the movement. According to Y Sok, one of the most active committee members was Y Ngong Nie (currently one of the Communist leaders in the highlands), who had been one of the group sent to Saigon for medical training. Another was his younger brother Y Wang Nie, an elementary school teacher. Two more from the medical training group, Y Tlam K'buor and Y Nue Buon Krong, also were on the committee, as were Y Bih Aleo and civil servant Y Blieng Hmok. In Buon Ho district north of Ban Me Thuot, the new Viet Minh leader was Y Wang Mlo, a male nurse, and he was assisted by Y Jonh (also spelled Joen or Jon) Nie Kdam, a respected teacher. Another Rhadé from Buon Ho named Y Yon Ecam joined the Viet Minh (later he sang Rhadé songs on Radio Hanoi propaganda broadcasts).

According to Y Tuic Mlo Duon Du (5.6), who had served in the French and Japanese military forces, the Viet Minh followed the Japanese pattern of organizing highland military personnel into newly formed units. Y Tuic was appointed commander of a battalion, the same rank he had held in the Japanese-organized unit. Y Tuic's brother, Y Toeh Mlo Duon Du (5.1), noted that he and other school teachers were not bothered by the Viet Minh although they made some changes in the curriculum, such as deleting French language training and emphasizing instruction in Vietnamese.

Ton That Hoi (the Quan Dao who had been named province chief by the Japanese) was taken prisoner by the Viet Minh and sent to Vinh, where he was tried before a "people's court." He was accused of "oppressing" the villagers in Darlac province. But he testified in his own defense that members of the Viet Minh who had been in the Ban Me Thuot political prison bore witness to the fact that he had been concerned with the welfare of the inmates. Ton That Hoi was therefore acquitted, but instead of returning to the highlands he settled in his ancestral village outside Hue.

According to Y Thih Eban, the only highlanders executed by the Viet Minh were Y Say Ktla (former secretary of the résident and one of those who had devised the Rhadé roman alphabet) and his son Y Lak Eban. Y Say was known as the wealthiest Rhadé in the Ban Me Thuot area. He and his son were accused of stealing land and forcing villagers to labor for the French without pay.

Noting that the Viet Minh forces that occupied Kontum were Vietnamese, Nguyen Huu Phu said that the first thing they did was to organize a Temporary Administrative Committee (like the one in Ban Me Thuot). Tran Quang Tuong, a school teacher from Saigon who belonged to no political group, was named chairman of the committee. Then the Viet Minh began reorganizing the various military units. The Garde Indigène, for example, bec..me the Liberation Militia (Giai-Phòng Quân). One of the Bahnar who joined the Viet Minh was Phem (1.17), son of Ber, the first highlander civil servant. Phem's former wife Rou (1.14) told of her father Mohr, the noted Bahnar chief, being forced by the Viet Minh to leave Kontum and return to Plei Bong. Since he was quite elderly, he fell ill after reaching the village and died soon after.

Early in September 1945 the Viet Minh occupied Cheo Reo. Rcom Rock (3.11), a member of the elite Rcom clan, explained that he had been studying at the Franco-Jarai School in Pleiku when the Japanese took over and that he had made his way back to Cheo Reo on foot. The Viet Minh cadre, all of them Vietnamese, immediately launched a propaganda campaign aimed primarily at teachers and students. As in Ban Me Thuot, the main theme of the propaganda was that the Viet Minh would expel the French from the highlands and then the highlanders would enjoy autonomy. Rock noted that the cadremen treated everyone well.

One of the first to rally to the Viet Minh side was Nay Der (2.12), the talented schoolmaster and son-in-law of the Jarai chief Nay Nui. In keeping with the Jarai preference for matrilateral cross-cousin marriage, Nay Der had arranged a marriage between his daughter Rcom H'trul and his sister's son Nay Phin (2.19) in 1942; they too joined the Viet Minh. Rcom H'trul is remembered in Cheo Reo as an unusually bright girl who was first in her class at the Kontum primary school. She also was the first female highlander to receive the Primary Studies Certificate. Her husband Nay Phin, a school teacher in Cheo Reo, was born around 1916 in the village of Buon Oi Nu, the same birthplace as Nay Der. Nay Phin also was an outstanding student in primary school, and at the Collège de Qui Nhon he excelled in languages, learning to speak French fluently. Rcom Rock recalls that Nay Phin was a "courageous man" as well as an excellent soccer and volleyball player.

Others who followed the Viet Minh were Rcom H'trul's sister Rcom H'dit and Siu Ken, a teacher from Buon Ju Plei Hjai near Cheo Reo. Later, H'dit and Ken were married. Another supporter was Rcom Briu (2.20), a teacher. According to a Communist source, Rcom Briu was born in June 1922 at Buon Ama Knik, close to Cheo Reo, and while a teacher in Pleiku brought about the removal of a French inspector of education (who was *particulièrement odieux*), prompting his dismissal from his position.[106] With the Viet Minh takeover in Cheo Reo, Briu was elected to the Peoples' Council for Pleiku province, charged with the Youth Organization for Cheo Reo district. His younger brother Rcom Pioi (2.21) was also a teacher and member of the Viet Minh but was less active. Their cousin (mother's sister's son) Rcom Brim (2.22), also a teacher, married the sister of Nay Phin.

Rcom Hin and Nay Luett named other teachers won over to the Viet Minh as Siu Nang and Ksor Ni, a particularly intelligent man who was first in his class at Ban Me Thuot Normal School. Rcom Yonh of Bon Sam, Kpa Yan of Plei Kli, and Rcom Thep of Pleiku also rallied to the Viet Minh.

When Touprong Hiou (4.4) reached his natal village of Labouille in the Danhim valley after being released in Saigon by the Viet Minh, he found the movement in control of the whole area. The Viet Minh were Vietnamese from the Haut Donnai area, but they quickly began to recruit among the young highlanders, particularly the Roglai. As in the other areas, the Viet Minh organized an Administrative Committee, and Touneh Han Din (4.3), son of Chru leader Touneh Han Dang (4.1), was named head. Another son of Han Dang, Touneh Han Tin (4.13), was also on the committee, as was Ya Yu Sahau, a teacher. Touprong Hiou was appointed Health Commissioner and subsequently named Representative of the Minority People for the region, a position he held for two months.

Hiou's younger brother Touprong Ya Ba (4.9), who had been held in forced labor on a plantation with other highlanders from the French military forces, also returned and joined the Viet Minh. He was given command of a company of troops. According to Touneh Han Tho (4.2), his father, who earlier had resigned from his position in the French administration, was asked by the Viet Minh to assume a role in their local government. Han Dang refused and retreated into the forest. Han Tho's kinsmen Banahria Ya Don (4.6), son-in-law of the Chru leader Banahria Ya Hau (4.8), responded to the Viet Minh call. Ya Don had studied

106. Commission des Relations Extérieures du Front National de Libération du Sud-Annam, *Personnalités du Mouvement de Libération du Sud-Vietnam*, 1962.

nursing, but rather than practice his métier he had become secretary to his father-in-law when Ya Hau was Tri Huyen. When the Viet Minh approached the village, Ya Hau fled into the forest and remained there until the French returned.

11 A PEOPLE IN BETWEEN: THE INDOCHINA WAR, 1945–1954

The Japanese takeover of the administration on 9 March 1945 and the subsequent August Revolution of the Viet Minh ended forever the relative isolation of the highlands and plunged its inhabitants into a long night of conflict. They now became "a people in between." On one side were the French, seeking to restore their rule, and on the other the Viet Minh, attempting to establish their authority in Indochina. The result was the Indochina War, and while the central highlands were not the main scene of battle—the northern mountains were—highlanders nonetheless were caught up in the struggle, fighting in the forces of both sides. But essentially the war was political, and the central highlands became an important pawn in French strategy. Initially it was a classical divide-and-rule strategy, and one aspect of it was to declare the central highlands an "autonomous zone." Later there was the façade of independence with the "Bao Dai solution" in which the highlands became a "crown domain" under the emperor. In the political struggle most highlanders remained neutral, although there were those who supported the French—who finally began referring to them as Montagnards rather than as Mois—and those who favored the Viet Minh.

These developments had a profound effect on highland leadership and the crystallization of a highlander ethnic identity. When highland teachers and civil servants joined the ranks of the Viet Minh, it was the first time that any highland people had participated in a nationalist political movement. While many of them left the movement (precipitating a significant division in highland leadership), they nonetheless were imbued with a nationalist spirit that would have a long-lasting effect.

With the formation of the Crown Domain in 1950 there was an upsurge in efforts by the administration to produce a larger, educated, pro-French elite among the highlanders. Young men from the elite families already described (those among the Ban Me Thuot Rhadé, the Kontum Bahnar, the Cheo Reo Jarai, and the Chru) joined other young men from elites of other ethnic groups (such as the Lat, Sre, Maa, and Mnong Rlam) at the improved schools in Kontum and Ban Me Thuot. Most converged at the Collège Sabatier in Ban Me Thuot, where they received advanced training, learned to speak Rhadé (which later became a lingua franca among highland leaders), formed close friendships, and shared the identity of being highlanders. This resulted in an increase in marriages among the elite families and marked a significant phase in the development of a sociopolitical network that increasingly cut across ethnic lines, vastly reinforcing the common identity of being highlanders.

THE WAR BEGINS

A declaration issued in Paris on 25 March 1945 made it clear that the French intended to restore their rule in Indochina once the war in the Pacific ended. Furthermore, in speaking of the "five states of Indochina," it let it be known that the French intended keeping Vietnam divided into Tonkin, Annam, and Cochinchina. Indochina would be given a federal government and an assembly with the right to pass on the federal budget. This assembly would have both French and indigenous members and would be responsible to the French governor general. This declaration was unanimously denounced by all Vietnamese nationalist groups. Nevertheless, on 16 August 1945, just after the war ended, French troops were ordered to proceed from France, Madagascar, and Calcutta to Indochina under the command of General Leclerc, who had become a military hero in the European war. The following day Admiral Thierry d'Argenlieu was named high commissioner (not governor general) of Indochina.

The Viet Minh forces which moved into Saigon following the Japanese surrender initially joined members of the United National Front, a coalition of religious sects (Cao Đài and Hòa Hảo) and various political groups (Đại Việt and Phục Quốc), to take control of the city. On 22 August the Viet Minh and United National Front delegations entered into negotiations, but the next day the latter withdrew, leaving the Viet Minh

Provisional Executive Committee for the South in control of the administration. Meanwhile a French negotiator, Jean Cédile, who had been named Commissioner of the Republic by Paris, had been parachuted from a Royal Air Force Dakota near Tay Ninh city on 22 August. He was taken to Saigon by the Japanese and there talked to Bocquet, the planter who had organized a resistance movement. Afterward he met with Viet Minh leaders.

Talks between Cédile and the Viet Minh leaders led nowhere, and by the beginning of September the squabbling among Vietnamese political groups was weakening Viet Minh control. At the Potsdam Conference following the German surrender the previous spring it had been agreed that the British would occupy Vietnam south of the 16th parallel as the Japanese were being disarmed while the Chinese Nationalists performed that task in the north. On 12 September 1945 the first British troops (a battalion of Gurkhas) and a company of French troops landed at Tan Son Nhut airport near Saigon. The following day General Douglas Gracey arrived to take command. Gracey set about restoring French control of the Saigon administration, a move that threw the city into confusion. The Viet Minh proclaimed a general strike on 17 September, to which Gracey responded by closing down all Vietnamese newspapers, finally declaring martial law on 22 September.

That same day the British released some 1,400 French troops, who immediately turned on the Vietnamese, killing many in the streets. As the French troops occupied police stations, the security police headquarters, the city hall, treasury, and post office, the Viet Minh Committee for the South fled Saigon. Soon after, it called for another general strike, during which the electric works were crippled, fires broke out in the central market, and fighting erupted throughout the city. Bui Van Luong, who later served in the cabinet of Ngo Dinh Diem, recalls that the shooting began without warning. Suddenly, in front of his villa on Bui Chu Street, Gurkhas appeared behind trees and opened fire on the Viet Minh nearby. Caught unaware, many Saigonese like Mr. Luong were trapped in their houses for days without food.

The Vietnamese nationalist forces moved from the center of Saigon and blockaded the city. On 5 October, General Leclerc arrived at the Saigon riverfront on board the cruiser *Gloire* to lead the French armies back into Indochina. In the middle of the arrival ceremony, the sun was obscured by a thick pall of black smoke from a rubber depot set afire by the Viet Minh.

Leclerc soon made it clear that he had no interest in the political negotiations which Cédile and Gracey were attempting to reestablish with the Viet Minh Committee for the South. His mission as he saw it was to clear the "insurgents" from Saigon, break the blockade, and defeat the Viet Minh in the rural areas.

By 12 October 1945 the British had occupied Gia Dinh and Go Vap just outside of Saigon, while French units took suburban Phu My. The arrival of French reinforcements, including armored units, gave Leclerc the wherewithal to move more rapidly. The first thrusts were southward along Colonial Route 4 to My Tho on the Mekong river, where the Viet Minh had taken refuge. The French armored columns next moved into Vinh Long and Can Tho in the Mekong river delta. Early in November, Tay Ninh (center for the Cao Daist sect) was captured, and the armored units, led by General Massu, swung northward to occupy the plantation areas at Hon Quan, Loc Ninh, and Bu Dop in the Stieng country.[1]

On 1 December the 5th Colonial Infantry Regiment under Commandant Rivier occupied Ban Me Thuot, which had been functioning as a Viet Minh arms center and relay station between southern Annam and Cochinchina. Y Sok Eban, Y Toeh Mlo Duon Du, and other Rhadé informants report that the Viet Minh dispersed quickly, most of them moving eastward along Route 21 and then into the mountains to the northeast. With them went teachers Y Plo Eban, Y Wang Nie Kdam, and Y Jonh Nie Kdam; civil servant Y Blieng Hmok; and a group from the medical service that included Y Wang Mlo Duon Du, Y Tlam K'buor, Y Nue Buon Krong, and Y Ngong Nie Kdam. Others who had supported the Viet Minh, however, particularly military personnel, now rallied to the French (see below), and the noted chief Khunjanob, wearing his Chevalier de la Légion d'Honneur medal, greeted the French troops arriving in Ban Me Thuot.[2]

The 5th Colonial Infantry sent elements north to Buon Ho, but they were ordered to go no farther. At the same time a battalion of the 6th Colonial Infantry Regiment landed at Nhatrang to protect the approximately 500 French civilians there. At Dalat the commander of a Japanese

---

1. Bernard Bourotte, "Essai d'histoire des populations Montagnardes du Sud-Indochinois jusqu'à 1945," *BSEI* 30, no. 1 (1955): 102–03; Joseph Buttinger, *Vietnam: A Dragon Embattled*, 2 vols. (New York: Frederick A. Praeger, 1967), 1: 308–13, 325–32; Philippe Devillers, *Histoire du Viet-Nam de 1940 à 1952* (Paris: Editions du Seuil, 1952), pp. 153–65.

2. Jean Marchand, *Dans le jungle "Moi"* (Paris: J. Peyronnet, 1951), pp. 33–50.

battalion received a formal order to guarantee the protection of French civilians in that city.

Meanwhile Leclerc's forces plunged deeper into the Mekong river delta. Long Xuyen was captured on 9 January 1946, Chau Doc and Ha Tien on 20 January, and Rach Gia on 26 January. Attention then turned again to the highlands and the coast of central Vietnam, where the Viet Minh were holding out in the Khanh Hoa citadel near Nhatrang. Operation Gaur was mounted to capture this redoubt. General Massu led the Colonial Infantry Regiment of Morocco and other units, including elements of the 9th Colonial Infantry Division, units of the 21st and 23rd Colonial Infantry Regiments, a battery of 105 mm pieces and five engineering sections, along Route 20 from Bien Hoa into the mountains. They sped through Blao and Djiring, occupying Dalat on 26 January 1946. From there they descended to the Danhim valley and moved on to Phan Rang and the Khanh Hoa citadel, which they captured.[3] According to Touprong Hiou, the Viet Minh in the Danhim valley made hasty preparations to retreat when news reached them of the French advance up Route 20. Hiou was scheduled to leave for Hanoi in four days when the French troops appeared in Dran. He and his brother Ya Ba quickly returned to their home village of Labouille but were arrested by the French (see below).

On 25 January a detachment of the 2nd Armored Division and a battalion of the 21st Colonial Infantry Regiment left Ban Me Thuot along Route 21 in the direction of the coast. At M'drak they encountered a small pocket of Viet Minh resistance and, after coping with it, continued to Ninh Hoa. At the same time units of the 1st Far Eastern Brigade and the 2nd Armored Brigade moved from Bien Hoa along Route 1 through Xuan Loc to Ham Tan, linking up with French elements that had continued southward from Nhatrang. In a press conference on 5 February 1946, General Leclerc stated that the pacification of southern Annam and Cochinchina was complete.[4]

According to General Marchand, the Viet Minh forces in the highlands were composed for the most part of Vietnamese, some of them highland residents and laborers from the plantations.[5] There also were some highlanders in secondary roles and some Japanese deserters. The Viet Minh

3. Jean Marchand, *L'Indochine en Guerre* (Paris: Les Presses Modernes, 1954), p. 108.
4. Joseph Buttinger, *Vietnam: A Political History* (New York: Frederick A. Praeger, 1968), pp. 226–27; Devillers, *Histoire*, p. 176; Marchand, *L'Indochine en Guerre*, pp. 105–08.
5. Marchand, *Dans le jungle*, pp. 44–45.

reaction to the swift military moves by the French with their sophisticated equipment was to resort to guerrilla tactics. As Y Thih Eban put it, "The Viet Minh were like tigers in the forest, hidden and quiet, but capable of savage attacks." They regrouped in more remote areas to train their cadres, increase their recruitment among the highlanders, and work out a strategy based on surprise and maneuverability. Their military methods included interdicting roads by blowing up bridges, building barricades, and setting ambushes. They also began attacking small military posts and engaging in terrorism and assassinations. Industrial and agricultural installations became targets too.

When the French returned to the southern portion of the central highlands, they found that the Viet Minh had destroyed many of the buildings and much of the machinery in the estates. They also were faced with a severe shortage of workers, since most of them had fled with the Viet Minh. A great many Vietnamese civil servants and teachers also had departed with the dissidents. The result was an effort at recruiting additional highland plantation laborers, civil servants, and teachers.[6]

Soon after the French occupied Ban Me Thuot, their former military personnel began to apply for reentry into service. Y Sok Eban, who had joined the military in 1921, went back to the army and was put in charge of reconstruction of the damaged camp at Poste du Lac. Y Tuic Mlo Duong Du (5.6), who had remained in the military forces of the Japanese and Viet Minh, rejoined the French army but subsequently was accused of having been sympathetic to the Viet Minh. Sentenced to one year in jail, he was released after six months and took a position as cook for the French résident. Y Pem Knuol, who had been in the French navy when the Japanese struck, had returned to Ban Me Thuot and was accepted in the French army and assigned to the 5th Far East Infantry Battalion. In describing this, he noted that this unit was formed of highlander volunteers. Y Bih Aleo, who had supported the Viet Minh, was allowed to rejoin the French army.

It was noted above that when the French moved into the Danhim valley, Touprong Hiou (4.4) and his brother Ya Ba (4.9) were jailed for having been in the Viet Minh. Ya Ba, who had been in the French army, was sent to Nhatrang but was released early in 1947 and given the rank of sergeant in the newly formed *partisans*, a local militia. Hiou was sentenced to one year in jail but released after six months and given a position in the

6. M. D., "En pays Moi (P.M.S.I.)," *France Indochine*, no. 47 (1948), p. 148.

provincial health service. Other Chru who had supported the Viet Minh were allowed to return to their former jobs. Touneh Han Din (4.3) and Ya Yu Sahau went back to teaching and Banahria Ya Don (4.6) was given a position in the forestry service.

Vigneras records that the newly formed highlander military units were given the mission of securing the province of Darlac where Viet Minh guerrilla harassment had begun by early 1946.[7] The highlander units proved effective, and with French support (primarily artillery and reconnaissance) a large part of Darlac and adjacent provinces were free of Viet Minh by September.

Admiral d'Argenlieu had arrived in Saigon on 31 October 1945 to assume his role as high commissioner, installing himself in the Norodom Palace. By early February 1946 d'Argenlieu had become convinced that the military pacification of the south was complete and that, as in the original conquest of Vietnam, the south would provide a base from which the French could move northward to establish their authority in Annam and finally Tonkin.[8]

This view was not shared by Sainteny, who had arrived in Hanoi on 22 August 1945 and immediately made contact with Vo Nguyen Giap, the Viet Minh minister of the interior. This led to talks between Sainteny (assisted by his political adviser Léon Pignon and General Alessandri) and Ho Chi Minh. The result was the Franco-Vietnamese Preliminary Convention signed on 6 March 1946 by Sainteny, General Salan, and Vo Nguyen Giap. The French agreed to recognize the Republic of Vietnam as a free state with its own parliament, army, and finances. The Vietnamese agreed that this state would be part of the Indochinese Federation and the French Union. There would be a referendum in the three parts of Vietnam (north, center, and south) to determine their political future. The annex also provided for a limit to the number of French troops in the country and their final withdrawal by 1952.

News of the agreement elicited a very strongly negative reaction from the French in Indochina, particularly the military, who considered it a sellout. Admiral d'Argenlieu, who had been in France during the negotiations, was highly critical, saying that he was shocked that such a fine

---

7. Marcel Vigneras, "The Montagnards of South Viet Nam: Their Military Value to the French before 1954," mimeographed (Saigon, 1964), pp. 6–7.

8. Le Thanh Khoi, *Le Viêt-Nam: histoire et civilisation* (Paris: Les Editions de Minuit, 1955), pp. 468–69.

expeditionary force would rather negotiate than fight. There also was dissatisfaction among the Vietnamese nationalists and the Viet Minh cadre. Nonetheless, on 7 March, before a large gathering in Hanoi, Giap defended the agreement.

In order to discuss their different views, the French and Vietnamese agreed to send delegations to a conference set for 17 April 1946 in Dalat. The Vietnamese delegation was led by Nguyen Tuong Tam, foreign minister and head of the VNQDD party, and it included Vo Nguyen Giap. The French representatives included Max André (former director of the Franco-Chinese Bank), Pierre Messmer, Pierre Gourou (a scholar who had done a classical study of human geography in the Red river delta), and Marcel Ner (another scholar, who had been inspector for education in the highlands).[9] The meeting ended in deep disagreement, but the participants promised to take up the whole matter at a later date in Paris. Giap emerged from the conference room convinced that war was inevitable, but Ho Chi Minh was still moderate, hoping for a negotiated end to the differences.[10]

On 19 April 1946, two days after the Dalat meeting, the Viet Minh convened a Congress of the Southern National Minorities (the Viet Minh officially designated all the minorities as Các Dân-Tộc Thiểu-Sô Anh-Em or "Fraternal Minority Peoples") at Pleiku, which still was under their control. At this gathering a letter from Ho Chi Minh was read in which he referred to the Kinh (the Viet Minh term of reference for the Vietnamese, the ethnic majority) as "blood brothers and sisters" of the "Djarai, Ede, Sedan, and Bana," i.e., the Jarai, Rhadé, Sedang, and Bahnar.[11] He emphasized that Vietnam was their common country and that the reason the majority and minority people had not been close in the past was

9. In a conversation concerning this meeting, Truong Cam Ninh, who was at the Lycée-Albert Sarrault in Hanoi in 1935 when Vo Nguyen Giap was a student, related that Pierre Gourou and Marcel Ner both were on the teaching staff. Giap was an outstanding student, particularly in history (the brightest student in history was Pham Huy Thong, who has since become a well-known historian), with a special interest in the French Revolution. A diligent student, Giap studied late at night and, since he was of a family with very modest means, often did not have money for breakfast in the morning. One day he fainted in Ner's philosophy class, and Ner began to give him breakfast in his home. As a result, Giap became Ner's protégé. Ninh pointed out that the French understood the respect that students are expected to accord their former teachers, and it was undoubtedly because of this that Ner and Gourou were in the Dalat delegation.

10. Buttinger, *Vietnam: A Political History*, pp. 238–50; Devillers, *Histoire*, pp. 219–26, 256–66; Jean Sainteny, *Histoire d'une paix manquée: Indochine 1945–1947* (Paris: Amiot-Dumont, 1953), pp. 85–86, 178–96.

11. Ho Chi Minh, "Letter Sent to the Congress of the Southern National Minorities, Pleiku, 1946," in *Ho Chi Minh on Revolutions: Selected Writings, 1920–1966*, ed. Bernard Fall (New York: New American Library, 1967), p. 156.

"people who sowed discord and division among us." At one point he also made mention of a "Department for National Minorities."

According to Nguyen Huu Phu, in May 1946 the Viet Minh organized elections in Kontum. Because the Catholics voted for him, Phu was elected president of the Administrative Committee. A Vietnamese was elected vice president, and Huk, a Bahnar catechist, was elected second vice president.

The forces of opposition to any negotiation with the Viet Minh (d'Argenlieu was usually cast as the leader) were actively trying to thwart further discussion. On 12 March Commissioner Cédile assured the colonels in Saigon that the 6 March agreement did not apply to Cochinchina, calling it a "regional arrangement" between Hanoi and the French for Tonkin and northern Annam. Two days later Marius Moutet, the Socialist minister of overseas territories, reiterated this, stating that Cochinchina would remain a "free state." [12]

On 16 May 1946 d'Argenlieu went to Ban Me Thuot for the Oath Ceremony, the first to be held since 1945. According to Y Thih Eban, the old chiefs Nay Nui, Y Ut Nie Buon Rit, and Khunjanob sat before the hundreds of local chiefs brought together for this occasion. D'Argenlieu sat on a stand erected in the middle of the town and the ceremony was conducted as it had been in 1926, with the chiefs touching the admiral's bracelet while they swore loyalty to France. [13] On 27 May 1946 d'Argenlieu issued an ordinance declaring that the provinces of Darlac, Haut Donnai, Lang Bian, Pleiku, and Kontum would form a Special Administrative Circumscription that would bear the title Commissariat of the Federal Government for the Highlander Populations of South Indochina. [14] The commissioner of this new administrative entity would be responsible to the high commissioner of France for Indochina. Because of certain military considerations, however, it was necessary for the provinces of Haut Donnai and Lang Bian to remain temporarily under the Commissioner of the Republic for South Annam. The ordinance indicated that the administrative center for this new highland circumscription would be Ban Me Thuot.

12. Buttinger, *Political History*, pp. 245–50; Devillers, *Histoire*, pp. 219–26.

13. Marchand, *Dans le jungle*, pp. 57–58.

14. T. d'Argenlieu, "Ordonnance fédérale du 27 Mai 1946 portant création d'un Commissariat du Gouvernement Fédéral pour les populations Montagnardes du Sud Indochinois," *Journal Officiel de la Fédération Indochinoise*, no. 23, 6 June 1946, p. 325.

This ordinance marked the beginning of a period during which the highlands would be a pawn in French political strategy. It appears to have been intended as a means of drawing the highlands into the orbit of French control by putting the new administrative circumscription under the high commissioner of France. At the same time it detached the highlands from South Annam and the possibility of the mountain region being affected by any implementation of the 6 March agreements.

On 1 June 1946 before a large gathering in Saigon, d'Argenlieu proclaimed the "autonomous Republic of Cochinchina." Soon after, upon his arrival in Paris for the proposed discussions on the 6 March agreements, Ho Chi Minh was informed of this development by Sainteny. Ho also was told that the planned conference would have to be postponed a month or two. The Vietnamese delegation went to Biarritz and returned to Paris on 19 June, when Georges Bidault became head of the new government. On 21 June, in another violation of the annex to the 6 March agreements fixing the strength and location of French garrisons, d'Argenlieu launched a new military campaign to bring the remainder of the central highlands under French control.[15]

On 21 June 1946 the 1st Far East Brigade held a defense line from M'drak (on Route 21 east of Ban Me Thuot) westward to Bokeo in Cambodia. The operation to reoccupy the remaining parts of the central highlands was organized in two phases involving two columns of the Far Eastern Brigade. The first column was concentrated in Ban Me Thuot and included the 5th Highlander Riflemen Battalion accompanied by armor, artillery, and engineer units. The second, composed only of the 4th Highlander Battalion, was located in Bokeo. A reserve unit in Ban Me Thuot was to be deployed in the final phase of the operation.

When the signal to move came on 21 June, the first column proceeded up Route 14 toward Pleiku. Since the French had taken Ban Me Thuot in December 1945, the Viet Minh had been active in cutting deep trenches into Route 14, cleverly camouflaging them with woven bamboo over which a thin layer of soil had been spread. They also arranged armed positions hidden among the rock formations in the forest along the route. Brenn gun carriers led the way as the column moved along and periodically skirmishes took place. Intense fighting occurred at the Chu Dreh pass,

---

15. Buttinger, *Political History*, pp. 250–51; Devillers, *Histoire*, pp. 266–75; Le Thanh Khoi, *Le Viêt-Nam*, pp. 468–71; Sainteny, *Histoire*, pp. 196–211.

almost midway between Ban Me Thuot and Pleiku, but the column continued on its way.

Meanwhile the second column was moving from Bokeo in a northeast direction along Route 19. It encountered no resistance, and south of Pleiku it joined with the first column. The main force of the Far Eastern Brigade continued northward, passing the sprawling Catecka tea plantation to enter Pleiku on 25 June. The town was in flames and the 4,000 Vietnamese inhabitants had taken to the road. The elderly, women, and children, all carrying what they could salvage of their belongings, crowded down Route 19 in the hope of reaching coastal Binh Dinh. Some of the armed units swiftly moved down Route 7 in a southeasterly direction into the Apa river valley and the town of Cheo Reo.[16]

By the time the French units reached Cheo Reo, the Viet Minh had fled. Nay Der (2.12), his daughter Rcom H'trul and her husband Nay Phin, as well as Der's other daughter Rcom H'dit and her future husband Siu Ken all left with the Viet Minh. According to several Jarai informants, in 1953 it was reported in Cheo Reo that the French had mounted a "clearing operation" in the Phu Phong area near An Khe and the Viet Minh were forced to flee their mountain redoubt. Among them were Nay Phin and Rcom H'tul, who was in an advanced state of pregnancy. She fell ill and died. Two other Jarai teachers who remained with the Viet Minh were Ksor Ni (who was first in his class at Ban Me Thuot) and Siu Nang.

R'mah Huen, who was born in 1909 and received technical training in Hue, recalled that when the Viet Minh occupied Cheo Reo, Nay Moul (2.17), the son-in-law of chief Nay Nui and one of the first Jarai to join the French army, cooperated with them. When news came that the French forces had moved on Pleiku, the Viet Minh made preparations to retreat. Nay Moul rounded up some 125 Jarai (including Huen) and with six Viet Minh cadremen they were marched northward. When the group reached Plei Tonia, midway between Cheo Reo and An Khe, Huen and some of the Jarai overcame their captors. All of them fled westward until they reached the French troops.

Meanwhile the main French force moved eastward along Route 19 through the Mang Yang pass to An Khe, where they encountered considerable resistance from the Viet Minh. At the same time other French units proceeded northward from Pleiku along Route 14 to Kontum. An

---

16. Marchand, *L'Indochine en Guerre*, pp. 105–08; idem, *Dans le jungle*, pp. 62–77.

artillery barrage of the north bank of the Dak Bla preceded the entry of tanks. The Viet Minh fell back in the direction of the coast by way of Kon Brai and Kon Phong. Some French units continued along Route 14 to Dak To and Dak Sut. French priests who had left Kontum when it was occupied by the Japanese in March 1945 accompanied the French troops and were welcomed by the population.[17]

Nguyen Huu Phu recalled that, after the French occupied Kontum, Cesarini, the chief of post who had hidden in the mountains when the Japanese took over on 9 March 1945, returned and was acclaimed a hero. Once in Kontum, he went immediately to the house of Vo Gia Du, a collaborator with the Japanese who had informed on where the French were hiding. Without saying a word, Cesarini shot Du dead, dragged his body to the garden, and dumped it into the well.

At An Khe the fighting continued, and on 1 July a break in the rainy season weather permitted the French air force to bring Spitfires to conduct air strikes on the Viet Minh positions. The following day, with their positions being shelled and hit by continued air strikes, the Viet Minh retreated into the nearby mountains. The French established positions farther east at the Deo Mung pass, but they had orders not to go beyond that point.[18]

In France the stalled conference finally opened at Fontainebleau on 6 July 1946. As at the Dalat meeting, Max André headed the French delegation, and the Vietnamese group was led by Pham Van Dong. The meetings began badly and ambled along without making significant progress.

On 1 August 1946 d'Argenlieu convened a second conference at Dalat. It had the expressed purpose of discussing the organization of the Indochinese Federation but clearly was aimed at undermining the Vietnamese position at Fontainebleau. Contending that the problems of Indochina would not be settled by conferences attended only by delegations from Hanoi, d'Argenlieu included in the new Dalat meetings representatives from Laos and Cambodia, both states solidly controlled by the French, the "Republic of Cochinchina," the "PMSI" (Populations Montagnards du Sud-Indochinois), and a delegation from an administrative entity that hitherto had not existed—South Annam. According to Touprong Hiou (4.4), the delegation from the PMSI consisted of himself,

17. Marchand, *Dans le jungle*, pp. 77–79.
18. Ibid., pp. 79–84.

his fellow medical technician Rhadé Y Djak Ayun (who was killed by the Viet Minh in a 1948 attack near Ban Me Thuot), and Hiou's kinsman Touneh Han Dang (4.1). Hiou said they had nothing to do but observe; they did not participate in any discussions.

Hiou also related that after this conference d'Argenlieu traveled in the highlands, first going to Ban Me Thuot where he was welcomed by Rigal, Commissioner of the Republic. Later they met with a delegation of Rhadé chiefs, and on 12 August 1946 in Kontum d'Argenlieu presided over a gathering of 3,000 Bahnar, Jarai, and Sedang chiefs who swore loyalty to France. Subsequently a similar ceremony took place in Pleiku, where Bahnar and Jarai chiefs had convened.[19]

News of the second Dalat conference almost brought the Fontainebleau discussions to a halt. But, although the talks continued into early September, they ended inconclusively with no decisions concerning Vietnamese independence, the status of Cochinchina, and the Vietnamese military and diplomatic organizations. On 13 September 1946 the Vietnamese delegation sailed for Vietnam, and the following day Ho Chi Minh and Marius Moutet signed a modus vivendi which dealt with economic and cultural rather than basic political matters. It nonetheless represented a concession by the Vietnamese to the French and a temporary truce as well.

Ho Chi Minh resumed the presidency on 20 October 1946, and on the 29th the National Assembly opened in Hanoi. It included members of the major political groups—the Viet Minh, the Marxist VNQDD, Vietnam Socialist party, Democratic party, and Đồng Minh Hội. On 8 November the assembly voted overwhelmingly in favor of a constitution. It created the Democratic Republic of Vietnam consisting of Bắc Bộ (north), Trung Bộ (center), and Nam Bộ (south) with the capital at Hanoi and a national flag displaying a five-pointed gold star on a red background.[20]

Hammer reports that among the assembly that drew up the constitution were members of the ethnic minorities from northern and central Vietnam.[21] The final document explicitly mentioned them, stating that "besides enjoying full and equal rights, the ethnic minorities are to receive every help and encouragement to enable them to reach the common level of advancement as speedily as possible." The minorities were also promised

19. "D'un moi à l'autre, pays Moi," *Indochine Française*, no. 24 (1946), p. 149.

20. Devillers, *Histoire*, pp. 295–310.

21. Ellen Hammer, *The Struggle for Indochina* (Stanford: Stanford University Press, 1954), pp. 178–81.

the right to study their own languages in primary schools and to use their native languages in the law courts. In parliamentary elections, the number of representatives from the minorities would be determined by law.

According to Célérier, there were in Hanoi at this time five representatives from the central highlands: "John, Ouek, Nay Phiu, Y Ngong, and Y Wang." [22] "John" probably is Y Jonh Nie Kdam, "Y Wang" is Y Wang Mlo Duon Du, and "Y Ngong" is Y Ngong Nie Kdam—all three Rhadé. Y Wang was a teacher and Y Ngong a medical technician, and both stayed with the Viet Minh when the French occupied Ban Me Thuot in December 1945. "Nay Phiu" probably is Nay Phin (2.19), a Jarai teacher from Cheo Reo who joined his father-in-law Nay Der (2.12) in following the Viet Minh. Célérier also notes that Y Ngong participated in the National Assembly and in the Permanent Commission.

By December 1946 the situation had deteriorated in spite of efforts by individuals on both sides to revive negotiations. Finally, a series of incidents between the French military forces and the Viet Minh in Hanoi touched off fighting on 19 December. On 20 December the French occupied Ho's house in Hanoi, but he and other Viet Minh leaders had fled. The following day Nguyen Binh, leader of the Viet Minh in the south, launched an offensive. While many consider 19 December 1946 the day the First Indochina War began, Le Thanh Khoi holds that it should be the day the war, which had begun on 23 September 1945 in the south, spread to the rest of Vietnam. [23]

As the fighting erupted in Haiphong and Hanoi, the Viet Minh attacked Tourane and Hue. Ton That Hoi, who had been Quan Dao at Ban Me Thuot and had been tried by the Viet Minh, recalled that he was in Hue when the Viet Minh assaulted the city. He accompanied the Queen Mother (Bao Dai's mother) to his ancestral village in the countryside. While they hid there, the royal palace and other buildings in the citadel were reduced to rubble.

THE HIGHLANDS BECOME A POLITICAL PAWN

Political events in Paris at this time became intense and determined to a great extent the course of the conflict in Vietnam. Minister for Overseas

22. Pierre Célérier, *Menaces sur le Viet-Nam* (Saigon: Imprimerie d'Extrême-Orient, 1950), pp. 113–14.
23. Le Thanh Khoi, *Le Viêt-Nam*, p. 472.

Territories Marius Moutet was sent to Indochina by Léon Blum.
Afterward Blum commented that "before any negotiations, it is necessary
to have military decisions." This view was shared by d'Argenlieu and
General Valluy, who had replaced General Leclerc as commander of the
French forces. Blum then sent Leclerc to view the situation in Indochina.
The former commander concluded that the war could not be won militarily unless there was a commitment of massive military might, adding
that "the major problem from now on is political." Léon Blum was
replaced by Ramadier and there was increased talk of negotiation, but the
French cabinet and legislature were deeply split. There was also the difficult
question of with which political faction would the French negotiate. By
early 1947 there gradually emerged a scheme to unite all of the anti-
Communist nationalist groups behind Emperor Bao Dai, who in March
1946 had gone to Hong Kong. If this were achieved, the French government could negotiate a settlement with this new government. General
Leclerc warned, "Anti-Communism will remain a useless tool as long as
the problem of nationalism is not solved."

In March 1947 d'Argenlieu was recalled and replaced by Emile Bollaert,
a civilian and member of the Radicals. When the new high commissioner
arrived in April, he brought with him as political advisor Paul Mus, an
expert on Far Eastern civilizations and former political adviser to General
Leclerc, a position Mus had left to become director of the Ecole de France
d'Outre-Mer. Since he had been born in Vietnam and had many friends
among the Vietnamese, Mus was sent on a special mission to contact Ho
Chi Minh. The terms of the French for any meaningful negotiation were
unacceptable, however, to the Viet Minh leader, so the talks led nowhere.
Equally unfruitful at this time were attempts by Mus and Bollaert on
separate trips to Hong Kong to gain the support of Bao Dai for a new,
French-sponsored, nationalist government.

Bollaert then settled on a scheme that he hoped would break the political
deadlock. It was the calling of a unilateral cease-fire to begin on 15 August
1947. This dramatic move, it was hoped, would set the stage for negotiations with the Viet Minh. It drew a very negative response from the
French in Saigon and also from General Valluy, who had been making
plans for a large-scale military offensive. Valluy immediately flew to Paris
where he convinced War Minister Coste-Floret and former Premier
Georges Bidault that his planned offensive would soon bring about a
"military solution" to the struggle. His mission succeeded, and the cease-
fire was cancelled.

On 10 September 1947 Bollaert declared in a speech that the French would offer the Vietnamese "liberty within the French Union" but that the French would retain control of the army, diplomacy, and the "federal services." If they so desired, the people of Cochinchina could rejoin Tonkin and Annam, but the high commissioner would remain "arbiter" in relations among the three regions of Vietnam. Finally, the ethnic minorities would be given a "special status," which in effect meant that the French would retain control of the upland regions of Vietnam.[24]

Although it may not have been related to political developments in Vietnam, the French government at this time sponsored the first ethnographic study of highlanders to be conducted by a professional anthropologist. After studying in Paris, Georges Condominas arrived in Vietnam in November 1947 to do research for the Centre des Recherches Scientifique et Coloniale. Following brief periods in the vicinity of Djiring and among the Mnong Rlam in Poste du Lac in southern Darlac, Condominas settled in the Mnong Gar village of Sar Luc at the end of November 1948, remaining there until the end of 1949. His research resulted in two books and numerous articles.[25]

By the end of 1947 the military situation began to become an important consideration in the attempts at organizing political negotiations. General Valluy's promised offensive against the Viet Minh began with operations between the Red and Black rivers in September 1947 and north of Hanoi in October. His claims of success reinforced French reluctance to make any concessions to Bao Dai regarding independence. On 7 December Bao Dai met with Bollaert on a French warship in the Bay of Along, and without any promise of independence the emperor signed a "protocol" specifying the conditions for collaboration. This produced sharp criticism from the Vietnamese nationalists and, in a discouraged mood, Bao Dai left Hong Kong for Geneva in what has been described as a "quest for pleasure."

By early 1948 a political impasse had developed in which the French refused to make any concessions to the Vietnamese and neither right nor left wing politicians in Paris were ready to accept Bao Dai.[26]

24. Buttinger, *Political History*, pp. 290–92; Devillers, *Histoire*, pp. 377–412; Hammer, *Struggle for Indochina*, pp. 206–14; Le Thanh Khoi, *Le Viêt-Nam*, pp. 472–73.

25. The books are *Nous avons mangé la forêt de la Pierre-Génie Goo* (Paris: Mercure de France, 1952) and *L'Exotique est quotidien: Sar Luk, Viet-nam central* (Paris: Plon, 1965). Several articles have already been cited. An early article on the Sar Luk research is "La marmite, le canif, et le tigre," *Sud-Est*, no. 3 (1949), pp. 56–57.

26. Buttinger, *Dragon Embattled*, 2: 710–12.

In February Bollaert officiated at the Oath Ceremony held at Ban Me Thuot in the presence of some 3,371 chiefs representing "twenty-five or thirty" different groups. Accompanied by Léon Pignon, Bollaert addressed the chiefs, calling for their oath of loyalty to France. After the elephants "saluted" them, the two French leaders sipped some alcohol from a few of the more than two hundred jars lined up for the occasion.[27]

In March 1948 the French announced the formation of a Thai Federation to include all the Tai-speaking ethnic groups of the northern Vietnamese highlands. It purported to grant these groups autonomy under the Great Thai Council composed of their principal notables. Hammer points out that there was little evidence of any real Thai autonomy movement, and this new "federation" would seem to have been another step in a strategy marked by such actions as the separate Cochinchinese "republic" and the special administrative zone that had been declared for the highlanders.[28] Hammer adds that "it seems to indicate a French desire to weaken any government which came to power in Viet Nam, under the cloak of protecting ethnic minorities."

French Socialist leader Louis Caput was highly critical of this move, relating it to the previous action by the d'Argenlieu administration in forming a "special administrative zone in the central highlands." In a letter to the French Socialist party he recalled that:

> the French authorities have long been exploiting the Moi particularism of the High Plateaux. The mountain people of these regions include numerous primitive and unorganized tribes (Rhadés, Djarais, Bahnars, Kohos, etc.) who certainly did not like the enterprising Vietnamese, but are beginning to detest singularly the French who recruit them as soldiers, subject them to exactions, and impose forced labor upon them. As a result, there has been a growing malaise, and abandonment of work and land, a retreat into the forest, and the least that one can say is that the situation in the High Plateaux of South Indochina begins to become very disquieting.[29]

Also, Caput noted that "the Moi question has moreover been one of the principal reasons for the bitter-sweet discussions between Bollaert and Bao Dai, the latter refusing to abandon these regions which France intends to turn into its central fief."

27. G. Gayet, "Evolution récente des populations Montagnardes du Sud-Indochinois," *Education* (Rectorat d'Académie, Bureau des Affaires Culturelles, Saigon), 1949, p. 79.
   28. Hammer, *Struggle for Indochina*, pp. 219–20.
   29. Ibid., p. 221.

Bao Dai met with representatives from Tonkin, Annam, and the government of Cochinchina in Hong Kong on 29 April 1948 to form a provisional central government with the initial goal of liquidating Cochinchinese separatism. They also approved General Nguyen Van Xuan's scheme for a new central government, and Bao Dai presented the national flag: three horizontal red stripes representing northern, central, and southern Vietnam against a background of yellow, the imperial color (it later became the flag of the Republic of Vietnam). On 5 June Bao Dai, General Xuan, and Bollaert signed an agreement that held that France would publicly and solemnly recognize the independence of Vietnam while retaining control of the armed forces and foreign policy. Immediately after the signing, Bao Dai departed for Europe and on 11 July announced that he was disengaging from the agreement. Xuan's proclamation of a provisional central government of Vietnam stirred no enthusiasm, and Xuan had difficulty getting capable people for cabinet positions. In addition, the French right wing successfully blocked the liquidation of the separatist regime in Cochinchina. Then it was revealed that the French were to retain control over the enclaves of Hanoi, Haiphong, Tourane, and the two "autonomous zones" in the highlands (the Special Administrative Area in the central highlands and the more recently formed Thai Federation in the north).[30]

Through the remainder of 1948 Vietnamese-French negotiations made no progress. Bollaert and the French government blamed the weakness of the Xuan administration on the refusal of Bao Dai to associate himself with it. The former emperor made it clear, however, that he would not return to Vietnam until he had an agreement from the French on unity and independence. On 2 September Bollaert announced that he would not request a renewal of his mandate as high commissioner, and on 21 October Léon Pignon, who had been political adviser to Admiral d'Argenlieu and had maneuvered behind the scenes at Fontainebleau to sabotage the French negotiations with the Viet Minh, was named as his replacement.

In January 1949 the Chinese Communists captured Peking and thereby altered the situation in Vietnam, as now an ally of the Viet Minh controlled the northern border. Buttinger points out that this raised the possibility of a Chinese Communist expansion into Southeast Asia, something the United

30. Buttinger, *Dragon Embattled*, 2: 713–19; Devillers, *Histoire*, pp. 425–36; Hammer, *Struggle for Indochina*, pp. 221–26.

States feared.[31] Sooner or later Washington would see its way clear to extend aid to the French in their containment of Communism. Such aid, however, could only be forthcoming if it were in the interest of the "free world," which would mean that Vietnam would have to be in fact independent and not a French colony. Still, those who decided French policy had no intention of giving up control of Indochina, and Buttinger notes that since they could not let their real intentions be known they had to engage in a "systematic deception" both at home and abroad.

As a result, early in 1949 negotiations between Bao Dai and the French began in earnest, with Pignon going to Cannes to consult with the former emperor. An exchange of letters between Bao Dai and French president Vincent Auriol led to the Elysée Accords of 8 March 1949 in which the independence of Vietnam and its status as an associated state of the French Union were reconfirmed. Bao Dai, however, agreed to numerous limitations on his sovereignty. Defense remained in the hands of the French, with a French Union Army to be stationed in Vietnam. A national army would be created but it would be under French command, with French military advisers. Foreign relations would be under French control, and there would be a special status for French citizens in Vietnam—for example, they could not be tried by Vietnamese law. For the first time, the French agreed to the abolishment of Cochinchinese separatism, and they relinquished the administrations in Hanoi, Haiphong, and Tourane. The French, however, retained their hold on the "autonomous" areas created for the minority groups in the highlands of northern and central Vietnam.[32]

The Elysée Accords contained a clause stating that the "non-Vietnamese populations" whose traditional habitat was situated on Vietnamese territory that "traditionally has been under the Vietnamese crown" would be the object of a "special regulation" agreed to by Bao Dai with "representatives of these populations." This regulation would be determined in cooperation with the French government and would guarantee "the eminent rights of Vietnam and the free evolution of these populations in relation to their traditions and customs."[33]

---

31. Buttinger, *Political History*, pp. 308–09.
32. Hammer, *Struggle for Indochina*, pp. 234–36.
33. These clauses were contained in "Lettre du Président de la République, Président de l'Union Française, en date du 8 Mars 1949" as published in *Viêt-Nam: une nouvelle étape* (Saigon: Imprimerie Saigonnaise, 1949), pp. 29–37. The text reads:

It was clear at this point that the French were willing now, as they had been at the end of the nineteenth century, to recognize the hegemony of the court of Hue over the central highlands on the basis of such thin evidence as Vietnamese settlements in places like An Khe and the tributary relations that existed between the Hue rulers and the King of Fire and the King of Water. This argument, however, was not limited to the French. Some Vietnamese legal scholars also had been claiming historical Vietnamese hegemony over the highlands. In 1942, for example, Tran Chanh Thanh based his case for this hegemony on historical Vietnamese settlement in the hinterlands of Annam and on French legislation concerning the administration of the highland provinces, though he did not invoke the tributary relations between the court of Hue and the Kings of Fire and Water.[34]

On 23 April the Cochinchinese Territorial Assembly voted to end separatism, and two days later Bao Dai returned to Vietnam. He went to Dalat to await the French Assembly's vote on a bill to have Cochinchina rejoin the rest of Vietnam. On 2 June 1949 Bao Dai, wearing a white suit, appeared with Léon Pignon, also in a white suit, for the Oath Ceremony at Ban Me Thuot. After two thousand chiefs had pledged loyalty to France in the bracelet-touching gesture that by now had become traditional, Bao Dai addressed them, stating that he would honor the "special regulation" of the Elysée Accords. These would, he added, permit the highland people to be free to develop in accordance with their own customs. Afterward High Commissioner Pignon spoke, declaring that the French would support Bao Dai's promises. The Rhadé chiefs then presented Bao Dai with gifts, including some elephant tusks, after which he drank some alcohol from the jars.[35]

The awaited bill rejoining Cochinchina to Vietnam was passed on 4 June. On the 13th Bao Dai went to Saigon, but his reception by the

---

L'administration des populations non vietnamiennes dont l'habitat historique est situé sur le territoire du Viêt-Nam tel qu'il vient d'être défini et qui ont toujours relevé traditionnellement de la Couronne d'Annam, fera l'objet de status particuliers, consentis aux représentants de ces populations par S. M. l'Empereur. Ces statuts seront déterminés en accord avec le Gouvernement de la République Française qui a, sur ce point, des obligations particulières vis-à-vis de ces populations. Ils devront garantir à la fois, les droits éminents du Viêt-Nam et la libre évolution de ces populations dans le respect de leurs traditions et de leurs coutumes.

34. Tran Chanh Thanh, "Statut politique et juridique des plateaux Mois du Sud-Annam," *La Revue Indochinoise Juridique et Economique*, no. 17 (1942), pp. 118–32.

35. "Le Mois en Indochine (25 Mai–25 Juin 1949)," *Sud-Est*, no. 2 (1949), p. 66.

population was remarkably indifferent. At the end of the month he accepted the resignation of the Cochinchina government and set about forming his national government. On the premise that the people would have to decide whether Vietnam would be a monarchy or republic, Bao Dai referred to himself as chief of state, although he "retained the title" of emperor. In June 1949 the U.S. Department of State welcomed the formation of "a new unified state of Vietnam" with the hope that the Elysée Accords of 8 March would "form the basis of the progressive realization of the legitimate aspirations of the Vietnamese people."

During this period the Viet Minh was aligning more and more with international Communism. Since the beginning of the war the Viet Minh had stood more or less alone, but with the Chinese Communists' sweeping victory in 1949 the Viet Minh could look to an ideological ally on its northern border who also could provide military aid. In December 1949 the Chinese Communists planted their flag at the international bridge linking Mon Cay with Tunghing. Soon after, the Viet Minh recognized the new Chinese regime, which reciprocated, recognizing the Viet Minh. On 30 January 1950 the Russians also recognized the Viet Minh.

This was a time when the Bao Dai regime succeeded in gaining support from the west, particularly the United States. Late in January 1950 the French government ratified treaties with Vietnam, Laos, and Cambodia which purported to grant them independence in accordance with the Elysée Accords. Newly named Prime Minister Nguyen Phan Long asked for economic and military aid from the Americans, specifically stating that it should be given direct to the Vietnamese, not through the French. It was, he said, necessary to build a Vietnamese army that could occupy areas taken over from the Viet Minh. He claimed that with $146 million in aid he could defeat the Viet Minh in six months; the French managed to remove Nguyen Phan Long in May 1950, replacing him with Tran Van Huu. On 7 February 1950 the United States recognized the three Indochinese states. Subsequent meetings between Secretary of State Dean Acheson and French Foreign Minister Robert Schuman resulted in an American decision to extend military aid to the French and some direct economic aid to the Indochinese States. The first military aid delivery was made on 20 June 1950. On 27 June, following the outbreak of the Korean War, President Truman announced that the United States would accelerate military assistance to the "forces of France and the Associated States in Indochina" and dispatch a military mission to provide close working relations with these forces. This was the beginning of the Military Assistance Advisory Group Indochina (MAAG Indochina), the first American military presence in Vietnam.[36]

There was at this time a significant change in the status of the central highlands. Ordinance Number 6 dated 15 April 1950 attached to Bao Dai personally all provinces and territories inhabited by non-Vietnamese populations and traditionally under the court of Hue. This in effect reiterated the French position, formulated in the late nineteenth century and contained in the Elysée Accords, that the existence of some Vietnamese settlements in the highlands and the tributary relations that existed between the court of Hue and the Kings of Fire and Water provided a basis for claiming Vietnamese hegemony over the central highlands. A subsequent decree dated 25 July 1950 created in the central highlands a Special Administrative Division, which was designated the Crown Domain of the Southern Highlander Country (Domaine de la Couronne du Pays Montagnards du Sud), and the region now was usually referred to as the Pays Montagnards du Sud (PMS). This made the central highlands a Crown Domain directly under the authority of Bao Dai.[37]

At the urging of General de Lattre de Tassigny, Bao Dai in 1951 began to form a national army, naming General Nguyen Van Hinh, son of politician Nguyen Van Tam, as chief of staff. According to General Hinh, the real beginning of the Vietnamese army was the 10,000-man Guard of the Autonomous Republic of Cochinchina, organized in 1946.[38] Since that time it had been the policy to train Vietnamese officers in France. However, in December 1948 a new military academy was founded in Hue. In 1950 it was relocated to Dalat and renamed the Ecole Militaire Inter-Armes. The following year a Vietnamese navy was created with the establishment of a naval center in Nhatrang. The opening in Nhatrang that same year of the Ecole de l'Air marked the beginning of a Vietnamese air force. In addition, also in 1951 at the suggestion of General de Lattre, Bao Dai and Prime Minister Tran Van Huu inaugurated the national conscription.

At this time security in the central highlands began to deteriorate. The

36. Buttinger, *Dragon Embattled*, 2: 727–34, 807–08.

37. *Annuaire des Etats Associés: Cambodge-Laos-Vietnam* (Paris: Editions Diloutremer et Havas, 1953), p. 68.

38. Nguyen Van Hinh, "Naissance d'une Armée Nationale," *Indochine Sud Est Asiatique*, no. 5 (1952), pp. 34–38.

intensification in the war in northern Vietnam and in the lowlands caused the French to withdraw most of their forces from the highlands. By 1950 there also had been an increase in the *pourissement* ("rotting away") of French control over large areas as small Viet Minh units and propaganda teams moved into the region. There was an increase in road ambushes and mining and attacks on outposts. The town of Ban Me Thuot was threatened, and a network of outposts was constructed around the outer perimeter to prevent any assaults.

To cope with this situation, it was decided in March 1951 to form the 4th Vietnamese Light Infantry Division, better known as the "Division Montagnarde" because most of its personnel were from such upland ethnic groups as the Rhadé, Jarai, Bahnar, Mnong, Sedang, Maa, and Hre. General Lecoq assumed the task of organizing the division, which was to have an enormous area of operation stretching from Dak Pek in the north to the highlands west of coastal Phan Thiet in the south. The division ultimately had 9,000 men with three infantry battalions (the 1st, 2nd, and 7th) composed exclusively of highlanders and one battalion (the 28th) of mixed Vietnamese and highlander personnel. The commandant was Colonel Le Van Kim, who had been trained at the Ecole d'Etat-Major de France and later would be involved in land development in the highlands and politics in Saigon. The other officers were French and Vietnamese, but the officer training school at Dalat already had graduated 75 highlander *aspirants* and the newly established Ecole Militaire Régionale du Lac at Lac Thien in southern Darlac was training another 50 aspirants. By the beginning of 1951 the division was operational, and as of the end of the year it claimed to have killed over 1,000 Viet Minh and captured some 600.[39]

The 5th Battalion had among its personnel many Rhadé and Jarai, including Nay Moul (2.17), a sous–lieutenant who had been one of the first Jarai to join the French army; Rcom Hin; and Rcom Pioi (2.21), a former school teacher from Cheo Reo whose brother Rcom Briu (2.20) had joined the Viet Minh. Other Jarai in the battalion were Nay Honh (2.23), a graduate of the Académie Militaire; Rcom Ko (3.9); Nay Dai; and Siu Nay. The Rhadé included Y Jao Nie Buon Rit, who was married to Rcom H'bu, the eldest daughter of the famous Jarai chief Nay Nui (2.11). In keeping with Rhadé and Jarai custom, Y Jao lived at his wife's long-

39. Simon Mays, "La quatrième division Vietnamienne," *Indochine Sud Est Asiatique*, no. 7 (1952), pp. 46–52.

house, and he is remembered as having owned a very large elephant. Other Rhadé were Y He Buon Ya, who also was married to a Jarai woman and lived in Cheo Reo, and Y Pem Knuol.

The 7th Battalion, whose symbol was a highlander machete and an elephant's head, was composed for the most part of men from the ethnic groups in Haut Donnai province. According to Touneh Han Tho, most were Chru, Sre, and Maa. The commander was Touprong Ya Ba (4.9), brother of Touprong Hiou. Ya Ba had joined the French army in 1941 and for a brief time had supported the Viet Minh. Other officers were Touneh Han Tin (4.13), half-brother of Touneh Han Tho, and two Sre aspirants, K'sau and K'nam. Among the noncommissioned officers were Touneh Ton (4.14) and K'tu, a Sre.

Han Tho also points out that the French and Vietnamese military leaders at this time dropped use of the term Moi in favor of Sơn Cước (*sơn* is Sino-Vietnamese for "mountain" and *cước* is "region"), a literary term for the highlanders which had long been used in novels and songs in northern and central Vietnam. The battalions with highlander personnel, for example, were called *Thiều Đoàn Sơn Cước*. For ceremonial occasions, there also was a Cờ Sơn Cước ("highlander flag") emblazoned with a laurel wreath crown against a blue background.

Y Pem and Rcom Hin both pointed out that the formation of the 4th Division brought together highlanders from different ethnic groups, resulting in an exchange of information about their respective customs and languages, with Rhadé becoming their lingua franca. For the younger men, all from villages, it broadened their view of the world—the first time most of them had worn western garb and cut their hair—and it also generated a feeling of common highlander identity. It also resulted, however, in many young highlanders being killed and wounded in a war from which their people would not benefit one way or another.

In its operations the 4th Division was aided by smaller highlander military units such as guard units, which served as security forces in specific areas, and Détachements Légers de Brousse (Light Brush Detachments) for reconnaissance and ambushes in more remote areas. There also were self-defense units, responsible for security and resupply of villages and maintaining intervillage communications. In mid-1951 the French began or-

Bahnar tomb carvings depicting French soldiers

ganizing "commando" units, which Marcel Vigneras points out should properly be called "Maquis" units, since they were organized to carry the war to the enemy's rear.[40] But, whereas commandos return to their home base, these fighters, like the Maquis in France during the German occupation, remained in the field, living off the land while they disrupted Viet Minh communications, destroying weapon and food stocks, and gathering intelligence.

The recruits for this Maquis were of various ethnic origins but most were highlanders. As the Maquis units grew in mid-1952, for logistical reasons they were grouped into one large organization called the Groupement de Commandos Mixtes Aéroportés (Composite Airborne Command Group). Each Maquis unit comprised from 10 to 1,000 riflemen with an average of 400. Depending on its size, it was commanded by a French lieutenant, a senior noncommissioned officer, or a corporal. After preliminary indoctrination at the guerrilla warfare school at Cap St. Jacques, the French cadremen joined their Maquis units to live with them in villages or in the forest. Vigneras estimates that by mid-1954 the Maquis throughout Indochina numbered between 20,000 and 25,000, but Fall puts the total at 15,000.[41]

Bao Dai signed a decree on 21 May 1951 at Dalat promulgating the "special regulation" for the central highlands that was promised in the Elysée Accords. This document reiterated the Crown Domain status for non-Vietnamese populations living in the Southern Highlander Country (PMS). It then noted that this decree constituted a *statut particulier*, and it repeated the words contained in the Elysée Accords that it would guarantee "the eminent rights of Vietnam and at the same time the free evolution of these populations in accordance with their traditions and customs." Article 3 called for the participation of a larger number of "Montagnards" in the administration of affairs in the PMS and the following article specified such roles as district and province advisers, sector, canton, and village chiefs, and representatives in various assemblies and in the highlander courts. The decree noted that an economic council would be formed

40. Vigneras, "Montagnards," pp. 7–12.
41. Ibid., pp. 9–10; Bernard Fall, *Street without Joy: Insurgency in Indochina* (Harrisburg, Pa.: Stackpole, 1961), pp. 241–42. Fall noted that recruiting of French personnel was difficult because an officer would be cut off from his parent unit, which among other things meant missing promotions. In addition, being in these units required one to live with the highlanders, learn their language, eat their food, and rely completely on them for security. One account of a French soldier's experiences in the Maquis is found in René Reisen, *Jungle Mission*, trans. James Oliver (London: Hutchinson, 1957).

of representatives most qualified to lend advice on agricultural, industrial, and commercial projects for the PMS.

The decree specified that the highlander law courts would continue. A commission also would be formed to study the matter of legislation in the highlands that would embody some Vietnamese and French laws pertinent to the region. Article 7 guaranteed the rights of the highlanders to own land; purchases, sales, or rentals of such lands would be reviewed by the administrative authorities and local chiefs and would be conducted in accordance with pertinent traditions. Medical and education programs would be improved. Medical programs would be organized in conformity with regulations established by the World Health Organization. In education, training in native languages would continue, while instruction in French and Vietnamese would be determined by particular situations. Finally, highlanders would not be drafted to serve in military units outside the highlands and would only be employed in the defense of their own territories.[42]

As a result of this decree the existing High Commissioner's Delegate for the central highlands (a role created by d'Argenlieu's ordinance dated 27 May 1946 when the central highlands became a "Special Administrative Circumscription") became an Imperial Delegate, but the post was still filled by a French official. A similar arrangement was made for the "autonomous" zone in the highlands of northern Vietnam. A decree dated 24 April 1952 created a single delegate for both highland zones, and Nguyen De, director of cabinet for Bao Dai, was named to this post. For both highland zones, however, there was a secretary general, and both were French. A Social and Economic Council for the Southern Highlander Country was formed (see below), and in June 1952 it produced a plan for socioeconomic development of the central highlands, which was elaborated in a booklet published in June 1953 under the authorship of Nguyen De.[43]

This plan first described the 500,000 highlanders as suffering famine and ill health because they clung to "agricultural methods dating from the early history of man." It also noted that there were 30,000 Vietnamese from the

---

42. Y Bham Enuol, "Extraits de l'histoire des Hauts-Plateaux du Centre Viet-Nam" (Pays Montagnards du Sud-Indochinois)" (Zone d'Organisation, 1965), pp. 1–12.

43. Nguyen De, *Plan d'action sociale pour les Pays Montagnards du Sud du Domaine de la Couronne* (Saigon: Editions de la Délégation Impériale du Domaine de la Couronne, 1953), pp. 5–10, 18–39, 42–47.

overcrowded coastal areas installed in the highlands and described them as pioneers in opening the gates for economic development of the upland areas. The plan envisaged two major goals. One was to "struggle against the depopulation" of the region by transforming the highlanders from people "who depend on the forest" for their livelihood to people living in "fixed stable communities" by introducing among them modern agriculture and animal husbandry. The other goal was to open the highlands to Vietnamese migration from the overpopulated coastal provinces.

In many respects the plan reflected the same prejudices that had characterized the Vietnamese view of the highlanders since they first had contact. For the Vietnamese, the highlanders still were dark-skinned, half-naked savages, badly nourished and housed, prone to innumerable ailments, and generally wallowing in primitive misery. In spite of the fact that highlanders practiced paddy farming in many areas where they had contact with the Vietnamese, there still was the persistent notion that the upland people used swidden methods exclusively. This gave rise to the equally mistaken idea that the mountain people were nomadic or seminomadic.

In the new plan, economic development would take place through exploitation of the agricultural potential by means of large-scale projects. This would involve concentrating on expansion of tea, coffee, rubber, rice, and sugarcane production. Estates already functioning would be enlarged, and new estates would be established. Related to this would be public works projects to supply more irrigation and electricity. New roads, bridges, and airstrips would improve communication and movement of products. Financing would be by the administration and increased investments by the private sector.

Within this framework, the highlanders would be "modernized." There would be large-scale regrouping of their villages; the plan noted that this was something the French military authorities were already doing to achieve better "security." This would enable the administration to introduce a range of programs to transform the highlanders' way of life. "Family projects" would introduce sewing, use of furniture, oil lamps, and use of soap, while accompanying "village projects" would bring modern tools, sewing machines, masonry, and bicycles to the villagers. In the area of medicine, "scientific therapy" would replace the reliance on shamans. The plan outlined the organization of a new Social Service to implement these programs in the highlands.

The major source of labor for the economic development of the highlands woud be provided by Vietnamese migrants brought from the coast and settled in planned communities on land cleared by bulldozers. These settlements would be accessible to the estates, and each family would have its house and plot on which it could arrange a garden. Each community would have its school, infirmary, market, communal house, and shops.

In spite of the changes in status that the central highlands had undergone since 1946, the French still were in control in 1953, and the highlanders had little voice in their own affairs. Until the declaration of the "special regulation" in 1951, most of the changes in the highlands following the return of the French had been due to the war, and many of these changes were not favorable to the French. Vigneras notes that by the early 1950s the Viet Minh had made impressive inroads in the central highlands through their propaganda, which played upon highlander discontent caused by the presence of the French army.[44] Corvée, the "leprosy of the highlands," was now directed not only at road maintenance but also at cutting new strategic trails through forests, building emergency airstrips, and transportation of supplies. In a similar vein, Touneh Han Din (4.3) reports that the war years were hard for the highlanders, who were pressed into service without pay by the French army to carry food and ammunition.[45] Many highlanders, he adds, died of sickness on the roads. Vigneras also points out that the French army's regrouping of villages for tactical purposes was unpopular with the highlanders, particularly when it resulted in destruction of rice stocks, loss of cattle, and abandonment of family tombs.[46] Then, too, as was indicated earlier, the drawing of many highland village men into the French military forces had mixed effects. While it increased the awareness of a common highlander identity, many died or were wounded.

A GROWING HIGHLAND ELITE

Another development during this period that contributed to the intensification and spread of a common highlander identity, particularly among

44. Vigneras, "Montagnards," pp. 8–9.

45. Touneh Han Din, "Dran-Canrang-Don Duong hay cánh đồng Danhim trước chương-trình tân-thiết" (Dran-Canrang-Don Duong or the Dran Valley in the Process of Development), *Địa phương chí tỉnh Tuyên Đức* (Tuyen Duc Province Bulletin), 1962, p. 2.

46. Vigneras, "Montagnards," p. 9.

the elite families of highland leaders, was the improvement of secondary education in Kontum and Ban Me Thuot. Young highlanders of different ethnic groups converged on these centers, particularly on Ban Me Thuot. This produced some changes in the educated highland leadership which had been emerging since the early decades of the century. These changes accompanied some other innovations that were taking place at this time and were most graphically manifest in Ban Me Thuot, Kontum, Cheo Reo, and Dalat.

Ever since the return of the French to the highlands, Ban Me Thuot had been gaining the reputation of being the unofficial "capital" of the region. (When d'Argenlieu declared the central highlands a Special Administrative Zone in May 1946, Ban Me Thuot was declared the seat of the commissioner.) Dalat was larger and more developed, but it was regarded as essentially a French city with a large Vietnamese population. Outside of Dalat, modern influences were felt more strongly at Ban Me Thuot than at any other place in the highlands. By 1950, for example, some of the Rhadé living close to the town had installed electricity in their longhouses, and there was the beginning of commercial activity among them. Y Bih Nie Kdam cites the example of a Rhadé named Y Cuc (an employee of one of the planters) who purchased a truck and became the first Rhadé to engage in the transport business.[47]

Ban Me Thuot also had become the center for the medical programs being organized for the highlands by the French. During the 1942–1944 period, a program for expanding medical facilities throughout the region was begun with a model hospital in Ban Me Thuot. Another hospital was constructed in Kontum, and dispensaries were opened in Djiring, Dran, and An Khe. During the confusion that accompanied the events from March to the end of 1945, all the medical facilities were looted. The program was started again, and by the end of 1946 there were six French doctors working the highlands in addition to Catholic nursing orders serving in Kontum, Djiring, and Dalat. At Ban Me Thuot, Y Djac Ayun (one of the highlanders who had been sent to Saigon for training in 1942) organized a nursing training program that by the end of 1946 had produced twenty-seven male nurses.[48]

---

47. Y Bih Nie Kdam, "Evolution culturelle des populations Montagnardes du Sud-Indochinois," *Education* (Saigon), 1949, pp. 88–89.

48. B. Jouin, "Les services sanitaires des populations Montagnardes du Sud-Indochinois," *Education* (Saigon), 1949, pp. 91–102.

As was indicated earlier, when the French reoccupied the southern portion of the highlands late in 1945, they found that most of the Vietnamese who had worked in the administration had fled with the Viet Minh, so more highlanders had to be trained for a wide range of positions. Pierre Yuk (1.12) recalled that the French quickly organized a one-year Cours de Formation Professionelle Accélérée to replace the defunct Cours de Pédagogie that had begun in 1943. The new course included training not only of teachers but also of secretaries, clerks, and technicians for the provincial services (agriculture, medicine, and public works). Some highlanders who had been in the administration and had left with the Viet Minh returned and were reappointed to their former positions, although some had to serve jail sentences first. Y Blieng Hmok, a civil servant who with medical technician Y Nue Buon Krong went with the Viet Minh, reached Hanoi before deciding to return to Ban Me Thuot. Jailed by the French, he was released in 1949 and became secretary to the résident.

As part of the scheme to train more highlanders for the administration, other educational facilities at Ban Me Thuot were expanded. The Collège Sabatier, which had opened with a one-year program in January 1945 but closed in March, was reopened in 1947 to offer a two-year program in advanced education. The Groupe Scholaire Antomarchi was refurbished and opened again. By 31 March 1949 the results of the restoration of the primary education system in the highlands could be seen. Whereas in 1937 there had been a total of 1,072 students in 29 classes, there now were 3,486 students in 338 schools. In 1937 there had been only a handful of highland teachers, but in 1949 there were 87. There also were large Ecoles de Plein Exercice in Ban Me Thuot (12 grades), Kontum (9 grades), and Cheo Reo (4 grades).[49]

The improvement in education during this period also was apparently aimed at producing a large pro-French elite among the highlanders. Since

49. F. P. Antoine, "L'Ecole Montagnarde," *Indochine Sud Est Asiatique*, no. 29 (1954), pp. 36–37; "L'Enseignement chez les populations Montagnardes du Sud Indochinois," *Education*, 1950, pp. 133–34. According to Touneh Han Tho, the normal primary school education program began with the Cours Enfantin, a two-year curriculum that included reading and writing in the mother tongue and in French as well as some drawing. The third year (Cours Préparatoire) involved training in arithmetic, French language, history of France, geography of Indochina (with emphasis on the highlands), health (cleanliness, proper diet, importance of boiling water), "moral studies" (duties toward parents and the state), and sports. The following four grades (élémentaire, première année, deuxième année, and cours supérieur) offered further instruction in French language, history and geography of France and Indochina, arithmetic, health, and moral studies. In addition, the student had travaux pratiques, which for the boys meant carpentry and for the girls some household skills (cooking and sewing). Both boys and girls worked in the gardens that provided food for the school.

most of the existing schools in the late 1940s had only two or three grades, those students who wished further training had to go either to Kontum or to Ban Me Thuot. Both places attracted the children of the elite, and the French administration subsidized their education and board. Among the students trained at Ban Me Thuot between 1947 and 1955 were many future leaders. From among the Rhadé were Y Thih Eban (5.2); Y Ju Eban, who along with Y Thih would be active in a later ethnonationalist movement; Y Chon Mlo Duon Du, later a leader in highland affairs; and Y Kdruin Mlo (2.24), a flamboyant young leader who called himself Philippe Drouin. Other Rhadé were Y Mo Eban (5.7); Y Klong Adrong, who now lives in California; and Y Jut Buon To (1.19), who later also would become a leader. The Jarai students included Rcom Anhot (3.12) and Nay Blim (2.25), both of whom would serve in the National Assembly; and Nay Luett (2.26), son-in-law of Nay Moul and later Minister for Development of Ethnic Minorities. Others were Rcom Pioi (2.21), a teacher who became an army officer; Ksor Dun (5.8), a medical technician, and Cheo Reo leader Rcom Perr (3.13). Hiup (1.20), who became a Kontum leader, was one of the new Bahnar students. The Mnong Rlam future leaders were known by the Rhadé names they had assumed, Y Tang Phok and Y Char Hdok (who would receive a degree in the United States). Another was Bun Sur, who went to Paris for further study and was appointed a province chief in Cambodia. Sar Lang was the only Mnong Chil student. The Chru students included Touneh Han Tho (4.2), a primary informant for this study who was to become the first highlander to complete the full course at the National Institute of Administration and study in Belgium, and his kinsmen Touneh Yoh (4.10) and Touneh Ton (4.14). Lat students were Lieng Hot Ngeo, K'Po, Ya Kiang, and K'Te. From among the Sre came the two brothers Toplui Pierre K'Briuh (4.11) and Toplui K'Broi (4.12), both of whom would receive degrees in the United States.

This drawing together of young future leaders in Ban Me Thuot was to have a profound effect on the development of highland leadership and of a common highlander ethnic identity. These students from different ethnic groups became friends, leading to many interethnic group marriages (as the various charts indicate). All of them learned to speak Rhadé, which increasingly became the lingua franca for the upland elite.

In 1952 Bao Dai began a program of granting young qualified high-lander students scholarships to the Lycée Yersin in Dalat. Among those who obtained scholarships were Touneh Yoh (4.10) and Banahria K'Sret, both Chru, and a group from the Collège Sabatier which included Ksor Dun, Nay Luett, Rcom Anhot, Touneh Han Tho, Bun Sur, Hiup, Toplui K'Briuh, and Toplui K'Broi.

Another development that affected the growth of an elite in the Ban Me Thuot area was the reestablishment of the Protestant Mission after the French returned to the highlands. The Reverend Gordon Smith, who had founded the mission in the 1930s, had left with his family just before the war in the Pacific began. Early in 1947 the Smiths returned to Saigon en route to Ban Me Thuot. Laura Smith describes going from Tan Son Nhut airport into nearby Saigon with an armed escort because of the insecurity even that close to the city.[50] The Smith family also rode in a convoy from Saigon to Ban Me Thuot, where they found their small chapel, which had been used by the Japanese to store ammunition, still standing. Their struggling congregation had continued to hold services, led by a Vietnamese pastor who from time to time had to flee into the forest to avoid the fighting near the mission.

Gordon Smith moved his family back into the Bourgery house and set about getting the mission functioning as it had been before the war. By 1950 the congregation had grown, with many converts in Buon Ale-A just south of Ban Me Thuot on Route 14. There Gordon Smith built a new chapel and designed three "Italian villas" on a hill overlooking the village for the missionaries. He also began construction of a leprosarium at Buon Ea Ana. One of his helpers was a newly converted Rhadé, Y Tuic Mlo Duon Du (5.6), by now a veteran of the French, Japanese, and Viet Minh armed forces.

Two marriages at this time within the mission congregation created kin bonds among some future leaders who were completing their educations at the Collège Sabatier. In 1951 Y Thih Eban (5.2) married H'wik Nie Hrah, daughter of Y Toeh Mlo Duon Du (5.1), one of the first primary school teachers in Ban Me Thuot (and brother of Y Tuic). Y Toeh's son was Y Ham Nie Hrah (5.4), Smith's most adept bible student and later the first highlander pastor. About the same time Ksor Dun (5.8), a Jarai from Cheo Reo studying at the Collège Sabatier, married H'chioh Nie Hrah, another daughter of Y Toeh. Following Rhadé and Jarai custom, Ksor Dun took up residence with his wife's family in Buon Ale-A and began calling himself Y Dun Ksor.

50. Laura Smith, *Farther into the Night* (Grand Rapids, Mich.: Zondervan, 1954), pp. 16–35.

An intensification of Viet Minh activities around Kontum during this period slowed orderly progress at the Catholic Mission and in the schools, a situation reflected in the fact that in 1939 there were reported to be 25,212 Catholics, most of them in the Kontum area, and by 1949 this figure had only risen to 25,255.[51] Three districts of the mission area already were under Viet Minh control, and in 1949 three more were invaded by them. In addition, some twenty-nine villages could be visited by the priests only rarely. The courage of these priests was sorely tested as they moved down the back trails, and on some occasions they had to have a small armed escort. By 1950 the situation had worsened and, as the mission report put it, the Viet Minh "took on the form of an almost invisible shadow" that threatened to encircle Kontum.[52] The Viet Minh stepped up their propaganda around Kontum, Pleiku, An Khe, Ban Me Thuot, and Attopeu, and the mission attributed it to the presence in the highlands of Duong Bach Mai, a Viet Minh agitator from Kontum.

At Kontum during this period there also were marriages among the highlander elite and between some of the Bahnar and the Rhadé of the Ban Me Thuot area. It was noted previously that in 1940 Phem (1.17), the son of Ber (1.10), had married Rou (1.14), daughter of Mohr (1.6), but they were divorced in 1942. Rou then married Nhep, a Rengao, while Phem married Lan, a Bahnar. It also was pointed out earlier that Phem had followed the Viet Minh in 1945 but supported the French after their return to Kontum in June 1946. In the late 1940s, however, fearing retaliation by the Viet Minh, Phem went to Ban Me Thuot and married H'bum Eban (1.21) from an elite family in Buon Ko Tam. Following Rhadé custom he took up residence in her longhouse.

In 1935 Pher (1.22), daughter of Ber, married Siu Hyin, member of the aristocratic Siu clan among the Jarai (the King of Fire must be of the Siu clan). As a small boy, Hyin had been taken to France by one of the colonial administrators and received his education there. After returning to Kontum, he worked at the province hospital where he met Pher. The couple followed Bahnar custom by establishing their own household, and their children were not given any surname. Siu Hyin's brother Siu Kioh also worked at the province hospital, and he married Nhao, sister of Bahnar leader Pierre Yuk (1.12). Yuk and his sister are of an old line of

---

51. Société des Missions-Etrangères, *Compte rendu des travaux de 1939* (Paris: Séminaire des Missions-Etrangères, 1940), p. 150; idem, *Compte rendu des travaux de 1949* (Paris: Séminaire des Missions-Etrangères, 1950), p. 108.

52. Société des Missions-Etrangères, *Compte rendu des travaux de 1950* (Paris, 1951), p. 86.

Bahnar Catholics that has produced civil servants and some military personnel. Yuk himself had been a seminarian between 1932 and 1938, and in 1941 he became a primary school teacher. In 1946 he was appointed secretary for Antoine, the French inspector for education in the highlands.

Siu Hyin's sister Siu H'lir married a Jarai, Ksor Tun, and their son is Siu Plung (1.23), who was captured in Pleiku by the Viet Minh in 1945 and held until 1947. Siu Hyin's younger brother Siu Hloaih (1.24) married a Jarai woman of the Rahlan clan. She had been married previously, and her son Rahlan Beo (2.14) was a well known civil servant. After the noted schoolmaster Nay Der (2.12) went with the Viet Minh in 1946, there was fear that the French might arrest his wife Rcom H'but (2.13), so a marriage was arranged between her and Rahlan Beo. This in effect created a somewhat weak link between the two elite kin networks in Cheo Reo (charts 2 and 3). A stronger link between the Cheo Reo elite (chart 3) and Kontum elite (chart 1) was formed when Siu Hyin's other younger brother Siu Khoa married Rcom H'klo (3.14).

In 1956 Pher and Siu Hyin's daughter Hium (1.25) married Paul Nur (1.13), a young schoolteacher who later became the first minister for development of ethnic minorities. Nur's mother was Kyat, a sister of Hiar (1.7), a schoolteacher and local Bahnar leader who has been cited frequently as a source on Kontum. Nur's father, however, was not of the Kontum elite. The father's mother, a Bahnar, while still a young girl was accused of being a *goh deng* (a much feared type of sorceress capable of injecting bullet-like stone or metal objects into a person's body, causing debilitating illnesses). Her family wished to be rid of her, so they sold her to a wealthy Vietnamese merchant who took her into his house to work as a domestic. When she had grown older, she met a Vietnamese laborer. They married and had a son who in 1926 married Kyat. The following year Kyat gave birth to Nur, who later was given the Christian name Paul. He attended the Vietnamese school, studying with his uncle Hiar, and later went to the Collège de Qui Nhon, after which he became a schoolmaster in Kontum. In 1943 he married Rum, a Sedang girl from Dak To whose father was a local leader. They had four children. In 1956 Nur left her to marry Hium.

About the same time Hiup (1.20), son of Pher and Siu Hyin, completed his studies at the Collège Sabatier and married H'met Eban, a Rhadé girl from Buon Ko Tam and sister of H'bum Eban (1.21), who had married Hiup's uncle Phem (1.17). Since Hiup was assigned as a teacher in Kontum, the couple went to live near the house of his parents.

Cheo Reo being only a district capital, the need for highlander administrators following the return of the French in 1946 was not acute. However, most of the school teachers had left with the Viet Minh, creating a shortage. When Siu Plung (1.23) was released by the Viet Minh in 1947, he was immediately appointed a teacher in the primary school. Late in 1946 Rcom Briu (2.20), one of the teachers who had followed the Viet Minh, returned to Cheo Reo but was jailed by the French. According to Nay Luett (2.26), after the French released him to allow him to teach, Rcom Briu was denounced by Rahlan Tai, a local notable, so he rejoined the Viet Minh, becoming a general in the North Vietnamese army. None of the other teachers who fled with the Viet Minh came back to Cheo Reo, and, as was noted above, Nay Der's wife Rcom H'but married Rahlan Beo. Her sister Rcom H'ban (2.18) recalled that H'but was a very dynamic woman, the first Jarai to start a transport business, with a truck bought in 1945.

According to Nay Luett, his father-in-law Nay Moul also had a transport business, carrying goods between Cheo Reo and Pleiku. In 1954, however, a convoy composed of several of his trucks was bombed by the French, ruining his business. Luett claims that this was the doing of a "bad man" named Ama H'nga who, seeking revenge against Nay Moul, reported to the French that the trucks were carrying material for the Viet Minh. Luett described Ama H'nga, Ama H'truick, and Ama Roo Bong as informers for the French who used their positions to extort money from the Jarai. Ama H'nga was finally forced to leave Cheo Reo.

During this period there were changes in the residence patterns of the elite Rcom clan as marriages took place. It was pointed out previously that two Rcom sisters, Rcom H'bem (2.3) and Rcom H'lok (2.4), ancestors of many of the Rcom now found in the vicinity of Cheo Reo, had established separate households when an epidemic struck. The descendants of H'bem (which includes the Rcom women married to leaders Nay Nui and Nay Moul) were centered in present Cheo Reo, while the descendants of H'lok split into two villages close to one another. H'lok's daughter Rcom H'pok and her husband founded the village that came to be called Buon Ama Knik. Rcom H'kuet (3.2) and her husband began the village of Buon Ama Djong. Their daughter Rcom H'areng (3.3) married Ksor Seng, bearing five daughters and six sons. As the sons married, they moved in keeping with Jarai custom to the longhouses of their wives, while the daughters and their families remained in the maternal house. It was noted that the eldest daughter, Rcom H'nher (3.4), married Ksor Wol, who became a local leader and assistant to the King of Fire, and that two other daughters, H'kra (3.6) and H'dla (3.8), married Jarai chief R'mah Dok. By the early 1950s Rcom H'nher and her husband Ksor Wol had established their own household, as did H'kra, H'dla, and their husband R'mah Dok. This left the parents and the two sisters H'ca (3.15) and H'pun and their families in the maternal house.

Not long after, Ksor Seng died and his role as village chief passed to Ksor Wol, husband of the eldest daughter H'nher (3.4). The widow H'areng (3.3) and the youngest daughter H'pun with her family then moved into the house of H'nher and Wol. H'ca, the last remaining daughter in the maternal house, had it dismantled and moved next to H'nher's longhouse so they could all live in proximity. Meanwhile, R'mah Dok died and his two widows remarried. Since Dok had no brothers, the levirate rule was applied to Dok's sister's son R'mah Hlin, who wed H'kra in spite of his being only sixteen as against her forty-five or so.

Some of the sons of H'areng and Ksor Seng became well known figures in the highlands. Rcom Rock (3.11) studied at the Franco-Bahnar School in Kontum from 1932 to 1937, continuing for three years at the Collège de Qui Nhon. He then taught from 1940 until 1945 at Pleiku, fleeing to Cheo Reo when the Japanese struck. After the French returned, he studied nursing at the Grall Hospital in Saigon, then practiced nursing with Dr. Jouin at Ban Me Thuot. His first wife R'mah H'djak was from Cheo Reo, but after she had borne two sons Rock left her to marry a Vietnamese, by whom he had seven sons. Rcom Kek (3.16) was a well known civil servant in the highlands; Bek (3.17) became a teacher; and Anhot (3.12) graduated from the National Institute of Administration and was elected to the National Assembly.

Between the early 1940s and the mid-1950s various French investigators provided some information, the first since the beginning of the century, concerning the King of Fire and the King of Water. In 1940 Ezzaoui, relying on a Bahnar informant, reported another of the many legends concerning the King of Fire's sacred saber.[53] Ezzaoui also revealed that, prior to his death, the King of Fire throws his bracelet into the stream where the residents of his village Plei M'tao bathe, and the male who emerges with the bracelet is the new King of Fire. Ezzaoui notes that when

53. J. Ezzaoui, "Une version de la légende des deux Sadets (le roi de l'eau et le roi du feu)," *IIEH* 3 (1940): 169–74.

the old king is near death his successor plunges the sacred saber into his neck. Writing in 1941, Guilleminet mentions briefly that the King of Fire enjoys considerable authority among the Bahnar and Jarai (who can readily list his predecessors) although this authority is of a mystical rather than of a temporal nature.[54] The King of Water, on the other hand, is not well known.

In a 1951 article Jouin, using Rhadé and Jarai sources, reported another legend concerning the origin of the sacred saber.[55] A young man named Y Thih—it will be recalled that one Jarai legend describes a man named Thih who came to possess the saber—forged a saber that manifested magical qualities. The saber was stolen by a Lao named K'bang and the renowned "chief of the Yang Prong Cham tower," who threw it into a highland lake. As news of this spread, the Lao and Vietnamese joined Y Thih in trying to retrieve the saber. Plunging into the lake, Y Thih managed to find the blade, the Vietnamese retrieved the sheath, and the Lao found the hilt.

On the basis of his information, Jouin concluded that Y Thih was the only true King of Fire and that those who succeeded him should more properly be called "Guardians of the Saber." Jouin also contends that the role of the King of Water only came into being following the death of Y Thih. The successors of the King of Water, however, have a right to bear that title, and they have more authority than the Guardians of the Saber.

In 1955 Bourotte, whose informants appear to have been Bahnar, related that, after the members of the King of Fire's entourage "aid him to die," the young warriors gather in the communal house to sleep.[56] While they sleep, one of the elders demands, "Who will be Bok Redau?" (Bok Redau is a Bahnar designation for the King of Fire.) When one of them responds, "It is I," a member of the Ksor clan places a string bracelet around his wrist. The new king then selects his assistants.

In the early 1950s French anthropologist Pierre Lafont began research on Jarai laws with the goal of codifying them. He began this task in October 1953, continuing until March 1954. Between January and June 1956 he completed his work, which was published in 1963.[57]

In the Dalat area, the return of the French produced much the same effect

54. Paul Guilleminet, "Recherches sur les croyances des tribus du Haut-Pays d'Annam, les Bahnar du Kontum et leurs voisins les magiciens," *IIEH* 4 (1941): 26–28.

55. B. Y. Jouin, "Histoire légendaire du Sadet du Feu," *BSEI* 26, no. 1 (1951): 73–84.

56. Bourotte, "Essai des populations Montagnardes," p. 33.

57. Pierre-Bernard Lafont, *Toloi Djuat: Coutumier de la tribu Jarai* (Paris: Ecole Française d'Extrême-Orient, 1963), pp. 12–13.

it did in Ban Me Thuot. A great many of the Vietnamese civil servants and teachers followed the Viet Minh when they departed, so highlanders were named to more positions in the administration than they had previously held. It was indicated earlier that Touprong Hiou (4.4) and his brother Ya Ba (4.9) were initially jailed by the French because they had been in the Viet Minh but were soon released. Hiou went into the health service and Ya Ba became a sergeant in the newly organized partisans. Among the others who had supported the Viet Minh, Touneh Han Din (4.3) and Ya Yu Sahau returned to teaching, and Banahria Ya Don (4.6) was given a post in the forestry service (although, according to Touneh Han Tho, he retained his sympathy with the Viet Minh cause).

The French asked Touneh Han Dang (4.1) to participate in the administration, and in 1947 he accepted the position of judge in the highlander law court, a position he had held in the 1930s. In 1949, after Bao Dai returned to Vietnam, Han Dang became a member of his cabinet, serving as adviser for highland affairs. Another Chru leader, Banahria Ya Hau (4.8), also became an adviser, and periodically the two met with Bao Dai. Han Dang, Ya Hau, and such other Chru leaders as Touprong Hiou and Touneh Han Din were often summoned to various gatherings of highland chiefs in what was supposed to be a show of support for the French. Early in February 1948, for example, they received a notice from the résident of Haut Donnai that they should gather at Dran to be transported to Ban Me Thuot for an Oath Ceremony on 21 February (as was described earlier, High Commissioner Bollaert and Léon Pignon were the honored guests).[58] The notice specified "national costume obligatory, Montagnard blankets, with lances or crossbows for the chiefs"—Han Dang and the other "chiefs" usually wore western clothes at this time.

In 1949 the French began to appoint local highland leaders as sector chiefs (assistants to the French district chiefs) to deal with the local highland populations. Touprong Hiou was named chief of the Dran sector. As was indicated before, Hiou had been born in 1917 (although he liked to say he was born around 1904 so that everyone would think him young for his age) and in 1942 he had been sent for medical training in Saigon. A very flamboyant figure with his wide smile and glinting eyes, Hiou had the reputation of being a very shrewd businessman—the Vietnamese in the

58. Résidence du Haut Donnai, *Note de Service*, 13 February 1948, personal papers of Touneh Han Dang, Saigon.

Danhim valley called him "the old fox"—and an inveterate Romeo. He laughingly recalled that once when he was young he had had an affair in Dalat with the wife of a highlander in the Garde Indochinoise. One night the husband returned home unexpectedly. As the outraged man brandished his gun, Hiou leapt out of a window and fled, only to fall into an open latrine. But he made good his escape, "with worms in my trouser cuffs," as he put it.

In 1941 he married Touneh Ma Preh, a Chru woman who died in a 1947 epidemic, and in 1945 he took a second wife, a "Koho" woman. One day in 1948 he took a fancy to a Chil girl who had just been married and over the protests of her husband (he wept) took the girl to his village, where she bore him six children. Eventually, Hiou had five wives and twenty-six children, all of whom he delivered himself. (On one occasion two wives gave birth the same day, keeping him very busy.)[59]

As sector chief, Hiou served as intermediary between the French district chief of Dran and the highland villagers. He transmitted orders, passed on complaints of the population to the district chief's office, and was responsible for implementing some administration programs. For example, one order dated 24 June 1949 and signed by Hiou directed the village authorities to build a communal house in each village and equip it with a large drum that would be struck to herald the daily work schedule at harvest time (starting time, lunch, quitting time).[60] It also noted that some women should be free to prepare meals and that there be no drinking from the alcohol jars during the work week. Another circular sent to the villages by Hiou concerning village hygiene called for everyone to bathe daily with soap, comb their hair, and wash their hands at least three times a day.[61] Women were advised to sweep their houses several times a day, using something called *crésyl*. He also played the role of arbiter in village disputes. For example, one communication dated 19 October 1949 transmitted the complaint of thirty-nine residents of a Chru village against two men of the same village they accused of "sorcellerie empoisonneuse" (poisonous sorcery).[62]

59. During one interview in 1967 at his village of Labouille, when asked how many children he had Hiou and his five wives had to round up the children in the house for a head count. The result: 18 in the house and 6 away at school.

60. Touprong Hiou, Chef de District Montagnard, à Messieurs les Conseillers du District de Dran, 24 June 1949, personal papers of Touneh Han Dang, Saigon.

61. Touprong Hiou, "Circulaire: Objet: L'Hygiène collective dans les communautés Montagnardes, Dran, 3 Novembre 1952," personal papers of Touneh Han Dang, Saigon.

62. Touprong Hiou, Président du Conseil de District Montagnard de Dran à Messieurs le Conseiller de l'Assemblée Représentative et le Président du Tribunal Coutumier de Dran, Dran, 18 October 1949, personal papers of Touneh Han Dang, Saigon.

Dalat at this time became the residence of Bao Dai and the "political capital" of Vietnam. He and his family lived in a sumptuous mansion built in the late 1930s style and located on a mountainside. Bao Dai was an avid hunter, and in addition to his duties as sector chief Touprong Hiou served as Bao Dai's hunting guide and interpreter when the emperor visited villages. According to Hiou, Bao Dai was a "grand chasseur" with numerous hunting lodges. At Ban Mc Thuot he built a large hunting lodge and, for guests, the "Grand Bungalow," an impressive structure consisting of three separate sections connected by covered walks. Built on piling in the Rhadé fashion, the bungalow was of local hardwood with roof shingles of precious *sao* (Hopea sp.: Dipterocarpus). There was another lodge at Poste du Lac (Lac Thien) in southern Darlac, and at Dai Kai, closer to Dalat, he had a small house where he hunted in the surrounding forest, fished in the nearby stream, and raised some baby elephants. Hiou recalled that Bao Dai would often take French military officers as guests on hunting parties, and sometimes he would bring his concubines. When there were guests, the hunting party would wait in a tree house while the big game came to devour small game that had been staked out in a clearing. Hiou grimaced when he described how the concubines chattered and loudly complained how uncomfortable they were, scaring the big game away. He noted, however, that Bao Dai's "second wife," a Chinese lady named Mong Diep, was a very adept hunter.

During this period Dalat grew in size and became a favorite place to hold conferences. Also, the number of educational institutions increased. Among the new educational facilities was the Ecole Nationale d'Administration, founded on 1 January 1953 to train Vietnamese cadre for higher positions in the administration.[63]

The Social and Economic Council promised in the *statut particulier* of May 1951 was created by a decree dated 11 February 1952 and signed by Bao Dai. It was explicitly to be concerned with the development of agriculture, commerce, and industry in the central highlands (PMS) as well as with the improvement of living standards, i.e., education, health, workers' needs, youth organizations, and sports. The decree called for a membership composed of four French, four Vietnamese, and four highlanders in addition to six supplementary members (two from each group).[64]

---

63. Nguyen Thieu Nguyen, "Dalat ville de rêve," *Indochine Sud Est Asiatique*, no. 30 (1954), pp. 36–42.

64. Sa Majesté Bao Dai, Chef de l'Etat, *Ordonné No. 25, QT-TD*, Dalat, 11 February 1952, personal papers of Touneh Han Dang, Saigon.

The highlanders named to the council were two Chru leaders, Touneh Han Dang (4.1) and Banahria Ya Hau (4.8), the old Jarai leader Nay Nui (2.11), and his son-in-law Nay Moul (2.17). There also was a Rhadé named Y Ju. Ton That Hoi, the mandarin who had been Quan Dao at Ban Me Thuot and who had been tried by the Viet Minh, was made president of the council. Among the French members were four planters, and the Vietnamese members included one entrepreneur.

At the first meeting, held on 11 May 1952 at Ban Me Thuot in the presence of Minister of the Crown Nguyen De, the first matter discussed was the problem of recruitment of Vietnamese labor for the highland estates. It was agreed that the highlanders could not supply the needed labor, so a commission would be appointed to study the possibility of finding laborers in Tonkin. "Social matters" included discussion of sanitation problems in the plantations and the housing of war refugees in the highlands.[65]

On 16 December 1952 the Economic and Social Council met at the Hotel du Lac in Dalat, with Han Dang, Ya Hau, Hiou, and Nay Moul present. The subjects on the agenda included the creation of a cadastral service in the highlands, collection of statistics (particularly census data on the highlanders), reorganization of the agricultural and economic services, diffusion of the Vietnamese language, and the matter of labor for the plantations. Regarding this last item, the secretary general of the Planters' Association reported that on a recent trip to Nhatrang he had received approval from the local authorities to recruit Vietnamese war refugees for plantation labor. Han Dang interjected that the highlanders were willing to work on the estates but would have to receive the same pay as the Vietnamese and have proper work contracts specifying such things as daily rice allotment, a grass hat, blankets, clothes, and a sleeping mat. Other highlanders seconded this proposal, and the council agreed.[66]

In 1952 the first American aid program was organized in the highlands. During an interview in Washington in November 1976, Dr. Herman Marshall recalled how in 1952 he organized a public health program in Dalat under the sponsorship of the American Special Technical and

65. Jeannin, *Procès-verbal de la Session inaugurale du Conseil Economique et Social des P.M.S. tenue à Banmethuot le 11 Mai 1952*, Ban Me Thuot, 11 May 1952, personal papers of Touneh Han Dang, Saigon.

66. Jeannin, *Procès-verbal des séances du Conseil Economique et Social des P.M.S., Session du 4ème trimestre 1952, Dalat, 26 Décembre 1952*, personal papers of Touneh Han Dang, Saigon.

Economic Mission (the name of the aid program at that time). He and another public health doctor took up residence in Dalat, visiting Kontum, Pleiku, and Ban Me Thuot to establish programs for nursing training, public hygiene, village health projects, and the use of basic medicines such as aspirin, iodine, and malaria pills.

While the French continued to rely on the "Bao Dai solution" in their political struggle, the Viet Minh underwent some political changes. The Communist party, officially dissolved on 11 November 1945, continued a clandestine existence and grew in numbers. On 3 March 1951 at a congress held in Viet Minh-controlled territory, Truong Chinh announced the formation of the Lao Động Đảng (Workers party), a new label for the Communist party. At the same time the Viet Minh attempted to broaden its political base by merging with the Lien Viet, the national front that had been formed in 1946. The Viet Minh radio now claimed that eight million people were in the new front.[67]

Early in 1953 the Viet Minh mustered all six available battalions of regular troops in Quang Ngai province and moved them into the uplands between Kontum and An Khe where the 4th Division elements were dispersed in a dozen posts supported by artillery. Much of the Vietnamese population in this area was already heavily infiltrated by the Viet Minh. After a diversionary attack in the vicinity of Kontum on 13 and 14 January, the Viet Minh struck at the 4th Infantry Division posts. Those at Thu Thuy and Cuu An were penetrated, and two companies of the 4th Division sent to aid these posts were ambushed with heavy losses. The defenders of the post at Kannak, realizing that they were threatened with encirclement, evacuated to An Khe. On the 21st, the post at Deo Mang on Route 19 retreated, after putting their artillery out of order. Finally on 24 January the French sent in three battalions of parachutists and an artillery unit, and by February 6, with the aid of additional reinforcements and air support, the tide began to turn as the Viet Minh moved back into the mountains. Marchand points out that the success of the Viet Minh in their initial attacks illustrated the extent to which a *pourissement* (rotting away) had taken place along Route 13 between An Khe and Kontum.[68]

By 1953 there was growing antiwar sentiment in Paris. In May the government of René Mayer fell, and a month later Joseph Laniel, a

---

67. Buttinger, *Political History*, pp. 335–37; Hammer, *Struggle for Indochina*, pp. 252–54.

68. Marchand, *L'Indochine en Guerre*, pp. 265–66; idem, *Le Drame Indochinois* (Paris: J. Peyronnet & Cie., 1952), pp. 207–09.

conservative Independent, was elected premier. He named Maurice Dejean high commissioner, and Marc Jacquet became secretary of state in charge of relations with the Associated States of Indochina. On 3 July Laniel informed the three states that France was prepared to "perfect" their independence and offered to turn over to them the various functions that remained in the hands of the French.

The results of this move varied in Indochina. Norodom Sihanouk, head of the Cambodian government, negotiated a military accord with the French. On 22 October, King Sisavang Vong of Laos signed a treaty of friendship and association with France. Laos was recognized as a "fully independent and sovereign state," and its government reaffirmed its membership in the French Union. In Vietnam an announcement by Bao Dai and Nguyen Van Tam that they soon would enter into negotiations with the French precipitated a burst of political activity. On 6 September 1953 a group of Vietnamese nationalists convened a Congress of National Unity and Peace in Cholon. Among the organizers were Ngo Dinh Nhu (younger brother of Ngo Dinh Diem), Madame Huynh Cong Bo (mother of Huynh Phu So, founder of the Hoa Hao religious movement), and Pham Cong Tac (leader of the Cao Daist Tam Ky sect, centered in Tay Ninh). The congress called for unconditional independence for Vietnam, the immediate summoning of a national assembly, freedom of the press, and reforms in the army and administration.[69]

The strong stand taken at this congress prompted Bao Dai to call a similar gathering of his own in October. Of the 200 seats, political parties were given 15, Cao Daists 17, Hoa Hao and Catholics 15 each, Binh Xuyen 9, Buddhists 5, and the highlanders 5 seats. According to Nay Moul, who at this time was serving as a sous-lieutenant in the 4th Division, he and R'mah Bar represented Pleiku province, Kontum was represented by Phem (1.17), and Y Ut Nie Buon Rit (the first highland schoolteacher) was the delegate from Darlac. The congress met for two days and chose 20 men from whom Bao Dai would select a delegation of 6 to carry on negotiations with the French.[70]

On 20 November 1953 General Navarre launched Operation Castor to recapture the post at Dien Bien Phu in the remote uplands of northwestern Vietnam. The Viet Minh abandoned the post, but at the same time the

69. Hammer, *Struggle for Indochina*, pp. 300–07.
70. Nguyen Phut Tan, *A Modern History of Vietnam (1802–1954)* (Saigon: Khai Tri, 1964), pp. 601–02.

French gave up Lai Chau, which the Viet Minh immediately occupied. They then began construction of a road from their supply depots near the Chinese border down to Lai Chau, terminating at Tuan Giao just northeast of Dien Bien Phu. By January 1954 the Viet Minh had completed the encirclement of the valley where the Dien Bien Phu post was located.[71]

FRENCH DEFEAT IN THE HIGHLANDS

Although very much overshadowed by the drama unfolding at Dien Bien Phu, the events in the central highlands at this time had considerable effect on the course of the Indochina War. It was noted previously that in the early 1950s the Viet Minh had been building up its forces in the region north of Kontum. Vigneras points out that during this time the Viet Minh had formed units of highlanders sympathetic to their cause, and the French found them to be formidable opponents.[72] In February 1953 the Viet Minh 325th Division was formed in the mountains near An Khe and began to operate in conjunction with smaller units in the region. This resulted in a steady contraction of French-controlled areas. Fall observed that the strategic value of the highlands became clear at this juncture: Viet Minh control of the central highlands would render a prolonged defense of southern Laos impossible as well as open Cambodia to Viet Minh invasion.[73] At the same time it would put the Viet Minh in a position to threaten French enclaves at Hue, Tourane, and Nhatrang.

In December 1953 the French high command began to strip the central highlands of French forces as the buildup took place at Dien Bien Phu. This left the 4th Division, the widely dispersed Maquis units, and the Vietnamese Mobile Group 11 (based in An Khe) to defend the entire region. The northern anchor of the defense perimeter was Kontum, and there was a string of posts from Dak To to Plateau Gi. Ban Me Thuot formed the southern anchor of defense. In order to reinforce the existing units, the French decided to redeploy Mobile Group 100 from Saigon to the highlands. This group had been formed on 15 November 1953 of some French battalions that had fought with the U.S. Army in Korea, in addition to several commando units, two Vietnamese companies, an

71. Buttinger, *Political History*, pp. 352–53.
72. Vigneras, "Montagnards," p. 9.
73. Fall, *Street without Joy*, p. 169.

artillery regiment, and an infantry battalion of the 43rd Colonial Infantry (a mixed unit made up of seasoned French and Cambodian troops).[74] According to Y Pem Knuol (who at this time was serving in the 5th Battalion of the 4th Division), the 1st, 2nd, and 3rd Infantry Battalions in Mobile Group 100 were composed of highlanders (this is not mentioned by Fall or other authors) recruited after the group reached the mountains. Most of these troops were Rhadé, Jarai, Bahnar, Sedang, and Chil. By 17 December 1953 Mobile Group 100 had begun operating in the vicinity of Buon Ho, along Route 14 north of Ban Me Thuot.

At this time the Viet Minh made a sudden thrust into central Laos. On 20 December two Viet Minh regiments moved from the vicinity of Vinh across mountain paths into Laos where they attacked and captured the Mekong river town of Thakhek. This in effect severed north-south communications and isolated the French air base at Seno, east of Savannakhet, necessitating its resupply by air. On 4 January 1954 the Viet Minh began launching assaults on Seno but were continually repulsed. To reinforce the garrison at Seno, a French mobile group was dispatched from Hue. However, as it moved over Route 9 through the Ai Lao pass—the ancient invasion corridor—it was ambushed and almost wiped out.[75]

Meanwhile, Pathet Lao and Viet Minh forces were on the move in the highlands of southern Laos. On 30 December 1953 they defeated a French battalion in the vicinity of Attopeu on the Boloven plateau and occupied the town. Following this, the Viet Minh 108th Regiment moved into the area north of Kontum, overrunning a string of French outposts. At the same time the 803rd Regiment swung farther southeast to menace the town of Cheo Reo and French positions along the Apa river. On 1 January 1954 Mobile Group 100 was sent to reinforce Cheo Reo, arriving four days later.[76]

On 20 January 1954 General Navarre launched large-scale Operation Atlante, aimed at clearing the coastal area of Viet Minh elements. According to Y Pem Knuol, Mobile Groups 41 and 42 (composed of highland personnel) were formed at this time to participate in the operation. The main force, made up of French and Vietnamese units and Mobile Group 41, staged at Nhatrang and then began moving up Route 1 (the

74. Ibid., pp. 169–70.
75. Marchand, *L'Indochine en Guerre*, pp. 300–01.
76. Fall, *Street without Joy*, pp. 172–73; Vo Nguyen Giap, *Dien Bien Phu* (Hanoi: Foreign Language Publishing House, 1964), pp. 68–69.

Mandarin Route) along the coast. The Viet Minh used small units to harass the French, and it took six weeks for the main force to reach Qui Nhon. Meanwhile Mobile Group 100 was ordered to open Route 7 between Cheo Reo and Tuy Hoa. They made slow progress due to land mines and destroyed bridges, finally reaching the coast on 28 January.[77]

General Vo Nguyen Giap writes that, when Operation Atlante began, the Viet Minh in the Fifth Zone (part of which was affected by the operation) moved their main forces into the highlands where the French forces were relatively depleted.[78] On 26 January 1954 they launched their offensive, overrunning the Mandel subsector north of Kontum city. On the 28th the 1st Korea Battalion of Mobile Group 100 was ordered to reinforce Pleiku, while two rifle companies and one battery of the 2nd Korea Battalion were sent to Kontum. By 1 February, however, the situation around Kontum had become grave. The Viet Minh captured Dak To, north of the city. According to Fall, the highland Maquis in the area put up no resistance either because they withdrew into the forest or (probably because of Viet Minh propaganda) turned on their French officers.[79] At Kon Brai, northeast of Kontum, a patrol of the 2nd Korea Battalion fell into an ambush and was almost completely destroyed. All of Mobile Group 100 was ordered to Kontum.

On 2 February the Viet Minh attacked all of the French positions around Kontum, and in spite of air support from Nhatrang and Seno most of the posts were captured. The Viet Minh 803rd Regiment was rapidly encircling the city, blowing up bridges on Route 14. The French high command elected not to defend Kontum, and on 7 February all French civilians and Vietnamese civil servants were evacuated. Mobile Group 100 remained at Pleiku, which now became the northern perimeter of the defense system.[80]

Pierre Yuk recalled that the French evacuation sent a wave of fear through the town, and the highlander civil servants (like himself) gathered their families to flee across the Bla river into the surrounding villages. Schoolteacher Hiu (1.16) added that three French priests went into the forest with some of the highlanders. Two of them were Father Brish (who later was at Kon Horing) and Father Renaud (who returned to France).

77. Fall, *Street without Joy*, pp. 172–73.
78. Giap, *Dien Bien Phu*, pp. 69–70.
79. Fall, pp. 174–75.
80. Ibid., pp. 175–76.

Until the cease-fire the following July, they and the refugees subsisted on bamboo shoots and wild plants. Hiu pointed out that there were few highlanders among the Viet Minh troops that occupied the town; most were Vietnamese from Quang Ngai province. Quang Van Hoang, their commander (also from Quang Ngai), became province chief. Hiu noted that their most intensive activity was a propaganda campaign against the French. (At the time of the Geneva Conference, they organized a large anti-French demonstration.)

Bahnar leader Hiar (1.7) said that in April 1954 Nay Der (2.12), the talented schoolteacher from Cheo Reo who had followed the Viet Minh in 1946, appeared in Kontum, staying for three days at the house of the Bahnar leader Mohr, who had died in 1945. He invited all the local highland leaders to attend a pig sacrifice in the front yard of the house. There, under the watchful eye of the Viet Minh guards, Nay Der extolled the virtues of the Viet Minh movement while all drank from the jars.

General Giap assesses the significance of the fall of Kontum in the following passage:

> The Kontum victory was another great success of our army and people in the Winter-Spring campaign. In the Fifth Zone, we foiled the threat of the enemy upon the rear of Quang Nam and Quang Ngai provinces, liberated the whole of the important strategical base in the north of the Western Highlands. Our free zone ran from Quang Nam and Quang Ngai sea coast to the Vietnam-Laos frontier, linked with the liberated southwestern part of the Boloven Highland of friendly Laos.[81]

Colonel Barrou, commander of Mobile Group 100, settled on a plan to expand the Pleiku perimeter so as to avoid crowding his troops into an area too small to allow maneuver. The command post was established at the sprawling Catecka tea plantation near Pleiku, and reinforcements were sent to Dak Doa, northeast of the town. Artillery was dispatched eastward to the vital Mang Yang pass, through which Route 19 runs on its way to the coast. Additional units (Vietnamese Mobile Group 11 and the Highlander Mobile Group 42) were massed at Pleiku. Meanwhile the Viet Minh continued its offensive, and two companies of their 803rd Regiment ambushed a patrol of the 2nd Korea Battalion, inflicting heavy casualties. On 11 February the Viet Minh made a thrust at Dak Doa, and the following day a relief column of two reinforced platoons from Mobile

81. Giap, p. 70.

Group 11 was sent to aid the post. It was ambushed on the road by a strong Viet Minh force, and when elements of Mobile Group 42 went to the rescue they too were assaulted by the Viet Minh. Both French units lost heavily, and on 17 February the Viet Minh overwhelmed the garrison at Dak Doa with a loss of eighty French troops, including three officers and fifty highlander Maquis.[82]

Meanwhile, at Dien Bien Phu, it was clearly Giap's intention to have a showdown with the French, and Navarre made the decision to accept the challenge. The battle of Dien Bien Phu began on 13 March 1954 with five days of strong Viet Minh artillery fire, followed by massive ground assaults on the French positions. The fierce fighting lasted until mid-afternoon 7 May when the Viet Minh attacked the remaining French concentration and white flags appeared everywhere. By 5:30 P.M. de Castries' headquarters was occupied.[83]

While these military events were taking place in Vietnam, international interest in a negotiated settlement to the war was rising rapidly. By the beginning of 1954 antiwar sentiment in France was very widespread, and individuals and groups of all political stripes clamored for an end to the fighting. Even with heavy American military aid to the French forces in Indochina, the cost of the war was seriously retarding the postwar economic recovery of France. Military costs in Indochina constituted more than 10 percent of the French national budget and 33.5 percent of its military budget. In 1953, with the United States paying almost half the cost of the war, the expenses of the French remained nearly as high as they had been in 1952. The initial steps for a conference to negotiate a peace were taken when the Big Four—Great Britain, the United States, France, and Russia—met late in January 1954 at Berlin to seek a solution to the East-West conflict over Germany.

That same month Bao Dai named his cousin Prince Buu Loc, a noted scientist, prime minister and they announced that they would negotiate with France for recognition of the "total independence" of Vietnam. In Saigon, nationalist groups called for the French to quit Vietnam so that the American-supported Vietnamese Army could carry on the fight against the Viet Minh. In April, Bao Dai went to Paris to convince the French leaders that they must save anti-Viet Minh nationalism from total extinc-

---

82. Fall, pp. 174–79; Vigneras, "Montagnards," p. 9.
83. Giap, pp. 110–36.

tion. Nothing came of these efforts, as the French were already thinking in terms of partition and had ideas about retaining some measure of control over the non-Viet Minh part of Vietnam. It was agreed by the great powers that late in April a conference would be held to discuss reunification of Korea and Indochina. The Geneva Conference convened on 26 April 1954 with nine states represented: France, the United States, Britain, the Soviet Union, the People's Republic of China, Cambodia, Laos, Bao Dai's State of Vietnam, and Ho Chi Minh's Democratic Republic of Vietnam. Initial discussion centered on the reunification of Korea, but this was put aside, and on 8 May, twenty-four hours after the garrison at Dien Bien Phu had surrendered, the conference began focusing on the subject of Indochina.[84]

While the discussions went on in Geneva, the war continued. Navarre informed Paris that in order to avoid a military disaster 30,000 additional troops were needed; between 1 May and the end of June only 9,000 new troops were sent from France. On 18 May, Generals Ely, Salan, and Pelissier arrived in Saigon with a plan for Navarre to concentrate his forces at Haiphong, which, in effect, would leave Hanoi and the Red river delta in Viet Minh hands. Knowing that the French were spread thinly, the Viet Minh attacked everywhere. The month of May, however, was quiet in the highlands because Operation Atlante, which had been halted in March, began again, and this drew Viet Minh forces to the coastal plain. But during the third week of June the French high command, anticipating a major Viet Minh assault on An Khe, ordered it abandoned. All of the forces there were to pull back to Pleiku. An airlift was organized to fly out some equipment and many civilians, but Mobile Groups 11 and 100 were to return to Pleiku via Route 19, a distance of 80 kilometers.

Mobile Group 42 (composed mostly of locally recruited highlanders) and Airborne Group No. 1 took up positions at Mang Yang pass. When reports indicated that a large Viet Minh force (possibly all of the 803rd Regiment) were deploying north of Route 19, Captain Vitasse and his Bahnar Maquis spread out in the area to detect any Viet Minh movement. Early on the morning of 24 June the large convoy moved out of An Khe, and in the afternoon a strong Viet Minh force attacked it, taking heavy casualties. At the Mang Yang pass, Mobile Group 42 received the battered column, and all of the forces now moved in the direction of Pleiku. On 27

84. Buttinger, *Dragon Embattled*, 2: 789–99, 812–13, 824–25; Hammer, *Struggle for Indochina*, pp. 321–22.

June at a point 30 kilometers from Pleiku where the forest gives way to a wide plain, the Viet Minh 108th Regiment, reinforced by the elite 30th Independent Battalion, attacked. As the situation was becoming dire for the French units, B-26 bombers from Nhatrang caught the Viet Minh in the open plain, dropping napalm on them while strafing. The Viet Minh units broke and retreated.

The French units straggled into Pleiku on 29 June. The 1st Korea Battalion had suffered more casualties in five days of fighting on Route 19 than it had in two years of combat in Korea. Nonetheless Mobile Group 100 assumed responsibility for the defense of Pleiku, and its first task was Opération Myosotis (Operation "Forget-Me-Not"), aimed at clearing the Pleiku-Ban Me Thuot section of Route 14. The clearing force consisted of three highlander battalions of Mobile Group 42, the 4th Vietnamese Artillery Group, the 1st Korea Battalion, and a reinforced armored platoon of the 3rd Squadron of the 5th Armored Cavalry. On 4 July the column moved southward. When it reached the Chu Dreh pass it was ambushed, but suddenly the Viet Minh forces scattered into the woods.[85]

At Geneva the discussions were moving in the direction of resolving the political struggle through some kind of partition. It also was becoming increasingly clear that the non-Viet Minh part of Vietnam would have to have a government of nationalists unsullied by any collaboration with the French and that all traces of colonialism would have to be eliminated. It also appeared that the United States would have the task of supporting any new nationalist regime. On 3 June representatives of France and the Bao Dai government initiated a treaty which recognized Vietnam as "a fully independent and sovereign state." On 16 June, Bao Dai accepted the resignation of Prince Buu Loc and invited nationalist Ngo Dinh Diem to form a new government. Diem accepted, and the new government became official on 7 July 1954. Meanwhile in France the Laniel government fell on 12 June. The new cabinet was headed by Pierre Mendès-France, who for years had denounced French policy in Indochina, advocating direct negotiations with the Viet Minh.

By early July the Geneva conference had reached a point where a settlement on the basis of partition had become certain. Diem received the news with a shock, since he apparently believed the National Army capable of continuing the war once the French withdrew. His foreign

85. Fall, *Street without Joy*, pp. 189–222.

minister, Dr. Tran Van Do, the representative at Geneva, called the decision "catastrophic and immoral." When they were concluded, the Geneva Agreements consisted of two parts. The first was devoted to the implementation of a cease-fire, and it was the only document signed at Geneva—signed by military representatives of the French and Viet Minh. The cease-fire provided for a "temporary" division of Vietnam at the 17th parallel with regroupment of the Viet Minh in the north and the French in the south within 300 days. Any civilian who desired to move from one zone to the other would be allowed to do so before 18 May 1955. Execution of the cease-fire would be achieved by an International Control Commission (ICC) composed of representatives of India, Canada, and Poland. The chairman was to be an Indian.

The second part of the agreements, the Final Declaration, consisted of a formal endorsement of the stipulations for ending the hostilities. It also attempted to spell out how the cease-fire provided for in the first part would come to an end, specifying that the military demarcation line at the 17th parallel was to be provisional and not to be considered a political or territorial boundary. This would be done through general elections to be held on 21 July 1956 "in order to insure that sufficient progress in the restoration of peace has been made, and that all the necessary conditions obtain for the expression of the national will." This section mentioned "competent representative authorities," but it did not make clear who they might be in the south. No representatives signed this part of the agreements. On 21 July 1954 the final session of the Geneva Conference was held. It marks the day the Indochina War ended.[86]

In spite of the armistice, some fighting continued in parts of the central highlands, due, according to the Viet Minh, to the poor communications between some scattered units and their regional command. Positions of Mobile Group 100 at Pleiku were attacked on 27 July and an outpost on Route 19 was shelled. Finally, on 1 August 1954 the cease-fire became effective. On 13 August the remnants of Mobile Group 100 moved from Saigon to Cap St. Jacques, and on 1 September the group was dissolved. The Indochina War had now ended in the highlands.[87]

The peace that came to the highlands in the wake of the Geneva Agreements soon proved to be only an interlude, a brief cease-fire as

86. Buttinger, *Dragon Embattled*, 2: 824–39.
87. Fall, *Street without Joy*, p. 222.

provided for in the only document that was signed at the conference. The Communists who now controlled that part of Vietnam north of the 17th parallel had not attained their goal of a unified nation, and their efforts at fulfillment would soon lead to a new phase of guerrilla warfare that would spread like a lengthening shadow in the highlands. It was only a matter of time before the violence of war would again return to the highlands, but no one dreamed in 1954 that it would take on the fury that it did.

At the same time, the period following the Geneva Agreements would be one marked by a heightened sense of highlander ethnic identity. A consolidation of leadership was rapidly taking place as younger members of elite families established contact and intermarried. Among them there increasingly was the realization that the "sons of the mountains," the highland people, were one, with a common past, pride, and identity. It soon became apparent, however, that the Ngo Dinh Diem government in Saigon regarded the highland people as a somewhat insignificant and bothersome "ethnic minority" that would have to be assimilated into the Vietnamese cultural sphere so that national integration could be realized. The result was the Unified Struggle Front for the Oppressed Races, an ethnonationalist movement that persisted through the devastation of the Vietnam War and exists today in the face of the authoritarian Communist regime's attempts to achieve what Ngo Dinh Diem failed to do.

APPENDIX A

Highland Population Figures

A 1921 census in the French protectorate of Annam where most highlanders were located—there were some in Cochinchina—reported a total of 405,888.[1] It also revealed that in Darlac province there were 5 French and 20 Vietnamese and in Kontum province 27 French and 7,000 Vietnamese. Lang Bian province had 24 French and 600 Vietnamese; Haut Donnai province had 20 French and 500 Vietnamese.

The highlander population of Darlac in 1921 was reported to be 98,000. In 1930, however, Monfleur estimated that the highlander population was closer to 150,000.[2] In 1931 a French government source reported for the first time that the highlander population in the colony of Cochinchina was 100,000, all in the eastern uplands.[3]

In 1943 an official census gave a total of one million highlanders.[4] It also listed the Vietnamese population in the highlands as 42,267: the distribution was 4,000 in Darlac; 10,000 in Haut Donnai; 7,000 in Kontum; 21,000 in Pleiku; and 267 in Dalat. The French population totaled 5,090, concentrated mostly in Darlac (199), Haut Donnai (141), Kontum (141), Pleiku (70), and Dalat (4,461).[5] In that same year the French administrator

1. Gouvernement Général de l'Indochine, Direction des Affaires Economiques, Service de la Statistique Générale, *Annuaire Statistique de l'Indochine* (Hanoi: Imprimerie d'Extrême-Orient, 1927), 1: 42.

2. A. Monfleur, *Monographie de la province de Darlac* (Hanoi: Imprimerie d'Extrême-Orient, 1931), p. 32.

3. Gouvernement Général de l'Indochine (Société des Etudes Indochinoises), *Cochinchine 1931* (Saigon: P. Géstaldy, 1931).

4. *Annuaire des Etats-Associés: Cambodge-Laos-Vietnam* (Paris: Editions Diloutremer et Havas, 1953).

5. Ministère de l'Economie Nationale, *Annuaire Statistique du Vietnam* (Saigon, Institut de la Statistique et des Etudes Economiques du Vietnam, vol. 1 (1949–1950), 1951, p. 24.

Guilleminet estimated that there were 60,000 Rhadé, 150,000 Jarai, and 80,000 Bahnar—a total of 290,000 for these three largest of the highland groups.[6]

In 1953 the Social Action Plan prepared by the Bao Dai regime used a total of 500,000 for highland people in the Crown Domain (not including the highlanders in central Vietnam or in the Cochinchina area) and stated that there were an estimated 30,000 Vietnamese living there.[7]

6. P. Guilleminet, "Ebauche d'une classification des Moi au point de vue culturel," *Indochine*, no. 169 (1943), p. 26.

7. Nguyen De, *Plan d'action sociale pour les Pays du Sud du Domaine de la Couronne* (Saigon: Editions de la Délégation Impériale du Domaine de la Couronne, 1953).

APPENDIX B
Additional Ethnographic Data

The selection of a site for a new swidden is never haphazard. To judge the relative fertility of the soil, highlanders rely upon a knowledge of the forest and soils passed down through generations. Bru, Katu, and Sedang informants report that they look for black or brown soil, avoiding red soil. On the other hand, the Cua prefer red soil for rice and black soil for maize. The Rhadé also consider red soil good for rice, but they avoid sandy soil. The Rengao judge a greyish soil to be best for upland dry rice. The Bru and Katu also view the presence of large trees to be a sign of soil fertility, as do the Halang and Sedang, who, in addition, regard some species of bamboo to be an indication of good soil. Among the Chrau-speaking people the practice is to feel the soil; if it "sticks together" it is considered good for rice cultivation. The Mnong Chil combine their careful scrutiny of the soil with divination; some of the men sleep on the prospective site, and if they have a "favorable dream" then they will farm the area. Among the Maa of the Blao plateau, the heads of the village households select the site for the communal swidden in which each family will receive a parcel. Eight days before the clearing begins they make a ritual visit to the site, and afterward, if no one has an inauspicious dream or presage of any kind, they will go ahead and farm the area.[1] The Jarai regard the presence of excrement from a certain type of worm as an indication that the soil is suited for rice farming, but if a specific type of monkey abounds in the area it is taboo for agriculture.

1. Jean Boulbet. "Le *miir* culture itinérante avec jachère forestière en pays Maa," *BEFEO* 52, no. 1 (1066): 79–80.

Preparation of the fields takes place during the dry season. For those highlanders located in areas affected by the southwest monsoon this would be in January, February, and March, while for those in the path of the northeast monsoon it would be in June, July, and August. Men fell the trees—large trees are usually left standing—while the women and children cut the brush. The wood is left to dry, and the men rake the debris into piles and burn it. The logs also are set ablaze, and the fires are controlled as much as possible. After the rains have begun and the soil is dampened, the crops are planted. Men make holes with dibble sticks while the women follow to plant the seed. The maturing periods for upland dry rice vary, usually from three to six months. During the growing period the fields are weeded and temporary shelters are constructed nearby to house the young men who protect the crop from marauding animals (particularly porcupines and wild boar). Some of the Maa construct sturdy enclosures around their swiddens.[2]

There are numerous varieties of upland dry rice cultivated by the highlanders. The Stieng have ten different types as do the Sedang, who distinguish them by the color of the husk and kernel. For example, one type of dry rice called *koang* has a yellow husk and white kernel while *khom* has a grey husk and grey kernel. Among some groups the duration of swidden use determines which of the varieties of dry rice will be cultivated. Farming a swidden for three years, the Rhadé Kpa will plant any of the four best types of rice during the first year in the belief that quality rice requires particularly fertile soil. Only one type of lesser quality rice is planted the second year, and the two varieties cultivated in the third year are thought to be better for rice alcohol preparation than for eating.

Swidden use and fallowing periods vary with the fertility of the soil. On the basis of available information, it appears that most highlanders farm their fields from one to three years. The Cua cultivate the swiddens for one year, as do the Bru, unless the soil is adjudged to be very fertile, in which case the period is extended to three years. Three years is normal for the Maa, Roglai, Sedang, Halang, Jarai Arap, Jeh, Bahnar, and Mnong Chil. The Rhadé Kpa cultivate from two to eight years, and Chrau-speaking informants report that some of the farmers in their area use the swiddens from three to ten years. Among most groups, the fallowing period that permits a substantial new growth is around ten years. Cua informants

2. Ibid., p. 81.

report that for them it is six years, and some Sedang and Rengao note that in certain areas north of Kontum city the bamboo that predominates the flora grows rapidly enough to permit recultivation in alternate years.

In recent times, cash-cropping has been on the increase among highlanders located near some of the towns. With experience gained while working on the French-owned coffee estates in Dac Lac province, some of the Rhadé Kpa have established their own small plantations. By 1971 there were 326 registered Rhadé coffee planters with a total of 531 hectares and a median holding of 1.0 hectare per plantation. Their coffee crops are sold to Chinese dealers in Ban Me Thuot who transport the coffee to Saigon. There also are some examples of kitchen gardening evolving into truck gardening. Some of the Chru farmers in the Danhim valley have begun cultivating crops not normally found in highland gardens (such as radishes, artichokes, potatoes, cauliflower, escarole, celery, chinese cabbage, beets, white beans, butter beans, and bean sprouts) for sale in Nhatrang and Phan Rang.

Hunting, trapping, and fishing traditionally have been sources of important food supplements in the highlanders' diets. Some of the game also have been included in the items traded with the lowlanders. In addition to the forest products among the gifts sent by the Cham kings to the Chinese court, Maspéro also reports that there were elephants, rhinoceroses, white quails, peacocks, parrots of variegated colors, as well as ivory and rhinoceros horns. As noted previously, Van Wusthoff recorded that deer skins were among the things the Chinese traders brought back to Sambok. Wild life abounds in the highlands, and informants have provided the names of much of the game they hunt and trap. (Another source is the work on hunting and game in Indochina by de Monestrol, who lists many of the Latin zoological names.[3])

The game includes elephants, tapirs, and several varieties of rhinoceroses (*Rhinoceros sondaicus* and *Rhinoceros sumatrensis*), although no rhinoceroses have been seen since the early 1940s and they are thought to be extinct in the highlands. There also are tigers; leopards; and panthers (*Felis uncia* and *Felis nebulosus*); several kinds of wild oxen, including gaurs and koupreys; various types of bear, among them the black bear and honey bear. Deer are plentiful and include small musk deer and barking deer. Other common game are wild boars, porcupines, jackals, otters, mongooses, hares, skunks,

---

3. H. de Monestrol, *Chasses et faune d'Indochine* (Saigon: Edition A. Portail, 1952), pp. 135–40.

and squirrels, including flying squirrels. Traps are placed near granaries to catch rats, which are roasted and eaten. There are many different kinds of wild cats, and among them are three types of civet—madagascar civets, binturongs, and palm civets. There also are langurs (*Semnopithecus Franciosi, Semnopithecus polyocephalus, Semnopithecus nigripses,* and *Semnopithecus nemoeus*), macaques (*Macacus cynomolgus, Macacus erthoeus,* and *Macacus Harmandii*), gibbons (*Hylabates leucogenys* and *Hylobates pileatus*), and the common Rhesus monkey. Crocodiles are found on the edges of some lakes and rivers, and other reptiles include several kinds of lizard, pythons (*Python molurus, Python reticulatus,* and *Python curtus*), and cobras. There also is a great variety of birds in the highlands, among them numerous kinds of pheasants (including Grey Peacock and Germain's Peacock pheasants), quails, falcons, herons, ducks, hawks, eagles, vultures, harriers, cranes, rails, coots, painted snipes, and owls.[4]

Although the disruptions due to the war have rendered it very difficult for the highlanders to search for forest products (rattan, wood, and bamboo), they still continue producing artifacts, most weapons, tools, mats, baskets, and cloths in the villages. In the past, crossbows, spears, sabers, and knives were used in warfare and in hunting. Now, any highlanders engaged in military activities use modern weapons provided from the outside, but they continue to use crossbows, sabers, and knives in hunting. Although it is expected that a man be able to make a crossbow, there usually are certain men in every village who are considered particularly adept at carving the hardwood and balancing it so as to produce a crossbow of excellence. Small crossbows are for hunting birds and larger ones for stalking big game.

Spears continue to be used for hunting in some of the more remote areas, but among most highlanders they are only carried on ceremonial occasions. Among some groups a buffalo being offered to the spirits is slaughtered with spears and/or sabers, and the Katu use long spears on blood hunts.

Village men make a variety of traps and snares for capturing wild game. They also fashion fish traps of split bamboo and rattan; nets are made in the village or purchased in nearby market towns. Some highlanders use poisons and drugs in both hunting and fishing. The Stieng, for example,

---

4. Philip Wildash, *Birds of South Vietnam* (Rutland, Vermont and Tokyo: Charles E. Tuttle Co., 1968), passim.

are particularly skilled at producing drugs and poisons from roots, leaves, and bark. Stieng informants contend that one of their deadly poisons, which they smear on the top of a large arrowhead, will kill a sizable tiger within minutes. Other preparations will stun animals, which are then captured or killed. The Stieng have periodic group fishing efforts in which all available villagers gather downstream from a point where men squeeze a milky substance from the root of a particular tree into the water. It kills small fish and stuns the larger ones. Laughing and rushing about, men, women, and children with baskets hurriedly gather up the catch which is shared by all.

The artifact most commonly encountered in the highlands is a long-handled ax with a small, very sharp blade used by the men to fell trees, split wood, hew timber, cut and shave rattan, dig out roots in the fields, clear brush, and break earth. Highlanders carry these axes with them as they move through the forest both for protection and for cutting any wild edible fruit or vegetable they may encounter. Village men also make farm tools, including various types of hoes, rakes, and in some cases plows.

Many highland villages have one or more specialists in metalworking, and this métier is especially developed among the Sedang and Halang. Normally the metals are purchased from Vietnamese or Chinese merchants, but during the Vietnam War metals from American army junk piles were used. Also, in some areas, the villagers dug metal out of craters left by artillery shells and aerial bombs. Among many groups, a double-piston bellows is used in forging the metal. These usually consist of two bamboo tubes with plungers fashioned from rags tied to the ends of two sticks to force the air through the tubes into the fire. It is these metalworkers who produce the spearheads, knives, sabers, ax blades, plowshares, and other metal parts of farm tools.

Mats and baskets are made by the men in most highland groups. The mats are used for sleeping, and they are spread on the floor or on wooden beds for guests to sit upon. All highlanders use a type of basket with shoulder straps that permit it to be carried on the back like a knapsack. Since the highlanders rarely use vehicles or beasts of burden, these baskets are the major means of transporting rice, garden produce, firewood, gourds of water for the house, and a host of other things. They also are placed along the walls of the sleeping areas in the houses to store clothes and personal possessions. Flat, round baskets of different sizes have many uses, such as drying rice and other foods and for winnowing. Other baskets are used for preparing, serving, and storing food. Pottery is rare among the highlanders, and what there is tends to be rudimentary.

In addition to taking care of the house and children, women maintain the kitchen gardens and tend the goats, pigs, chickens, and ducks while the men look after the cattle and water buffalos. While an ever-increasing number of highlanders are purchasing cloth, village women continue to weave material for skirts, tops, shirts, loincloths, blankets, and slings for carrying infants. Generally the colors are rich shades of red, blue, and yellow contrasted with black, white, and grey, worked into stripes or geometric motifs. Particularly intricate patterns, each of which has a distinct name, are favored by the Stieng. The Jarai Arap combine traditional designs of such things as deer, fish, lizards, and birds with what one woman described as "the things we see around us." In the early 1970s this included various kinds of helicopters, jet fighter bombers, Americans, and M-16 automatic rifles.[5]

Among some highland groups the services of the talented woodcarvers are sought to produce symbolic designs for the houses and figures to grace the tombs. The Rhadé favor having female breasts on the plank stairway leading to the house and on the central beam of the house frame along with a buffalo horn design. The Katu house carvings include hunting and fishing scenes, sacred animals, geometric designs, phalli, stylized cocks, toucans, fish, snakes, and iguanas.[6] Around some highland tombs there are carvings depicting humans and animals. Contemporary motifs also inspire some of the woodcarvers. Carvings done in the late 1940s and early 1950s often were of Frenchmen, particularly soldiers, while more recent carvings depict American military personnel, notably those in the Special Forces.

5. Dr. Mattiebelle Gittinger, Research Associate for Southeast Asian Textiles at the Textile Museum, Washington, D.C., did the following analysis of a piece of Jarai Arap cloth.

This is an all cotton textile length which has a tubular form created by continuous warp elements. Its warp-faced plain weave structure contains narrow warp stripes of commercially spun and brightly dyed yarns which alternate with broad bands of black, handspun yarns. Additional colored stripes concentrate about two decorative bands on one edge of the cloth. The commercial yarns of the warp are Z-spun 2-plied-S and the handspun are single Z-spun elements. Black Z-spun 2-plied-S yarns also make up the weft. The outermost decorative band shows a white on black diamond pattern that is created by white yarns interlacing in variable lengths in the manner of 2/2 diamond twill. A second decorative stripe shows multicolored figures on a white ground. These designs are paired supplementary wefts which are continuous through the width of the white band and laid in with the ground weft when not in use. 20 warp/cm. 9 weft/cm. 396 × 68 cm.

6. J. Le Pichon, "Les chasseurs de sang," *Bulletin des Amis du Vieux Hué* 25 (1938): 359–64.

Also, some Jarai tomb carvings are of American military cargo aircraft and jet bombers.

Although their gongs are obtained from the lowland people (see below), the highlanders make all of their other musical instruments, which include a wide range of string and woodwind instruments. The Stieng fabricate "singing kites" that now are made with rattan and paper. A bow, which is tuned by swinging it in a circle, is tied to the bottom of the kite and, as it dips and soars, the wind passing through the bow strings produces pleasant musical sounds.

Items of adornment also are produced in the villages. Brass or copper bracelets are worn by men and women alike; while some highlanders regard them as decorations, others use them to symbolize a betrothment or an alliance between individuals. Ankle bracelets are worn by Stieng women to indicate wealth, and they also wear ivory ear plugs. An ear plug of the mother is rubbed on a newborn female and the father's pipe is rubbed on a male infant while the protection of the spirits is invoked. Lat women distend their ear lobes with large ivory or bone rings, and the women of the Monom have long nail-like earrings. Many highland women wear strings of small multicolored beads, and in some cases they claim that the beads are of unknown origin and have been passed down for many generations, so they are considered extremely valuable. Traditionally, long hair was favored by highland men, and this still is the case with the Stieng and Katu and in more remote villages among other groups. The Stieng continue to make metal combs with which buns are held in place, and among the High Katu, for ceremonial occasions, many men employ combs and sticks to arrange elaborate hairdos reminiscent of Japanese geisha coiffures.

The Bru are the only highland people who blacken their teeth. Both men and women do this using a black lacquer. Tattooing also is found among the Bru and the Katu. Prior to marriage, young Bru men tattoo their foreheads with a row of dots. The Katu favor more elaborate designs such as sunbursts, a dancing woman, a stylized monkey, a Greek cross or a swastika on the forehead, chest, arms, wrists, and above or below the knees.[7]

Historically, the highlanders traded with the lowland people to obtain commodities which they needed but could not produce in the highlands. For garnishing food they desired salt, Vietnamese fish sauce, and soy sauce,

---

7. L. Bezacier, "Notes sur quelques tatouages de Moi 'Ka-tu'," *IIEH* 2 (1942): 117–25.

and they needed metals for making weapons and farm tools. They also traded for various kinds of manufactured items, the most important of which were jars for making alcohol and gongs. Both gongs and jars traditionally have been considered prestige items among the highlanders and reflections of one's wealth. In more recent times most of these desired commodities have been available in Chinese and Vietnamese shops which are part of the market centers. But many highland villages have not been accessible from these towns, and until the mid–1960s it was not uncommon to see small groups of highlanders in coastal market towns selling their wares for cash with which to buy salt, metal, cooking pots, and cloth. In 1957 small bands of Katu were staying at Gordon Smith's World Evangelization Crusade compound in Danang while they made sales and purchases in the market. Often, however, they complained that the Vietnamese would taunt them because of their long hair and their brief loincloths.

Jars for making alcohol vary in size as well as in quality. Generally, the older jars are considered to be of great value and many of them are said to date "from the time of the ancestors." Most of these have a worn dark brown or black glaze, and some would surely command a good price in the world antique market. Occasionally one also encounters large blue and white porcelain jars, some of which also appear to be of value. The Rhadé differentiate between "male" and "female" old jars, and both the Rhadé and Bahnar have myths that describe the ancient jars as once having been live animals that lived in swampy areas. Upon being struck with arrows, they were transformed into jars. Normally the old jars never leave the house, but the Stieng often include highly valued *srung* jars in the bride price, with some resultant movement of these from one family to another. Newer jars usually have a light brown glaze and a dragon motif on the side. They are produced in kilns in coastal cities by the Vietnamese and are shipped to the highlands in trucks.

Jar alcohol normally is produced by fermenting rice, but occasionally some highlanders use maize. During the Vietnam War, it was discovered that the bulgur wheat distributed through the American aid program made quite palatable alcohol. Among the Rhadé Kpa, the first step in alcohol preparation is to mix a ferment (*k'pei*) consisting of white rice flour, wild ginger root, and bark from two kinds of local trees. These ingredients are ground to a powder to which some water is added so as to attain a pasty consistency. The mixture is then rolled into balls about the size of a thumb and placed on a shelf over the cooking hearth to dry. The second step in the process begins with the boiling of partially husked rice, which is then spread on a large circular flat basket and placed on the veranda to dry in the sun. After the cooked rice is dried, some of the ferment is powdered and mixed with it. One piece of ferment is sufficient for a small jar of alcohol but four are needed for a large jar.

In the third phase, a mixture of rice bran and broken husks is placed on the bottom of a deep basket, and the mash of cooked rice and ferment is poured over it. The remainder of the basket is filled with more bran and husks, and the basket is left to stand for at least one day. The contents of the basket are then poured into a jar, which is sealed with banana leaves. A week is considered the minimum period for the mixture to ferment into an acceptable alcohol. With the arrival of the ritual occasion at which the jar of alcohol will be included among the offerings, the banana leaf seal is opened and fresh leaves stuffed into the jar. For the ceremonial drinking, some water is poured into the jar and a bamboo drinking tube inserted for the drinker to draw up the alcohol. Those invited to drink are expected to consume a specified amount; in the past among the Rhadé Kpa the measures used were buffalo horns but now are more likely to be tumblers or beer cans. These measures are filled with water that is poured into the jar as the drinker draws fluid through the bamboo tube, lowering the level.

The rather haunting sound of gongs in a highland village can signal any kind of occasion from a solemn funeral ritual to a joyful fete marking the end of an abundant harvest. The Rhadé Kpa have three types of gongs, all of metal with upturned rims. There is the very large gong called *char* that gives off a resonant sound when struck with the wooden hammer. Smaller in size but similar in appearance are the *knah* gongs that are always used in sets of six, with each gong having a name that indicates its relative size. When they are stored with one inside the other, they form concentric circles. The third type is called *ching*, which has a circular indentation in the center where the gong is struck. These gongs are always found in sets of three and like the *knah* have names to indicate relative size. Informants report that in the past these gongs were obtained in Cambodia and Laos; those made in Cambodia are called *ching kur* while those of Lao manufacture are known as *ching lao*. In recent times the Rhadé have bought only Vietnamese-made gongs (*ching yuan*), which they consider inferior in both strength and sound.

KINSHIP AND MARRIAGE PATTERNS

Matrilineal Descent Groups

Most of the groups with matrilineal descent have exogamous matrilineal clans (i.e., those related through the female line are members of the same clan, identified in these instances by a name and, in some cases, a common food taboo). For members of the same clan to marry is considered incestuous. In addition to having clans regulate marriage, one group, the Rhadé, have two phratries into which all of the clans are grouped, and marriage within each phratry is forbidden. Among all of them there is a preference for marriage with either the mother's brother's daughter (matrilineal cross cousin) or the father's sister's daughter (patrilateral cross cousin) and, after marriage, residence is at the girl's parent's house (matrilocal residence).

On the basis of present research it appears that the kinship systems of the Jarai subgroups vary from east to west. The Jarai Arap and the Jarai Tabuan, both located east of Pleiku city, have bilateral descent systems (which will be discussed later) while the other Jarai subgroups to the east all have matrilineal descent as well as exogamous matrilineal clans, cross-cousin marriage, and matrilocal residence after marriage.

Dournes reports that while there appear to be ten clans among the Jarai—the Kosor, Rahlan, Rocom, Nai, Kopa, Romah, Siu, Roo, Hyao, and Puih (Dournes' transliteration)—the Roo actually are a subclan of the Nei, and the Hyao and Puih are subclans of the Rahlan and Kopa respectively.[8] This would leave seven clans, and most of these are divided into subclans. Within the Nei there are the Roo, Nei-Asuk, Nei-conang, Nei-tobbany. The subclans of the Kopa and Rahlan are indicated above. The Kosor is divided into Kosor-prong (Big Kosor) and Kosor-ddet (Little Kosor), and a similar dichotomy is made within the Siu and Rocom clans. Dournes also reports that the Rocom clan in the area of Cheo Reo originated with the Rocom clan of the Hroy-Cham, which Dournes considers a mixed Cham and Hroy subgroup of the Hroy.[9]

Jarai informants report that the clans found among the subgroups east of Pleiku city are the Siu, Rcom, Ksor, Nay, Rahlan, Romah, Ro-o, Kpa,

8. Jacques Dournes, *Coordonnées structure Jörai familiales et sociales* (Paris: Travaux et Mémoires de l'Institut d'Ethnologie, 1972), pp. 50–55.

9. Jacques Dournes, "Recherches sur le Haut Champa," *France-Asie* 14, no. 2 (1970): 157.

and Puih (these are transliterations according to the Jarai orthography commonly used by the Jarai themselves and will be used throughout this work). They point out that in the vicinity of Pleiku city there also are two small clans—the Hiao and Roban—among the Jarai Hodrung.

These Jarai groups have preferential cross-cousin marriage, and informants note that this usually is matrilateral cross-cousin marriage, i.e., for a boy to marry his mother's brother's daughter (for a girl it would be patrilateral cross-cousin marriage where she marries her father's sister's son). In one sample of twenty-five marriages, Dournes found that eleven (44 percent) adhered to the preference rule.[10] Among these groups residence is matrilocal. They also have the levirate and sororate. As previously stated, levirate rule is that a male is either obliged or expected to marry his older brother's widow. If the younger brother is already married, he can take the widow as a second wife. It is taboo, however, for a man to marry his younger brother's widow. The rules of the sororate are similar, with a girl offering to marry the widower of her deceased older sister.

All of the Rhadé have matrilineal descent and exogamous matrilineal clans. Further, Rhadé clans are organized into two phratries and marriage between those in the same phratry is forbidden. One phratry is called Nie, and the name is equated with the Nay clan among the Jarai so that there is an interdiction against anyone from the Nay clan marrying a member of the Nie phratry. The Rhadé clans that comprise the Nie phratry are the Nie Kdam, Nie Buon Dap (also called Buon Dap), Nie Buon Rit, Nie Blo, Nie Buon Ya, Nie Enuol, Nie Sieng, Nie Trei, Nie Krieng, Nie Ale, Nie Drieng, Nie Ksor (which also is equated with the Ksor clan among the Jarai), Nie Hrah, Nie Adrong, Ecam (equated with the Rcom clan of the Jarai), and Buon To. The other phratry is called Eban, and it is equated with the Rahlan clan of the Jarai, restricting marriage between members of that clan and the Eban phratry. The member clans are the Eban Buon Kang, Eban Buon Lang, Eban Buon Sut, Eban Rahlan, Eban Kat Hla Jue, Hmok, Ayun, Hdrue, Buon Krong (some of which are called Buon Krong Pang), Mlo (one branch of which is called Mlo Duon Du), Hdok, Kbuor, Kdoh, Knul, and Hwing.

With the exception of a taboo against marriages between members of the Buon To and Mlo Duon Du clans, those in the Nie phratry are free to marry anyone from the Eban phratry. As indicated above, each phratry is

---

10. Dournes, *Coordonnées structures Jörai*, pp. 164–65.

exogamous, but for the Eban phratry the rule varies in its rigidity. For example, marriages between any of the Eban clans and the Ayun and Hmok, as well as marriages between the Ayun and Hmok, are allowed if prescribed offerings to the spirits of the ancestors are made.

As among the Jarai, the Rhadé prefer cross-cousin marriage, and there appears to be a predominance of marriage with the mother's brother's daughter (matrilateral cross-cousin marriage). Some informants note that a boy has a close relationship with his mother's brother, particularly her eldest brother, and it is desirable to arrange a marriage with his daughter. In the vicinity of Ban Me Thuot, it is the pattern for males of the Eban clans to marry Nie Kdam females. The first overtures for courtship are made by the girl's parents through an intermediary, and they must pay a dowry before the marriage. Residence is at the girl's longhouse, where the couple occupies one of the compartments. The Rhadé have the levirate and the sororate.

Like the Jarai and Rhadé, the Chru have matrilineal descent and exogamous matrilineal clans. Informants list some thirteen clans: the Touneh, Touprong, Yolong Prong, Yolong Ade, Banahia, Sahao, Charau-Ale, Kobao-Vonu (Fighting Buffalo), Mohi, Chru-Yang, Gonong-Sang (House Post), Yango, and Yanang-Roc. In addition to having corporate functions such as mutual aid and mutual hospitality, all members of the same clan in a village are buried in a common tomb.

According to Touneh Han Tho, until 1962, when most of the Chru became Catholics, it was traditional for all males to marry their father's sister's daughter (patrilateral cross-cousin). Fuller and Boju Jrang note that this pattern, which also means that a female marries her mother's brother's son (matrilateral cross-cousin), is reflected in the kin terminology.[11] The kin terminology also reveals the Chru preference for exchange marriage wherein a brother and sister of one family marry a sister and brother of another family. Chru informants point out that residence is matrilocal for the eldest daughter and her husband, but the other daughters and their spouses only reside matrilocally for a limited period, after which they establish their own households nearby. When the parents are advanced in age, they normally leave the maternal house to go and live with the youngest daughter.

---

11. E. Fuller and Boju Jrang, "Cross-Cousin Marriage as Revealed in Chru Kinship Terminology," mimeographed, Summer Institute of Linguistics (Saigon, 1974), pp. 1–22.

Patrilineal Descent Groups

All of the highland groups with patrilineal descent have languages of the Mon Khmer stock. The Bru, Pacoh, and Katu languages are of the Katuic branch, while the Cua language is of the North Bahnaric branch, and the Stieng and Maa languages are of the South Bahnaric branch.

The Bru have patrilineages (*sau*) that are traced through an indefinite number of ascending generations, and membership includes all of those who are related through the male line. According to informants, each patrilineage is known by the name of the head, who is selected by the adult members of the patrilineage. For example, one informant was a member of *sau achua Angi* or "patrilineage of the grandfather of Angi." The head of the patrilineage has the title Cuai Yong Asiau or "the Person Who Possesses the Blocks," a reference to two blocks flat on one side and rounded on the other. One of the functions of the head is to make the prescribed offerings to the spirits of the ancestors, and these blocks are used in a divination ritual to determine whether the offerings have been accepted by the ancestral spirits. In addition to accepting donations from members of the patrilineage for these ritual offerings, the head also maintains a spirit house (*dong soc*), a small model of a Bru house. On the death of a member of the patrilineage, the head places a stick in the spirit house, and periodically there is a large celebration to make a final offering to the ancestors represented by the collection of sticks. If the divination block ritual indicates that the offerings are accepted, the head burns the spirit house, after which a new spirit house is prepared and the cycle is renewed.

Miller reports that the Bru also have kindreds that extend an individual's kin ties to other clans through marriage; members of those clans from which the members of an individual's clan have taken wives are referred to by him as *cuya*, and members of those clans whose members have taken wives from his clan are referred to as *khoi*.[12] Relations with those who are cuya and khoi involve such things as mutual assistance in house construction or the accumulation of a bride price and, in times of stress, the procurement of food. Both clan and kindred regulate marriage. It is forbidden to marry within the clan. Nor can a man marry any member of a clan with which he has a khoi relationship. The preference is for a boy to marry his mother's brother's daughter, but Miller notes that this occurs infrequently. It is forbidden, however, to marry the father's sister's daugh-

---

12. John Miller, "Bru Kinship," *SA* 2, no. 1 (1972): 62–70.

ter. After marriage the couple either resides at the boy's house or constructs a new house nearby.

Information from Katu informants indicates that they have patrilineal descent and patrilineages (*kabuh hama*), the members of which occupy one longhouse in a village. There also appear to be kindreds similar to those found among the Bru and Pacoh. The term *shuhya* designates members of those patrilineages from which males in one's patrilineage have taken wives, while the term *cha chaau* indicates members of those patrilineages into which females of one's patrilineage have married. There is a preference for a boy to marry his mother's brother's daughter, and residence is patrilocal. The Katu have the levirate and sororate, but neither is obligatory.

According to Boulbet, the Maa have patrilineal descent and two kinds of lineages (*nao*)—the great lineages (*nao kuang*) and small lineages (*nao koon*)—and there are some families unaffiliated with any lineage (*cau goe*).[13] The great lineages are those that trace their ancestry to primordial times when the universe was coming into being, and their genealogies are preserved in poetic chants that are sung on ritual occasions. Their "hero ancestors" (*paang*) are associated with a pantheon of supernatural beings who were involved in the origin of the universe. The head of a great lineage (*cau kuang*) is what Boulbet calls a "*personnage important*" in that he is expected to be an individual highly motivated to maintain the lineage as a viable social group, and he also must have the economic means to continue the lineage religious functions. This involves maintaining a lineage altar (*nao*, the same word for "lineage"), at which prescribed rituals are held. The lineage head also is the keeper of the magic plants and the sacred stones that symbolize lineage continuity as well as a special alliance with the *krong*, which are spirits associated with the village territory.

In these great lineages the role of the chief normally passes from father to son, but if the individual succeeding to the role is not of the right character it goes to another son. Should it happen that the lineage head has no male offspring, it is possible to arrange a marriage between the chief's eldest daughter and the youngest son in another great lineage. This son is adopted into the lineage and he can assume the role of lineage head. Boulbet points out that these great lineages function as an aristocracy with "clients" from

---

13. Jean Boulbet, *Pays des Maa domaine des génies Nggar Maa, Nggar Yaang* (Paris: Ecole Française d'Extrême-Orient, 1967), pp. 132–37.

the small lineages or those families without lineages. Traditionally, it was the members of the great lineages who led the Maa in war.

The small lineages do not trace their lineages beyond a few ascending generations, and many of them tend to fragment. Unlike the great lineages, they do not have the genealogical chants and scrupulously observed rituals that reiterate ancestral affiliations.

Bilateral Descent Groups

The ethnic groups with bilateral descent are the Bahnar, Rengao, Sedang, Halang, Jeh, and Hre—all of whom have languages of the North Bahnaric branch of the Mon Khmer family—and the Austronesian-speaking Tabuan and Arap, subgroups of the Jarai.

The Bahnar have bilateral descent, and it is forbidden to marry anyone related through the great grandparents. When a marriage has been agreed upon, the families exchange gifts, and Jolong informants report that following the wedding the couple will remain at the girl's house for two years, after which they reside at the boy's house. Bahnar Golar informants describe residence as initially patrilocal and then matrilocal. Among all the Bahnar groups the couple eventually remain with the boy's or girl's parents, depending on where their presence is needed, or establish their own household (neolocal residence). The descent rules and marriage patterns among the Rengao, Sedang, and Halang are very similar to those of the Bahnar. All have bilateral descent, and Rengao informants report that it is taboo to marry any consanguineal kin, so the grandparents on both sides are consulted first in order to ascertain that no blood relationship exists. The Sedang are forbidden to marry any kin with the same grandparents, while among the Halang there is an interdiction against marrying anyone related through the great, great grandparents. As among the Bahnar, in all three groups postmarriage residence is temporarily ambilocal, after which the couple settles with the boy's or girl's parents if they do not establish their own household.

Unlike the other Jarai subgroups described already, the Arap and Tabuan have neither matrilineal descent nor exogamous matrilineal clans. Rather, they both have bilateral descent. There are no family names, and informants indicate that it is taboo to marry "close kin," i.e., kin whose consanguineal affiliation can be traced. Residence after marriage is determined by whether it is more advantageous for the couple to remain with the boy's or girl's parents.

Lai Chau

Ha Tuyen

Bac Thai

Cao Lang

Hoang Lien Son

Quang Ninh

Vinh Phu

Ha Bac

Son La

Hanoi

Hai Hung

Ha Son Binh

Haiphong

Thai Binh

Ha Nam Ninh

Thanh Hoa

Nghe Tinh

Binh Tri Thien

17th Parallel (Former DMZ)

Quang Nam-Da Nang

Nghia Binh

Gia Lai-Cong Tum

Phu Khanh

Dac Lac

Song Be

Lam Dong

Tay Ninh

Long An

Thuan Hai

Dong Thap

Dong Nai

An Giang

Ho Chi Minh City (Saigon)

Ben Tre

Ho Chi Minh

Kien Giang

Tien Giang

Hau Giang

Cuu Long

Minh Hai

0   250

KM

1. Provinces of the Socialist Republic of Vietnam

2. Indochinese States

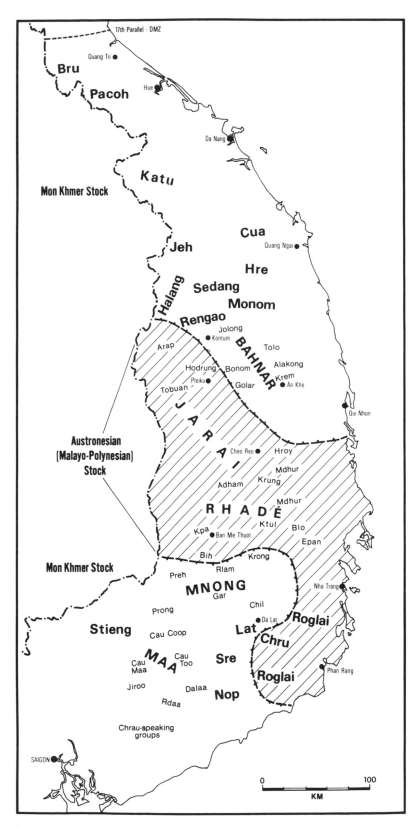

Map labels:

17th Parallel - DMZ

Bru

Pacoh

Quang Tri

Hue

Da Nang

Katu

Mon Khmer Stock

Cua

Jeh

Quang Ngai

Hre

Halang

Sedang

Monom

Rengao

Jolong

Arap

Kontum

Tolo

BAHNAR

Hodrung

Bonom

Alakong

Tobuan

Pleiku

Golar

Krem

An Khe

Qui Nhon

Austronesian
(Malayo-Polynesian)
Stock

J A R A I

Cheo Reo

Hroy

Mdhur

Adham

Krung

Mdhur

R H A D É

Ktul

Blo

Kpa

Ban Me Thuot

Epan

Bih

Krong

Mon Khmer Stock

Preh

Rlam

MNONG

Gar

Nha Trang

Prong

Chil

Roglai

Stieng

Cau Coop

Da Lat

Lat

Chru

MAA

Cau
Too

Sre

Cau
Maa

Jiroo

Dalaa

Nop

Roglai

Phan Rang

Rdaa

Chrau-speaking
groups

SAIGON

0   100

KM

3. Ethnolinguistic Groups

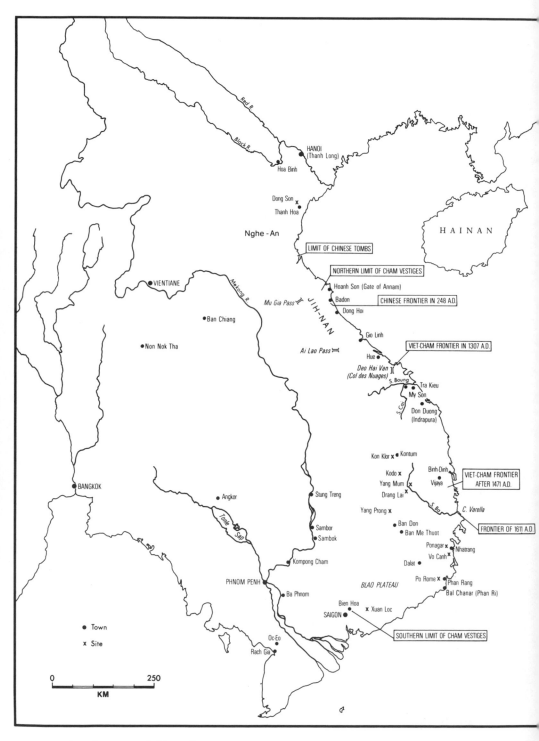

4. Prehistoric and Cham Sites

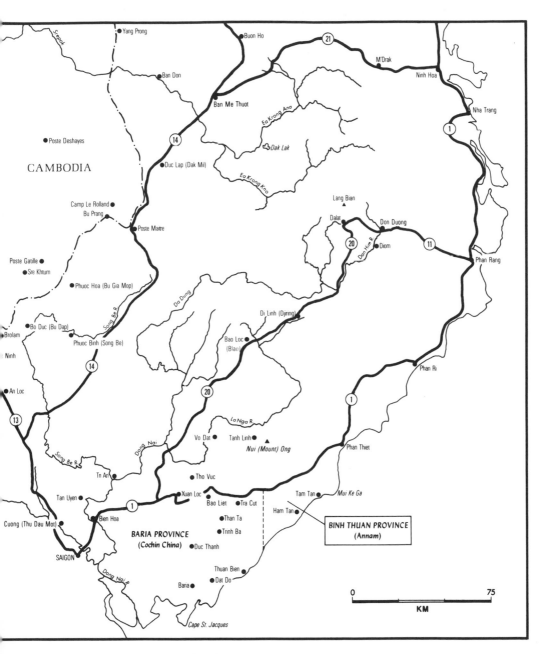

5. Southern Portion of the Highlands

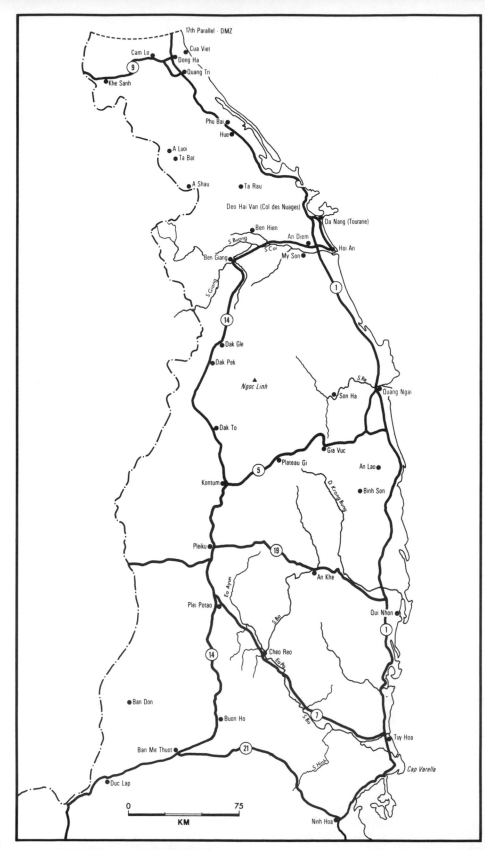

6. Northern Portion of the Highlands

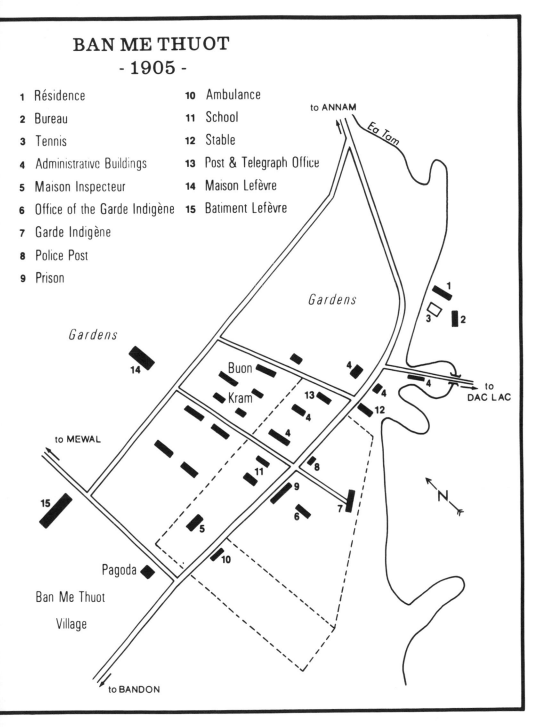

BAN ME THUOT
- 1905 -

1 Résidence
2 Bureau
3 Tennis
4 Administrative Buildings
5 Maison Inspecteur
6 Office of the Garde Indigène
7 Garde Indigène
8 Police Post
9 Prison

10 Ambulance
11 School
12 Stable
13 Post & Telegraph Office
14 Maison Lefèvre
15 Batiment Lefèvre

to ANNAM

Ea Tam

Gardens

Gardens

Buon

Kram

to MEWAL

to DAC LAC

N

Pagoda

Ban Me Thuot

Village

to BANDON

7. Ban Me Thuot, 1905

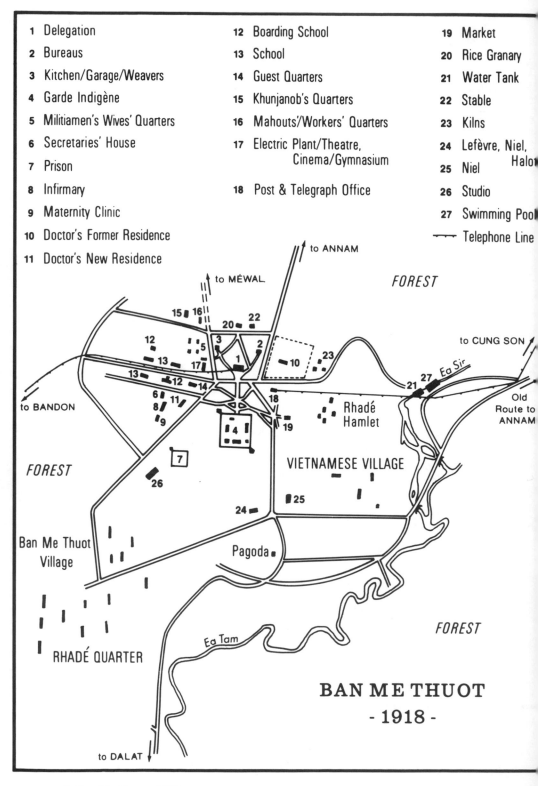

Legend:

1 Delegation
2 Bureaus
3 Kitchen/Garage/Weavers
4 Garde Indigène
5 Militiamen's Wives' Quarters
6 Secretaries' House
7 Prison
8 Infirmary
9 Maternity Clinic
10 Doctor's Former Residence
11 Doctor's New Residence

12 Boarding School
13 School
14 Guest Quarters
15 Khunjanob's Quarters
16 Mahouts'/Workers' Quarters
17 Electric Plant/Theatre,
Cinema/Gymnasium

18 Post & Telegraph Office

19 Market
20 Rice Granary
21 Water Tank
22 Stable
23 Kilns
24 Lefèvre, Niel, Halo
25 Niel
26 Studio
27 Swimming Pool
⎯ Telephone Line

to ANNAM
to MÉWAL
FOREST
to CUNG SON
Ea Sir
to BANDON
Rhadé
Hamlet
Old
Route to
ANNAM
FOREST
VIETNAMESE VILLAGE
Ban Me Thuot
Village
Pagoda
FOREST
Ea Tam
RHADÉ QUARTER

BAN ME THUOT
- 1918 -

to DALAT

8. Ban Me Thuot, 1918

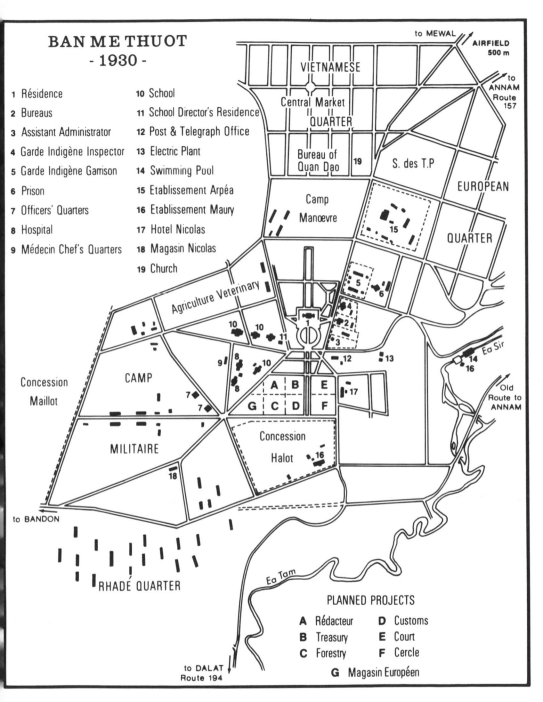

BAN ME THUOT
- 1930 -

1 Résidence
2 Bureaus
3 Assistant Administrator
4 Garde Indigène Inspector
5 Garde Indigène Garrison
6 Prison
7 Officers' Quarters
8 Hospital
9 Médecin Chef's Quarters

10 School
11 School Director's Residence
12 Post & Telegraph Office
13 Electric Plant
14 Swimming Pool
15 Etablissement Arpéa
16 Etablissement Maury
17 Hotel Nicolas
18 Magasin Nicolas
19 Church

to MEWAL
AIRFIELD 500 m
to ANNAM Route 157

VIETNAMESE
Central Market
QUARTER

Bureau of Quan Dao

S. des T.P

EUROPEAN

QUARTER

Camp Manœuvre

Agriculture Veterinary

Concession Maillot

CAMP

MILITAIRE

Concession Halot

Ea Sir

Old Route to ANNAM

to BANDON

Ea Tam

RHADÉ QUARTER

to DALAT Route 194

PLANNED PROJECTS

A Rédacteur   D Customs
B Treasury   E Court
C Forestry   F Cercle
        G Magasin Européen

9. Ban Me Thuot, 1930

CHART 1

ELITE KIN NETWORK IN THE DAK TO-KONTUM-PLEIKU AREA

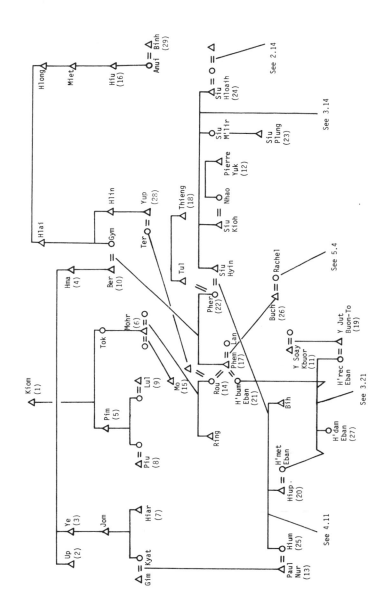

CHART 2

SEGMENT A OF THE ELITE KIN NETWORK AT CHEO REO

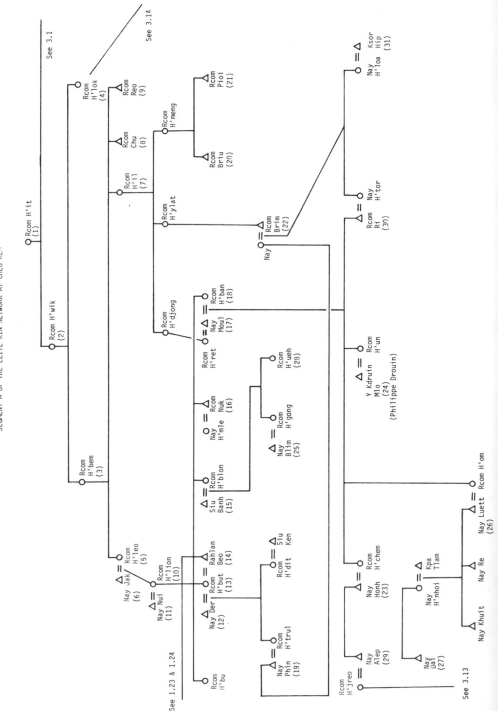

SEGMENT B OF THE ELITE KIN NETWORK AT CHEO REO

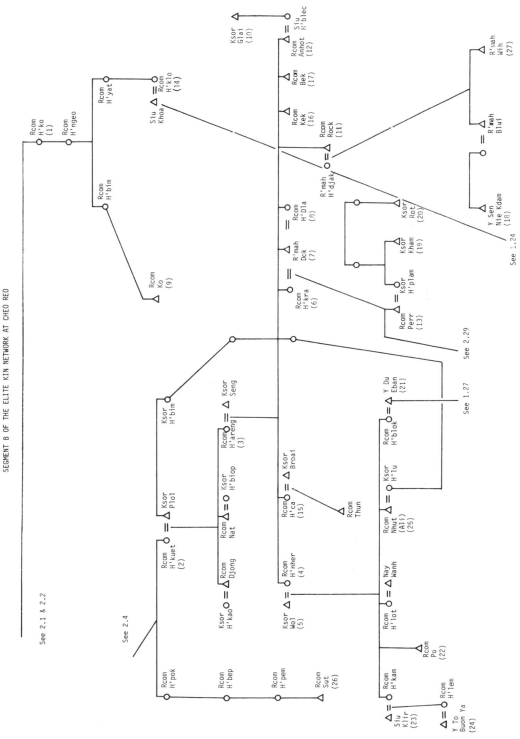

CHART 4

CHRU-LAT-SRE KIN NETWORK

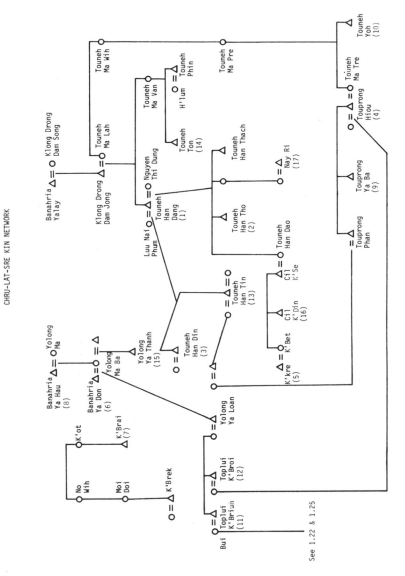

See 1.22 & 1.25

CHART 5

RHADÉ KIN GROUP IN THE BAN ME THUOT AREA

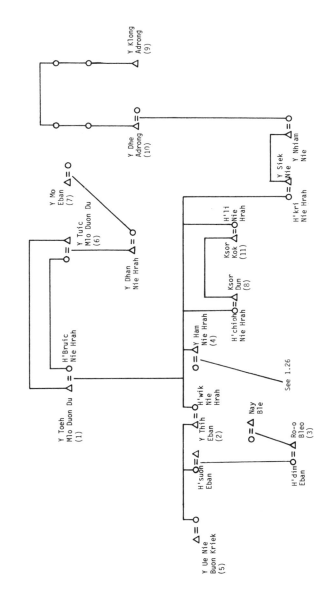

A NOTE ON BIBLIOGRAPHY

Documentary sources on the central highlands from the prehistoric period to 1954 vary considerably not only in quality but also in length (some consist of only a few pages or paragraphs). Those deemed valuable for this study have been recorded in the footnotes. For the interested reader, however, the following is designed to provide a selection of works which were found to be of particular value. To a great extent they represent the wide range of sources on this subject, including historical studies, explorers' accounts, colonial administrative and military records, legal treatises, ethnographic articles (usually in obscure journals), several dictionaries, a few polemical writings, works on flora and fauna, and a modern anthropological monograph. Regardless of length, all of these sources are highly informative and most of them strongly reflect the historical emphasis of the French scholastic tradition.

Two useful works dealing with the general history of the region are Henri Maitre, *Les Jungles Moi* (Paris: Larose, 1912) and the more recent study by Bernard Bourotte, "Essai d'histoire des populations Montagnardes du Sud-Indochinois jusqu'à 1945," *BSEI* 30, no. 1 (1955): 1–116. A specific treatment of relations between some highland groups and the early kingdom of Lin Yi is found in Rolf A. Stein, "Le Lin-Yi," *Han-Hiue: Bulletin du Centre d'Etudes Sinologiques de Pékin* 2 (1947): 1–321. There were numerous accounts written during the latter half of the nineteenth century and the early part of the twentieth century which shed a great deal of light on the history of the highlands. Events surrounding the founding of the French Catholic mission at Kontum can be found in the polemical work by J. B. Guerlach, *"L'Oeuvre néfaste," réplique du Père J. B. Guerlach, missionaire apostolique au F. Camille Paris, colon en Annam* (Saigon: Imprimerie Commerciale, 1905) and in Pierre Dourisboure's *Les Sauvages Bah-Nars (Cochinchine Orientale): souvenirs d'un missionaire* (Paris: Pierre

Taqui, 1922). A translation of the latter work is included in Pierre Dourisboure and Christian Simonnet, *Vietnam: Mission on the Grand Plateaux* (Maryknoll, New York: Maryknoll Publications, 1967).

Most French explorers of the late nineteenth century published accounts. Two articles by Jules Harmand are "De Bassac à Hué (Avril–Août 1887)," *Bulletin de la Société de Géographie*, January 1879, pp. 71–104; and "Rapport sur une mission en Indo-Chine de Bassac à Hué (16 Avril–14 Août 1877)," *Archives des Missions Scientifiques et Littéraires* 5 (1879): 247–62. Jules Harmand's private papers, many of which contain data on the highlanders, can be found in the Harmand Collection, Olin Library, Cornell University, Ithaca, New York. Paul Néis and Lt. Septans recorded their explorations in "Rapport sur un voyage d'exploration aux sources du Dong-Nai," *Excursions et Reconnaissances*, no. 10 (1881), pp. 15–80. Paul Néis also published "Rapport sur une excursion scientifique faite chez les Mois de L'Arrondissement de Baria du 15 Mai au 15 Juin 1880," in Gouvernement de la Cochinchine, *Variétés sur les pays Mois* (Saigon, 1935), pp. 1–30. Amédée Gautier described his highland explorations in "Voyage au pays des Mois," *Excursions et Reconnaissances*, no. 14 (1882), pp. 219–49, and "Voyage au pays des Mois accompli en Février, Avril, Mai et Juin 1882," in Gouvernement de la Cochinchine, *Variétés sur les pays Mois*, pp. 31–59. An additional work on his trips is found in Maurice Dubourg, "Une tentative de colonisation en pays Moi: la mission d'Amédée Gautier," *Revue d'Histoire des Colonies* 37 (1950): 101–38. Paul Nouet's account of his exploration is contained in "Excursion chez les Mois de la frontière nord-est," *Excursions et Reconnaissances*, no. 19 (1884), pp. 5–26. Similarly, M. R. Humann's report is published in "Excursion chez les Moi indépendants," *Excursions et Reconnaissances*, no. 19 (1884), pp. 27–42, and E. Navelle's is in "De Thi-Nai au Bla," *Excursions et Reconnaissances* 13, no. 30 (1887): 211–342.

The bizarre expeditions of Charles David, better known as Mayréna, are described and analyzed by Jean Marquet in "Un aventurier du XIXe siècle: Marie Ier Roi des Sedangs (1888–1890), " *Bulletin des Amis du Vieux Hué* 14, nos. 1–2 (1927): 1–135; and Marcel Ner's review of the Marquet work and Maurice Soulié's *Marie Ier Roi des Sedangs, 1888–1890* (Paris: Marpon et Cie, 1927) in *BEFEO* 27 (1928): 308–17. An expedition in the highlands as part of the Pavie Mission is described by Captain Cupet in *Voyages au Laos et chez les sauvages du sudest de l'Indo-Chine*, the third volume of the eleven-volume report by Auguste Pavie, *Mission Pavie en Indochine,*

1879–1895 (Paris: Ernest Leroux, 1900). A general work on Dr. Alexandre Yersin is Noël Bernard's *Yersin: Pionnier, Savant, Explorateur (1863–1943)*, with preface by Pasteur Vallery-Radot (Paris: La Colombe, 1955). Yersin also recorded his expeditions in "Sept mois chez les Mois," in *Variétés sur les pays Mois*, pp. 166–70, as well as in a series of articles in the journal *Indochine*; "Premier contact avec les pays Mois de l'Annam," no. 99 (1942), pp. 1–3; "Rencontre avec des pirates sur le plateau Moi," no. 100 (1942), pp. 9–10; "Premières reconnaissances du plateau du Lang-Bian," no. 101 (1942), pp. 4–6; "Voyage de Nhatrang à Stung-Treng par les pays Mois," no. 103 (1942), pp. 4–7, no. 104 (1942), pp. 3–7; "Un mois chez M'Siao (Juillet–Août, 1893)," no. 117 (1942), pp. 3–8; and "De Nhatrang à Tourane par les plateaux Moi," no. 137 (1943), pp. 3–9, no. 146 (1943), pp. 5–9, and 150 (1943), pp. 4–8. Works of the early twentieth century include M. A. Lavallée, "Notes ethnographiques sur diverses tribus du Sud-Est de l'Indo-Chine," *BEFEO*, no. 4 (1901), pp. 291–311; and Prosper Odend'hal, "Itinéraires d'Attopeu à la mer," *Revue Indochinoise* 9 (1908): no. 78, pp. 399–413, no. 79, pp. 499–513, no. 80, pp. 575–89, no. 81, pp. 684–88, no. 82, pp. 742–58, and no. 83, pp. 835–48.

Some late nineteenth century ethnographies are M. Silvestre, "Rapport sur l'esclavage," *Excursions et Reconnaissances*, no. 14 (1880), pp. 95–144; H. Azémar, "Les Stiengs de Brolam," *Excursions et Reconnaissances*, no. 27 (1886), pp. 147–60; no. 28 (1886), pp. 215–50; M. Brière, "Notice Sur les Moi du Binh Thuan et du Khanh Hoa," *Excursions et Reconnaissances*, no. 32 (1890), pp. 235–72. Similar works of the early twentieth century are E. M. Durand, "Les Mois du Son-Phong," *Bulletin de Géographie Historique et Descriptive*, nos. 1–2 (1900), pp. 284–322; M. Brière, "Culture et commerce de la cannelle," *Bulletin Economique de l'Indochine* 6, no. 33 (1904): 935–50; H. Haguet, "Notice ethnique sur les Mois de la région de Quang-Ngai," *Revue Indochinoise* 1 (1905): 1410–26; H. Besnard, "Les populations Moi du Darlac," *BEFEO* 7, no. 1 (1907): 61–86; Trinquet, "Le poste administratif du Lang-Ri (Quang-Ngai)," *Revue Indochinoise* 10 (1908): 346–82; and J. E. Kemlin, "Alliances chez les Reungao," *BEFEO* 17 (1917): 1–119.

Sources dealing with the historical roles of the King of Fire and the King of Water are Adhemard Leclère, "Légende Djarai sur l'origine du sabre sacré par le Roi du Feu," *Revue Indochinoise*, no. 6 (1904), pp. 366–69; J. B. Guerlach, "Quelques notes sur les Sadet," *Revue Indochinoise*, no. 1 (1905), pp. 184–88. Nun Suon, "Le roi de l'eau et le roi du feu," Document

63003, 15 June 1944, Commission des Moeurs et Coutumes, Institut Buddhique, Phnom Penh; B. Y. Jouin, "Histoire légendaire du Sadet du Feu," *BSEI* 26, no. 1 (1951): 74–84; and Charles Meyer, "Les mystérieuses relations entre les Rois du Cambodge et le 'Pôtao' des Jarai," *Etudes Cambodgiennes*, no. 4 (1965), pp. 11–26. Two Vietnamese sources by French-trained scholars describing relations between the Kings of Fire and Water and Vietnamese rulers are Nghiêm Thẩm, "Tìm hiểu đồng bào thượng" (Understanding the Highland Compatriots), *Quê Hương*, no. 31 (1962), pp. 133–48, and *Nhu viễn trong Khâm-định Đại Nam hội-điển sự lệ* (Foreign Relations in the Collection of Official Administrative Regulations of Đại Nam), 2 vols., trans. into modern Vietnamese by Tạ Quang Phát, rev. and ed. by Bưu Cầm (Saigon, Bộ Văn-Hóa Giáo-Dục, 1965).

Three sources that contain information on the French administration in the highlands during the 1930s are Léopold Sabatier, *Palabre du serment du Darlac* (Hanoi: Imprimerie d'Extrême-Orient, 1931); and Nyo, "Pénétration Française dans les pays Mois," *BSEI* 12, no. 2 (1937): 45–67. Official colonial administration reports on the Python God movement that swept the highlands in the late 1930s can be found in *La Question Moi* Papers, Department of Manuscripts and University Archives, Cornell University, Ithaca, New York. Ethnographic works published during the 1930–1954 period include J. Le Pichon, "Les chasseurs de sang," *Bulletin des Amis du Vieux Hué* 25 (1938): 357–409; P. Huard and A. Maurice, "Les Mnong du plateau central Indochinois," *IIEH* 2 (1939): 27–148; Paul Guilleminet, "Recherches sur les croyances des tribus du Haut-Pays d'Annam, les Bahnar du Kontum et leurs voisins les magiciens," *IIEH* 4 (1941): 9–33; A. Maurice, "L'habitation Rhadé," *IIEH* 5, fasc. 1 (1942): 87–106; L. Bezacier, "Note sur quelques tatouages de Moi 'Ka-tu'," *IIEH* 5, fasc. 2 (1942): 117–25; Dr. Queguiner, "Notes sur une peuplade moi de la Chaine Annamitique sud: les Cau S're," *IIEH* 6 (1943): 395–402; B. Jouin, *La mort et la tombe: L'abandon de la tombe* (Paris: Institut d'Ethnologie, 1949); P. Guilleminet, "La tribu Bahnar du Kontum," *Actes du XXIᵉ Congrès des Orientalistes* (Paris: Imprimerie Nationale, Société Asiatique de Paris, 1949), pp. 383–84; B. Y. Jouin, "Les traditions des Rhadé," *BSEI* 25, no. 4 (1950): 357–400; P. Guilleminet, "La tribu Bahnar du Kontum," *BEFEO* 45 (1951–52); 393–561; Georges Condominas, *Nous avons mangé la forêt de la Pierre-Génie Goo* (Paris: Mercure de France, 1952); and A. Maurice and G. Proux, "L'âme du riz," *BSEI* 29 (1954): 129–258.

Some compendiums of highland indigenous laws were prepared by French scholars prior to 1954. The best of these are D. Antomarchi, *Recueil de coutumes Rhadées du Darlac* (Hanoi: Imprimerie d'Extrême-Orient, 1940); Jacques Dournes, *Nri, recueil des coutumes Sre du Haut-Donnai* (Saigon: Editions France-Asie, 1951); T. Gerber, "Coutumier Stieng," *BEFEO* 45 (1951): 228–69; and Paul Guilleminet, *Coutumier de la tribu Bahnar des Sedang et des Jarai de la Province de Kontum,* 2 vols. (Paris: Ecole Française d'Extrême-Orient, 1952). Dictionaries of highland languages compiled by the French include Mgr. Cassaigne, *Dictionnaire Koho* (Saigon: Imprimerie de l'Union, 1936); and T. Gerber, *Lexique Français-Stieng* (Saigon: Imprimerie du Théâtre, 1937). A work on big game and hunting in the highlands is Henri de Monestrol, *Chasses et faune d'Indochine* (Saigon: Edition A. Portail, 1952), and forests are described in R. Champsoloix, *Rapport sur les forêts des P.M.S., République du Viet-Nam* (Saigon: Ministère de la Réforme Agraire et de Développement en Agriculture et Pêcherie, 1952).

INDEX

479